THE BRITISH YEAR BOOK OF INTERNATIONAL LAW

THE
BRITISH YEAR BOOK OF
INTERNATIONAL LAW
1983

FIFTY-FOURTH YEAR OF ISSUE

OXFORD

AT THE CLARENDON PRESS

1984

Oxford University Press, Walton Street, Oxford OX2 6DP

London   New York   Toronto
Delhi   Bombay   Calcutta   Madras   Karachi
Kuala Lumpur   Singapore   Hong Kong   Tokyo
Nairobi   Dar es Salaam   Cape Town
Melbourne   Auckland

and associated companies in
Beirut   Berlin   Ibadan   Mexico City   Nicosia

Oxford is a trade mark of Oxford University Press

© *Unless otherwise stated, Oxford University Press 1984*

ISBN 0-19-825508X

ISSN 0068-2691
The British Year Book of International Law is an annual
journal, starting with Volume 52 (1981). Subscriptions £50
(U.S. $105 for subscribers in the U.S.A., £45 for those in the
U.K.), postage included. Subscriptions should be sent to
Journals Subscriptions Department, Oxford University Press,
Walton Street, Oxford OX2 6DP, U.K., or placed through a
subscription agent or bookseller.

Printed in Great Britain
at the University Press, Oxford
by David Stanford
Printer to the University

Editorial Communications should be addressed as follows:

Articles and Notes:
PROFESSOR IAN BROWNLIE
All Souls College, Oxford, OX1 4AL.

Books for Review:
PROFESSOR D. W. BOWETT
Queens' College, Cambridge, CB3 9ET.

The Editors and members of the Editorial Committee do not make themselves in any way responsible for the views expressed by contributors, whether the contributions are signed or not.

CONTENTS

Book Reviews (*cont.*)

THE INTERNATIONAL COURT OF JUSTICE
AS SEEN FROM BAR AND BENCH*

By JUDGE SIR HUMPHREY WALDOCK

Late President of the International Court of Justice

THE International Court of Justice has probably seemed to many of you—at any rate until today—a somewhat remote and esoteric tribunal, almost like some body in outer space. The work of the Court, by its very nature, is unlikely to make any meaningful impact in the day-to-day practice of the average solicitor or member of the Bar. Certainly when I was called to the Bar by Gray's Inn, between the wars, it never occurred to me that the work of the International Court might touch me personally.

The Court, although designated by Article 7 of the Charter as one of the six principal organs of the United Nations, and by Article 92 as its principal judicial organ, has its seat not at the main centres of United Nations activity in New York but some 3,000 miles away in The Hague. This may help to insulate the Court from the political pressures to which it might be exposed in New York but it has the drawback that, except when electing judges, the General Assembly and the Security Council all too easily forget the existence of the Court and the use that might be made of it in the handling of disputes. The tendency to view the Court as something extraterrestrial also stems from the fact that under Article 34 of the Court's Statute only sovereign States or intergovernmental organizations may appear before it. Inevitably, lawyers do not as a matter of course think of the International Court as an integral part of their own legal systems even in the way that European lawyers are increasingly beginning to think of the E.E.C. Court in Luxembourg and the Human Rights Commission and Court in Strasbourg as part of their own legal systems.

The main difficulty comes from the categorical provision in Article 34 of our Statute that only States may be parties in cases before the Court and from a provision in Article 96 of the Charter which restricts use of the Court's advisory jurisdiction to the General Assembly, Security Council and certain other bodies authorized by the General Assembly. As a result of these provisions neither individuals nor companies, however multinational these may be, can either institute or defend proceedings in this Court. This is not, however, to say that the interests of individuals or companies may not be the subject of proceedings here. On the contrary,

* © Estate of the late Sir Humphrey Waldock. The text which is printed originally formed an address given by Waldock in The Hague to a group of English lawyers on 11 April 1980. The copy found in his papers does not bear a title, and the Editors have supplied the title which appears at the head of this page. This title in fact appears at the head of a slightly different text of the same address which was also with Waldock's papers.

the interests of individuals or companies have constituted the subject-matter of a large proportion of the cases. The true victims of direct violations of a State's rights under treaties or general international law have, not infrequently, been individuals or companies, when the principal object of the international proceedings is naturally to obtain redress for their injuries rather than for that of the State itself. The same is the case even more obviously when the claim is one for denial of justice, that is for an injury to a foreign national or foreign company by treatment incompatible with minimum standards as these are laid down by general international law. But in all these cases, although the true victim is the individual or the company, in law it is the State's own rights that are involved, and it is the international claim of the State itself that alone may be made the subject of the proceedings before the Court. As examples of cases concerning the interests of individuals, I may mention the *Ambatielos* case involving a claim by Greece against the United Kingdom on behalf of a Greek businessman; the *Nottebohm* case involving an attempt by Liechtenstein to bring a claim on behalf of an alleged Liechtenstein national, and a case between the Netherlands and Sweden concerning the guardianship of a Dutch infant girl. Company cases have been numerous and include the *Anglo-Iranian Oil Company*, the *Barcelona Traction Company* and *Interhandel* cases. I may add that the claims of individuals have been the whole object of some of the cases submitted to the Court's advisory jurisdiction. These have been claims by international civil servants for wrongful dismissal or some similar injury which have already been before either the United Nations or the I.L.O. Administrative Tribunal, and the reference to the Court's advisory jurisdiction is really a delicately worked-out form of appeal. I say delicately worked out because the procedure has to skate round the individual's lack of any *locus standi* before the Court.

States before the Court, even when litigating in the interest or on behalf of their nationals, are normally represented by their Foreign Office Legal Advisers, their government Law Officers, and by counsel who, when they doff their robes, prove to be professors of international law. International organizations, on the few occasions they have appeared in Court, have always been represented by officials from their Legal Departments. The Court's Rules, I must make clear, contain no provisions regulating the qualifications of the person entitled to appear before the Court, and it has never been called on to pronounce on the question. Manley Hudson, in his book on the Permanent Court, said that it had at one time considered the desirability of regulating the question but had concluded that it would be impossible to frame provisions which would take account of the varying conditions of practice in the different countries. Truth to tell, this is no real problem at The Hague as self-interest and a sense of responsibility to the Court alike ensure that governments and organizations choose only persons with adequate qualifications to appear on their behalf.

True, Article 42 of the Statute speaks of the agents of the parties having the assistance of 'counsel or advocates', and these words may seem to indicate specifically *legal* qualifications. But the provision is broadly interpreted and parties not infrequently include political or scientific advisers in their lists of persons appearing in the case; moreover, on occasion scientific advisers have even addressed the Court, not as expert witnesses, but pleading as counsel. In the *Icelandic Fisheries* cases, for example, a German fisheries expert, speaking from counsel's podium, gave us a fascinating account of the methods of procreation of the various fish stocks around Iceland; and I can well recall Commander Kennedy, R.N., in the *Anglo-Norwegian Fisheries* case, similarly trying—though in vain—to get the Court to understand the geometrical method by which mariners have always determined the seaward boundary of the territorial sea. Naturally, however, the great majority of those who plead before the Court are highly qualified lawyers; and these, by custom, appear either in the professional dress of their own countries, wigs included where these form part of it, or in academic robes.

My own introduction to the Peace Palace was in 1948 in the *Corfu Channel* case, the very first case before the present Court; and it was at any rate made in good company. Richard, now Lord, Wilberforce and Hersch Lauterpacht were my fellow Juniors and we were led by Eric Beckett, Legal Adviser to the Foreign Office, and Hartley Shawcross, then Attorney-General. Those proceedings were—characteristically!—on a preliminary objection by the respondent, Albania, and Wilberforce and I also appeared for the United Kingdom at the second stage of that case, and again in the *Anglo-Norwegian Fisheries* case. In the *Anglo-Iranian Oil Company* case I shared the position of Junior with Harry Fisher, now President of Wolfson College, and afterwards acted as Counsel for India, Spain, Denmark and the Netherlands in cases before the Court as well as for other countries in arbitrations outside the Court. These are, as it were, my credentials for speaking to you today. I would emphasize, however, that it is the Court's own custom and discipline which governs appearance before the Court, not the rules or custom of any individual country. This you will easily understand when I say that so far as this Court is concerned, a solicitor has just as good a right of audience as a member of the Bar. Francis Mann of Herbert Smith & Co. proved that by addressing the Court in the *Barcelona Traction Company* case in 1969, when it so happens I appeared against him. Whether any significance is to be attached to the fact that, on the one occasion a solicitor has addressed the Court, he did so on behalf of the Belgian, not the British, Government I must leave to you.

A factor which inevitably affects the choice of counsel is the provision in Article 39 of the Statute that French and English shall be the official languages of the Court. Although, upon request, the Court will authorize the use of another language, proficiency in one of the official languages is almost a *sine qua non* for counsel. However, the majority of international lawyers perforce acquire such a proficiency at conferences or in meetings with foreign colleagues; and, even if there has been some disposition to employ lawyers from French- or English-speaking countries, this factor is not so restrictive as might at first sight appear. What does certainly count is experience in international cases, and some counsel tend to be found on one side or another in several cases so that there is the making of an international Bar. Indeed, the number of foreign counsel sometimes instructed by governments almost breeds a suspicion that the primary object may be to ensure that they will not be found on the other side.

International litigation has its own special features. In our domestic proceedings the written pleading is brief and economical to the point of being uninformative as to the parties' cases, which are fully exposed only in the oral arguments of counsel. In international proceedings, on the other hand, the written pleadings are usually somewhat long, and are full to the point of disclosing virtually the whole of each party's case; but even so, there is full oral argument which not infrequently repeats much of what is contained in the written pleadings. Clearly, this may involve some waste of time as judges are not so obtuse as some counsel appear to think. But both as counsel and judge I have been struck by the way in which the successive stages of the pleading have helped to clarify and crystallize the issues. The cases are, moreover, usually of considerable importance legally or politically and governments not unnaturally tend to leave no stone unturned in their arguments. You must also remember that counsel find themselves confronted by no less than fifteen inscrutable figures on the Bench, coming from different parts of the world and with different legal backgrounds. Counsel's position, therefore, is a little like that of a salmon fisherman: he can never be quite sure what legal fly will attract each judge and tends to try them all.

Do not be deceived by the somewhat theatrical *mise-en-scène* of the Peace Palace. It conceals a thoroughly professional Court, with some fifty years' experience of arbitral litigation behind it, and a markedly efficient staff and organization. It is fully capable, if given sufficient opportunities, to make a valuable contribution both to the settlement of disputes and to the development of international law.

The contribution of the Court to the modern law of the sea has, for example, been both considerable and, in the idiom of today, progressive, without departing from the Court's judicial character. This is true conspicuously of the *Corfu Channel*, *Anglo-Norwegian Fisheries* and *North Sea Continental Shelf* cases. In its judgments in those cases the Court performed the classic function of a court in determining and clarifying what it conceived to be the existing law. In doing so, however, it threw fresh light on the considerations and the principles on which the law was based in a manner to suggest the path for its future development. In that way and by those judgments the Court has materially influenced the actual development of the modern law of the sea, and not merely its formulation.

In short, although the major factors in determining the shape of the new law of the sea may have been the immense developments in technology of recent years and the aspirations of the newly independent States, the judicial role of the International Court of Justice has also played its part.

The Court's task, as you will appreciate, can be a somewhat delicate one in these times, when many branches of international law are undergoing rapid evolution. In the *Icelandic Fisheries* case, for example, the Court itself recognized that its pronouncements on the law might prove to have only transient value and thought it necessary to underline that it was not its function to anticipate the law before the legislature had laid it down.

Clearly, the Court cannot make its full contribution to the development of international law and the settlement of international disputes until greater use is made of it by States and by the United Nations. As you know, the jurisdiction of the Court in any given case depends on the consent of the States concerned, given either *ad hoc* or in some instrument beforehand. States, unfortunately, still remain extremely shy of submitting themselves to judgment by the Court. Regrettable as this may be, it is one of the facts of international life at the present time. We in the Peace Palace do not live in an ivory tower, we are aware of the turmoil and change going on in almost every part of the world. We are aware of the new social problems, the economic aspirations, and conflicts of interests which advances of science and technology are bringing. We also recognize the prejudicial effects of the general tension in the international community on the willingness of governments to come before the Court. Accordingly, we may have to accept that the Court will not be able to play its full role until a larger measure of stability has been achieved in the world's affairs. This I believe makes it all the more important that use of the judicial process should never be lost sight of whenever an appropriate opportunity presents itself. Ultimately, the effective working of the international judicial process is surely essential to the achievement and maintenance of a peaceful world order. It would be disastrous if in the turmoil of our present times we lost the habit of its use.

THE CALLING OF THE INTERNATIONAL LAWYER: SIR HUMPHREY WALDOCK AND HIS WORK*

By IAN BROWNLIE[1]

I. INTRODUCTION

HUMPHREY WALDOCK was the only international lawyer to have been at one time or another the President of the International Court of Justice at The Hague, Chairman of the International Law Commission in Geneva, President of the European Commission of Human Rights at Strasbourg and President of the European Court of Human Rights at Strasbourg. His high professional standards and capacity for hard work carried him through a career which covered every aspect of international legal experience except that of Legal Adviser in the Foreign Office—though his wartime service at the Admiralty involved responsibilities which were similar.

The purpose of the present study is to pay tribute to a friend and colleague and to do so by building upon the variety and substance of Waldock's professional life in order to produce a useful picture of the roles which international law and those who practise it may play. All too often the novice and the layman find public international law mysterious and remote and lack a ready means of correcting such impressions. Waldock was always sensitive to the need to make the subject more fathomable for the non-specialist, not least because, as common lawyer (and a pupil of Stallybrass), he understood the sceptical attitudes of those whose paths lie outside the confines of government, foreign policy and the small international law Bar. Thus no other means of commemoration of Sir Humphrey Waldock and his work could be more appropriate than a sort of geography of the terrain of international law based upon his career.

II. BEGINNINGS

Claud Humphrey Meredith Waldock was born in Ceylon, as it was then known, on 13 August 1904. He was educated at Uppingham School and Brasenose College, Oxford, where he was a pupil of a common lawyer, W. T. S. Stallybrass, who was best known as the editor of the seventh to the tenth editions of *Salmond on Torts*, and was reputed to be a good tutor.[2] There can be no doubt that Waldock's professional formation was within

---

* © Professor Ian Brownlie, 1984.
[1] Q.C., D.C.L., F.B.A.; Chichele Professor of Public International Law in the University of Oxford.
[2] See Lawson, *The Oxford Law School 1850-1965* (1968), pp. 121, 129-30.

the common law, and in this respect his subsequent career was in keeping with the English tradition that an international lawyer should be in the first instance a *lawyer*, who had come to specialize in a certain area of problems. Such a background produced a professional attitude which did not see public international law as wholly set apart from the general stock of legal concepts and techniques.

At Oxford Waldock completed Classical Moderations (1925), the Final Honour School of Jurisprudence (1927) and the Degree of Bachelor of Civil Law (1928). He was called to the Bar at Gray's Inn in 1928, joined the Midland Circuit and practised for a time. However, in 1930 he was elected a Fellow of Brasenose College and, apart from the war years, remained a college tutor until 1947, when he was elected to the Chichele Chair of Public International Law at Oxford, and consequently became a Fellow of All Souls College.

The apparently well-established pattern of academic life was to be disturbed by the outbreak of war and Waldock's work at the Admiralty in the years 1940–5. That translation was to bring him into constant contact with international law, but in the years before the war Waldock's interests lay within the subjects of equity, real property and the law of mortgages. However, he taught international law in tutorials attended by Brasenose and Oriel men. In 1938 there was published *The Law of Mortgages*, which Waldock had written in conjunction with Harold Greville Hanbury, subsequently to succeed to the Vinerian Chair of English Law. In a generous supplement to the preface, Hanbury recorded the fact that the part dealing with mortgages of land (three-quarters of the whole) had been written by Waldock. The book was very well received, appeared in a second edition in 1950 over Waldock's name alone,[3] and remains to this day as a classic account and a testament of its author's craftsmanship.

Soon after the outbreak of war Waldock went to work in Military Branch I, a branch of the Admiralty, and his duties involved heavy and continuous involvement with international relations and matters of international law. The connection with international law was continued and reinforced in the decade after the end of the war. Waldock went back to Oxford,[4] but continued to carry out commissions for the United Kingdom Government. In 1947 he was elected to the Chichele Chair of Public International Law at Oxford.[5] In 1950 he was elected an *Associé* of the Institute of International Law, such election constituting recognition of the candidate's professional standing by the international fraternity of senior colleagues. In the same year Waldock returned to practice at the

---

[3] See the reviews of the second edition in the *Law Quarterly Review*, 67 (1951), p. 112 (S. J. Bailey) and the *Modern Law Review*, 13 (1950), p. 533 (A. D. Hargreaves).

[4] It is interesting to note that in the academic year 1946–7 Waldock lectured in each term, twice weekly, on real property: he gave no other lectures.

[5] The first Professor was elected in 1859, and until 1947 the Chair was described as of 'International Law and Diplomacy'. Waldock's predecessors were Mountague Bernard (1859–74), Thomas Erskine Holland (1874–1911), Sir Henry Erle Richards (1911–22) and James Leslie Brierly (1922–47).

English Bar and went into chambers in the Temple at 2 Hare Court. In this period his practice quickly developed, a good deal of work coming from the British Foreign Office, and in 1951 he was appointed Queen's Counsel.

Thus by the early 1950s Waldock's course was set. The pattern was visible and important elements in it were the practical experience of international law and the regular provision of professional services to his own government, always referred to in lectures and in conversation as 'H.M.G.'[6] At the same time Waldock continued to play an active role in the affairs of the Oxford Law Faculty, the University,[7] Gray's Inn[8] and All Souls College. His home circumstances were favourable: his beloved wife, Beattie, shared his life and his thoughts for over fifty years, and was an abiding source of strength.

III. The Royal Navy's Foreign Relations: The Admiralty, 1939-45

In the war years Waldock joined a branch of the Admiralty called Military Branch I, of which he became the head, and attained the grade of Principal Assistant-Secretary.[9] This role called for heavy and continuous service advising on both legal matters and matters of an administrative nature. The work related to the highest levels of policy-making and involved the Cabinet Office. Advice was proffered to the First Sea Lord, the professional head of the Service, but in fact the questions in issue were of political significance and concerned the First Lord of the Admiralty, an important cabinet post held from September 1939 until May 1940 by Mr. Winston Churchill. The issues were often of critical importance and the war at sea, and problems with neutrals, were prominent features of the darkest days of the war. The early phase of the war saw France defeated, Dunkirk, the campaign in Norway and the struggle for control of Atlantic shipping routes. The United States and the Soviet Union remained on the sidelines.[10]

This period in Waldock's life has been well described by Judge Sir Robert Jennings, as he now is:[11]

I did not know Waldock then, but a colleague of mine, Professor C. H. Wilson, who worked in Military Branch I under Waldock, has told me how Humphrey,

---

[6] He was awarded the O.B.E. (1942), and C.M.G. (1946), and was in due course knighted (1961).

[7] He was a member of Hebdomadal Council, 1949-61, and Assessor of the Chancellor's Court, 1947-72. In the years 1967 to 1970 he was Chairman of the Commission of Inquiry into the University Press, which produced important proposals for the future of the Press.

[8] Of which Waldock became a Bencher in 1957 and Treasurer in 1971.

[9] At the end of 1945 he was invited to remain in the Admiralty as an Under-Secretary, but elected to return to Oxford.

[10] See, generally, Captain S. W. Roskill, *The War at Sea 1939-1945*, I: *The Defensive* (1954); Martin Gilbert, *Finest Hour: Winston S. Churchill 1939-1941* (1983).

[11] An address delivered on the occasion of the Memorial Service at the University Church of St. Mary the Virgin, Oxford, 17 October 1981.

whose family was then in the United States, slept in a bunk in the Admiralty air raid shelters, rose at 7 or 7.10, and, except for a short lunchtime walk in St. James's Park, and an occasional dinner at the United Universities Club, worked till 2 or 3 every morning; though every *other* Sunday, he would have what he called 'a long lie in' till 10.30 or 11.00, before rising to work all day Sunday and into the night. He abandoned all other interests till the war was over. His concentration on his department was total. Whereas Military Branch I might so easily have been just another of many Admiralty sub-departments, under Waldock it became of the first importance and was respected, admired, and sometimes feared, throughout Whitehall; or, at least, the Head of it was. The department occupied one small room overlooking Horse Guard's Parade, next to the First Lord's own room and Private Office. It was badly damaged by bombs twice; once when they were there and once when they were not.

The work was, in a word, the Royal Navy's foreign relations; and Waldock realized that what the Navy was doing would need to be explained to the world, not just as an Admiralty matter, but as part of Britain's foreign policy in the widest sense. This work inescapably involved questions of international law of the first importance; neutral waters, the *Altmark*, the French fleet at Alexandria, the disputes over French passage via Gibraltar, various cases of hot pursuit, rights over Gulf oil. And what better way could there be of becoming an international lawyer, than through the exigencies of practical situations of grave importance where often an irreversible answer had to be given within hours? I remember his telling me years later how over and over again, faced with a question of the right action to take in a practical situation, the only real help he found was in the rules propounded in old international law text books on the laws of war, supposed in the mid-30s to have been obsolete.

This long immersion in high State affairs and international law revealed to Waldock the interest and significance which attached to a subject previously outside his ken. His career in international law had begun.

There was at least one other lawyer heavily engaged in naval matters at this time. Gerald Fitzmaurice, subsequently to be first Legal Adviser at the Foreign Office and a Judge of the International Court, was seconded from the Foreign Office, where he was third Legal Adviser, to the Ministry of Economic Warfare from 1939 to 1943. In this office Fitzmaurice became an expert on contraband control and his duties involved co-operation with the Admiralty, and in that connection with Mr. Waldock of Military Branch I.[12] Both Fitzmaurice and Waldock produced articles for the *British Year Book* which stand as memorials of these episodes in their professional lives. The work of the former provided the basis of a major article on 'Some Aspects of Modern Contraband Control and the Law of Prize',[13] and the latter produced an account[14] of the facts and legal issues attending the release of British prisoners on board the *Altmark*, a German Naval Auxiliary, steaming through Norwegian territorial waters at a time when Norway was neutral, by the action of British destroyers under

[12] Reference to the period occurs in the obituary of Waldock written by Master Sir Gerald Fitzmaurice for *Graya*, 85 (1981), p. 54 at p. 55.

[13] See this *Year Book*, 22 (1944), p. 73.   [14] Ibid. 24 (1947), p. 216.

Captain Vian.[15] The First Sea Lord and the Foreign Secretary were directly concerned in the decision-making at the most critical juncture.[16] Apart from illustrating the foreign policy implications of naval operations, the *Altmark* incident had a considerable emotional impact and caught the public imagination. As Roskill puts it: '. . . the cry of the *Cossack*'s boarding party to the prisoners confined in the ship's holds, "The Navy is here", rang throughout the length and the breadth of the nation.'[17]

To regard the work that advisers like Waldock and Fitzmaurice were called upon to do during a particularly dramatic period of British naval history as exceptional, like the history of those years itself, would be a gross error. It is, however, the kind of error likely to be made by those ignorant of the role of law in naval staff planning and thus in the designing of the rules of engagement supplied to naval operational commanders. This role has been described in some detail by the late Professor O'Connell,[18] who was able to build upon experience in advising the naval staffs of two nations at least. The ability to appreciate the role of law in naval staff planning, and in the decision- and policy-making of governments overall, is adversely affected by the fashionable views of the academic world, views the narrowness and myopia of which are preserved by the fluent complacency of the legal theory which pervades law schools. Legal theory commonly produces models which, however refined, assume that *in fact* law is an *external* phenomenon both in terms of formulation and efficacy. In so far as such models are based upon actual legal experience, a very narrow range of decision-making is referred to and vast areas of experience are totally ignored.

The legal theorist does not trouble to get the facts right and there is at times the strong suspicion that he is not interested in facts which might invalidate his suppositions about 'law', in terms of his preferred theoretical model. In many contexts of decision-making by governments international law provides the syntax, the very fabric, of the subjects to which decisions relate. The law is in practice not external, coercive and alien, but internal, logically necessary and familiar.[19] In Military Branch I Waldock the official had to deal with a range of topics, many of which involved categories and definitions to which only legal sources had given attention.[20]

---

[15] The incident took place on 16 February 1940.

[16] See Captain S. W. Roskill, op. cit. above (p. 9 n. 10), pp. 151–3; W. S. Churchill, *The Second World War*, vol. 1 (1st edn., 1948), pp. 443–6. See further, James Cable, *Gunboat Diplomacy* (1971), pp. 23–32, 235–6 (bibliography); *Correspondence between His Majesty's Government in the United Kingdom and the Norwegian Government respecting the German Steamer 'Altmark', London, 17th February–15th March, 1940* (H.M.S.O.), Cmd. 8012 (Norway, No. 1 (1950)); and MacChesney, *Northwestern University Law Review*, 52 (1957), p. 320.

[17] Roskill, op. cit. above (p. 9 n. 10), p. 153.

[18] See this *Year Book*, 44 (1970), p. 19; *The Influence of Law on Sea Power* (1975).

[19] See further the present writer, this *Year Book*, 52 (1981), p. 1 at p. 5.

[20] For example: neutral rights, merchant ships, contraband, prisoners of war, questions of surrender and armistice.

IV. The Settlement of International Disputes

(a) *The Commission of Experts for the Investigation of the Italo-Yugoslav Boundary, 1946*

In the nature of things the professional international lawyer will in his practice be concerned with the peaceful settlement of disputes, and more especially the more 'legal' and 'formal' methods of settlement by means of adjudication and arbitration. These more formal methods, involving the settlement of specified issues in accordance with the principles of international law, are but part of a spectrum, a set of options, of methods for the settlement of disputes between States.[21] The options include negotiation, mediation and good offices and conciliation. These labels are but a poor guide to the range of procedural possibilities revealed by diplomatic history. Thus the term 'mediation' has been used in respect of a variety of proceedings. Negotiation and its fellows are often described as 'political' methods of settlement and so they are. At the same time such proceedings, like the process of decision-making by individual governments, necessitate consideration of legal issues or, at least, the use of legal expertise in order to analyse and structure the issues, making them more manageable and ensuring that definitional and like problems are confronted at the right time.

Waldock's association with the British government service, and his success in his work at the Admiralty, meant that he was at times called upon to play a role in the settlement of international disputes in the political forum. The preparation of the Italian Peace Treaty by the Council of Foreign Ministers in 1945 and 1946 involved the question of the status of Trieste and the determination of an appropriate Italo-Yugoslav boundary in the region of Venezia Giulia.[22] The Council of Foreign Ministers set up a Commission on which Waldock was a representative of the United Kingdom: the Commission of Experts for the Investigation of the Italo-Yugoslav Boundary.[23]

The task of the Commission was to prepare a report and recommendations for the Foreign Ministers' Deputies on fixing the boundary, which was to be 'in the main an ethnic line leaving a minimum population under

---

[21] For a survey, see the David Davies Memorial Institute for International Studies, *International Disputes: The Legal Aspects* (1972).

[22] For the background, see Arnold and Veronica M. Toynbee (eds.), *Survey of International Affairs 1939–46: The Realignment of Europe* (R.I.I.A. 1955), pp. 463–76; Donelan and Grieve, *International Disputes: Case Histories 1945–1970* (David Davies Memorial Institute, 1973), pp. 23–7; *Foreign Relations of the United States 1946*, vol. 2 (1970); Whiteman, *Digest of International Law*, vol. 3 (1964), pp. 50–109.

[23] Waldock was also appointed to the Special Commission on the Statute of the Free Territory of Trieste: see *Foreign Relations of the United States 1946*, vol. 4 (1970), pp. 844–7. At this time his path ran parallel to that of Fitzmaurice, who was legal adviser to the U.K. Delegation to the Paris Peace Conference: see Fitzmaurice, *Graya*, 85 (1981), p. 54 at p. 56, who remarks that 'they shared a common admiration and affection for that best of men, Ernest Bevin, then Foreign Secretary'. See further Fitzmaurice, 'The Juridical Clauses of the Peace Treaties', *Recueil des cours*, 73 (1948–II), pp. 259–367.

alien rule'. However, the special economic and geographical features of the areas to be investigated were also to be taken into consideration. Intricate questions of fact were involved and the exercise was virtually a continuation of a procedure for implementing the principle of self-determination, which principle had been recognized in the peace-making of 1919 but not very carefully implemented in certain cases.[24] In the Istrian or Julian hinterland the Croat and Slovene elements predominated whilst Italians were concentrated in Trieste and certain coastal towns. The Soviet Union proposed a line which left virtually the entire province to Yugoslavia. Other proposals called for various divisions more or less favourable to Italy or Yugoslavia, the French line being the most ethnically orientated.

The process was in substance political and the framework was the multilateral procedure for establishing a Peace Treaty within the Council of Foreign Ministers and the Paris Peace Conference. At the same time the essence of the matter was a boundary dispute between Italy and Yugo-slavia. Moreover, whilst the issues were not presented in legal terms, particular matters of fact were to be established by means of investigation and expert appraisal. In the event, the Council of Foreign Ministers accepted the French line as the boundary but decided that the area included within the city and environs of Trieste was to be placed under an international regime as the Free City of Trieste. The status of Trieste was not successfully regulated by the Italian Peace Treaty and was the subject of an eventual bilateral agreement between Italy and Yugoslavia.[25]

(b) *The Secretary-General's Mission to Peking, 1955*[26]

In January 1955 the Secretary-General of the United Nations, Dag Hammarskjøld, embarked upon a highly significant and spectacular mission to Peking for talks with Mr. Chou En-lai, the Chinese Prime Minister and Minister for Foreign Affairs. The party which accompanied the Secretary-General included Waldock as sole legal adviser.

The background to this episode calls for elucidation. In 1950 the Korean War had broken out and the People's Republic of China had intervened to assist North Korea at a point of crisis in that war. The Chinese and North Korean Commands faced a United Nations Command, which in terms of command structure was under the operational control of the United States, at a time when the United States and its allies had a marked preponderance of power in the United Nations. The Korean War (and the United States protection of Formosa (Taiwan) at the end of the Chinese Civil War) constituted a high point of tension in the relations of the new

---

[24] See Harold Nicolson, *Peacemaking 1919* (rev. edn. 1943), *passim*.

[25] The Treaty signed at Osimo on 10 November 1973; see Caggiano, *Italian Yearbook of International Law*, 2 (1976), p. 248.

[26] See Folliot (ed.), *Documents on International Affairs 1954* (R.I.I.A. 1957), pp. 335-40; *Yearbook of the United Nations*, 1955, pp. 54-5; Urquhart, *Hammarskjøld* (1972), pp. 94-131.

Government of China and the United States. After a bloody conflict the Korean Armistice Agreement[27] was signed on 27 July 1953, an agreement which was rather more structured and definitive than its nomenclature would suggest. In the difficult process of drawing up the Armistice Agreement, the issue of repatriation of prisoners of war was a particularly delicate question.

On 23 November 1954 a Chinese military tribunal sentenced eleven officers and men of the United States armed forces to terms of imprisonment for spying. Two American civilians were also sentenced for the same offence. The eleven officers and men had been captured in January 1953. The circumstances of the capture of the two civilians were to remain mysterious. The American reaction was sharp and took the form of a protest note of 26 November 1954 and a complaint of a violation of the Korean Armistice Agreement to the General Assembly. In the view of the United States the personnel concerned had been on combat missions over Korea and were prisoners of war: consequently, their detention and sentencing involved serious breaches of the Armistice Agreement, which provided for the repatriation of prisoners of war not later than 25 September 1953.

The General Assembly adopted a resolution[28] on 10 December which agreed with the substance of the contentions of the United States and requested 'the Secretary-General, in the name of the United Nations, to seek the release, in accordance with the Korean Armistice Agreement, of the eleven United Nations Command personnel, and all other captured personnel of the United Nations Command still detained'. The response of the Chinese Prime Minister, Mr. Chou En-lai, was a firm contradiction.[29] In the opinion of the Chinese Government the personnel had intruded into Chinese airspace and the evidence was that they had conducted espionage activities. The conviction of such spies was an internal affair and had 'nothing to do with the question of prisoners of war in Korea'.

As Secretary-General, Dag Hammarskjøld was on a number of occasions to take important initiatives at times of crisis and this forward approach was of particular significance at a period when the Security Council was more or less incapacitated.[30] In the circumstances prevailing in the years 1953 to 1955 this readiness to engage in personal diplomacy and mediation was the more valuable since the Government of the People's Republic of China was not represented in the United Nations. In face of the General Assembly's request to seek the release of the American personnel, Hammarskjøld decided on a visit to Peking to establish direct contact with the Chinese Government,[31] and Mr. Chou En-lai agreed on

[27] Folliot (ed.), *Documents on International Affairs 1953* (R.I.I.A. 1956), p. 386.
[28] Ibid., p. 337.   [29] Ibid.
[30] See Whiteman, *Digest of International Law*, vol. 13 (1968), p. 806.
[31] See the Secretary-General's Reports: *General Assembly Official Records*, Ninth Session, Annexes, Agenda Item 72, Doc. A/2891 (31 December 1954); ibid., Tenth Session, Supplement No. 1, Doc. A/2911 (Annual Report); U.N. Doc. A/2954 (9 September 1955), *Documents on International Affairs 1954* (R.I.I.A. 1957), p. 339.

arrangements for the mission.[32] The mission itself was followed by sustained contacts with Mr. Chou En-lai and the eleven American personnel who had been sentenced were released on 4 August 1955, four other detained airmen having been released in May.

In his final report on the question, Hammarskjøld stated that the visit was 'aimed primarily at clarifying the substantive and legal aspects of the matter'. Waldock's role was to provide the Secretary-General with legal appraisals of the issues, and particularly the question of the qualification of personnel as lawful combatants and the characterization of the flying missions concerned as lawful operations of the Korean war. However, it was undoubtedly the factual aspects which were the more prominent, and Waldock was able to provide guidance to his principal on the evaluation of the evidence, rather in the fashion of a judge reviewing the evidence for the benefit of a jury. It is clear that the legal aspects were played down in the conversations with Mr. Chou En-lai, but it is equally clear that the background of legal evaluation assisted the Secretary-General in determining the approach to his diplomatic task. On such occasions legal advice can be of great value, without being heavily technical. Certain it is that Hammarskjøld enjoyed a cordial relation with Waldock and was very grateful for his assistance, to which he referred in a letter as 'a most splendid co-operation'.[33] The entire episode was a model of careful diplomacy on the part of Hammarskjøld and entailed constant involvement with matters of fact and matters of proof. The legal approach was in the event more relevant to the question of *proof* (on the issue of espionage especially), and was only contingently concerned with the issues of legal principle. In practice this focus provided the better vehicle for successful diplomacy.

V. The Practice of International Law: Advising and the Conduct of Litigation

(a) *Generally*

Between June 1950, when he became a member of chambers at 2 Hare Court,[34] and February 1973, when he began his term as a Judge of the International Court, Waldock conducted a substantial practice in public international law. During this period he was a member of the European Commission of Human Rights (1954–61) and subsequently of the European Court of Human Rights (1966–74).

In effect Waldock's practical experience in international law matters had begun with his work at the Admiralty and his first experience in

---

[32] For a description of the mechanics of the visit: U.N. Dept. of Public Information, Note to Correspondents No. 1024 (14 January 1955).

[33] On 30 May 1961 the Secretary-General delivered a lecture to the Congregation of Oxford University under the title 'The International Civil Servant in Law and in Fact', published by the Clarendon Press, 1961. See further, Urquhart, op. cit. above (p. 13 n. 26), p. 531.

[34] Of which John Foster, K.C., was a member.

international litigation began in 1947, when the proceedings in the *Corfu Channel* case were set in train. The United Kingdom Government employed Waldock as Counsel in three cases before the International Court of Justice: the *Corfu Channel* case, the *Anglo-Norwegian Fisheries* case and the *Anglo-Iranian Oil Company* case.[35] This experience, and his taking silk in 1951, together with his capacity for good legal work, laid the foundations for a successful practice as a member of the English Bar specializing in international law.

(b) *Advising*

Both lawyers and laymen commonly see practice in terms of litigation, and Waldock had a substantial quantity of such work. However, practice may also involve advising the client on a course of conduct, in short, on policy-making, planning, operations, disposition of resources and the making of transactions. In international relations litigation, and its prospect, often grows out of the normal flow of State affairs. Thus the work of the adviser may be fairly constant, varied in content, concerned with courses of action, and not focused exclusively upon the paraphernalia of claims and disputes. Of course, the possibility of adjudication, and especially the 'unilateral' resort to an existing jurisdictional clause, is on a number of occasions an inevitable aspect of the overall development of relations between the States concerned: and it may be noted in passing that any realistic assessment of 'the role of international tribunals' should include research into the occasions on which resort to an international tribunal was one of the 'political' options available and which consequently played a part in the evolution of the relevant diplomacy as a whole.

Waldock's practice was based on classical international law with a certain emphasis on territorial disputes, a wide range of law of the sea questions, jurisdictional issues, and the relations between foreign investors or concession holders and the territorial sovereign as host State. Some of the clients were corporations, but the generality were Governments. Waldock's clients included not less than seventeen States, involving all the continents except Africa. The pattern of work was fairly consistent, but there were some less usual commitments, including the Hammarskjøld mission to Peking, already adverted to, and a mediation.

(c) *International Litigation*

Waldock was Counsel in the following cases:

1947–9   The *Corfu Channel* case[36]
1949–50   *Petroleum Development (Qatar) Ltd.* v. *Ruler of Qatar*[37]
1949–51   The *Fisheries* case (*United Kingdom* v. *Norway*)[38]

---

[35] See further below.
[36] (*Preliminary Objection*) I.C.J. Reports, 1947–8, p. 15; (*Merits*) ibid. 1949, p. 4.
[37] 18 I.L.R. 161.   [38] I.C.J. Reports, 1951, p. 116.

1949–51   *Petroleum Development (Trucial Coast) Ltd. v. Ruler of Abu Dhabi and its Dependencies.*[39]

1951–2   The *Anglo-Iranian Oil Company* case (*United Kingdom v. Iran*)[40]

1954–5   *Arbitration Concerning Buraimi and the Common Frontier between Abu Dhabi and Saudi Arabia*[41]

1955–60   The *Right of Passage* case (*Portugal v. India*)[42]

1962–70   The *Barcelona Traction Company* case (New Application, 1962) (*Belgium v. Spain*)[43]

1964–6   *Arbitration of a Controversy between the Argentine Republic and the Republic of Chile* (The *Palena* case)[44]

1967–9   The *North Sea Continental Shelf* cases (*Federal Republic of Germany/Denmark*; *Federal Republic of Germany/Netherlands*)[45]

1967–73   *Beagle Channel Arbitration* (*Argentine Republic/Republic of Chile*) (to the close of the first phase of the written pleadings)[46]

The volume of work involved in major cases between States in respect of delimitation of maritime or land boundaries or other significant subject-matter is enormous. When States do litigate—an unusual procedure—the scale of the pleadings, and especially the written pleadings, will tend to match the importance of the issues. It is not always sufficiently appreciated that in the classical delimitation cases—such as the *Anglo-Norwegian Fisheries* case or the *Beagle Channel Arbitration*—the issue is that of the permanent *status*, the sovereignty, title and control, of territory and waters. The subject-matter may involve valuable resources, such as fisheries, but the issue of *rights*, of entitlement as such, is commonly of primary importance. It is a considerable error to think that the term 'rights' is a mere legalism, a technicality, even when used in a legal context. Governments and public opinion readily appreciate the significance of rights, and many legal terms, such as 'sovereignty', are linked to important national symbols and create strong political reverberations.

In proceedings before the International Court, or an *ad hoc* Court of Arbitration set up on the basis of a bilateral treaty, the exchanges of written pleadings and the subsequent oral hearings may occupy a period

[39] 18 I.L.R. 144.

[40] (*Preliminary Objection*) I.C.J. Reports, 1952, p. 93.

[41] No award was given. For an account see J. M. Kelly, *Eastern Arabian Frontiers* (1964), *passim*. The interest of Abu Dhabi was represented by the United Kingdom.

[42] (*Preliminary Objections*) I.C.J. Reports, 1957, p. 125; (*Merits*) ibid. 1960, p. 6.

[43] (*Preliminary Objections*) ibid. 1964, p. 6; (*Second Phase*) ibid. 1970, p. 4.

[44] *Award of Her Majesty Queen Elizabeth II* (H.M.S.O. 1966); 38 I.L.R. 10; *Reports of International Arbitral Awards*, vol. 16, p. 109.

[45] I.C.J. Reports, 1969, p. 4.

[46] *Award of Her Britannic Majesty's Government*, 18 April 1977 (H.M.S.O.); *Controversy Concerning the Beagle Channel, Award* (Republic of Chile, bilingual edn., 1977); 52 I.L.R. 93.

of between two and three years. In the *Anglo-Norwegian Fisheries* case, which was initiated by means of a unilateral Application filed by the United Kingdom, the pleadings spanned a period of two years from the date of the Application. The extensive written pleadings[47] consisted of the United Kingdom's *Memorial* and *Reply*, and Norway's *Counter-Memorial* and *Rejoinder*. The oral hearings occupied five weeks.

In cases of this type, given the importance of the issues and the fact that the clients are Governments, the work is the responsibility of a team, consisting of the Agent, one or more of the Law Officers of the Government concerned, one or more of the lawyers working in the Foreign Office (who may combine the roles of Agent and Counsel), and a number of members of the legal profession, who are usually, but not necessarily, members of the Bar. There may also be technical experts in the team. Thus in the *Corfu Channel* case (*Merits*) the United Kingdom was represented at the oral hearings by Sir Eric Beckett, Legal Adviser to the Foreign Office, as Agent and Counsel, Sir Hartley Shawcross, the Attorney-General (replaced at a certain point by Sir Frank Soskice, the Solicitor-General), Humphrey Waldock, Richard Wilberforce, Mervyn Jones and M. E. Read. It must be borne in mind that the written pleadings would be prepared with the assistance of other advisers within the Foreign Office.

Waldock was fortunate in that his experience was to encompass matters which were nearly all properly described as leading cases. Five of these will be examined with the aid of the perspective which the passage of time provides and with particular reference to the role played by the pleadings.

1. Corfu Channel *case* (Merits)[48]

In the final stages of the Second World War elements of suspicion and tension began to emerge in the ranks of the coalition fighting the Axis powers. In the Adriatic the Governments of Yugoslavia and Albania, newly liberated from German occupation, and political associates of the Soviet Union, adopted an unfriendly attitude towards the Western powers. In 1944 civil war had broken out in Greece and both sides of the conflict received varying degrees of external patronage. It was against this background that a catastrophic incident took place in 1946, in which forty-four British naval personnel lost their lives and forty-two were injured.

On 15 May 1946 two British cruisers using the officially approved[49]

---

[47] See International Court of Justice, *Pleadings, Oral Arguments, Documents, Fisheries* case (*United Kingdom* v. *Norway*), 4 vols.

[48] *I.C.J. Reports*, 1949, p. 4. It is worth recalling that the first phase of the case (*I.C.J. Reports*, 1947-8, p. 15) (the Preliminary Objection phase) produced some interesting technical points concerning *forum prorogatum* and the possibility of the Court's exercising jurisdiction on the basis of informal consent: see Waldock's article in the *International Law Quarterly*, 2 (1948), p. 377. For comment on the main phase of the case by Waldock see the Cornelis van Vollenhoven Memorial Lecture, delivered in 1979: *The International Court and the Law of the Sea* (T.M.C. Asser Institute, The Hague), pp. 4-8.

[49] By the British Navy, which had first swept the North Corfu Channel in 1944, and check-swept in 1945.

'swept channel' through the North Corfu Channel were fired upon by Albanian shore batteries. This episode provoked diplomatic correspondence relating to the right of innocent passage through the North Corfu Channel, but there was no further development in the ensuing six months. The correspondence was inconclusive and, in view of the possibility of the establishment of diplomatic relations with Albania, the United Kingdom Government decided to ascertain 'whether the Albanian Government have learnt to behave themselves', in other words, to recognize the right of innocent passage.[50] On 22 October 1946 the cruisers *Mauritius* and *Leander*, together with the destroyers *Saumarez* and *Volage*, were sent through the North Corfu Strait with the purpose of testing Albania's attitude. Outside the Bay of Saranda the *Saumarez* struck a mine and was badly damaged and, whilst towing the *Saumarez*, the *Volage* struck a mine and had her bows blown off. *Volage* nevertheless succeeded in making Corfu with *Saumarez* in tow.

The mining took place in Albanian territorial waters. The evidence available did not establish the identity of the authors of the mine-laying, and the court was unwilling to employ a presumption of knowledge on the part of Albanian authorities on the basis that the mining had occurred within Albanian territorial waters. At the same time, the indirect evidence[51] led to 'the conclusion that the laying of the minefield which caused the explosions on October 22nd, 1946, could not have been accomplished without the knowledge of the Albanian Government'.[52]

The case went before the International Court on the basis of a Special Agreement, by the first part of which the following question was submitted to the Court:

Is Albania responsible under international law for the explosions which occurred on the 22nd October 1946 in Albanian waters and for the damage and loss of human life which resulted from them and is there any duty to pay compensation?

The Court's conclusion was this:[53]

The obligations incumbent upon the Albanian authorities consisted in notifying, for the benefit of shipping in general, the existence of a minefield in Albanian territorial waters and in warning the approaching British warships of the imminent danger to which the minefield exposed them. Such obligations are based, not on the Hague Convention of 1907, No. VIII, which is applicable in time of war, but on certain general and well-recognised principles, namely: elementary considerations of humanity, even more exacting in peace than in war; the principle of the freedom of maritime communication; and every State's obligation not to allow knowingly its territory to be used for acts contrary to the rights of other States.

[50] *I.C.J. Reports*, 1949, pp. 27–8, 30–1.
[51] Ibid., pp. 18–22. For example, the mines were part of a carefully laid pattern, and had been recently laid in a channel which had been previously swept.
[52] Ibid., p. 22.
[53] Ibid., pp. 22–3.

In fact, Albania neither notified the existence of the minefield, nor warned the British warships of the danger they were approaching.

But Albania's obligation to notify shipping of the existence of mines in her waters depends on her having obtained knowledge of that fact in sufficient time before October 22nd; and the duty of the Albanian coastal authorities to warn the British ships depends on the time that elapsed between the moment that these ships were reported and the moment of the first explosion.

On this subject, the Court makes the following observations. As has already been stated, the Parties agree that the mines were recently laid. It must be concluded that the minelaying, whatever may have been its exact date, was done at a time when there was a close Albanian surveillance over the Strait. If it be supposed that it took place at the last possible moment, i.e., in the night of October 21st–22nd, the only conclusion to be drawn would be that a general notification to the shipping of all States before the time of the explosions would have been difficult, perhaps even impossible. But this would certainly not have prevented the Albanian authorities from taking, as they should have done, all necessary steps immediately to warn ships near the danger zone, more especially those that were approaching that zone. When on October 22nd about 13.00 hours the British warships were reported by the look-out post at St. George's Monastery to the Commander of the Coastal Defences as approaching Cape Long, it was perfectly possible for the Albanian authorities to use the interval of almost two hours that elapsed before the explosion affecting *Saumarez* (14.53 hours or 14.55 hours) to warn the vessels of the danger into which they were running.

In fact, nothing was attempted by the Albanian authorities to prevent the disaster. These grave omissions involve the international responsibility of Albania.

The Court therefore reaches the conclusion that Albania is responsible under international law for the explosions which occurred on October 22nd, 1946, in Albanian waters, and for the damage and loss of human life which resulted from them, and that there is a duty upon Albania to pay compensation to the United Kingdom.

The Special Agreement also submitted to the Court the question whether the acts of the British vessels on 22 October 1946 violated Albania's sovereignty. The Court concluded that they did not.[54] The Albanian Government contended that passage of warships through the Strait could only take place with the previous authorization of that Government, since the Strait was not in legal terms an 'international strait'. The Court held that the North Corfu Strait fell within the class of international straits; that the passage of warships 'through straits used for international navigation between two parts of the high seas' without the previous authorization of the coastal State, was in accordance with international custom, provided that the passage was innocent;[55] and that on the facts the passage was innocent.[56]

In addition, the Court had two other tasks: the construction of the terms of the Special Agreement in order to decide whether the Court had jurisdiction to assess the amount of compensation due to the United

---

[54] *I.C.J. Reports*, 1949, pp. 26–32.   [55] Ibid., pp. 28–30.   [56] Ibid., pp. 30–2.

Kingdom,[57] and the question whether a minesweeping operation on 12 and 13 November 1946 (in the channel where the mining had occurred) constituted a violation of Albanian sovereignty.[58] Both questions were answered affirmatively.

The relatively compact judgment of the Court refers to a considerable number of important issues of international law, every one of which has great practical significance.[59] The questions related to the law of State responsibility, the law of international straits, problems of evidence in international law, the principles of the law of damages, the law concerning the use of force by States, and the interpretation of treaties. An unusual aspect of the case was the oral testimony by a total of ten witnesses and a general issue of evaluation of evidence.

The passages of the judgment concerning Albania's responsibility for the mining of the British warships on 22 October 1946 are often cited, and are of great interest.[60] The conditions under which a State may become responsible for sources of harm to other States arising within its territory have a wide range of reference. Problems arising from pollution, pirates and terrorist groups fall within the broad concept, familiar to English lawyers, of the 'adoption' of a nuisance. The case also shows how in the sphere of responsibility the law of evidence, and especially thinking about standards and burdens of proof, forms an important part of the judicial approach. It is worth recalling, by way of example, that the rule in *Rylands* v. *Fletcher* of common law systems can be stated in the form of a shifting of the burden of proof to the defendant. In this context the Court's pronouncements on recourse to inferences of fact and circumstantial evidence, indicating a half-way house between fault and strict liability, are notable.

Certain aspects of the Court's reasoning are open to doubt. This is particularly the case with the findings of the Court as to the 'innocence' of the British passage on 22 October 1946, and the Court's apparent assumption that it had to make an affirmative finding on the nature of the passage in order to justify the responsibility of Albania. The passage involved the affirmation of a right which was the very question in issue between the United Kingdom and Albania: the right of innocent passage through a strait, the North Corfu Strait, the legal status of which was the subject of controversy between Albania and the United Kingdom.[61] The mode of 'affirmation' was inevitably a form of self-help, and the Court's handling of this aspect of the episode wanted finesse.

---

[57] Ibid., pp. 23–6.

[58] Ibid., pp. 32–5.

[59] See Hersch Lauterpacht, *The Development of International Law by the International Court* (1958), pp. 87–90; Mervyn Jones, this *Year Book*, 26 (1949), pp. 447–53; Brownlie, *International Law and the Use of Force by States* (1963), pp. 283–9.

[60] See Brownlie, *System of the Law of Nations: State Responsibility*, i (1983), ch. iv.

[61] See Brüel, *Festschrift für Rudolf Laun* (1953), p. 259 at pp. 273–6.

2. Fisheries *case*[62]

The *Fisheries* case, brought by the United Kingdom against Norway by means of a unilateral application by virtue of the Statute of the International Court, was the second major piece of litigation since the war involving the United Kingdom, and once again Waldock was Counsel, together with Sir Eric Beckett, Sir Frank Soskice, Richard Wilberforce and David Johnson. The Norwegian team was led by Sven Arntzen (as Agent and Counsel) and Maurice Bourquin.

The twentieth century has seen two major international cases arising from disputes over access to fisheries. The first was the *North Atlantic Fisheries Arbitration*[63] of 1910 and the *Fisheries* case was the second. The role of the latter in the development of the customary law of the sea has been of the highest significance. In consequence, the decision of the International Court enjoys prominence in published works[64] and is frequently invoked in pleadings. It is the leading case in the law of the sea apart from the jurisprudence relating to the continental shelf. As the pleadings in the *Fisheries* case[65] indicate, it involved a great deal of law and, at the same time, a considerable volume of historical and other evidence. Expert advisers on hydrographic and other questions were in service on both sides.

In the course of the nineteenth century, competition in the North Sea fisheries grew sharper and in 1906 British steam trawlers first appeared off the coasts of Norway. As early as 1869 Norway had begun to extend her coastal jurisdiction by means of the use of straight baselines. This development culminated in a decree of 1935 which established a comprehensive system of straight baselines drawn between forty-eight specified base points either on the mainland or on islands and rocks. Eighteen of the baselines exceeded fifteen miles in length and one was forty-four miles long. In September 1948 the Norwegian Government began the strict enforcement of the decree of 1935 and this precipitated the United Kingdom application to the International Court.

Both sides entertained the possibility of claims for compensation arising from the facts of the case, but the case in fact proceeded on the single issue of the validity of the Norwegian system of baselines in terms of general international law. In English law terms it was an action for a declaration. The United Kingdom did not seek to contest the four-mile breadth of the

---

[62] *I.C.J. Reports*, 1951, p. 116. For commentary see Waldock, this *Year Book*, 28 (1951), p. 114; Fitzmaurice, ibid. 30 (1953), p. 8, and 31 (1954), p. 271; Johnson, *International and Comparative Law Quarterly*, 1 (1952), p. 145; Bourquin, *Acta Scandinavica Juris Gentium*, 22 (1952), p. 101; Evensen, *American Journal of International Law*, 46 (1952), p. 609; Wilberforce, *Grotius Society Transactions*, 38 (1952), p. 151; Lauterpacht, *The Development of International Law by the International Court* (1958), pp. 190-9. See also Waldock in the Cornelis van Vollenhoven Memorial Lecture, op. cit. above (p. 18 n. 48), pp. 8-10.

[63] *Reports of International Arbitral Awards*, vol. 11, p. 167.

[64] See O'Connell, *The International Law of the Sea*, vol. 1 (ed. Shearer) (1982), list of cases.

[65] International Court of Justice, *Pleadings, Oral Arguments, Documents, Fisheries* case (*United Kingdom v. Norway*), 4 vols.

Norwegian jurisdiction. Moreover, whilst the decree referred to a fisheries jurisdiction, in their arguments both parties assumed that it delimited the territorial sea. The litigation was exclusively concerned with the boundary between the high seas and the maritime territory of the coastal State,[66] and it was thus determinative of the permanent *status* of maritime territory and its economic value. In such litigation the public law or property aspect is dominant and matters of the highest significance become justiciable. No mere action for damages is involved.

The United Kingdom case was essentially as follows.[67] The extent of the territorial sea is regulated by general international law and the breadth of the territorial sea must be measured from the low-water mark on the land as the normal baseline. Certain exceptions to the low-water mark rule are recognized: in the case of bays with a closing line of ten miles or less and, otherwise, only in the case of bays and straits which can be claimed on historic grounds.[68] These positions on the substance of the law were accompanied by two sets of refined technical arguments. First, arguments were raised concerning the burden of proof on various issues.[69] Secondly, the United Kingdom produced carefully fashioned reasoning to demonstrate the practicality of establishing the *outer* limit of the territorial sea, as a belt of uniform breadth, on a rugged coast not by means of an exact image, the *tracé parallèle* method, but by the use of envelopes of arcs of circles, the *courbe tangente*.

The Norwegian position consisted in part of an attack on the legal rules invoked by the United Kingdom and their standing as rules of general international law. The positive aspect of the Norwegian case took the form of the formulation of certain vague principles governing delimitation: that 'a State's maritime territory is restricted to adjacent waters, namely to those waters which may be considered as accessory to the land'; and that 'waters accessory to the land are those waters which the coastal State has power to appropriate or occupy and in regard to which its legitimate interests justify its appropriation'.[70] The Norwegian case was also bolstered by the argument that the claim to waters affected by the decree of 1935 was in any case justified on the basis of historic title.[71] This position did not sit very happily with Norway's general strategy, which came close to denying the existence of any legal principles relating to delimitation of the territorial sea, since the role of historic title can only subsist against a background of *general* rules. The Norwegian reasoning in a sense avoided this logical difficulty by invoking the concept of occupation.[72]

[66] But there was also the question of the status of various areas as internal waters rather than territorial sea.

[67] For Waldock's part in the oral hearings see the *Pleadings*, vol. 4, pp. 394–418.

[68] For the fairly complex conclusions presented at the end of the oral reply by the Agent of the U.K. Government, see *I.C.J. Reports*, 1951, pp. 121–2.

[69] See Wilberforce, loc. cit. above (p. 22 n. 62), pp. 156–7; and Waldock, in reply to Norway, *Pleadings*, vol. 4, pp. 394–8.   [70] Norwegian counter-memorial, paras. 238–42.

[71] Ibid., paras. 537–75.   [72] See ibid., para. 242.

The Court was faced with two radically opposed conceptions of maritime delimitation. The United Kingdom view, expressed simply, involved insistence upon the territorial sea as a belt of uniform breadth, appurtenant to the coast as a geographical fact. Exceptions to this principle were to be kept within a narrow range. In particular, straight baselines could only be drawn across bays and could not be longer than ten miles. The Norwegian conception would give the coastal State a very wide discretion and involved criteria which were difficult to define objectively. Moreover, the Norwegian arguments, both generally and with reference to historic title, invoked geographical, economic and security considerations.[73] Judge Sir Arnold McNair in his dissenting opinion[74] referred to 'the difference between the subjective and objective views of the delimitation of territorial waters'.

The judgment of the Court was decisively in favour of Norway: her *system* of straight baselines was in accordance with general international law and, moreover, the *individual baselines* were held to be compatible with the system validated as such. The ten-mile rule for bays, supported by the United Kingdom, had 'not acquired the authority of a general rule of international law'.[75] The drawing of straight baselines was permissible provided certain conditions were fulfilled and, in particular, 'the drawing of baselines must not depart to any appreciable extent from the general direction of the coast'.[76] As to the outer limit of the territorial sea, the Court found that the arcs of circles method was 'not obligatory by law'.[77]

It cannot be doubted that the decision involved judicial legislation[78] and the principles governing straight baselines, somewhat tightened, are to be found in the Territorial Sea Convention of 1958 and the Law of the Sea Convention of 1982. In its reasoning the Court gave weight to two policies. On the one hand, the Court emphasized that delimitation of sea areas 'cannot be dependent merely upon the will of the coastal State as

---

[73] Norwegian counter-memorial, paras. 571–5.

[74] *I.C.J. Reports*, 1951, p. 169.

[75] Ibid., p. 131 (and see p. 129).

[76] Ibid., p. 133.

[77] Ibid., p. 129.

[78] But see Waldock's emollient view expressed in the Cornelis van Vollenhoven Memorial Lecture, op. cit. above (p. 18 n. 48), at p. 10: 'It is difficult to quarrel with Lauterpacht's view that the Court's pronouncements amounted to judicial legislation in that the law had never been formulated in such a way before. Even if at the 1930 Conference coastal archipelagos had been recognised as presenting a special problem, there is no indication of any proposal to deal with it on the lines adopted by the Court. On this point, however, the Judgment does not seem to be judicial legislation in the sense of travelling outside the proper scope of the judicial function. The written pleadings in the case had revealed a sufficiently impressive body of practice in regard to the use of straight base-lines on indented or island-fringed coasts to make Counsel alert the United Kingdom Government to the possibility that the Court might find in it evidence of a general practice. This was indeed the reason why the United Kingdom ultimately conceded that Norway might claim the benefit of a historic title to the waters of its fjords and sunds, as the Court would not then need to pronounce upon the general law regarding bays and islands. Accordingly, in deducing a general rule of customary law from the practice, the Court appears only to have exercised the normal function of an international tribunal, even if it may have done so in what some might call a "progressive" manner.'

expressed in its municipal law'.[79] At the same time the Court spoke of 'the close dependence of the territorial sea upon the land domain', and the requirement that baselines must not depart to any appreciable extent from the general direction of the coast.[80] On the other hand, the Court gave a significant role to 'geographic realities'[81] and 'adaptation rendered necessary by local conditions'.[82] In this same mode the Court invoked 'local requirements' and the consideration of 'certain economic interests peculiar to a region, the reality and importance of which are clearly evidenced by a long usage'.[83]

In a survey of the evolution of the law of the sea published in 1972, Judge Sir Robert Jennings, as he now is, wrote the following:

Looking back one can see very clearly that the turning point was the judgment of the International Court of Justice in the *Anglo-Norwegian Fisheries Case*; for the effect of that decision in loosening the grip of the old law about sea boundaries can hardly be overestimated. That judgment had the effect of detaching the territorial sea from the coast by making a major breach in the old tide-mark rule. It is true that the straight baseline method of delimiting the territorial sea was confined in its application to localities which were either deeply indented or having a fringe of islands; but this raises questions of degree and hence leaves room for subjective appreciation: a subjective appreciation which must, in the first place at least, be one for the coastal state itself to exercise. Moreover, by sanctioning in certain kinds of locality an egregious extension of internal waters, enclosed by straight baselines, the judgment laid the essential foundations for the present archipelago claims, which would make vast areas of seaway into internal waters with the result that even the inner limit of the territorial sea might be many miles out to sea.[84]

It is, of course, unfair to judge the advocacy in such a case in terms of the outcome. The United Kingdom did badly in many respects, losing both the fisheries and having some favourite legal principles discounted. However, the United Kingdom faced at least two difficulties. In the first place, she was the claimant procedurally. Secondly, the particular subject-matter—the geography of the Norwegian coast—presented special features which led the Court to favour a relatively flexible regime of delimitation. Given this penchant for flexibility, it may be that the United Kingdom arguments at least deterred the deployment of principles even more favourable to the coastal State. Certain it is that it is difficult to raise effective arguments before a tribunal which in fact is minded to produce significant innovations.

Before leaving this extraordinary case, two other facets of the judgment may be noticed. The judgment places significance upon 'geographical realities'[85] and 'the peculiar geography of the Norwegian coast'.[86] The

---

[79] *I.C.J. Reports*, 1951, p. 132.
[80] Ibid., p. 133.
[81] Ibid., p. 128; see also p. 139.
[82] Ibid., p. 133.
[83] Ibid.; see also p. 142.
[84] *Cambridge Law Journal*, 31 (1972B), p. 32 at p. 34.
[85] *I.C.J. Reports*, 1951, p. 128.
[86] Ibid., p. 139.

fact that a court refers to highly relevant background elements, such as geography, is hardly a matter for surprise. The difficulty which arises lies in the assumption that the geography of coasts, islands, straits and so on consists, so to speak, of mere data, which has an automatic and obvious relevance. On occasion this will be so, as in the case of the course of a navigational track in relation to a maritime boundary. More often it is not, and the reference to 'geographical' realities or circumstances is a confusing shorthand. 'Geographical realities' is a phrase containing assumptions about the *legal* relevance of coastal formations. In the context of delimitation, and especially maritime delimitation, the *realities* consist of the political, social and economic implications of the geography of an area: and it would be helpful if geography were not so readily invoked as a substitute for more precise and open analysis of a problem.

Another element which figures at critical junctures in the Court's reasoning is the attitude of third States, and 'the general toleration of the international community',[87] in face of the Norwegian system, embodying a method which 'had been consolidated by a constant and sufficiently long practice'.[88] These persistent references are unobjectionable in so far as they are part of an inquiry into the status of the Norwegian system in relation to general international law. Yet the tenor of the passages might lead to the conclusion that a certain prescriptive element is present and that the 'toleration' of third States is a diluted version of the historic title which had figured prominently in the Norwegian pleadings. This impression is enhanced by the reference to 'certain economic interests peculiar to a region, the reality and importance of which are clearly evidenced by long usage'.[89]

In an article in this *Year Book* Waldock produced a critique of the judgment.[90] In particular, he complained that the twenty-seven pages of judicial reasoning showed too great an economy in the treatment of important matters both of law and of fact, and he remarked that 'by erecting subjective factors into primary tests of claims to inland waters, the Court has materially strengthened the "will" of the coastal State as an element in the law and correspondingly weakened the "will" of other States as a check upon its claims'.

3. Barcelona Traction *case* (Second Phase)[91]

The litigation between Belgium and Spain began in 1958 when the Belgian Government first filed an application with the International Court

---

[87] *I.C.J. Reports*, 1951, pp. 136–7, 138–9.

[88] Ibid., p. 139.

[89] Ibid., p. 133. See also the passage relating to the Lopphavet, at p. 142.

[90] Vol. 28 (1951), p. 114; in particular at pp. 166–71.

[91] *I.C.J. Reports*, 1970, p. 3. For comment see Briggs, *American Journal of International Law*, 65 (1971), pp. 327–45; Lillich, ibid., pp. 522–32; Metzger, ibid., pp. 532–41; Caflisch, *Zeitschrift für ausländisches öffentliches Recht und Völkerrecht*, 31 (1971), pp. 162–96; C. de Visscher, *Revue belge de droit international*, 7 (1971), pp. 1–6; id., *Théories et réalités en droit international public* (4th edn.,

against the Spanish Government seeking reparation for damage allegedly caused to the Barcelona Traction, Light and Power Company, Limited, on account of acts said to be contrary to international law. These proceedings ended with a discontinuance. After failure of negotiations among the private interests, the Belgian Government submitted a new application in 1962, this time claiming in respect of damage allegedly sustained by Belgian nationals who were shareholders in the Barcelona Traction Company. The Spanish Government raised four preliminary objections to the Belgian application and in 1964 the International Court rejected two of the preliminary objections and joined the third and fourth to the merits.[92]

The written pleadings occupied some four years, and in 1969 oral hearings took place which occupied sixty-four public sittings.[93] In a judgment given in 1970 the Court held the Belgian claim to be inadmissible. The case was one of great dimension and this in several respects. The proceedings were lengthy, the documentation massive, and the written and oral pleadings very substantial. The facts were of great complication and the legal issues were of the first importance and related both to questions of admissibility and to issues of substantive law. The claim itself was for 200 million dollars and related to a group of companies worth more than this figure. The case produced considerable controversy both in respect of the application of the law by the Court and in respect of the procedure, which involved advocacy focused to a considerable extent on issues which the Court would set on one side.

Waldock was fortunate enough to be involved in this unusual litigation as Counsel for Spain. At the oral hearings in 1969, Belgium was represented by thirteen counsel and Spain by eighteen counsel or advocates. The private conclaves of practitioners are often enlivened by the reminiscences of those who took part in the *Barcelona Traction* case, the scale and complication of which achieved legendary proportions.

The leading roles in the controversy which led up to the international proceedings were taken by the Spanish Government and the group of foreign companies headed by Barcelona Traction. However, the allegations of fact included the assertion that a private group of Spanish nationals, including the industrialist Juan March, had been allowed to take advantage of the erroneous application of Spanish law by the Spanish courts, together with other favourable opportunities presented by the Spanish administrative authorities. The outcome—according to the Belgian Government—was the transfer of control of the group of

---

1970), pp. 303–5; Higgins, *Virginia Journal of International Law*, 11 (1971), pp. 327–43; various items, *Revista española de derecho internacional*, 23 (1971), nos. 2–3; Seidl-Hohenveldern, *Österreichische Zeitschrift für öffentliches Recht*, 22 (1971–2), pp. 255–309; Grisel, *Annuaire suisse de droit international*, 17 (1971), pp. 31–48; Mann, *American Journal of International Law*, 67 (1973), pp. 259–74.

[92] *I.C.J. Reports*, 1964, p. 6.

[93] International Court of Justice, *Pleadings, Oral Arguments, Documents, Barcelona Traction, Light and Power Company Limited* (New Application, 1962), 10 vols.

companies to Spanish interests, leading to the 'total despoliation' of the group. On this view of the circumstances, what occurred was a parallelism of action between the Spanish organs of State and certain private interests resulting not in expropriation to the Spanish State but in a despoliation of foreign assets in favour of Spanish private interests.

The Barcelona Traction Company was incorporated in Canada in 1911 and had its head office in Toronto. The company was a holding company and formed a number of subsidiary companies for the purpose of developing the production and distribution of electric power in the Spanish province of Catalonia. Some of the subsidiaries were incorporated under Canadian law and had registered offices in Canada; the others were incorporated under Spanish law and had registered offices in Spain. In the Belgian contention by the time of the outbreak of the Second World War the share capital of Barcelona Traction was in large part held by Belgian nationals, the principal shareholder being a Belgian company called Sidro.[94] During the Second World War large blocks of shares were transferred to nominees and were vested in a trustee, but in the Belgian Government's view these remained Belgian.

In the immediate post-war period the Spanish authorities refused to authorize foreign currency transfers to service sterling bonds which had been issued by the Barcelona Traction Company. As a consequence in 1948 three Spanish holders of recently acquired bonds brought bankruptcy proceedings in the court of Reus in the province of Tarragona. Within a matter of days a judgment was obtained declaring the company bankrupt. In fact the company had not received a judicial notice of the proceedings and was not represented before the Reus court. After an immense judicial battle, involving over 500 judgments, Barcelona Traction Company and the subsidiary companies failed to invalidate the declaration of bankruptcy. Eventually the Spanish trustees in bankruptcy sold the shares (in the form of newly created share certificates) to a newly formed company.

The despoliation of the assets of the Barcelona Traction group was completed in 1952. Apart from the incredible network of proceedings in the Spanish courts, what other recourse was available? Diplomatic representations were made by several foreign governments and by the Canadian Government in particular. Negotiations among the private interests concerned were also undertaken but without success.

At the level of diplomatic protection the Canadian Government clearly had *locus standi* in accordance with international law, since the Barcelona Traction Company was incorporated in Canada and had its head office in Toronto. A key point in the history is the reluctance of Canada to take any effective action after 1952. The result, given the failure of negotiations, was the application by the Government of Belgium acting on behalf of the

---

[94] The principal shareholder in Sidro was another company, Sofina, in which, it was alleged, Belgian interests were preponderant.

Belgian holders of shares in the Barcelona Traction Company. The proceedings were expected to deal with the merits but two preliminary objections were outstanding from the earlier phase of the case. The Spanish preliminary objections raised two issues: the proof of Belgian *locus standi* to act in respect of the shareholders in a non-Belgian company; and the failure of the company to exhaust local remedies. In addition, it was possible for Belgium to fail on the basis that she had not come up to proof on the Belgian character of the shares.[95]

The Court, by fifteen votes to one, held that as a general issue of law, Belgium had no legal capacity to act on behalf of the shareholders and, as a consequence of that finding, made no determination of any other legal issues or contentions of fact. The decision on the conditions in which the national State of shareholders in a foreign company may exercise diplomatic protection on their behalf was of the greatest importance. The Belgian Government had mounted some interesting arguments, based in part on conceptions of equity.[96] The Court was adamant in its insistence that the mechanism of the limited liability company should be respected: when the company is harmed what is affected is not the *rights* of the shareholders but a simple interest. The shareholders must look to the company and thence to the national State of the company for action. The shareholders would receive separate diplomatic protection only in two situations: (*a*) when the act complained of was aimed at the direct rights of the shareholder as such (for example, the right to a dividend); and (*b*) when the corporation had ceased to exist in law. The Court also referred to the possibility of diplomatic protection in the case where the corporation has the nationality of the defendant State but did not commit itself on the validity of this view of the law.[97]

The judgment was as to its reasoning supported by twelve judges but, in spite of this broad support, it provoked doubts and criticism. For example, Judge Sir Gerald Fitzmaurice had voted with the majority in holding the Belgian claim to be inadmissible, but expressed considerable reservations on significant issues of principle in a substantial separate opinion.[98] Fitzmaurice, with others, would have preferred to have wider bases of diplomatic protection in the case of shareholders. Moreover, he castigated 'the unsatisfactory state of the law that obliges the Court to refrain from pronouncing on the substantive merits of the Belgian claim, on the basis of what is really—at least in the actual circumstances of this case—somewhat of a technicality'.[99]

Aside from the two preliminary objections joined to the merits in the

---

[95] See the separate opinion of Judge Jessup, *I.C.J. Reports*, 1970, p. 161 at pp. 202 ff.

[96] For the Court's reaction: *I.C.J. Reports*, 1970, pp. 48–50, paras. 92–101. It may be noted that the oral arguments in the *Barcelona Traction* case were subsequent to judgment in the *North Sea* cases on 20 February 1969.

[97] *I.C.J. Reports*, 1970, p. 48.

[98] Ibid., pp. 64–113.

[99] Ibid., p. 64.

1964 proceedings, the Court was expected to deal with the merits of the Belgian claim. In the event and in the light of its finding that the applicant had no *jus standi*, there could be no findings on the substance of the complex and dramatic contentions to be found in the Belgian pleadings. The Belgian Government had faced the task of relating the highly sophisticated machinations ascribed to the Spanish judicial and administrative authorities, in conjunction with Spanish private interests, to established categories of international responsibility. The categories employed were as follows: abuse of rights (the improper, arbitrary and discriminatory attitude of certain administrative authorities); usurpation of jurisdiction (the exercise of jurisdiction in bankruptcy in respect of a Canadian company);[100] denials of justice *lato sensu* (manifest errors by the Spanish courts in the application of Spanish law); and denials of justice *stricto sensu* (disregard of the rights of the defence in the bankruptcy proceedings). The written and oral pleadings in the *Barcelona Traction* case form a rich mine of material on some important issues of State responsibility, prepared as they were by able counsel.

This heroic piece of litigation has many remarkable aspects. The economy of the case is much debated. For the Court the wrong applicant had appeared, in the face of clearly adverse indications in the law. For some the case was an embarrassment to advocates of judicial settlement, an exercise in futility. The case contains many difficult points of pleading and procedure, including the problem of the proper relation of the merits and the preliminary objections.[101] The proceedings provide a useful reminder that international disputes do not always fall along the simple polarities of a 'bipolar world'. Many States, including the applicant and respondent States in this case, are both exporters of capital and to a substantial degree also hosts to foreign capital. It is commendable to seek to identify the 'interests' lying behind the legal categories, but such interests may be complex and perhaps finely balanced. In any event many recent bilateral treaties relating to the protection of investments have stipulated for obligations directly related to the interests of shareholders.[102]

The decision in the *Barcelona Traction* case stirred up controversy, most of which was focused upon the issues of admissibility and the diplomatic protection of shareholders. Relatively neglected, and unjustifiably so, was the fascinating and important technical problem of the causes of action.[103] The Belgian Government had clearly faced some difficult problems in articulating the four causes of action which were intended to be applicable to various aspects of the conduct attributed to the respondent State. It is to be noted that the formulations in the written pleadings and in the final submissions during the oral proceedings show

---

[100] See the argument of Waldock, *Pleadings*, vol. 9, pp. 103–89.

[101] See Jiménez de Aréchaga, *American Journal of International Law*, 67 (1973), p. 1 at pp. 11–21; and Hambro, in Gross (ed.), *The Future of the International Court of Justice* (1976), p. 365 at p. 370.

[102] See Mann, this *Year Book*, 52 (1981), p. 241, for reference to recent British practice.

[103] For a general account of the problem see Brownlie, this *Year Book*, 50 (1979), p. 13.

some interesting variations. The tactical problems were numerous. Thus the reparation claimed was integral to the claim as a whole: aliquot parts were not related to different aspects of the four causes of action. Again, the placing of abuse of rights alongside other delictual categories is hazardous, since the assertion of abuse of rights involves a preliminary acceptance of the prima-facie legality of conduct, subject to the applicant's ability to prove *abuse*, which is no easy thing to do.

4. North Sea Continental Shelf *cases*[104]

The Governments of the Netherlands and the German Federal Republic, and of Denmark and the German Federal Republic, submitted issues concerning delimitation of the continental shelf in the North Sea to the International Court on the basis of their respective Special Agreements. The Court was not asked to draw a line but to decide 'what principles and rules of international law' were applicable to the delimitation of the shelf. The two cases were consolidated and the judgment which ensued was of enormous importance, forming the groundwork of the law relating to delimitation—and, indeed, to the entitlement of the coastal State—in respect of continental shelf. Waldock appeared as Counsel representing both the Netherlands and Denmark. The German agent was Professor Jaenicke.

The written pleadings in the *North Sea* cases[105] were of high quality and have been given close attention by counsel engaged in the conduct of international litigation. The oral proceedings were equally lively and, like the written pleadings, involved considerable and effective use of sketch-maps.

Although the *North Sea* cases concerned the particular situation of three adjacent States located on a concave coast, the pronouncements of the Court on the general legal philosophy of the continental shelf and other matters constituted a major contribution to the development of the law. The Special Agreement had provided that the German Federal Republic would submit a memorial and that would be followed by counter-memorials from Denmark and the Netherlands, and so forth. Thus the scene was set for the very attractive and innovative German argument. In the first place the German side asserted that the equidistance method was not a rule of customary law. This contention was buttressed by careful technical work to establish that in certain geographical circumstances the equidistance method produced unacceptable results. As to the content

[104] *I.C.J. Reports*, 1969, p. 3. For comment see Jennings, *International and Comparative Law Quarterly*, 18 (1969), pp. 819-32; Brown, *Current Legal Problems*, 23 (1970), pp. 187-215; Münch, *Zeitschrift für ausländisches öffentliches Recht und Völkerrecht*, 29 (1969), pp. 455-75; Monconduit, *Annuaire français de droit international*, 15 (1969), pp. 213-44; Friedmann, *American Journal of International Law*, 64 (1970), pp. 229-30; Grisel, ibid., pp. 562-93; Eustache, *Revue générale de droit international public*, 74 (1970), pp. 590-639; Goldie, *New York Law Forum*, 16 (1970), pp. 315-77.

[105] International Court of Justice, *Pleadings, Oral Arguments, Documents, North Sea Continental Shelf* cases, 2 vols.

of the law—since the Continental Shelf Convention of 1958 was not applicable between the parties—the German team argued that the State practice since 1945 showed that 'the principle of the just and equitable share was regarded as the overriding principle governing the delimitation of the continental shelf', and thus there should be a 'just and equitable apportionment' of the shelf in accordance with certain criteria. Various geographic and other factors were to be taken into account in order to achieve an 'equitable solution'.

For Denmark and the Netherlands, Waldock and his colleagues argued firmly that there was a mandatory rule of customary law, reflecting Article 6 of the Convention, according to which all continental shelf boundaries must be drawn by means of an equidistance line, unless special circumstances exist. The reference to special circumstances constituted an *exception* to the general rule, and such circumstances could only arise if *some exceptional feature*, such as a promontory, gives the State concerned an extent of continental shelf abnormally large in relation to the general configuration of its coast. In the contention of the Danish and Dutch counter-memorials there were no 'special circumstances' justifying a departure from the equidistance principle.

When the *dispositif*,[106] the operative part, of the judgment is perused

---

[106] *I.C.J. Reports*, 1969, p. 53, para. 101:

'101. For these reasons,

THE COURT,

by eleven votes to six,

finds that, in each case,

(A) the use of the equidistance method of delimitation not being obligatory as between the Parties; and

(B) there being no other single method of delimitation the use of which is in all circumstances obligatory;

(C) the principles and rules of international law applicable to the delimitation as between the Parties of the areas of the continental shelf in the North Sea which appertain to each of them beyond the partial boundary determined by the agreements of 1 December 1964 and 9 June 1965, respectively, are as follows:

(1) delimitation is to be effected by agreement in accordance with equitable principles, and taking account of all the relevant circumstances, in such a way as to leave as much as possible to each Party all those parts of the continental shelf that constitute a natural prolongation of its land territory into and under the sea, without encroachment on the natural prolongation of the land territory of the other;

(2) if, in the application of the preceding sub-paragraph, the delimitation leaves to the Parties areas that overlap, these are to be divided between them in agreed proportions or, failing agreement, equally, unless they decide on a régime of joint jurisdiction, user, or exploitation for the zones of overlap or any part of them;

(D) in the course of the negotiations, the factors to be taken into account are to include:

(1) the general configuration of the coasts of the Parties, as well as the presence of any special or unusual features;

(2) so far as known or readily ascertainable, the physical and geological structure, and natural resources, of the continental shelf areas involved;

(3) the element of a reasonable degree of proportionality, which a delimitation carried out in accordance with equitable principles ought to bring about between the extent of the continental

and compared with the German pleadings, it can be seen that the Court had been strongly attracted by the German arguments. Certainly, the Court rejected the 'just and equitable share' approach and insisted that the coastal State has an inherent entitlement to its 'natural prolongation', and not merely a right to a share of an as yet unapportioned whole. In the same context the Court pointed out that it was only 'areas of convergence' or 'marginal areas' that would require delimitation in accordance with equitable principles,[107] and emphasized that it was 'not a question of totally refashioning geography'.[108] None the less the Court essentially adopted the German view of the equidistance method and the role of equitable principles. The test is the Court's discounting of 'special circumstances' as an exception: once it ceased to be 'legally necessary' to prove the existence of special circumstances in order to justify not using the equidistance method, the equidistance method no longer ranks as a rule.[109] Thus equitable principles had been confirmed in place of the 'equidistance–special circumstances' rule put forward by Waldock on behalf of Denmark and the Netherlands.

The principles propounded by the Court in the *North Sea* cases are not easy to apply in practice. In spite of the rejection of the 'just and equitable share' approach, the Court has created an unresolved tension between the geographical data (no refashioning of geography) and the possibility of some level of adjustment on grounds of equity. The scale of such adjustment is controversial. If proportionality is employed as a dominant element, then the result appears to be an 'equitable apportionment'. Moreover, the superficial student may believe that the judgment writes down equidistance more than it really does. The same kind of tension can be detected in the relationship of the concept of natural prolongation, according to which rights arise *ipso facto* and *ab initio*, and the idea of equity.

As in the *Anglo-Norwegian Fisheries* case, Waldock had pleaded on the basis of the law as he saw it—and as many others at the relevant time also saw the law—when the Court was minded to make a change of direction, or at least to change the balance of the normative elements already in existence.[110] There can be little doubt that the Court let loose some unruly horses, and among these were the concept of natural prolongation, the role of equitable principles in maritime delimitation and the very loose concept of the 'balancing up' of the considerations 'which

shelf areas appertaining to the coastal State and the length of its coast measured in the general direction of the coastline, account being taken for this purpose of the effects, actual or prospective, of any other continental shelf delimitations between adjacent States in the same region.'

[107] Ibid., p. 49, para. 89; p. 52, para. 99; p. 53, para. 101, C (2).
[108] Ibid., p. 49, para. 91.
[109] Ibid., p. 45, para. 82.
[110] For some comment on the decision see the lecture given by Waldock for the Cornelis Van Vollenhoven Foundation, op. cit. above (p. 18 n. 48), at pp. 11-15.

States may take account of for the purpose of making sure that they apply equitable procedures'.[111]

It is a tribute to Waldock's professionalism and ability to be objective that, when in the *Anglo-French Continental Shelf* case the United Kingdom presented arguments very similar to those he had made as Counsel in 1969, Waldock, as arbitrator, rejected them.[112]

5. Beagle Channel *arbitration*[113]

In the years 1971 to 1976 the written and oral arguments took place in a major arbitration concerning the boundary between Chile and Argentina in the region of the Beagle Channel. The *Compromiso* or jurisdictional instrument was signed by representatives of the Governments of the United Kingdom, Chile and Argentina. The *Compromiso* provided for a Court of Arbitration consisting of five judges of the International Court (on an *ad hominem* basis).[114] The pleadings were extensive and were built upon substantial documentary and cartographic evidence. The issue was the interpretation of the first three articles of the famous Boundary Treaty of 23 July 1881, and the material relating to the negotiation of the Treaty and the subsequent conduct of the parties was complex.

The Chilean counsel at the outset of the case consisted of Waldock, Elihu Lauterpacht, Q.C., and Prosper Weil, and the distinguished agents were H. E. Señor Alvaro Bunster and H. E. Señor Don José Miguel Barros. This case was to be the last of Waldock's practice prior to his becoming a Judge of the International Court, and he was to leave the team at the end of the memorial stage of the pleadings, which were conducted on the basis of simultaneous exchange of written pleadings. The *Memorial of the Government of Chile*,[115] dated 1973, was to provide the framework of the Chilean presentation throughout the case, its strength deriving from the successful identification of key categories and the careful marshalling of a vast amount of detailed evidence. The soundness of the Chilean case was in due course to be confirmed by the decision and report of the Court of Arbitration in 1977. On 10 July 1978 the Court of Arbitration, in accordance with the *Compromiso*, declared that the award stood 'fully and materially executed' and repeated the view that the claim of the Argentine Government to reject the award was to be regarded 'as itself inadmissible and invalid'.[116]

---

[111] *I.C.J. Reports*, 1969, p. 50, para. 93.   [112] See below.

[113] Award of 18 April 1977: *Award of Her Britannic Majesty's Government* (H.M.S.O.) (Report and Decision of the Court of Arbitration); 52 I.L.R. 93; *International Legal Materials*, 17 (1978), p. 632; *Controversy Concerning the Beagle Channel Region, Award* (bilingual edn., Republic of Chile, 1977).

[114] Judges Dillard, Sir Gerald Fitzmaurice, Gros, Onyeama and Petrén. The Court elected Sir Gerald Fitzmaurice as its President.

[115] This consisted of three volumes: vol. i, *Memorial*; vol. ii, *Annexes*; vol. iii, *Documents relating to Acts of Jurisdiction*. In addition there was an impressive *Atlas*, which is a major contribution to the cartography of Latin America, and a volume entitled *Some Remarks Concerning the Cartographical Evidence*.

[116] *International Legal Materials*, 17 (1978), pp. 738, 1198, 1203.

VI. The European Commission of Human Rights, 1954–61: The Pioneer Stage of the European Convention on Human Rights

The European Convention on Human Rights was signed in Rome on 4 November 1950 and entered into force on 3 September 1953.[117] The Convention constituted a set of treaty standards which was in effect a Bill of Rights for those Members of the Council of Europe who became parties.[118] The guarantees of human rights were implemented by machinery consisting of the European Commission of Human Rights, the European Court of Human Rights and the Committee of Ministers of the Council of Europe. The most striking element in this machinery is the possibility of recourse to the Commission by means of applications by individuals in respect of alleged breaches of the Convention by Governments, provided the Government concerned has by declaration recognized the competence of the Commission. The Commission first acquired such competence on 5 July 1955, the right of individual recourse having been recognized by six countries with effect from that date.

Waldock had been elected as the United Kingdom member for a six-year term which expired in May 1960.[119] He was re-elected for a further term, but resigned in December 1961.[120] In December 1955 he was elected President of the Commission, and remained in the office until he left the Commission. His period of office coincided with the years when the Commission was picking up the threads of its responsibilities and solving various administrative and technical problems. The flow of individual applications was to increase gradually—and eventually became a flood. In addition, there was the possibility of proceedings brought by States against other parties to the Convention and, in the context of civil strife in Cyprus, the Government of Greece was to bring two sets of complaints against the United Kingdom. The size of the work-load which resulted is evident from Waldock's own papers and other sources, and it is to be recalled that the Commission has a duty to exercise good offices in order to effect a conciliation between the parties.

The European Convention and its machinery for the effective guarantee of standards of human rights has been a remarkable and wholly successful experiment. For the first time[121] individuals were provided with effective

---

[117] For references to the literature see Brownlie, *Basic Documents on Human Rights*, 2nd edn. (1981), p. 242.

[118] See Waldock in this *Year Book*, 34 (1958), p. 356 (speech, as President of the Commission, in Brussels on 3 September 1958).

[119] Membership of this body involved him in litigation on one occasion: see *Zoernsch* v. *Waldock*, [1964] 1 W.L.R. 675, an authority on the legal status of the Commission as an 'organ' of the Council of Europe. See further Bowett, this *Year Book*, 40 (1964), p. 372.

[120] He had been co-opted as a member of the International Law Commission earlier that year.

[121] An earlier experiment, the Central American Court of Justice, was less successful: see Hudson, *The Permanent Court of International Justice 1920–1942* (1943), pp. 42–70. The Central American Court was in existence from 1908 until 1918.

recourse against their own governments (and this without restriction on the basis of nationality). The decisions of the Commission and the Court would impart greater precision to the rights conferred and the derogations recognized. However, the perspective of 1983 is not the perspective of 1955, when the Commission began to function. In spite of the derogations included in the text, the arrangements for individual recourse seemed rather daring in the early days and some governments were apprehensive. Thus, the United Kingdom did not accept the competence of the Commission in respect of complaints by individuals until 1966. Such caution should not be viewed with the condescension which goes with hindsight. It is a notable characteristic of systems of recourse, such as that provided by the European Convention, that the resulting level of justiciability is inevitably high. Human rights standards, however modest they may be, involve the risk of putting in issue situations of the highest constitutional and political significance. During the early life of the Commission this proposition was exemplified by the Greek applications concerning British policies in Cyprus.[122] In later years the *Belgian Linguistics* case,[123] the complaints of the Republic of Ireland against the United Kingdom,[124] and of Cyprus against Turkey,[125] illustrate the same theme. The suggestion sometimes made by 'political scientists', that international law is only concerned with marginal issues, is based on ignorance.

No doubt Waldock's appointment to the Commission stemmed from the confidence which the Foreign Office had in him. In the event, it was a shrewd appointment. In its early years the Commission had to prove itself, both by being sufficiently effective to justify its existence, and at the same time by avoiding a stance which was too far ahead of the political market, thus deterring the appearance of new declarations accepting the competence of the Commission. To his tasks as President, Waldock brought great professionalism and a will to make the experiment work.[126] The results were good, and in later years the Commission built on this success, guided by another able British President, James Fawcett. The Commission and its work provide evidence of the specific contribution which lawyers can make to the protection of the rule of law by converting the airy and often prejudiced enthusiasms of politicians into practical and even-handed ways and means.

In the seven-year period of Waldock's membership, the Commission produced a store of experience which prefigured many of the elements in the later patterns of its work; but above all the first years involved problems of organization and working methods. Thus the Commission had to complete and adopt its rules of procedure, to urge the Council

---

[122] See below, p. 37.

[123] European Court of Human Rights, judgment of 23 July 1968, 45 I.L.R. 136.

[124] European Court of Human Rights, judgment of 18 January 1978, 58 I.L.R. 190.

[125] Decision of the Commission on admissibility, 10 July 1978, 62 I.L.R. 5.

[126] For Waldock's assessment of the work of the Commission in a speech of 1958, see this *Year Book*, 34 (1958), p. 356 at pp. 359-61.

of Europe to deal with the question of the privileges and immunities of its members,[127] and to keep the organization and operation of the Secretariat of the Commission under careful review.

(a) *The* Cyprus *Cases: emergency powers*

In connection with the civil strife in Cyprus and the response of the British authorities thereto, the Greek Government introduced two applications complaining of violations of the Convention for which the United Kingdom was responsible.[128] These two applications involved serious charges and a great deal of difficult work for the Commission on questions such as the legality of collective punishment. Both applications, having been declared admissible, were referred to a Sub-Commission of seven members, charged with ascertaining the facts and seeking a 'friendly settlement' in accordance with Articles 28 and 29 of the Convention. In both cases the United Kingdom appointed Waldock as 'a person of its choice' by virtue of Article 29.

As in earlier episodes in his professional life, the *Cyprus* cases involved very hard work in fact-finding and the first case led to a strenuous visit to the island. Apart from the fact-finding, the cases called for the resolution of significant issues of principle. Article 15 of the Convention operates 'in time of war or other emergency threatening the life of the nation' and authorizes a government to take measures derogating from certain of its obligations under the Convention to the extent strictly required by the exigencies of the situation. The provisions of Article 15 were extensively in issue in the *Cyprus* cases and the Commission had no doubt that it was competent to inquire into the United Kingdom Government's appreciation of the extent of the emergency and of the measures required to meet it.[129]

The Commission was also called upon to examine the justification of emergency powers in the *De Becker*[130] and *Lawless* cases.[131] In both the *Cyprus* case of 1956 and the *Lawless* case the Commission accepted that the respondent government had 'a certain measure of discretion', or 'a certain margin of appreciation' in assessing the means of responding to the exigencies of the situation.[132]

---

[127] And also of agents, advocates and advisers of the parties, witnesses and experts.

[128] European Commission of Human Rights, *Documents and Decisions*, 1955–7, p. 128; *Yearbook of the European Convention on Human Rights*, 2 (1958–9), pp. 174, 182 (Application No. 176/56), 178, 186 (Application No. 299/57).

[129] See Waldock, this *Year Book*, 34 (1958), p. 356 at p. 357.

[130] *Yearbook of the European Convention on Human Rights*, 2 (1958–9), p. 214.

[131] Ibid., p. 308 (decision on admissibility); ibid. 4 (1961), p. 438 (European Court). For the Report of the Commission see the *Lawless* case: *Publications of the European Court of Human Rights*, Series B, *Pleadings, Oral Arguments, Documents*, 1960–1, p. 9.

[132] See further Rosalyn Higgins, this *Year Book*, 48 (1976–7), p. 281 at pp. 296–301, and citations therein.

(b) *The* Lawless *Case: the role of the Commission before the European Court*[133]

In the course of the proceedings in the *Lawless* case, Waldock was associated with a major procedural innovation in the presentation of cases which are referred to the European Court of Human Rights by the Commission.

The European Court of Human Rights was set up at Strasbourg on 21 January 1959. Only States parties to the Convention, and the Commission of Human Rights, can bring cases before the Court (Articles 46–8) and its jurisdiction is compulsory only for those States making express declarations of acceptance (Article 46). The Committee of Ministers is an alternative instance in the scheme. The individual does not have access to the Court, yet he is, in substance, an interested party, a complainant, and obviously his case must be presented to the Court as well as that of the government against which he has brought his petition. The problem as to how this should be done was raised in the course of hearing preliminary objections in the first case brought before the Court, that of the petition of Lawless, an Irish citizen, against his government. This raised an important question as to the interpretation of Article 15 of the Convention, which gives States the right of derogating from their obligations under the Convention 'in time of war or other public emergency threatening the life of the nation'. In determining the questions of interpretation the Commission was divided and decided to refer the case to the Court for an authoritative decision in addition to transmitting its report to the Committee of Ministers. The Court had now to decide what was the role of the Commission in these circumstances. *Inter alia*, was the Commission to appear as a party to the proceedings? Was the Commission to act as the advocate of the individual applicant? And if it was not to act as his advocate, by what means, if at all, was the point of view of the applicant to be put to the Court?

In accordance with the rules of court and the Commission's rules of procedure the Commission appointed delegates to take part in the consideration of the case before the Court. Waldock acted as the principal delegate of the Commission, and in his opening address to the Court in the *Lawless* proceedings, he stated that it was impossible for the Commission to depart from its objectivity and impartiality or to identify itself either with the government or with the individual. On 30 March 1960 the Commission had adopted a new Rule 76 of its rules of procedure. Under this rule, when a case brought under Article 25 is subsequently referred to the Court, the Secretary of the Commission shall immediately notify the applicant, and, unless the Commission shall otherwise decide, the Secretary shall also in due course communicate to him the Commission's report, informing him that he may, within a time limit, submit to the

---

[133] The text of this account is taken from Brownlie, *Principles of Public International Law* (3rd edn., 1979), pp. 586–8.

Commission his written observations on the said report. The Commission will then decide what action to take in respect of the observations. In the *Lawless* proceedings the Commission communicated its report to the applicant and invited his observations thereon, with a view to transmitting them, if this was considered appropriate, to the Court as one of the Commission's documents in the case. In its memorial the Commission asked the Court to give leave for this to be done and also to give directions as to the right of the Commission to communicate to the Court the comments of the applicant in regard to matters arising in the proceedings. The Irish Government strongly objected to the procedure proposed and stated that the Commission 'attempts by a subterfuge to bestow on the individual the quality of a party before the Court'. The Court gave judgment on a variety of preliminary objections and questions of procedure on 14 November 1960. It accepted, implicitly at least, the validity of Article 76 of the Commission's rules of procedure. On the request of the Commission for leave to communicate to the Court the applicant's observations on its own report and on other points arising in the proceedings, the Court reserved the right to make a decision on these questions at a later date, as it had not at that time been able to examine the merits of the case. It did, however, remark that 'it is in the interests of the proper administration of justice that the Court should have knowledge of and, if need be, take into consideration, the applicant's point of view'.

Judgment on the merits was delivered on 1 July 1961. On the questions of procedure raised in a submission by the principal delegate of the Commission the Court gave judgment on 7 April 1961. *Inter alia*, the Court stated:[134]

Whereas in its judgment of 14th November 1960 the Court declared that there was no reason at this stage to authorise the Commission to transmit to it the written observations of the Applicant on the Commission's Report:

Whereas in the said Judgment . . . the Court has recognised the Commission's right to take into account [*de faire état*] the Applicant's views on its own authority, as a proper way of enlightening the Court;

Whereas this latitude enjoyed by the Commission extends to any other views the Commission may have obtained from the Applicant in the course of the proceedings before the Court;

Whereas, on the other hand, the Commission is entirely free to decide by what means it wishes to establish contact with the Applicant and give him an opportunity to make known his views to the Commission;

Whereas in particular it is free to ask the Applicant to nominate a person to be available to the Commission's delegates;

Whereas it does not follow that the person in question has any *locus standi in judicio*.

For these reasons,

[134] *Publications of the European Court of Human Rights*, Series A, *Judgments and Decisions*, 1960–1; see 31 I.L.R. 290 at pp. 291–2.

Decides unanimously:

... that at the present stage the written observations of the Applicant ... are not to be considered as part of the proceedings in the case;

... that the Commission has all latitude, in the course of debates and in so far as it believes they may be useful to enlighten the Court, to take into account the views of the Applicant concerning either the Report or any other specific point which may have arisen since the lodging of the Report;

... that it was for the Commission, when it considered it desirable to do so, to invite the Applicant to place some person at its disposal (in order to make known to the Court the Applicant's point of view on any specific points arising in the course of the debates), subject to the reservations indicated above.

VII. The International Law Commission: the Codification of the Law of Treaties

With effect from the thirteenth session in 1961, Waldock became a member of the International Law Commission of the United Nations, and was re-elected on three occasions, eventually ceasing to be a member in 1972 on his election as a Judge of the International Court. He was appointed General Rapporteur of the Commission[135] in 1963 and Chairman in 1967. In the years 1961 to 1966 he was Special Rapporteur on the Law of Treaties and was appointed Expert Consultant at the United Nations Conference on the Law of Treaties held at Vienna in 1968 and 1969. In 1967 Waldock was appointed Special Rapporteur to deal with State Succession in respect of Treaties.

He found himself on the Commission at a time when that body had the benefit of a particularly significant agenda and was enjoying what may come to be seen as its heyday, encompassing major projects in the codification and progressive development of international law. At this period the Commission had a conspicuously distinguished membership, with a preponderance of persons well qualified in public international law and with significant practical experience.[136] The Commission[137] had had a rather poor start in 1949, focusing on an agenda of unpromising subjects, but had picked up considerably later on, preparing, *inter alia*, the drafts on

---

[135] The General Rapporteur is elected each session to prepare the Report on the work of the session, which as a matter of practice is submitted to the General Assembly of the United Nations.

[136] In 1962 the membership was as follows: Mr. Roberto Ago (Italy); Mr. Gilberto Amado (Brazil); Mr. Milan Bartoš (Yugoslavia); Mr. Herbert W. Briggs (U.S.A.); Mr. Marcel Cadieux (Canada); Mr. Erik Castrén (Finland); Mr. Abdullah El-Erian (United Arab Republic); Mr. Taslim Elias (Nigeria); Mr. André Gros (France); Mr. Eduardo Jiménez de Aréchaga (Uruguay); Mr. Victor Kanga (Cameroon); Mr. Manfred Lachs (Poland); Mr. Liu Chieh (China); Mr. Antonio de Luna García (Spain); Mr. Luis Padilla Nervo (Mexico); Mr. Radhabinod Pal (India); Mr. Angel Paredes (Ecuador); Mr. Obed Pessou (Dahomey); Mr. Shabtai Rosenne (Israel); Mr. Abdul Hakim Tabibi (Afghanistan); Mr. Senjin Tsuruoka (Japan); Mr. Grigory Tunkin (U.S.S.R.); Mr. Alfred Verdross (Austria); Sir Humphrey Waldock (U.K.); Mr. Mustafa Kamil Yasseen (Iraq) (*Yearbook of the International Law Commission*, 1962, vol. 1, p. vii).

[137] See generally Briggs, *The International Law Commission* (1965); id., *Recueil des cours*, 126 (1969-I), pp. 242–316; Ramcharan, *The International Law Commission* (1977).

which were based the Law of the Sea Conventions of 1958 and the Vienna Convention on Diplomatic Relations of 1961.

The Commission is undoubtedly the most useful mechanism for the revision of international law ever devised. It has been far more successful than the procedures of codification employed by the League of Nations.[138] Drafts are carefully prepared, and considerable effort is made to take into account the views of governments on the provisional draft. As a consequence the practical aspect of things, and the working context, are faced up to and the subsequent diplomatic conference is provided with a set of realistic and well-prepared articles, accompanied by helpful commentaries which represent the collective view of the Commission.

In this procedure the role of the Special Rapporteur is obviously critical. A number of Waldock's colleagues on the Commission have given the writer accounts of Waldock's ability to draw a diversity of views together and to isolate particular areas of difficulty. His output was prodigious and the six Reports on the Law of Treaties prepared by Waldock,[139] together with the final Report of the Commission to the General Assembly,[140] constitute Waldock's principal published work, and remain as a major source of the law of treaties. It is to be recalled that Waldock succeeded Fitzmaurice as Special Rapporteur and was able to produce drafts which had a markedly more practical aspect than the impressive but highly involved work of his predecessor.

When it finally emerged, the Vienna Convention on the Law of Treaties was the culmination of a sustained and arduous process to which Waldock made the key contribution, being able to bring to it a rare combination of legal scholarship, practical sense and diplomatic skill.[141] An important part of Waldock's success on the Commission undoubtedly lay in his capacity to reconsider his first view and to avoid insisting on some preconceived personal or national viewpoint. Everything had to be hammered out on the anvil of practice and principle. Thus in the context

---

[138] See the excellent article by Rosenne, this *Year Book*, 36 (1960), p. 104, especially at pp. 144–8.

[139] *Yearbook of the International Law Commission*, 1962, vol. 2, p. 27; 1963, vol. 2, p. 36; 1964, vol. 2, p. 5; 1965, vol. 2, p. 3; 1966, vol. 2, p. 1; ibid., p. 51.

[140] Ibid., 1966, vol. 2, p. 169 at pp. 173–274.

[141] Judge Sir Robert Jennings has observed: 'He made a major contribution to the development of international law, not only in his teaching and writing. He was always a practical man, interested first and last in results. Anyone further removed from the stage image of the don as a talker and arm-chair commentator, it would be difficult to imagine. And it must be a question whether any other individual has, so to speak with his own hands, made so important a contribution to the practical development of international law, as Waldock did; to take only one example, in the Vienna Convention on the Law of Treaties. Certainly the groundwork was splendidly laid down by his three distinguished British predecessors who were Special Rapporteurs on the Law of Treaties to the International Law Commission. But it was Waldock who moved the machine into producing practical results, first as Special Rapporteur to the International Law Commission from 1962–6, and then as Expert at the Vienna Conference on the Law of Treaties 1968 and 1969. The exercise involved at least two highly politicised questions that were strenuously disputed between governments. But the Convention emerged, and even before it came formally into operation it was generally regarded as the primary source of law on the subject.' (An Address delivered on the occasion of the Memorial Service at the University Church of St. Mary the Virgin, Oxford, 17 October 1981.)

of the law of treaties the position adopted by Waldock was by no means a reflection of received British opinion, either academic[142] or official.[143] In assessing the achievement involved in the adoption of the Vienna Convention on the Law of Treaties, it must be remembered that certain significant facets of the instrument, as of the draft articles of the Commission, involved matters with important political implications.[144] This was true, in particular, of the provisions relating to the invalidity, termination and suspension of the operation of treaties and the procedure for the settlement of disputes.

In 1967 Waldock began his work as Special Rapporteur on succession of States in respect of treaties, and he presented five reports on the subject.[145] He was eventually replaced on the Commission by Sir Francis Vallat, who also became Special Rapporteur in his place.[146] The work led in due course to a diplomatic conference, which adopted the Vienna Convention on Succession of States in respect of Treaties on 22 August 1978.[147] This subject is notoriously recalcitrant and the solutions produced by the Commission have been the object of criticism in some quarters.[148] The difficulties of the topic are indicated by the fact that the thinking of Waldock (and the Commission) and the 'opposition' consisting of O'Connell (and the International Law Association) evolved in such a way as to achieve certain similarities. The 'clean slate' approach favoured by the Commission at an earlier stage was replaced by a greater inclination toward a regime of treaty continuity in 'non-colonial' contexts.[149] At the end of the day both the 'clean slate' school and the 'continuity' school had to attempt to come to terms with the need for a certain flexibility. It may well be that O'Connell was justified in his view that the subject was not yet suitable for codification.[150]

Waldock's time on the Commission included the year 1969, which was a sort of *annus mirabilis* for him, for in the spring and summer of that year he was coping with his tasks as a member of the Commission, his appointment as Expert Consultant at the Vienna Conference on the Law of Treaties, his duties as Counsel for the Government of Spain in the *Barcelona Traction* case[151] and his duties in Oxford.

[142] Cf. Brierly, *Law of Nations* (5th edn., 1955), pp. 243-72.
[143] See the views of the U.K. Government, reported in Sinclair, *The Vienna Convention on the Law of Treaties* (1973), *passim*.
[144] See the *United Nations Conference on the Law of Treaties*, Second Session, Vienna, 9 April–22 May 1969, *Official Records, Summary Records of the Plenary Meetings and of the Meetings of the Committee of the Whole* (1970).
[145] *Yearbook of the International Law Commission*, 1968, vol. 2, p. 87; 1969, vol. 2, p. 45; 1970, vol. 2, p. 25; 1971, vol. 2 (pt. i), p. 143; 1972, vol. 2, p. 1.
[146] Ibid., 1974, vol. 2 (pt. i), p. 3.
[147] *International Legal Materials*, 17 (1978), p. 1488.
[148] For example, Brownlie, *Principles of Public International Law* (3rd edn., 1979), p. 666; and O'Connell in Bos (ed.), *The Present State of International Law and other Essays* (1973), pp. 331–8.
[149] This evolution is traced by Crawford, this *Year Book*, 51 (1980), p. 1 at pp. 31–44.
[150] Quoted by Crawford, loc. cit. (previous note), p. 44.
[151] See the *Pleadings* in the *Barcelona Traction* case, vol. 9, p. 103.

VIII. On the Bench: I. The European Court of Human Rights

Waldock was elected a Judge of the European Court of Human Rights in 1966, becoming its Vice-President in 1968 and President in 1971.[152] This high judicial office was not full-time, and was not regarded as incompatible with the discharge of other duties. It was Waldock's first judicial experience, although it had been prefigured by his membership of the European Commission of Human Rights. The Court had started to function in 1959, and Lord McNair had been the first British Judge and also the first President of the Court.

During the seven years which coincided with Waldock's office the Court decided eight different cases, although certain of these were dealt with at more than one procedural phase. A proportion of the cases were considered by a chamber which did not include Waldock. In the cases of *Delcourt*[153] and *Ringeisen* (Interpretation of Judgment)[154] the chambers constituted included President Waldock. At no juncture did Waldock deliver or participate in a separate or dissenting opinion.

It is true to say that it has been since 1974, when Waldock's term expired, that the Court has had the most striking calendar of business, including inter-State and other cases affecting the United Kingdom Government. In the earlier period of its existence the tempo was slow and, apart from the *Belgian Linguistics* case,[155] the cases were not of great interest. At the same time some important work was done. In a series of cases the Court asserted the incompatibility of certain long-tolerated forms of pre-trial detention with the European Convention.[156] The fair trial guarantee of Article 6 of the Convention was in issue in several cases,[157] and for the first time the application of the compensation provisions of Article 50 was considered.[158] The Court also gave attention to the question of simplifying the procedure set up by the Convention, and for this purpose a Working Party, of which Waldock was a member, was set up in 1972.

In retrospect the two most significant cases were the *Belgian Linguistics* case[159] and the *Vagrancy* cases.[160] The former case demonstrates the way in which the statement of the rights of the individual inevitably renders justiciable very large and sensitive questions involving the legal and political status of whole communities. The applicants had raised specific

---

[152] His term of office expired on 20 January 1974.
[153] *Publications of the European Court of Human Rights*, Series A, No. 11.
[154] Ibid., No. 16.
[155] Ibid., Nos. 5, 6.
[156] *Wemhoff*, ibid., No. 7; *Neumeister*, ibid., No. 8; *Stögmüller*, ibid., No. 9; *Ringeisen*, ibid., No. 13. See also *Matznetter*, ibid., No. 10.
[157] *Delcourt*, ibid., No. 11; *Ringeisen*, ibid., No. 13.
[158] *Vagrancy* cases, ibid., No. 14; *Ringeisen*, ibid., No. 15; *Neumeister*, ibid., No. 17.
[159] Ibid., Nos. 5, 6.
[160] Ibid., No. 12.

matters concerning the equality of provision for the education of children in the language of the family: in the Belgian context this involved the largest issue in national political life, the relationship of the Walloon and Flemish linguistic communities. Belgium as respondent invoked a preliminary objection to the Court's competence *ratione materiae* in a case which, on any view, raised the issue of the reserved domain of domestic jurisdiction in a striking form.[161] The Court rejected the Belgian objection in these words:[162]

Whereas, furthermore, resort to the notion of the reserved domain, which the Belgian Government has put forward as another aspect of the same preliminary objection of incompetence (second memorial, paras. I, 5 and II, 2), equally concerns the merits and therefore cannot lead to any different result; whereas the Government seeks, in fact, by invoking this notion, to demonstrate the absence in this case of any factor relating to the Convention; whereas the Court is unable to agree with this reasoning; whereas the Convention and the Protocol, which relate to matters normally falling within the domestic legal order of the Contracting States, are international instruments whose main purpose is to lay down certain international standards to be observed by the Contracting States in their relations with persons under their jurisdiction (Article 1 of the Convention); whereas the jurisdiction of the Court extends to all cases concerning the interpretation and application of those instruments (Article 45 of the Convention); whereas, as explained above, the present case concerns the interpretation and application of those instruments; whereas, therefore, the Court cannot in the circumstances regard the plea based upon the notion of reserved domain as possessing the character of a preliminary objection of incompetence; . . .

In its decision on the merits in the *Linguistics* case the Court analysed the concept of discrimination in terms of certain articles of the Convention, making a major contribution to the jurisprudence of human rights.[163] In the *Vagrancy* cases the Court gave careful consideration to the application of the provisions of paragraph 4 of Article 5 of the Convention, according to which 'everyone who is deprived of his liberty by arrest or detention shall be entitled to take proceedings by which the lawfulness of his detention shall be decided speedily by a court and his release ordered if the detention is not lawful'.[164]

From its inception the Court had to give thought to the general approach to the interpretation of the Convention. On this question Waldock gave expression to his views in a paper published in 1980, and the key passages are as follows:[165]

The first is the question whether we are to regard the Convention primarily as a treaty or as a form of 'constitution'—a question apparently at the root of some

[161] *Publications of the European Court of Human Rights*, Series A, No. 5.
[162] Ibid., p. 19.
[163] For a convenient source: 45 I.L.R. 136 at pp. 163–6, 173–4, 180–1, 186, 199–201, 216–17.
[164] *Publications of the European Court of Human Rights*, Series A, No. 12, pp. 39–44.
[165] *Human Rights Law Journal*, 1 (1980), p. 1 at pp. 2–5. See also Waldock in *Mélanges offerts à Paul Reuter* (1981), p. 535 at pp. 542–7.

recent differences in the interpretation of certain provisions. The true answer, I suspect, is that the nature of the Convention is ambivalent. In 1958, on Council of Europe Day at the Brussels Exhibition, it fell to me as President of the Commission to deliver a speech reviewing the operation of the Convention up to that time.[166] In that speech, I laid stress upon the Convention as a European Bill of Rights, maintaining that it was this aspect of the Convention which was supremely important. I added however: 'But the very word "Convention" serves as a warning that our Bill of Rights may have the features more of European international than of European constitutional law.' I did so, of course, because the treaty-basis of the instrument finds clear and even sharp expression in some of its provisions: notably, in the optional nature of the provisions concerning acceptance both of the right of individual petition and of the compulsory jurisdiction of the Court, in the obligation to renounce recourse to other procedures for the settlement of disputes, and in the provisions regarding signature, ratification, reservations, denunciation and the depositary functions of the Secretary-General.

On the other hand, as the Commission expressly held in the *Pfunders* case[167] between Austria and Italy in 1961, the objective, constitutional character of the great bulk of the dispositive provisions of the Convention is equally evident in their language and in that of the Preamble. *Inter alia*, the Commission there stated that:

> 'the obligations undertaken by the High Contracting Parties in the Convention are essentially of an objective character, being designed rather to protect the fundamental rights of individual human beings from infringement by any of the High Contracting Parties than to create subjective and reciprocal rights for the High Contracting Parties themselves'.

That statement, in the framing of which I had some hand, is not, I believe, controversial. As I understand them, the differences of opinion that have appeared in some recent cases relate rather to the conclusions to be drawn from that finding when interpreting the Convention, and more especially the rights and freedoms in Section 1.

The differences of approach to the interpretation of the Convention have arisen in two separate, if related, contexts. One is the question of the effect to be given to an evolution in European legal or social concepts in determining the meaning and scope of any particular right or freedom at any given time. The other is the conditions under which a secondary or ancillary right or freedom, not referred to in the Convention, may properly be regarded as 'necessarily inherent' and therefore 'implied' in one of the rights or freedoms specifically mentioned in Section 1. In these contexts appeal has been made to the rules for the interpretation of treaties set out in Articles 31 and 32 of the Vienna Convention on the Law of Treaties in support of both approaches: that is, both to support giving primacy to the actual terms of the Convention and to support a 'dynamic' interpretation of its provisions by reference to its object and purpose. But these articles do not give primacy either to the text or to the object and purpose. On the contrary, they unequivocally require that the text shall be taken together, and in conjunction,

---

[166] Reproduced in this *Year Book*, 34 (1958), pp. 356–63.
[167] *Yearbook of the European Convention on Human Rights*, 4 (1961), pp. 138–42.

with the object and purpose. The terms of the treaty are to be interpreted in good
faith in their context and in the light of its object and purpose.

The Vienna Convention does not deal specifically either with the effect of an
evolution in legal concepts, the so-called inter-temporal law, or with the limits
within which terms may properly be implied in a treaty as necessarily inherent
in it. The International Law Commission's commentary,[168] however, which I
myself wrote, stated that, in its view, both these points are to be considered as
covered by the requirement of interpretation 'in good faith'. With regard to both
points, it explained that so much depends on the particular context, and on the
intention of the parties in the particular treaty, that it would be difficult to lay
down any general rules. In other words, these questions can be resolved only
through the normal interpretation of the terms of the treaty in good faith in the
light of its object and purpose.

The recent differences of opinion can hardly therefore have their source in the
principles of interpretation laid down in the Vienna Convention. Indeed, the
principle that the content of a right or freedom may evolve with a change in legal
and social concepts within the Council of Europe does not seem, in itself, to be in
dispute. Applied specifically by the Court as a basis of its decisions in the *Tyrer*[169]
and *Marckx*[170] cases, its general relevance seems also to have been recognised in
cases like *Engel*[171] and *Airey*.[172] The principle of implying secondary or ancillary
rights, as being inherently necessary to the effectiveness of a right or freedom set
out in the Convention, has likewise been acted on by the Court in a whole series of
cases beginning with the *Belgian Linguistic case*[173] in 1968. In regard to both principles, the differences of opinion seem rather to concern the legitimacy of their
application in particular contexts in certain cases. The instances I have in mind
are the differences as to the consequences to be drawn in the *Tyrer* and *Marckx*
cases from the evolution of legal concepts regarding respectively corporal punishment and the treatment of illegitimacy and the differences in the *Golder* and *Airey*
cases regarding the propriety of implying from the right to a fair hearing
secondary rights, in the one case, to see a solicitor, and in the other, to receive legal
aid. Underlying the differences of opinion in these cases, however, there does
seem to be a divergence of view concerning the acceptable limits of the judicial
function in interpreting the Convention. Critics of the decisions in those cases
argue that in them the Court transgressed the boundary between interpretation
and legislation. In the Court's view, on the other hand, those decisions justify
themselves as interpretations of the provisions in question in the light of the object
and purpose of the Convention.

It is no part of my purpose to make any comment upon the correctness or otherwise of the interpretation arrived at by the Court and the Commission in those
cases. My concern to-day with the dynamic approach of the Commission and the
Court to the interpretation of the Convention in those cases is merely as an aspect
of the distribution of functions and powers between the Court and the national

[168] *Yearbook of the International Law Commission*, 1966, vol. 2, pp. 219, 222.
[169] Series A, No. 26, pp. 15–16.
[170] Series A, No. 31, pp. 19–20.
[171] Series A, No. 22, p. 30.
[172] Series A, No. 32, pp. 14–15.
[173] Series A, No. 6, p. 31; see also *Golder*, Series A, No. 18, pp. 16–18; *National Union of Belgian
Police*, Series A, No. 19, p. 18; *Swedish Engine Drivers' Union*, Series A, No. 20, p. 15; *Schmidt and
Dahlström*, Series A, No. 21, p. 15; *Airey*, Series A, No. 32, pp. 13, 15–16.

authorities of Member States under the Convention. I should, however, like to stress that the position adopted by the Commission and the Court in those cases in regard to interpretation of the Convention can be fully appreciated only in the light of their whole approach to the distribution of functions and powers between them and national authorities.

The Court has constantly disclaimed any power to determine the particular measures which should be taken in national systems to comply with the Convention. In the *Belgian Linguistic* case[174] the Court underlined 'the subsidiary nature of the international machinery of collective enforcement established by the Convention' and the impropriety of its attempting to 'assume the rôle of the national authorities'. It then observed:

'The national authorities remain free to choose the measures which they consider appropriate in those matters which are governed by the Convention. Review by the Court concerns only the conformity of these measures with the requirements of the Convention'.

Similar observations occur in some other cases,[175] but it is in connection with the doctrine of the State's 'margin of appreciation' that the Court has most fully developed its ideas concerning its relation to national authorities under the Convention.

It should be recalled that Waldock's successor on the bench of the European Court, Sir Gerald Fitzmaurice, was to have very strong reservations in face of the Court's judicial policy and believed that a proper balance had not been achieved in the application of the standards of the Convention.[176]

IX. On the Bench: II. The International Court of Justice

Waldock took up his office as Judge of the International Court in 1973, leaving behind a substantial practice and laying down his work as a member of the International Law Commission, as Chichele Professor at Oxford, and as Editor of this *Year Book*. The completion of his nine-year term on the Court in 1982 was prevented by his sudden death at The Hague on 15 August 1981. He became President of the Court in 1979. His translation to the Court was a fitting and natural development in his career as an international lawyer, and he was to discharge his responsibilities in accordance with the best standards. At the time of his death the written pleadings in the *Tunisia–Libya Continental Shelf* case[177] had been completed and the oral hearings were awaited. At the same period it was in the wind that Waldock would be asked to act as President, should a

[174] Series A, No. 6, pp. 34–5.

[175] e.g. *National Union of Belgian Police*, Series A, No. 19, p. 20; *Swedish Engine Drivers' Union*, Series A, No. 20, p. 15; *Schmidt and Dahlström*, Series A, No. 21, p. 16.

[176] See *Golder*, Series A, No. 18; *National Union of Belgian Police*, ibid., No. 19; *Marckx*, ibid., No. 31; and further in Bernhardt (ed.), *Festschrift für Hermann Mosler* (1983), p. 203.

[177] *I.C.J. Reports*, 1982, p. 18.

chamber of the Court be constituted to hear the *Gulf of Maine* case between Canada and the United States.

It is difficult and, indeed, artificial to attempt to quantify the contribution of an individual to the performance of what is by definition a collegiate activity, more especially as Waldock did not persistently produce separate or dissenting opinions. In spite of a strong character, his inclination was, without doubt, to produce a well-supported judgment of the Court which would carry the necessary authority and persuasiveness. Nor can it be doubted that in his role as President he did his best to develop cohesion and a reasoned consensus.

President Elias has described his colleague on the Court in these terms:[178]

All those who had the opportunity of working with him in The Hague admired his enormous industry, his direct grasp of the issues in a case, and his gift of lucid exposition and drafting. Despite the traditional anonymity surrounding the drafting of the Court's decisions, no reader of Sir Humphrey's vigorous separate or dissenting opinions will doubt the extent of his contribution to the formulation of the Court's decision in cases where he was on the side of the majority.

Behind the orderly process of discussion and debate which he was the first to safeguard and promote, one could always detect from the look, the posture—and occasionally a sigh—a chafing eagerness to press on.

The institution of which Waldock had become a part is 'the principal judicial organ' of the United Nations. As such the Court has to lead two lives. In one manifestation it renders services to the organs of the United Nations and the specialized agencies by way of advisory opinions, and is in some sense integrated in the organization.[179] In its other role it is an independent international tribunal, which is the reference in many jurisdictional clauses and also in Special Agreements (*Compromis*) on the basis of which inter-State disputes are referred to the Court. It is common knowledge that the Court exists in an unfavourable climate.[180] For long it was fashionable to assume that the reasons for this lay within the Court; and thus critics focused upon the regional and cultural elements represented on the Court and the possibilities of procedural reform. However, in the 1970s the composition of the Court was difficult to fault on regional and cultural grounds, and the Rules of Court had been revised in 1972 and again in 1978.[181] The fact is that the true causes of non-recourse to the Court lie in the non-judicial habit of States and the general conditions of international relations.[182]

---

[178] A Tribute by Acting President Elias, on the occasion of the Memorial Service at the University Church of St. Mary the Virgin, Oxford, 17 October 1981.

[179] See Judge Lachs, *Liber Amicorum Adolf F. Schnitzer* (1979), p. 269.

[180] See generally Gross (ed.), *The Future of the International Court of Justice* (1976), 2 vols.

[181] *International Legal Materials*, 11 (1972), p. 899, and 17 (1978), p. 1286. See further International Court of Justice, *Note by the Registry on the Revised Rules of Court* (1978).

[182] See Kearney, Rovine and Fitzmaurice in Gross, op. cit. above (n. 180), pp. 105, 313, 461, respectively.

In general the role of the International Court, and of international adjudication in general, is as substantial as States allow it to be. Far too much is expected of judicial activity and most international law is naturally applied out of court. At the same time international tribunals, including the Court, deal with a calendar of major cases, especially concerning delimitation, the subject-matter of which would rarely be justiciable within national legal systems.[183] Much useful and difficult work is done but is ignored more or less totally by the media.

The basic conditions of existence of the International Court do not change much from decade to decade, but in the period from 1973 to 1981 the life of the Court was in some ways particularly fraught, and Waldock's service on the bench occurred at a very testing time. Instead of having a calendar of disputes which both parties genuinely wished to have decided on the merits, the Court was bedevilled by a set of circumstances and a series of episodes which, looked at in retrospect and cumulatively, reveal a large element of sheer bad luck.

(a) The 'Non-appearing' Defendant State

In the nine years beginning in 1972, seven cases[184] were commenced by unilateral application in which the defendant State refused to take part in the proceedings before the Court, although the views of the States concerned were transmitted by indirect means. This raised technical issues relating to the application of the provisions of Article 53 of the Statute which are of considerable interest.[185] Article 53 provides:

1. Whenever one of the parties does not appear before the Court, or fails to defend his case, the other party may call upon the Court to decide in favour of its claim.

2. The Court must, before doing so, satisfy itself, not only that it has jurisdiction in accordance with Articles 36 and 37, but also that the claim is well founded in fact and law.

The Court's reaction to the practice of non-appearance has been uniform and is exemplified by the following passage from the judgment in the *Aegean Sea Continental Shelf* case:[186]

15. It is to be regretted that the Turkish Government had failed to appear in order to put forward its arguments on the issues arising in the present phase of the proceedings and the Court has thus not had the assistance it might have derived

---

[183] See Brownlie, this *Year Book*, 42 (1967), p. 123.

[184] *Fisheries Jurisdiction* case (*United Kingdom* v. *Iceland*), *I.C.J. Reports*, 1974, p. 3; *Fisheries Jurisdiction* case (*Federal Republic of Germany* v. *Iceland*), ibid., p. 175; *Nuclear Tests* case (*Australia* v. *France*), ibid., p. 253; *Nuclear Tests* case (*New Zealand* v. *France*), ibid., p. 457; *Case Concerning Trial of Pakistani Prisoners of War*, ibid. 1973, pp. 328, 347; *Aegean Sea Continental Shelf* case, ibid. 1978, p. 3; *United States Diplomatic and Consular Staff in Tehran*, ibid. 1980, p. 3.

[185] See the studies by Sinclair, *International and Comparative Law Quarterly*, 30 (1981), p. 338; Fitzmaurice, this *Year Book*, 51 (1980), p. 89. See also Merrills, *Cambridge Law Journal*, 39 (1980), p. 137 at pp. 161–3.

[186] *I.C.J. Reports*, 1978, pp. 7–8.

from such arguments or from any evidence adduced in support of them. Nevertheless, the Court, in accordance with its Statute and its settled jurisprudence, must examine *proprio motu* the question of its own jurisdiction to consider the Application of the Greek Government. Furthermore, in the present case the duty of the Court to make this examination on its own initiative is reinforced by the terms of Article 53 of the Statute of the Court. According to this provision, whenever one of the parties does not appear before the Court, or fails to defend its case, the Court, before finding upon the merits, must satisfy itself that it has jurisdiction. Before proceeding further, however, the evolution of the main events leading to the bringing of this dispute before the Court must be outlined.

In this connection Waldock was not inclined to choose a different course, although there are some significant considerations of principle— not least that of fairness to the applicant State, which finds itself virtually in an adversary position *vis-à-vis* a Court leaning over backwards to appreciate the elements in the defendant's case (had it been presented)—in favour of a procedure which would give fewer tactical advantages to the non-appearing State.[187] However, there are no less significant considerations of a practical character which seem to justify both the maintenance of Article 53 in its present form and the cautious response of the Court to the cases of non-appearance.[188]

(b) *Cases Involving a High Level of Justiciability*

In the period under examination the Court was fated to be asked to deal with issues of the highest political significance.[189] The various cases all concerned legal issues and in that sense they were justiciable and could be decided in accordance with law. However, it is obvious that all the issues of substance involved either the vital interests of the defendant State or political issues of great magnitude.[190]

The catalogue is as follows:

(i) The *Nuclear Tests* cases involved the national security of France and an activity which had been indulged in for a long period without previous condemnation by Australia, which State had indeed co-operated in the carrying out of tests on her own territory.[191]

The French Government had conducted a series of nuclear weapons

---

[187] See Fitzmaurice, loc. cit. above (p. 49 n. 185), pp. 93, 113, 116, 120-1. At pp. 105-6 there is a critical reference to the Court's attitude 'even during Sir Humphrey's term on the Court'. There is also an acknowledgment that in the *Fisheries Jurisdiction* case, *I.C.J. Reports*, 1973, p. 3 (at p. 35, paras. 21 and 22 of his separate opinion) the writer had himself avoided taking a strong line when on the bench.

[188] See Thirlway, *Non-appearance before the International Court of Justice* (The Hague, 1983: paper made available to the Institute of International Law, to be published in due course by Cambridge University Press).

[189] For a most interesting survey of the *actual* role of the Court and its predecessor, see Virally, *Revue générale de droit international public*, 87 (1983), p. 281.

[190] See Fitzmaurice, loc. cit. above (p. 49 n. 185), pp. 99-105.

[191] See the dissenting opinion of Judge Gros, *I.C.J. Reports*, 1974, p. 276, at pp. 279-89; and the separate opinion of Judge Petrén, ibid., p. 298, at pp. 302-7.

tests in the atmosphere at Mururoa Atoll in the Pacific. The Australian and New Zealand Governments were opposed to the tests in part because of the belief that contaminated material would be deposited on territory under their sovereignty. Claims were brought before the International Court based upon various apparently appropriate causes of action. Apart from the insistence by the applicants upon the illegality of nuclear tests *tout court*—a source of great difficulty—the case would have been a straightforward attempt to impose State responsibility for creating a nuisance. There were, however, at least two problems facing the applicants. In the first place, it was only in the recent past that the Australian and New Zealand Governments had come to the view that atmospheric nuclear tests were illegal; and, secondly, the proof of actual damage was no easy matter on the facts. At a late phase of the proceedings the Court held that the claims were inadmissible, since they had ceased to have an object in view of a French undertaking to discontinue the tests.

(ii) The *Fisheries Jurisdiction* cases concerned the principal element in the Icelandic economy and related not simply to access to the fisheries but to the very existence of stocks threatened by overfishing. In a Note dated 29 May 1972 the Government of Iceland expressly stated that 'the vital interests of the people of Iceland are involved'.[192] Moreover, in the Exchange of Notes between Iceland and the United Kingdom in 1961 the United Kingdom had acknowledged 'the exceptional dependence of the Icelandic nation upon coastal fisheries for their livelihood and economic development'.[193]

(iii) *The Western Sahara* case[194] involved the Court's rendering an advisory opinion at the request of the General Assembly of the United Nations. The request was couched in the form of two questions drafted in highly abstract and unhelpful terms.[195] The substantial issues consisted of a complex of questions relating to the principle of self-determination, the issue of title to the territory of Western Sahara at a particular time, and the existence of 'legal ties' between the territory and the Kingdom of Morocco and between the territory and the Mauritanian entity. In spite of the highly artificial nature of the questions put to the Court in the request for the advisory opinion, the real issue was the contemporary legal status of Western Sahara. The essence of the matter was well expressed in the forthright separate opinion of Judge Dillard.[196] Some of the Judges,

---

[192] *I.C.J. Reports*, 1973, pp. 6–7.

[193] Ibid. 1974, pp. 12–13.

[194] Ibid. 1975, p. 12.

[195] They were as follows:

'I. Was Western Sahara . . . at the time of colonisation by Spain a territory belonging to no one (*terra nullius*)?

'If the answer to the first question is in the negative,

'II. What were the legal ties between this territory and the Kingdom of Morocco and the Mauritanian entity?'

[196] *I.C.J. Reports*, 1975, p. 116.

including Gros[197] and Petrén,[198] had grave doubts as to the legal nature of the questions raised by the General Assembly.

(iv) *The Aegean Sea Continental Shelf* case.[199] This case concerned the delimitation of continental shelf areas, a question which is notoriously *justiciable*. However, in the Turkish view the Greek claims involved a serious threat to the territorial balance established by the Lausanne Peace Treaty of 1923.[200]

(v) *Case Concerning United States Diplomatic Staff in Tehran.*[201] The seizing of United States diplomatic and consular personnel in Tehran and elsewhere subsequent to attacks by mobs on the embassy in Tehran and the consulates in Tabriz and Shiraz gave rise to a major international crisis with many facets. Amongst the measures taken by the United States Government was an application to the Court which asked for a declaration in the following terms:

The United States requests the Court to adjudge and declare as follows:

(a) That the Government of Iran, in tolerating, encouraging, and failing to prevent and punish the conduct described in the preceding Statement of Facts, violated its international legal obligations to the United States as provided by

—Articles 22, 24, 25, 27, 29, 31, 37 and 47 of the Vienna Convention on Diplomatic Relations,

—Articles 28, 31, 33, 34, 36 and 40 of the Vienna Convention on Consular Relations,

—Articles 4 and 7 of the Convention on the Prevention and Punishment of Crimes against Internationally Protected Persons, including Diplomatic Agents, and

—Articles II (4), XIII, XVIII and XIX of the Treaty of Amity, Economic Relations, and Consular Rights between the United States and Iran, and

—Articles 2 (3), 2 (4) and 33 of the Charter of the United Nations;

(b) That pursuant to the foregoing international legal obligations, the Government of Iran is under a particular obligation immediately to secure the release of all United States nationals currently being detained within the premises of the United States Embassy in Tehran and to assure that all such persons and all other United States nationals in Tehran are allowed to leave Iran safely;

(c) That the Government of Iran shall pay to the United States, in its own right and in the exercise of its right of diplomatic protection of its nationals, reparation for the foregoing violations of Iran's international legal obligations to the United States, in a sum to be determined by the Court: and

(d) That the Government of Iran submit to its competent authorities for the purpose of prosecution those persons responsible for the crimes committed

---

[197] *I.C.J. Reports*, 1975, pp. 69–70.
[198] Ibid., pp. 107–12.
[199] Ibid. 1978, p. 3.
[200] Turkish *Notes Verbales*, 18 November 1975 and 15 March 1976: *Pleadings, Oral Arguments, Documents, Aegean Sea Continental Shelf* case, pp. 40, 44.
[201] *I.C.J. Reports*, 1980, p. 3.

against the premises and staff of the United States Embassy and against the premises of its Consulates . . .

The highly charged and tense atmosphere attending these proceedings is easily recalled and the completion of the proceedings was anticipated by the disastrous attempt at a rescue operation by armed forces of the United States. In the Iranian view the hostages question was linked with the entire package of grievances against the United States.[202]

It is obvious that the Court did not invite the arrival of this high tide of issues, which washed up against the limits of justiciability. Moreover, in a number of cases the Court found reasons for not dealing with the merits. But in two cases the Court, or a major section of the Court, was clearly reluctant to turn business away even when the custom offered was not a little eccentric. Thus in the *Nuclear Tests* cases,[203] Waldock and three other Judges were prepared to find that a jurisdictional basis existed and, further, that the claims were admissible. Similarly, in the *Western Sahara* case the majority of the Court was unwilling to consider refusing to accede to the request for an advisory opinion, inauspicious though the circumstances were.

The view that the Court has been exposed too much by its receiving highly political business can easily be sustained.[204] During the years 1973 to 1981 the Court may be thought to have tried too hard to oblige once work turned up. Waldock would have rejected such doubts. His strongly held view was that the Court had a duty to cope with the issues placed before it.

(c) *Resort to Recondite Jurisdictional Clauses*

In the years in which Waldock was on the bench the 1928 General Act for the Pacific Settlement of International Disputes was invoked as a basis of jurisdiction in no less than four cases: the *Case Concerning Trial of Pakistani Prisoners of War*,[205] the *Nuclear Tests* cases[206] and the *Aegean Sea Continental Shelf* case.[207] In each case the Court found that it was not necessary to deal with the technical problems relating to the General Act, for example, whether it had survived the demise of the League of Nations.[208] In the *Nuclear Tests* cases Waldock joined with Judges Onyeama, Dillard and Jiménez de Aréchaga in a dissenting opinion in each case.[209] In that dissenting opinion is to be found a trenchant defence of the continuing validity of the General Act and a rejection of the argument based upon desuetude.[210]

---

[202] Fitzmaurice, loc. cit. above (p. 49 n. 185), p. 104.

[203] *I.C.J. Reports*, 1974, pp. 312, 494.

[204] See Skubiszewski, in *Festschrift für Hermann Mosler* (1983), p. 891 at pp. 901–2.

[205] *I.C.J. Reports*, 1973, pp. 328, 347.   [206] Ibid., pp. 99, 135.

[207] Ibid. 1976, p. 3; 1978, p. 3.

[208] See Merrills, *Cambridge Law Journal*, 39 (1980), p. 137; and Johnson, *Australian Yearbook of International Law*, vol. 7, p. 309.   [209] *I.C.J. Reports*, 1974, pp. 312, 494.

[210] Ibid., pp. 327, 509. See also Fitzmaurice, this *Year Book*, 51 (1980), p. 89 at pp. 99–100.

Whatever the outcome of the argument over the continuing validity of the General Act, the fact remains that it was, at least in a political sense, a dormant and obscure source of jurisdiction.[211] The Court was undoubtedly placed in a difficult position as a consequence of the ingenious attempts of applicant States to rely upon recondite clauses. As Judge Gros observed:[212]

The cause of international adjudication has not been furthered by an attempt to impose the Court's jurisdiction, apparently for a formal reason, on States in whose eyes the General Act was, quite clearly, no longer a true yardstick of their acceptance of international jurisdiction.

(d) *Impending or Very Recent Changes in General International Law*

It is well known that the merits stage of the *Fisheries Jurisdiction* cases[213] coincided with a period of rapid transition in the law relating to fisheries jurisdiction. The United Kingdom and the Federal Republic of Germany were complaining of an extension of Icelandic jurisdiction to fifty nautical miles from the baselines. In fact in the 1970s many States were adopting fishery limits and also exclusive economic zones of 200 miles in extent. In 1976 the United States proclaimed a 200 miles fishery conservation zone and the European Economic Community adopted such a limit for fishing zones of Member States with effect from 1 January 1977.[214] Moreover, in the *Nuclear Tests* cases Judge Gros explained his position on the justiciability of the dispute on the basis that the view of Australia and other States as to the illegality of nuclear weapons testing was the result of a sudden change of policy, and what was involved as between France and Australia was no more than a conflict of political interests.[215]

(e) *The* Nuclear Tests *Cases as a Controversial Episode in the Life of the Court*

For a number of reasons the *Nuclear Tests* cases constituted a certain crisis in the life of the Court and raised questions about its proper functioning. In the first place, the Court was seriously divided in face of the issues with which it was confronted. The decision as to admissibility was by nine votes to six:[216] and the earlier decision as to interim measures of protection was taken by eight votes to six.[217] In the decision on admissibility Waldock and three colleagues participated in a strong joint dissenting opinion.[218] Secondly, several judges expressed strong doubts about the order of the consideration of key issues by the Court and, in

---

[211] See the separate opinions of Judge Gros, *I.C.J. Reports*, 1974, pp. 296, 482.

[212] Ibid., p. 297.

[213] Ibid., pp. 3, 175.

[214] *International Legal Materials*, 15 (1976), p. 1425.

[215] *I.C.J. Reports*, 1974, pp. 277–89 (separate opinion); ibid., pp. 480–2 (separate opinion relating to the New Zealand application).

[216] Ibid., pp. 272, 478.   [217] Ibid. 1973, pp. 106, 142.   [218] Ibid. 1974, p. 312.

particular, the postponed consideration of the questions of jurisdiction and admissibility.[219] Waldock referred to this problem in a declaration, couched in rather formal terms, made at the time of the order for interim measures of protection in 1973.[220] Thirdly, in the context of the proceedings on interim measures of protection there was a serious breach of the requirement that the deliberations of the Court 'shall take place in private and remain secret'. The result of the proceedings relating to interim measures of protection became known prior to the Court's announcement of its decision. Apart from the disclosure (in a public statement by the Prime Minister of Australia) as such, there were differences within the Court concerning the extent of the inquiry which was carried out by the Court and which was closed without having identified any specific source of the statements published.[221] Five Judges, including Waldock, made a joint declaration in which they expressed the view that the Court had taken all the steps necessary in dealing with the problem of disclosure.[222]

It is to be borne in mind that, alongside the features recorded above, the *Nuclear Tests* cases also involved some difficult questions of substantive law and a non-appearing defendant State. Like other cases which were sought to be placed before the Court at this period it was on the margins both of justiciability and of jurisdiction.

(f) *Competition from Other Instances*

In the last thirty years a significant number of international disputes have been adjudicated by *ad hoc* courts of arbitration.[223] There is at present perhaps a 50 per cent chance of disputes being submitted to such courts of arbitration, set up by the parties and expressly empowered to deal with a particular dispute, rather than to the International Court. This tendency is by no means to be deplored, and all reasonable avenues to peaceful settlement of disputes should be kept in service. In the recent past the Court has responded to the competing practice of arbitration by amending its Rules in order to induce States to have resort to chambers constituted by the Court in consultation with the parties. These changes were made in the revised Rules of 1972 and confirmed in the Rules of 1978. The Governments of Canada and the United States have agreed to place the *Gulf of Maine* case before a chamber of the Court constituted under the 1978 Rules.[224]

It remains to be seen whether the use of chambers will be popular with States and whether the procedure as such will work satisfactorily. A more

---

[219] Separate opinions of Judge Gros, ibid., pp. 289, 480; and Petrén, ibid., pp. 298, 483.

[220] Ibid. 1973, pp. 108, 144.

[221] See the declaration of President Lachs, ibid. 1974, p. 273; and the separate opinion of Judge Gros, ibid. pp. 293–6.

[222] Ibid., p. 273.

[223] See Johnson, *Year Book of World Affairs*, 34 (1980), p. 305.

[224] *I.C.J. Reports*, 1982, p. 3 (order for constitution of the chamber).

serious form of competition for jurisdiction has appeared in the work of the Third United Nations Conference on the Law of the Sea and the Law of the Sea Convention of 1982—the International Tribunal for the Law of the Sea and provisions for the constitution of arbitral tribunals within the framework of the Convention.[225] The appearance of arrangements for peaceful settlement of disputes in an important multilateral convention is normal and not open to criticism. However, the provisions of the Convention envisage a certain separation of law of the sea matters from the general materials of international law and this is by no means a healthy development.

There can be no doubt that members of the International Court have reservations about the tendencies revealed in the Law of the Sea Conference.[226] Waldock, as President of the Court, was asked to deliver the first Cornelis van Vollenhoven Memorial Lecture, and his title was 'The International Court and the Law of the Sea'.[227] He used the occasion to assert the role of the Court in diplomatic but absolutely clear terms:[228]

> The contribution of the Court to the modern law of the sea has, it is believed, been both considerable and, in the idiom of to-day, progressive, without departing from the Court's judicial character. This is true conspicuously of the *Corfu Channel, Anglo-Norwegian Fisheries* and *North Sea Continental Shelf* cases, and in its Judgments in those cases the Court performed the classic function of a court in determining and clarifying what it conceived to be the existing law. In doing so, however, it threw fresh light on the considerations and the principles on which the law was based in a manner to suggest the path for its future development. In that way and by those Judgments the Court has materially influenced the actual development of the modern law of the sea, and not merely its formulation. In short, although the major factors in determining the shape of the new law of the sea may have been the immense developments in technology of recent years and the aspirations of the newly independent States, the judicial role of the International Court of Justice has also played its part.

If and when the Third Conference on the Law of the Sea completes its work, it is manifest that the need for the interpretation and application of the law through the judicial process will remain, and even increase, as the Negotiating Text

---

[225] See Annexes VI, VII and VIII of the Convention.

[226] See Judge Lachs in Kalshoven, Kuyper and Lammers (eds.), *Essays in Memory of Haro F. van Panhuys* (1980), p. 21 at pp. 43-4, where speaking of possible innovations in the Rules of the International Court, he states: 'The other type of Chamber I would gladly welcome, is a Chamber for the Law of the Sea. While I write these lines, the Conference on the Law of the Sea is still dealing with the subject of the settlement of disputes, and is envisaging the establishment of a law-of-the-sea tribunal. This idea has been very much advanced, and many views have been expressed in favour of the establishment of such a tribunal. Regrettably, I cannot share these views. The International Court of Justice has had a long experience in dealing with maritime matters; some of its decisions have paved the way to changes in the law of the sea. A new tribunal would create competing jurisdiction and jurisprudence, and even a split within the law. It may pose special problems of harmonisation where disputes straddling both areas, the sea and the land, are concerned. What would become of the organic unity of the law?' Similar views are expressed by Judge Oda, *Indian Journal of International Law*, 19 (1979), p. 157 at p. 165.

[227] Published in 1979 by the T.M.C. Asser Institute, The Hague.

[228] At pp. 16-17.

expressly recognises. This Court, by its past contributions to the law of the sea, its long tradition of judicial proceedings and its position as the principal judicial organ of the United Nations, is peculiarly equipped to play its part in that work. Indeed, the next case on the Court's list—between Tunisia and Libya—concerns the delimitation of the continental shelf, while another case of a similar kind may be brought before a Chamber of the Court under a treaty recently concluded between Canada and the United States.

(g) *Waldock's Role on the Court*

There can be no doubt that Waldock served the Court well during a difficult period. His inclination was always to do his best to make things work, to try to foster a consensus, and to aim at institutional effectiveness. Both as a Judge, and later as President, he would prefer broadly based and therefore authoritative decisions. Consequently, his approach would not involve a succession of separate and dissenting opinions. At the same time he would not pursue a collegiate policy at any price, and in the *Nuclear Tests* cases[229] Waldock participated in a densely reasoned joint dissenting opinion which showed a willingness to grasp nettles not always evident in the policies of the majority in those cases. In other controversial and difficult cases—the *Fisheries Jurisdiction* cases (*Merits*),[230] the *Western Sahara* advisory opinion[231] and the *Aegean Sea Continental Shelf* case[232] —Waldock voted with the majority.[233]

It may be surmised—and this not merely on the basis that Waldock was President of the Court at the time—that certain majority judgments owe a great deal to Waldock's drafting. This would seem to be true of the *Aegean Sea* case[234] (when he was not President), the *Hostages* case (*Interim Measures*),[235] the *Hostages* case (*Merits*),[236] the advisory opinion on *Interpretation of the Agreement of 25 March 1951 between the W.H.O. and Egypt*,[237] and the application by Malta to intervene in the *Tunisia–Libya Shelf* case.[238] In these five proceedings the voting was as follows: 12 votes to 2 (*Aegean Sea*); unanimously (*Hostages* case, *Interim Measures*); by 13 votes to 2, 13 votes to 2, unanimously, unanimously, 12 votes to 3, and 14 votes to 1 (*Hostages* case, *Merits*); by 12 votes to 1, 12 votes to 1, 11 votes to 2 (advisory opinion on *Interpretation*); unanimously (Malta's application to intervene). Waldock's well-recognized ability to produce a certain disciplined enlightenment was less evident in the advisory opinion proceedings of 1980, which produced a long tally of separate opinions.

[229] *I.C.J. Reports*, 1974, pp. 312, 494.
[230] Ibid., pp. 3, 175 (but he wrote a separate opinion in each case).
[231] Ibid. 1975, p. 12.
[232] Ibid. 1978, p. 3.
[233] He also voted with the majority in the Interim Measures stage of the *Nuclear Tests* cases, ibid. 1973, pp. 99, 135; and the advisory opinion proceedings, *Application for Review of Judgment No. 158 of the U.N. Administrative Tribunal*, ibid., p. 166, among others.
[234] Ibid. 1978, p. 3.
[235] Ibid. 1979, p. 7.
[236] Ibid. 1980, p. 3.
[237] Ibid. p. 73.
[238] Ibid. 1981, p. 3.

Waldock made two contributions to the jurisprudence of separate opinions, the first two of which were exclusively his own and were induced by the *Fisheries Jurisdiction* cases (at the Merits stage).[239] In the case between the United Kingdom and Iceland Waldock was in 'general agreement' with the operative part and the reasoning of the judgment of the Court, but stated that he considered that certain aspects of the case 'should have received more prominence in the Judgment'.[240] In his view 'the starting point for determining the rights and obligations of the Parties in the present case has to be the 1961 Exchange of Notes' as a valid agreement applicable to the extension of Iceland's fishery jurisdiction.

Having carefully placed the 1961 Exchange of Notes within the diplomatic history, Waldock analysed the compromise which that agreement represented. In his view the clause providing for notice of an extension of fisheries jurisdiction around Iceland, and reference to the Court in case of a dispute related to such an extension, was not 'a mere compromissory clause' but 'a basic condition of the settlement'.[241] As a consequence the extension of the twelve-mile limit agreed to in the treaty of 1961 was not opposable to the United Kingdom 'if that extension does not comply with the conditions laid down in the compromissory clause'.[242] The result was the fundamental invalidity of the extension of jurisdiction under general international law and not simply a matter of validity under maritime international law: 'Consequently, I do not think that it would be correct to regard Iceland's total refusal of the Court's jurisdiction as having the effect only of exposing her to a judgment in default of appearance under Article 53 of the Statute'.[243] In the remainder of the opinion Waldock discussed the ambit of the compromissory clause with special reference to the Court's competence in respect of preferential rights and conservation.[244]

In the case between the German Federal Republic and Iceland, Waldock produced a separate opinion on the same general grounds.[245] However, in this separate opinion he made some interesting observations concerning the issue of State responsibility and the German claim to compensation for alleged acts of harassment of its vessels by Icelandic patrol vessels.[246]

In the *Nuclear Tests* case[247] between Australia and France Waldock joined with Judges Onyeama, Dillard and Jiménez de Aréchaga in a substantial dissenting opinion of sixty pages. The dissent was carefully reasoned and of wide scope, as the conclusion indicates:[248]

---

[239] *I.C.J. Reports*, 1974, pp. 3, 175.   [240] Ibid., p. 105.
[241] Ibid., p. 144, para. 22.   [242] Ibid., p. 115, para. 24.
[243] Ibid., pp. 117–18, paras. 29–30   [244] Ibid., pp. 120–5, paras. 37–46.
[245] Ibid., pp. 227–9.   [246] Ibid., pp. 229–33, paras. 6–13.
[247] Ibid., p. 312. A similar joint dissenting opinion was delivered in the case involving New Zealand and France: ibid., p. 494.
[248] Ibid., p. 371.

Since we are of the opinion that the Court has jurisdiction and that the case submitted to the Court discloses no ground on which Australia's claims should be considered inadmissible, we consider that the Applicant had a right under the Statute and the Rules to have the case adjudicated. This right the Judgment takes away from the Applicant by a procedure and by reasoning which, to our regret, we can only consider as lacking any justification in the Statute and Rules or in the practice and jurisprudence of the Court.

It would be pointless to summarize the opinion, which contains a great wealth of material on the General Act of 1928 and other subjects. The particular quality of the opinion is the careful attention which it devotes to certain highly significant questions of principle: the meaning and scope of the declaratory judgment, the desuetude of treaties, the compatibility of treaties bearing upon the same subject-matter, the concept of a reservation, the problem of characterizing issues as having a 'preliminary' or 'non-preliminary' character, the distinction between 'political' and 'legal' disputes, and the concept of 'legal interest'.

This modest description of Waldock's work on the Court may be completed by a reference to the role he fulfilled, even among other very experienced professional colleagues, of setting an example of high standards of performance. Hard work was a part of this example, but there was the other part, and it has been reported upon vividly by Sir Francis Vallat:[249]

Throughout his long and distinguished judicial career, starting as a member of the European Commission of Human Rights in 1954 and ending as President of the International Court of Justice in 1979, Humphrey Waldock insisted on maintaining both the appearance and the reality of strict judicial impartiality. To such an extent did he carry this attitude that, during the hearings before the Human Rights Commission on the Greek allegations of torture in Cyprus brought against the United Kingdom, he was unwilling to speak to British counsel.[250] In later years, he relaxed a little, but always maintained an impenetrable attitude of impartiality.

X. On the Bench: III. The Anglo-French Court of Arbitration

On 10 July 1975 the Governments of France and the United Kingdom concluded an Arbitration Agreement by the provisions of which a Court of Arbitration was constituted in order to decide the question: 'What is the course of the boundary (or boundaries) between the portions of the continental shelf appertaining to the United Kingdom and the Channel Islands and to the French Republic, respectively, west of 30 minutes west of the Greenwich Meridian as far as the 1000 metre isobath?' This question was to be decided 'in accordance with the rules of international law applicable in the matter as between the Parties'.

---

[249] *Graya*, 85 (1981), p. 57 at p. 59.   [250] Of whom Sir Francis was one.

The Court was composed of five Judges of whom one, having been nominated by the United Kingdom Government, was Waldock. André Gros was appointed by the French Government (instead of Paul Reuter, who resigned for reasons of health). The other members were Erik Castrén of Finland (who was President), Herbert Briggs of the United States and Endre Ustor of Hungary.

Thus composed and for other reasons this Court of Arbitration was a fine example of the small family of distinguished *ad hoc* tribunals which in recent years have been empowered to decide particular disputes affecting important interests.[251] The decision of the Court on 30 June 1977[252] forms a major part, together with the *North Sea Continental Shelf* cases[253] and the *Tunisia–Libya Continental Shelf* case,[254] of the jurisprudence relating to the delimitation of continental shelf areas as between opposite or adjacent States—a subject which is likely to remain of great practical significance.

The general quality of the decision of the Court is undeniable, although the enclaving of the Channel Islands inevitably gave rise to criticism in some quarters. The Court was required to draw a precise line[255] (in contrast to the task of other Courts in recent maritime delimitation cases) and the delimitation involved three separate regions: the English Channel as such, the Channel Islands region within the rectangular gulf formed by the coasts of Normandy and Brittany, and the Atlantic region (the portions of shelf lying immediately to the westward of the Channel as far as the 1,000-metre isobath). In a real sense three separate issues were involved. Moreover, aside from the issues concerning delimitation, the Court had to consider some difficult questions relating to the sources of international law and the law of treaties.[256]

The reasoning of the decision of 30 June 1977 is full and more or less exhaustive. The sophistication and coherence of structure of the drafting tends to be characteristic of the decisions of such *ad hoc* tribunals. The Anglo-French Court of Arbitration had a distinguished membership and such bodies work on collegiate lines. However, it is very probable that the actual text of the decision was drafted by Waldock, and it bears all the marks of his work. If this view be correct, the decision stands as a significant monument to Waldock's capabilities as judge and arbitrator. It may be compared with the decision of the Court of Arbitration in the *Beagle*

---

[251] See Johnson, *Year Book of World Affairs*, 34 (1980), p. 305.

[252] For the text: H.M.S.O. Misc. No. 15 (1978) (Cmnd. 7438); 54 I.L.R. 6.

[253] *I.C.J. Reports*, 1969, p. 3.

[254] Ibid. 1982, p. 18.

[255] The decision of 30 June 1977 was marred by a technical problem as to the precise course of the boundary. The error was corrected, but only in relation to the Channel Islands, by the decision of 14 March 1978, and the question of uncorrected error was the subject of the separate opinion delivered by Waldock.

[256] Generally on the issues in the case see Bowett, this *Year Book*, 48 (1976-7), p. 67; and 49 (1978), p. 1; Brown, *San Diego Law Review*, 16 (1979), p. 461; and McRae, *Canadian Yearbook of International Law*, 15 (1977), p. 173.

Channel case,[257] which was decided in the same year. The Court in that case was similarly composed of five highly qualified persons (who had been Judges of the International Court at the time of appointment), and Sir Gerald Fitzmaurice acted as President.[258] The reasoning of the decision in the *Beagle Channel* case is impressive, and it is probable that much of the text was drafted by Fitzmaurice. The world of international adjudication is, in one sense, a small one and the *Anglo-French* and *Beagle Channel* cases caused timetabling problems, since Judge Gros was a member of both Courts, in addition to his duties at The Hague.

The decision of the Court in the *Anglo-French* case built upon the judgment of the Court in the *North Sea* cases. In particular, it was emphasized that the equidistance/special circumstances rule was to be seen as an expression of the 'fundamental norm' that 'delimitation must be in accordance with equitable principles',[259] and that 'the appropriateness of the equidistance or any other method for the purpose of effecting an equitable delimitation is a function or reflection of the geographical and other relevant circumstances of each particular case'.[260] There is much of interest, and the substantial text calls for careful study. Particularly striking features, not always sufficiently appreciated, are the division of the subject-matter into distinct regions for the purpose of delimitation, and the concept of primary delimitation,[261] to be followed by a second stage of reasoning involving abatement or adjustment of the 'primary boundary' in the light of local geographical eccentricities. The Court also makes important statements about the application of Article 6 of the Continental Shelf Convention of 1958, the relevance of islands to the process of delimitation, the nature of relevant circumstances, the significance of fault zones and the concept of proportionality.

The task of the Court in the *Anglo-French* case was one of peculiar difficulty. For the first time a tribunal was required *to establish an actual boundary* on the basis of equitable principles: whereas in the *North Sea* cases the Court had not been asked to do more than state 'what principles and rules of international law' were applicable to the delimitation in the course of negotiations. It is notoriously difficult to justify every aspect of a land boundary on the basis of precise evidence and legal reasoning. The justification of the various sectors of a continental shelf delimitation in the form of a boundary line is equally difficult. The borderland between unacceptable discretion and the proper judicial application of equitable principles to varying geographical circumstances is full of traps. It may

---

[257] 52 I.L.R. 93.

[258] After his retirement from the Court in 1973 Sir Gerald returned to legal practice in the Temple. It was in this way that he appeared, as a member of Malta's team, in the *Malta Intervention* proceedings in 1981 (*Tunisia–Libya Continental Shelf* case), *I.C.J. Reports*, 1981, p. 3, before a Court of which his successor, Waldock, was then President.

[259] Decision, para. 97. See also paras. 194, 195, 239–41.

[260] Ibid., para. 97.

[261] Ibid., paras. 199, 201–2.

be that the distinction between 'refashioning geography' (which is forbidden) and abatement or adjustment of a primary boundary on grounds of equity is ultimately one of scale.

The decision in the *Anglo-French* case is carefully reasoned, but in certain aspects the reasoning is in truth not much more than the reporting of an exercise of discretion. It is inherently difficult to describe the application of equitable principles in highly articulate fashion. For example, the Court gave the Scilly Isles 'half effect' in drawing a modified equidistance line in the Atlantic region,[262] gave full effect to Ushant in doing so,[263] and gave the Channel Islands a restricted and enclaved area of shelf.[264] These elements in the reasoning are justified by use of phrases such as 'an appropriate abatement of the inequitable effects of the distorting geographical feature',[265] 'a radical distortion of the boundary creative of inequity'[266] and 'an inequitable distortion of the equidistance line'.[267]

Too insistent a criticism of the use of judicial discretion can only succeed in being facile. The application of the relevant principles must always involve a certain measure of flexibility, since the geographical circumstances vary greatly from case to case. Moreover, the decision in the *Anglo-French* case is careful to stress certain elements of control or discipline in the process of delimitation. In several passages it is stressed that delimitation takes place within the framework of legal rules and that consideration must be given not only to 'the particular geographical and other circumstances' but also to 'any relevant considerations of law and equity'.[268] The injunction of the *North Sea* cases judgment against distributive justice (and the refashioning of geography) is repeated on several occasions;[269] and there are several important passages explaining the concept of proportionality and insisting that its role in the *North Sea* cases was exceptional.[270] Finally, where an 'inequitable' distortion or 'disproportionate' effect is detected, the outcome is 'abatement'[271]—in other words, a *moderate* level of adjustment.

It should also be pointed out that in the most difficult phase of the delimitation—in the Channel Islands region—the Court gave very considerable care to the reasoning and the outcome is impressive.[272] The content of the reasoning makes clear the fact that the Court was very far from treating dependent islands *in general* as counting for less for purposes of shelf delimitation. There can be little doubt that two factors—neither connected with islands as a class—were particularly influential. The first was the location of the Channel Islands within the Golfe Breton-Normand,[273] 'not only "on the wrong side" of the median line[274] but

---

[262] Decision, paras. 243–51.

[263] Ibid., paras. 248–51.

[264] Ibid., paras. 196–202.

[265] Ibid., para. 251.

[266] Ibid., para. 199.

[267] Ibid., para. 243.

[268] Ibid., paras. 191, 194.

[269] Ibid., paras. 101, 195, 248.

[270] Ibid., paras. 98–101, 246–51.

[271] Ibid., para. 249.

[272] Ibid., paras. 145–203.

[273] Ibid., paras. 183, 196.

[274] Strictly speaking, this should be read as the wrong side of the *mainland coast* median line.

wholly detached geographically from the United Kingdom'.[275] The second factor was the equitable considerations relating to 'navigational, defence and security interests in the region', which tended 'to evidence the predominant interest of the French Republic in the southern areas of the English Channel . . .'.[276]

XI. TEACHING AND WRITING

It must be obvious that a major part of Waldock's intellectual and professional output was in the realms of practical activity. In academic circles it is common for such as Waldock to be evaluated in terms of 'published' work. The considerable output of opinions, draft pleadings and other material—much of it of a standard certainly no less than the standards of ordinary publication and carrying heavy responsibilities— would not be appreciated. Waldock's chief works were his Reports for the International Law Commission on the Law of Treaties and on Succession of States in Respect of Treaties, published in the *Yearbook* of the International Law Commission,[277] and his contribution to the drafting of the judgments of international tribunals.

In any case, Waldock's 'ordinary' literary output in public international law was not at all inconsiderable. Apart from some substantial articles, he produced a very successful sixth edition of Brierly's *Law of Nations*,[278] and gave the General Course at The Hague Academy of International Law in 1962.[279] He also edited this *Year Book* from 1955 until 1973: he was the successor to Sir Hersch Lauterpacht, and was responsible (from 1959 in conjunction with Sir Robert Jennings) for fifteen volumes.

Waldock always expounded his views with great clarity and careful ordering of the material. The development of a subject would be related to the relevant experience, including the practice of States, and the account would be informed and enlivened by his practical experience. There was in fact a synthesis—so successful that it was not noticed—between Waldock's teaching, writing and practice. He was a keen observer of the behaviour of States and was well aware of the underlying issues of policy, which were brought into play quite naturally. He was thus one of the best reporters of the workings of the law. His wavelength was a good balance of optimism and scepticism, and he did not badger students with any special brand of idealism or with fashionable ideas borrowed from that most vacuous of spheres, political science. His teaching and his work were always broadly based and above all informative and comprehensive.

Waldock's particular forte as a writer and teacher was the application of legal analysis, in his own form of non-sectarian positivism, to the new and

---

[275] Ibid., para. 199.
[276] Ibid., para. 188. See also paras. 163 and 175.
[277] See above.
[278] 1963. This edition appeared in a Portuguese edition (the fourth in that language) in 1979.
[279] *Recueil des cours*, 106 (1962–II), pp. 1–250.

extensive developments in the years after the Second World War. This ability is seen to great advantage in his General Course on public international law delivered in 1962 and published by the Hague Academy. Many international lawyers found difficulty in recognizing, and especially in assimilating, the work of the United Nations, the proliferation of international organizations in general, changes in the position of the individual in international law and the appearance of standards of human rights. Waldock was adept at relating the new and extensive material to the existing matrices of the law and recognizing the development of new rules of customary law. Moreover, his craft was that of *general* international law and he would not consider the law of the sea, for example, as a 'special subject' to be fenced off from the remainder of international law, but rather as a major area of a coherent subject.

Both in his writing and in his work as teacher and judge, Waldock was always sensitive to the problem of finding a balance between imposing an exacting level of obligation on governments, which the 'political market' could not bear at the particular time, and solving the efficacy problem by simply drawing the line of legality at the mark set by the lowest common denominator. This problem of balance is constantly faced by the legislator within national legal systems and is particularly acute in rapidly changing fields, such as human rights and—in part—the law of the sea. It is faced by international tribunals interpreting jurisdictional clauses and multilateral standard-setting treaties, concerning human rights matters.

Waldock's approach was to accept the need for flexibility, and the possibility of a changing content of obligations related to changes in social and economic conditions. Thus he approved[280] of the recognition by tribunals of the 'evolution' of treaty obligations as, for example, in the following passage from the decision of the European Court of Human Rights in the *Marckx* case:[281]

The Government concede that the law at issue may appear open to criticism but plead that the problem of reforming it arose only several years after the entry into force of the European Convention on Human Rights in respect of Belgium (14 June 1955), that is with the adoption of the Brussels Convention of 12 September 1962 on the Establishment of Maternal Affiliation of Natural Children (see paragraph 20 above).

It is true that, at the time when the Convention of 4 November 1950 was drafted, it was regarded as permissible and normal in many European countries to draw a distinction in this area between the 'illegitimate' and the 'legitimate' family. However, the Court recalls that this Convention must be interpreted in the light of present-day conditions (*Tyrer* judgment of 25 April 1978, Series A, No. 26, p. 15, § 31). In the instant case, the Court cannot but be struck by the fact that the domestic law of the great majority of the member States of the Council

---

[280] *Mélanges offerts à Paul Reuter* (1981), p. 535 at pp. 544–5.
[281] *Publications of the European Court of Human Rights*, Series A, *Judgments and Decisions*, No. 31, p. 19, para. 41.

of Europe has evolved and is continuing to evolve, in company with the relevant international instruments, towards full juridical recognition of the maxim '*mater semper certa est*'.

Admittedly, of the ten States that drew up the Brussels Convention, only eight have signed and only four have ratified it to date. The European Convention of 15 October 1975 on the Legal Status of Children born out of Wedlock has at present been signed by only ten and ratified by only four members of the Council of Europe. Furthermore, Article 14 § 1 of the latter Convention permits any State to make, at the most, three reservations, one of which could theoretically concern precisely the manner of establishing the maternal affiliation of a child born out of wedlock (Article 2).

However, this state of affairs cannot be relied on in opposition to the evolution noted above. Both the relevant Conventions are in force and there is no reason to attribute the currently small number of Contracting States to a refusal to admit equality between 'illegitimate' and 'legitimate' children on the point under consideration. In fact, the existence of these two treaties denotes that there is a clear measure of common ground in this area amongst modern societies.

As always he recognized the problem of finding the proper balance and did not offer a monolithic view of the question under review. Thus, with reference to the practice of the European Court and in the context of his approval of the 'evolutionary' approach, he sums up in this fashion:[282]

The line between a judicial determination that the meaning of a provision of the Convention has evolved in response to changed conditions and judicial *legislation* may, clearly, be a fine one, and views may sometimes differ as to precisely when interpretation ceases and legislation begins. Indeed, in a dissenting opinion in the *Marckx* case Judge Fitzmaurice made it plain that he believed the Court to have abandoned interpretation for legislation in that case. In the *Tyrer* case the Court itself recognised that 'evolutionary' interpretation by reference to modern conditions has its limits and could not justify the recognition of a general right to legal aid in civil proceedings in evident conflict with the original intention of those who drew up the Convention. The cases here discussed appear, however, now to have established that, within those limits,[283] the meaning and content of the provisions of the Convention will be understood by the Commission and Court of Human Rights as intended to evolve in response to changes in legal or social concepts. That this approach to the construction of the Convention is in harmony with the general principles governing the interpretation of treaties seems clear from the pronouncements already cited of the International Court of Justice, in analogous contexts in the *Aegean Sea* and *Namibia* cases.[284] Indeed, the approach adopted by the Commission and Court may also be considered to be inherent in the character of the Convention as an instrument designed to be the Council of Europe's 'Bill of Rights';[285] for such an 'evolutionary', or in the modern idiom 'progressive',

[282] Waldock in *Mélanges offerts à Paul Reuter* (1981), p. 535 at p. 547.

[283] The duty to respect the limits of the interpretative process is strongly emphasized by Judge Fitzmaurice in a separate opinion in the *National Union of Belgian Police* case (1975), Series A, No. 19, pp. 30 ff.

[284] *I.C.J. Reports*, 1978, pp. 32–4, and ibid. 1971, pp. 31–2, respectively.

[285] Waldock, this *Year Book*, 34 (1958), pp. 356–63; F. A. Mann, *Law Quarterly Review*, 94 (1978), pp. 512–33.

approach has certainly been manifested by the Supreme Court over the years in its interpretations of the guarantees of individual rights in the United States Constitution.[286]

A particular quality of Waldock's approach was his common sense. Lawyers often pretend that, if the correct formulation is discovered, a rule can be applied with greater success. Sometimes this is true, but rules are by nature general and ultimately they have to be *applied*—on the basis of the 'appreciation' of the decision-maker. Waldock did not insist that all difficulties were the outcome of villainy or bad drafting—there often remains an area of genuine difficulty. Similarly, he accepted that tribunals inevitably make law whenever they apply rules, however familiar, to new sets of facts. He also avoided the irritating habit of trying to have things both ways in criticism of tribunals: that is to say, of accusing them on one occasion of conservatism and on another of judicial legislation.

A good proportion of Waldock's published work grew out of his practical experience. This is particularly true of his articles in this *Year Book* on the release of the *Altmark*'s prisoners,[287] the disputed sovereignty in the Falkland Islands Dependencies,[288] the *Anglo-Norwegian Fisheries* case,[289] and the 'decline of the Optional Clause'.[290]

Overall Waldock's published works reflect recurrent themes in his practice, and thus mirror the major concerns of international law in a twenty-five years period beginning in 1947. An important subject for Waldock was the law relating to acquisition of territory. His article relating to the disputes with Chile and Argentina over sovereignty in respect of the Falkland Islands Dependencies remains a classic on the subject. It conveys the essence of the concept of title very well and the subject-matter responds to the common lawyer's capacity to connect principles and circumstantial and symbolic evidences of title. The acquisition of title to territory is often regarded—in academic circles—as theoretical, out of date and, in short, non-existent. The truth is that in the world of diplomacy and practice the subject has great importance. Disputes over title are numerous, though not always publicized. Moreover, disputes regarded as merely of 'historical' interest may suddenly come alive: and the Falklands dispute is an illustration of the contingent importance of many disputes. The relevance of territorial disputes is marked by the incidence of adjudications, including the *Temple* case,[291] the *Palena* case,[292] the *Rann of Kutch* arbitration,[293] the *Western Sahara* advisory opinion[294] and the *Beagle Channel* arbitration.[295] Other adjudications

---

[286] e.g. on questions of racial discrimination and, interestingly enough, on questions of legal aid. See 'Partners in Law', a B.B.C. radio broadcast of a conversation between Lord Scarman and Professor Archibald Cox of Harvard University, recorded in *The Listener* of 7 February 1980.

[287] Vol. 24 (1947), p. 216.

[288] Vol. 25 (1948), p. 311.

[289] Vol. 28 (1951), p. 114.

[290] Vol. 32 (1955-6), p. 244.

[291] *I.C.J. Reports*, 1962, p. 6.

[292] 38 I.L.R. 10.

[293] 50 I.L.R. 2.

[294] *I.C.J. Reports*, 1975, p. 12.

[295] 52 I.L.R. 93.

wait in the corridors of confidential diplomacy. It may be recalled that the writings of Sir Gerald Fitzmaurice[296] and Sir Robert Jennings[297] indicate the significance of the problems of proving title to territory.

From his early contact with international law at the Admiralty until the end of his career Waldock was interested in and involved with the law of the sea in its various aspects. His wartime experience was obviously focused upon the law of naval warfare and questions of neutrality, and this surfaced in his article on the release of the *Altmark*'s prisoners. A considerable amount of his legal practice was concerned with delimitation problems in respect of territorial sea fisheries zones and continental shelf areas. The quantity of this practice is not reflected in his publications. The chief outcome was the important critique of the judgment in the *Anglo-Norwegian Fisheries* case.[298] During his term on the International Court he delivered a lecture on 'The International Court and the Law of the Sea',[299] and at a much earlier period he was Chairman of the International Committee of the I.L.A. on Rights to the Seabed and Subsoil, which reported to the Edinburgh Conference in 1954.[300]

Both in his teaching and in his writing Waldock exhibited an abiding interest in the practical problems of the maintenance of peace, including the issues of collective security and the definition of aggression. He was involved in the work of several non-governmental bodies on the problems of revision of the United Nations Charter, at a stage when it was still fairly widely believed that Charter revision was the way forward.[301] Not long before his death Waldock wrote a review of the *Collected Papers of Hersch Lauterpacht*,[302] in which he singled out Lauterpacht's papers (written in the years 1941–3) entitled 'The Principles of International Organization' and 'Sovereignty and Federation in International Relations'. Waldock shows a strong sympathy for the practical idealism which inspired Hersch Lauterpacht's thinking on such matters as the creation of machinery for peaceful change and 'the principle of majority rule' in international organization. The ideas expressed by Lauterpacht and admired by Waldock may seem threatened by the rough seas of contemporary international relations: yet it has proved impossible to find better basic designs and it is difficult to accuse those whose adult lives coincided with

---

[296] See, in particular, this *Year Book*, 32 (1955–6), pp. 20–76, and *Recueil des cours*, 92 (1957–II), pp. 129–50.

[297] See his monograph: *The Acquisition of Territory in International Law* (1963).

[298] This *Year Book*, 28 (1951), p. 114. See also *International Relations*, published by the David Davies Memorial Institute of International Studies (1956), pp. 163–94: 'International Law and the New Maritime Claims.'

[299] The Cornelis Van Vollenhoven lecture, 22 May 1979, published by the T.M.C. Asser Institute, The Hague.

[300] *Report of the Forty-Sixth Conference* (1954), p. 425.

[301] This approach has not disappeared from view: see President Carter's Report on the *Reform and Restructuring of the United Nations System*, submitted to Congress on 2 March 1978.

[302] Edited by E. Lauterpacht, 4 vols. 1970–8. The review appears in this *Year Book*, 52 (1981), p. 255.

the Second World War and its associated disasters for civilian populations of a lack of realism. The events of the War—and more, the full knowledge of those events which Waldock and his contemporaries had—gives a particular authority to the views they formed about the future of international organization.

The logical adjunct of the problems of international organization and collective security is the study of the legal regulation of the use of force by States. Waldock's first experience of international law—his service at the Admiralty—involved the law of war, and especially of naval warfare, and his role as Counsel in the *Corfu Channel* case[303] falls into this pattern. There was also the preparation of a revised British *Naval Prize Manual* in the aftermath of the Second World War, a project which must have been much to his taste. His publications, aside from his article on the *Altmark* incident,[304] were not related to the law of war, the *jus in bello*, but rather to the *jus ad bellum*, the legality of the use of force by individual States. He gave a course of lectures on this subject at the Hague Academy in 1952,[305] and the issues figured prominently in his lectures at Oxford. More succinct treatments appear in his General Course of lectures delivered at The Hague Academy in 1962,[306] and in the ninth chapter of Waldock's edition of Brierly's *Law of Nations*,[307] which was written entirely by Waldock and replaced Brierly's short chapter on the subject.

Waldock's views on the use of force by States were expounded with characteristic lucidity and have been influential, not least in the practice of the United Kingdom.[308] Whilst in all his writing he was at pains to relate the law of the United Nations and other new developments to classical international law, in the present context he tended to give considerable play to the pre-existing customary law on the basis that Article 51 of the Charter constituted a reservation of the former customary law rules.[309] Waldock was not alone in this view, which is shared by Bowett[310] but not by the present writer.[311]

As the paradigm of international adjudication—or at least the *modern* paradigm, since *ad hoc* courts of arbitration used to be the standard—the International Court of Justice stands at the centre of the world of the professional international lawyer. The role of the Court in the settlement of disputes rests upon the consent of States and the expression of this consent is the subject of a specialized body of knowledge relating to the Optional Clause in the Statute of the International Court.

---

[303] See above.
[304] See above.
[305] *Recueil des cours*, 81 (1952–II), pp. 455–517.
[306] Ibid. 106 (1962–II), p. 1 at pp. 230–46.
[307] 6th edn. (1963), pp. 397–432.
[308] See this *Year Book*, 50 (1979), p. 384.
[309] See *Recueil des cours*, 81 (1952–II), pp. 495–503; 106 (1962–II), pp. 232–7.
[310] *Self-Defence in International Law* (1958), pp. 182–99.
[311] See this *Year Book*, 37 (1961), p. 183; *International Law and the Use of Force by States* (1963).

The expression of consent is limited by means of reservations and in the *Right of Passage* case (*Preliminary Objections*)[312] Waldock (as Counsel for India) was much concerned with this complex world of tactics affecting the jurisdiction of what is strictly speaking a *juge d'exception*. In fact the first case in which he had been engaged as Counsel, the *Corfu Channel* case (*Preliminary Objection*),[313] had given rise to issues of jurisdiction.

The jurisdictional questions affecting the Court provoked a series of articles by Waldock which have remained classic expositions of the subject. The first, though short, provides a very useful discussion of the question of *forum prorogatum*—that is, the conditions under which jurisdiction may be obtained as a result of a unilateral summons to appear before the Court, and the subsequent informal acceptance of jurisdiction by the defendant State.[314] The second and third articles were concerned with the more general question of the working of the system of consensual jurisdiction existing by virtue of the Statute of the International Court. In the second article Waldock examined the plea of domestic jurisdiction before international tribunals.[315] The piece is Waldock at his best: all the relevant elements are carefully analysed and a balanced judgment is given. Moreover, the jurisdictional issue is related to the fundamental question of the ambit of the reserved domain of jurisdiction in terms of general international law.

The third article, entitled 'The Decline of the Optional Clause',[316] is particularly well known. It makes a frank and incisive study of the technical weaknesses of the Optional Clause. The result is the following prognosis:[317]

That there has been a sensible decline in the quality of State practice under the Optional Clause is manifest. If the tendencies discussed in the present article continue, the large majority of declarations will become terminable either immediately or on short notice, while a number will contain particular escape clauses. There appears even to be some danger that the attitude of States towards the Optional Clause may degenerate into one of pure opportunism, declarations being made, cancelled and varied as the immediate interests of each State may dictate.

In general terms the picture has remained the same,[318] although the famous 'automatic' form of reservation[319] has fallen out of fashion to some extent.[320] Indeed, the evidence of the malaise which caused concern to

---

[312] *I.C.J. Reports*, 1957, p. 125.

[313] Ibid. 1948, p. 15.

[314] *International Law Quarterly*, 2 (1948), p. 377.

[315] See this *Year Book*, 31 (1954), p. 96.

[316] Ibid. 32 (1955–6), p. 244.

[317] Ibid., p. 283.

[318] See the study by Merrills, ibid. 50 (1979), p. 87.

[319] '. . . Provided, that this declaration shall not apply to . . . (b) disputes with regard to matters which are essentially within the domestic jurisdiction of the United States of America as determined by the United States of America . . .'

[320] See Crawford, ibid., p. 63.

Waldock has increased dramatically with the phenomenon of the non-appearing defendant State, to which reference has already been made.[321] Seen in a long perspective, the problems of reservations and escape clauses in acceptances of jurisdiction constitute the symptoms but not the disease itself: although it is still useful to criticize some of the more abusive attempts to appear virtuous whilst retaining considerable liberty of action. The problems are, of course, ultimately political, and Waldock, always realistic, was quick to recognize this. Thus, in his General Course given at the Hague Academy in 1962, the chapter devoted to the 'Judicial process in international law' concludes as follows:[322]

> In general, the judicial process has stood still and the reasons for it are not far to seek. The tensions of the cold war and the violent changes taking place in the political structure of the world community create a climate unfavourable to the working of the judicial process. The regular and effective functioning of the judicial process in any community is the result rather than the cause of stable political conditions.

There is perhaps an element in the picture which should be added. In spite of the weaknesses of the system of the Optional Clause, and by a paradox, States still do find the need to resort to adjudication by international tribunals in order to settle disputes, most of which involve important subject-matter by any standards of informed judgment. Since 1981 the following cases have been referred to the International Court: the *Tunisia–Libya Continental Shelf* case, the *Gulf of Maine* case (Canada–United States), the *Malta–Libya Continental Shelf* case and *Mali* v. *Upper Volta*. At the time of writing the more or less arcane knowledge of practitioners extends to at least three other disputes which may go either to the Court or to an *ad hoc* court of arbitration. Thus the system of the Optional Clause is by no means an index of resort to adjudication. It is the case that States prefer a very specific and recent, and therefore 'politically focused', consensual basis of jurisdiction.

Incidentally, it is to be noted that the view of Waldock as to the legal effect of the 'automatic reservation' has received strong criticism in a carefully reasoned article by Professor James Crawford.[323] Waldock shared the views of Judge Sir Hersch Lauterpacht and others[324] to the effect that the 'automatic reservation' was incompatible with Article 36 of the Statute of the International Court.[325] Crawford provides attractive reasons for thinking that, undesirable though the 'automatic reservation' may be, and of that he has no doubt, there are three ways in which such

---

[321] See above.

[322] *Recueil des cours*, 106 (1962–II), p. 120. See also the conclusion to the article on the Optional Clause, loc. cit. above (p. 66 n. 290), pp. 286–7.

[323] See this *Year Book*, 50 (1979), p. 63.

[324] For the citations: ibid., pp. 64–5.

[325] See Waldock, ibid. 31 (1954), pp. 131–7; ibid. 32 (1955–6), p. 277; *Recueil des cours*, 106 (1962–II), pp. 111–12.

a reservation may be valid and compatible with Article 36 of the Statute. Thus Crawford argues, *inter alia*:[326]

If treaty reservation rules are to be applied, then the general acquiescence of States parties in the making of automatic reservations would appear to be effective, under the customary equivalent of Article 20 of the Vienna Convention, to make automatic declarants parties to the Optional Clause, unless the Court would be prepared to substitute a contrary view of its object and purpose. It has shown little inclination to do so.

During his term on the International Court Waldock delivered a number of occasional lectures on the work of the Court.[327] One of these, noticed earlier in the present study, took the form of an examination of the contribution made by the Court to the development of the law of the sea.[328] In 1976 Waldock gave the fourth of the Gilberto Amado Memorial Lectures and chose as his subject the advisory jurisdiction of the International Court.[329] The concluding passages are of considerable interest, not least because they follow express reference to the *Namibia*[330] and *Western Sahara*[331] cases. They are as follows:[332]

Clearly, the Court has moved quite a distance beyond the decidedly reserved attitude of the Permanent Court towards issues of fact in advisory cases. In this, as in other matters, it has tended to assimilate advisory to contentious proceedings. But to assimilate is not to convert into the same thing. In advisory proceedings, even where a Request relates to an existing dispute, the States concerned are not parties to a contentious *case*; only parties to a dispute in connection with which the requesting organ has asked for an opinion. On matters of fact their relation to the Court is on a different basis from that of parties in contentious proceedings. They are not normally under any obligation to participate in the proceedings, so that their failure to do so is not therefore equivalent to a default of appearance. When they do so, they strictly speaking furnish information to the Court rather than evidence and proof. Similarly, the primary responsibility of the Court is to the requesting organ rather than to the individual States, however specially interested these may be in the questions referred to the Court. These differences, which are not merely technical, indicate that, in the Court's treatment of issues of fact, there may be limits to the process of assimilation.

The two Courts, largely by the process of assimilation, have developed the advisory jurisdiction into a flexible instrument capable, if the will is there, of fulfilling almost any judicial purpose. In the past the purposes for which it has been used have been very varied: constitutional questions, bilateral legal disputes, appeals from judicial or quasi-judicial tribunals, legal issues arising before

---

[326] Loc. cit. above (p. 70 n. 323), p. 85.

[327] One of these lectures is printed in this *Year Book*, p. 1.

[328] The Cornelis van Vollenhoven Memorial Lecture, *The International Court and the Law of the Sea* (1979): and see above, pp. 56-7, for the conclusions.

[329] *Aspects of the Advisory Jurisdiction of the International Court of Justice*, lecture delivered on 3 June 1976 (published by the United Nations, 1976).

[330] *I.C.J. Reports*, 1971, p. 16.

[331] Ibid. 1975, p. 12.

[332] At pp. 12-13 of the lecture as published.

international organisations. Indeed, it is because of the varied character of advisory cases that the Court has kept its Rules of Procedure for these cases comparatively short and adaptable to their particular circumstances. Under the United Nations, as I have indicated, there has been an increasing tendency for requests to concern the activities of the requesting organ and yet closely involve the specific interests of particular States. This makes it all the more important for the Court to maintain the strictly judicial character of its advisory function, from whatever body the Request may emanate and whatever the nature of the questions put to the Court.

The part which Waldock played in the European Commission of Human Rights in putting human rights to work in the context of the European Convention of Human Rights has been examined earlier in this study. It is clear that his influence was that of the decision-maker and as a member of the Commission in its early, pioneer, phase. Consequently, it would be an error to measure his contribution in terms of his publications on the subject of human rights. However, his writing provides clear evidence of his interest in and commitment to the legal methods of implementation of the standards of human rights referred to in the Universal Declaration of Human Rights of 1948 and the European Convention of 1950.[333] His particular ability was to see the need to assimilate the new concepts to the mainstream of general international law. The process has still not been completed and some lawyers have not yet even perceived the problems. Waldock always saw things as a whole, as a practitioner should. Without great elaboration he saw the connections between the new standards and the problems of diplomatic protection and nationality of claims.[334] He was also concerned to explain the significance which the Universal Declaration *could have* as a result of developments in the practice of States.[335] Indeed, he went so far as to write in 1962 that:

. . . it may now be possible to regard the Declaration as an authoritative expression of the customary international law of to-day in regard to human rights or, at least, the customary law of the United Nations on that subject.[336]

In the same connection Waldock, in two essays, examined the problems of treaty interpretation arising from the work of the European Court of Human Rights.[337] As it has already been seen, he gave general approval to the 'evolutionary' approach of the Court to the construction of the

---

[333] For his account of the functioning of the European Convention see this *Year Book*, 34 (1958), p. 356; *La Comunitá Internazionale* (1975), p. 3.

[334] See his General Course at the Hague Academy: *Recueil des cours*, 106 (1962-II), pp. 192-211; and in British Institute of International and Comparative Law, *The European Convention on Human Rights*, *International and Comparative Law Quarterly*, Supplementary Publication No. 18 (1965), p. 1 at pp. 2-3.

[335] *Recueil des cours*, 106 (1962-II), pp. 32-3, 198-9; British Institute publication (previous note), pp. 2-3.

[336] *Recueil des cours*, 106 (1962-II), pp. 32-3.

[337] See *Mélanges offerts à Paul Reuter* (1981), p. 535; *Human Rights Law Journal*, 1 (1980), p. 1.

.European Convention.[338] Like Sir Gerald Fitzmaurice, Waldock found it necessary to place the issues concerning human rights within the general framework of international law and to analyse the problems within that broad technical perspective.

XII. Envoi

Much of Waldock's professional life is documented, often, but by no means always, in publications readily available in most libraries. Apart from such sources, the writer has made some use of unpublished material, but this has called for a necessary discretion. A further source has been personal knowledge of Waldock's views and attitudes gained in the course of the writer's life in Oxford, whether as an undergraduate attending Waldock's lectures, as a postgraduate preparing a doctoral thesis under his supervision, as his colleague within the Law Faculty for ten years, or as a member of the Bar. Both as supervisor and, later, as a colleague, he was helpful, always approachable, and a source of careful and undogmatic criticism.

His attitude toward theory is to be remarked. He had no deep interest in theory as such. This is not to suggest that he neglected it, and his lectures and writings would contain incisive analysis of the principal theories attending such subjects as the relation of national and international law, and the recognition of States. Waldock's penchant was to analyse the existing experience and to probe behind the façade of concepts. Analysis and legal technique were his chosen instruments. In this he was not unlike other British lawyers of his generation, and his writing compares well with the productions of those writers whose ambitious superstructures of theory do nothing to improve objectivity and tend to divert attention from the existing stock of experience. It should also be said that, in general, attachment to theory has little or no connection with interest in *ideas*, that is to say, the political and moral concepts and standards at work in society and which influence law-making. As his writing on human rights shows, Waldock was by no means indifferent to the world of ideas.

The object of this study has been to commemorate Waldock by setting out a sort of geography of the terrain of international law based upon his career. The account could only be more or less biographical in relation to the many important episodes which involved collegiate activity and work within institutions, especially in the case of the European Commission of Human Rights, the European Court of Human Rights, the International Law Commission, and the International Court. This condition of the study can be the more tolerated once it is understood that the general intention has been commemorative and not biographical. Moreover, what Waldock did, others did, and that is why his career is an appropriate basis

---

[338] See above.

for describing a substantial sample of the work of the international lawyer. The particular features of Sir Humphrey Waldock's career were the unique curriculum vitae, the high standards which he applied in the various offices which came his way, and his dedication to the practical science of the peaceful settlement of disputes between States.

INTERNATIONAL LAW AND FOREIGN SOVEREIGNS: DISTINGUISHING IMMUNE TRANSACTIONS*

By JAMES CRAWFORD[1]

I. INTRODUCTION

IN the hubbub of decision, enactment and debate on the subject of foreign sovereign immunity and foreign act of State in the last decade,[2] one thing at least remains puzzlingly clear. It is confidently asserted what sovereign immunity is not, and—unlike the situation earlier this century—these assertions, if we ignore for the moment the insistence of the Soviet Union and certain other countries that the State is indivisible, have a comforting air of uniformity. Sovereign immunity is not absolute. It is—another way of asserting the negative—restricted. But what is clear is that we lack a rationale, a connected explanation, for this state of affairs, an articulated set of criteria which would enable us to draw the distinction between cases in which States or their transactions are entitled to immunity from the jurisdiction of other States[3] as a matter of international law and cases in which they are not.[4]

---

* © Professor James Crawford, 1984.

[1] Professor of Law, The University of Adelaide; Commissioner, Australian Law Reform Commission. The author is Commissioner in Charge of the Australian Law Reform Commission's Reference on Foreign State Immunity. The views expressed here are personal, and do not necessarily represent those of the Commission. The author wishes to thank Mr. S. R. Curran, Senior Law Reform Officer with the Commission, for his assistance and insight.

[2] The literature on both topics is vast. Earlier works which remain valuable are Fitzmaurice, this *Year Book*, 14 (1933), pp. 100–24; Fawcett, ibid. 25 (1948), pp. 24–51; Lauterpacht, ibid. 28 (1957), pp. 220–72; Brandon, *Cornell Law Quarterly*, 39 (1954), pp. 425–62; Garcia-Mora, *Virginia Law Review*, 42 (1956), pp. 335–59; Sucharitkul, *State Immunity and Trading Activities in International Law* (1959). More recent literature on State immunity includes Lissitzyn, in Friedmann, Henkin and Lissitzyn (eds.), *Transnational Law in a Changing Society. Essays in Honor of Philip C. Jessup* (1972), pp. 188–201; Sucharitkul, *Recueil des cours*, 149 (1976–II), pp. 89–215; Johnson, *Australian Yearbook of International Law*, 6 (1978), pp. 1–51; Brownlie, *Principles of Public International Law* (3rd edn., 1979), pp. 321–44; Schreuer, *Comparative Law Yearbook*, 1978, pp. 215–36; Sinclair, *Recueil des cours*, 167 (1980–II), pp. 113–284; Hill, *Fordham Law Review*, 50 (1981), pp. 155–238; Ress, in Bothe and Vinuesa (eds.), *International Law and Municipal Law* (1982), pp. 67–94; and the essays collected in the *Netherlands Yearbook of International Law*, 10 (1979). See also United Nations Legislative Series, *Materials on Jurisdictional Immunities of States and their Property* (ST/LEG/SER.B/20, 1982). The literature on act of State is directed mostly to particular municipal law versions of the doctrine, with occasional comparative flurries. See, e.g., Van Panhuys, *International and Comparative Law Quarterly*, 13 (1964), pp. 1193–1213; Greene, *Cornell International Law Journal*, 8 (1975), pp. 273–89; Kindred, *Revue de droit de l'Université de Sherbrooke*, 10 (1979), pp. 271–88; Rich, *Virginia Journal of International Law*, 19 (1979), pp. 679–89; Singer, *American Journal of International Law*, 75 (1981), pp. 283–323; Lloyd Jones, *Virginia Journal of International Law*, 22 (1982), pp. 433–79; Fraser, *Fordham Law Review*, 51 (1983), pp. 722–46.

[3,4] [*Footnotes 3 and 4 overleaf.*]

Obviously enough, the set of explanations presently offered will not do. For example, section 1602, the central finding specified in the Foreign Sovereign Immunities Act 1976 (U.S.A.), asserts that

> Under international law, states are not immune from the jurisdiction of foreign courts insofar as their commercial activities are concerned, and their commercial property may be levied upon for the satisfaction of judgments rendered against them in connection with their commercial activities.

But the Act's appeal to 'commercial activities' does not account for the lines it draws between immune and non-immune transactions. For example, if the ambassador of a foreign State in the United States protests against the exercise by United States courts of antitrust jurisdiction with respect to a commercial activity of an instrumentality of that foreign State abroad, it is difficult to see how (except in a sense of 'commerce' that renders the asserted distinction meaningless) the ambassador engages in 'commercial activity'. Yet on the literal interpretation of section 1605 (a) (2) ('an act performed in the United States in connection with a commercial activity of the foreign state elsewhere') this is precisely what he does.[5] Similarly, if the ambassador orders an assassin to kill an enemy of his government in the forum and the assassin succeeds, the foreign State commits a non-immune tort within the jurisdiction.[6] Yet the assassination is hardly a commercial transaction, whether or not the assassin is paid.

The distinction is sometimes put another way: foreign 'governmental' transactions are immune; foreign 'non-governmental' ones are not. But what is it, in acts of a government, that renders them governmental or otherwise? Only some general theory of government, that is, of the functions peculiar to or distinctive of government—or, alternatively, only some conventional test of what is to count as 'governmental'—could provide an answer. Yet it is trite to say that, internationally, there is no agreement between different ideologies on this question.[7] Indeed, there is little agreement on it even within many Western countries.

A third distinction, between 'governmental' and 'commercial' trans-actions, compounds the fallacies of the other two, since it assumes not merely that the terms are complementary but also that they are, taken together, comprehensive. It would be remarkable enough if the two

---

[3] In fact attention has been devoted almost exclusively to immunity from judicial jurisdiction, to the neglect of other forms of State jurisdiction. But see, e.g., Brower, *American Journal of International Law*, 71 (1977), pp. 438–60.

[4] To similar effect cf. Brownlie, loc. cit. above (p. 75 n. 2); Higgins, *Netherlands International Law Review*, 29 (1982), pp. 265–76; Triggs, *Monash University Law Review*, 9 (1982), pp. 74–113; Sornarajah, *International and Comparative Law Quarterly*, 31 (1982), pp. 661–85.

[5] On the divergent interpretations of these provisions see O'Neil, *Journal of International Law and Economics*, 13 (1979), pp. 633–49; Wheeler, *New York University Journal of International Law and Politics*, 13 (1981), pp. 571–615; Pell, *Cornell International Law Journal*, 14 (1981), pp. 97–115; Johnson and Worthington, *Georgia Journal of International and Comparative Law*, 12 (1982), pp. 209–30.

[6] Cf. the facts of *Letelier* v. *Chile*, 488 F. Supp. 665 (1980) (though it was not suggested that the Ambassador was involved in that case); below, p. 110.   [7] See below, p. 89.

notions did not overlap; to claim that they fit precisely to cover the field is not to analyse but to stipulate. When we are told that 'by definition, acts in connection with a commercial activity are not acts which give effect to the public interest'[8] (sc. are 'governmental') we had better abandon the attempt at definition and go back to first principles.

This is not to say that the developing law of restrictive State immunity is necessarily insecure or radically defective. But it is the case that its foundations are poorly articulated. And unless the underlying principles are better articulated, they are not going to persuade doubters, or assist in drawing distinctions in difficult cases. Incoherent articulation may indeed lead to a breakdown in the law altogether, with (presumably) a consequent extension of national jurisdiction. Such a process of disintegration is familiar in other contexts (e.g. the extension of coastal jurisdiction in the law of the sea). But in a matter as fundamental as jurisdiction over foreign sovereign acts, it is very much a last resort. Indeed, if international law cannot regulate this conflict of sovereignties its own claims to coherence must be questioned.

The need for articulation is, it is true, not a new one. The simple assertion, *par in parem non habet jurisdictionem*, which is said to underlie the principle of jurisdictional immunity,[9] is itself question-begging. In a world in which some States are equal to anything, with respect to which issues (if not all) are States to be regarded as *pares*, equals—and hence, presumably, susceptible to coercive jurisdiction only with their consent? The notion that a foreign State defendant was always an equal in this sense, while it may have simplified matters, was itself unsatisfactory. Why should not a forum State assume jurisdiction to do justice in a matter occurring within its boundaries and governed by its law? The simple assertion of local competence, of fairness to plaintiffs, is at the root of the breakdown of the old law.[10] But it too does nothing to solve the problem—short of universal territorial competence, which is not a principle of immunity.

In response to these difficulties it is sometimes said that the distinction between immune and non-immune transactions is not drawn by international law but by municipal law, so that if the distinction varies between States (as it does) this is merely a reflection of differences in the municipal law of each State—no new phenomenon.[11] Of course, the detailed working

---

[8] Haworth, *Rutgers Law Review*, 34 (1982), pp. 538–66 at p. 564 n. 140.

[9] Cf. *The Schooner Exchange* v. *M'Faddon*, 7 Cranch 116 (1812).

[10] Thus in *The Philippine Admiral*, [1977] A.C. 373, once it was established that neither international law nor domestic precedent required immunity to be accorded, jurisdiction was asserted as a matter of fairness to the plaintiff: see at pp. 402–3 ('the restrictive theory is more consonant with justice').

[11] See, e.g., *Claim Against the Empire of Iran* case (1963), 45 I.L.R. 57 at p. 80; repeated by the Federal Constitutional Court in its *Philippines Embassy* decision of 13 December 1977, *Zeitschrift für ausländisches öffentliches Recht und Völkerrecht*, 38 (1978), p. 242 at p. 278, where the Court stated that 'the classification of a State's function (according to the legal nature of the act) as governmental or non-governmental must be determined according to current domestic law, as international law does

out of any distinction may depend to a considerable extent on the substantive law of the forum State: for example, whether it has, as some civil law jurisdictions do but common law ones do not, a ready-made distinction between the capacities in which the forum government (and thus perhaps, by analogy, a foreign government) acts.[12] Even more important, it must depend on the procedural and remedial law of the forum State. There is certainly room for divergences here, quite apart from the point that a State need not exercise jurisdiction with respect to a foreign State defendant, but may accord immunity as a matter of comity, deference or strategy.[13]

But this response must go further. The claim must be that international law (once the theory of absolute or general immunity is disposed of) does not *require* immunity to be accorded to foreign State defendants or to their transactions or property in any case.[14] For, as soon as it is conceded that (special rules apart) international law does require some such immunity, then international law distinguishes to that extent between immune and non-immune transactions, and the question becomes on what basis it is doing so. The difficulty with the sceptical response to the problem is that there is virtually universal agreement that a State is entitled to immunity with respect at least to some transactions.[15] This agreement might perhaps be illusory, in that the formulae used to embody this 'hard core' of immune transactions may turn out on analysis to be empty of content or devoid of meaning. But the point is that one cannot simply assume either possibility. The initial assumption should be that international law does allow such distinctions to be drawn, that it does not leave them to the uneven discretion of forum States. But that assumption requires first an investigation of the different senses in which States and their transactions might be said to be immune from local jurisdiction.

II. State Immunity, Act of State, Choice of Law

There are at least four levels at which a municipal court might respond to a foreign State transaction or activity presented directly to it as the subject of litigation. This is quite apart from those cases where the foreign

---

not, as a rule, include criteria for such a delineation'. Similarly, Article 3 of the resolution of the Institut de Droit International in 1954 stated that 'la question de savoir si un acte n'est pas de puissance publique relève de la lex fori': *Annuaire de l'Institut de Droit International*, 46 (1954), pp. 301–2.

[12] For criticism of the terminology in common law systems see Harlow, *Modern Law Review*, 43 (1980), pp. 241–65.

[13] Cf. the position taken by the State Immunity Act 1978 (U.K.) in the case of foreign central banks: below, p. 118.

[14] Lauterpacht went close to adopting this position, but having rejected most of the orthodox bases of immunity he apparently allowed a quite extensive area of immunity in, as it were, through the back door: loc. cit. above (p. 75 n. 2) at pp. 237–9. For an 'abolitionist' view see Falk, *The Role of Domestic Courts in the International Legal Order* (1964), pp. 139–69.

[15] See, e.g., the replies to the I.L.C. Questionnaire, in U.N.L.S., *Materials* (above, p. 75 n. 2), pp. 559–648.

State's involvement can be distinguished, or treated as subsidiary or indirect or as not arising. First, the court might decline to deal with the case simply on the ground of the foreign State's involvement. Secondly, the court might decline to adjudicate on the State transaction or activity, while attempting as far as possible to deal with the case apart from the transaction or activity. Thirdly, the court might recognize the transaction as valid (or invalid) under the relevant law, and decide the case accordingly, while refusing to carry out or implement the transaction in any active way. Fourthly, the court might implement or enforce the transaction by its own adjudication and enforcement powers.[16] Plainly, State immunity issues arise at the first level only; the second level (and to some extent the third) involve the so-called act of State doctrine (and a related non-justiciability rule), while the third and (in the absence of some authoritative direction to enforce foreign State acts irrespective of their validity under the relevant law or laws) the fourth involve the range of issues usually classified as ones of the conflict of laws.[17]

The peculiarity of the first level, as distinct from the other three, is that it alone depends on the identity of the parties to the case. State immunity is an issue only where the defendant is a foreign State or an entity identified with a foreign State.[18] In orthodox terms, it is an immunity *ratione personae*, not *ratione materiae* (though the shift to restrictive immunity is tending to obscure the distinction). It is relatively easy to see how international law might be regarded as influencing or even controlling the substantive law that a court should apply in cases involving acts of a foreign State. Thus if State B has authority under international law to determine a particular matter (e.g. the nationality of a person sufficiently connected with State B, or whether a person is entitled to vote in State B), it may well be that the courts of State A should not decline to recognize that authority.[19] *A fortiori*, if international law itself prescribes the substantive rule, it is easy to see that a particular State should not be allowed to apply an inconsistent rule.[20] But it is harder to see how international law requires the forum State to decline jurisdiction on the basis of the 'sovereign' identity of the defendant.

There is, however, one international law rule which might be regarded

---

[16] On the distinction between 'recognition' and 'enforcement' of foreign State acts see, e.g., Dicey and Morris, *The Conflict of Laws* (10th edn., 1980), vol. 2, pp. 1035–43.

[17] The term has an expanded meaning here since the conflict might be one between international law and one of the municipal laws involved.

[18] Or where the State is 'indirectly impleaded' by an action affecting its property: cf. *United States of America* v. *Dollfus Mieg et Cie.*, [1952] A.C. 582; *Juan Ysmael & Co. Inc.* v. *Government of the Republic of Indonesia*, [1955] A.C. 72.

[19] They may, of course, decline to enforce a claim based on a foreign 'act of State', e.g. on the ground that it involves a penal, revenue or 'public' law: cf. *Attorney-General of New Zealand* v. *Ortiz*, [1982] 2 Lloyd's Rep. 224 (C.A.), decided by the House of Lords on other grounds: [1983] 2 Lloyd's Rep. 265.

[20] The State could avoid doing so by applying either the international law rule itself or some rule of municipal law consistent with it.

as precluding the exercise of jurisdiction on such a ground: that is, the rule that a State cannot be required to submit to international adjudication without its consent.[21] This 'international dispute settlement rule' (as it will be called for convenience) is a rule about parties, not about the content of the law, and it is the nearest direct analogue in international law to the rule of State immunity.[22] One difficulty is that municipal courts are not obviously engaged in 'international adjudication' in the sense of the rule, since they do not necessarily apply international law, and since the defendant State is not necessarily bound by the judgment in international law. Moreover, the direct application of the rule to domestic courts would produce an unqualified rule of absolute immunity. This cannot be accepted, since at least some transactions are by international law presumptively referred to the authority of the forum State—that is to say, transactions occurring within its territory and jurisdiction and not excluded from it by any special rule. There is no consensus that the defendant's identity as a State is as such the basis of any such exclusionary rule.[23]

The distinction between international and municipal adjudication may be accepted, but it does not exhaust the force of the international law rule about adjudicating against foreign States. With respect to transactions not within the jurisdiction of the forum State under international law, how is the forum State in a *better* position than an international judicial forum in asserting compulsory jurisdiction against a foreign State defendant? It could be said that the difference lies in the municipal court's application of its municipal law to the defendant, thus avoiding determining the international issue. But it is a curious justification for adjudicatory authority that the defendant *ex hypothesi* does not accept the rule to be applied. It could be said that the difference lies in the absence of any international obligation on the part of the defendant State to comply with the judgment, but it is a curious justification for adjudicatory authority that the defendant is not obliged under international law to accept the result but may attempt to reverse it by acts of self-help. An exercise of jurisdiction could be justified simply as an extension of law-making authority, on the basis of an acknowledged jurisdiction to prescribe the law, but on the present hypothesis that jurisdiction is precisely not acknowledged; and in any event the judgment is itself regarded as a reason for enforcement action, including execution against State property.[24] In short, although the international law rule prohibiting adjudication against foreign States without their consent may not apply directly to municipal courts, it has

---

[21] Cf. *Monetary Gold removed from Rome in 1943*, *I.C.J. Reports*, 1954, p. 19. The rule was described by the Court in the *Western Sahara* opinion as a 'fundamental rule, repeatedly reaffirmed in the Court's jurisprudence': ibid. 1975, p. 12 at p. 23.

[22] Like the foreign State immunity rule it depends on the absence of consent of the 'defendant' State. The application of choice of law rules does not in principle depend on the defendant's consent.

[23] Cf. below, pp. 86–8.

[24] Cf. below, p. 116.

much force as an analogy, with respect to the matters it covers. But in municipal forums, the international dispute settlement rule covers a relatively narrow range of issues. This does not include matters specifically referred to the authority of the forum (e.g. acts of violence perpetrated on its territory).[25] Nor does it include transactions under a municipal law system with non-State parties: in the absence of special circumstances such transactions are not matters of 'international jurisdiction' in the sense of the rule. They are matters initially of municipal jurisdiction, subject to the 'exhaustion of local remedies' rule.[26]

It has been argued so far that the distinction adopted by international law between international and municipal jurisdictions, and the well-established international dispute settlement rule with respect to the former, provides strong support by analogy, if not directly, for a rule of foreign State immunity in the rather limited areas governed by that jurisdictional rule.[27] But it could be argued that, for the most part at least, a domestic court could act consistently with this requirement if it applied an act of State or non-justiciability doctrine to transactions of the kind described. So it might be said that the international law rule identified here only suggests or requires *some* rule of deference, not a rule of State immunity.[28]

The answer to proposals along such lines takes several forms. It might simply be said that State immunity is a well-established technique of deference in this context, with which courts and States are reasonably familiar, and one whose outright abolition would undoubtedly cause serious concern to many States. Further, given a proper level of articulation in other respects, it is a relatively straightforward and predictable technique—certainly one that is better developed and more certain than the vague, conflicting and disputable act of State and non-justiciability rules with which the United States Supreme Court and the English House of Lords have been grappling in recent years.[29]

More fundamentally, a State immunity rule is more consistent with the international dispute settlement rule, and with the juristic integrity of a municipal system which asserts at least some capacity to apply international law as part of the law of the forum. By contrast neither act of State nor non-justiciability fits these requirements well. The central point is that the State immunity rule is defeasible with the defendant's consent. The act of State doctrine is either a rule treating foreign State acts as valid,

---

[25] It is true that international law in general prohibits such acts of violence by other States. But it does not deprive the forum State of authority (including adjudicatory authority) over them.

[26] Cf. below, p. 84.

[27] Cf. Crawford, *American Journal of International Law*, 75 (1981), pp. 820–69 at pp. 854–8 for an earlier version of the argument.

[28] Cf. Falk, op. cit. above (p. 78 n. 14), for the most persuasive version of this argument.

[29] Cf. *Banco Nacional de Cuba* v. *Sabbatino*, 376 U.S. 398 (1964); *First National City Bank* v. *Banco Nacional de Cuba*, 406 U.S. 759 (1972); *Alfred Dunhill of London Inc.* v. *Republic of Cuba*, 425 U.S. 682 (1976), with *Buttes Gas and Oil Co.* v. *Hammer*, [1982] A.C. 888, noted this *Year Book*, 53 (1982), pp. 259–68.

or as if valid, because they were performed or effected within the foreign State's jurisdiction (whether or not they possess intrinsic validity), or it is a rule about the relative competence of executive and judiciary in matters relating to foreign affairs. If the former, why should the consent of an organ or entity of the defendant State to the exercise of adjudicatory jurisdiction be treated as a denial of that State's assumed competence to act?[30] If the latter, why should the division of governmental power within the forum State be affected or set aside simply at the instance of a defendant State?[31] More subtle act of State theories allow the assertion of local jurisdiction where the relevant international law rules are clear and undisputed.[32] This may be a reasonable response, *ratione materiae*, by a court which seeks to apply international law in cases within its authority: amongst other things it acknowledges the subordinate but still important role domestic courts can play in the international system. But the international dispute settlement rule precludes certain exercises of jurisdiction *ratione personae*, and it is not conditioned on the clarity or certainty of the international law rule being applied.

A vaguer non-justiciability rule is no better. How does a dispute the substance of which cannot be resolved by the application of 'available legal standards'[33] become resolvable because the defendant State consents to its resolution? Either the legal standards exist or they do not: if their availability to the court depends on the consent of a party, the rule is better formulated as a rule of personal immunity. Similarly, a court is placed in an invidious, if not incoherent position if in one context it asserts jurisdiction on the basis that international law is in some sense available to it,[34] while in a related context it denies the justiciability of transactions governed by international law, indeed in some cases the very existence of that law.[35]

It can be concluded that, at least in limited circumstances, the international dispute settlement rule indicates, if it does not require, the adoption of a rule of deference by a municipal court, and that this rule is most coherently treated as an immunity *ratione personae* of foreign States from adjudicatory jurisdiction. It is true that difficulties and uncertainties arise in translating the international dispute settlement rule into a

[30] In a developed State the organ or entity before the court is unlikely to be the organ or entity responsible for the 'act of State', unless all State organs are to be lumped together for this purpose.

[31] For a case where, at the instance of both parties, a U.K. court purported to determine a matter which was probably non-justiciable, see *R.* v. *Secretary of State for Foreign and Commonwealth Affairs, ex parte Indian Association of Alberta*, [1982] 2 All E.R. 118, especially at pp. 130–1 *per* Kerr L.J.

[32] Falk, op. cit. above (p. 78 n. 14). There are, at least, traces of this approach in the Court's decision in *Sabbatino*, 376 U.S. 398 (1964) at pp. 427–8.

[33] Cf. *Buttes Gas and Oil Co.* v. *Hammer*, [1982] A.C. 888 at p. 938 *per* Lord Wilberforce.

[34] Cf. *Trendtex Trading Corporation* v. *Central Bank of Nigeria*, [1977] Q.B. 529.

[35] Cf. *Occidental of Umm al Qaywayn Inc.* v. *A Certain Cargo*, 577 F. 2d. 1196 (1978), cert. den. 442 U.S. 928 (1979). There the Circuit Court of Appeals stated, *inter alia*: 'In their external relations, sovereigns are bound by no law ... Because no law exists binding these sovereigns and allocating rights and liabilities, no method exists to *judicially* resolve their disagreements' (at pp. 1204–5, emphasis in original).

municipal foreign State immunity rule, not least because the international transactions which are the primary subject-matter of the former do not often arise in municipal courts, at least in a direct form. But other rules and requirements of international law assist in making this translation, and in limiting the discretion of the forum State in adopting a foreign State immunity rule.

In particular, the distinction between international and municipal jurisdiction, which the international dispute settlement rule implies, is accompanied by a distinction *between* municipal jurisdictions, a distinction usually, though somewhat misleadingly, encapsulated in the term 'domestic jurisdiction'.[36] The term is ambiguous because a jurisdiction may cease to be 'domestic' *vis-à-vis* an international forum such as the United Nations General Assembly, while remaining domestic *vis-à-vis* another municipal legal system—and vice versa. Thus the existence of a rule of international law which provides a basis for legitimate criticism in an international forum of the acts of State B within its territory (acts which would otherwise be within State B's domestic jurisdiction) does not as such prevent those acts being matters of State B's domestic jurisdiction *vis-à-vis* the courts of State A. For example the qualification under the law of State B of a person for appointment as a judge in State B's court is a matter of domestic jurisdiction *vis-à-vis* State A, notwithstanding that the fact that the appointment was a deliberate act of racial discrimination would give the General Assembly a title to discuss and criticize it consistently with Article 2 paragraph 7 of the Charter.[37]

For present purposes, the 'domestic jurisdiction' of a State extends to those transactions—typically, transactions within the community of a particular State—which international law refers primarily or exclusively to the competence of that State. Examples include the conferment of nationality on persons sufficiently connected with the State, the disposition of armed forces within the jurisdiction, and the exercise of legislative power over nationals resident within the State. For the most part such matters involve special powers exercised by the State or special relationships of State nationals with the State: in such matters the community of the State is autonomous, an autonomy which would disappear if authority with respect to such matters was to be exercised by the courts (or other governmental organs) of other countries.

Again, it can be argued that sufficient deference to matters of domestic jurisdiction in this sense can be shown through act of State or choice of law rules. Certainly, the domestic jurisdiction rule so described is not obviously analogous to a rule of immunity *ratione personae*, and such transactions could arise between private parties where on any view foreign

---

[36] Much of the discussion of 'domestic jurisdiction' in the literature is vitiated by the failure to appreciate its relative character, not only as to issues but also as to forums.

[37] Cf. Brownlie, op. cit. above (p. 75 n. 2) at pp. 291–7; Higgins, *The Development of International Law through the Political Organs of the United Nations* (1963), pp. 58–130.

State immunity would not be available as a technique of deference. None the less, given the need, already established, for some version of a State immunity rule, and the existence of a range of issues particularly affecting the government of a foreign State and the relations between that government and its subjects, it is appropriate to link the two to provide a degree of secure protection against intervention in State transactions by foreign courts.

A third rule of international law which is at least analogous to or suggestive of a rule of immunity *ratione personae* is the exhaustion of local remedies rule, as it relates to 'private law' claims against the foreign State. Where a foreign State is said to have violated the rights of a private party in its own territory, then in general the private party is required to exhaust local remedies in the foreign State before the matter can be taken up on the diplomatic level by the aggrieved party's own government.[38] In this sense the exhaustion of local remedies rule is a corollary of the international dispute settlement rule; significantly, it too can be waived by the 'defendant' State. The point for present purposes is that it is hardly consistent with the exhaustion of local remedies rule to allow the claimant's State to assert jurisdiction on the basis of nationality to determine the claim against the foreign State. As against the claimant State, the foreign State is surely entitled by the rule to assert that available local remedies be first tried. No such assertion could be made by a private party injuring a national abroad: in such cases the question is merely the well-known one of the proper basis for asserting civil jurisdiction over extraterritorial acts. If such jurisdiction is proper, choice of law issues arise, but no issues of personal immunity. Thus the exhaustion of local remedies rule is, to say the least, consistent with a restricted immunity rule allowing immunity to a defendant State with respect to transactions between that State and private persons in its territory. The analogy is reinforced by the fact that both rules can be waived.

It may be objected that reliance on the exhaustion of local remedies rule proves too much, since if directly applicable in this context it might seem to require immunity to be granted to a foreign State—with a corresponding opportunity being afforded to that State to do justice to the claimant in its own courts—in all cases. But the exhaustion of local remedies rule does not apply to all disputes between private parties and foreign States. Other exceptions aside (e.g. where there is no local remedy or where such a remedy would be manifestly futile),[39] the rule probably applies only to disputes arising in the defendant State's territory or jurisdiction. Thus if State B injures Smith, a national of State A (or State C) or the territory of State A, the exhaustion of local remedies rule does not restrict Smith to the remedies provided by the courts of State B. But the exhaustion of local remedies rule does suggest a need for restraint in asserting jurisdiction

---

[38] Brownlie, op. cit. above (p. 75 n. 2) at pp. 495–505.
[39] Ibid., at pp. 498–9.

over the disputes of a foreign State with private parties, and it emphasizes the appropriateness of that restraint being embodied in the waivable form of immunity *ratione personae* in cases where on ordinary principles such jurisdiction may not exist.

To summarize, distinguishing between cases in which foreign States are immune from local jurisdiction and those in which they are not by a rule of immunity *ratione personae* is more consistent with various international law rules distributing competence between international and municipal forums, and as between municipal forums, than alternative proposals based exclusively on the act of State doctrine, on choice of law rules or on notions of non-justiciability.[40] But these rules do not require a municipal court to decline jurisdiction where a foreign State is a party in all or even most cases: in particular, local jurisdiction may be asserted where the transaction occurred within the forum State, or where it does not involve a matter specifically within the domestic jurisdiction of the defendant State, or alternatively governed by the international dispute settlement rule. These 'structural' rules of international law do not support claims to absolute immunity: they support neither universal defendant State jurisdiction, nor universal claimant's State jurisdiction. But so far no trace of a distinction, such as is commonly asserted, between 'commercial' and 'non-commercial', 'governmental' and 'non-governmental', or 'governmental' and 'commercial' transactions has emerged. It may be that the practice supports some such distinction with sufficient clarity and definiteness to establish it as a positive rule of international law, just as consistent practice might establish a rule of absolute immunity. Whether either, or some other more variegated principle applies, must depend on a more detailed account of the practice.

III. Principles Underlying a State Immunity Regime

Determining the existence and content of a rule of international law when practice and opinion conflict requires the adoption (tacit or otherwise) of a theory of the nature and sources of international law. Obviously, to set out such a theory in full would require a separate study: the discussion here is based upon certain assumptions which will be briefly stated without any extended argument in support.

To establish a rule of law requires either a sufficiently general consensus on the existence of the rule as such (universal agreement is not required), together with some agreement on key aspects of its formulation, or it requires that the rule be inducible by recognized methods of reasoning from other clearly established rules; in the latter case support for the

---

[40] This is of course not to say that the other techniques or rules may not be relevant at a later stage of a case. Cf. *International Association of Machinists* v. *Organization of Petroleum Exporting Countries*, 477 F. Supp. 533 (1979) (decided on State immunity grounds); affirmed on act of State grounds, 649 F. 2d 1354 (1982), cert. den. 102 S. Ct. 1036 (1982).

induced rule can be taken to exist in the absence of clear indications to the contrary. Rules can thus be 'isolated' or 'positive', or they can be structural or systematic, deriving part at least of their validity from the assumption that international law is a system, not merely a set of primary norms.[41] A 'positive' rule can, if sufficiently established, contradict the rule which would otherwise be induced or inferred from more basic 'structural' rules.[42] But such a rule is relatively 'brittle' or unstable, in the sense that it requires the sustenance of a continued consensus to support it. Where there is sustained disagreement over a rule, but agreement that the area is in principle subject to legal regulation, the presumption is that the 'structural' rule represents the law, a presumption which depends for its strength on the inferential or inductive links between that rule and other accepted rules. The effect of rules so established on dissenting States also depends on the relationship between the rule in question and other rules or principles. For example, a State is in general entitled to assert a rule so established against a dissenting State if the subject-matter of the rule would otherwise be within the acknowledged jurisdiction of the asserting State.

(a) *General Immunity from Jurisdiction: a Structural or Positive Rule?*

It can plausibly be argued that the rule of general immunity of foreign States from the jurisdiction of municipal courts was an established rule of international law in, say, 1920.[43] It is not inconsistent with that proposition that exceptions to the rule may have existed—e.g. title to local land, or the arrest of State-owned merchant ships—since these could be accommodated as exceptions and did not necessarily undermine the basic rule.[44] On the other hand, there is no doubt whatever that there is no general consensus supporting such a rule now. On the one hand, the Soviet Union,[45] at least some Eastern European countries,[46] the People's

---

[41] For an application of this distinction between 'inherent' and 'positive' norms see the *North Sea Continental Shelf* cases, *I.C.J. Reports*, 1969, p. 3 at pp. 29–32.

[42] Rules can be structural or systematic in certain other ways. Similarly, some of what are referred to here as 'rules' may be 'principles' in one sense or another. There is no need to examine these questions here.

[43] Cases such as *The Porto Alexandre*, [1920] P. 30, *Duff Development Co. v. Government of Kelantan*, [1924] A.C. 797, and *Berrizzi Bros. Co. v. S.S. Pesaro*, 271 U.S. 562 (1926), represent the high-water mark of the absolute immunity theory in the English-speaking world. The position in Europe at that time also tended towards absolute immunity, though there were notable exceptions: see Lauterpacht, loc. cit. above (p. 75 n. 2), at pp. 250–72.

[44] An exception for disputes over title to local land was an expression of the widely held view that the *lex rei sitae* had exclusive jurisdiction in such cases: cf. *British South Africa Co. v. Companhia de Moçambique*, [1893] A.C. 602.

[45] See Osakwe, *Virginia Journal of International Law*, 23 (1982), pp. 13–52; Boguslavskii, *Netherlands Yearbook of International Law*, 10 (1979), pp. 167–77. But for the Soviet treaty practice, which is difficult to reconcile with this view, see Crawford, *American Journal of International Law*, 75 (1981), pp. 820–69 at pp. 827–9.

[46] Cf. Enderlein, *Netherlands Yearbook of International Law*, 10 (1979), pp. 111–24 (German Democratic Republic) with Varady, ibid., pp. 85–95 (Yugoslavia).

Republic of China[47] and some third world countries support a general immunity rule. On the other hand, the weight of international treaty practice,[48] legal opinion and the practice of many other States (including most States before whose courts issues of immunity actually arise) supports restrictive immunity in some form or another.[49] Confronted with divergent opinions the Special Rapporteur of the International Law Commission on the topic has rightly declined to treat absolute immunity as an established rule in its own right, let alone a norm of *jus cogens*.[50] As he pointed out in his Fourth Report:

> the challenge to 'trading or commercial activities' as an exception to State immunity has come from certain quarters as a matter of policy or principle without any evidence in terms of judicial decisions. . . . [T]he Special Rapporteur is not expected to supplement want of judicial decisions with his own inventions or speculations.[51]

It has been argued already that neither the general principle of State equality, nor its specific embodiment in the context of judicial settlement of disputes, the international dispute settlement rule, implies or entails a general immunity of foreign States from local jurisdiction. The principle of equality does not do so, since to assert that State A is 'equal' to State B with respect to State A's transactions on the territory or within the jurisdiction of State B is not merely to beg the question: it is to assert a form of 'co-sovereignty' of State A on State B's territory to the extent that State A chooses or is permitted to act there. This contradicts an obvious principle of international law, viz. that State B is exclusively sovereign with respect to its territory. Chief Justice Marshall in *The Schooner Exchange* v. *M'Faddon*[52] avoided the fallacy, since he regarded immunity as an inference to be drawn as to the terms on which State A was permitted to enter State B's territory, an inference which was limited to certain kinds of 'entry', and could be varied by State B.[53]

Similarly, the 'international dispute settlement rule' does not imply a general immunity, since it applies only to transactions integrally governed

---

[47] See Carlson, *Columbia Journal of Transnational Law*, 15 (1976), pp. 254–76; Theroux and Peele, *China Law Reporter*, 2 (1983), pp. 129–150.

[48] See, e.g., the multilateral and bilateral instruments cited by Crawford, loc. cit. above (p. 86 n. 45), pp. 821–31.

[49] See the extensive account of State practice and legal opinion in the Reports of I.L.C. Special Rapporteur Sucharitkul: First Report, A/CN.4/323 (1979) (general survey); Second Report, A/CN.4/331 (1980) (introductory and definitional articles); Third Report, A/CN.4/340 (1981) (jurisdictional problems; political subdivisions, organs, agencies and instrumentalities of a foreign State); Fourth Report, A/CN.4/357 (1982) (relation between general principle and exceptions; trading and commercial activity); Fifth Report, A/CN.4/363 and Add. 1 (1983) (contracts of employment; personal injuries and damage to property; ownership, possession and use of property).

[50] As suggested by the U.S.S.R. delegate in the Sixth Committee: U.N. Doc. A/C.6/37/SR.39, para. 28 (1982).

[51] Fourth Report (above, n. 49), p. 39.

[52] 7 Cranch 116 (1812).

[53] Cf. ibid. at pp. 137, 143–5.

by international law; it is certainly not the case that transactions between private parties and States are, in general, so governed. By contrast a number of established international law rules can be regarded as underlying the notion of restrictive immunity. These include the international dispute settlement rule, which implies that certain disputes involving States are to be settled on the international plane, not by subjecting the defendant State to the compulsory jurisdiction of some municipal court; the principle of domestic jurisdiction (i.e. the principle that some matters are exclusively or primarily matters for a particular State to determine: a number of these matters relate particularly to the organization and legal relations of the State); and the rule of exhaustion of local remedies, viz. that some claims against foreign States may not be pursued by the claimant's State before local remedies in the foreign State have been tried without success.[54]

With respect to matters arising within the forum State or otherwise properly subject to its jurisdiction, a rule of absolute foreign State immunity would be an 'isolated' or 'positive' rule not supported by other established rules. Whatever the situation may have been earlier in the century, there is plainly now no consensus sufficient to support such a rule. It follows that it no longer exists (if it ever did) as a rule of general international law.

(b) *A Single Restrictive Rule:* Acta Iure Imperii/Acta Iure Gestionis?

It does not follow from the rejection of an absolute immunity rule that international law prescribes an alternative rule, at least in any detail. The older rule could, of course, simply have been 'repealed' without a replacement.[55] But it has been argued already that there is at least good analogical argument for some version of a restrictive rule. It is quite frequently claimed that a restrictive rule is indeed established as a matter of international law—viz. a rule distinguishing, or requiring the forum to distinguish, the 'public' acts of foreign States (*acta jure imperii*) from their 'private' acts (*acta jure gestionis*), and precluding the forum from exercising jurisdiction with respect to the former. This approach seems to have been adopted by the House of Lords in *I Congreso del Partido*.[56] It also appears to underlie the European Convention on State Immunity of 1972.[57] That Convention does not, in terms, embody a single distinction between 'public' and 'private' acts. It lays down in Articles 1–14 a series of restrictions on immunity of a relatively precise kind. But apart from these

---

[54] Cf. Brownlie, op. cit. above (p. 75 n. 2), at p. 324.

[55] Although the point is sometimes overlooked, there is nothing to prevent States by uniform practice from abolishing a rule without replacing it. Art. 53 of the Vienna Convention on the Law of Treaties, which asserts the contrary with respect to norms of *jus cogens*, fails to distinguish the processes of 'disestablishment' of an old rule and creation of a new one.

[56] [1983] A.C. 244 at p. 262 *per* Lord Wilberforce.

[57] *United Kingdom Treaty Series*, No. 74 (1979).

provisions, Article 24 (1) allows contracting States to expand the categories of local jurisdiction

to the extent that its courts are entitled to entertain proceedings against States not Party to the present Convention. Such a declaration shall be without prejudice to the immunity from jurisdiction which foreign States enjoy in respect of acts performed in the exercise of sovereign authority (*acta jure imperii*).

The implication is, apparently, that all States are immune from local jurisdiction in respect of acts performed 'in the exercise of sovereign authority'.

The point has already been made that there is no international consensus as to a single distinction, however phrased, between governmental and non-governmental transactions of governments; and the distinction has no inherent plausibility. It may well be workable within (as of course it derives historically from) those legal systems with a tradition of, and rules and techniques for, distinguishing private from public law. But not every legal system contains such a distinction, at least in any developed form: this is true, for example, of the common law.[58] Deprived of such contextual support, the distinction is radically defective and cannot claim to represent general international law. How can it be said that international law requires a distinction to be drawn between 'sovereign' and 'private' activities of States, when it is clear that there is no international consensus on the 'proper' scope of governmental acts in many fields? According to Brownlie

there is a logical contradiction in seeking to distinguish the 'sovereign' and 'non-sovereign' acts of a state. The concept of acts *iure gestionis*, of commercial, non-sovereign, or less essential activity, requires value judgments which rest on political assumptions as to the proper sphere of state activity and of priorities in state policies.[59]

Similarly the United States Supreme Court in 1926 pointed out that there was

no international usage which regards the maintenance and advancement of the economic welfare of a people in time of peace as any less a public purpose than the maintenance and training of a naval force.[60]

It should be noted that this criticism applies most directly to the concept of 'public' or 'governmental' activity as the criterion for immunity. Its force is much less as applied to specific exceptions to immunity such as 'wrongful damage to local property', or 'supervision of local arbitrations'. The emphasis here is on the reasonableness of the assertion of local

---

[58] Cf. above, p. 78 n. 12.
[59] Op. cit. above (p. 75 n. 2), at pp. 330-1. To similar effect Fitzmaurice, loc. cit. above (p. 75 n. 2), at p. 121; Lauterpacht, loc. cit. above (p. 75 n. 2), at pp. 224-6.
[60] *Berrizzi Bros.* v. *S.S. Pesaro*, 271 U.S. 562 (1926) at p. 574, cited in *The Philippine Admiral*, [1977] A.C. 373 at p. 349.

jurisdiction, not on the defendant State's motivation. Even the notion of 'trading' or 'commercial activity' as one amongst a number of exceptions to immunity is not radically incoherent, since the concept of trade and commerce is a reasonably autonomous one when it is not presented as the other part of a universe of State activities from which the 'sovereign' or governmental part is excluded. The point is that the more work concepts such as 'private' or 'commercial' have to perform in distinguishing non-immune from immune cases, the more difficult and intractable these concepts become.

Moreover the generality of and lack of guidance provided by concepts such as 'governmental' or 'public' makes them easily manipulated, whether by plaintiffs or courts seeking to achieve a particular result or by foreign States seeking to avoid local jurisdiction. If the test of 'public acts' is to be literally applied, a recalcitrant government has considerable latitude to manipulate its acts to give them the appearance of 'public' acts. In that sense the test puts a premium on deliberate repudiation of obligations. The point can be illustrated from the disagreement between the majority and minority in respect of the *Marble Islands* in *I Congreso del Partido*. The majority emphasized that the Cuban Government's acts in disposing of the sugar (by gift to the Democratic People's Republic of Vietnam) were ostensibly carried out in the exercise of private law powers.[61] Presumably it would have been easy for the Government to have carried out the gift in the exercise of 'public' powers (e.g. by decree). Yet the reality of the matter would have been no different.[62] It is true that, in some cases at least, such manipulation may reflect unfavourably on the State (if or when its acts become known). To some extent this may deter States from manipulating the rules. But this is speculative, and is certainly not a sound basis for establishing liability over foreign State defendants.

A further objection to such a categorical distinction is that it results in immunity being accorded to foreign State activities classified as public or governmental in particular cases even though there may be good reasons for asserting local jurisdiction in such cases. This may be so, for example, with respect to some torts within the jurisdiction and some local contracts of employment.[63] Moreover, there are some cases which can hardly be classified as 'public' or 'private' but which may well justify the assertion of local jurisdiction. This is true, for example, of the forum's supervisory jurisdiction over local arbitrations (which need not depend on the commercial character of the underlying dispute), or over local violations of industrial property rights (whether or not the violation involves 'commercial activity').

Confronted with these difficulties, it cannot seriously be argued that

---

[61] [1983] A.C. 244 at pp. 273-6 *per* Lord Diplock; at p. 278 *per* Lord Keith; at p. 279 *per* Lord Bridge.

[62] Cf. ibid. at pp. 271-2 *per* Lord Wilberforce; at pp. 276-7 *per* Lord Edmund-Davies.

[63] Cf. below, pp. 109-13.

a distinction between 'public' or 'governmental' and 'private' or 'non-governmental' transactions exists as a matter of positive international law. Nor does any single distinction emerge from the underlying rules which, it has been argued, support at least analogically the adoption of a restrictive immunity rule for foreign States. Not all 'public' acts of State are directly governed by international law or are matters of domestic jurisdiction of that State *vis-à-vis* other municipal systems. The distinctions suggested are of a more diffuse or varied kind, and this characteristic is closely reflected in recent legislation embodying restrictive State immunity, as an examination of the more important 'exceptions' will show.

(c) *The Definition and Scope of 'Commercial Transactions'*

As we have seen, there are many difficulties with the notion of 'commercial activity' as *the* central or distinguishing concept in a regime of restrictive immunity (that is, as sharing with the notion of 'governmental activity' the universe of State transactions). As such a classification it is both simplistic and incomplete. Not all State activities can be described either as 'governmental' or 'commercial': indeed, very many cannot. The ownership of vacant land, driving a car, operating a lift, dispensing cups of tea, burning rubbish: many such relatively undistinguished activities would be classified as 'neutral' or colourless (unless in a particular case one could say that they acquired a 'colour' or 'classification' from their context). Even if the driving of diplomats on official business or the burning of secret documents are 'governmental' activities, they may be indistinguishably mixed with activities which are not—the diplomat's wife on a shopping expedition, or miscellaneous rubbish in the incinerator. And the damage they cause, and the resulting claim, may have nothing to do with the 'governmental' aspect of the activity: chauffeurs may be equally negligent on the way to a government office as to a shopping centre.

On the other hand, it is suggested that the notion of commercial or trading activity as one among a number of exceptions to immunity presents no such radical difficulties. Consistently with the general theory of restrictive immunity presented here, 'commercial transactions' in the ordinary sense, even where a State is a party, are not matters within the domestic jurisdiction of that State (provided at least that ordinary jurisdictional links with the forum State exist). Nor are they matters integrally governed by international law in the sense outlined above. The exhaustion of local remedies analogy might indicate that the defendant State should be given the opportunity to do justice in its own courts, but as we have seen that rule is not treated in international practice as an exception to ordinary jurisdictional rules with respect to civil claims. Sufficient respect is shown for that rule by deference to express choice of law or choice of forum clauses in the transaction, and by the availability of a *forum non conveniens* discretion (conditioned, *inter alia*, upon the availability of more suitable remedies elsewhere).[64] On this basis it is presumptively appropriate for States to assert jurisdiction over commercial transactions of foreign States within accepted jurisdictional limits, and this presumption is supported rather than rebutted by the extensive international practice allowing such claims.[65] On this basis, although the forum State must be accorded some flexibility in the definition of 'commercial transactions', these may be defined as contracts or related industrial or commercial activities, not being transactions governed by international law (such as treaties or public international arbitrations), and not being matters recognized as within the domestic jurisdiction of the foreign State. This latter consideration points to the desirability of distinguishing commercial transactions from contracts of employment: in some respects at least the relations between a State and its employees or servants are matters within its domestic jurisdiction.[66]

Of course difficulties of application can still arise, especially in the classification of complex transactions. Rather different approaches have been taken to these in the United Kingdom and the United States Acts. The United Kingdom Act tries to resolve by stipulation a number of the difficulties of classification that have arisen; as often happens such stipulations can present their own problems. Thus the principal extension beyond Articles 1–14 of the European Convention in the United Kingdom Act is section 3 (1) (a), conferring local jurisdiction over 'a commercial transaction entered into by the State'. 'Commercial transaction' is defined in section 3 (3) to mean:

(a) any contract for the supply of goods or services;
(b) any loan or other transaction for the provision of finance and any guarantee or indemnity in respect of any such transaction or of any other financial obligation; and
(c) any other transaction or activity (whether of a commercial, industrial, financial, professional or other similar character) into which a State enters or in which it engages otherwise than in the exercise of sovereign authority.

As it stands, the description in section 3 (3) (c) ('otherwise than in the exercise of sovereign authority') applies only to 'other' transactions or activities, and not to the transactions covered by section 3 (3) (a) or (b). Even if those transactions are engaged in 'in the exercise of sovereign

---

[64] The availability of a judicial remedy in the defendant State's courts is relevant to the exercise of a general *forum non conveniens* discretion. Cf. *Thai-Europe Tapioca Service Ltd.* v. *Government of Pakistan*, [1975] 1 W.L.R. 1485 at p. 1492 *per* Lord Denning M.R.

[65] Cf. Sucharitkul, Fourth Report (above, p. 87 n. 49), at pp. 25–77.

[66] The State Immunity Act 1982 (Can.) makes no specific provision for contracts of employment and thus asserts jurisdiction over all such contracts as would be regarded as 'commercial transactions' on the basis, e.g., that there was a breach of contract within the jurisdiction. The difficulty is that in some respects (e.g. payment of wages due) such contracts may be 'commercial transactions'; in other respects (e.g. placement or removal of public servants) they may impinge significantly on the internal administration of the defendant State. Cf. Sucharitkul, Fifth Report (above, p. 87 n. 49), at pp. 12–23.

authority', they are not immune, despite the express guarantee in Article 24 (1) of the European Convention. For example, a dispute over a loan between the I.B.R.D. and a State would be a 'commercial transaction' as defined in section 3 (3) (b) and within local competence unless the loan agreement specified otherwise.[67] Similarly, it could perhaps be argued that the Ugandan Government's ambiguous statutory undertaking to compensate for expropriated debts, in *Uganda Holdings*, would be a 'guarantee or indemnity in respect of any . . . financial obligation' within section 3 (3) (b) and thus not immune under the Act, even though Donaldson J. regarded it as 'a classic example of an act which is jus imperii'.[68] Other examples could no doubt be given. Whether section 3 (3) (b) would be given a more restrictive meaning because of Article 24 of the European Convention is an open question.[69]

The definition of commercial transaction which occupies a similarly central place in the United States Act is much less elaborate: the intention was to leave the matter substantially for the courts to decide.[70] Under section 1605 (a) a foreign State is not immune in any case

. . . in which the action is based upon a commercial activity carried on in the United States by the foreign State; or upon an act performed in the United States in connection with a commercial activity of the foreign state elsewhere; or upon an act outside the territory of the United States in connection with a commercial activity of the foreign state elsewhere and that act causes a direct effect in the United States.

Section 1603 (d) defines 'commercial activity' as 'a regular course of commercial conduct or a particular commercial transaction or act', and adds that:

The commercial character of an activity shall be determined by reference to the nature of the course of conduct or particular transaction or act, rather than by reference to its purpose.

In fact most of the difficulties with section 1605 (a) have arisen over its jurisdictional nexus requirements.[71] But a good example of the problems of classification raised by the term 'commercial transaction' is

---

[67] The I.B.R.D. is not a 'State' for these purposes (s. 3 (2)), nor could it be certified as such under s. 21 (a), since such a certificate is only conclusive in respect of something that is in truth a 'country'. Cf. note, *Columbia Law Review*, 69 (1969), pp. 886–905.

[68] [1979] 1 Lloyd's Rep. 481 at p. 487.

[69] The Court of Appeal in *Alcom Ltd.* v. *Republic of Colombia*, [1983] 3 W.L.R. 906, was clearly unsympathetic to attempts to read down the broad language of s. 3 (3).

[70] *Jurisdiction of U.S. Courts in Suits against Foreign States*, Hearings on H.R. 11315 before Sub-Committee on Administrative Governmental Relations of the House Committee on the Judiciary, 94th Congress, 2nd session, at p. 5 (1979) (Mr. Monroe Leigh, Legal Adviser, State Department). See also House Report No. 94—1487 (Foreign Sovereign Immunities Act of 1976), *U.S. Code Congressional and Administrative News*, 1976, p. 6604; in U.N.L.S., *Materials* (above, p. 75 n. 2), at p. 98.

[71] For discussion of section 1605 (a), see, e.g., Cosby, *Baylor Law Review*, 34 (1982), pp. 295–308; Schloss, *Journal of International Law and Economics*, 14 (1979), pp. 1163–73.

Yessenin-Volpin v. *Novosti Press Agency*,[72] a libel action against Novosti and others in respect of articles published in the Soviet Union defaming the plaintiff. The court held that the publication was an expression, in official Soviet journals, of material representing an 'official commentary of the Soviet government'.

> By collaborating in the publication . . . Novosti . . . was engaged not in 'commercial activity' but in acts of intra-governmental co-operation of a type which apparently constitutes much of Novosti's . . . activity. Such action was not in connection with a contract or other arrangement with a non-governmental or foreign party, which activity would be found commercial under most circumstances.[73]

It is of interest that all but one of the State Immunity Acts passed since 1978 have adopted the English definition of 'commercial transaction': the exception is the Canadian Act of 1982 which preferred the flexibility of the United States Act.[74] But whichever approach is adopted, problems of application will arise, in particular where the litigation arises in the highly controversial area of resource development,[75] or in the context of 'strategic' decisions about public works.[76] Labelling such transactions as 'commercial' or otherwise can obviously be acutely difficult. It is suggested that three different questions need to be distinguished if confused or question-begging decisions are to be avoided.

1. *Individuation*

An initial step which, although it may not solve all problems of classification, materially assists in isolating and thus clarifying issues is one of individuation. Given that some only of the complex activities of foreign States are amenable to local jurisdiction, it is essential to locate, to identify with precision, the act or series of acts giving rise to the particular claim, so that *that* particular act or series of acts can be classified. Under a restrictive theory it is not enough to attach a classification to a complex network of foreign State acts, some aspects only of which are in issue (and indeed such a complex fact situation will often be impossible to classify satisfactorily). This is not to say that the surrounding facts may not be relevant in making the classification, although their role is likely to be secondary. But what is important is to isolate the particular acts in virtue of which the State is said not to be immune, and to identify their relationship

---

[72] 443 F. Supp. 849 (1980).

[73] Ibid., at p. 856.

[74] State Immunity Act 1982 (Can.), ss. 2 (definition of 'commercial activity'), 5. See Molot and Jewett, *Canadian Yearbook of International Law*, 20 (1982), pp. 79–122 at pp. 96–104.

[75] Cf. *International Association of Machinists and Aerospace Workers* v. *O.P.E.C.*, 477 F. Supp. 557 (1979); affirmed on act of State grounds, 649 F. 2d. 1354 (1981); cert. den. 102 S. Ct. 1036; *In re Sedco Inc.*, 543 F. Supp. 561 (1982).

[76] e.g. *Ferranti-Packard Ltd.* v. *Cushman Rentals Ltd.* (1979), 26 O.R. (2d.) 344 (design of freeway system); *Amanat Khan* v. *Fredson Travel Inc.* (*No. 2*) (1982), 36 O.R. (2d.) 17 (provision of airport security).

with the plaintiff's claim.[77] In fact this problem of individuation seems to have two aspects, which correspond with two ways in which the identification of particular transactions can be difficult. The first, perhaps most obvious, one is the aspect of *remoteness*. A particular act usually has ramifications forward in time, is part of some larger activity or purpose. The acceptance of an offer may entail the conclusion of a contract on particular terms for the purchase of concrete for use in building barracks to house an army increased in size for particular foreign policy purposes. Secondly, a single act usually has various descriptions, depending on the aspect which is relevant to the particular enquiry: this can be described as a question of *breadth*. In law, if not in life, one is concerned with particular acts for specific purposes rather than at large, and it is the purpose at hand which will usually suggest the preferable characterization of the act in point of breadth. The fact that a diplomat is being driven on official business is irrelevant if the claim arises out of a collision with the car: it may be a relevant or overriding aspect in a different context. But here the aspect of remoteness may intrude. It may be that the accident was caused by the car's being driven at excessive speed (say, under police escort) in order for the diplomat to confer urgently with the foreign minister on a matter of pressing importance. At this level a value-judgement, indeed almost an exercise of discretion, seems inevitable.

In the literature and also, to some extent, in the practice the problem is addressed by the 'distinction' between the nature of the transaction and its purpose.[78] But the notion that human activity can be classified, or even described, without referring to its purpose is a delusion. Any particular act can be described in a variety of ways: for example, as fulfilling a contract of employment, pumping water, replenishing the water supply, making a particular noise, poisoning the inhabitants of the house (if there is poison in the water), murder (if the person pumping knows of the poison), assisting a revolution (if the inhabitants are the political leaders of the country), and so on.[79] Similarly a single act might be described as publishing a journal, defaming the plaintiff, co-operating with the State authorities, or fulfilling the defendant's statutory mandate, or as striking

[77] Cf. *I Congreso del Partido*, [1983] A.C. 244 at p. 263 *per* Lord Wilberforce. The same analysis is required for other exceptions to immunity, but usually not so acutely.

[78] Cf. Foreign Sovereign Immunities Act 1976 (U.S.A.), s. 1603 (d) ('The commercial character of an activity shall be determined by reference to the nature of the course of conduct or particular transaction or act, rather than by reference to its purpose'); State Immunity Act 1982 (Can.), s. 2 ('any . . . conduct . . . that by reason of its nature is of a commercial character'). The I.L.C. Special Rapporteur had earlier adopted a similar test (see Second Report (above, p. 87 n. 49), pp. 24–6), but in the version provisionally adopted by the Drafting Committee it is a distinct hybrid. Draft Art. 3 (2) provides: 'In determining whether a contract for the sale or purchase of goods or the supply of services is commercial, reference should be made primarily to the nature of the contract, but the purpose of the contract should also be taken into account if in the practice of that State that purpose is relevant to determining the non-commercial character of the contract' (*35th Report of the International Law Commission, General Assembly Official Records*, 38th Session, Supplement No. 10 (A/38/10)) (1983), pp. 76–8). 'That State' is, apparently, the defendant State.

[79] The example is taken from Anscombe, *Intention* (2nd edn., reprinted 1972), pp. 37–41.

at the enemy, giving one's own company a monopoly, stealing the property of another, returning to the people control over (part of) the economy, and so on. Within limits, *each* of these may be an accurate description. Certainly each involves notions of purpose, so that the 'correct' description cannot be found by ignoring purpose. Picking between purposes might seem arbitrary or question-begging: by what criterion does one prefer the description that emphasizes commercial purpose to that which emphasizes governmental?

As with other aspects of the law of foreign State immunity, repeated formulas have tended to blind rather than bind. The terminology of the 'nature/purpose' distinction is untenable. Its intent, on the other hand, seems to be to distinguish the narrower from the broader aspects or descriptions of a transaction. In the interests of the clarity and certainty, indeed the viability, of a restrictive immunity rule, this seems entirely legitimate. One might recast the 'nature/purpose' distinction in the following form: in assessing foreign State immunity with respect to a particular transaction, identify the transaction as precisely and narrowly as is reasonably possible having regard to the factual and legal issues. If, so described, the transaction can fairly be classified as a 'commercial transaction' (or, in the case where the claim arises in virtue of a particular aspect or qualification of the transaction, that aspect can be so classified), then the transaction will not lose that character or classification because extraneous facts or aspects surrounding the individual transaction suggest or would attract a different classification.[80]

The point was well made by Hank D.J. in *International Association of Machinists and Aerospace Workers* v. *Organization of Petroleum Exporting Countries*, an antitrust claim against O.P.E.C. and its thirteen member States. After referring to the United States Act's definition of 'commercial activity', the Court said:

These standards are somewhat nebulous, however, in the context of a particular factual situation . . . [T]he determining factor is how the court defines the act or activity. An act or activity can be defined broadly, such as 'hiring of employees', an activity carried on by private parties, and thus, 'commercial', or it can be defined narrowly, such as, 'employment of diplomatic . . . personnel', a governmental activity. It was suggested that in determining whether to define a particular act narrowly or broadly, the court should be guided by the legislative intent of the FSIA, to keep our courts away from those areas that touch very closely upon the sensitive nerves of foreign countries. This Court agrees that this 'commercial activity' should be defined narrowly. This determination, while based partially on the factor mentioned above, is premised primarily on the recognition that a court must base its ruling on specific facts. By basing a ruling

---

[80] One difficulty here is that the plea of sovereign immunity, which goes to the jurisdiction of the court and is therefore usually taken at a preliminary stage, may be more or less closely related to the merits, and is often dependent on findings of fact (cf. *I Congreso del Partido*, [1983] A.C. 244, at p. 279 *per* Lord Bridge). The power to join the immunity issue to the merits (as the International Court can join a plea of domestic jurisdiction to the merits of a claim) may occasionally be useful.

on a *generalised* view of the evidence, a court may be basing its ruling on half-truths. This Court is required to make its ruling upon the *specific* evidence presented . . . From the evidence . . . it is clear that the nature of the activity engaged in by each of these OPEC member countries is the establishment by a sovereign state of the terms and conditions for the removal of a prime natural resource . . . from its territory.[81]

It is not suggested that all the problems that arise can be solved merely by this process of individuation. But many confusions can be avoided, and the actual questions for decision exposed with greater clarity. A good example of a case where this did not happen, with resulting confusion, is *American International Group Inc.* v. *Islamic Republic of Iran.*[82] There it was held that the Islamic Republic's failure to compensate for the expropriation of the plaintiff's insurance interests was an act performed 'in connection with a commercial activity of defendants'. But the only relevant commercial activity was that of the Central Insurance of Iran, a separate Iranian instrumentality. The Islamic Republic's expropriation was an act apparently independent of Central Insurance's activities (though it resulted in a monopoly for them).[83] The decision might perhaps have been justified by treating Central Insurance as indistinguishable from Iran, yet that issue was not addressed; and indeed the distinction between the Government and its commercial instrumentalities was clearly affirmed in the Iranian Treaty (on which the Court relied to avoid the act of State doctrine).[84] Even if, in certain circumstances, the commercial character of an instrumentality's activities could colour the acts of a central Government directed at those activities, the court did not enquire as to the independence or otherwise of Iran's expropriation and Central Insurance's commercial transactions. The term 'in connection with' in section 1605 (a) (2) was apparently interpreted so broadly as to avoid this need. So interpreted, it would attract jurisdiction over all governmental acts which had an effect on State-owned commercial instrumentalities, irrespective of whether the acts were performed for general governmental purposes. This is an impossibly wide interpretation.

A rather similar problem—of foreign State action directly affecting the

---

[81] 477 F. Supp. 553 at p. 567 (1979). Cf. ibid. at p. 569 n.: 'The fact that a nation owns and operates an airline company, does not mean that all government activities regulating the use of airspace . . . are commercial activities. Accordingly, we must look to the specific activity in which the defendants engage.' On appeal in that case Choy D.J. said: 'a critical step in characterizing the nature of a given activity is defining exactly what that activity is. The immunity question may be determined by how broadly or narrowly that activity is defined': 649 F. 2d. 1354, 1357 (1981); cert. den. 102 S. Ct. 1036. Similarly in *In re Sedco Inc.*, 543 F. Supp. 561 at p. 565 (1982), O'Conor D.J. emphasized the need to 'focus on the specific acts made the basis of the claim, not on D's general character or activities'. To similar effect, *Arango* v. *Guzman Travel Advisors Corp.*, 621 F. 2d. 1371 at p. 1379 (1980). Not all courts have been so careful: cf. *In re Rio Grande Transport Inc.*, 516 F. Supp. 1155 at p. 1162 (1981).

[82] 493 F. Supp. 522 at p. 525 (1980).

[83] The monopoly resulted from the expropriation rather than the failure to compensate, but clearly the court was in no mood for refined analysis.

[84] For the U.S.–Iranian treaty of 15 August 1955 see [1955] 8 *United States Treaties*, p. 899.

commercial transactions of separate State instrumentalities—arose in
I Congreso del Partido,[85] and here again it was essential to distinguish
carefully the particular State transactions giving rise to the claim. This
was an Admiralty action in respect of two ships operated by a Cuban State
instrumentality (Mambisa) and carrying sugar to Chile under a contract
with another Cuban instrumentality (Cubazucar). The Chilean importer,
IANSA, owned and had paid for the sugar. In response to the overthrow
of the Allende government in Chile, the Cuban Government broke off
diplomatic relations and ordered the two ships not to proceed with their
contractual voyage. (One ship, the *Playa Larga*, was already in a Chilean
port unloading its cargo; the other, the *Marble Islands*, was still on its way
to Chile.) IANSA sued the Cuban Government and Mambisa[86] for breach
of contract, conversion and detinue.

In each of the lower courts, the problem was treated broadly, as one
of classifying the Cuban Government's acts performed apparently for
political reasons, but performed in relation to commercial transactions.
But it is clear that this approach, which raised the *jure gestionis/jure imperii*
distinction in its most baffling form, was too general, and that it ignored
important factual and legal distinctions between the two cases. In the case
of the *Playa Larga*, the Republic of Cuba was the owner, and it was at least
arguable that the Republic of Cuba was contractually liable for the
carriage under the bills of lading.[87] In the case of the *Marble Islands*, the
Republic of Cuba only became owner after the coup, and after the Cuban
decree freezing Chilean assets 'located on Cuban territory' (which may or
may not have included the sugar here). Moreover, it could not be argued
that the Republic of Cuba was contractually liable for the carriage of the
sugar in the *Marble Islands*.[88] It followed that the transaction to be classified in respect of the *Playa Larga* was either the breach of the bills of lading
by the Cuban directive (if Cuba was contractually liable under the bills of
lading) or at least the wrongful detention of the sugar in a State-owned
ship by virtue of powers which *could* have been powers of ownership rather
than of governmental decree. In respect of this transaction the House of
Lords held unanimously that the Cuban Government was not entitled to
immunity.[89]

The position of the *Marble Islands* was quite different. No question of
contract arose, nor of IANSA 'doing business with' a Cuban-owned ship.
The only claim could be tortious, for detinue and conversion of the sugar,
and it could only be made against *Cuba* in respect of commercial transactions performed by it after it became owner of the ship. What was crucial

---

[85] [1983] A.C. 244. The various stages of the case are noted in this *Year Book*, 49 (1978), pp. 262–7;
50 (1979), pp. 224–7; 52 (1981), pp. 314–19.
[86] The action against Mambisa failed for technical reasons: see this *Year Book*, 49 (1978), pp. 266–7.
[87] On the evidence so far available it is very doubtful whether this is so. On this point the writer
would agree with Lord Wilberforce rather than Lord Diplock: see [1983] A.C. 244 at pp. 267, 273.
[88] Ibid., at p. 269 *per* Lord Wilberforce, at p. 273 *per* Lord Diplock.
[89] See below, p. 100.

then was a close analysis of the acts performed by Cuba after this time, in their factual and legal context. On this underlying distinction there was no disagreement in the House of Lords, although there was strong disagreement on the result of that analysis, with the majority holding (Lords Wilberforce and Edmund-Davies dissenting) that here too the Republic of Cuba was not entitled to immunity.[90] The point here is that, difficult as it may have been, an analysis of the legal effect of the specific acts performed by the Cuban Government after it became owner of the ship was a task considerably better suited for judicial decision than some more general classification of the Government's overall motive or purpose in the complex series of transactions following the coup.

This need for individuation is not confined to State immunity problems. It is equally necessary in cases where the plea of foreign act of State is relied on, as the case of *Buttes Gas and Oil Co.* v. *Hammer* (*Nos. 2 and 3*) shows.[91] And the same approach is necessary under the immunity legislation, as is made clear if one applies the United Kingdom Act to the fact situation in *Congreso*. Under section 10 of the Act, a State is not immune with respect to actions *in rem* or *in personam* relating to Admiralty claims in connection with a ship belonging to the State which 'at the time when the cause of action arose . . . was in use or intended for use for commercial purposes'. Although section 10 does not say so explicitly, it is clearly necessary that the ship be owned by the State at that time (unless the State in purchasing the ship takes it subject to a maritime lien or similar liability, a possibility which is not relevant to the situation in *I Congreso*). The *Playa Larga* was 'in use . . . for commercial purposes' when the cause of action arose and it was then a State-owned ship. It would not therefore have been immune under section 10. But the *Marble Islands* was not then owned by the State, and there was no 'commercial transaction' relating to the *Marble Islands* into which the State (as distinct from its separate enterprises, Mambisa and Cubazucar) had entered. In a case such as the *Marble Islands* the State would accordingly be immune unless a distinct claim within the scope of Admiralty jurisdiction and arising 'in connection with' the ship had arisen after its acquisition by Cuba. This was precisely the issue in *I Congreso*.[92]

[90] Cf. [1983] A.C. 244 at pp. 271–2 *per* Lord Wilberforce, at pp. 275–6 *per* Lord Diplock.

[91] [1982] A.C. 888. In that case there was a claim for defamation (a slander committed within the jurisdiction) and a counterclaim for conspiracy arising out of the same general fact situation, but in which the crucial facts had occurred outside the jurisdiction. Lord Wilberforce declined to distinguish between the two claims, holding the conspiracy claim and the plea of justification in respect of the libel both non-justiciable. For criticism, see this *Year Book*, 53 (1982), pp. 259–68.

[92] Under s. 10 of the 1978 Act it is also necessary for the ship to have been 'in use *or* intended for use for commercial purposes'. Although the sugar was eventually donated by Cuba to Vietnam, it was not argued that the *Marble Islands* had then ceased to operate for 'commercial purposes'. In fact in *Congreso* the House expressly declined to draw analogies from the Act: see [1983] A.C. 244 at p. 260 *per* Lord Wilberforce: 'If one state chooses to lay down by enactment certain limits [to immunity], that is by itself no evidence that those limits are generally accepted by states. And particularly enacted limits may be (or presumed to be) not inconsistent with general international law—the latter being in a state of uncertainty—without affording evidence what that law is.'

2. *Classification*

Even when the process of individuation has been carried out, and the precise act or transaction the basis of the claim isolated, problems of classification of that act or transaction may remain. For the transaction, or the aspect of the transaction relevant to the claim, may still be a mixed or indistinguishable transaction, plausibly commercial or not. A good example is *Yessenin-Volpin* v. *Novosti Press Agency*,[93] where the court was required to classify certain acts of publication as 'commercial activity' or as 'inter-governmental cooperation'.

In classifying State transactions in difficult cases such as these, much will depend on the particular facts—for example, whether the defendant was acting directly as agent for the State where the State itself was on any view exercising governmental functions (e.g. in the context of immigration control),[94] or whether the particular action *could* have been performed by the defendant in the exercise of contractual or proprietorial powers. In *Congreso*, the latter consideration was important at least to Lord Wilberforce. As owner of the *Playa Larga* the Cuban Government *could* have ordered the departure of the ship from Chile.

> It may well be that those instructions would not have been issued . . . if the owner of the *Playa Larga* had been anyone but a State: it is almost certainly the case that there was no commercial reason for the decision. But these consequences follow inevitably from the entry of states into the trading field . . . It may be too stark to say of a state 'once a trader always a trader'; but, in order to withdraw its action from the sphere of acts done *jure gestionis*, a State must be able to point to some act clearly done *jure imperii*.[95]

In the result his Lordship, 'with much hesitation', concluded that this could not be shown.[96]

Once a particular transaction has, through the State's involvement in affairs, taken on a 'commercial' aspect it may be reasonable to apply an onus of proof in this way: a similar presumption was applied by the United States Supreme Court in the *Dunhill* case.[97] But it is an insecure way of deciding sensitive questions. And it assumes that a foreign State may, by action taken independently of its contractual or proprietary powers, repudiate commercial transactions for reasons of policy. This seems to confound the very distinction on which the law is said to be based: if States retain the capacity to act *jure imperii* with respect to their *jure gestionis* transactions then the 'commercial transactions' rule is reduced to an 'inadvertent transactions' rule, allowing recovery against States for 'honest

---

[93] Above, p. 94.

[94] *Arango* v. *Guzman Travel Advisors Corp.*, 621 F. 2d. 1371 (1980).

[95] [1983] A.C. 244 at pp. 268–9.

[96] Ibid., at p. 269. Lord Diplock, who thought that the Cuban Government was also contractually liable for the carriage, had even less difficulty: ibid., at p. 276. The other members of the House simply agreed.

[97] 425 U.S. 682 (1976).

mistakes' but not for deliberate repudiation. Again the single broad distinction between acts *jure imperii* and acts *jure gestionis* which the House of Lords purported to apply (and which Lord Wilberforce did in fact apply) in *Congreso* leads to uncertainty and confusion.

Once the assertion of jurisdiction over commercial transactions is made, then the rationale for limited jurisdictional immunity suggested here provides no ground for withdrawing that assertion (i.e. for according immunity) merely because the State's repudiation of its commercial obligation was deliberate or 'public'. At the level of jurisdictional immunity, the question is what is the transaction into which the State has entered? If that transaction is a commercial one—e.g. a commercial contract—then jurisdiction can be asserted on that basis, whatever the reason for repudiation. On the other hand, a State's act does not become commercial merely because performed with respect to a commercial transaction between other parties.[98] Otherwise the State becomes the guarantor of all private transactions affected by its acts (whether through illegality, frustration or otherwise).[99]

The apparent confusion in *Congreso* arose from two complicating features: first, the fact that in the case of both ships the transaction interfered with (the bill of lading) was a transaction with a State instrumentality, and secondly that (at least as far as the *Playa Larga* was concerned) the repudiation was performed by the use of a State-owned ship in circumstances giving rise to an Admiralty action *in rem*. As to the first, the question is whether the commercial acts of an instrumentality are to be attributed to the States, and as the State Immunity Act 1978 confirms the answer is that, except in special circumstances, they are not.[100] (The separate instrumentality may, of course, be liable itself with respect to the cargo: that is a separate issue.[101]) As to the second question, the delineation of a 'commercial ships exception' is by no means the same as a 'commercial transactions exception'—indeed at common law the first preceded the second by some years.[102] The internationally acceptable scope of a

---

[98] Cf. above, p. 97.

[99] In the litigation arising from the *Congreso* affair it was accepted that Cuba's acts had had the effect of frustrating the long-term sugar contract. The issue was the fate of the two shipments in progress for which payment had been made. See *Empresa Exportadora de Azucar* v. *Industria Azucarera Nacional S.A.*, [1982] 2 Lloyd's Rep. 171 at pp. 187–9 *per* Ackner L.J. Cf. the very similar situation in *Dunhill* (above, p. 100 n. 97).

[100] Just as, conversely, the independent acts of a State cannot be attributed to a State instrumentality: cf. *C. Czarnikow Ltd.* v. *Centrala Handlu Zagranicznego Rolimpex*, [1979] A.C. 351. Generally on State instrumentalities and State immunity see Kincaid, *Journal of World Trade Law*, 10 (1976), pp. 110–28; Thompson, *Vanderbilt Journal of Transnational Law*, 12 (1979), pp. 165–84.

[101] Cf. *Empresa Exportadora de Azucar* v. *Industria Azucarera Nacional S.A.*, [1983] 2 Lloyd's Rep. 171.

[102] Between *The Cristina*, [1938] A.C. 485, and *The Philippine Admiral*, [1977] A.C. 373, the position of actions *in rem* against State-owned ships remained uncertain. At the same time, it was regarded as settled that in actions *in personam* (even where these could have been Admiralty actions), absolute immunity prevailed: cf. ibid. at pp. 402–3 *per* Lord Cross; *Thai Europe Tapioca Service Ltd.* v. *Government of Pakistan*, [1975] 3 All E.R. 961.

jurisdiction with respect to State trading ships is reasonably clearly delineated in treaties such as the Brussels Conventions of 1926 and 1952,[103] and is inferentially confirmed by the Geneva Conventions of 1958[104] and the European Convention of 1972.[105] The question is simply whether a claim properly within the scope of Admiralty jurisdiction arose when the ship in question was in use for commercial purposes. Although a generalized 'commercial transactions' analysis would usually achieve the same result, the former analysis is both more straightforward and avoids confusing the different jurisdictional bases for commercial transactions and Admiralty actions.[106]

To summarize, once a more specific rather than a more general jurisdictional basis is established, and once the particular act or transaction which is the foundation of the claim is singled out or identified, the process of classification will usually not be difficult. It is assisted by a reformulated distinction (as we have seen, usually stated as a distinction between 'nature' and 'purpose') between the immediate or proximate and remote or ulterior purpose or aim of the transaction: the sale of army boots or the borrowing of money on which interest is payable are as such commercial transactions notwithstanding that the boots are for the army or the money is for munitions. Once an identified transaction which is the basis of the suit is properly classified as commercial it does not lose that classification because extraneous facts or aspects surrounding the individual transaction suggest a different classification.[107]

3. Jurisdiction

Finally, there is a question whether special jurisdictional requirements have to be specified before jurisdiction can be asserted over a foreign State on the basis of a particular transaction. Here again, the precision to be achieved by distinguishing different grounds for asserting jurisdiction contrasts favourably with the generalized formulae necessary to resolve this problem under an immunity regime which depends on distinguishing *acta jure gestionis* from *acta jure imperii*.[108] For present purposes it is sufficient to deal in detail with two kinds of commercial claims already distinguished, maritime claims and commercial transactions.

[103] Below, p. 103 nn. 110–11.

[104] Below, p. 103 nn. 112–13.

[105] Below, p. 104 n. 115.

[106] The need for distinct limits on arrest of State public ships is not attended to in the U.K. Act: cf. the references to 'intended use' in ss. 10 and 13 (4).

[107] Cf. above, p. 96.

[108] The Swiss courts have been perhaps the most consistent supporters of a jurisdictional link requirement in the context of a distinction between *acta iure imperii* and *acta iure gestionis*: cf. *Libya* v. *Libyan American Oil Co.*, *International Legal Materials*, 20 (1981), p. 152, citing the earlier cases going back to *Austrian Minister of Finances* v. *Dreyfus*, 44 A.T.F. I 49 (1918). And see Lalive, *Netherlands Yearbook of International Law*, 10 (1979), pp. 153–66. In fact most of the cases have concerned State bonds: in that context the Swiss rule is satisfied if performance is required to be or is in fact made within the jurisdiction: *Banque Centrale de la République de Turquie* v. *Weston Cie. de Finance et d'Investissement S.A.*, 104 A.T.F. Ia 367 (1978).

(i) *Maritime claims.* The propriety of arresting State-owned ships (other than warships and other public ships) in aid of maritime claims is now well established, even when the maritime claim has no particular nexus with the jurisdiction. This situation perhaps derives from the origins of Admiralty jurisdiction in a mercantile and marine custom which was thought to be common to different nations.[109] In any event the modern position is clear. Article 1 of the 1926 Brussels Convention for the Unification of Certain Rules concerning the Immunity of State-owned Ships provides:

Sea-going ships owned or operated by States, cargoes owned by them, and cargoes and passengers carried on State-owned ships, as well as the States which own or operate such ships and own such cargoes shall be subject, as regards claims in respect of the operation of such ships or in respect of the carriage of such cargoes, to the same rules of liability and the same obligations as those applicable in the case of privately-owned ships, cargoes and equipment.[110]

The liability to arrest of State-owned commercial ships on the same basis as privately owned ships is affirmed, by implication at least, in the 1952 Brussels Convention relating to the Arrest of Sea-going Vessels.[111] It is also expressly contemplated by Article 21 of the Geneva Convention on the Territorial Sea of 1958, which applies to government ships operated for commercial purposes the general rules applicable to innocent passage of merchant ships in Articles 18 to 20 of the Convention. Article 20 provides that the qualified prohibition from arrest of merchant ships engaged in innocent passage through the territorial sea is 'without prejudice to the right of the coastal State, in accordance with its laws, to levy execution against or to arrest, for the purpose of any civil proceedings, a foreign ship lying in the territorial sea, or passing through the territorial sea after leaving internal waters'.[112] The International Law Commission proposed that, by Article 21, these powers of execution and arrest be extended to State-owned commercial vessels since the rules of the 1926 Brussels Convention 'followed the preponderant practice of States', and this view was accepted.[113] Articles 20–32 of the United Nations

---

[109] That this conception is still capable of influencing judges is clear from the joint dissent of Lords Salmon and Scarman in *Bankers Trust Ltd.* v. *Todd Shipyards Corp.*, [1981] A.C. 221 at pp. 242–4, 250.

[110] *League of Nations Treaty Series*, vol. 176, p. 199. Art. 2 subjects such ships to the same 'rights of action and procedure' as private ships. Art. 3 exempts ships of war and other ships used exclusively on 'Government and non-commercial service'; these are exempt from 'seizure, arrest or detention by any legal process' (including actions *in rem*). There are approximately twenty-three parties to the Convention and its Protocol of 1934.

[111] *British and Foreign State Papers*, vol. 159, p. 368. The Convention deals with 'sea-going ships' in general. Art. 2 provides for liability to arrest in respect of a 'maritime claim', but Art. 3 allows arrest of any sister ship owned by the same 'person', and 'person' is defined to include 'Governments, their Departments and Public Authorities' (Art. 1 (3)).

[112] *United Nations Treaty Series*, vol. 516, p. 205. Nine countries have made reservations to Art. 21, and eleven have objected to those reservations.

[113] *Report of the International Law Commission on its 8th Session* (1956), *General Assembly Official Records*, 11th Session, Supplement No. 9, at p. 22.

Convention on the Law of the Sea of 1982 are to similar effect.[114] The European Convention on State Immunity of 1972[115] reserves the question of claims relating to State-owned ships, on the basis that the matter is regulated already by these general conventions.

This consistent practice is reflected in the position at common law. In *I Congreso del Partido* the only connection between the forum and the dispute was the arrest of a sister-ship of the two ships in question within the jurisdiction. It was argued that this was an insufficient nexus for the purpose of exercising jurisdiction over a foreign State. The argument was rejected by Mr. Justice Goff. He said:

> The arrest of ships is a procedure widely recognised throughout the world, though the court may thereafter decline to proceed with the case on the ground that there exists elsewhere a more appropriate forum for the trial of the dispute or on some other more limited principle of a similar kind . . . The possibility of arrest of state-owned ships is expressly recognised by the Brussels Convention of 1926: claims arising from the operation of such ships are within article 1 of the Convention, which presumably include claims arising from collisions on the high seas. I find it difficult to accept that, in an appropriate case, the English courts should not assert jurisdiction by an action *in rem* against a state-owned ordinary trading ship in a case arising from a collision with another foreign ship on the high seas. Furthermore, article 1 of the Convention contemplates the possibility of arrest in a case concerned with carriage of cargo; once again, I find it difficult to accept that the English courts should not be able to assert jurisdiction in an action *in rem* against a foreign state-owned trading ship in such a case, even though the contract of carriage had no connection with the territorial jurisdiction of the English court. Jurisdiction asserted by means of an arrest of a ship is not an exorbitant jurisdiction. By allowing his ships to trade a foreign sovereign must be taken to have exposed his ships to the possibility of arrest, a procedure which is widely accepted among maritime nations and which is regulated to some extent by international convention, in the case of state-owned ships by the Brussels Convention of 1926, and in the case of other sea-going ships by the Brussels Convention of 1952.[116]

Both the Court of Appeal and the House of Lords agreed on this point: as Lord Wilberforce said, the claim was 'an Admiralty claim in which territoriality is not a requirement for jurisdiction'.[117]

(ii) *Commercial transactions.* A more difficult question is whether some special nexus with the jurisdiction ought to be required in the case of commercial transactions. In *Rahimtoola* v. *Nizam of Hyderabad* Lord Denning stated that:

if the dispute concerns, for instance, the commercial transactions of a foreign government (whether carried on by its own departments or agencies or by setting

---

[114] *International Legal Materials*, 21 (1982), p. 1261.
[115] European Convention (above, p. 88 n. 57), Art. 30; Council of Europe, *Explanatory Report on the European Convention on State Immunity and the Additional Protocol* (Strasbourg, 1972), at p. 39.
[116] [1978] Q.B. 500 at p. 543.
[117] [1983] A.C. 244 at p. 272. Cf. [1980] 1 Lloyd's Rep. 23 at p. 30 *per* Lord Denning M.R.

up separate legal entities), and it arises properly within the territorial jurisdiction of our courts there is no ground for granting immunity.[118]

That the reference to matters 'properly within the territorial jurisdiction of our courts' was not simply a reference to the ordinary jurisdictional rules was confirmed by *Thai-Europe Tapioca Service Ltd.* v. *Government of Pakistan.*[119] This was a claim between German owners and the Government of Pakistan pursuant to a bill of lading incorporating the terms of a charter-party between the owners and Polish charterers, for demurrage incurred at Karachi. In an action *in personam*, leave to serve outside the jurisdiction was granted on the basis that the bill of lading was governed by English law. A majority of the Court of Appeal dismissed the claim, applying a rule of general immunity.[120] Lord Denning M.R. agreed, but only on the ground that the dispute lacked any sufficient connection with the forum. After referring to his speech in *Rahimtoola* he said:

> I would stress particularly the necessity that the dispute should arise properly within the territorial jurisdiction of our courts. By this I do not mean merely that it can be brought within the rule for service out of the jurisdiction under RSC Ord 11, r 1. I mean that the dispute should be concerned with property actually situate within the jurisdiction of our courts or with commercial transactions having a most close connection with England such that, by the presence of parties or the nature of the dispute, it is more properly cognisable here than elsewhere. But none of the exceptions applies in the present case. None of the transactions here occurred within the territorial jurisdiction of these courts . . . I can see no possible justification for these courts asking the Government of Pakistan to come here to contest the claim. That sovereign has offered to let the case be decided by the courts of Pakistan. Seeing that the delay occurred at Karachi, that is a very proper forum.[121]

Later cases have left this question open, although Mr. Justice Goff in *I Congreso del Partido* observed that 'on the evidence before [him] there appears to be no international consensus on the requirement of territorial connection'.[122] On the other hand, Mr. Justice Steele in the Ontario Supreme Court dismissed a claim against the Government of Pakistan arising out of allegedly inadequate security precautions at Karachi airport, in part on grounds that the case involved 'the failure of a sovereign state to perform acts within its own territorial limits',[123] although it is true that the acts in question were classified as public or non-commercial.

---

[118] [1958] A.C. 378 at p. 422.

[119] [1975] 3 All E.R. 961, noted this *Year Book*, 47 (1974–5), pp. 362–4.

[120] [1975] 3 All E.R. 961 at pp. 967–8 *per* Lawton L.J., at pp. 969–70 *per* Scarman L.J.

[121] At pp. 966–7.

[122] [1978] Q.B. 500 at p. 534. On appeal Lord Wilberforce expressly left this question open: [1983] A.C. 244 at p. 272.

[123] *Amanat Khan* v. *Fredson Travel Inc.* (*No. 2*) (1982), 36 O.R. (2d.) 17. The second defendant, Pakistan Airlines, did not plead immunity to the contractual claim against it. The contract had been made within the jurisdiction by the first defendant as its agent, so that no problem of nexus arose in that respect.

On this issue it is significant that the international instruments and municipal legislation take no consistent position. Both Articles 4 and 7 of the European Convention of 1972 require relatively close connections with the forum, although to some extent this arises from the Convention's emphasis on recognition and enforcement of judgments.[124] Section 1605 (a) 2 of the Foreign Sovereign Immunities Act 1976 (U.S.A) is also, as we have seen, based on the view that some special nexus with the jurisdiction is required. The House Report on the Act comments that the definition 'is intended to reflect a degree of contact beyond that occasioned simply by US citizenship or US residence of the plaintiff', and that 'substantial contact' with the United States is specified.[125] In practice, the nexus requirements of section 1605 (a) 2 have generated a large and rather divergent case law,[126] and have been one reason for the great emphasis placed on waiver under the Act (in the context of commercial transactions with no sufficient nexus). As one District Court judge remarked,

section 1605 (a) (2) is most deceptive. Great difficulty often inheres in determining the locus of the act sued upon.[127]

In general, however, the jurisdictional requirements have been liberally construed: in doubtful cases the courts have inclined strongly towards

---

[124] The *Explanatory Report* on the Convention (above, p. 104 n. 115) states that the various exceptions to immunity incorporate

'a series of connecting links, which are designed to prevent proceedings being instituted against a State in the courts of another State where the dispute is not sufficiently closely related to the territory of the State of the forum to justify the exercise of jurisdiction by a court in that State. These links are also necessary to establish bases of jurisdiction which would be accepted when the foreign judgment comes to be submitted for recognition and enforcement' (at p. 10).

On Art. 4 the Report states:

'In principle, immunity should not be granted to a State with respect to any contracts it has concluded. The article compensates to a certain degree for the relatively narrow scope of Article 7 ... According to the procedural law of some States, the jurisdiction of a court depends on the place where the disputed contractual obligation arose or where it was discharged or falls to be discharged. Other States do not recognise this basis of jurisdiction or do so only in special circumstances. The connecting link in Article 4 therefore represents a compromise' (at p. 14).

Art. 7, it states:

'covers the principal activities of a State *iure gestionis*. Had the Convention dealt simply with questions of jurisdictional immunity, it might have been possible to frame the article in more general terms so as to extend it to cover all cases where a State engages in industrial, commercial or financial activities having a territorial connection with the State of the forum. As the Convention requires States to give effect to judgments rendered against them, it was necessary to insert a connecting link to found the jurisdiction of the courts of the State of the forum, namely the presence on the territory of this State of an office, agency or other establishment of the foreign State. This limitation is counter-balanced by the broad terms of Article 4: most industrial, commercial or financial activities carried on by a State on the teritory of another State where it has no office, agency or establishment would probably give rise to contractual obligations which are dealt with by Article 4' (at p. 17).

The compromise nature of these Convention articles, and of the jurisdictional links they require, is clear.

[125] House Report (above, p. 93 n. 70), in U.N.L.S., *Materials* (above, p. 75 n. 2), p. 98 at p. 108.

[126] See the works cited above, p. 76 n. 5.

[127] *Gibbons* v. *Udaras na Gaeltachta*, 549 F. Supp. 1094, at p. 1112 (1982) *per* Ward D.J.

allowing actions to proceed.[128] In the light of this case law the apparent emphasis in section 1605 (a) (2) on jurisdictional nexus loses some of its significance. By contrast, section 3 (1) (a) of the State Immunity Act 1978 (U.K.) simply removes immunity with respect to 'a commercial transaction entered into by the State'. There is no special requirement of a jurisdictional nexus in the Act, or in its Singapore,[129] Pakistan,[130] South African[131] or Canadian[132] equivalents.[133] Initially the State Immunity Bill 1977 did provide for such links, along the lines of those in the European Convention on which it was modelled. But these were deleted in the House of Lords after criticisms especially from Lords Wilberforce and Denning. Lord Wilberforce was clearly of the view that no special links were necessary or desirable.[134] Lord Denning, despite his earlier judicial views, appeared to agree.[135] In the result all that is required to claim jurisdiction over commercial transactions of foreign States is compliance with the ordinary requirements for service of process in the Rules of Court. In the context of actions against foreign States (as distinct from separate State corporations), involuntary service within the jurisdiction is most unlikely to be available. The service provisions of the Act are expressed to be without prejudice to any requirement to obtain leave to serve process

---

[128] Cf. *Gilson* v. *Republic of Ireland*, 682 F. 2d. 1022, at p. 1028 (1982): 'it ought to be difficult for defendants engaged in commercial activity with substantial American contact . . . to invoke successfully sovereign immunity when sued for underlying commercial misdeeds.'

[129] State Immunity Act 1979, s. 5 (1) (a).

[130] State Immunity Ordinance 1981, s. 5 (1) (a).

[131] Foreign State Immunities Act 1981, s. 4 (1) (a).

[132] State Immunity Act 1982, s. 5.

[133] Section 3 (1) (b) of the U.K. Act does require such a nexus: it applies to any 'obligation of the state which by virtue of a contract (whether a commercial transaction or not) falls to be performed wholly or partly in the United Kingdom'. This sub-paragraph does not apply 'if the contract (not being a commercial transaction) was made in the territory of the State concerned and the obligation in question is governed by its administrative law'. But it is difficult to think of convincing cases of contracts falling within s. 3 (1) (b) that would not be commercial transactions under s. 3 (1) (a). In some respects this result is curious. After the first round of amendments during passage through Parliament the position was that all contracts made in the exercise of sovereign authority fell under what is now s. 3 (1) (b): see text of clause 3, *Hansard*, H.L. Debs., vol. 389, col. 1501 (16 March 1978). This was regarded as necessary if the Act was to comply with the requirements of international law: 'The jurisdiction with regard to contracts which may be exercised on other grounds under Order 11 of the Rules of the Supreme Court is considered in many foreign countries to be excessive. It is not without doubt whether we could justify the assumption of jurisdiction so widely over contracts of a sovereign nature. There will, for instance, be no immunity if the contract is to build a fighter plane or a battleship and the construction takes place in the United Kingdom. But, I submit, there would be no basis in public international law for the assumption of jurisdiction where the construction was to take place elsewhere, unless the foreign State had agreed on jurisdiction by the United Kingdom courts. Contracts not concluded in the exercise of sovereign authority will in the main be commercial transactions as defined in subsection (3), for which I submit, no jurisdictional link is necessary' (ibid., cols. 1503-4 (Lord Chancellor)). But as enacted *all* contracts for goods, services or finance, whether made in the exercise of sovereign authority or not, are subject only to the jurisdictional links required by Order 11 of the Rules of Court. A contract for fighter planes which is to be performed outside the jurisdiction can be litigated in the U.K. if the requirements of Order 11 can be satisfied.

[134] *Hansard*, H.L. Debs., vol. 380, cols. 66-7 (17 January 1978); vol. 389, col. 1506 (16 March 1978).

[135] Ibid., vol. 388, cols. 71-3 (17 January 1978).

outside the jurisdiction.[136] In effect therefore, the United Kingdom Act asserts jurisdiction over commercial transactions in any case where leave to serve outside the jurisdiction is available and is granted. In England and Wales, apart from the discretionary element in obtaining leave, this includes actions in respect of 'any contract which was made within the jurisdiction by or through an agent trading or residing within the jurisdiction on behalf of a principal trading or residing out of the jurisdiction or is governed by English law or in respect of a breach within the jurisdiction of a contract wherever made'.[137] Thus under the Act the courts could assert jurisdiction over the Government of Pakistan if the facts of the *Thai-Europe Tapioca*[138] case were to recur, because the contract there was governed by English law.

Draft Article 12 provisionally adopted by the International Law Commission does not stipulate jurisdictional links with respect to commercial contracts: it is sufficient that 'by virtue of the applicable rules of private international law, difficulties relating to the commercial contract fall within the jurisdiction of a court of another State'. The commentary states that:

It is common ground among the various approaches to the study of State immunities that there must be a pre-existing jurisdiction in the courts of the foreign State before the possibility of its exercise arises and that such jurisdiction can only exist and its exercise can only be authorized in conformity with the internal law of the State of the forum, including the applicable rules of jurisdiction, particularly where there is a foreign element involved in a dispute or differences that require settlement or adjudication. The expression 'applicable rules of private international law' is a neutral one, selected to refer the settlement of jurisdictional issues to the applicable rules of conflict of laws or private international law, whether or not uniform rules of jurisdiction are capable of being applied. Each State is eminently sovereign in matters of jurisdiction, including the organization and the determination of the scope of the competence of its courts of law or other tribunals.[139]

The cogency of this reasoning is not improved by the formulation of Draft Article 12 in terms of implied consent, or by the assertion that a State is 'eminently sovereign' in matters of jurisdiction. A State cannot unilaterally determine the scope of its jurisdiction as against other States. But the Draft Article tends to confirm the view that no special jurisdictional links are required for commercial transactions.

---

[136] State Immunity Act 1978 (U.K.), s. 12 (7).

[137] R.S.C. O. 11 r. 1 (1) (f) and (g). Another possibility is where the foreign State is a necessary or proper party to an action against a person duly served within the jurisdiction (e.g. an agent of the State in respect of the transaction): O. 11 r. 1 (1) (j). Cf. *Derby and Co. Ltd.* v. *Larsson*, [1976] 1 W.L.R. 202, *Union Bank of the Middle East Ltd.* v. *Clapham*, *The Times*, 20 July 1981. Generally on these provisions see Dicey and Morris, op. cit. above (p. 79 n. 16), pp. 203–13.

[138] Above, p. 105 n. 119.

[139] *35th Report of the International Law Commission* (above, p. 95 n. 78), p. 53. The Special Rapporteur's proposed Draft Article had required that the commercial activity be carried out 'partly or wholly' in the forum State.

It can be concluded that there is no consensus in international practice on the need for closer connections with the forum in the case of commercial transactions with foreign States than can properly be asserted for commercial transactions generally[140] where the party to be sued is outside the jurisdiction. (That States, as distinct from State instrumentalities, are 'resident' outside the jurisdiction is a corollary of the State independence which is the basis of restrictive immunity.)

(d) Non-Commercial Transactions

In addition to asserting jurisdiction over commercial transactions on this basis, all the more recent Acts assert jurisdiction over a range of transactions or acts which may not qualify as 'commercial' in the sense outlined above. The question is on what basis this can be justified, given the orthodox emphasis upon commerial transactions as *the* exception to foreign State immunity.[141] A number of such exceptions illustrate the way in which legislative practice has escaped the bounds of the 'theories' of immunity usually presented: the provisions dealing with local personal injury or damage to property provide the best example of these.

1. 'Torts within the jurisdiction': local personal injury or damage to property

All but one of the State immunity Acts enacted since 1976 assert jurisdiction over a range of 'torts' within the jurisdiction causing certain specified kinds of damage:[142] similar assertions are made in the European Convention of 1972[143] and in the International Law Association's Draft Articles,[144] and a proposal to similar effect has been made by the International Law Commission's Special Rapporteur.[145] Thus under section 5 of the United Kingdom Act

A State is not immune as respects proceedings in respect of—

(a) death or personal injury; or
(b) damage to or loss of tangible property,

caused by an act or omission in the United Kingdom.

Apart from verbal differences[146] section 5 differs from the European Convention in avoiding a requirement that 'the author of the injury or damage' should have been present in the forum when 'the facts which occasioned

---

[140] Though care should be taken not to define retrospectively the consequences of submission to local law. This is one of the vices in the decision in *Jackson* v. *People's Republic of China*, 550 F. Supp. 869 (1982); see Theroux and Peele, loc. cit. above (p. 87 n. 47).

[141] Cf. above, p. 76.

[142] The exception is the Pakistan Ordinance of 1981.

[143] European Convention (above, p. 88 n. 57), Art. 11.

[144] International Law Association, Montreal Draft Articles for a Convention on State Immunity (1982), Art. III F.

[145] Fifth Report (above, p. 87 n. 49), pp. 5–17.

[146] The terms 'death' and 'loss' were added to section 5 *ex abundanti cautela*. Cf. *Fothergill* v. *Monarch Airlines Ltd.*, [1981] A.C. 251.

the injury or damage occurred'. Similarly there are minor verbal differences with respect to the *locus delicti* in the Acts based on the British Act.[147] The United States Act adopts a different approach, though the end result may not differ markedly. Section 1605 (a) (5) removes immunity in any case (not covered by the 'commercial transactions' exception)

in which money damages are sought against a foreign state for personal injury or death, or damage to or loss of property, occurring in the United States and caused by the tortious act or omission of that foreign state or of any official or employee of that foreign state while acting within the scope of his office or employment; excepting this paragraph shall not apply to:

(A) Any claim based upon the exercise or performance or the failure to exercise or perform a discretionary function regardless of whether the discretion be abused, or

(B) any claim arising out of malicious prosecution, abuse of process, libel, slander, misrepresentation, deceit, or interference with contract rights.

Only the United States provision covers claims of damage to 'nontangible' property as such, presumably necessitating the various exceptions in paragraphs (A) and (B). The result, however, is similar: each applies to actions for death or injury to persons or property within the jurisdiction, without any specification of the nature of the State act which causes the death or injury. Yet it is easy to imagine State acts which are on any view *jure imperii*, causing death or damage locally. The principal purpose of section 1605 (a) (5), apparently, was to deal with motor accident and similar claims in which foreign State vehicles were involved,[148] but none of the provisions is so limited.

This is illustrated in a striking way by *Letelier* v. *Chile*.[149] Orlando Letelier was a former Chilean ambassador and foreign minister granted asylum in the United States. Letelier and a companion were assassinated by a car bomb in Washington. Representatives of the victims sought damages against Chile and various agents on the ground that this was a deliberate political assassination carried out on the instructions of the Chilean Secret Service. In the event substantial damages were awarded.

At the jurisdictional hearing, Chile, while denying responsibility for the deaths, claimed that if it was responsible this was a classical example of an act *jure imperii*, entitled to immunity. The argument, faced with the explicit statutory language, failed. The Court said:

Subject to the exclusion of these discretionary acts defined in subsection (A) and the specific causes of action enumerated in subsection (B), neither of which have been invoked by the Republic of Chile, by the plain language of section 1605 (a) (5) a foreign state is not entitled to immunity from an action seeking money

---

[147] The State Immunity Act (Can.), s. 6 requires that the death, damage, etc., occur in Canada, irrespective of where the act causing it was performed. Thus manufacturers' liability cases could be brought where the relevant damage has occurred.

[148] House Report (above, p. 93 n. 70), in U.N.L.S., *Materials* (above, p. 75 n. 2), p. 98 at p. 112.

[149] 488 F. Supp. 665 (1980). See Collums, *Virginia Journal of International Law*, 21 (1981), pp. 251-68; Petri, *Harvard International Law Journal*, 21 (1980), pp. 793-8.

damages 'for personal injury or death caused by the tortious act or omission of that foreign state' or its officials or employees. Nowhere is there an indication that the tortious acts to which the Act makes reference are to only be those formerly classified as 'private', thereby engrafting onto the statute, as the Republic of Chile would have the Court do, the requirement that the character of a given tortious act be judicially analysed to determine whether it was of the type heretofore denoted as *jure gestionis*, or should be classified as *jure imperii*. Indeed, the other provisions of the Act mandate that the Court not do so, for it is made clear that the Act and the principles it sets forth in its specific provisions are henceforth to govern all claims of sovereign immunity by foreign states.[150]

Whatever result would have been achieved by a court applying a *jure gestionis*/*jure imperii* analysis, this is plainly a correct interpretation of the provision: the same result would be reached under the European Convention and the United Kingdom Act. The basis for the assertion of jurisdiction over 'governmental torts' such as these is equally plainly not a distinction between 'governmental' and 'non-governmental' acts, but an assertion of local control over (i.e. jurisdiction over) obvious forms of harm or damage. Deliberately to cause such harm or damage on the territory of another State by an act of 'public power' is, in the absence of some special exception, a plain violation of international law, whether the harm is caused by assassination or invasion. The exercise of local jurisdiction in such cases is an assertion of the forum's right, acknowledged by international law, to deal with the consequences of unlawful acts on its territory. This helps to explain the exclusion by the various texts of the 'economic torts', where the location of damage tends to be much less clear, and the link between act and effect is much less direct than in cases of death or personal injury. Other exclusions can be justified on other grounds. Conspiracy is an amorphous tort which is easily capable of calling in question acts of foreign States within their domestic jurisdiction. Indeed, in the *Buttes* case conspiracy was the vehicle for calling in question a transaction plainly covered by the international dispute settlement rule.[151] Defamation is presumably excluded because publication, and damage to reputation, can occur as a result of statements issued anywhere in the world. For State A to assert jurisdiction over the (non-commercial) statements of State B published in State A or causing injury to reputation there would be, in effect, to set up State A's courts as censors of State B. The fact that the assertion would probably be unenforceable does not add to the attractiveness of making it. The exclusion of defamation is also a recognition of the very powerful public interest in freedom of speech at the international level.

The assertion of local jurisdiction over foreign State acts causing physical

---

[150] 488 F. Supp. 665 at p. 671. The court held that the 'discretionary function' exception in s. 1605 (a) (5) (A) did not apply, since 'a foreign country . . . has no "discretion" to perpetrate conduct designed to result in the assassination of an individual . . ., action that is clearly contrary to the precepts of humanity as recognized in both national and international law': at p. 673.

[151] Above, p. 81 n. 29.

damage within the jurisdiction which are lawful under international law (for example, where the acts are performed by way of self-defence or pursuant to a Security Council resolution under Chapter VII of the Charter) appears more difficult to justify. If the 1976 Mogadishu raid (performed by West German commandos with the consent of the Somali Government) had occurred under one of the State Immunity Acts the local courts would have had jurisdiction to award damages against West Germany for losses necessarily caused in the rescue.[152] Similarly, Argentinian courts could have awarded damages for Israel's kidnapping of Eichmann if some physical 'injury' had been occasioned during the kidnapping, even though the illegality was subsequently repaired in the Security Council.[153] The answer is, surely, that the legality of such transactions can be distinguished from the propriety of exercising jurisdiction over them. Provided that the forum's courts have the relevant international law rules available to them, whether through some general rule of incorporation, or the specific implementation of a relevant treaty or otherwise, it is not obviously inappropriate that jurisdiction be exercised in such cases. On the other hand, at least in common law countries, the rules with respect to visiting forces and local acts of belligerents are obscure and ill-defined, in large part because the case law is scanty.[154] This is one of a number of areas where the parameters of the 'restrictive theory' remain obscure, and it results in part at least from the connection, not often perceived, between jurisdictional immunity and substantive law (including 'choice of law') in certain cases. But clearly enough the resolution of such exceptional cases need not obscure the point that the assertion of local jurisdiction in these cases does not depend on any conception of 'governmental' or 'commercial' acts.

2. Other 'non-commercial' exceptions

Most of the recent State immunity Acts follow the pattern of the European Convention in asserting local jurisdiction over a range of other matters that are not, or at least need not necessarily involve, 'commercial transactions' or activities. These include disputes relating to local immovable property (and in certain cases to movable property also),[155] violations of local industrial and intellectual property rights, irrespective of the character of the violation,[156] liabilities for certain local

---

[152] Collums, loc. cit. above (p. 110 n. 149), at p. 267 instances the U.S. rescue mission in Iran, and asserts that 'the collateral legality of the use of force' under the Charter would distinguish the case from *Letelier*. Of course, this assumes, *inter alia*, that Iranian courts would apply the Charter!

[153] Subsequent consent or reparation is particularly difficult, as the expropriation cases (above, p. 81 n. 29) indicate.

[154] Cf. *Wright* v. *Cantrell* (1943), 44 S.R. (N.S.W.) 45; *Chow Hung Ching* v. *R.* (1948), 77 C.L.R. 449. In practice the matter is usually regulated by treaty: cf. Brownlie, op. cit. above (p. 75 n. 2), pp. 367–71, but this may not cover exceptional situations.

[155] e.g. State Immunity Act 1978 (U.K.), s. 6. See Sucharitkul, Fifth Report (above, p. 87 n. 49), pp. 17–29.

[156] e.g. State Immunity Act 1978 (U.K.), s. 7.

taxes[157] and (in the case of the United States only) disputes over expropriated property.[158] Some of the Acts follow the United Kingdom example in asserting jurisdiction in general terms over proceedings relating to arbitrations.[159] These provisions suffer from uncertainty about when a dispute 'relates to' an arbitration: for example, do proceedings to enforce an arbitral award do so?[160] Where the arbitration results from an agreement to arbitrate which is a commercial transaction, or where the dispute itself is of a civil or commercial character, the commercial transactions exception is likely to cover much of the ground. In this respect the European Convention of 1972 reveals greater clarity of thought: its arbitration provision deals only with the forum's 'supervisory' jurisdiction over arbitrations, on the basis that the substance of civil or commercial arbitrations is covered by other provisions.[161] Yet that supervisory jurisdiction—over the fairness and legality of the arbitral procedure, over the misconduct of arbitrators, etc.—is an expression of local public policy with respect to settlement of disputes, a concern which is not intrinsically 'commercial' or 'private' at all. The same is true of the provisions dealing with State participation in local associations, corporations or partnerships.[162] Again the assertion of jurisdiction over foreign States escapes the confines of a single distinction or exception. On the other hand, the assertion of local jurisdiction over public international arbitrations would be another matter, since such arbitrations are, in general, governed by the 'international dispute settlement rule' rather than any particular municipal system. The United Kingdom Act avoids most such matters by excluding all arbitrations between States (unless the arbitration agreement otherwise provides): this does not quite cover the field since public international arbitrations can occur between States and other international entities.[163] A similar problem exists for 'public international corporations', that is to say, international organizations with separate legal personality.[164]

---

[157] Ibid., s. 11; cf. European Convention (above, p. 88 n. 57), Art. 12.

[158] Foreign Sovereign Immunities Act 1976 (U.S.A.), s. 1605 (a) (3).

[159] State Immunity Act 1978 (U.K.), s. 9. There are similar provisions in the Singapore, Pakistan and South African Acts.

[160] A provision which would have excluded enforcement of awards from s. 9 was deleted in the House of Lords: *Hansard*, H.L. Debs., vol. 389, cols. 1516–17 (16 March 1978). However, it is very unlikely that this would be used to assist in interpreting the Act: cf. *Davis* v. *Johnson*, [1979] A.C. 264.

[161] European Convention (above, p. 88 n. 57), Art. 12; cf. *Explanatory Report* (above, p. 104 n. 115), p. 21.

[162] State Immunity Act 1978 (U.K.), s. 8.

[163] Cf. above, p. 93 n. 67. On the status of I.C.S.I.D. arbitrations under the U.S. Act cf. *Maritime International Nominees Establishment* v. *Republic of Guinea*, 693 F. 2d. 1094 (1982).

[164] There have been significant problems of interaction between foreign State and international organization immunity, in part because of the significant number of intergovernmental agencies acting in effect as State organs. See, e.g., *Rios* v. *Marshall*, 350 F. Supp. 351 (1981); *Velidor* v. *L.P.G. Benghazi & Compagnie Algero-Libyenne de Transport Maritime*, 653 F. 2d. 812 (1981); *Tuck* v. *Pan American Health Organisation*, 668 F. 2d. 547 (1981); *Burnell* v. *International Joint Commission* (1976), 71 D.L.R. (3d.) 725. See, e.g., Glenn, Kearney and Padilla, *Virginia Journal of International Law*, 22 (1982), pp. 247–90.

IV. Conclusions

In the present state of international practice and opinion, it is clear that neither an absolute or general immunity nor any particular distinction between immune and non-immune transactions can claim to represent general international law. But it does not follow that States are free to abandon all forms of a State immunity rule and to assert jurisdiction over foreign States on the basis of ordinary jurisdictional requirements. In fact, despite certain suggestions to this effect, no State has adopted this course of action.

On the other hand, although there has been a tendency to assert the existence of a rule of restrictive immunity predicated on a distinction between 'private', 'commercial' or 'non-governmental' acts of States and their 'public', 'non-commercial' or 'governmental' acts there is in international practice no consensus on any such distinction. Indeed, the better view is that, in the absence of a worked-out distinction between 'public' and 'private' law as part of the *lex fori*, such a distinction is incoherent. Nor does it reflect the actual distinctions drawn between immune and non-immune transactions in any of the recent international texts or municipal Acts. The better approach is to deal with the specific categories or classes of case that have arisen in practice and to elaborate specific rules for each such category, taking into account the reasons for extending immunity or asserting jurisdiction in that context. This is essentially the approach adopted in the United Kingdom Act and its counterparts, in the European Convention and (though to a rather lesser extent) in the United States and Canadian Acts.[165] In this process it is necessary to have regard to the underlying reasons for extending immunity *ratione personae* to foreign States: in particular, the immunity from local jurisdiction of States with respect to transactions essentially within their domestic jurisdiction, or governed directly by the international dispute settlement rule. Of course it is also necessary to respect specific immunities established in international practice: in particular, the immunities of diplomatic and consular personnel and premises and of foreign public ships from arrest.[166] Considerations of comity and reciprocity are also relevant, though the specific guidance they provide is, as usual, limited.

It is an interesting question whether common law courts, in the absence of State immunity legislation, could have arrived independently at the nuanced or variable results achieved by that legislation in different contexts. Special rules probably already existed for local real property,[167]

---

[165] These Acts omit a number of categories dealt with in the British Act, and thus place a great deal more stress on the category of 'commercial transaction' or 'activity'.

[166] Cf. below, p. 116.

[167] *Larivière* v. *Morgan* (1872), L.R. 7 Ch. App. 550, reversed on the facts (1875), L.R. 7 H.L. 423; *Strousberg* v. *Republic of Costa Rica* (1881), 44 L.T. 199. Similar considerations applied to the administration of estates in England, to interests in property as *bona vacantia*, and to the winding up of companies: cf. *Re Russian Bank for Foreign Trade*, [1933] Ch. 745 at pp. 769-70.

the administration of trusts[168] and Admiralty actions.[169] Employment contracts may have presented special difficulties. A 'commercial transactions' rule at common law had achieved acceptance by 1981, but in such relatively broad terms that it may have swallowed up the more specific exceptions. The position with respect to local non-commercial torts, perhaps the most interesting field of non-immunity, remains unclear.[170] The question is now speculative, the Parliaments of half a dozen common law countries having preferred the relative certainty of statute to the flexibility (and consequent, at least interim) uncertainty of the common law. That process, having commenced, is likely to continue, supported by the argument that common law development has now been substantially cut off in the more important jurisdictions. It remains to be seen whether the adoption of a satisfactory set of Draft Articles by the International Law Commission will substantially resolve the disagreements at the international level.

In the meantime, certain important questions remain. One such question is whether legislation on foreign State immunity, to be consistent with international law or practice, should include a residual prohibition preventing the exercise of jurisdiction over foreign States in respect of their acts 'in the exercise of sovereign authority', notwithstanding that the case falls within one of the defined exceptions from immunity. It is clear that neither the international texts nor the overseas legislation adhere strictly to any distinction between *acta jure imperii* and *acta jure gestionis*, or between commercial and governmental transactions, however these may be defined. At the same time there is no precedent for a residual prohibition in respect of *acta jure imperii* or governmental transactions in any of the texts,[171] although that seems now to be the effect of the common law rule.[172]

Despite statements to the effect that international law does not allow local jurisdiction to be exercised over foreign States in respect of their acts of sovereign authority, it is suggested that this is not an accurate or comprehensive statement of the relevant principles. It has already been suggested that the various distinctions drawn between immune and non-immune transactions are the result not of a single rule or principle but of a balance of principles and considerations. It follows that, provided local legislation reasonably reflects that balance, no further safeguard or prohibition is required. However, it does not follow from the fact that

---

[168] The point was fully argued, but left open by the Privy Council in *Sultan of Johore* v. *Abubakar Tunku Aris Bendahar*, [1952] A.C. 318 at pp. 343–4. It was also described as 'open' by Barwick C.J. in *Chang* v. *Registrar of Titles* (1976), 8 A.L.R. 285 at p. 289.

[169] Cf. above, p. 101 n. 102.

[170] Cf. above, p. 105.

[171] Arts. 24 (1), 27 (2) of the European Convention preserve 'the immunity . . . which foreign States enjoy in respect of acts performed in the exercise of sovereign authority', but only in respect of extensions beyond the specific cases listed in Arts. 1–14: cf. above, p. 89.

[172] Above, pp. 88–91.

a foreign State is not immune that appropriate respect should not be shown to its governmental acts. Thus the effects of a foreign State's legislative, executive or judicial acts may be recognized by the courts of the forum, either affirmatively pursuant to rules of the conflict of laws, or as foreign acts of State on which the courts will not adjudicate. There is, however, no precedent for regulating such matters in legislation on foreign State immunity. They involve questions of substantive law, not jurisdictional immunity, and they apply irrespective of whether the foreign State is itself a party to the litigation.[173] The point for present purposes is that the protection accorded to a foreign State's public or governmental acts is another reason why no special residual provision is needed in legislation on State immunity.

A second area of concern is, of course, that of State immunity from execution or enforcement. This has been a subject of increasing study and litigation over the past decade as the rules of jurisdictional immunity have been reshaped.[174] In one sense it can be argued that execution is a correlative to jurisdiction. The jurisdiction of a State, for present purposes, is precisely a power to determine what should be done by the parties to a dispute in accordance with the relevant law. It is not merely an advisory jurisdiction, or a jurisdiction to establish what the law is (a 'jurisdiction to prescribe'). Presumptively, therefore, adjudicatory jurisdiction carries with it the power to enforce any resulting judgment.[175] This presumption could of course be rebutted by establishing a general immunity of foreign States from execution independent of any immunity from jurisdiction. Again there was, earlier in this century, strong support for this position, but this is no longer so. Apart from the recent municipal legislation, the courts of a number of States have concluded that foreign State property in use 'for commercial purposes' is liable to attachment and execution.[176] The international treaty practice, on the whole, supports the same position.[177]

On the other hand, there are dangers in simply equating jurisdiction and execution immunities. For one thing, there are special rules immunizing from seizure certain classes of foreign State property—especially certain diplomatic and consular property, and State warships and public ships assimilated to warships.[178] But perhaps more importantly many of the

[173] Cf. above, p. 79.

[174] See Crawford, loc. cit. above (p. 86 n. 45) and works there cited.

[175] Ibid., at pp. 859–60. Cf. *Alcom Ltd.* v. *Republic of Colombia*, [1983] 3 W.L.R. 906 at p. 912 *per* Sir John Donaldson M.R.: 'If the State is amenable to the jurisdiction of the English courts in accordance with [section 3 (1)], there seems no logical reason why its money should not be attachable in satisfaction of a judgment.'

[176] See especially the decision of the West German Federal Constitutional Court in the *Philippines Embassy* case (above, p. 77 n. 11), and its decision of 12 April 1983 in the *National Iranian Oil Co.* case. For a review of the case law see Crawford, loc. cit. above (p. 86 n. 45), at pp. 834–52. A recent French case supports this position also: see Oppetit, *Journal de droit international*, 110 (1983), pp. 145–52.

[177] Crawford, loc. cit. above (p. 86 n. 45), at pp. 821–32.

[178] Ibid., at pp. 861–3.

techniques available to help in classifying State transactions for jurisdictional purposes are not available in the context of execution. The fact
situation which is the subject of the litigation can, as we have seen, provide
a focus and a 'purpose' which materially assist in classifying that situation.
Where the question is simply whether property was 'in use' (or, more difficult still, 'intended for use') for commercial purposes then this focus is
almost entirely lacking. One solution is to limit execution to the property
the subject of the dispute, or which was 'used' in carrying on the commercial transaction in question, as the United States Act does. But, apart
from the severe limitations this imposes on the availability of execution
against foreign States,[179] this still does not resolve the difficulties. When is
property 'used' for the purposes of a commercial transaction? The problem is particularly difficult in the case of funds in an account: these may be
available in some sense to meet liabilities in respect of a transaction
(though they will rarely be 'set aside' for the transaction in any particular
way) but while in the account the 'funds' (strictly, the debt or chose in
action represented by the account) are hardly being 'used' for a commercial activity (unless perhaps they are interest-bearing). The problem is
exacerbated if the definition of 'commercial purpose' or 'commercial use'
for the purposes of execution is simply equated with 'commercial transaction', as it is in the United Kingdom Act.[180] The point was rather vividly
demonstrated by the Court of Appeal's decision in *Alcom Ltd.* v. *Republic
of Colombia*. There the court was unable to discern *any* use of an account
established substantially to maintain the Colombian Embassy which was
not for the purpose of a commercial transaction, as defined by the Act.[181]
Yet it is strongly arguable that accounts maintained substantially for the
purposes of an Embassy should be immune from execution, and the West
German Federal Constitutional Court in 1977, in a very careful judgment,
affirmed that international law contains a requirement to that effect.[182]

The difficulties of the specific classification of State property, especially
in the context of 'mixed accounts' or 'mixed purposes', suggest the need
for a rather different approach to the question of execution. Particular
classes of property, the seizure of which would raise sensitive foreign
relations problems, may have to be immunized from execution; this is the
case under the existing legislation for military property and for all or some
foreign central bank property.[183] The essentially pragmatic character of

---

[179] See Metzger, *Netherlands Yearbook of International Law*, 10 (1979), pp. 131–41; del Bianco,
Yale Studies in World Public Order, 5 (1978), pp. 109–46.
[180] State Immunity Act 1978 (U.K.), s. 17 (1).
[181] [1983] 3 W.L.R. 906.
[182] Above, p. 77 n. 11.
[183] e.g. State Immunity Act 1978 (U.K.), ss. 14 (4) (central bank or monetary authority); Foreign
Sovereign Immunities Act 1976 (U.S.A.), s. 1161 (b) (1) (central bank or monetary authority), (b) (2)
(military property). Other examples can be imagined. Thus on the reasoning in *Alcom* v. *Republic of
Colombia* (above, n. 181), an item of a State's cultural or historical heritage being exhibited within the
jurisdiction would, if a fee was charged for entry to the exhibition, be 'in use for commercial purposes'
and subject to execution.

these exemptions is demonstrated by the United Kingdom Act's exclusion of central bank property, which is treated more favourably than that of separate State entities (indeed, more favourably than much *State* property), despite the fact that many foreign central banks are substantially privately owned, and many that are not would not, on the authority of *Trendtex Trading Corporation* v. *Central Bank of Nigeria*, be treated as State agencies at common law.[184] This can only be explained on the basis of a policy decision on the part of the United Kingdom authorities to extend an immunity to foreign central banks which was not justified on the basis of any 'principle' underlying the Act, in order not to discourage such banks from maintaining reserves in the United Kingdom. That policy may well represent a valid assessment of the forum's interest in the matter; but it should not be presented as a consequence of any basic principle of foreign State immunity.

At the same time as particular property is immunized from execution, the remainder of a State's property within the jurisdiction might well be made subject to execution, unless at least it can be shown to be substantially in use for protected purposes such as the maintenance of an embassy, visiting force or visiting mission. This is particularly so with funds or similar liquid assets, which can (assuming the State's solvency) be readily replaced, and which can only with difficulty be said to be 'in use' for particular purposes unless specifically designated or set aside. An alternative solution—again foreshadowed by the European Convention—would be an undertaking by foreign States to comply with judgments against them in cases where it was agreed that no immunity from jurisdiction existed (and subject to the usual requirements of valid service, etc.) in return for an extended immunity from execution. Such an arrangement would need to be embodied in bilateral or multilateral agreements: the question is a particularly important one for the International Law Commission if it is to formulate balanced provisions on execution. Insistence on general immunity from execution, in the absence of an arrangement along these lines, is likely to be unacceptable to those States which now assert that the jurisdiction to determine disputes involving foreign States entails at least some capacity to enforce the resulting adjudication. At the same time the formula that links jurisdiction with execution, without an appreciation of the real difficulties and differences between them, is likely to be abandoned—one of the many formulae which, in this field, have for so long been treated as a substitute for careful and particular analysis.

---

[184] [1977] Q.B. 529. And cf. the caustic criticism by Mann, this *Year Book*, 50 (1979), pp. 43–62 at pp. 61–2.

SOME OBSERVATIONS ON THE DOCTRINE OF CONTINUITY AND FINALITY OF BOUNDARIES*

By KAIYAN HOMI KAIKOBAD[1]

I. INTRODUCTION

THE international political system appears to grant a considerable degree of importance to rights in respect of territory. While States are normally highly cautious and sensitive about questions of territorial sovereignty, they attempt to safeguard what they consider to be their rights to territory not only on the basis of political facts but also on grounds of law and justice. One of the fundamental concerns for a State in this regard is the maintenance of a maximum degree of territorial stability. The function of a boundary between States is the attribution of territory, and, accordingly, a frontier regime is closely connected with questions of territorial extent and sovereignty: the precise limits to the exercise of territorial sovereignty can only be determined by knowledge of the location of the alignments enclosing a State on all relevant sides. In most cases, boundary changes imply the diminution and enhancement of territory for the States on either side of it, with all the attendant escalations in friction and tension between them. States, therefore, have come to appreciate the importance of stable boundaries, the finality of frontier settlements and the general continuity of alignments. Generally speaking, States seek to deny to their adjacent entities a continuously available process whereunder they can call into question the status of an alignment settled on the basis of either an express settlement or the operation of a set of legally valid criteria. It is this need which has found expression in the rule of law which, in general terms, is to the effect that a boundary established in accordance with law attains a compelling degree of continuity and finality.

This general rule in respect of boundaries was perhaps first stated by the Permanent Court of Arbitration in October 1909 when it held in the *Grisbadarna* case[2] that 'it is a settled principle of the law of nations that a state of things which actually exists and has existed for a long time should be changed as little as possible'.[3] In the *Eastern Greenland* case,[4]

---

* © Dr. K. H. Kaikobad, 1984.

[1] B.A. (Punjab), LL.B. (Karachi), LL.M. (London), Ph.D. (London); Advocate, Punjab Bar Council, Pakistan.

[2] Scott, *Hague Court Reports* (1916), p. 122.

[3] Ibid., at p. 130. This was a statement of the *quieta non movere* doctrine. In 1925, the Permanent Court held in the *Mosul* case that 'the very nature of a frontier and of any convention designed to establish frontiers between two countries imports that a frontier must constitute a definite boundary line throughout its length': *P.C.I.J.*, Series B, No. 12, at p. 20. See below, pp. 137 ff.

[4] *P.C.I.J.*, Series A/B, No. 53, p. 22.

the Permanent Court of International Justice ruled in favour of Denmark's claims to title to Greenland on the grounds, *inter alia*, that she had maintained territorial sovereignty over the disputed territory for a period of time sufficient in law to invest her with title thereto.[5] In this context, Sir Hersch Lauterpacht observed that a decision in favour of *terra nullius* 'would have been contrary to those principles of finality, stability and effectiveness . . . which have characterised the work of the Court'.[6] Latterly, the rule has been expressed in the *Temple* case[7] where the International Court of Justice held that in general when two countries establish a frontier between themselves one of the primary objectives is to achieve finality and stability. This would be impossible, the Court continued, if the line so established could at any given moment and on the basis of a continuously available process be called in question, and its rectification claimed, whenever any inaccuracy by reference to a clause in the parent treaty was discovered.[8] Similarly, in the recent *Beagle Channel* case[9] the Court of Arbitration observed in respect of the Argentina–Chile Boundary Treaty of 1881:

. . . [T]he regime set up by the Treaty, and no other, was meant thenceforth to govern the question of boundaries and title to territory . . . and it was meant to be definitive, final and complete, leaving no boundary undefined, or territory then in dispute unallocated or . . . left over for some future allocation.[10]

The recurrence of the principle of finality and stability, and its appearance in different forms in frontier matters, prompts the suggestion that it constitutes one of the more fundamental and important precepts in the corpus of the rules relating to boundaries and that, to some extent, it is a doctrine in the general principles of international law. The purpose of this work is to elicit some of the more important manifestations and implications of this rule.

II. Manifestations of the Doctrine

An account of the manifestations of this doctrine may fairly be preceded by a brief statement in respect of some of its general implications. The general rule or, in certain cases, presumption is that a boundary between two States is, in all the appropriate circumstances, to be regarded as being a definitive attribution of territory. One of the appropriate circumstances is, of course, mutual consent: that is to say, where two States agree, whether expressly or otherwise, to modify the location of the alignment

---

[5] *P.C.I.J.*, Series A/B, No. 53, at pp. 46, 54.
[6] Lauterpacht, *The Development of International Law by the International Court* (1958), p. 241.
[7] *I.C.J. Reports*, 1962, p. 6.
[8] Ibid., at p. 34. Also see the *Frontier Land* case (*I.C.J. Reports*, 1959, p. 209) in the matter of the Convention of 1843 and the determination of the status quo: pp. 221–2 and 217–22.
[9] Award of 18 April 1977: H.M.S.O. 1977; *International Legal Materials*, 17 (1978), p. 632.
[10] Award, H.M.S.O. 1977, p. 12.

existing between them, the doctrine of finality and continuity clearly has no relevance. More important, however, is the question of validity. It may be emphasized that the doctrine of continuity of boundaries does not imply that in principle an illegal or invalid frontier must be perpetuated.[11] A boundary regime can be regarded as being subject to this rule of finality only where either of the States can establish its legal credentials. However, it is clear that in most cases, the heart of the legal issue in a boundary dispute between States may well be the question of the *validity* of the alignment claimed by one State against the other. To some extent, therefore, it may appear as if the doctrine were begging a question essential to the determination of the dispute, in so far as it is concerned with the matter of deciding which of the two (or more) States has, on the basis of the law and evidence of the case, succeeded in establishing her territorial and boundary-related claims. It is also to be noted that the doctrine and all its various implications are not in any way unique, for clearly any regime or arrangement existing between States, be it territorial, commercial or diplomatic, is, in all the appropriate circumstances, to be regarded as continuing and binding upon the States parties to the arrangement.

This view, it is submitted, is not unsound, but the important point throughout is that it is this very doctrine or rule which is, and has been, relied upon by States to prove the validity of a frontier line established in legally controversial or doubtful circumstances. In other words, States have been known to advocate the continuation of a boundary line on the basis, *inter alia*, of the need for maintenance of the territorial status quo. The doctrine, thus, is employed as a validating criterion. This aspect of the matter will be elaborated elsewhere,[12] and it may be sufficient to note here that judicial decisions have on various occasions been consistent with this general theme of reasoning.

(a) *Acquiescence and Recognition of Boundaries*

The rules relating to acquiescence and recognition of boundaries are essentially an application of the general principles of acquiescence in respect of title to territory. This, however, must be qualified by stating that many of the sources of the rules in respect of title to territory are related to boundary disputes, and this is especially true of judicial decisions. The questions of territory and frontiers are quite interrelated and at times it may be difficult, and perhaps serve no useful purpose, to determine whether a boundary dispute is in fact a territorial one, or vice versa, inasmuch as the relevant legal criteria are applicable to either class of dispute. It follows, therefore, that there is no value in dwelling on the view that the notion of acquiescence in respect of boundaries is an especial

---

[11] On many occasions, an 'illegal' frontier *is* perpetuated, but that is so on account of the operation of various legal factors, including the doctrine of finality and stability. See below, and pp. 123–5 for detailed discussion.

[12] Below, pp. 123–5.

development of the law relating to title to territory, for both are parts of the same body. Nevertheless, the general principles of acquiescence and estoppel do have particular relevance to matters of boundaries, and, speaking in broad terms, the rule in this respect is that long and uninterrupted maintenance of a boundary by one State against another will preclude the latter from contesting the validity or location of that line at a subsequent period of time, provided that she had knowledge of such administration, or was in a position to have acquired such knowledge, but failed to reserve her rights to the location of the alignment or the territory attributed by it. Such reservation of rights may take on various forms, one of which is the issuance of a protest to the administering State.

This rule is central to the doctrine of stability and finality. While variations to this general concept are considerable, they all reflect the general norm, i.e. that a continuously available process which allows States to question an established and respected alignment should be denied them in the interests of stability. In the *Temple* case the International Court held that the Annex 1 map, which was not an official map annexed either to the boundary treaty or to the proceedings of the boundary commission, had virtually acquired treaty status inasmuch as Thailand, by failing to protest, had implied that she had accepted the map as representing the work of the commission, and thereafter she was precluded from protesting against the depiction contained therein.[13]

Similarly, in the *Anglo-Norwegian Fisheries* case,[14] the International Court of Justice ruled in favour of the Norwegian system of delimitation of the territorial sea. It observed that Britain had remained silent in the face of the development of this system for a period of about sixty years, and that the international community of States had also exhibited 'general toleration' in the enforcement of the straight baseline system.[15] These facts precluded them from challenging the validity of the system subsequently. In terms, thus, the Court ruled in favour of the maritime boundary delineated by Norway.[16]

The general rule of acquiescence in respect of boundary regimes has also been upheld by municipal courts, prominent among which is the Supreme Court of the United States. In *Indiana* v. *Kentucky*,[17] the question was whether the southern or northern channel of the Ohio River in the region of Green River Island constituted the boundary between these two States. Kentucky argued that she had exercised dominion and

---

[13] *I.C.J. Reports*, 1962, p. 32. See separate opinion of Judge Alfaro for a fairly detailed statement of the law on the matter, pp. 39–51.

[14] Ibid. 1951, p. 116.

[15] Ibid., at p. 138.

[16] Ibid., at pp. 136–9. See also the Guyana–Surinam boundary and the question of the 'true' source of the Corentyne; and especially Lord Salisbury's statement in respect thereof: Menon, 'International Boundaries—A Case Study of the Guyana–Surinam Boundary', *International and Comparative Law Quarterly*, 27 (1978), p. 738 at p. 757.

[17] 136 U.S. 479.

control over Green River Island for a long period of time without encountering protest from Indiana and, accordingly, the true dividing line was formed by the northern channel.[18] 'It is', the Court ruled, 'a principle of public law universally recognised, that long acquiescence in the possession of territory and in the exercise of dominion and sovereignty over it, is conclusive of the nation's title and rightful authority.'[19]

Cognate with this aspect of acquiescence and recognition in respect of boundaries is the application of the rule in question to those cases where the precise location of the line is either clearly in contradiction with the terms of a provision contained in a boundary treaty or is surrounded by legally controversial circumstances. The general principle in such regimes appears to be in favour of maintaining rather than of upsetting the territorial status quo. In the *Rann of Kutch* arbitration[20] between India and Pakistan, the latter argued that the vertical line, which delineated part of the western sector of the borderlands, was an invalid alignment. She argued that the agreement of 1914, concluded between the State of Kutch and the British Indian Province of Sind, was limited to the territory which fell on either side of the Sir Creek and the 'blue-dotted' east–west line which ran between the northern end of the creek and the western terminus. The vertical line, she said, was demarcated in excess of powers vested in the boundary demarcation commission. While the Chairman of the Tribunal accepted the contention that the vertical line was not, in principle, encompassed by the agreement of 1914, he ruled that the Sind Administration and higher authorities had accepted the vertical line without censure or challenge, and that it was 'not open to the Tribunal to disturb a boundary settled in this manner by the British Administration and accepted and acted upon by it, as well as the State of Kutch, for nearly a quarter of a century'.[21]

In *State of South Australia* v. *State of Victoria*[22] the Judicial Committee of the Privy Council was called upon to determine the legal status of the line demarcated by a joint commission on the basis of the Letters Patent of 1836 and the Act of 1938 which provided for a boundary along the 141st meridian of east longitude. South Australia discovered subsequently that the demarcated line lay about $2\frac{1}{4}$ miles to the east of the stipulated meridian. The Judicial Committee observed that while certain sectors of the boundary had been formally proclaimed and acknowledged, other sectors had not received 'formal and public recognition' and had not been

---

[18] Ibid., at p. 503.

[19] Ibid., at p. 510. Also see *Virginia* v. *Tennessee*, 148 U.S. 503, at pp. 520–7; *Maryland* v. *West Virginia*, 217 U.S. 1, at pp. 40–5.

[20] 50 I.L.R. 1; *Reports of International Arbitral Awards*, vol. 17, p. 1.

[21] 50 I.L.R. 475. In the *Temple* case, the line depicted in the Annex 1 map was, in the contention of Thailand, in contravention of the Treaty of 1904, which delineated the boundary along the watershed of the Dangrek range. The Court gave precedence to the former alignment for reasons described above, p. 122.

[22] [1914] A.C. 283.

ordered, carried out and accepted in precisely the same way that the other sectors had been. Nevertheless, it held that there was no 'difference between the two portions of the boundary in respect of their authority and finality', and declined to hold the demarcated line invalid.[23]

Similarly, in *Virginia* v. *Tennessee*,[24] the former contended that the boundary established between Tennessee and herself by virtue of mutual recitals contained in their respective legislative acts was invalid inasmuch as the recitals constituted an agreement between States of the Union. The U.S. Constitution, it was argued, prohibited the conclusion of compacts between States of the Union without consent of Congress, and therefore the alignment established as a result of this compact was null and void. The Supreme Court, however, refused to accept this argument and held that independently of any effect caused by the compact, the line, which had been located and marked out and subsequently recognized by the parties, would be conclusive even if it were ascertained that it varied from the course given in the original grant.[25]

State practice, in this regard, is also indicative of the emphasis States place on the maintenance of boundary regimes which have been in existence for a considerable period of time. The frontier between Uganda and Tanzania is one example.[26] The basis of this line was laid down in Article 1 of the Anglo-German Heligoland Treaty of 1890 which defined the limits of the spheres of influence of either State's possessions in East Africa. The boundary was delineated along the 1° of south latitude. In July 1906 the parties signed an agreement which represented the work of the demarcation commission. The agreement, however, was not ratified. In 1914, the same line was described by the parties in a draft treaty, the formal conclusion of which was held up on account of the war of 1914–18. The alignment, nevertheless, was maintained and continued by Britain after she had succeeded to Germany's East Africa possessions as mandatory power. It was this alignment which the two sovereign States, Uganda/Tanganyika and Tanzania, succeeded to in 1962 and 1964 respectively.[27] Although there are difficulties of precise location, it appears that no dispute exists in principle between the two States. In his learned study of African boundaries, Professor Brownlie points out that '[a]s a matter of international law, the practice of the States concerned has involved the adoption of the alignment in spite of the absence of a formal agreement'.[28] Similarly, in the matter of the difficulties related to the precise position

---

[23] [1914] A.C. 283, at p. 310. Also *New Mexico* v. *Colorado*, 267 U.S. 30, *in re* the Darling line which was not strictly along the 37th parallel of north latitude, at pp. 34–5; *Michigan* v. *Wisconsin*, 270 U.S. 295, *in re* the Burt alignment, which the former contended was void for 'excusable ignorance' on her part: p. 308. Both lines were held to be valid, and were continued: ibid.

[24] 148 U.S. 503.

[25] Ibid., at p. 522.

[26] See, generally, Brownlie, *African Boundaries: A Legal and Diplomatic Encyclopaedia* (1979), pp. 1011–16; McEwen, *International Boundaries of East Africa* (1971), pp. 265–82.

[27] Brownlie, loc. cit. (previous note).

[28] Ibid., at p. 1013.

of the demarcated boundary and the stipulated 1° line, he states: 'Legal and other considerations dictate a principle of finality and stability: the actual alignment acquiesced in by the States concerned should prevail.'[29]

Further, in the matter of the eastern sector of the boundary dispute between India and the People's Republic of China, the latter contends that the MacMahon Line of 1914, which delimited the boundary between parts of India and Burma from Tibet, is not a valid frontier. She argues that the Simla Agreement, which forms the basis of the line, was void on account of the fact that Tibet, a vassal of China, concluded the treaty without her consent, and could not therefore create any lawful territorial rights in favour of either party.[30] Even so, it appears that China at one time reconciled herself to the 1914 alignment, and in a letter to the Prime Minister of India, written in January 1959, she stated:

In view of the various complex factors . . . the Chinese Government on the one hand finds it necessary to take a more or less realistic attitude towards the MacMahon Line, and, on the other hand, cannot but act with prudence and needs time to deal with this matter.[31]

Finally, reference may be made to Britain's attitude in the frontier question between Venezuela and British Guiana (now Guyana). The boundary, which was established by way of the award of an arbitral tribunal in 1899 and demarcated by the parties in June 1905, was challenged by Venezuela in 1962 on the grounds that the award itself was invalid.[32] In statements to the U.N. General Assembly and the Special Political Committee, the United Kingdom, which was then exercising control over British Guiana, replied that the members of the Committee should consider the implications of bringing into dispute an alignment which had been settled for fifty-seven years. Mr. Crowe, the British representative, said: 'It has always been the keystone of British policy, and I believe the vast majority of other member States of the United Nations, that respect for international agreements freely concluded is not only essential to world stability but axiomatic if the rule of international law is to survive.'[33]

While there can be little doubt that law and State practice clearly support the doctrine of finality, it must be emphasized that boundaries are not in any way sacrosanct. Before a boundary line can be continued on the

[29] Ibid., at pp. 1015-16. See also the Exchange of Notes between Australia and the Netherlands of 1936 wherein it was decided that the boundary demarcated on the ground 'shall continue to be the boundary whether or not subsequent surveys should indicate that [the boundary monument established was] in fact situated somewhat to the east or west of the 141st meridian of east longitude': *British and Foreign State Papers*, vol. 140 (1936), pp. 130-2.

[30] See, generally, Ministry of External Affairs, Government of India, *Report of the Officials of the Governments of India and China on the Boundary Question* (1961), p. CR-19 to p. CR-32.

[31] Ministry of External Affairs, Government of India, *Notes, memoranda and letters exchanged and agreements signed between the Governments of India and China, 1954-59, White Paper I*, pp. 52-4 at p. 53. Also see Indian Letter to China, 14 December 1958, *White Paper I*, pp. 48-51.

[32] E. Lauterpacht, *The Contemporary Practice of the United Kingdom in the Field of International Law* (1962), pt. ii, pp. 161-2.

[33] U.K. Reply (pp. 163-75), at p. 173.

basis of acquiescence, all the surrounding legal and factual circumstances will have to be taken into consideration. In other words the principle of finality has to be seen in conjunction with, and subject to, various factors. One of these is the rule that acquiescence is not to be lightly presumed. In the *Palena* case,[34] the Court of Arbitration rejected the argument that the correspondence conducted between Argentina and Chile between 1913-15 and 1952 had yielded a common understanding, express or implied, in respect of the location of the frontier.[35] Similarly, it rejected Argentina's contention that Chile had acquiesced in the deliberations of the Mixed Commission which had, in the opinion of the Court, offered a 'friendly solution' to the boundary problem between the two States.[36] In the *Frontier Land* case,[37] the International Court gave full weight to the fact that Belgium was placed in a geographically disadvantageous position in respect of the detection of encroachments by the Netherlands over the disputed enclaves, and declined to rule in favour of the Dutch contention that Belgium had acquiesced in and recognized the former's jurisdiction and control over the territory in question.[38] In the *Rann of Kutch* arbitration, the Chairman of the Tribunal rejected India's contention that the depiction of a boundary line along the northern edge of the Rann on the map annexed to the 1914 agreement precluded Pakistan from contending that the boundary in the Rann was essentially an unsettled matter. '[T]he Resolution [i.e. the 1914 agreement]', he ruled, 'and the map are recognized as a binding determination only of the portion of the boundary up to the Western Trijunction.'[39] In general terms, therefore, where recognition of an alignment is being claimed by one party against another, there must be a definite and positive connection between the alignment and all the facts of the situation. Where this is not in evidence, the claims of acquiescence and recognition will remain inconclusive and disproved. In other words, each situation relating to acquiescence has to be examined individually with due consideration of all the facts regarding it, the doctrine of finality and stability of frontiers notwithstanding.

(b) *State Succession and Boundary Treaties*

The general rule of customary international law in this matter is that, in principle, a State succeeds to the territorial limits of her predecessor: she gains no more and no less territory upon succession. The opinions of

---

[34] *Reports of International Arbitral Awards*, vol. 16, p. 111.

[35] Ibid., at p. 166. See also separate opinion of Judge Basdevant in the *Minquiers* case (*I.C.J. Reports*, 1953, p. 47) on the implications of the fishery incidents and the *démarche*. He found neither renunciation nor acknowledgement of the rival claim: p. 81. See also *Chamizal* case, *Reports of International Arbitral Awards*, vol. 11, p. 316 at pp. 328-9.

[36] Ibid., vol. 16, at p. 171.

[37] *I.C.J. Reports*, 1959, p. 209.

[38] Ibid., at pp. 227-30, especially p. 229.

[39] 50 I.L.R. 1 at p. 476.

writers, both old and modern alike, favour the rule cited above. Wharton, Hall and Oppenheim[40] have all acknowledged the rule of continuity of territorial regimes and boundaries in the event of State succession. To some extent, the doctrine of *uti possidetis* of the Latin American States was, and continues to be, rooted in this principle. In the *Costa Rica* v. *Panama* arbitration,[41] the former State relied heavily upon this doctrine, and in her argument said: 'It is a principle universally admitted, that when a colony gains its independence, it gains at the same time so much of the territory covered by it under the old sovereign as is wrested from his possession.'[42] Among the modern writers, Professors Verzijl, McNair and Brownlie have expressed views in favour of this rule.[43]

The rationale behind the rule of presumption of continuity lies in the theory that, in general terms, a boundary regime or treaty remains and runs with the land. A frontier agreement, it is said, acts as a conveyance and it is the objective regime which the agreement creates which is of paramount importance. In 1968, at its fifty-third Conference, at Buenos Aires, the International Law Association passed a resolution relating to the succession of new States to treaties and other obligations. Resolution No. 8 stipulated:

When a treaty which provides for the delimitation of a national boundary between two States has been executed in the sense that the boundary has been delimited and no further action needs to be taken, the treaty has spent its force and what is succeeded to is not the treaty but the extent of national territory so delimited.[44]

It is clear that these propositions reflect the general acknowledgement among States that executed boundary agreements and existing frontier lines are best left undisturbed.

The same emphasis on continuity was apparent when the International Law Commission deliberated upon the question of State succession to, *inter alia*, boundary treaties. At the 1968 session, when Sir Humphrey Waldock introduced draft article 4, which specified, in general terms, that boundary treaties and rights and obligations established by those treaties remained unaffected by the occurrence of a succession of States, the greater number of members of the Commission expressed their agreement

---

[40] Wharton, *A Digest of the International Law of the United States*, vol. 1 (1887), pp. 26–7; Hall, *A Treatise on International Law* (8th edn., 1924), pp. 119–24, especially pp. 120, 123; Oppenheim, *International Law*, vol. 1 (8th edn., 1955), pp. 925–9. Also Harvard Draft Article 26 on the Law of Treaties, *American Journal of International Law*, 29 (1935), Supplement, pp. 1066–7.

[41] *Reports of International Arbitral Awards*, vol. 11, p. 528.

[42] *Argument of Costa Rica* (Washington, 1913), pp. 39–40.

[43] Verzijl, *International Law in Historical Perspective*, vol. 7 (1974), pp. 171, 303; McNair, *Law of Treaties* (1961), pp. 656 ff.; Brownlie, *Principles of Public International Law* (3rd edn., 1979), pp. 666–7; Udokang, *Succession of New States to International Treaties* (1972), pp. 377 ff.; Okoye, *International Law and the New African States* (1972), pp. 93–4.

[44] *Report of the 53rd Conference* (1968), p. 589, at p. 598; commentary, p. 603. Also see I.L.A. publication, *The Effect of Independence on Treaties, A Handbook* (1965), pp. 361–7.

with the general principles specified therein.[45] The same broad general consensus is discernible from the records of the session of 1972.[46] In his First Report as Special Rapporteur on Succession of States in respect of Treaties, Sir Francis Vallat referred to the various underlying notions and principles of the continuity of frontier regimes in the event of State succession.[47] 'Moreover', he said, 'to allow a succession of States in itself to provide a ground for unilateral rejection of settled boundaries or of territorial rights and obligations would tend towards uncertainty and instability, and would not, generally speaking, be in the interests of the maintenance of international peace and security.'[48]

In its definitive form, Article 11 specifies that

A succession of States does not as such affect

(a) a boundary established by a treaty; or
(b) obligations and rights established by a treaty and relating to the regime of a boundary.[49]

Brief reference may also be made to the practice of States. At Cairo in July 1964, the heads of States members of the Organization for African Unity declared in a resolution that they had agreed to 'respect the borders existing on their achievement of national independence'.[50] At Cairo in October of the same year, States attending the Non-Aligned Summit Conference, which had representation from Asia, Africa and Latin America, pledged in their Final Declaration 'to respect frontiers as they existed when the States gained independence'.[51] These facts clearly establish the importance States attach to the maintenance of the maximum degree of stability in matters of territorial limits and the rejection of conditions which tend to disturb the equilibrium established by pre-independence alignments.

The above statement on the law must be qualified. First, it is to be emphasized that the succession of States does not imply that the territorial limits of the succeeding State are, from the moment of succession, to be regarded as final and not open to question merely on the basis of the fact that a succession of States has occurred. A change of this kind is not to be regarded as a process of legitimization whereby boundaries established

---

[45] *Yearbook of the International Law Commission*, 1968, vol. 2, pp. 92–3; and vol. 1, pp. 130–46; see Castrén at p. 134.

[46] Ibid. 1972, vol. 1, pp. 247–54.

[47] Ibid. 1974, vol. 2, pt. 1, p. 83; and commentary to draft Articles 11 and 12, pp. 197–208.

[48] Ibid. Also commentary to Article 59 of the Final Report of the International Law Commission to the General Assembly on the Law of Treaties, *Yearbook of the International Law Commission*, 1966, vol. 2, pp. 259–60.

[49] Vienna Convention on Succession of States in respect of Treaties: U.N. Document A/CONF.80/31 (22 August 1978); *International Legal Materials*, 17 (1978), p. 1488.

[50] Text, Brownlie, *Boundaries* (above, p. 124 n. 26), pp. 10–11, commentary at pp. 9–12; McEwen, op. cit. above (p. 124 n. 6), pp. 21–7 (and pp. 27–31). See also Preamble to the O.A.U. Charter of 1963: *United Nations Treaty Series*, vol. 479, p. 70.

[51] Text: *Indian Journal of International Law*, 4 (1964), p. 589, pt. v, at p. 610. Certain Latin American States and Finland were represented by observers.

unlawfully or in legally controversial circumstances acquire validity and finality—providing, of course, there are no countervailing considerations of acquiescence and recognition. The fact is that a State succeeds not only to all the territorial rights of her predecessor, but also to all the limitations and liabilities that are connected therewith. Therefore, all claims in relation to the status and location of the boundary existing prior to succession will also be deemed to continue. Secondly, the doctrine in question does not imply that States are bound to maintain a particular alignment after succession even if there is agreement between the relevant States in favour of modifying the line; or, that they are not free to agree to make modifications in the boundary regimes after there has occurred a succession of States. The rule against changes after succession is confined to situations in which either one of the parties unilaterally claims modifications in the boundary or status of the territory attributed by it.

(c) *The Doctrine of* Rebus Sic Stantibus *and Boundary Treaties*

Customary international law provides that where a fundamental change of circumstances has occurred between States in the context of certain treaty relations between them, the treaty establishing such relations may be regarded as void and the two States are thereafter released from their (mutual) treaty obligations.[52] It is also a well-established rule of law that boundary treaties are, generally speaking, exempt from the operation of this doctrine.[53] These rules were stated in Article 62 of the Vienna Convention on the Law of Treaties. Paragraph 2(a) of this article stipulates:

A fundamental change of circumstances may not be invoked as a ground for terminating or withdrawing from a treaty:

(a) if the treaty establishes a boundary . . .[54]

As in the case of the principle predicated in Article 11 of the Vienna Convention on the Succession of States to Treaties, members of the Commission were generally in favour of including a proviso consistent with the continuity of frontiers.[55]

The assumptions underpinning this proviso to the doctrine of *rebus sic stantibus* are cognate with those mentioned in respect of the continuity

---

[52] See, generally, Fitzmaurice, *Yearbook of the International Law Commission*, 1957, vol. 2, pp. 56–65; Waldock, ibid. 1963, vol. 2, pp. 79–85; McNair, *Law of Treaties* (1961), pp. 681–91; Brownlie, *Principles* (above, p. 127 n. 43), pp. 616–18; O'Connell, *International Law* (1970), vol. 1, pp. 278–80; Harvard Draft Article 28 on the Law of Treaties, loc. cit. above (p. 127 n. 40), pp. 1096–1126; Haraszti, *Recueil des cours*, 146 (1975-III), p. 7.

[53] Waldock, *Yearbook of the International Law Commission*, 1963, vol. 2, p. 85; ibid. 1966, vol. 2, pp. 42–4; Commentary to Draft Article 59, ibid., p. 259; O'Connell, *State Succession in Municipal Law and International Law* (1967), vol. 2, p. 273; Udokang, op. cit. above (p. 127 n. 43), p. 380. Cf. Zemanek, *Recueil des cours*, 116 (1965-III), pp. 239–44.

[54] *United Kingdom Treaty Series*, No. 58 (1980) (Cmnd. 7964).

[55] See *Yearbook of the International Law Commission*, 1963, vol. 1, pp. 136–58, especially Lachs, p. 140, and Ago, p. 154; ibid. 1966, vol. 1, pt. 1, pp. 75–87, and vol. 2, pp. 39–44.

of frontiers in the event of State succession. It will be sufficient, therefore, to say that a boundary treaty, once agreed to, is exhausted and remains evidence of the transfer and attribution of territory to the States concerned. As such, boundary stipulations impart a lasting effect upon the territory, an effect which is transferred to the succeeding State.[56] It is not, however, essential for the treaty to be executed. In the Shatt-al-Arab boundary dispute between Iraq and Iran, the latter renounced the Frontier Treaty of 1937 on the basis of the doctrine *rebus sic stantibus*. In his analysis of the legal aspects of this dispute, Al-Izzi commented upon the irrelevance of this doctrine to the Frontier Treaty, and remarked that 'boundary treaties regulate positions characterised by permanence and finality and are, as such, unaffected by changing circumstances'.[57] Changed conditions, he said, could not be invoked to invalidate such treaties because they are immediately effective and establish an immutable regime of a permanent and final nature.[58] In the dispute between Peru and Ecuador in respect of the Rio de Janeiro boundary protocol concluded in January 1942, it was contended by the Government of Peru that the said protocol was not binding upon her inasmuch as it was invalid.[59] The United States, one of the four guarantor States, challenged Ecuador's contentions, and in a telegram to Peru she maintained that it was a basic principle of international law that the unilateral will of one of the parties was not sufficient to invalidate a boundary treaty or to liberate it from the obligations imposed therein.[60] She went on to stress the fact that the line had been demarcated in almost all its course.

(d) *Traditional Boundaries*

International law recognizes that, in certain circumstances, a customary and traditional frontier, i.e. a frontier which exists, not on the basis of a treaty or an internationally relevant municipal instrument,[61] but primarily and essentially upon the basis of custom and tradition, is to be regarded as a lawful boundary, capable of creating valid territorial rights in favour of both parties. In the *Rann of Kutch* arbitration, both India and Pakistan were agreed that there was no comprehensive boundary treaty delimiting their territories and argued on the basis of the existence of an ancient traditional and customary frontier which had always divided their

---

[56] Above, pp. 126–9.

[57] Al-Izzi, *The Shatt-al-Arab River Dispute in Terms of Law* (1972), p. 102.

[58] Ibid.

[59] Whiteman, *Digest of International Law*, vol. 3 (1964), pp. 676 ff.

[60] Ibid., pp. 679–80. See also Cukwurah, *The Settlement of Boundary Disputes in International Law* (1967), pp. 119–21.

[61] Reference is here being made to decrees and orders issued by the Metropolitan Powers in Africa and Asia in respect of internal administrative divisions. In certain cases these orders have continued as the bases of allocation of territory after the separation of these units and their emergence as sovereign States. See, for example, the administrative measures which constitute the bases of the Algeria–Niger frontier, Brownlie, *Boundaries* (above, p. 124 n. 26), pp. 85–6; and the Order in Council of 1 February 1926 which forms the basis of the Kenya–Uganda frontier, ibid., pp. 941–3.

predecessor entities.[62] The dispute, therefore, was not one in which either of the parties challenged the principle or validity in international law of customary frontiers, but in which the Tribunal was called upon to determine the location of the alleged boundary. The Tribunal gave full importance to traditional criteria,[63] and Judge Lagergren, the Chairman of the Tribunal, focused his inquiry initially upon discovering whether or not a historic line had indeed existed in the region.[64] Although his conclusions were negative in this regard,[65] it is amply clear that had he discovered a customary frontier, it would have formed the basis of the award; and effectively a line based upon facts of history and tradition would have been continued and employed to allocate territory between two modern States. As Judge Ales Bebler, a Member of the Tribunal, observed in his dissenting opinion, 'Yet they [i.e. traditional boundaries] do exist. Described or not, depicted or not, they exist. They have an international legal existence in all cases—described and depicted in treaties or not. They are universally considered as binding the neighbours.'[66]

Similarly, in the boundary case between *Honduras and Nicaragua*,[67] the Arbitrator, King Alphonso XIII of Spain, observed that '. . . from what is inferred from all the foregoing, the point which best answers the purpose by reason of historical right, of equity and of a geographical nature, to serve as a common boundary on the Atlantic Coast between the two contending States, is Cape Gracias á Dios for the Atlantic Coast, and . . . this Cape fixes what has practically been the limit or expansion or encroachment of Nicaragua towards the north and of Honduras towards the south . . .'.[68]

In the *Honduras Borders* case, the Special Arbitral Tribunal was required to determine the *uti possidetis* line of 1821 between Honduras and Guatemala. In the southernmost sector of the boundary the Tribunal observed that there was no royal rescript or other executive order which formed the basis of allocation of territory, and therefore took into consideration certain traditional factors, including repute of the inhabitants of the area. In respect of Rio Frio, the Tribunal observed that the Guatemalans, who lived north of the river, had protested against the issue of Honduran land grants on their side of the Frio. They claimed that 'from

---

[62] Award, 50 I.L.R. 1 at pp. 22-6.

[63] Ibid., at pp. 474-94; dissenting opinion of Judge Bebler, at pp. 405-15; pp. 424 ff.

[64] Ibid., at p. 474.

[65] Ibid., at pp. 493-4.

[66] Ibid., at p. 408. It is to be noted that in his view the legal force behind traditional boundaries lies in the principles of acquiescence and recognition, which is, on this view of the matter, a subject closely related to but quite apart from traditional boundaries.

[67] *Reports of International Arbitral Awards*, vol. 11, p. 111.

[68] Ibid., at p. 115. In respect of Cape Camarón, the Arbitrator noted that there was no evidence that Nicaragua had ever extended her influence to the aforementioned Cape, 'and there is no reason, therefore, to select said Cape as a frontier boundary with Honduras on the Atlantic coast as is claimed by Nicaragua...' (p. 114). See, further, the *Guiana Boundary* case (ibid., p. 21) in which the Arbitrator held: '. . . it does not appear . . . that there are historical and legal claims on which to found thoroughly determined and well-defined rights of sovereignty in favour of either . . . [party] . . .': p. 22.

time immemorial their forefathers, natives of Esquipulas, had possessed and worked the lands of Las Granadillas mountain . . .'.[69] Part of the line was subsequently drawn along the Rio Frio.

Traditional considerations were also present, to some extent, and in respect of certain parts of the border, in the *Costa Rica* v. *Panama* arbitration.[70] The arbitrator, Mr. White, Chief Justice of the Supreme Court of the United States, observed, in respect of the Saxiola river, that Panama's description and claims of a boundary river corresponded with the Saxiola,[71] and that Colombia, her predecessor, had always regarded the eastern bank as 'the line of its jurisdiction of that country'.[72] One indication of this was that Colombian settlements were limited to the east bank of the Saxiola, while Costa Rica's settlements extended up the west bank. These facts, among others, were taken into account in the determination of the definitive line.[73]

Finally, it may be noted that in the *Temple* case, both parties made, *inter alia*, claims of history, religion and tradition in respect of the boundary.[74] Thailand claimed that the high ground in the Dangrek range had been Thai territory since the thirteenth century, although she admitted that during certain periods she had extended to the south of the range.[75] 'But never', said Mr. Pramroj, Counsel for the Government of Thailand, in his oral argument, 'have we been forced beyond the ramparts of the Dangrek range of mountains'.[76] While the majority opinion dismissed these contentions as being legally indecisive,[77] the late Sir Gerald Fitzmaurice said:

> Such matters may have some relevance in a case about territorial sovereignty which turns on the weight of factual evidence that each party can adduce in support of its claim, and not on any more concrete and positive element, such as a treaty.[78]

Thus, on his view, since the Treaty of 1904 governed the rights and obligations of the parties in respect of the frontier, these 'extraneous factors' had only an 'incidental relevance in determining where today, as a matter

---

[69] *Reports of International Arbitral Awards*, vol. 2, p. 1307 at p. 1354. See also observations in respect of the area east of the Motagua valley, p. 1359, and Guatemala's claims in respect of the Merendon range: 'Nature herself seems to have been interested in establishing an ideal boundary between Guatemala and Honduras which during the colonial period and the greater part of her independent life has served as a limit for a development of the two neighbour countries': *Counter-Case of Guatemala* (Washington, 1932), p. 461. Cf. Award, ibid., pp. 1357–8.

[70] *Reports of International Arbitral Awards*, vol. 11, p. 528.

[71] Ibid., at p. 529.

[72] Ibid., at p. 533.

[73] Award, ibid., pp. 545–6. See *Palena* case where the Court of Arbitration observed that 'Tradition dictates the names of rivers, and sound evidence of traditional nomenclature—indigenous names or names given by first discoverers—would be decisive': loc. cit. above (p. 126 n. 34), p. 177.

[74] *I.C.J. Pleadings, Temple of Preah Vihear*, vol. 1, pp. 170–2, 437, 547–8.

[75] Ibid., p. 171. 'Phra Viharn', she said, 'has thus been connected historically with Thailand for some six hundred years': ibid.

[76] *Pleadings*, vol. 2, p. 212.

[77] *I.C.J. Reports*, 1963, p. 6, at p. 15.

[78] Ibid., at p. 53.

of law, it does run'.[79] In other words, even in these circumstances, traditional and historical considerations may not be completely ruled out.

Before conclusions are drawn, a word on State practice in this regard will not be inappropriate. Several States in Asia have given great emphasis to traditional boundaries in both the conclusion of treaties and the pursuance of claims. In the Sino-Pakistan Boundary Treaty of 2 March 1962, Article 1 states that 'the two Parties agree to delimit [the frontier] on the basis of the traditional customary boundary line, including natural features'.[80] Similarly, in the Boundary Treaty between China and Nepal concluded on 5 October 1961, Article 1 states that '[t]he Contracting Parties basing themselves on the traditional customary boundary line . . . hereby agree on the following alignment . . .'.[81] These treaties are all the more interesting when viewed in light of the fact that the States in question were not animated by a desire either to redraw or to change boundaries existing on the basis of 'colonial' treaties, but by a reasonable need for the precise and modern delimitation of lines which had in fact existed in administrative measures over the years preceding independence.[82] In the Sino-Indian boundary dispute, both parties have relied extensively on traditional criteria, and a customary basis has been found for each of the three, i.e. the western, middle and eastern, sectors of the frontier.[83]

There is evidence that certain international frontiers in Africa have also been influenced by historic and traditional factors, notwithstanding the fact that 'the colonial partition overrode traditional boundaries for the most part'.[84] As Professor Brownlie has pointed out, it would not be entirely correct to say that ethnological, tribal and traditional considerations were always ruled out in the settlement of boundary questions.[85] A substantial part of the northern sector of the frontier between Botswana and Zimbabwe is based on the Pandamentaka (or Hunters) Road which has served traditionally and administratively as a separating entity.[86] In Europe, too, customary frontiers abound, and it may be fitting to quote Professor Verzijl on this aspect who observed that 'the actual *tracé* of many boundaries still dates back to feudal times . . . They appear to display

[79] Ibid. See also, in passing, the *Jaworzina* case, *P.C.I.J.*, Series B, No. 8, pp. 20, 21. In respect of title to territory and historical considerations, see the *Minquiers* case (*I.C.J. Reports*, 1953, p. 47) and the *Western Sahara* advisory opinion (ibid. 1975, p. 12).

[80] Text: *Indian Journal of International Law*, 2 (1962), p. 547.

[81] Text: ibid. 1 (1960–1), p. 704. See also Article 5 of the Sino-Burmese Boundary Treaty, ibid., p. 695, at p. 696. Further see Lamb, *Asian Frontiers: Studies in a Continuing Problem* (1968).

[82] This, however, is not entirely true of the Burma-China boundary inasmuch as the Conventions of 1894 and 1897 and subsequent demarcation protocols governed most of the boundary regime. It is, however, true of the sector between N. lat. 25° 35' and 28°.

[83] *Report of the Officials of the Governments of India and China*, loc. cit. above (p. 125 n. 30), pp. 41–50, 71–83, 101–2, 103–9. Chinese Report, p. CR-7; CR-33 to 74.

[84] Brownlie, *Boundaries* (above, p. 124 n. 26), p. 8.

[85] Ibid., pp. 5–9.

[86] Ibid., pp. 1082–4. See also the Burundi–Rwanda, Chad–Sudan and Angola–Zambia (the *Western Boundary of the Barotse Kingdom* case) frontiers, ibid., pp. 739–43, 617–39, 1041–72.

a curious character of sacrosanctity which forbids their elimination even today.'[87]

A word of caution must be added here. The above discussion on the importance of traditional boundaries, it must be emphasized, is grounded on the proposition that wherever other legal factors, viz. treaty stipulations and the principles of acquiescence and recognition, are operative, customary frontiers, wherever they are inconsistent with the territorial effects and implications of these principles, have diminished legal importance. In other words, where the law relating to, for example, acquiescence points in the direction of a line different from a customary frontier, it is the former which supersedes the latter. The same is true for treaty stipulations. It is with this point in view that conclusions may be drawn. It is clear that international law recognizes the legal importance of traditional criteria and historic and customary frontiers. Where a State can establish the existence of a traditional boundary, she can, in all the appropriate circumstances, claim valid title to territory on the basis of the attribution of the line in question. In very real terms, the continuation of traditional boundaries in modern conditions constitutes a latter-day confirmation of the status quo and an acknowledgement that ancient divisions of territory are not without legal effects, and are not, therefore, to be lightly disturbed. The adoption, therefore, by international law of rules and propositions in favour of the continuation of customary frontiers is, on this view of the matter, a further indication of the importance the law assigns to the continuity of frontiers in general.

(e) Coercion and Boundary Treaties

The doctrine of finality also has relevance in certain matters of essential validity of treaties. One of the general rules in this regard is that a treaty is void if consent thereto has been secured by way of coercion by one State against the other.[88] This rule, however, has emerged relatively late in the international legal system and represents a change from the earlier period when the validity of treaties could not in principle be challenged on the ground of coercion.[89] This transition in the law has important implications for those treaties which were not only concluded in that earlier period but

---

[87] International Law in Historical Perspective, vol. 3 (1970), p. 517. See also Whiteman, op. cit. above (p. 130 n. 59), vol. 3, p. 32; Cukwurah, op. cit. above (p. 130 n. 60), p. 19; Boggs, International Boundaries (1940), p. 100.

[88] Generally, see McNair, Law of Treaties (1961), pp. 206–11; Lauterpacht, Yearbook of the International Law Commission, 1953, vol. 2, pp. 147–52; Waldock, ibid. 1963, vol. 2, pp. 51–2; Verzijl, International Law in Historical Perspective, vol. 6 (1973), pp. 78–9; Brownlie, International Law and the Use of Force by States (1963), pp. 404–5; Harvard Draft Article 32 on the Law of Treaties, American Journal of International Law, 29 (1935), Supplement, pp. 1148–61.

[89] For traditional views, see Hall, A Treatise on International Law (8th edn., 1924), pp. 381–2; Hyde, International Law, Chiefly as Interpreted and Applied by the United States (2nd edn., 1945), vol. 2, pp. 1379–81; O'Connell, International Law (1970), vol. 1, pp. 239–41; Harvard Draft Article 32, loc. cit. (previous note), pp. 1148–59; Fitzmaurice, Yearbook of the International Law Commission, 1958, vol. 2, pp. 38–9.

were also permanent and constitutive in character, and certain boundary treaties may well be included in this category. The problem, therefore, is related to the reconciliation between two opposite effects of the law. One answer is clearly to resort to the principle of intertemporal law which requires a legal situation to be evaluated in light of the law prevailing at the time the situation came into existence. In terms, therefore, a boundary treaty would be valid if it were established that at the time of its conclusion, coercion was not, in international law, an invalidating factor.

The International Law Commission deliberated upon these matters in the proceedings which led to the conclusion of the Vienna Convention on the Law of Treaties. It is apparent from the records of the proceedings that certain members of the Commission appreciated the importance of abstaining from the settlement of a rule which would sanction the re-examination of settled boundary matters on the basis of arguments relating to 'invalid and unequal treaties'.[90] 'The more general formulation [on the invalidity of treaties the consent of which had been secured by coercion]', said Mr. J. de Aréchaga, 'might result, for instance, in long-standing treaties concerning frontiers being called in question on the ground that they had been secured by coercion . . . That might encourage a move towards revision beyond what was reasonable and justified.'[91]

A further complicating fact which arose in this context was the rule of *jus cogens*, predicated in Article 53 of the Convention. Thus it could be argued that a boundary treaty was void *ab initio* inasmuch as its conclusion was not consistent with the principles of *jus cogens*. When, in 1966, the Commission debated the consequences of the nullity or termination of a treaty conflicting with a peremptory norm of general international law, it was pointed out by Mr. Reuter, the Member from France, that 'certain rules of jus cogens were not only based on justice, but must also take acçount of questions of stability'.[92] He went on to query whether a colonial frontier treaty could be challenged on grounds of coercion and *jus cogens*. 'It would', he said, 'be agreed that nullity of that kind could not be extended into the past *ad infinitum*.'[93] Thus Article 64 of the Vienna Convention provides that if a peremptory norm of general international law *emerges* any *existing treaty* in conflict with that norm becomes void and terminates. The commentary to draft Article 50 explained that the 'words "becomes void and terminates" make it quite clear the Commission considered that the emergence of a *new* rule of *jus cogens* is not to have retroactive effects on the validity of a treaty'.[94] Further, in an apparent attempt to safeguard, *inter alia*, certain boundary and territorial regimes, Article 71 (2) (b) provides that a treaty which becomes void and terminates under Article 64 'does

[90] See de Aréchaga and Luna, *Yearbook of the International Law Commission*, 1964, vol. 1, pp. 34, 37; and Reuter, de Aréchaga and Ago, ibid. 1966, vol. 1, pt. 2, pp. 17, 22, 23.
[91] *Yearbook of the International Law Commission*, 1964, vol. 1, p. 34.
[92] Ibid. 1966, vol. 1, pt. 2, p. 17. See also Waldock, ibid. 1963, vol. 2, p. 52.
[93] Ibid.
[94] Ibid. 1966, vol. 2, pp. 248-9. Special Rapporteur's Observations, pp. 19-20.

not affect any right, obligation or legal situation of the parties created through the execution of the treaty prior to its termination'.[95]

It is clear from the foregoing that international law recognizes the virtues of territorial stability. Plainly, a rule of law which does not inhibit the reopening of frontier questions, settled in an earlier period of time, on charges of coercion would not only constitute an invitation for fresh boundary claims, but would be inconsistent with the general underlying notions of continuity of boundaries presented in the context of State succession to boundary treaties and the proviso to the doctrine *rebus sic stantibus*. The rule, however, in favour of the continuation of boundary treaties concluded in controversial circumstances at an earlier period of time emphasizes the view that boundary treaties and regimes have lasting effects and underlines again the importance of the doctrine of finality.

III. CONCLUSIONS

The several classes of proposition presented above represent one major strand of the law, which is that boundary regimes are to be viewed with a maximum degree of continuity and a minimum of change. While this is the general rule, it is the case that certain exceptions, which have been elicited above, do exist. Nevertheless, three major implications of this rule need to be pointed out. First, where a State can adduce evidence which prima facie establishes the existence of a definite boundary line in the border region, a presumption in favour of continuing the line in question may arise, provided that the other disputant State fails to show the existence of countervailing considerations which rebut the presumption so raised. A reference to the existence of a definite boundary line in the border region is meant to imply any alignment which exists either in proven administrative acts and measures taken in respect of the boundary line as such, i.e. acts of general control, for example, border patrolling, and the establishment of frontier posts and pickets; or in the evidence of records, maps and other documents, and instruments with or without the accompaniment of administrative activity. It would be out of place to enter here into a discussion on the position of the law on this aspect of the question, and it will therefore be sufficient to state that, for purposes of this analysis, as well as the law on the matter, a boundary line which exists essentially in 'theory' as it were, i.e. a line which is not administered on the ground, is susceptible of being regarded as a frontier in law. The positive aspect of this proposition is that it throws the burden of proof on to the State which seeks either to challenge a well-established line or to disturb a previously unchallenged attribution of territory. Since States are not, as a rule, to be allowed a continuously available process with which they may seek to raise questions about the status and location of a frontier line,

---

[95] See also commentary to draft Article 66, *Yearbook of the International Law Commission*, 1966, vol. 2, pp. 265–6.

it does not appear unreasonable to place the burden upon the State which seeks to question the status quo.

The difficulty, however, with this interpretation is that in the majority of cases, States are prepared to adduce evidence to establish what they consider to be the 'true' and legal boundary. In other words, it is the case that States do not confine their objections to questions of invalidity of the prevailing frontier, but try, on the other hand, to establish that the alignment claimed by them constitutes the 'true' and legal boundary. Where both States approach the dispute with this kind of claim it may be difficult, and perhaps undesirable, to attempt to admit a rebuttable presumption in favour of either position. It follows therefore that this proposition is significant primarily in those cases where the main assertion of a State disputing an alignment is related to dissent against an established boundary on the basis of, *inter alia*, a technically invalidating feature, as, for example, an unratified treaty or an incorrect boundary demarcation. Notwithstanding its limited applications, the presumption advanced above may have important implications for certain outstanding boundary disputes. While it is not intended here to offer even a provisional view on these complex boundary and territorial problems, it may be appropriate to point out that matters elaborated above have particular significance for the Venezuela–Guyana, Iran–Iraq and Afghan–Pakistan frontier disputes.

The second implication is a composite of various considerations, the underlying notion of which is that the international political and legal orders abhor, as it were, the continued existence of territorial and boundary-related controversies. The Permanent Court hinted at this in the *Mosul* advisory opinion[96] when it held that 'the very nature of a frontier and of any convention designed to establish frontiers between two countries imports that a frontier must constitute a definite boundary line throughout its length'.[97] The proposition now being advanced is that in view of the paramount interests of territorial sovereignty, States may be considered legally bound to resolve, in a conclusive manner, all territorial and frontier disputes. This proposition is being put forward not unmindful of the fact that it constitutes an extension, or a further development, rather than a representation of the doctrine of finality. The principle discussed in the preceding pages was based on the notion that the law disfavours the creation of *new* territorial and boundary difficulties where evidence shows that no uncertainties existed. It is acknowledged that it is quite a different thing to propose that States should be considered legally bound to settle conclusively all existing problems. Nevertheless, in so far as the doctrine in question reflects the general abhorrence of territorial uncertainties, it does not appear entirely inappropriate to extend the operation of the doctrine to the compulsory settlement of boundary disputes.

[96] *P.C.I.J.*, Series B, No. 12 (1925).
[97] Ibid., at p. 20.

There appears to be some justification for this view. It is recognized that the received principle is that in general there is no obligation in international law in favour of the compulsory settlement of disputes,[98] and that there is no rule of law which supports compulsory adjudication and arbitration.[99] Nevertheless, it is submitted with respect that there is something to be said in favour of the contention that the law has to some extent been developing in the direction of imposing a broad general duty upon States to settle their disputes peacefully and by use of all the appropriate processes and instrumentalities provided for in the prevailing legal order.[100] Article 2 (3) of the Charter of the United Nations stipulates that: 'All Members shall settle their international disputes by peaceful means in such a manner that international peace and security, and justice, are not endangered.'[101] In the Report presented by the Study Group set up by the David Davies Memorial Institute which investigated the legal aspects of international disputes, it was observed that the obligation to settle disputes was not limited to circumstances in which there were possibilities of a breach of international peace. 'On the contrary', the Report added, 'the Charter makes the obligation of Members to settle their disputes by peaceful means an autonomous and fundamental rule of the organisation'.[102] One of the most important and useful means resorted to by States is clearly the conduct of negotiations and, interestingly, the International Court observed in the *North Sea Continental Shelf* cases[103] that there was an international legal obligation to negotiate, and that this was predicated, *inter alia*, in Article 33 of the Charter.[104] It is submitted

[98] See Verzijl, *International Law in Historical Perspective*, vol. 8 (1976), pp. 33, 73; Brownlie, *Principles* (above, p. 127 n. 43), p. 705; Fitzmaurice, 'The Contribution of the Institute of International Law to the Development of International Law', *Recueil des cours*, 138 (1973-I), p. 211 at p. 249; Brierly, *The Law of Nations* (6th edn. by Waldock, 1963), p. 368; Waldock, 'General Course on Public International Law', *Recueil des cours*, 106 (1962-II), p. 5 at p. 108; de Aréchaga, 'General Course in Public International Law', ibid. 159 (1978-I), p. 9 at p. 143; *Eastern Carelia* case, *P.C.I.J.*, Series B, No. 5 (1923), at p. 27.

[99] Verzijl, op. cit. (previous note), p. 73; De Visscher, *Theory and Reality in Public International Law* (Corbett trans., 1968), pp. 360ff.; Briggs, 'Reflections on the Codification of International Law . . .', *Recueil des cours*, 126 (1969-I), p. 241 at pp. 294–309, regarding the failure to achieve consensus at the Vienna Conference on the Law of Treaties on compulsory adjudication of disputes in respect of invalidity of treaties.

[100] Report of the Study Group, David Davies Memorial Institute of International Studies, *International Disputes: The Legal Aspects* (1972), pp. 6–14; Darwin, 'General Introduction' in Memoranda to Report, ibid., pp. 62–4; Schwarzenberger, *International Law as applied by International Courts and Tribunals*, vol. 1 (3rd edn., 1957), p. 307; Mosler, 'The International Society as a Legal Community', *Recueil des cours*, 140 (1974-IV), p. 17 at p. 283.

[101] See also General Assembly Resolution No. 2625 (XXV): Declaration on Principles of International Law concerning Friendly Relations and Cooperation among States (24 October 1970). Text: *International Legal Materials*, 9 (1970), p. 1292.

[102] Report, op. cit. above (n. 100), p. 9. Cf. Mosler, loc. cit. above (n. 100), p. 287.

[103] *I.C.J. Reports*, 1969, p. 3.

[104] Ibid., p. 47. Also, de Aréchaga, loc. cit. above (n. 98), p. 147. In the *Mosul* case, the Permanent Court took account of Article 3 of the Treaty of Lausanne which provided, *inter alia*, that the frontier between Turkey and Iraq was to be 'laid down in friendly arrangement' between the former and Great Britain, and that in the event of a failure to reach agreement the dispute was to be referred to the Council of the League of Nations. The Court observed that third-party intervention seeking

that whether or not compulsory peaceful settlement is *de lege ferenda*, there can be little doubt that it has particular significance and relevance for boundary and territorial problems. On the one hand, it will have especial relevance in those cases where the boundary has been settled in principle but cannot be implemented on account of difficulties in the interpretation of the relevant instrument or treaty. Here compulsory settlement could be invoked by either side either to initiate or to maintain the momentum of negotiations. On the other hand, the problem of boundary disputes of particularly long standing cannot be overstated. As a rule of political fact, albeit not of law, the longer the duration of a period in which a party exercises territorial control over disputed tracts, the greater the entrenchment of interests therein, and in some cases, the greater the probability of hostilities between the disputing States.[105] While the State out of possession may duly protest or reserve her rights by agreeing, for example, to consider an alignment in question a provisional one maintained without prejudice, the boundary may nevertheless acquire over an extended period of time a degree of permanence, and the State in possession real rights. When the provisional status quo begins to acquire an element of inviolability, as many lines of this kind do, the gap between law and political fact will have become wide: the practical difference between an alignment in law and in fact may become difficult to assess. It must, however, be emphasized that it is not being contended that the unlawful but effective maintenance of a line in the face of protest will or can create lawful territorial rights. What is being stressed is that unresolved territorial problems tend towards great political and legal uncertainty. It appears reasonable, therefore, to support a proposition which attempts to arrest a decline into a situation which, with the passage of time, attracts greater uncertainty and becomes politically more intractable. Accordingly, the doctrine of finality of boundaries may be invoked by States as a means of providing support and argument for the assertion that the disputing States are legally obliged to settle their frontier disputes amicably. By so doing States may be able to reduce the hiatus between law and fact.

The emphasis, of course, is upon the incident rather than the particular mode or process of settlement. Thus States may prefer to adopt a solution which does not concentrate upon delimitation, but upon a 'freezing' of territorial rights and claims and/or upon mutual compromises. Reference here is being made to the settlements which resulted in the regime established by the Antarctica Treaty of 1959, and which, by virtue of Article IV, reserved the rights of all the disputing States to the disputed

---

a definitive solution was a matter in contemplation of the States parties to the treaty, not only because of the provisions of Article 3, but also on account of the 'very nature of a frontier'—i.e. that the existence of a frontier between two countries imports that it must constitute a definite boundary line throughout its length: *P.C.I.J.*, Series B, No. 12, at p. 20.

[105] The Falkland Islands conflict of 1982 is but one example.

regions of Antarctica;[106] to the Neutral Zone created by treaty in 1922 between Saudi Arabia and Kuwait in respect of the disputed areas between their alignments;[107] and to the Protected Zone in the Torres Strait between Australia and Papua New Guinea, a zone which attempts to 'acknowledge and protect' the traditional way of life and livelihood of the inhabitants of the area.[108]

This leads on to the third and final feature of the doctrine under consideration. It is submitted that where States resort to adjudication or arbitration in respect of the settlement of their boundary and/or territorial disputes, it may not be unreasonable to assume that international tribunals are ready to place great emphasis on the question of resolving conclusively and definitely all the rights and claims of the parties. To some extent this perspective is covered by the doctrine of *non liquet*,[109] but both the nature of the law under discussion and the attitude adopted by international tribunals justifies, on this view of the matter, a separate statement in respect thereof. A perusal of the claims and submissions made by States, in the process of either diplomacy or adjudication, reveals that on various occasions evidence relied upon by them happens, in fact, to be either conflicting and inconsistent and/or incomplete in various ways. Further, States have been known to rely upon criteria which in different circumstances would be categorized as political and not legal considerations. In this category are included the facts of traditional and customary rights and limits of control, claims of political expediency as, for example, the need to avoid the outbreak of hostilities and friction, and exigencies of security and defence. In such circumstances, the task of the tribunal will acquire complexity inasmuch as it will be required to determine the precise location of an alignment in the absence of convincing evidence in respect of each and every sector of the boundary. The task of the tribunal will be made even more difficult if it is required to determine the exact position of the alignment in a 'weight of claim' type of case. In all or any combination of these circumstances, the primary task of the tribunal will continue to be the precise allocation of territory, for a decision which rejects either State's claims on the basis of absence either of law or of precise criteria which would enable it to evaluate the claims, *and also* fails to delineate a line or to elicit the principles on which the disputed territory is to be delineated, would not only constitute a departure from accepted doctrine, but would

---

[106] Text: *British and Foreign State Papers*, vol. 164 (1959–60), pp. 189–97.

[107] See El-Ghoneimy, 'The Legal Status of the Saudi-Kuwaiti Neutral Zone', *International and Comparative Law Quarterly*, 15 (1966), p. 690.

[108] Treaty on Sovereignty and Maritime Boundaries in the Area between the Countries (18 December 1978): *International Legal Materials*, 18 (1979), p. 291, Art. 10.

[109] Lauterpacht, *The Function of Law in the International Community* (1933), pp. 63–9; 'Some Observations on the Prohibition on "*Non-Liquet*" and the Completeness of the Law', *Symbolae Verzijl* (1958), p. 196; Brierly, op. cit. above (p. 138 n. 98), pp. 66–8, 368–9; Gross, 'Limitations upon the Judicial Function', *American Journal of International Law*, 58 (1964), p. 415, at pp. 423–31; Higgins, 'Policy Considerations and the International Judicial Process', *International and Comparative Law Quarterly*, 17 (1968), p. 58 at pp. 66–71.

also fail to achieve what is paramount in the matter of boundaries: the termination of dispute and the final and conclusive attribution of territory between States.

While it is beyond the scope of this short work to describe in detail the various occasions on which tribunals were faced with this problem, and the attitudes adopted by them, it is necessary to state that in the United Kingdom/France *Continental Shelf* case,[110] the Court of Arbitration declined to rule out the considerations of defence and security in the matter of the delineation of the continental shelf boundary between the United Kingdom and France.[111] In the *Rann of Kutch* arbitration and the *Western Sahara* advisory opinion,[112] considerations of traditional and customary control were of determinative significance,[113] and in the *Honduras Borders* case,[114] the Special Arbitral Tribunal relied upon a variety of criteria in order to determine the *uti possidetis* line.[115] Furthermore, it is interesting to note that at times, tribunals have had to 'invent' a boundary, i.e. describe an alignment which either the States had not claimed or was based on considerations neither of the States had urged. Thus the line awarded by the Court of Arbitration for part of the frontier in the *Palena* arbitration,[116] and the straight lines drawn along the 'jagged coastline' of the north-eastern part of the Rann in the *Kutch* case are illustrations of this situation.[117] It may not, therefore, be unreasonable to conclude that international tribunals have in certain circumstances adopted a less restrictive approach in the matter of admitting certain facts and considerations which are not at first sight susceptible of being classified as legal criteria. They have also exhibited a similar attitude in describing lines where precise evidence in respect thereof is absent. It is submitted in conclusion, therefore, that this attitude adopted by tribunals is a measure of the importance they bestow upon the conclusive and definitive nature of boundaries, and thereby confirms the prominent status of the doctrine of finality and continuity of alignments in the law relating to boundaries.

[110] H.M.S.O., Misc. No. 15 (1978) (Cmnd. 7438); *International Legal Materials*, 18 (1979), p. 397.

[111] H.M.S.O., Misc. No. 15 (1978), p. 91. Britain had urged: 'Zonal defence arrangements ... have little or nothing to do with national frontiers, and much less with continental shelf boundaries': p. 87.

[112] *I.C.J. Reports*, 1975, p. 12.

[113] For the *Rann of Kutch* arbitration, see 50 I.L.R. 1 at pp. 474–94; and for the *Western Sahara* case, see *I.C.J. Reports*, 1975, p. 12 at pp. 41–9 and 57–68. See also separate opinion of Judge Ammoun at pp. 92–102. See also Verzijl, *International Law in Historical Perspective*, vol. 3 (1970), pp. 611–12, and especially *Brazil–British Guiana Boundary* arbitration, *Reports of International Arbitral Awards*, vol. 11, p. 21 at p. 22; and De Visscher, op. cit. above (p. 138 n. 99), pp. 394–5.

[114] *Reports of International Arbitral Awards*, vol. 2, p. 1307.

[115] Ibid., *passim*.

[116] Ibid., vol. 16, p. 111 at pp. 180–1.

[117] 50 I.L.R. 1 at p. 521; also see, in the matter of the two deep inlets, p. 520.

OBSERVATIONS ON THE REVISION OF THE 1949 GENEVA 'RED CROSS' CONVENTIONS*

By B. A. WORTLEY[1]

I. THE OBJECTS OF THE REVISION

THE General Assembly of the United Nations had adopted twenty-three resolutions relating to the protection of human rights in armed conflicts when, in 1974, the Swiss Federal Council called a diplomatic conference to supplement the four Geneva Red Cross Conventions of 1949. The Argentine and the United Kingdom were among the 124 States which attended the first session to draft what were to become the two Protocols to these Conventions; the Argentine and the United Kingdom also took part in the second session of 120 States, the third session of 107 States and the fourth session of 109 States.[2]

The object of the Conference was to study two draft additional protocols prepared after official and private consultations by the International Committee of the Red Cross and intended to supplement the Four Geneva Conventions of 12 August 1949,[3]

thereby attempting further protection of human rights in times of armed conflict.

These two Protocols were summarized two days after signature by Her Majesty's Government by Mr. Evan Luard, M.P. in the House of Commons in these words:

The two protocols were opened for signature on 12th December 1977. Protocol I relates to the protection of victims of international armed conflicts and Protocol II to the protection of victims of non-international armed conflicts. Signature of both protocols on behalf of the United Kingdom took place on 12th December.

The Government consider that, overall, the two protocols mark a valuable advance in humanitarian law applicable in armed conflicts. In Protocol I we particularly welcome the increased protection for the sick and wounded and for medical aircraft; the improved arrangements for information on persons reported missing; the protection of the civilian population against direct attack, and the

---

* © Emeritus Professor B. A. Wortley, 1984.

[1] C.M.G., O.B.E., Q.C., LL.D., Hon. Dr. de Strasbourg et de Rennes, Hon. D.C.L. (Durham), Member of the Institute of International Law. This article is part of research conducted as a Leverhulme Fellow.

[2] See *Final Act of the Diplomatic Conference on the Reaffirmation and Development of International Humanitarian Law Applicable in Armed Conflicts, with Protocol I, Protocol II and Resolutions adopted at the Fourth Session*, Misc. No. 19 (1977) (Cmnd. 6927), pp. 5–9.

[3] Ibid., at p. 5; and see Draper, 'The Implementation and Enforcement of the Geneva Conventions of 1949 and of the Two Additional Protocols', *Recueil des cours*, 164 (1979–III), pp. 9–54.

new provisions on implementation and enforcement both of the protocol and the Geneva Conventions. Protocol II provides the minimum standards of conduct to be observed by both sides in civil wars, a field previously covered only by a single article in each of the four 1949 Geneva Conventions. We welcome the fundamental guarantees provided by Protocol II, in relation to, e.g., accused and detained persons, protection of the wounded and sick and medical personnel and protection of the civilian population.[4]

United States Ambassador George Aldrich noted

significant advances in Protocol I; the protection of civilians, the first codification of the customary rule of proportionality; and due prohibition of starvation of civilians as a method of warfare; special protection of dams, dikes and nuclear power stations; the restriction of target area bombardment of cities; and the protection of the natural environment against methods or means of warfare that may be expected to cause wide-spread, long-term and severe damage.[5]

Article 1 (2) of the 1977 Protocol I makes it clear that

in cases not covered by this Protocol or by other international agreements, civilians and combatants remain under the protection and authority of the principles of international law derived from established custom with principles of humanity and from the dictates of public conscience.[6]

Those professionally engaged in military or police operations are usually the first to insist on a legal regulation of force, not only to protect the public, but also to maintain discipline in the law-enforcers themselves.

II. The Elaboration of the Protocols of 1977

The texts of the two Protocols submitted to the fourth session of the Geneva Conference on 8 June 1977 had taken three years to prepare. They were in Arabic, English, French, Russian and Spanish.

The situation of China, the most populous State in the world, must be mentioned here. China, an original member of the United Nations, with the right of veto in the Security Council, ratified the four Geneva Conventions of 1949 (with reservations) in 1956; she exploded her first atomic bomb in October 1964 and her first hydrogen bomb in 1967. She attended only the first (1974) session of the Conference on the Protocols to the Geneva Conventions.[7]

---

[4] *Hansard*, H.C. Debs., vol. 941, Written Answers, col. *236* (14 December 1977).

[5] *American Journal of International Law*, 75 (1981), p. 764 at p. 778.

[6] A one-page statement, in seven propositions, of these rules has been attempted 'to facilitate the dissemination of knowledge' of this topic. For the text, see Roberts and Guelff, *Documents on the Laws of War* (1982), p. 466. By recommendation 945 (1982) the Assembly of the Council of Europe stressed the need to disseminate the texts of the Geneva Conventions of 12 August 1949 and their Protocols in the armed forces and among the civilian population.

[7] 'China' was taken by the United Nations to mean the People's Republic of China, though this Government was not recognized by the U.S.A. until 1 January 1979, and by Ireland and Portugal in June of that year. The Chinese text of the Protocols has now been agreed by the Swiss and Chinese Governments. China has not signed the Protocols, but, as we shall see, she may accede to them.

Some treaties create legal obligations by mere signature: the *procès-verbal* of 1936 on submarine warfare was one such. The Geneva Protocols, however, like most multilateral treaties, require ratification or accession, though, as we shall see, even in these cases, signature can have some legal consequences,[8] but to understand all the legal implications of the work of the Conference on Protocols I and II we must consider, step by step, the unusual procedures adopted, for they are a minefield of complexity.

(a) *The Expression of Consensus of 8 June 1977*

The 1977 texts of Protocols I and II to the Geneva Conventions in five equally authentic languages became available on 8 June 1977, and were then adopted by the Conference, by consensus, i.e. 'by agreement, accord, sympathy, common feeling'.[9] This consensus prepared the way for 'signing' the Final Act two days later. It merely indicated 'the mind' of those present—a useful show of unanimity and goodwill, and it may prove to be of importance when customary law becomes a subject for discussion.

(b) *The Signing of the Final Act of the Protocols by Participants at the Conference on 10 June 1977 to Adopt the Text*

The Final Act of the Conference, setting out the five available texts of the two Protocols, was produced on 10 June 1977, two days after the consensus had been expressed by the Conference.

Representatives of 104 States 'signed' on 10 June 1977, and by Conference Resolution 3 (1) certain 'national liberation movements recognized by the regional intergovernmental organizations concerned' were invited to participate in the Conference, 'it being understood that only delegations representing *States* were entitled to vote'.[10] These liberation movements were certainly not States, nor were they parties to the Geneva Conventions. No less than eleven 'national liberation movements' had been invited to participate without vote in the deliberations of the Conference and its main committees; three of these 'movements', the Palestine Liberation Organization, the Pan-Africanist Congress of South Africa and the South West Africa People's Organization, were the only ones to 'sign' the text of the Protocols on 10 June 1977 and, at the time, it was stated that 'signatures' of liberation movements 'were without prejudice to the position of participating States on the question of precedent'.

---

[8] See below, p. 147, and Jones, *Full Powers and Ratification* (1948), pp. 132–3; and Fitzmaurice in this *Year Book*, 15 (1934), p. 117. See also the Vienna Convention on the Law of Treaties, which came into force as a treaty on 27 January 1980, Articles 11–14 (especially Article 12). On the whole, the Vienna Convention states the customary law.

[9] *Oxford English Dictionary*, and see Meyrowitz, 'La Stratégie nucléaire et le Protocol I', *Revue générale de droit international public*, 83 (1979), pp. 905–61.

[10] Cmnd. 6927, p. 9.

Indeed, 'liberation movements' had been invited to the Conference only as being 'recognized by regional intergovernmental organizations', not as States, nor yet as bodies which held 'belligerent rights'. 'Special groups' given 'observer status' at the Conference were not even empowered to sign on 10 June 1977; the list of 'observers' started with the Council of Europe and ended with the world Y.W.C.A.

What then was the purpose of the 'signing' on 10 June 1977 of the five texts of the Protocols adopted by consensus two days previously? The object seems to have been 'the adoption of a text of the Protocols' by the consent of all the *States* and the three liberation movements participating in its 'drawing up'. The States were adopting the text under the customary rule expressed in Article 9[11] of the Vienna Convention on the Law of Treaties of 1969.[12] The adoption of the text on 10 June 1977 was a step beyond the informal consensus expressed on 8 June 1977 by the Conference as a whole; between the consensus on 8 June and the adoption on 10 June there was a delay in which, presumably, any clerical mistakes in the five language texts could have been corrected.

But even this 'signature' of the Protocols by States for 'adoption of the text' (Article 9 of the Vienna Convention on the Law of Treaties) did not import that the text was binding on the States signatories, nor on the 'liberation movements'. The 'signature' by a State party to the Geneva Conventions (to which the Protocols are adjuncts) to adopt the text can, it is submitted, merely create an estoppel to prevent a State from denying that the text exists and in the terms adopted.[13]

(c) *The Second 'Signature' by States only in December 1977*

A second signing or 'signature' by States only in December 1977 was needed to authenticate the text 'adopted' at the Final Act on 10 June 1977 and to prepare the way for parties to be bound by the Protocols as treaties. Article 92 of Protocol I and Article 20 of Protocol II are identical:

This Protocol shall be open for signature by the Parties to the Conventions [i.e. the Geneva Conventions] six months after the signing of the Final Act [i.e. six months after 10 June 1977, that is, from 10 December 1977] and will remain open [for signatures] for a period of twelve months [i.e. until 10 December 1978].

Until a further 'signature' to a Protocol by two qualified States during the period allowed, i.e. from 10 December 1977 until 10 December 1978, the Protocol was 'an escrow', and was not 'in force', i.e. it could not be ratified or acceded to by other States. In fact, sixty-eight States signed Protocol I, and sixty-four of them also signed Protocol II in the time allowed.[14] Forty-

---

[11] On Article 9, see Sinclair, *The Vienna Convention on the Law of Treaties* (1973), pp. 34–5.

[12] This Convention did not come into force until 27 January 1980.

[13] The subject of estoppel has already been well ventilated by Professors Bowett and MacGibbon in this *Year Book*, 33 (1957), p. 176, and 31 (1954), p. 143.

[14] See Roberts and Guelff, op. cit. above (p. 144 n. 6), pp. 459–60.

seven of these States signed Protocol I on 12 December 1977—almost the first available date, though four of them did not sign Protocol II. The signatures to both Protocols included the United Kingdom, Albania, Afghanistan, France and Turkey, but the Argentine did not sign at all. The effect of a signature to authenticate was to give the State signing the right, but not the duty, to ratify in the time allowed, if it wished to do so; to accede was an option for those States that did not ratify.

The coming into force of the Protocols did not oblige any State to ratify or to accede to them. It merely raised a *hope* that signatories might take a next step to be bound by the Protocols, which were, after all, adjuncts to the Geneva Conventions already binding on them: meantime, the substance of the Protocols was at this stage only binding on States, signatories and non-signatories to the Protocols alike, in so far as the Protocols represented customary developments in international law, or illustrated 'general principles of law'.

The analogy between signing the Protocols and the delivery of a deed 'in escrow'[15] in English law is not complete, but it is not irrelevant. When a deed is delivered in escrow it will not become effective to bind the parties until an agreed condition has been fulfilled. In the case of the signature of the Protocols 'for authentication' under Article 92 of I or Article 20 of II, the signature of two qualified States, within the time allowed, had to occur before the Protocols could come into being as treaties capable of being ratified or acceded to.[16] The signature for authentication of a treaty *does*, however, from the time of signature, import a *negative* obligation towards other *signatories* (Article 18 of the Vienna Convention on the Law of Treaties), i.e. to 'refrain from acts which would defeat the object and purpose of a treaty when it has signed the treaty subject to ratification, acceptance or approval, until it shall have made its intention clear not to become a party to the treaty . . .'. States which only signed to adopt the text in June 1977, and not 'for authentication', were possibly not caught by Article 18.

(d) Ratification or Accession

The Protocols entered into force *as treaties six months after two instruments* of ratification 'or accession' had been deposited with the Swiss Federal Council.[16] Ghana ratified on 28 February 1978 and Liberia on 7 June 1978, and thus were constituted the two ratifications needed to bring the Protocols 'into force' so that they were, and other parties could become, in due course, bound by the Protocols by ratification or accession. Neither of these two first ratifying States made any reservation. Each State party to the Protocol became bound six months after deposit of its instrument of ratification or accession.[17]

---

[15] 'A scrowl or writing which is not to take effect as a deed till the condition be performed': *Coke on Littleton*, § 36a.

[16] Arts. 95 (1), Protocol I, and 23 (1), Protocol II.

[17] Arts. 95 (2), Protocol I, and 23 (2), Protocol II.

Signature to authenticate is then a preliminary to ratification, but signature is not necessary for accession to the Protocols, so that a State party to the Geneva Conventions but which has not signed the Protocols may accede thereto, because Article 94 of Protocol I and Article 22 of Protocol II open the Protocols to accession by non-signatories. By 7 October 1982 some twenty-six States had ratified or acceded to the Protocols, eight of them with reservations or declarations.[18]

What was the object of this complicated 'four-step' procedure used to revise the text of the four 1949 Geneva Conventions to which only States were parties? So far as States were concerned these first two steps, the expression of consensus (8 June 1977) and the first signature (10 June 1977), were not strictly necessary at all. What mattered was the signature in December 1977, followed by ratification and/or accession, and even here, as we next see, States made declarations on signature which may vitally affect their legal obligations. The expression of consensus of 8 June 1977 and the first signature of 10 June 1977 to adopt the text were gestures intended to draw the attention of States and of 'liberation movements' to the way hostilities may be rendered more civilized.

[18] The following States had ratified or acceded to the Protocols as at 7 October 1982:

State	Date of ratification or accession
Austria*	13 August 1982
Bahamas	10 April 1980
Bangladesh	8 September 1980
Botswana	23 May 1979
Cyprus (Protocol I only)	1 June 1979
Denmark*	17 June 1982
El Salvador	23 November 1978
Ecuador	10 April 1979
Finland*	7 August 1980
Gabon	8 April 1980
Ghana	28 February 1978
Jordan	1 May 1979
Lao People's Democratic Republic	18 November 1980
Libyan Arab Jamahiriya	7 June 1978
Mauritania	14 March 1980
Mauritius	22 March 1982
Niger	8 June 1979
Norway*	14 December 1981
Republic of Korea*	15 January 1982
St. Lucia	7 October 1982
Sweden*	31 August 1979
Switzerland*	17 February 1982
Tunisia	9 August 1979
Viet Nam (Protocol I only)	19 October 1981
Yugoslavia*	11 June 1979
Zaïre (Protocol I only)	3 June 1982

* Ratification or accession accompanied by a reservation and/or a declaration.

III. THE UNITED KINGDOM DECLARATION ON SIGNATURE FOR AUTHENTICATION IN DECEMBER 1977

This is an important indication of the attitude of the then Her Majesty's Government to many controversial problems raised by the Protocols: this declaration is printed at the end of this article[19] and will now be treated under separate heads.

(a) *Insurgency and Liberation Movements*

These are dealt with in paragraphs (a), (h) and (j) of the United Kingdom declaration. Dealing with (j) in the House of Commons, Mr. Luard[20] spoke of the general tenor of Protocol II, elaborating future rules to be observed 'by both sides in civil wars'. At that time (14 December 1977) Southern Rhodesia (now Zimbabwe) was in turmoil. Mr. Luard said:

. . . as with several recent international conventions, the Government have considered it necessary to reserve the right not to apply the Protocols in relation to Southern Rhodesia unless and until they are in a position to ensure that the obligations of the Protocols in respect of that territory can be fully implemented.

Certainly the United Kingdom declaration on signature paragraph (j) resembles a reservation in a treaty by a colonial power.

Paragraph (j) is now otiose: Zimbabwe is recognized as independent but has not yet signed or become a party to the Geneva Conventions, a condition precedent to acceding to the Protocols. The United Kingdom declaration proceeded to add *ex abundante cautela*, in a sentence after paragraph (j), that the United Kingdom 'had signed Protocol II [on civil wars] on the same understanding as in (j) above'.

Paragraphs (a) and (h) of the United Kingdom declaration raise the difficult political and legal problems of deciding who, besides the armed forces of recognized belligerents, may be given the benefit of the humanitarian rules of warfare. Prima facie, armed groups not recognized as being 'at war', nor as having the character and rights of belligerents, are liable to be dealt with by the States they attack as violent criminals; the fact that some foreign States may accord to some of them the status of political refugees, and refuse to allow them to be extradited, does not affect any liability under the *lex loci delicti*.

No doubt it is desirable to curb the acts of dissident armed bands in the general interest of humanity. No doubt, too, if States are prepared to grant formal recognition of belligerent rights[21] they will in effect treat insurgents

---

[19] At pp. 165–6, below.

[20] *Hansard*, H.C. Debs., vol. 941, Written Answers, col. *237* (14 December 1977).

[21] The recognition of belligerency, which was thoroughly discussed in books and articles and in this *Year Book* during the Spanish Civil War before the Second World War, traditionally is a matter for individual States to decide when their interests are affected by a civil war; recognition is a 'privilege' of non-belligerents and not a right of revolutionary bodies. See also the *Bibliography of International Humanitarian Law* of the International Committee of the Red Cross (Geneva, 1980), pp. 351–63.

as having the rights of combatants but, in the absence of such recognition, violent dissident groups prima facie run the risk of being treated as criminals engaged in fomenting anarchy. By Article 2, common to the four Geneva Conventions of 1949, their provisions apply to 'declared war or any other armed conflict . . . between two or more of the High Contracting Parties, even if the state of war is not recognized by one of them'.[22] This implies that belligerent rights may be granted by third States to combatants in a conflict which one side does not recognize as a war, as in the Sino-Japanese conflict of the 1930s.[23] Traditionally, the tests for the granting of belligerent rights included the effective occupation of territory seized, and the Geneva Conventions apply 'to all cases of partial or total occupation of the territory of a High Contracting Party, even if the said occupation meets with no armed resistance'.

Article 3, common to the 1949 Geneva Conventions, provides for 'minimum' humanitarian rules to be applied in non-international armed conflicts occurring in the territory of one of the High Contracting Parties. Insurgents may be granted recognition by States, but insurgents have no right to recognition.[24] The British *Manual of Military Law* (1958)[25] states:

> Whether or not the rebellion or insurgency amounts to an 'armed conflict' is a question of fact depending upon the circumstances of the case.

Article 3 represents a treaty obligation assumed by the High Contracting Parties to other High Contracting Parties; those revolutionaries who themselves fail to carry out humanitarian obligations must take the consequences; but even the observance of such obligations

> does not debar the lawful government from trying captured insurgents for treason or other offences, subject to the indispensable judicial guarantees and the requirements of humane treatment referred to in [Article 3 of the Geneva Convention].[26]

(b) *Extension of the Concept of Non-international Armed Conflicts*

Article 1 (4) of Protocol I would extend the operation of Article 2 of the 1949 Conventions relating to 'declared war or other armed conflicts'

to include armed conflicts in which *peoples* are fighting against colonial domination and alien occupation and against *racist* regimes in the exercise of their right of self-determination, as enshrined in the Charter of the United Nations and the Declaration on Principles of International Law concerning Friendly Relations

---

[22] Article 1 of the Regulations annexed to Hague Convention IV of 1907 extended the notion of a belligerent army to cover 'militia and volunteer corps' and Article 2 recognized as belligerents a spontaneous *levée en masse* 'if they carry arms openly and if they respect the laws and customs of war'.

[23] Oppenheim, *International Law*, vol. 2 (7th edn. by Lauterpacht, 1952), p. 369n. See also Brownlie, *International Law and the Use of Force by States* (1963), ch. 23.

[24] Castrén, *Civil War* (1966), pp. 115, 216.

[25] Pt. iii, p. 6.

[26] Ibid.

and Co-operation among States in accordance with the Charter of the United Nations.[27]

The terms 'people' and 'racist' are hardly legal terms of art.[28] However, Article 96 (3) of Protocol I provides for a most unusual procedure, whereby Article 1 (4) of Protocol I may not only apply to 'situations' referred to in the articles of the 1949 Conventions, but goes further. Article 96 (3) reads:

The authority [i.e. not the State] representing a *people* engaged against a High Contracting Party in an armed conflict . . . referred to in Article 1, paragraph 4, may undertake to apply the Conventions and this Protocol [to which 'the authority' is not a party] in relation to that conflict by means of a unilateral declaration addressed to the depositary . . .

i.e. just as if 'the authority' had been a party to the Conventions and the Protocols.

This would seem to be an attempt to obtain, unilaterally, the status of belligerents irrespective of any recognition by their opponents. It is not surprising therefore that paragraph (h) of the United Kingdom declaration on signature was made in these terms:

in relation to paragraph 3 of Article 96, that only a declaration made by an authority which genuinely fulfils the criteria of paragraph 4 of Article 1 can have the effects stated in paragraph 3 of Article 96, and that, in the light of the negotiating history, it is to be regarded as necessary also that the authority concerned be recognised as such by the appropriate regional intergovernmental organisation . . .

It will be recalled that the Palestine Liberation Organization, the Pan-Africanist Congress of South Africa and the South West Africa People's Organization 'signed' for the adoption of the text of the Protocols on 10 June 1977 and, at that time, it was stated that the 'signatures' 'were without prejudice to the position of participating States on the question of precedent'.

That terrorists and rebels may attempt unilaterally to bring themselves within the protection of Article 1 (4) of Protocol I was, no doubt, in the mind of Mr. Luard when he said to the House of Commons:

The provisions of Protocol I, including that on prisoner of war status for irregular fighters, apply only to international armed conflicts, which are now so

---

[27] Emphasis added.
[28] Mr. Freeland, for the United Kingdom, explained the United Kingdom attitude to Art. 1 (4). His delegation had abstained in the vote on Art. 1 as a whole and would have abstained on paragraph 4 if a separate vote had been taken on it. At the first session of the Conference the United Kingdom delegation had voted against the amendment to include the paragraph now appearing as paragraph 4, partly because it had seen legal difficulty in the language used, which seemed to be cased in political rather than legal terms. The main reason for its opposition, however, was that the paragraph introduced the regrettable innovation of making the motives behind a conflict a criterion for the application of humanitarian law. And see Levie (ed.), *Protection of War Victims*, vol. 1 (1979), p. 68, and Best, *Humanity in Warfare* (1982), p. 321.

defined by the protocol as to include certain self-determination conflicts. The Government have considered it desirable in this connection to place formally on record by means of an interpretative declaration their understanding of the meaning of the term 'armed conflict', which implies a high level of intensity of military operations, and their understanding of the requirements to be fulfilled by any national liberation movement which sought to invoke the protocol.[29]

'A high level of intensity' of a combat is one of the pragmatically ascertainable features which helps to determine whether a conflict is covered by the Geneva Conventions and Protocols. But this is not all. There is also the problem of what 'authority' may be considered to be 'representing a people' engaged in armed conflict, under Article 96 (3) of Protocol I, to enable it unilaterally to give the undertaking to the Swiss Federal Government to apply the rules of war and to assume the equivalent rights and duties of States parties to the non-international armed conflict.[30] The United Kingdom declaration paragraph (h) makes it clear that the United Kingdom has the sovereign right to decide whether a particular declaration is genuine and likely to be effective in fact and not just as a piece of political propaganda, and in 1977 Mr. Luard had the situation in Northern Ireland very much in mind when he said:

Neither in Northern Ireland nor in any other part of the United Kingdom is there a situation which meets the criteria laid down for the application of either protocol. Nor is there any terrorist organisation operating within the United Kingdom that fulfils the requirements which a national liberation movement must meet in order to be entitled to claim rights under Protocol I. There is, therefore, no question of any of the provisions of either protocol benefiting the IRA or any others who may carry out terrorist activities in peacetime.[31]

Article 1 (2) of Protocol II excepts internal disturbances and this is not limited to totalitarian States:

This Protocol shall not apply to situations of internal disturbances and tensions, such as riots, isolated and sporadic acts of violence and other acts of a similar nature, as not being armed conflicts.

And Article 3 protects the claims of sovereignty and again it is not limited to totalitarian States:

1. Nothing in this Protocol shall be invoked for the purpose of affecting the sovereignty of a State or the responsibility of the government, by all legitimate means, to maintain or re-establish law and order in the State or to defend the national unity and territorial integrity of the State.
2. Nothing in this Protocol shall be invoked as a justification for intervening, directly or indirectly, for any reason whatever, in the armed conflict or in the

---

[29] *Hansard*, H.C. Debs., vol. 941, Written Answers, col. *237* (14 December 1977).
[30] Schindler, in *Recueil des cours*, 163 (1979–II), p. 144, suggests that 'States which accede to Protocol I thereby implicitly recognize the legitimacy and legality of wars of liberation'.
[31] *Hansard*, H.C. Debs., vol. 941, Written Answers, col. *237* (14 December 1977).

internal or external affairs of the High Contracting Party in the territory of which that conflict occurs.

In general, the United Kingdom declaration on signature reflects the attitudes taken by the United Kingdom delegation during the Conference, which represent common-sense attempts to make the Protocols workable for commanders in the field and, above all, to make it clear that organized murder and terror by political enemies, operating covertly and not openly under responsible identifiable commanders, are not protected by Protocols I and II.

(c) The Nature of Military Attacks

Paragraphs (b) to (f) inclusive of the United Kingdom declaration deal with the nature of military attacks in relation to 'protected' persons and places. The following points must be stressed when considering these paragraphs, which are set out at the end of this article and which relate to Protocol I.

Military attacks must be carried out against the enemy and, says paragraph (b) of the United Kingdom declaration, *so far as is practical* in the circumstances at the time of the attack, with due regard to the safeguards in Protocol I (Article 41) to spare enemy *hors de combat* and (Articles 57 and 58) to spare *civilian* population and objects. *Prisoners of war* are to be respected, and by Article 44 of Protocol I, even if a combatant is not distinguished from the civilian population, he retains his status as a combatant provided he carries his arms openly when he is deployed, but this is only in respect of occupied territory or in conflicts covered by Article 1 (4) (above, pp. 150–1). Paragraph (c) of the United Kingdom declaration states that 'deployment' in Article 44 is held to be 'any movement towards a place from which an attack is to be launched'; this would not cover *individual* acts of assassination, which are still crimes in international law.

Articles 51 to 58 all deal with the protection of civilians and civilian objects, which are not the proper subjects of attack. Paragraph (d) of the United Kingdom declaration would allow the attackers to decide and to act on 'the information from all sources available' to them at the 'relevant time'. In the heat of battle they can do little else! There may, therefore, be a higher standard for the attacker with the more sophisticated means of information-gathering. Here science may help to protect civilians from the dangers of unintended harm. Incidental loss or damage to civilians or civilian objects is dealt with by Article 51 (5) (b). This must not be excessive in relation to the 'concrete and direct military advantage anticipated', and Article 57 (2) (a) (iii) requires the attacker 'to refrain from . . . any attack . . . excessive . . . in relation to the concrete and direct military advantage anticipated'; paragraph (e) of the United Kingdom declaration stresses that such advantage is to be seen 'from the attack considered as a whole and not only from isolated or particular parts of the attack'.

Paragraph (f) of the United Kingdom declaration relates to Article 52 of Protocol I (general protection of civilian objects) and this raises the question of 'area' or 'carpet' bombing thoroughly discussed by Dr. H. Blix in this *Year Book*.[32] Paragraph (f) would allow that a specific area of land may be a military objective (e.g. within Article 51) 'if, because of its location or other reasons specified in [Article 52] its total or partial destruction, capture or neutralisation in the circumstances ruling at the time [presumably of the attack] offers definite military advantage'. This, we suggest, must be read in connection with what we say later with regard to weapons of 'mass destruction'. Article 52 provides that civilian objects, and Article 53 that cultural objects and places of worship, are to be respected, and not to be the subject of reprisals. Paragraph (g) of the United Kingdom declaration, however, would forfeit this protection of Article 53 if the object is 'unlawfully used for military purposes . . .', presumably, for example, where a church steeple is used by snipers but not where the church is used as a temporary Red Cross hospital.

All the interpretative declarations by the United Kingdom must now be considered in relation to United Kingdom declaration paragraph (i) on nuclear warfare and, by implication, other weapons of potential mass destruction.

(d) *Nuclear Weapons and Weapons of Mass Destruction*[33]

The most important part of the United Kingdom declaration is paragraph (i), which has already brought into existence a considerable literature and which states:

the *new* rules[34] *introduced* by the Protocol are not intended to have any effect on and do not regulate or prohibit the use of nuclear weapons.[35]

The United States declaration states:

the *rules established* by this Protocol *were* not intended to have any effect on and *do not* regulate *or prohibit* the use of nuclear weapons.[35]

Dr. H. Meyrowitz has pointed out that the United Kingdom formula is the clearer one since it indicates that existing international law continues to regulate nuclear weapons.

---

[32] 49 (1978), p. 31.

[33] See the *Bibliography of International Humanitarian Law* (above, p. 149 n. 21), especially pp. 195–201 on nuclear weapons. See also Meyrowitz in *Revue générale de droit international public*, 83 (1979), pp. 905–61; *Europa Archiv*, Folge 22 (1981), pp. 689–96; *Annuaire français de droit international*, 27 (1981), pp. 87–125; *Österreichische Zeitschrift für öffentliches Recht*, 23 (1981), pp. 29–57; *Zeitschrift für ausländisches öffentliches Recht und Völkerrecht*, 41 (1981), pp. 1–68; *Journées d'études juridiques Jean Dabin*, 10 (1982), pp. 607–39; Andries, ibid., pp. 549–606; Roucounas, *Revue hellénique de droit international*, 31 (1978), pp. 57–153 (with bibliography, pp. 148–53); Rauch, ibid. 33 (1980), pp. 53–110; Aldrich, loc. cit. above (p. 144 n. 5), pp. 781–2 on the position of the United States.

[34] See Meyrowitz, *Journées d'études* (previous note), at p. 622 n.

[35] Emphasis added.

The introduction of new weapons or the development of existing weapons may require new interpretations of existing rules of law. So far as new weapons are concerned, i.e. weapons developed after the coming into force of the 1977 Protocol, Article 36 requires of States accepting Protocol I:

In the study, development, acquisition or adoption of a new weapon, means or method of warfare, a High Contracting Party is under an obligation to determine whether its employment would, in some or all circumstances, be prohibited by this Protocol or by any other rule of international law applicable to the High Contracting Party.

This is a wise provision that all States, parties or not to the Protocol, might well comply with. Professor D. W. Greig[36] has pointed out that substantial practical problems need to be overcome if non-nuclear States are to be assured that they will not suffer by nuclear tests or by proliferation of nuclear capacity. Weapons that cannot yet be controlled in their effects in time or in space are unlikely to comply with Article 51 (4) of Protocol I or the resolution of the Institute of International Law on indiscriminate weapons,[37] or with the customary law.

Complex problems are bound to arise from the development of new weapons; safety systems such as have been developed in relation to mines at sea (interception by laser beams directable by the attacked) need to be developed if new weapons are to be brought within the limits of international law and subjected to control by the launcher.

It has been said that 'nuclear weapons are revolutionary because familiar moral categories, ideas of right and wrong do not fit all-out nuclear war . . . war connotes some proportion between damage done and political goals'.[38] The aim of international lawyers is to prevent 'all-out' nuclear war. 'All-out' nihilists cannot call themselves lawyers and the task of lawyers is to attempt, by the control of force, to limit the force used even in armed conflict which, regrettably, still occurs. Sovereignty may seem to some 'an unbridgeable obstacle to disarmament'[39] but every valid treaty represents an attempt to control the exercise of sovereignty within the context of international law.

Can it be said by the United Kingdom, for example, that Article 35 (3) of Protocol I is a 'new rule' introduced in Protocol I? Is it declaratory of customary law when it states:

It is prohibited to employ methods or means of warfare which are intended, or may be expected, to cause widespread, long-term and severe damage to the natural environment.

---

[36] 'The Interpretation of Treaties and Article IV (2) of the Nuclear Non-Proliferation Treaty', *Australian Year Book of International Law*, vol. 6, pp. 77, 107.

[37] *Annuaire de l'Institut de Droit International*, 53 (1969), pt. 2, p. 377, Article 7.

[38] Mandelbaum, *The Nuclear Revolution* (1981), p. 4.

[39] Ibid., p. 25.

This clause was introduced expressly as a result of disastrous experiences with the use of poisonous substances affecting land in conflicts fought after the Second World War. Their use may well be covered by the customary law set out in paragraphs 1 and 2 of Article 35. The lawfulness of nuclear and other weapons of mass destruction[40] may well depend upon the understanding of the nature of the three concepts of terror, reprisals and genocide in the context of international law.

1. *Terror by 'wanton attack'*

We have seen that there is no presumption of legality in favour of terrorists. International law, however, proceeds on the assumption that States members of the United Nations are 'peace-loving' and that the onus is on those who would prove the contrary, i.e. on those who would allege aggression or other conduct on the part of a State.

Does the accumulation of modern weapons of mass destruction change this presumption? The discoveries of scientists cannot be 'unlearned' nor set aside, and it is therefore important to distinguish between the accumulation of weapons by States and their use.

Provided there is no breach of treaty or custom the *accumulation* of poison gas or of weapons of mass destruction is not in itself illegal: the usual explanation of such accumulation is the fear of being left without adequate means of reprisals if a possible enemy were to use such weapons.

In the 1969 discussions of weapons of mass destruction the late Professor Quincy Wright made it clear that it is the *use*, rather than the possession, of nuclear and other weapons of mass destruction that may be unlawful.[41] Deterrence by possession of weapons is not the same thing as terror.[42] Article 6 of the resolution of the Institute of International Law stated: 'Existing international law prohibits, irrespective of the type of weapon used, any action whatsoever designed to terrorize the civilian population.'[43]

Article 51 (2) and (3) of Protocol I states:

2. The civilian population as such, as well as individual civilians, shall not be the object of attack. Acts or threats of violence the primary purpose of which is to spread terror among the civilian population are prohibited.
3. Civilians shall enjoy the protection afforded by this Section, unless and for such time as they take a direct part in hostilities.

---

[40] For weapons of mass destruction, see the *Bibliography of International Humanitarian Law* (above, p. 149 n. 21), pp. 186–201.

[41] Of course, when possession is lost, liability under the *Trail Smelter* arbitration may occur: see Oppenheim, *International Law*, vol. 1 (8th edn. by Lauterpacht, 1955), p. 346, and the award in *American Journal of International Law*, 33 (1939), p. 182.

[42] *Annuaire de l'Institut de Droit International*, 53 (1969), pt. 2, p. 99.

[43] Ibid., p. 377 (English text). Pt. iii of the British *Manual of Military Law*, p. 171, para. 616, states: 'The extensive destruction of protected property and the property of protected persons carried out unlawfully and wantonly is prohibited . . . unless "justified by military necessity".' Note 2 to this statement instances the burning of 30,000 civilian houses among the charges for which Jodl was found guilty, even though the defence stated that the purpose was to deny housing to the allied invader.

This restates customary international law and therefore expresses a rule which binds all States, whether or not they are bound by that Protocol as a treaty, but civilians may forfeit the protection if they take a direct part in hostilities.

Professor Charles Rousseau, a former President of the Institute of International Law, in his new work, *Le Droit des conflits armés*,[44] says there is 'no general provision [i.e. by general treaty] on the production, possession *or use* of nuclear weapons . . .',[45] but only special treaties imposed on the defeated in the Second World War. It is submitted that customary law, irrespective of treaty law, forbids the use of *any* weapon, nuclear or otherwise, designed to terrorize civilians. Paragraph (i) of the United Kingdom declaration on signature of Protocol I[46] states:

The *new* rules introduced by the Protocol . . . do not regulate or prohibit the use of nuclear weapons.[47]

The United Kingdom reference to 'new rules'[48] must be taken to refer to rules which do not reflect the existing treaty, customary and general principles of international law. This is borne out by the British *Manual of Military Law* which, when made in 1958, stated:

There is no rule of international law dealing specifically with nuclear weapons. Their use, therefore, is governed by the general principles laid down in this chapter.[49]

For States without nuclear weapons, warfare between them will be governed by existing treaties and custom. A threat by an *ally* with nuclear weapons, however, may be a different matter. The U.S.A., the U.S.S.R.

---

[44] Pedone, 1983, at p. 127 (to be reviewed in the next volume of this *Year Book*).

[45] 'Le droit positif actuellement en vigueur ne renferme que des dispositions particulières interdisant la fabrication et la détention d'armes nucléaires aux Etats de l'Axe parties aux traités de paix de 1947 (Italie, Bulgarie, Roumanie, Hongrie et Finlande), à l'Autriche (en vertu du traité d'Etat du 15 mars 1955) et à la R.F.A. (en vertu de l'Annexe I au protocole n⁰ III du 23 octobre 1954 visant l'interdiction de fabrication mais non l'interdiction de possession des armes visées).

'Mais il n'existe aucune disposition juridique qui interdise d'une manière générale la production, la possession et l'emploi des armes nucléaires, en dehors de l'interdiction des essais nucléaires à des fins militaires résultant du traité de Moscou du 5 août 1963 (texte dans *R.G.D.I.P.*, 1964, pp. 300-302), auquel sont parties 105 Etats, à l'exception de la France et de la Chine. Les armes nucléaires ont été exclues du champ des débats de la Conférence qui a abouti à l'adoption des protocoles additionnels de 1977 et les trois grandes Puissances nucléaires (Etats-Unis, Grande-Bretagne et U.R.S.S.) ont confirmé par des déclarations unilatérales que les dispositions du protocole n⁰ I (section I du titre IV) ne devaient pas être interprétées comme s'appliquant à l'emploi des armes nucléaires (v. à ce sujet l'article précité d'H. Meyrowitz en 1979)' (i.e. in *Revue générale de droit international public*, 83 (1979), pp. 905-61).

[46] Declarations on signature have been discussed by McRae (see this *Year Book*, 49 (1978), p. 155) and by Bowett (ibid. 48 (1976-7), p. 67), who remarks that it 'is not the nomenclature but the effect a statement purports to have' that differentiates declarations from reservations (p. 68).

[47] Emphasis added.

[48] The United Kingdom reference to 'new rules' is relevant also to Article 36 of Protocol I which imposes a duty to consider rules affecting the use of 'new weapons' on the States accepting the Protocol.

[49] Pt. iii, at p. 42.

and the U.K. stated at the Security Council on 17 June 1968 that they would not *use* nuclear weapons against non-nuclear States signatories of the non-proliferation treaty.[50] There were similar declarations by China (1964/5) and India (1973). Action or threats of action by nuclear States *against each other* and against non-nuclear States may, as we shall see, raise the whole question of reprisals and the question of legitimate defence against aggression; this could, for example, involve the consideration of the use of anti-ballistic weapons operating to destroy in space an enemy's attempt at a nuclear 'first strike'.

In the British *Manual of Military Law*,[51] it is stated that the means of warfare

are restricted by international conventions and declarations and also by the customary rules of warfare . . . There are compelling dictates of humanity, morality, civilisation and chivalry, which must not be disregarded.[52]

This elaboration of Hague Rule 22 reflected in Article 35 of Protocol I is still sound and in harmony with the respect for human rights, and it is consistent with the right of a judge, or any international lawyer, to have recourse to 'the general principles of law' to fill apparent gaps in a legal system in order to prevent the plea of *non liquet* in international disputes.[53]

Article 1 (2) of Protocol I confirms this view, since cases not covered by Protocol I, i.e. not included in an operative text of the Protocol, remain under the existing law, and Article 35 (1) and (2) restates the customary law:

1. In any armed conflict, the right of the Parties to the conflict to choose methods or means of warfare is not unlimited.
2. It is prohibited to employ weapons, projectiles and material and methods of warfare of a nature to cause superfluous injury or unnecessary suffering.

2. *Reprisals*

Dealing with legal theory (doctrine) as opposed to 'legal enactment'— treaties and the like—Professor Rousseau states:

Legal theory [or teaching] is divided on the problem of the licitness or illicitness of the use of nuclear arms, even though the majority of authors declare for its illicitness. Some such as Schwarzenberger[54] admit they may be used exceptionally in legitimate defence, from necessity, for the right of [self] preservation or even

[50] Discussed by Furet, Martinez et Dorandeu, *La Guerre et le droit* (1979), p. 99 (reviewed in this *Year Book*, 53 (1982), p. 238).

[51] Pt. iii, at p. 40.

[52] According to the *Encyclopaedia Britannica* (15th edn., 1975), vol. 5, p. 893, after the Korean War 77,000 prisoners were returned by the United Nations forces and 12,700 by their opponents.

[53] Judge Lauterpacht's seminal work, *The Function of Law in the International Community* (1933), is discussed in Wortley, *Jurisprudence* (1967), pp. 377 ff.; see also Falk and Kim, *The War System* (1980), p. 628, and Fitzmaurice in this *Year Book*, 50 (1979), p. 1 at pp. 8–10.

[54] *The Law of Armed Conflict* (1968), pp. 105–6.

to exercise the right to prevent an attempt at world domination. The use of atomic weapons on the basis of reprisals is admitted by a large number of authors.[55]

Many conventional weapons can be devastating and some types of neutron bombs may be controllable. These things need to be considered before the use of a military weapon can be considered permitted as reprisals in international law:

(i) the technical limits of control;

(ii) the permissibility of the nature of the weapon in relation to treaties in force affecting its use, e.g. whether action offends the treaties covering poison gas, bacteriological, atomic and other weapons of mass destruction or likely to cause unnecessary suffering;

(iii) whether or not the action constitutes the crime of genocide.

For an international lawyer to judge whether or not the particular use of any weapon fulfils the tests laid down in the United Kingdom declaration, he needs evidence of the technical nature and capacity of any weapon used, and the accuracy in information-gathering arrangements. These are questions of fact relevant to any charge of reckless or inhuman conduct. Paragraphs (b) to (g) of the United Kingdom declaration relate to practical problems of the military in the field.

The claim to enforce reprisals arises when a delinquent State has not given adequate satisfaction by restitution or reparation, including where necessary the punishment of its own delinquent forces, and there is no other means of bringing home to the delinquent enemy the unlawfulness of his act. The measures taken in reply must not be excessive in severity; and such measures of reprisal are more easily judged when of the same quality and extent as those attributed to the enemy.[56] In the case of a State bound by the Protocols to the Geneva Convention the measures taken must not contravene the rules therein. They are rational attempts to protect human rights, and may prove to be evidence of what prima facie is not permitted by custom or legal principle.

Reprisals must not be excessive but they need not be of the same nature as the type of wrong that it is hoped to punish and to deter. Thus, subject to certain conditions, an unjustified attack by nuclear weapons may in theory be met by an equally devastating attack by conventional weapons.

States wishing to respect humanitarian rules will limit force, even when taking reprisals for attacks on civilians. Protocol I forbids direct attack upon enemy civilians: civilians are not to be treated as hostages of

---

[55] *Le Droit des conflits armés* (1983), p. 127: 'La doctrine est divisée sur le problème de la licéité ou de l'illicéité de l'emploi de l'arme nucléaire, encore que la majorité des auteurs se prononce pour son illicéité. Quelques auteurs comme Schwarzenberger admettent son utilisation au titre exceptionnel de la légitime défense, de l'état de nécessité, du droit de conservation, voire même du droit de prévention contre une tentative de domination mondiale. L'emploi de l'arme atomique au titre des représailles est admis par un grand nombre d'auteurs.' Rousseau adds a reference to 32 I.L.R. 626–42 for the Japanese view.

[56] See Schwarzenberger, *The Law of Armed Conflict* (1968), p. 453.

belligerents. Clearly reprisals as an institution may be irrelevant in a situation of complete breakdown of a State or after its total destruction, though if other civilized States remain in being, it may be possible for the United Nations forces (if any) and for allies of the State destroyed to embark on controlled reprisals to reply to an earlier unlawful act resulting in the destruction of that State. The United Kingdom declaration excluding from the *new* rules of the Protocol 'the use of nuclear weapons' poses practical problems of great complexity, not least in relation to reprisals. Some articles of Protocol I expressly exclude reprisals and prohibit them: Articles 51 (6) and 57 (5) (attacks on civilians and civilian objects), Article 53 (c) (attacks on objects of culture and religion), Article 54 (4) (attacks on things indispensable for civilian survival), Article 55 (2) (attacks on the natural environment) and Article 56 (1) and (4) (attacks on works and installations containing dangerous forces). Such attacks may, under customary law, amount to war crimes. They may also be 'grave breaches' under Article 85 of Protocol I, so far as it is accepted by parties to the Protocol. We have seen, however, that the United Kingdom declaration paragraph (g) would forfeit the protection of 'objects of culture and religion' when abused, i.e. it would allow counter-measures or reprisals.

The classic theory of reprisals demands a controlled response by whatever weapon[57] is employed in response to an unlawful attack. In other words, the licitness or illicitness of the use of nuclear weapons, if not covered by the treaties or the Protocols or custom, may well be governed by the general teachings (*la doctrine*) of the publicists mentioned in Article 38 (1) (d) of the Statute of the International Court of Justice. The use of force is lawful for the ends expressed in Article 1 of the United Nations Charter, to remove threats to the peace 'in conformity with the principles of justice and international law . . .'. Those who purport to use force in the service of justice cannot without contradiction refuse to limit that use in the interests of human rights. To use unlimited force, even in a lawful cause, is an 'abuse of right'. The Rapporteur at the 1969 Session of the Institute of International Law at Edinburgh, General Baron von der Heydte, took the view[58] that Article 7 of the Resolution of the Edinburgh Meeting in 1969[59] covered nuclear weapons, biological and chemical weapons and 'blind' weapons, such as the V1 and V2 bombs, on the grounds that their objectives could not be limited. The question of control is the vital one in connection with all reprisals.

One question must be asked: does a prior breach of the *new* rules, e.g.

---

[57] On the dangers of lack of discrimination when long-range unguided missiles are used, see O'Connell, *American Journal of International Law*, 66 (1972), pp. 785–94.

[58] *Annuaire de l'Institut de Droit International*, 53 (1969), pt. 2, p. 98.

[59] '7. Existing international law prohibits the use of all weapons which, by their nature, affect indiscriminately both military objectives and non-military objects, or both armed forces and civilian populations. In particular, it prohibits the use of weapons the destructive effect of which is so great that it cannot be limited to specific military objectives or is otherwise uncontrollable (self-generating weapons), as well as of "blind" weapons': ibid., p. 377. On the use of neutron bombs, see Meyrowitz, *Annuaire français de droit international*, 27 (1981), p. 87 at p. 117.

attacks against civilians (contrary to Protocol I), permit reprisals in kind by the State whose civilians have been deliberately exterminated? Dr. H. Blix[60] has indicated that Article 51 of Protocol I which would prevent indiscriminate attacks does not, according to a view of some States (including the United Kingdom), prevent bombardment of a specific area and the area's being considered as a military objective, and in fact paragraph (f) of the United Kingdom declaration accepts that the criterion is whether such bombardment 'offers a definite military advantage'. It is suggested that this view must be read also in the context of the need to be able to limit the area of an attack, e.g. in reprisals, and to avoid genocide.

The principle of not causing unnecessary suffering is reflected in what is now probably the customary law[61] and this, along with other humanitarian rules, must certainly be regarded as binding on those States accepting Protocol I and on armed forces of the United Nations. Indeed, the prohibition of genocide is now probably part of international case law.[62]

3. Genocide

Genocide was recognized as a crime against customary international law by the four allies at the Nuremberg trials. The law was subsequently embodied in the Genocide Convention 1948, signed and ratified by most States (but not yet by the U.S.A.). It came into force on 12 January 1951 and was ratified by the United Kingdom on 30 April 1970 after the passing of the Genocide Act 1969. Articles I and II of the Convention are as follows:

Article I

The Contracting Parties confirm that genocide, whether committed in time of peace or in time of war, is a crime under international law which they undertake to prevent and to punish.

Article II

In the present Convention, genocide means any of the following acts committed with intent to destroy, in whole or in part, a national, ethnical, racial or religious group, as such:

    (a) Killing members of the group;
    (b) Causing serious bodily or mental harm to members of the group;
    (c) Deliberately inflicting on the group conditions of life calculated to bring about its physical destruction in whole or in part;
    (d) Imposing measures intended to prevent births within the group;
    (e) Forcibly transferring children of the group to another group.

---

[60] See this *Year Book*, 49 (1978), pp. 31–69, at p. 68 (note 5).
[61] E. Hambro in his report to the Institute of International Law, *Annuaire de l'Institut de Droit International*, 56 (1975), pp. 112, 114.
[62] Green, *International Law through the Cases* (3rd edn., 1970), pp. 243, 408.

Genocide is a deliberate act, not an accidental one. It is not the same thing as killing recognized enemy forces or destroying military objectives when some civilians may be put at risk. The destruction of a 'specific area of land' is not necessarily the destruction of its population, but if it does destroy the population because no warning was given, or other possible precautions were not taken, then it may be deemed to be an unnecessary and unlawful use of force. A belligerent must attempt to distinguish between military and civilians and between military and non-military objects of attack.

Article 8 of the 1969 resolution of the Institute of International Law states:

Existing international law prohibits all attacks for whatsoever motive or by whatsoever means for the annihilation of any group, region or urban centre with no possible distinction between armed forces and civilian populations or between military objectives and non-military objects.[63]

This statement may be taken to relate to the crime of genocide.

The definition of aggression adopted by the General Assembly states:

The first use of armed force by a State in contravention of the Charter shall constitute prima facie evidence of an act of aggression although the Security Council may, in conformity with the Charter, conclude that a determination that an act of aggression has been committed would not be justified in the light of other relevant circumstances, including the fact that the acts concerned or their consequences are not of sufficient gravity.[64]

A first strike by any weapon will often be unlawful, but any reply by way of reprisals must take into account basic human rights, which should be respected if at all possible. Any action which results in Mutually Assured Destruction (M.A.D.) is nihilistic, the opposite of lawful. Even reprisals must stop short of this universal genocide.

The legality of attacks may well depend upon the technology of control, and the United Kingdom declaration does attempt to indicate measures to control an attack. The neutron bomb, for instance, may even be controllable,[65] as are many terrible 'conventional' weapons.

IV. The Problem of Cognoscibility and the Mosaic of Treaty Rules

In the case of a multilateral law-making group of treaties such as those under discussion which come into force for different States at different times, the business of sorting out the effect of these law-making treaties is complex, i.e. those responsible for conducting an armed conflict must find in any given case:

[63] *Annuaire de l'Institut de Droit International*, 53 (1969), pt. 2, p. 377 (9 September 1969).
[64] G.A. Res. 3314 (XXIX) (December 1974).
[65] Meyrowitz, *Annuaire français de droit international*, 27 (1981), p. 87 at p. 102.

(i) The time of acceptance of treaty obligations by a State, e.g. by ratification or accession or succession, or of denunciation (e.g. under Article 99 of Protocol I and Article 25 of Protocol II).

(ii) Which States have made reservations thereto, or declarations on signature, and how far these are valid.[66]

(iii) In the case of an armed conflict, the date when it started and between which States.[67] It will be recalled that in each of the World Wars, the Allies did not go to war against Germany at the same time and that the U.S.A. in the Second World War was not at war with Finland, and that the U.S.S.R., after being an ally of Nazi Germany, later became its enemy and only joined the war against Japan at a later stage.

We have seen that the Protocols do not become treaties on signature; they do, however, have a normative effect on the development of the customary law of war and therefore cannot be ignored by international lawyers and the military commanders in the field, for they are designed to protect human rights and good faith demands that this purpose should be borne in mind when they come to be used as criteria for conduct.

However, it cannot be said, even for States which have ratified or accepted the Geneva Conventions and the Protocols, that the exact obligations they impose towards other States are always easy to ascertain. How then can a statesman faced by sudden attack know the strict legal position?[68] Can modern communications make it possible to avoid this sort of situation in relation to the precise obligations due from each party to the Geneva Conventions and the Protocols? Presumably, one answer might be to set up a United Nations guided computer with subsidiary computers for all parties to the treaties on the law of war to enable the legal situations to be presented to armed forces at a moment's notice.[69] Until a legal state of belligerency has occurred between particular States, statesmen are justified, in the absence of a clear indication of aggression, in suspending judgment and in remaining neutral in a conflict. The Security Council can pronounce on aggression, provided of course it can produce a decision free from veto by one of the five powers with the veto, or by a group of powers with sufficient votes to prevent a decision; failing that, the General Assembly may, by an appropriate majority, authorize action under the 'Uniting for Peace' Resolution; but the Falklands experience shows that the point of time when an armed conflict starts is not always decided without delay.[70]

---

[66] For a list, see Roberts and Guelff, op. cit. above (p. 144 n. 6), pp. 331–7 and 461–3.

[67] The difficulties of settling the opening of hostilities are reviewed in Rousseau, *Le Droit des conflits armés* (1983), pp. 29–34.

[68] In the Battle of New Orleans the British were defeated by the Americans when in fact, as neither side knew, 'peace' had been made by the Treaty of Ghent of 24 December 1814.

[69] See Tabory, *American Journal of International Law*, 76 (1982), pp. 353–5, on computerization of treaties.

[70] On 30 March 1982 the Commons were told that the situation was dangerous; the Islands were

Protocol II relating to non-international armed conflicts is likely to raise even more problems in its attempt to apply the rules of the Geneva Convention and Protocols to the struggles of revolutionaries (envisaged in Article 1 of Protocol II) who may be too elusive to contact and whose 'responsible officers' may be hard to discern.

V. Conclusions

1. Jurisprudentially, there may be no legal positive *duty* on a State to implement a treaty which it has merely 'signed to adopt a text for authentication', that is, no legal duty will then have arisen for it *from that treaty*. This does not of course prevent a duty from arising from any customary rule of the law of war stated in the treaty.

2. Nevertheless, when a State has signed a treaty, for authentication, then the State must avoid any actions which 'defeat the object and purpose of a treaty' (and this includes Protocols I or II), in force between those States which have ratified or acceded to it.

3. A State, not yet bound by the Protocols, may nevertheless rightly and lawfully choose to observe the humanitarian precepts of customary law in the Protocols. A State may be under no treaty *duty* under the Protocols, but it may exercise a liberty to observe the terms of the Protocols in any conflict; there would then be no breach of international humanitarian law, nor would those army commanders observing the Protocols be under any *international* liability for doing so, even when not technically bound to do so. Whether such commanders might be liable to disciplinary proceedings in their own State will depend on the constitution there;[71] but if, in fact, international law is 'part of the law of England' it may prove difficult to press charges against the military when they have merely taken the liberty of exercising moderation and mercy in their operations within the spirit of the Geneva Conventions and Protocols, particularly when faced by the need for prompt defensive action, on the best evidence available, without having computerized information on the legal situation with regard to the relevant treaties.

4. Declarations on signature may well create estoppels when it comes to interpreting treaties.

5. The United Kingdom and United States declarations on nuclear warfare will need continuous study in the light of the growing body of special treaties on nuclear use and proliferation: technical advances may conceivably enable nuclear weapons to be destroyed after launching but before they arrive on target, and to be subject to well-defined control when they are employed.

taken by the Argentines on 2 April and this action was condemned by the Security Council on 3 April. A British task force set out on 5 April 1982.

[71] See A. Andries, Avocat général près la cour militaire, 'L'Obéissance militaire et les interdictions du droit international public', in *Licéité en droit positif et références légales aux valeurs, Journées d'études juridiques Jean Dabin*, 10 (1982), pp. 549–606.

No doubt when the United Kingdom accepts the new Protocols a new edition of Part III of the British *Manual of Military Law* will be made for those conducting hostilities on behalf of Her Majesty's Government. Nevertheless, just as ordinary citizens who act defensively with common sense, humanity and courage when attacked are not likely to infringe legal principles, soldiers who obey orders that are not flagrantly wrong[72] and commanders who act with humanity are not likely to be held to break the rules either.

A new manual on the law for armed conflict covering *all* armed services[73] is highly desirable and, if possible, the same for all member States of N.A.T.O.

To say, as does a recent contributor to the *Encyclopaedia Britannica*, that 'most international lawyers realistically accept that international law is . . . among rather than above States. It is according to legal doctrine, binding on States, but unenforceable . . .',[74] seems unduly pessimistic. After all, as the late Judge Baxter, an international lawyer of distinction with considerable military experience, observed:

> The law governing the conduct of warfare was not framed as a set of rules to permit the playing of a game of war . . . but arises from a much more fundamental humanitarian need.[75]

ANNEX

Text of the United Kingdom Declaration on Signature of the 1977 Geneva Protocols

(*a*) In relation to Article 1, that the term 'armed conflict' of itself and in its context implies a certain level of intensity of military operations which must be present before the Conventions or the Protocol are to apply to any given situation, and that this level of intensity cannot be less than that required for the application of Protocol II, by virtue of Article 1 of that Protocol, to internal conflicts;

(*b*) in relation to Articles 41, 57 and 58, that the word 'feasible' means that which is practicable or practically possible, taking into account all circumstances at the time including those relevant to the success of military operations;

(*c*) in relation to Article 44, that the situation described in the second sentence of paragraph 3 of the Article can exist only in occupied territory or in armed conflicts covered by paragraph 4 of Article 1, and that the Government of the United Kingdom will interpret the word 'deployment' in paragraph 3(*b*) of the Article as meaning 'any movement towards a place from which an attack is to be launched';

(*d*) in relation to Articles 51 to 58 inclusive, that military commanders and others responsible for planning, deciding upon or executing attacks necessarily have to reach decisions on the basis of their assessment of the information from all sources which is available to them at the relevant time;

---

[72] *The Times*, 4 December 1981, and Wortley, *Jurisprudence* (1967), ch. 21, especially pp. 449–51.

[73] e.g. the Italian 1938 *Legge di guerra e di neutralità*, and the Austrian *Grundsätze des Kriegsvölkerrechtes* (Abhang B: '*Der Truppen Führung*') (1965).

[74] 15th edn. (1975), vol. 19, at p. 547.

[75] Cited by Whiteman, *Digest of International Law*, vol. 10 (1968), p. 49.

(*e*) in relation to paragraph 5(*b*) of Article 51 and paragraph (2) (*a*) (iii) of Article 57, that the military advantage anticipated from an attack is intended to refer to the advantage anticipated from the attack considered as a whole and not only from isolated or particular parts of the attack;

(*f*) in relation to Article 52, that a specific area of land may be a military objective if, because of its location or other reasons specified in the Article, its total or partial destruction, capture or neutralisation in the circumstances ruling at the time offers definite military advantage;

(*g*) in relation to Article 53, that if the objects protected by the Article are unlawfully used for military purposes they will thereby lose protection from attacks directed against such unlawful military uses;

(*h*) in relation to paragraph 3 of Article 96, that only a declaration made by an authority which genuinely fulfils the criteria of paragraph 4 of Article 1 can have the effects stated in paragraph 3 of Article 96, and that, in the light of the negotiating history, it is to be regarded as necessary also that the authority concerned be recognised as such by the appropriate regional intergovernmental organisation;

(*i*) that the new rules introduced by the Protocol are not intended to have any effect on and do not regulate or prohibit the use of nuclear weapons; and

(*j*) that the provisions of the Protocol shall not apply to Southern Rhodesia unless and until the Government of the United Kingdom inform the depositary that they are in a position to ensure that the obligations imposed by the Protocol in respect of that territory can be fully implemented.

In addition, the UK declared that it had signed Protocol II on the same understanding as in (*j*) above.

NON-CONFIRMATION
OF PROBATIONARY APPOINTMENTS*

By C. F. AMERASINGHE[1] and D. BELLINGER[2]

I. INTRODUCTION

THIS article examines the decisions of international administrative tribunals pertaining to non-confirmation of probationary appointments based primarily upon unsatisfactory service.[3] Cases where probationary appointments are not confirmed because of a promotion or a transfer are not included. It may be noted that the type of appointment (i.e. permanent, indefinite or fixed term) generally appears to make no difference in probation cases.

The staff rules and regulations of the various international organizations require a probationary period for almost all appointments. Similarities exist in those rules and regulations which govern probation. The approaches taken by the different Tribunals in interpreting these rules and regulations have generally not been in conflict with each other. Hence, it is possible to deduce general underlying principles. However, it should be recognized that some decisions may depend on the particular content of the pertinent rules and regulations of the organization concerned.

II. GENERAL NATURE OF PROBATION

Staff rules and regulations contain principles governing probation. Tribunals review the legality of decisions terminating probationary appointments in terms of these principles and other relevant sources of law. In general, the organization has considerable discretionary authority in dealing with probationary appointments and Tribunals merely review

* © C. F. Amerasinghe and D. Bellinger, 1984.

[1] M.A., LL.B., Ph.D., LL.D. (Cantab.), LL.M. (Harvard), Ph.D. (Ceylon); Executive Secretary, World Bank Administrative Tribunal; Associé de l'Institut de Droit International.

[2] Lic.-en-droit (Grenoble), M.A. (Catholic University); Research Assistant, World Bank Administrative Tribunal.

The views expressed in this article are not necessarily those of the World Bank Administrative Tribunal nor of the World Bank Group.

[3] Forty-four decisions were identified as involving non-confirmation of probationary appointments. Twenty-four of these were judgments of the International Labour Organization Administrative Tribunal (ILOAT), eight were judgments of the United Nations Administrative Tribunal (UNAT), eight were judgments of the Court of Justice of the European Communities (CJEC), two were judgments of the World Bank Administrative Tribunal (WBAT), one was a judgment of the Organization of American States (OAS) and one was a decision of the North Atlantic Treaty Organization Appeals Board (NATO). Of the twenty-four ILOAT cases fourteen were brought by staff members of the World Health Organization (WHO), seven by staff members of the Food and Agriculture Organization (FAO) and one was brought by a staff member of the ILO. Of the eight UNAT cases, five were brought by staff members of the Secretariat of the United Nations.

and control the exercise of this discretionary power. The reason for the extensive discretion accorded to organizations in the matter of dealing with probationary appointments seems to be that probation serves mainly the interests of the organizations. The purpose of probation is really to give the organization a chance of finding out whether the probationer is suitable for employment. In *Mirossevich*[4] the Advocate-General stated that the probationary period was required in the interest of the administration which, before committing itself, legitimately wishes to be assured of the suitability of the probationer. In *Salle*[5] WBAT stated that it was of the essence of probation that the organization be vested with the power both to define its own needs, requirements and interests and to decide whether, judging by the staff member's performance during the probationary period, he does or does not qualify for employment with the organization. The administrative authority during the probationary period tests not only the probationer's professional ability but also whether he can adjust to the specific requirements of the organization. In *Molina*[6] ILOAT stated that the most important object of probation was to establish the probationer's suitability to the particular needs of the organization. It held that the evidence in the probationer's personnel file contained information concerning the probationer's suitability but was not conclusive in this regard; that the Director-General had the power additionally to evaluate the probationer's personality; and that the administrative authority further could assess the probationer's intellectual and moral qualities in determining whether he was suitable for his assigned post. Conversely, however, it cannot be denied that the probationer has an interest, which has been considered and cannot be ignored, in being definitely employed.

Certain rights accrue to the probationer at the very inception of his probationary appointment. He can legitimately expect guidance and training in order to qualify for employment. His duties must be well-defined and he should be given a fair chance to demonstrate his suitability. In *Johnson*[7] UNAT clearly referred to this aspect arising from the contract of employment.

The most important feature of probation is the provisional status conferred upon the probationer during the probationary period. During this period, it appears, the administration has the discretionary power to: (i) decide on the duration of probation, (ii) establish the standard of performance, (iii) define the interests of the international organization, and (iv) provide the rules of procedure. Tribunals, in the exercise of their power to review the exercise of discretionary power, will, as the cases

---

[4] CJEC Case 10/55 (1954-6).
[5] WBAT Decision No. 10.
[6] ILOAT Judgment No. 440.
[7] UNAT Judgment No. 213. See also *Mirossevich*, CJEC Case 10/55 (1954-6), and *De Bruyn*, CJEC Case 25/60 (1962).

show, intervene in order to (i) protect the limited rights of the probationer, (ii) review the legality of the procedure followed, which probably constitutes the most important safeguard for the probationer, and (iii) review the substantive legality of administrative decisions. In addition Tribunals determine which of the remedies available is most appropriate for the particular case. It should be noted that Tribunals exercise special caution in reviewing a decision not to confirm a probation in order to ensure that probation can serve its purpose as a trial period: *Molina*.[8]

III. THE PROVISIONAL STATUS OF PROBATION

The provisional status of probationers is confirmed in the decisions. Tribunals have been particularly explicit in affirming this provisional status, which derives from the nature and the purpose of probation. As a result, in their interpretation of the various staff rules and regulations, they deny to probationers many of the guarantees granted to confirmed staff members. In *Kersaudy*[9] and *Schawalder-Vrancheva*[10] ILOAT stated that probationers could not enjoy the same guarantees as staff members who were confirmed in fixed term or permanent contracts. Their appointments could be terminated at any time upon confirmation of their unsuitability. Additionally, their termination for unsatisfactory service might be regarded as a measure taken in the interests of the organization. In *Joyet*[11] the same Tribunal invoked Staff Rule 960 of WHO (see Annex 3) and the general principles of law applicable to the international public service in order to reaffirm the provisional status of probationers.

However, the guarantees granted to confirmed staff members are not always denied to probationers. In *Eskenasy*[12] the matter at issue was the establishment of the quality of the probationer's work or the determination of the degree of his efficiency. OASAT noted that, while the purpose of the determination was not the same, the nature of the determination was essentially the same for probationers as for confirmed staff members. The Tribunal referred in this regard to Staff Rule 104.5 (b) (i) of the OAS (see Annex 5) which provided that probationers enjoy all the benefits granted to permanent staff members. The approach taken by OASAT enhances the rights of probationers. It does not deny that probationers enjoy a provisional status but it goes considerably further than the ILOAT decisions in protecting the rights of probationers. The difference, however, may rest on the content of the relevant staff rules and regulations, although at the same time it may be true that probationers do enjoy some of the rights accorded to permanent staff members.

[8] ILOAT Judgment No. 440.   [9] Ibid., No. 152.
[10] Ibid., No. 226.   [11] Ibid., No. 318.
[12] OAS Judgment No. 40.

IV. The Duration of Probation

The duration of probationary appointments varies from one organization to another. Generally, staff rules and regulations provide, at least, for a maximum probationary period. Although probation is meant to be in the interests of the international organization concerned, probationers too have an interest in reducing to a minimum the period under which they are kept in a state of uncertainty. If a maximum period is provided in the rules and regulations, it must be adhered to. In *Lane*[13] UNAT found that the applicant irregularly remained twenty-two months in service beyond the expiration of his extended probationary period in violation of Article 104.12 of the UN Staff Rules. He was awarded compensation, although not specifically for the above irregularity. However, the Tribunal stated that there was no automatic conversion of a probationary appointment into a permanent one either by efflux of time or by an omission of the administration. On the other hand, in *Mange*,[14] where the applicant contested the actions of the organization on the basis that the probationary period had exceeded eighteen months which was the maximum time allowed by the WHO Staff Regulations in force at the time, ILOAT found that the period of probation did not exceed eighteen months and held, therefore, that it was not competent to award the indemnity asked for in spite of the promotion gained by the applicant during her probation and the good opinion of the Board of Enquiry and Appeals, which was even confirmed by the Director-General.

There is no minimum period of probation nor is there a specific date for its termination, except that it must come to an end at the latest when the maximum stated period comes to an end, as has been seen above. In *Mariaffy*[15] the applicant contended that he was on sick leave for five months out of twenty-one months of the probationary period. UNAT held that a probationary appointment had no specific expiration date and that the administrative authority had a wide margin of discretion in determining the end of probation. In *Sternfield*[16] the applicant complained that only five months after the beginning of his probation he was informed that he was not going to be confirmed. ILOAT held that there was no minimum period of probation required either by the Staff Rules of WHO or by any general rule of law. It held that a probationer's appointment could be terminated at any time after his unsuitability for the assigned post had been established. In *de Roy*[17] the applicant contended that her probation was curtailed because she took annual leave and because there was not enough work in the office. The CJEC said that not always was there work which was suitable for probationers and that the latter, during such periods, were expected to improve their skills. The Court concluded

[13] UNAT Judgment No. 198.   [14] ILOAT Judgment No. 8.
[15] UNAT Judgment No. 168.   [16] ILOAT Judgment No. 197.
[17] CJEC Case 92/75 (1976).

that Miss de Roy was given an adequate opportunity to show her abilities but failed to perform satisfactorily. The mere fact that the period of probation was shortened by her taking leave was not relevant.

V. EXTENSION OF THE PROBATIONARY PERIOD

The decision to extend the period of probation lies exclusively with the administrative authority. It appears that generally probationers should be informed about the decision to extend their probation. On the other hand, Tribunals have regarded tacit extensions as regular inasmuch as such extensions confer only benefits on probationers, who ultimately could refuse them: *Molina*[18] and *Lane.*[19] However, it is established that there is no such thing as a tacit confirmation of a probationer nor can there be an automatic conversion of a probationary appointment into a permanent one: *Lane.*[20]

An extension is normally granted if the performance of the probationer is not quite satisfactory: *Salle*,[21] *de Ungria*,[22] *Ghaffar*[23] and *Kersaudy*;[24] or if the probationer experiences difficulties in adjusting to the requirements of the service: *Vrancheva*[25] and *Nagels*,[26] in which the probationary appointment was extended twice. The fact that the probationary period is extended certainly does not mean that the probationer will or must ultimately be confirmed: *Salle.*[27]

Decisions extending the period of probation have been contested by probationers whose performance was rated satisfactory in their reports. In *Peynado*,[28] the probationary period was extended in spite of two entirely favourable reports and the approval by the Secretary-General of the UN of the decision confirming Mr. Peynado's appointment. UNAT did not explicitly hold irregular *per se* the extension of Mr. Peynado's probation for one more year, but it declared itself disturbed by a number of unsatisfactory features of the case, namely, *inter alia*, (*a*) the retroactive appraisal of earlier performance properly evaluated in two period reports one of which was signed by the same officer who subsequently changed his mind; and (*b*) the fact that, notwithstanding the Secretary-General's approval, the case was referred back to the Appointment and Promotion Board under Staff Rule 104.13 (c) (iii). The Tribunal awarded compensation for procedural defects. In *Johnson*[29] UNAT was more positive. The applicant's probationary appointment was extended in spite of an excellent periodic report covering the first nineteen months of her probation. The extension was requested by the applicant's new supervisor in order that she might demonstrate her adaptability to her new supervisor and

---

[18] ILOAT Judgment No. 440.
[20] Ibid., No. 198.
[22] UNAT Judgment No. 71.
[24] Ibid., No. 152.
[26] CJEC Case 52/70 (1971).
[28] UNAT Judgment No. 138.

[19] UNAT Judgment No. 198.
[21] WBAT Decision No. 10.
[23] ILOAT Judgment No. 320.
[25] Ibid., No. 194.
[27] WBAT Decision No. 10.
[29] Ibid., No. 213.

to the objectives of her new job description. The Appointment and Promotion Committee had to approve this extension retroactively, since the end of the probationary period had already occurred when the issue came up for consideration by the Committee. UNAT held that the extension was irregular and did not fulfil its purpose, i.e. of giving the probationer a chance to meet the required standards. In fact, the periodic report covering the extended probation was not taken into consideration when the applicant's candidacy for permanent employment was examined. The Tribunal held that in the circumstances the applicant was denied the opportunity to demonstrate her capabilities and awarded her compensation in lieu of specific performance. In a very early decision of ILOAT[30] the applicant's performance had been qualified as satisfactory and her supervisor had recommended her for permanent appointment, but the review body had extended the probationary period. ILOAT confirmed that the extension had been imposed upon the applicant but found, on the other hand, that she had not appealed against the decision. Thus, a decision to extend probation must also be appealed, if it is to be questioned later as being irregular or because the probationer's work was rated as satisfactory.

There are situations in which the respondent organization may justifiably refuse to extend the period of probation. In *Mariaffy*,[31] even though the applicant's supervisor had recommended extension of the probationary period on the grounds that Mr. Mariaffy's performance, although satisfactory, had not shown that he had actually contributed to the work of the Department, because of the five months' sick leave which he had taken, UNAT held that the respondent had no legal obligation to extend the probation in order to compensate for that sick leave. The shortening of the period of probation was attributable to the applicant, not to the respondent's fault. In *Crapon de Caprona*[32] the Tribunal stated that the respondent could refuse to extend the probationary period, if it appeared that the probationer's performance could not possibly improve with an extension. The Tribunal considered that the extension granted to Mr. Caprona at his request, in order to avoid having to move during the winter, was outside the scope of WHO Staff Rule 440 (now Rule 540—see Annex 3) pertaining to the end of probation and therefore was not really a regular extension of probation, which could justifiably have been refused in the case.

In *Loomba*,[33] ILOAT said that failure to notify the applicant of the decision extending the probationary period normally constituted an irregularity. However, the Tribunal concluded in that case that the applicant should have inferred that his probationary period had been tacitly extended because of the special circumstances of the case, i.e. at his own request an investigation was ordered and his probation was extended

---

[30] *Marsh*, ILOAT Judgment No. 10.   [31] UNAT Judgment No. 168.
[32] ILOAT Judgment No. 112.   [33] Ibid., No. 169.

awaiting the results of that investigation. Consequently, the Tribunal accepted the possibility of a tacit extension in appropriate circumstances. It also stated that the probationer must prove that he had suffered damage from any uncertainty in which he was kept as a result of an inappropriate tacit extension, if he was to qualify for compensation. In *di Pillo*,[34] however, the CJEC indirectly conceded that a tacit extension was irregular, after finding that the probation report was drawn up after a delay of three months in violation of Staff Rule 34 (see Annex 4). The Court, therefore, awarded compensation to Mr. di Pillo for being kept in a state of uncertainty. The purpose of ensuring that the probationer is aware of the extension of his probationary period is to give him a chance to defend himself, as appears from *Kersaudy*,[35] where it was held that, as the applicant was informed of the grounds for the decision to extend his probationary period, he had the opportunity to present his comments.

VI. TERMINATION IN THE INTERESTS OF THE ORGANIZATION

(a) *When Possible and Requirements*

The administrative authority can terminate a probationary appointment at any time during the maximum period of probation, as is provided in the staff rules and regulations of international organizations. Tribunals in their interpretation of the staff rules and regulations seem to concede that on the timing of the termination decision, which is left to the discretion of the administration, will depend whether the probationer has certain rights or not. Thus, a distinction is made between termination at the end of the probationary period and termination during probation. In addition, the timing of the termination assumes importance, particularly when the appointment is terminated in the interests of the organization. The time at which a decision to terminate a probationary appointment has been taken has been discussed in cases against the UN, the OAS and the FAO.

1. *UNAT approach*

Timing was first considered important by UNAT in *Cooperman*,[36] in which the Tribunal in its interpretation of Staff Regulation 9.1 (c), Staff Rule 104.13 (c) (iii) and Staff Rule 104.12 (a) (see Annex 1) said that when a probationary appointment was terminated at the end of the probationary period the employee's suitability for permanent appointment had to be reviewed by a review body, namely the Appointment and Promotion Board, in accordance with a well-defined procedure. This meant that a probationer whose employment was terminated at the end of his

---

[34] CJEC Cases 10/72 and 47/72 (1973).   [35] ILOAT Judgment No. 152.
[36] UNAT Judgment No. 93.

probationary period enjoyed an element of protection which was denied to those whose employment was terminated during probation. Mr. Cooperman's employment was terminated during probation without reference to the Board. The Tribunal held that the termination decision was valid, and that the appointment could be terminated during probation in the interests of the organization on the basis of Staff Regulation 9.1 (c). In addition, the Secretary-General could unilaterally define the interests of the UN Secretariat. The Tribunal could only examine the bona fides of the administrative authority in this situation. In *Mariaffy*[37] the applicant's appointment was terminated before the end of his probation on the basis, *inter alia*, of medical advice, although he had been away from the office as a result of an accident for five of twenty-one months. The Tribunal held that a probationer's appointment could be terminated in the interests of the organization at any time before the end of probation on the basis of an unfavourable opinion of the UN Medical Service because the standards required by Staff Rule 104.13 (a) (i) (see Annex 1) had not been met.

At the end of the probationary period, an appointment could only be validly terminated pursuant to Staff Regulation 9.1 (c) and Staff Rule 104.13 (a) (i) in accordance with the procedure specified in Staff Rule 104.13 (c) (i) and (iii) (see Annex 1): *de Ungria*,[38] *Chiacchia*[39] and *Johnson*.[40] In *Peynado*[41] the Tribunal held that, because the applicant's employment was terminated at the end of his period of probation, though in the interests of the organization, he was entitled to a fair and reasonable procedure before the Appointment and Promotion Board which examined his suitability for permanent employment. In addition, Mr. Peynado was entitled to all the guarantees provided in the Staff Rules and Administrative Instruction ST/AI/115, paragraph 13 (see Annex 1). The Tribunal pointed out that the fact that the decision not to confirm the probationer had been reviewed by the review body (the Appointment and Promotion Board) did not necessarily guarantee the validity of that decision. The Tribunal awarded compensation to Mr. Peynado for the injury caused by procedural defects in the termination of his probationary appointment. In *Lane*,[42] the Tribunal reaffirmed the principles stated in *Cooperman* and *Peynado*. It held that, because the appointment of Mr. Lane was terminated a long time after the expiry of his extended probation, he was entitled to a fair assessment of his suitability for permanent appointment. Mr. Lane's appointment was terminated in the interests of the organization because he failed to demonstrate his suitability for permanent appointment. The Tribunal awarded him compensation because there had been no appraisal report covering the twenty-two months of his irregularly extended probation.

---

[37] UNAT Judgment No. 168.
[38] Ibid., No. 71.
[39] Ibid., No. 90.
[40] Ibid., No. 213.
[41] Ibid., No. 138.
[42] Ibid., No. 198.

2. OASAT approach

In *Eskenasy*,[43] OASAT made the same distinction as has been made in the UNAT cases between termination of a probationary appointment during probation and termination at the end of such period. The Tribunal held that, if a probationary appointment had not been terminated in the interests of the General Secretariat during the probationary period or its extension, then the probationer should have been duly evaluated in the last month of his probation and given the opportunity to present his comments, in accordance with Staff Rule 104.5 (f) and (h) (see Annex 5). The Tribunal concluded that a probationary appointment could not be terminated at the end of the probationary period simply in the interest of the General Secretariat.

3. ILOAT approach

All ILOAT decisions rendered on this issue were the result of actions brought by staff members of the FAO. The Tribunal stated that the Director-General could unilaterally define the interests of the organization, and that judicial control would be exercised only in the case of misuse of power. The following ILOAT decisions show that administrative authorities possess a wide discretion in defining the interests of the organization.

In interpreting the FAO Staff Rules and Regulations as well as the FAO Administrative Manual, ILOAT has concluded that a probationer's appointment could be terminated at any time during or at the end of his probationary period on the grounds of *unsatisfactory service*. However, in *McIntire*,[44] the Tribunal held that in that event the reasons for the termination should be specific enough and should be communicated to the staff member. On the other hand, it was also said that the Director-General of FAO could terminate the appointment of a probationer by invoking *the interests of the organization* in accordance with Article IX, Section 301.0913 of the FAO Staff Regulations (see Annex 2).[45] In *Loomba*[46] the applicant's appointment was terminated in the interests of the organization under the above provisions, because of his character and his psychological unsuitability for international service which, moreover, was verified by the Tribunal itself from the content and tone of his correspondence. The Tribunal held that the respondent did not have to provide Mr. Loomba with a written statement of reasons, inasmuch as he was given a warning and was informed of his supervisor's intention to dismiss him. Consequently, he was sufficiently informed of the grounds of his termination. It was also said that in any case under the relevant provisions this procedure was not required to be followed. In *Guisset*,[47] where the applicant's probationary appointment was terminated in the interests of

---

[43] OASAT Judgment No. 40.   [44] ILOAT Judgment No. 13.
[45] See also *Kersaudy*, ibid., No. 152.   [46] Ibid., No. 169.
[47] Ibid., No. 396. See also *Al-Zand*, ibid., No. 389.

the organization, because of the incompatibility of temperament between himself and the Director-General of FAO, the Tribunal held that the Director-General had the power to define the interests of the organization and that there was no need to provide Mr. Guisset with a written statement of reasons because he was dismissed in the interests of the organization and the action was not a disciplinary one. In *Pini*,[48] the Tribunal held that it was not open to the Tribunal to reassess the evidence as was requested by Mr. Pini, *inter alia* because his probationary appointment was terminated in the interests of the organization under Article IX, section 301.0913 of the FAO Staff Regulations.

It appears from the decisions analysed that whenever the administrative authority has the right to and chooses to terminate a probationary appointment in the interests of the organization Tribunals are very reluctant to intervene. It should be mentioned that the Staff Rules and Regulations of the EEC and WHO do not provide for termination based upon the interests of the organization.

(b) *Grounds for Termination*

1. *Standard of performance*

Tribunals have recognized the discretionary power of the administrative authority to determine the professional qualifications of their staff members. In the case of probation the discretionary power of the administration is even wider because of the nature and purpose of probation. The administrative authority has the discretion to establish the standards which the probationer should attain before the appointment is confirmed. Tribunals do not express value-judgements on those standards, but exercise control over the legality of the administrative act by reference to facts which the administration has the right to select in reaching the relevant conclusion. The administrative authority has the discretion to evaluate the professional capabilities of the probationer and his moral and psychological fitness for the specific requirements of the service and to take the decision to confirm or not to confirm his appointment. The staff rules and regulations of several international organizations confer this discretion on the administration and Tribunals have consistently reaffirmed such power.

It would seem that seldom has a probationary appointment been terminated for unsatisfactory services *per se*. On the contrary, in the majority of cases probationers have failed to adjust to the special requirements of the given international organization. In *Cooperman*,[49] UNAT stated that Mr. Cooperman's record was a mixed one and that it did not have the power to pronounce upon the ratings given by various

---

[48] ILOAT Judgment No. 455.
[49] UNAT Judgment No. 193. The same principle was reaffirmed in *Peynado*, ibid., No. 138, and *Adler*, ibid., No. 267.

officers from time to time. In *Kissaun*,[50] *Crapon de Caprona*,[51] *Joyet*[52] and *Heyes*,[53] ILOAT stated that it would not substitute its own opinion for that of the Director-General of WHO as regards the suitability of the probationer concerned whether it be in respect of his performance or his conduct. In *Buranavanichkit*,[54] WBAT stated that the concept of unsatisfactory performance could be defined by the administration to include the probationer's character, personality and conduct generally in so far as they bear on ability to work harmoniously and to good effect with superiors and other staff members, and that the Tribunal would not review the merits of a decision taken by the administration as to unsatisfactory performance as thus defined except for the purpose of satisfying itself that there had not been an abuse of discretion.

It appears that satisfactory performance alone, evidenced in successive periodic reports during the probationary period, does not confer a right to permanent tenure. In *de Ungria*,[55] the applicant's appointment was terminated in the interests of the organization because he failed to meet the standards required for permanent appointment. UNAT held that, though Mr. de Ungria's performance was entirely satisfactory, his unauthorized outside activities disqualified him for permanent appointment. Similarly, in *Chiacchia*,[56] the applicant's work performance was fully satisfactory. However, her insubordination and lack of punctuality disqualified her for permanent appointment. In *Adler*,[57] the applicant's performance was rated as satisfactory in three successive periodic reports. However, his appointment was terminated in the interests of the organization under UN Staff Regulation 9.1 (c) (see Annex 1), because he failed to demonstrate his suitability as an international civil servant. In the same decision UNAT held that, though the applicant's supervisor recognized some of his qualities—in fact he only wanted his transfer, not termination of his appointment—the administrative authority had the discretion to decide whether or not the applicant should be given a permanent appointment.

In *Mange*,[58] the applicant not only performed satisfactorily but she was even promoted just before the termination of her appointment. The termination, which was upheld, was based upon her unsuitability for the environment of the organization. In *Milous*,[59] the applicant's unsatisfactory conduct (he communicated to the King of Jordan his supervisor's alleged hostility towards the King) made him unsuitable for international service.[60]

2. *Characterization of performance as unsatisfactory in spite of impeccable professional qualifications*

There are cases in which the professional qualifications of probationers

50 ILOAT Judgment No. 69.   51 Ibid., No. 112.   52 Ibid., No. 318.
53 Ibid., No. 453.   54 WBAT Decision No. 7.   55 UNAT Judgment No. 71.
56 Ibid., No. 90.   57 Ibid., No. 267.   58 ILOAT Judgment No. 8.
59 Ibid., No. 42.
60 See also *Kissaun*, ibid., No. 69, and *Loomba*, ibid., No. 169, to the same effect.

have not been questioned but, none the less, their performance has been described as unsatisfactory, either because they failed to adjust to the specific requirements of the organization or because they failed to perform some of their duties satisfactorily. Although Tribunals in such cases seem to be more cautious in accepting the standard of performance laid down by the administration as well as the choice of relevant facts by the administration, they have not been generally inclined to interfere with such choice of standards or facts. Also sometimes Tribunals have themselves examined pieces of the probationer's work in order to ascertain whether the evaluation of performance by the administrative authority was proper.

In *Crapon de Caprona*,[61] ILOAT said that the administrative authority might set *reasonable* standards. In *Kersaudy*,[62] although the same principle was reaffirmed, ILOAT nevertheless held that the standard set by the FAO was only one among many factors to be considered in the evaluation of the probationer's performance. The other factors were identified as being the difficulty of the work as well as the circumstances in which the work was performed. In the former case, the applicant had some fifteen years of experience as a translator. His appointment was, however, terminated on the grounds of unsatisfactory performance. The Tribunal, instead of relying on the evaluation of the applicant's performance by the administration, proceeded to examine his translations and found that in fact some of the corrections were disputable and possibly unjustified but that most of them were pertinent. In the end the Tribunal concurred with the opinion of the reviewers that the applicant's work was below the average standard required. It appears that ILOAT will interfere with an evaluation given by the administration only if it is abundantly clear that the applicant's work had in fact met the standards set by the organization. Similarly, in *Kersaudy* where the applicant's professional qualifications were not questioned, the Tribunal embarked on an examination of the applicant's translations and concluded that there were some doubts about the importance or value of the criticisms made of the quality of the translations. However, ILOAT took into consideration the applicant's insufficient work output (number of words translated) and declared that his low work output was one of the elements of his unsatisfactory performance. It appears that when there is an objective factor, such as an easily measured work output, ILOAT is more reluctant to question the administrative authority's evaluation of performance. The existence of such an objective factor makes it possible to confirm the value-judgement concerning the quality of the probationer's work made by the administration.[63]

[61] ILOAT Judgment No. 112.
[62] Ibid., No. 152.
[63] See also *Sternfield*, ibid., No. 197, for a similar decision.

3. *Unsuitability in spite of excellent professional qualifications*

In many cases ILOAT has upheld the termination of probationary appointments for unsuitability, although the professional skills of applicants have not been in question. In *Kraicsovits*,[64] the applicant failed to adjust to the conditions in which his work had to be done—he disliked field-work. The non-confirmation of his appointment was upheld.[65] In *Al-Zand*,[66] Mr. Al-Zand lacked practical experience and was, therefore, found to be unsuitable for the post to which he was assigned. ILOAT said in this case that 'unsuitable' meant 'unsatisfactory' and that Mr. Al-Zand's appointment was rightly terminated in the interests of the organization in accordance with FAO Staff Regulation 301.0913 (see Annex 2).[67] In *Heyes*,[68] Mr. Heyes was found unsuitable for international service and his appointment was terminated under WHO Staff Rule 1060 (see Annex 3). It should be noted that ILOAT held that Mr. Heyes's complaints about his working conditions and home accommodation were not sufficient reasons for concluding that he was unsuitable, because some of his complaints were justified and he did not persist in complaining. However, the Tribunal agreed that Mr. Heyes's working relations were unsatisfactory, itself determined his unsuitability from the tone of his correspondence, and declared that he was a difficult, if not an impossible person with whom to work.[69]

VII. THE SUBSTANTIVE OBLIGATIONS OF THE ADMINISTRATION DURING PROBATION

While the administration has discretionary power during the probationary period, probationers have certain rights. Probation results from the contract of employment which creates rights and obligations for both parties. Some of these obligations derive from the nature of probation. Furthermore, most of the staff rules and regulations of international organizations provide for some of the obligations the administrative authority owes probationers, such as the obligation to train and guide them. However, Tribunals have, in the absence of explicit provision, had recourse to general principles of law in determining the obligations of the administration and the rights of probationers.

In many decisions Tribunals have expressly referred to the obligations of the administration.[70] In *Eskenasy*,[71] OASAT referred to some of the

---

[64] Ibid., No. 140.
[65] See also *Schawalder-Vrancheva*, ibid., No. 226.
[66] Ibid., No. 389.
[67] For another FAO case of a similar character, see *Guisset*, ibid., No. 396.
[68] Ibid., No. 453.
[69] Ibid., No. 440.
[70] See, e.g., *Johnson*, UNAT Judgment No. 213; *Ghaffar*, ILOAT Judgment No. 320; *Heyes*, ibid., No. 453; *Eskenasy*, OASAT Judgment No. 40; *Salle*, WBAT Decision No. 10.
[71] OASAT Judgment No. 40.

duties the administrative authority had to perform in order to give the probationer a fair evaluation to which he had a right. Some of the necessary elements of the evaluation system were identified as being effective communication between supervisor and probationer, definition of the probationer's duties and responsibilities as derived from his job description, and specification of the manner in which such duties should be carried out. In *Heyes*,[72] ILOAT stated that WHO Staff Rule 530 (see Annex 3) provided for one of the obligations the respondent had to fulfil, namely, the obligation to provide guidance and instruction to the probationer, which included suggestions for improvement if performance was unsatisfactory. The CJEC has stated that there is a contractual obligation to give the probationer an opportunity to prove his ability.[73]

(a) *Duty to Provide Fair Conditions for Performance*

In *Chiacchia*,[74] the applicant contended that she had the right to work during her probationary period under favourable conditions. Although it did not explicitly deny this right, UNAT said that if the unfavourable conditions under which Ms. Chiacchia had worked during her probation had been known to the Secretary-General when he evaluated her and took the decision to terminate her appointment, Ms. Chiacchia's rights had not been infringed. Consequently, UNAT seems to be of the view that the knowledge of the situation by the Secretary-General exempts the administrative authority from this particular obligation. In *Ghaffar*,[75] however, ILOAT found that, when he took his decision to terminate the applicant's appointment, the Director-General of FAO had overlooked the difficult conditions under which Mr. Ghaffar had worked during his probation, inasmuch as the duties assigned to him were not in accord with his job description, and found fault with this omission.

(b) *Duty to Assign Duties within the Scope of the Job Description*

In *Johnson*[76] UNAT noted that in many instances the respondent had failed to carry out its obligations towards Ms. Johnson. For example, at the end of Ms. Johnson's second year of probation the complete reorganization of the department to which she had been assigned as well as the change of her supervisor resulted in a new job description for her. However, the administrative authority failed officially to inform her of these changes and her new supervisor was unable to make her understand what he was expecting of her in the new situation. The Tribunal found fault with this omission.[77] In *Nagels*,[78] on the other hand, where the applicant argued that

---

[72] ILOAT Judgment No. 453.
[73] See *Mirossevich*, CJEC Case 10/55 (1954–6), and *Nagels*, CJEC Case 52/70 (1971).
[74] UNAT Judgment No. 90.   [75] ILOAT Judgment No. 340.
[76] UNAT Judgment No. 213.   [77] See also *Ghaffar*, ILOAT Judgment No. 320.
[78] CJEC Case 52/70 (1971).

there was a discrepancy between the nature of the duties assigned to his post as described in the notice for the vacancy for which he had applied and the actual duties with which he was entrusted, the CJEC found that Mr. Nagels had failed to perform satisfactorily the administrative aspects of his duties, which in fact were very closely linked to the subject-matter as described in the vacancy notice. Furthermore, the Court noted that although a misunderstanding might have occurred because of the wording of the notice in Dutch (the applicant's mother tongue), discussions which took place with the department prior to his recruitment as to the nature of the position as well as his curriculum vitae, in which it was mentioned that he had administrative experience, indicated adequately that Mr. Nagels himself contributed to such misunderstanding. The Court held against Mr. Nagels but awarded him one half of his costs.

(c) Duty to Provide Guidance and Training

The obligations of the administration to provide guidance and training are generally found in the staff rules and regulations of the various organizations. Tribunals have taken into consideration the circumstances of the case whenever the enforcement of these obligations has been in issue. Thus, in *Crapon de Caprona*,[79] where the applicant contended that he did not receive adequate training during his probationary period, the Tribunal held that he had had fifteen years of experience as a translator and consequently did not need any special training.[80] In *Salle*,[81] WBAT pointed out that the relevant personnel manual statement required that the probationer be provided adequate supervision and guidance and also, in certain circumstances, adequate language training, but held that the administration had, in the circumstances of the case, discharged the obligation placed upon it.

(d) Duty to Warn about Shortcomings

In *Crapon de Caprona*[82] ILOAT stated that a probationer should be informed of his shortcomings. Similarly, in *Heyes*[83] in interpreting WHO Staff Rule 1060 (see Annex 3), the same Tribunal stated that only in a very exceptional case was it possible to terminate a probationer's appointment under that staff rule without previously giving him an opportunity to correct himself.

(e) Duty to Assist and Protect

In *Guisset*,[84] where the applicant contended that he had been persecuted

---

[79] ILOAT Judgment No. 112. See also *Kersaudy*, ibid., No. 152. In *Vrancheva*, ibid., No. 194, where the decision to terminate was quashed on the grounds of procedural irregularity, the Tribunal did not explicitly deal with the contention that the applicant had not received guidance.

[80] See also *Sternfield*, ibid., No. 197.   [81] WBAT Decision No. 10.

[82] ILOAT Judgment No. 112.   [83] Ibid., No. 453.   [84] Ibid., No. 396.

and a victim of a plot, ILOAT clearly stated that the administration had the duty, even in the absence of express provision, to respect the staff member's dignity and reputation, even when he was on probation. The Tribunal held that Mr. Guisset's professional position had not been damaged, although it was not entirely clear whether his dignity and reputation had not. The applicant had been reinstated in his country's foreign service.

(f) *Duty to Transfer*

It is not clearly established that the administration has a duty to transfer a probationer during probation. It is mentioned here, because probationers often refer to it. It appears that the decision to transfer a probationer during his probation lies exclusively with the administrative authority, which decides when and whether to take such action, but that if the administration decides to transfer the probationer, then the decision accrues to his benefit. However, there seems to be a difference of opinion on this subject. UNAT does not seem to recognize a right to transfer. ILOAT in a recent decision took a somewhat different approach.

In *Adler*[85] UNAT found that the applicant's supervisor had clearly stated that Mr. Adler had several talents but was unsuitable for the post to which he was assigned. Therefore, Mr. Adler's probation was extended in order to find a suitable position for him in another department. However, the efforts were fruitless. The Tribunal held that the administration had no obligation to transfer him. In a very early UNAT decision[86] the Tribunal affirmed that the probationer did not have the right to be given another chance by transfer when unsuccessful.

In *Al-Zand*[87] ILOAT held that the applicant whose performance was unsatisfactory had no right to ask for a transfer to another post. In a subsequent decision[88] pertaining to an action brought by an FAO staff member, ILOAT clearly stated the principle also mentioned in *Al-Zand* that before dismissing a staff member thought should be given to transferring him to some other post on trial, especially if he was junior in rank. But, in this particular case, the Tribunal excluded the possibility of transfer, since the applicant was hired for a specific post (Special Assistant to the Director-General) because of the friendship between himself and the Director-General. Consequently, ILOAT noted that when the applicant lost the Director-General's confidence he could no longer render to the organization the special services for which he had been hired and there was no reason to keep him any longer in the organization. In the two above-mentioned decisions there was no reference to FAO staff rules or regulations as such. The difference in approach between the two judgments may be explained by the fact that in *Al-Zand* the applicant was

[85] UNAT Judgment No. 267.   [86] *Chiacchia*, ibid., No. 90.
[87] ILOAT Judgment No. 389.   [88] *Guisset*, ibid., No. 396.

considered to be lacking pragmatism which rendered him unsuitable, and
'unsuitable' was held in this case to mean 'unsatisfactory', whereas in
Guisset Mr Guisset was found unsuitable because of the incompatibility of
temperament between himself and the Director-General and he was dismissed in the interests of the organization under FAO Staff Regulation
301.0913 (see Annex 2). It could be, therefore, that, depending upon the
circumstances, i.e. the type of unsuitability, a probationer might have, in
an appropriate case, a right to transfer. In *Molina*[89] ILOAT again
considered the issue of whether an unsuccessful probationer has a right to
gain a transfer. In this case, the applicant, a WHO staff member, contended that he should have been transferred for the remaining eleven
months of his two-year contract. The Tribunal held that there was no
reasonable possibility of transferring him to another unit because he had
specialized in computer science and could only work in the data processing
department. Mr. Molina's appointment was terminated under WHO Staff
Rule 1060 (see Annex 3) for unsuitability because he was incompatible in
the group to which he had been assigned. In *Gale*[90] unsuccessful efforts
were made to transfer Mr. Gale, a staff member of UNESCO, to another
post and the Appeals Board of UNESCO had even assessed the compensation to be offered to him as an alternative to his transfer to a suitable
post. ILOAT held that the compensation recommended by the Appeals
Board was adequate to compensate the applicant for any wrong done to
him. It seems that there is consistency in the ILOAT judgments. If a
probationer is found unsuitable but not unsatisfactory, then he may in
appropriate circumstances have the right to be transferred.

In *Johnson*,[91] where the applicant was transferred during her probation,
UNAT held that the periodic report covering the period after the applicant's transfer should have been considered when her assignment was
reviewed for the granting of a permanent appointment. The omission to
take into consideration the periodic report covering the period of probation after the transfer was declared irregular. Where the applicant is in
fact transferred, he must have the full benefit of the transfer. No clear
conclusion can be drawn from this case in regard to the right to transfer,
in so far as it is not clear from the case whether there were provisions in
the staff regulations and rules of the organization requiring transfer nor
whether the Tribunal would have regarded the applicant's rights as having
been violated if he had not been transferred.

VIII. OBLIGATIONS OF THE ADMINISTRATION RELATIVE TO
PROCEDURE AND MATTERS OF SUBSTANCE

Tribunals exercise a certain amount of judicial control over administrative decisions taken to terminate probationary appointments. Generally, the provisions relating to probationary appointments and their

---

[89] Ibid., No. 440.   [90] Ibid., No. 84.   [91] Ibid., No. 213.

termination are to be found in the staff rules and regulations of each international organization. When the texts are silent, Tribunals have had recourse to general principles of law, practices of the organization and similar sources of law in controlling the exercise of discretionary powers. Tribunals are particularly concerned as to whether the probationer was given a fair trial. Therefore, Tribunals are vigilant in exercising their control over the procedures pertaining to the termination of probationary appointments whether laid down in the staff rules and regulations of the organization or not. Although tribunals exercise some control over matters of substance, judicial control over procedure is in most cases ultimately the only protection available to the probationer. To some extent also the power of the administration to choose the relevant facts in certain situations may limit judicial control. The record shows that in the majority of cases, while Tribunals have examined the exercise of discretionary power, they have often found that the grounds for the decision were factually correct or that the decision was not tainted with prejudice or with procedural irregularities.

The NATO Appeals Board in its *Decision No. 90* held that the termination of a probationary appointment should be based on 'adequate' grounds and that it was for the Tribunal to determine whether the grounds adduced justified the termination decision. The CJEC in a very early case, *Mirossevich*,[92] stated that the administrative authority could at its discretion evaluate the capacities of probationers to carry out their duties, and the Court would review only the 'ways and means' which might have led to such evaluation. In *Adler*[93] UNAT declared that it would only review a decision if there were evidence that it was motivated by prejudice or based on extraneous factors. In *Kersaudy* ILOAT made a statement of general principle relating to the judicial power to review administrative decisions:

> The Tribunal is competent to review any decision of the Director-General to terminate the appointment of a staff member during or on the expiry of the probationary period if it is taken without authority, is in irregular form or tainted by procedural irregularities, or is taken on illegal grounds or based on incorrect facts, or if essential facts have not been taken into consideration or where there has been a misuse of authority, or if conclusions which are clearly false have been drawn from the documents in the dossier. But the Tribunal may not substitute its own judgment for that of the Director-General concerning the work or conduct of the person concerned or his qualification for employment as an international official.[94]

(a) *Procedural Matters*

The most common procedural irregularity is the infringement of what may be narrowly called the probationer's right to due process. The most important procedural irregularities so far identified relate to periodic

---

[92] CJEC Case 10/55 (1954–6).   [93] UNAT Judgment No. 267.
[94] ILOAT Judgment No. 152 at p. 5.

reports, the time limit for the submission of such reports, completeness of such reports, opportunities of rebuttal of such reports, competence of the person or persons entitled to draw up such reports, reference of the case to a review body, absence or nature of the warnings given to the probationer, the statement of reasons in the termination decision and notification of decisions. Generally, the procedural requirements from which these irregularities arose were mentioned in the various staff rules and regulations of the international organizations concerned. If the texts were silent then Tribunals explicitly or implicitly have had recourse to the general principles of law in ascertaining whether a fundamental right had been infringed.

1. *Periodic reports*

The objective of periodic reports or appraisal reports is to inform the probationer about the quality and quantity of his work and to point out his shortcomings and how he may improve. They are prepared periodically during the probationary period. Tribunals do not usually order the rectification of these reports, but they may apply sanctions to any errors that may be contained in them. Only in one case so far has a report been annulled. In *Molina*[95] the report of a first-level supervisor was annulled after prejudice was inferred from the whole dossier.

Tribunals do, however, attach importance to appraisal reports and have had to pronounce on the procedures relating to them. In a very early decision of ILOAT, *Marsh*,[96] the Tribunal stressed the importance of the procedure to be followed during the probationary period in regard to appraisal reports. The Tribunal noted a serious procedural irregularity, namely, that one of the applicant's supervisors had failed to evaluate her. Consequently, the Tribunal considered the report to be an incomplete document which had undeniably exercised a determining influence on the whole of the subsequent procedure, including the decision of the Director-General of ILO, and quashed the termination decision. The Tribunal further said that the time-limits for the submission of reports evaluating the probationer, as stated in the Staff Regulations, were conceived with a view to enabling the probationer to be informed of the contents of such reports on time and eventually to defend himself against criticism *before* the administration's decision to terminate his appointment was made. However, if a report were favourable to the applicant, then the disregard of the time-limit was not prejudicial to the probationer. The Tribunal found in the case that the second report was three months late and covered only two months of the six months' extended probation and that this was irregular.[97]

In *Johnson*,[98] in which there was no periodic report covering the

---

[95] Ibid., No. 440.
[96] Ibid., No. 10.
[97] See also *Adler*, UNAT Judgment No. 267, for a similar UNAT decision.
[98] Ibid., No. 218.

applicant's probationary period after her transfer, UNAT pointed out, among other irregularities, that the Appointment and Promotion Board had relied on an incomplete document in evaluating her performance. Similarly, in *Lane*[99] UNAT said that Mr. Lane, whose appointment had been terminated long after the expiry of his extended probation, had been denied due process on the grounds that the Appointment and Promotion Board had made its recommendation to the Secretary-General without examining his performance during the last twenty-two months of his probation. In fact, no periodic report had been prepared for that period. Consequently, the decision had been taken on the basis of incomplete information. This was a violation of Mr. Lane's right to due process.

In *Buranavanichkit*[100] WBAT held that the fact that the evaluation report did not include, as required by the personnel manual statement, the comments of two of the supervisors who had worked with the applicant for eleven and seven months respectively constituted a culpable procedural irregularity.

The CJEC has also had to address the issue of periodic reports. In *Luhleich*[101] the applicant's probation report was drawn up after a delay of one year. The Court declared that this delay constituted a procedural irregularity, inasmuch as it emerged from the evidence that a report prepared on time would have been favourable to the applicant. On the other hand, in *Prakash*[102] the Court held that the delay in the preparation of the probationer's report, although an irregularity *per se*, was not a vitiating element because his superior had intentionally delayed the drawing up of the report in order to give him a second chance. Therefore, a report prepared on time would not have been more favourable to Mr. Prakash. Similarly, in *di Pillo*[103] where the probation report had been drawn up after a delay of three months in violation of Article 34 of the Staff Regulations in force in 1971 (according to which the probationary report should be drawn up, at the latest, one month before the expiry of the probationary period), the Court held that the delay was an irregularity but was not of such a nature as to invalidate the decision not to confirm the probationer. In *Luhleich*[104] the Court found that two important sources of information had not been made available through the appraisal report to the Establishment Board (the review body). The first was the testimony of one of the applicant's supervisors and the second was the report prepared by the Consolo Committee which had made an investigation into the working conditions in the applicant's department. The Court held that the appraisal report was an incomplete document because it was based upon inaccurate or incomplete facts.

In *Eskenasy*[105] where OASAT had to decide whether a memorandum

[99] UNAT Judgment No. 198.   [100] WBAT Judgment No. 7.
[101] CJEC Case 68/63 (1965).   [102] CJEC Case 19 and 65/63 (1965).
[103] CJEC Case 10 and 47/72 (1973).   [104] CJEC Case 68/63 (1965).
[105] OASAT Judgment No. 40.

could formally be considered as an appraisal report, the Tribunal held that this memorandum addressed by the applicant's supervisor to the Personnel Department and merely stating that the applicant's performance was unsatisfactory and that therefore he should not be confirmed did not constitute an evaluation of performance in accordance with Staff Rule 104.5 (h) (see Annex 5). The Tribunal declared that this procedural irregularity was serious enough to entail the annulment of the termination decision and the reinstatement of the probationer.

From the decisions examined above it appears that the omission to cover in a report even a part of the probationary period always constitutes a serious procedural irregularity. However, the disregard of time-limits concerning appraisal reports may or may not constitute a serious procedural irregularity depending upon the circumstances. Also it is necessary that the comments of all the required supervisors should be included in these reports.

2. *Competence*

The staff rules and regulations of international organizations seldom specify the official who is competent to prepare the appraisal report. However, in *Sternfield*[106] ILOAT stated that in international organizations the appraisal report should normally be drawn up by the immediate supervisor of the staff member. In the same decision the Tribunal made an exception to this principle where the unit by its nature excluded a hierarchical line organization. This was the case of the Division of Public Information to which Mr. Sternfield was assigned. The Tribunal stated that, in this case, the Director himself had authority to draw up Mr. Sternfield's appraisal report instead of the Assistant Director, Mr. Sternfield's immediate supervisor.

In *De Bruyn*[107] the defendant contended that the (favourable) report drawn up by the Director of the Department did not constitute the appraisal report, and that the real report could only be made by the Secretary-General, and that since the Secretary-General could not address a report to himself, the termination decision taken by the Secretary-General was the probationary report. The Court replied that the report should have been made by the Director of the Department (the supervisor). Consequently, the report submitted by the Director of the Department constituted the probationary report. In *D'Auria*,[108] the applicant contended that the probationary report was vitiated by lack of competence. The CJEC replied that the staff regulations did not specify who the 'assessor' should be. However, the head of the medical service was more qualified to assess the abilities of the applicant than the Director of Personnel. Therefore, since the former had prepared the report, the Court refused to hold that there was an irregularity.

[106] ILOAT Judgment No. 197.   [107] CJEC Case 25/61 (1962).
[108] CJEC Case 99/77 (1978).

In *Adler*[109] UNAT found that, among other procedural irregularities, the periodic reports were signed by unauthorized officers in violation of administrative practices. This was a deficiency for which compensation was payable.

3. *Review body*

UNAT in its interpretation of Staff Rules 104.12, 104.13, 104.14 and Staff Regulation 9.1 (c) (see Annex 1) recognized that probationers whose employment was terminated at the end of the probationary period had some rights which were denied to those whose employment was terminated during probation. For example, as already pointed out, when a probationer's appointment is terminated at the end of the probation period, the administration must refer the case to a review body, i.e. the Appointment and Promotion Board. Where the review body examines the suitability of the probationer and follows the appropriate procedure, the rights of due process of the probationer are respected: *de Ungria*.[110] In *Peynado*,[111] however, the Tribunal held that the mere review of Mr. Peynado's appointment by the Appointment and Promotion Board did not mean that the procedure followed in terminating his appointment was necessarily valid. The Board had relied on a periodic report in regard to which the applicable procedure had not been followed. Hence, its recommendation was tainted, as was the subsequent decision of the Secretary-General to terminate Mr. Peynado's appointment. In *Cooperman*[112] UNAT held that a probationer whose employment had been terminated in the interests of the organization during his probationary period, i.e. under Staff Regulation 9.1 (c) (see Annex 1), was not entitled to have his suitability reviewed by the special review body provided for in Staff Rule 104.14 (see Annex 1).

4. *Rebuttal of the periodic report*

The right to rebut the appraisal report is an important element of the right to due process. In *Peynado*,[113] as already pointed out, UNAT held that the review of Mr. Peynado's appointment by the Appointment and Promotion Board did not constitute a guarantee that the procedure followed in terminating his appointment was valid. The Tribunal held that Mr. Peynado's right had been infringed because the Appointment and Promotion Board had based its recommendation to the Secretary-General on an incomplete document. The document was incomplete because Mr. Peynado's rebuttal of the third period report had not been duly investigated nor had the head of the department, in accordance with Administrative Instruction ST/AI/115, paragraph 13 (see Annex 1), recorded an appraisal in writing of this rebuttal. The Tribunal awarded

---

[109] UNAT Judgment No. 267.   [110] Ibid., No. 71.
[111] Ibid., No. 138.   [112] Ibid., No. 93.
[113] Ibid., No. 138. See also *Johnson*, ibid., No. 213.

compensation for procedural defects. In *Buranavanichkit*[114] WBAT found that reliance was placed in terminating a probationary appointment on problems relating to the applicant's employment by the Bank on a previous occasion. This information was not communicated to nor was available to the applicant. The Tribunal held that reliance on it was irregular and contrary to the principle of due process, since she did not have an opportunity to answer it. The same principle was affirmed by ILOAT in *Kissaun*.[115] In that case the Tribunal stated that the right to be heard existed even in the absence of special provisions in the staff rules and regulations of the organization. In *Vrancheva*[116] the applicant had requested an explanation of certain remarks on her performance before she defended herself. The request had gone unheeded. The Director-General's decision to terminate her employment had, thus, been made on insufficient grounds, because a proper right of rebuttal had been denied. Hence, that decision was quashed by ILOAT.[117]

It is sufficient that the probationer was given the opportunity to explain his case either orally or in writing,[118] though there is no obligation to hear him personally.[119]

The administration is under no obligation to give the probationer a chance to make a second rebuttal.[120]

5. *Warnings*

In *Crapon de Caprona*[121] and *Heyes*[122] ILOAT stated that the decision to terminate a probationer's appointment could not be taken without previously giving him a warning and an opportunity to correct himself. However, in *Heyes* ILOAT also held that such termination may be possible in a very exceptional case and it considered that the case of Mr. Heyes could be classified as an exceptional one. Mr. Heyes's faults were of manner, and given his age (in his 30s), it was very unlikely that he could correct them. Consequently, the Tribunal endorsed the opinion of the applicant's supervisor who believed that Mr. Heyes's shortcomings were not curable.

6. *Statement of reasons*

In *Vrancheva*[123] ILOAT stated that the omission to inform Dr. Vrancheva in advance of the exact reasons for her termination was an irregularity and an infringement of her rights, justifying the quashing of the termination decision. Similarly, in *De Bruyn*[124] where Ms. de Bruyn

---

[114] WBAT Decision No. 7.
[115] ILOAT Judgment No. 69.
[116] Ibid., No. 194.
[117] See also *Molina*, ibid., No. 440.
[118] See *Milous*, ibid., No. 42, and *Terrain*, ibid., No. 109.
[119] See *Sternfield*, ibid., No. 107, and *Prakash*, CJEC Case 19 and 65/63 (1965).
[120] *di Pillo*, CJEC Case 10 and 47/72 (1973).
[121] ILOAT Judgment No. 112.
[122] Ibid., No. 453.
[123] Ibid., No. 194.
[124] CJEC Case 25/60 (1962).

had been dismissed without a statement of reasons the CJEC held that the decision was invalid and awarded her compensation.

In *Kersaudy*[125] ILOAT found that, though what had happened before the case went to the Appeals Committee was not clear, Mr. Kersaudy was informed of the grounds of his termination before the Appeals Committee and was, therefore, given the opportunity to present his comments. This was held to be a sufficient statement of reasons. It appears, thus, that the infringement of the probationer's right to due process in this regard prior to the termination decision can be rectified during the proceedings before an appellate body.

7. *Notification of decisions*

The probationer must be notified in good time of the decision terminating a probationary appointment and of decisions extending the period of probation. In *Loomba*[126] ILOAT found that the omission of the administration explicitly to inform the applicant of the two successive extensions of his probation constituted a procedural irregularity.

The time-limit for notification of the termination decision is a matter that has been dealt with only by the CJEC. The Court noted that Article 34 of the Staff Regulations (see Annex 4) of the EEC did not provide for a time-limit. However, the Court endeavoured to define what would constitute a reasonable period of time between the date of the drawing up of the probation report and of the notification to the probationer of the initial decision to terminate, on the one hand, and the final decision to terminate on the other. In *Nagels*[127] sixteen days were considered to be a reasonable period of time; in *di Pillo*[128] seven weeks were considered to be a reasonable period; in *de Roy*[129] six days were considered to be a reasonable period; and in *D'Auria*[130] eight weeks were considered to be a reasonable period of time.

(b) *Matters Substantive to the Decision to Terminate*

Judicial control over the content and motives of administrative decisions terminating probationary appointments is generally very limited. Tribunals recognize the wide discretion of the administrative authority in this regard and have been very cautious in interfering with the actions of the administration. Tribunals have intervened where there is some evidence that discretionary power was exercised for reasons extraneous to the interests of the service, that there was an error in regard to the facts on which the decision was based, that clearly wrong conclusions were drawn from the facts, or that essential facts were not taken into consideration.

In *Chiacchia*[131] and *Adler*[132] UNAT stated that it would intervene

---

[125] ILOAT Judgment No. 152.   [126] Ibid., No. 169.   [127] CJEC Case 52/70 (1971).
[128] CJEC Case 10 and 47/72 (1973).   [129] CJEC Case 92/75 (1976).
[130] CJEC Case 99/77 (1978).   [131] UNAT Judgment No. 90.   [132] Ibid., No. 267.

only if the decision was based on erroneous information or was motivated by prejudice. In *Sternfield*,[133] *Joyet*[134] and *Crapon de Caprona*[135] ILOAT defined its power of review by limiting it to verifying whether:

(*a*) the decision of the administrative authority was tainted with illegality;

(*b*) the decision was based on incorrect facts;

(*c*) the administrative authority had failed to take account of essential facts; or

(*d*) the administrative authority had drawn from the evidence conclusions that were 'clearly false' or 'manifestly unfounded'.

The cases show that Tribunals very seldom openly find administrative decisions tainted with prejudice or improper motives. Frequently an irregularity as to the substance of the decision was coupled with some procedural irregularities and Tribunals almost always preferred to quash decisions on the ground of procedural irregularity.[136] In *McIntire*,[137] however, ILOAT could have quashed the decision for procedural irregularity (substitution of grounds) but preferred to base its decision on prejudice or misuse of power.

1. *Prejudice as a misuse of power*

Only two decisions have been found to have been decided clearly on the basis of improper motives as a misuse of power. In *McIntire*[138] ILOAT held that the administrative authority committed a misuse of power because the termination decision was not based on the applicant's unsatisfactory services but on personal considerations which had nothing to do with his performance. There was flagrant evidence that the termination decision was due to an extraneous factor, since Mr. McIntire one week prior to his termination had received the title of Chief of Section. The extraneous factor was identified to be a letter sent to the organization by the United States Government concerning Mr. McIntire. In *Ghaffar*[139] the same tribunal examined in great detail a decision not to confirm a probationary appointment. The Tribunal concluded that the decision of the Director-General of WHO was vitiated either because he drew wrong conclusions from the appraisal reports or because he relied exclusively on the opinion of the applicant's supervisor whose judgment was unreliable and volatile and could not be regarded as unbiased. The decision was quashed and the applicant reinstated.

In *De Bruyn*,[140] in which the decision to terminate the applicant's employment failed to specify any reason for the termination, the CJEC held that the decision was based on grounds not valid in law and was in open

---

[133] ILOAT Judgment No. 197.   [134] Ibid., No. 318.   [135] Ibid., No. 112.
[136] See *Johnson*, UNAT Judgment No. 213, *Vrancheva*, ILOAT Judgment No. 194, *Mirossevich*, CJEC Case 10/55 (1954–6), and *Luhleich*, CJEC Case 68/63 (1965).
[137] ILOAT Judgment No. 13.   [138] Ibid.   [139] Ibid., No. 320.   [140] CJEC Case 25/60 (1962).

contradiction to a positive appraisal report drawn up by the applicant's supervisor. The Court awarded the applicant compensation for non-material damage. This also appears to be a case in which the decision was based on improper motive.

In the majority of cases, tribunals have on the facts rejected the allegations of misuse of power based on improper motive. In *Chiacchia*,[141] for instance, the Appeals Board of the UN had found elements of *a priori* unfavourable attitudes toward the appellant on the part of her supervisors. However, the Appeals Board did not find sufficient evidence of prejudice but recommended to the Secretary-General that he consider giving the appellant a second chance. The Secretary-General did not change his decision. UNAT held that the applicant had failed to establish improper motive and rejected her application. In *Schawalder-Vrancheva*[142] the applicant contended that the non-confirmation of her probationary appointment was motivated by the animosity of her supervisor. ILOAT held that the supervisor's animosity toward the applicant was obvious but that the Director-General of WHO who took the final decision had not based his decision on the supervisor's criticism of the applicant. On the contrary, he had taken his decision after a thorough investigation of the facts, after consultation with several officials and taking into consideration the efficient running of the organization. Hence, the non-confirmation was held valid. In *Molina*[143] the applicant contended that the termination decision was taken for reasons not connected with his performance and based on the prejudice of his supervisor. ILOAT, however, held that the decision was not tainted with prejudice, that the Director-General of WHO did not draw wrong conclusions from the evidence submitted and that he took into consideration Mr. Molina's difficult working relations not only with his supervisor but also with other colleagues. None the less, ILOAT found the appraisal report written by the supervisor to be tainted with prejudice and ordered that the said report be annulled and removed from the files of the organization. This is a difficult decision, to say the least.[144]

2. *Wrong conclusions*

Though tribunals have admitted that the drawing of conclusions which are clearly false and manifestly unfounded from the facts is a ground for review,[145] no case has apparently held that a termination decision has been vitiated by such a fault. In *Crapon de Caprona*[146] ILOAT reviewed the applicant's translations and found that some of the corrections were 'debatable' and 'possibly unjustified' but most of them were pertinent.

[141] UNAT Judgment No. 90.   [142] ILOAT Judgment No. 226.   [143] Ibid., No. 440.
[144] For other decisions where no improper motive was found, see *Kraicsovits*, ibid., No. 140, *Kersaudy*, ibid., No. 152, *Mirossevich*, CJEC Case 10/55 (1954-6), *Prakash*, CJEC Case 19 and 65/63 (1965), *D'Auria*, CJEC Case 99/77 (1978).
[145] See, e.g., *Crapon de Caprona*, ILOAT Judgment No. 112, and *Sternfield*, ibid., No. 197.
[146] Ibid., No. 112.

The Tribunal also held that Mr. Caprona's linguistic skills were beyond doubt, but that it was not unreasonable to consider his work as unsatisfactory and that, therefore, the conclusions drawn by the Director-General of WHO were not manifestly unfounded. In *Kersaudy*,[147] the same tribunal, after examining Mr. Kersaudy's translations, held that although there were some doubts about the importance of the criticisms made of his work, the Director-General of WHO did not draw conclusions clearly contrary to the evidence in the dossier.[148]

3. *Error of fact*

Error of fact is a ground for review. This is where the evidence does not support a fact or facts on which a relevant conclusion is based. In two very similar decisions in which the applicants complained of error of fact the CJEC reached opposite conclusions. In *Luhleich*[149] the Court held that the most important criticisms made of the applicant were based on inaccurate or incomplete facts. The Court reached its conclusion after a thorough examination of the facts, and after considering the harsh attitude of the applicant's superior as well as the many organizational difficulties prevailing at that time in the ISPRA Center. The Court said that neither the finding that the applicant's conduct was inappropriate nor the finding that he had failed to adjust to the necessities of the service was well founded. In *Prakash*[150] the applicant contended that the decision to terminate was based on erroneous facts. The issue for the CJEC was whether the defendant's findings that Mr. Prakash had a tendency towards excess in preparing programmes and in calculating resources was accurate. The Court held that it could not substitute its own assessment of the applicant's contribution for that of the defendant, nor could it decide whether or not a particular apparatus was sufficient for undertaking a given piece of research. Nevertheless, the Court held itself competent to carry out a thorough examination of the facts leading to the defendant's finding. The Court mainly relied upon the testimony of the Director who basically confirmed the accusation of the first-in-line supervisor. The testimony of the Director was deemed acceptable to the Court, although the latter was not familiar with the applicant's work, because the Director was perfectly aware of the harsh attitude of the first-in-line supervisor towards his subordinates. Furthermore, the Court relied upon the information supplied by the applicant's former employer confirming some of the applicant's shortcomings. Finally, the Court held that the witnesses heard did not corroborate the applicant's allegation, nor was the applicant able to prove that he did not have enough resources and sufficient apparatus for the short-term project. Consequently, the Court held that the applicant did have a propensity toward excess and that there could be

---

[147] Ibid., No. 152.
[149] CJEC Case 68/63 (1963).

[148] See also *Sternfield*, ibid., No. 197.
[150] CJEC Case 19 and 65/63 (1965).

no serious doubts about the accuracy of the facts leading to the defendant's finding.

4. *Standards of judgment*

Tribunals will not substitute their own standards of judgment for those of the administration. Standards, unlike the establishment of facts, are solely within the discretion of the administrative authority. Thus in *Prakash*[151] the CJEC stated that in regard to performance the applicant might have been judged rather strictly. However, the Court said that should it describe that strictness as illegal it would be violating the rule of separation of the judicial and administrative powers. It was the administrative authority that had exclusive jurisdiction to decide upon the degree of severity chosen in assessing its employees.

IX. REMEDIES

It has been seen that in probation cases the discretionary power of the administration is wide and that judicial control is fairly limited. In regard to remedies, however, Tribunals have retained the right to choose among the different remedies available to them. In doing so Tribunals have not restricted themselves necessarily to the remedies referred to in their constitutive statutes but have resorted to their inherent powers in this regard. When Tribunals evaluate the amount of compensation, they seem to take into consideration the kind of appointment for which the probationer was hired. Thus the distinction between a fixed term and a permanent appointment has become relevant.[152] Also, Tribunals have addressed the issue of awarding compensation irrespective of whether the termination decision itself was illegal and was required to be quashed.

Tribunals have delineated several options in regard to the selection of the most adequate remedy. They may decide (i) to quash the decision and order reinstatement; (ii) to leave the choice between reinstatement and compensation to the administration; (iii) if the decision is tainted with some procedural irregularities, which, if corrected, would, however, not have a material bearing upon the probationer's rights because the substance of the decision would remain unchanged, to award compensation for the damage suffered; (iv) if the decision is found invalid but is not annulled either because the applicant does not request reinstatement or because reinstatement is not possible, as substantial changes have meanwhile taken place in the organization, to award compensation for procedural irregularities; (v) to remand the case; or (vi) although the decision is valid, to award compensation for irregularities or order specific performance in some respects.

[151] CJEC Case 19 and 65/63 (1965).
[152] See *Kissaun*, ILOAT Judgment No. 69; *Johnson*, UNAT Judgment No. 213; and *Loomba*, ILOAT Judgment No. 169.

(a) *The Termination Decision is Quashed and Reinstatement is Ordered by the Tribunal with or without Damages*

In *Marsh*,[153] ILOAT annulled the termination decision because it was based on incomplete information (the report was considered to be an incomplete document) and the Director-General of ILO relied upon it when he took the termination decision. ILOAT ordered the reinstatement of the applicant as a probationer for a period of six months. The Tribunal also ordered the payment of costs. In *Ghaffar*,[154] the same Tribunal quashed the non-confirmation decision and declared that Mr. Ghaffar should be retroactively reinstated because of (a) his eleven years of loyal service with the WHO; (b) his exemplary conduct under difficult circumstances; and (c) the moderation of his submission to the Tribunal. Furthermore, the Tribunal ordered that Mr. Ghaffar be paid fair compensation from the date of his dismissal until his reinstatement, taking into consideration any other revenues that he might have earned. The Tribunal on its own motion awarded $1,000 to the applicant as costs. In *Mirossevich*,[155] the CJEC annulled a termination decision on the grounds that the probation was not properly conducted and ordered the reinstatement of the applicant who was to enter on a new probationary period of six months according to the new staff regulations in force. However, the applicant's claim for compensation was rejected on the grounds that the outcome of the probation would have been uncertain, even if the probation had been conducted properly. In addition, Ms. Mirossevich's claim for non-material damages was rejected on the grounds that she was offered a new post with possibilities of promotion and this offer was similar to compensation. She was also awarded four-fifths of her costs.

(b) *The Termination Decision is Annulled, but the Administration is left with the Choice of either Reinstating or Paying Compensation to the Probationer*

In *McIntire*,[156] ILOAT rescinded the termination decision. However, the administration was given the choice of either reinstating the applicant or paying him (i) compensation equal to fifteen months' salary with interest at 4 per cent from the date at which the probationary period should normally have ended and until the actual payment of the claim; (ii) $3,000 for the material and moral damage he suffered from the date of the termination of his appointment to the date of the judgment; and (iii) $300 as costs. In *Kissaun*,[157] ILOAT quashed the termination decision and invited the administration to reopen the case and consider whether Mr. Kissaun should be reinstated. The Tribunal accepted the notion that the dismissal could incapacitate the staff member for a certain period of time.

---

[153] Ibid., No. 10.
[155] CJEC Case 10/55 (1954–6).
[156] ILOAT Judgment No. 13.
[154] Ibid., No. 320.
[157] Ibid., No. 69.

However, the amount of compensation which the applicant could claim, whether he was reinstated or not, was limited to the prejudice actually suffered and in time to the period from the date of the contested decision until the normal expiration date of his fixed-term contract. In *Eskenasy*,[158] OASAT found that the termination decision was invalid and ordered the retroactive reinstatement of Mr. Eskenasy and the reopening of the case. However, in accordance with paragraph 2 of Article VII of the Statute of the Tribunal, the Tribunal fixed compensation in the amount of one year's basic salary should the administration decide not to reinstate Mr. Eskenasy. He was also awarded $1,800 as legal costs.

(c) *The Decision is Tainted with some Procedural Irregularities which, if Corrected, will not have a Material Bearing on the Substance of the Decision and the Tribunal Awards Compensation for the Damage Suffered because of the Procedural Irregularities*

In *Peynado*,[159] UNAT found that the periodic report was an incomplete document. The respondent did not request the remand of the case for correction of procedure and UNAT awarded Mr. Peynado compensation in lieu of specific performance for the injury caused by the procedural defects in the amount of three months' net base salary. The same Tribunal in *Lane*[160] awarded the applicant compensation for 'fault of procedure' in the amount of six months' net base salary because, even if the procedural irregularities (no appraisal report was drawn up for the last twenty-two months of the irregularly extended probation) had been corrected, he would still not have been confirmed because his unsuitability for permanent employment had been evidenced in the appraisal report covering the first three years of his probation. Similarly, in *Adler*,[161] UNAT held that the compensation in the amount of six months' net base salary, as recommended by the Joint Appeals Board and ultimately awarded by the Secretary-General to Mr. Adler, was adequate to compensate him for the infringement of his right to due process.

In *Loomba*,[162] the applicant had not been officially notified of the two successive extensions of his probation and ILOAT confirmed that the compensation recommended by the Appeals Committee and granted by the Director-General was more than adequate to compensate Mr. Loomba for the damage suffered because he was kept in a state of uncertainty. He was compensated as if his appointment had been confirmed and then terminated. The amount of the compensation was six months' salary. The applicant was the holder of a one-year fixed-term contract with a six-month probation period.

In *di Pillo*,[163] where the dismissal decision was found lawful, the CJEC

---

[158] ILOAT Judgment No. 40.
[160] Ibid., No. 198.
[162] ILOAT Judgment No. 169

[159] UNAT Judgment No. 138.
[161] Ibid., No. 267.
[163] CJEC Case 10 and 47/72 (1973).

awarded Mr. di Pillo compensation for the procedural irregularity which resulted from the lateness in the drawing up of the probation report. The report required at the end of probation was due, at the latest, on 31 July 1971. However, the report was made and communicated to Mr. di Pillo only on 4 November 1971. The Court noted that Mr. di Pillo suffered damage, because after the expiry of his probation he was kept in a state of uncertainty as to his future in general, and fixed the amount of compensation at 200,000 Belgian francs, taking into consideration the post he had occupied.

In *Buranavanichkit*,[164] WBAT found that certain procedural and substantive irregularities had taken place but that rescission of the contested decision or specific performance was not an appropriate remedy in the circumstances. It awarded a sum equivalent to one-year's net base salary as compensation for the damage done and $1,250 as costs.

There are some other cases in which the same principle has been discussed and confirmed, although damages have not been awarded.[165]

(d) *Compensation is Awarded in Lieu of Specific Performance since, though the Termination Decision is Found Invalid, it is not Annulled either because the Applicant does not want Reinstatement or the Reinstatement is not Possible, as Considerable Changes have taken place in the Organization*

In *Johnson*,[166] UNAT found the termination decision invalid as a result of several procedural irregularities, and that Ms. Johnson had been deprived of permanent appointment by the fault of the respondent. However, because of the considerable structural changes which had taken place in the department to which the applicant had been assigned, it was impossible to require a new evaluation of the applicant's suitability. Consequently, the Tribunal awarded Ms. Johnson compensation in lieu of specific performance. The Tribunal noted that the applicant could have expected to remain in service until superannuation, i.e. till September 1983, seven years from the date of the judgment. Therefore, Ms. Johnson was awarded the maximum, namely the equivalent of two years' net base salary. She was also awarded $800 as costs.

In *De Bruyn*,[167] the applicant claimed only damages for breach of contract. The CJEC found the termination decision to be illegal and awarded the applicant damages of 40,000 Belgian francs for the non-material damage caused to her. In *Luhleich*,[168] the CJEC stated that, since the applicant did not seek reinstatement, there was no reason to examine whether to annul the decision and refer the matter back to the defendant. The Court found that the non-confirmation decision was illegal.

---

[164] WBAT Decision No. 7.
[165] See *Prakash*, CJEC Case 19 and 65/63 (1965), and *Guisset*, ILOAT Judgment No. 396.
[166] UNAT Judgment No. 213.
[167] CJEC Case 25/60 (1962).
[168] CJEC Case 68/63 (1965).

It awarded the applicant damages equivalent to nine times the monthly net emoluments received by him at the moment when the dismissal took effect. He was also awarded costs.

(e) *The Termination Decision is Found Unlawful and the Case is Remanded*

In *Vrancheva*,[169] the non-confirmation decision was quashed and the respondent was invited to reopen the case, investigate the facts, hear the applicant and decide if her probation could be terminated under WHO Staff Rule 960 (see Annex 3). ILOAT deferred the ruling on the request for compensation and costs. In the follow-up case,[170] after the remand, the termination of the probationary appointment was found lawful. Consequently, the applicant's request for compensation was rejected. However, the Tribunal awarded the applicant $3,000 as costs because the irregularities committed by the respondent gave rise to her application.

(f) *The Termination Decision is Found Lawful; none the less, the Tribunal Awards Compensation or Orders Specific Performance in some Respects*

In *Molina*,[171] the non-confirmation of the applicant was found lawful and consequently he was denied reinstatement and compensation. However, ILOAT ordered that the appraisal report written by the first-in-line supervisor be annulled and removed from the files of the organization because it was tainted with prejudice. In *Nagels*[172] the application was dismissed as unfounded. The CJEC, however, awarded Mr. Nagels one-half of his costs on the ground that the misunderstanding about the nature of his duties, which occurred at the time of his recruitment, gave rise to the proceedings.

X. CONCLUSION

The above analysis of the cases on probationary appointments reveals some interesting features of the practice of international administrative tribunals. Tribunals have accepted the fact that, in probation cases, the discretionary power of the organization is involved, but at the same time have not failed to recognize that the exercise of the discretion is not unfettered. Even in probation cases, discretion must not be exercised arbitrarily.

In controlling the exercise of discretion in this area, tribunals have primarily applied the written internal law of international organizations, to wit, charters, articles of agreement, resolutions, by-laws, regulations, rules and the like, but they have also gone further than this. First, they have often interpreted the written internal law where it is less than explicit by calling in aid functional principles and the criterion of reasonableness.

---

[169] ILOAT Judgment No. 194.   [170] Ibid., No. 226.
[171] Ibid., No. 440.   [172] CJEC Case No. 52/70 (1971).

Thus, in the case of the distinction made between non-confirmation in the interests of the organization and for unsatisfactory service, tribunals have clearly interpreted the written law so as to make sense of it and so as to implement the objective supposedly underlying the existence of the distinction. Secondly, the written law may also be interpreted in the light of general principles of law.

Tribunals have done more. They have had recourse to general principles of law and the practice of organizations where the written law is silent. As is generally known, these are also sources of the internal law of international organizations. The law that has evolved, for instance, in the area relating to procedural safeguards in cases involving the non-confirmation of probationary appointments, has been derived almost entirely from general principles of law. The general features of probation discussed in the earlier part of this article also show that tribunals are prepared to base their decisions on deductions inherent in the generalized concept of probation. Practice has been addressed less often but has also been relevant.

In the field of remedies, it has been found that tribunals appear even to have called in aid notions of equity. The practice of awarding compensation where reinstatement is not ordered or where the termination decision is lawful, even though the statute of the tribunal or the written law of the organization does not explicitly permit this, would seem to be traceable to this source.

In conclusion, it may be said that in the area examined, as in other areas, administrative tribunals have adopted an imaginative approach to their functions. They have played a creative role in the development of international administrative law both in the application of general principles of law and equity and in interpreting the written internal law of international organizations.

ANNEX 1

UNITED NATIONS
STAFF REGULATIONS AND RULES

1.   *Article IX*

Separation from Service

Regulation 9.1 (c)

In the case of all other staff members, including staff members serving a probationary period for a permanent appointment, the Secretary-General may at any time terminate the appointment, if, in his opinion, such action would be in the interest of the United Nations.

2.   *UN Staff Rule 104.12*

Temporary Appointments

(a) Probationary appointment

The probationary appointment may be granted to persons under the age of 50 years who are recruited for career service. The period of probationary service under such an appointment shall normally be two years. In exceptional circumstances, it may be reduced or extended for not more than one additional year.

At the end of the probationary service the holder of a probationary appointment shall be granted either a permanent or a regular appointment or be separated from the service.

The probationary appointment shall have no specific expiration date and shall be governed by the Staff Regulations and Staff Rules applicable to temporary appointments which are not for a fixed term.

3.   *UN Staff Rule 104.13*

Permanent and Regular Appointments

(a) Permanent appointment

   (i) The permanent appointment may be granted to staff members who are holders of a probationary appointment and who, by their qualifications, performance and conduct, have fully demonstrated their suitability as international civil servants and have shown that they meet the high standards of efficiency, competence and integrity established in the Charter.

(c) (i) Recommendations proposing the grant of permanent or regular appointments on the ground that a holder of a probationary appointment has met the requirements of this rule may be made to the Secretary-General by agreement between the Office of Personnel Services and the Department or Office concerned. Such agreements shall be reported to the Appointment and Promotion Board before submission to the Secretary-General.

  (iii) In the absence of an agreed favourable recommendation as provided in (c) (i) or (ii) above, the matter shall be referred to the Appointment and Promotion Board.

4.   *UN Staff Rule 104.14*

Appointment and Promotion Board

(f) Functions of the Appointment and Promotion Board

The function of the Appointment and Promotion Board shall be to make recommendations to the Secretary-General in respect of the following:

(i) Appointment

Proposed probationary appointments and other proposed appointments of a probable duration of one year or more, excluding the appointment of persons recruited specifically for service with a mission.

(ii) Review

(A) The suitability for permanent or regular appointment of staff members serving on probationary appointments, as may be referred to it in accordance with the provisions of rule 104.13 (c). Recommendations of the Board may include extension of the probationary period for one additional year or separation from the service.

5.   *Administrative Instruction ST/AI/115, para. 13*

If the staff member so desires, he may make a written statement in explanation or rebuttal of part or all of any report, which statement shall be joined to the report to which it refers. Where a staff member makes such a statement, the Head of the Department will investigate the case and will record his appraisal of it in writing. This record will be filed together with the report and the staff member's statement.

6.   *Article IV*

Appointment and Promotion

Regulation 4.5:

(b) The Secretary-General shall prescribe which staff members are eligible for permanent appointments. The probationary period for granting or confirming a permanent appointment shall normally not exceed two years, provided that in individual cases the Secretary-General may extend the probationary period for not more than one additional year.

ANNEX 2

FOOD AND AGRICULTURE ORGANIZATION (FAO)

STAFF REGULATIONS

(as of July 1979)

Article IX

301.09   Separation from service

301.091   The Director-General may terminate the appointment of a staff member who holds a continuing appointment (i) if the necessities of the service require abolition of the post or reduction of staff, or (ii) whose services prove unsatisfactory, or who is, for reasons of health, incapacitated for further service.

301.0912   The Director-General may terminate the appointment of a staff member with a fixed-term appointment prior to the expiration date for any of the reasons specified in Staff Regulation 301.091, or for such other reasons as may be specified in the letter of appointment.

301.0913   In the case of staff members serving a probationary period or holding any other type of appointment not referred to in Staff Regulations 301.091 and 301.0912, the Director-General may at any time terminate the appointment, on finding that such action would be in the interests of the Organization.

301.0913 (as of May 1970)

> In the case of all other staff members, including staff members serving a probationary period for a permanent appointment, the Director-General may at any time terminate the appointment if, in his opinion, such action would be in the interests of the Organization.

ANNEX 3

WORLD HEALTH ORGANIZATION (WHO)

STAFF RULES

(as of January 1980)

420.4 (Previously numbered 320.4)

> Any appointment of one year or more shall be subject to a period of probation, which shall be at least one year and may be extended up to two years when necessary for adequate evaluation of the staff member's performance, conduct and suitability to international service.

530. (Previously numbered 430) *Supervision and Performance Evaluation*

530.1 (Previously numbered 430.1)

> Supervisors shall be responsible for facilitating the adjustment of a staff member to his work by:

> > 530.1.1 Providing him with a clear statement of his duties and his official relationship;

> > 530.1.2 instructing and guiding him in performing his functions;

> > 530.1.3 introducing him properly to those staff members with whom he will be required to work;

> > 530.1.4 discussing his work with him at frequent intervals.

530.2 (Previously numbered 430.2)

> For staff at D.2 level and below, in addition to the normal work review and discussion with a staff member, supervisors shall periodically make a formal evaluation of the performance, conduct, and potentialities for greater usefulness of each staff member under their supervision. This evaluation shall be made at such intervals as the work situation or the individual's performance requires but in no case less frequently than once a year. Supervisors shall discuss their conclusions with the staff member and make specific suggestions for improvement in any aspects of performance which are not entirely satisfactory. If a staff member exercises supervisory responsibilities, the evaluation shall include an assessment of his performance as a supervisor.

530.3 (Previously numbered 430.3)

> The functions and activities performed by the staff member during the preceding year shall be summarized by him and shall be evaluated by his supervisors on an established form, in relation to the actual duties and responsibilities of the post. The form shall be signed by the supervisors and the staff member concerned who may, if he so wishes, attach a statement concerning any part of the report with

which he disagrees and this shall become a part of his performance report file.

530.4 (Previously numbered 430.4)

The evaluation of performance as reflected in these reports shall be the basis for assisting the staff member to make his most effective contribution to the work of the Bureau and for decisions concerning the staff member's status and retention in the Bureau.

540. (Previously numbered 440) *End of Probation*

540.1 (Previously numbered 440.1)

A performance evaluation report (see Rule 530.2) shall be made before the end of the normal probationary period (see Rule 420.4). On the basis of this report a decision shall be taken, and notified to the staff member, that his:

540.1.1 appointment is confirmed;

540.1.2 probationary period is extended for a specified period;

540.1.3 appointment is not confirmed and is to be terminated.

540.2 (Previously numbered 440.2)

In the case of either 540.1.2 or 540.1.3, the staff member shall be notified of the reasons. If the probationary period is extended, a further report and decision are required before the expiry of this additional period.

1060. (Previously numbered 960) *Non-Confirmation of Appointment*

If, during an initial or extended probationary period, a staff member's performance or conduct is not satisfactory, or if he is found unsuited to international service, the appointment shall not be confirmed but terminated. The staff member shall be given one month's notice. No indemnity is payable.

1210 (Previously numbered 1110) *Non-Confirmation of Appointment*

1210.1 A staff member may appeal against a decision taken under Rule 1060 not to confirm his appointment because of unsatisfactory performance or conduct, or because of unsuitability for international service, if he considers that such decision has been made for reasons not connected with his performance, conduct or suitability for international service. Such an appeal must be made in writing to the Director within fifteen calendar days of receipt of notice of non-confirmation. The Director's decision shall be final and none of the other appeal procedures described in this section shall apply, except as provided in Rule 1240.

STAFF REGULATIONS

1.5 Staff members shall conduct themselves at all times in a manner compatible with their status as international civil servants. They shall avoid any action and in particular any kind of public pronouncement which may adversely reflect on their status. While they are not expected to give up their national sentiments or their political and religious convictions, they shall at all times bear in mind the reserve and tact incumbent upon them by reason of their international status.

1.6 Staff members shall exercise the utmost discretion in regard to all matters of official business. They shall not communicate to any person any information known to them by reason of their official position which has not been made public, except in the course of their duties or by authorization of the Director. At no time shall they in any way use to private advantage information known to them by reason of their official position. These obligations do not cease with separation from service.

1.10 All staff members shall subscribe to the following oath or declaration: 'I solemnly swear (undertake, affirm, promise) to exercise in all loyalty, discretion, and conscience the functions entrusted to me as an international civil servant of the Pan American Sanitary Bureau, to discharge those functions and regulate my conduct with the interests of the Pan American Sanitary Bureau only in view, and not to seek or accept instructions in regard to the performance of my duties from any government or other authority external to the Bureau or the World Health Organization.'

ANNEX 4

EUROPEAN COMMUNITIES

STAFF REGULATIONS

(as of July 1975)

Article 34 (8)

1. Officials other than those in Grades A 1 and A 2 shall serve a probationary period before they can be established. The period shall be nine months for officials in Category A, in the Language Service or in Category B, and six months for other officials.

2. Not less than one month before the expiry of the probationary period, a report shall be made on the ability of the probationer to perform the duties pertaining to his post and also on his efficiency and conduct in the service. This report shall be communicated to the person concerned, who shall have the right to submit his comments in writing. A probationer whose work has not proved adequate for establishment in his post shall be dismissed.

A report on the probationer may be made at any time during the probationary period if his work is proving obviously inadequate. The report shall be communicated to the person concerned, who shall have the right to submit his comments in writing. On the basis of the report the appointing authority may decide to dismiss the probationer before the end of the probationary period, giving him one month's notice; this period of service may not, however, exceed the normal probationary period.

Except where he is entitled forthwith to resume his duties with the civil service to which he belongs a dismissed probationer shall receive compensation equal to two months' basic salary if he has completed at least six months' service and to one month's basic salary if he has completed less than six months' service.

The provisions of this paragraph shall not apply to officials who resign before the end of their probationary period.

ANNEX 5

ORGANIZATION OF AMERICAN STATES
STAFF RULES

Rule 104.5 Appointment

(b) Temporary appointments may be probationary, fixed-term or short-term.

   (i) Anyone less than 50 years of age who has been selected by the Secretary General to occupy a permanent post in the General Secretariat, who is to enter the international career service, shall be appointed for a probationary period. This period shall be for 12 months and, in exceptional circumstances, may be extended, but in no case for more than an additional six months. If an extension be granted, the interested party shall be notified at least 30 days before the expiration of the normal probationary period. During this time the staff member shall enjoy all the benefits granted to permanent staff members.

  (ii) Fixed-term appointments are those made for the carrying out of specific programs or purposes; they shall have a duration of one year or more, but may not exceed five, and the date of their expiration must appear in the notification of appointment. A fixed-term appointment does not carry with it the right to renewal or conversion into some other type of appointment. Persons who receive fixed-term appointments shall be subject to a probationary period of six months, which may not be extended.

(g) The Secretary General may terminate the services of a staff member who has not completed the probationary period referred to in paragraph (b) (i) and (ii) of this rule when he considers that this is in the interest of the General Secretariat.

The staff member concerned must be notified of such a decision at least 30 days before the end of the normal probationary period or of its extension, as the case may be. If appropriate, the General Secretariat must pay .... expenses of the individual concerned, including expenses of transferring .... and household effects.

(h) If the Secretary General does exercise the authority provided for in the foregoing paragraph an evaluation will be made of the staff member's work performance, within the last month of the normal probationary period or of its extension, as applicable, and, according to the findings of that evaluation, he shall be given a permanent appointment, his position shall be confirmed (if a fixed-term appointment is concerned), or his services shall be terminated.

Rule 105.9 Work performance evaluation

(a) All supervisors in the General Secretariat shall make a periodic review and evaluation at least once a year, of the work performance of the staff members under their supervision. The purpose of this evaluation shall be to determine not only the efficiency with which the staff member has performed his duties, but also his actual and potential capacities. Besides the points mentioned, the report shall also contain any comments or observations that the supervisor and staff member may wish to have included.

(b) Supervisors shall meet privately with each staff member under their supervision and review all aspects of the work. When the evaluation report has been completed, the original shall be signed by both the supervisor and the staff member. The report shall be sent to the department or office director and to the appropriate Executive Secretary or Assistant Secretary, with a copy and any pertinent appendices, so that it may be reviewed and approved. It will then go to the Director of Personnel to be added to the staff member's personnel record.

(c) The official work performance evaluation must be made at least one month before any consideration of the staff member's annual within-grade salary increase.

(d) In carrying out its duty as coordinator of the program for evaluating the work performance of the staff the Office of Personnel shall do the following:

    (i) Prepare a form for the work performance evaluation and see that the supervisors comply strictly with their duty under this rule to make the evaluation at least once a year;

    (ii) Render any necessary technical assistance and advice to ensure the use of uniform evaluation standards;

    (iii) Maintain a file of all the work performance evaluation reports;

    (iv) Present an annual report to the Secretary General, summarizing the findings of the program for evaluating the work performance of the staff;

    (v) See that the provisions of paragraph (c) above are met.

(e) A staff member shall receive a copy of each evaluation made of his work performance and may request copies of any that are in the possession of the General Secretariat. He shall have access to all documents concerning him that are in the Office of Personnel and that are presented or used against him.

NOTES

PRIORITIES OF CLAIMS IN PRIVATE
INTERNATIONAL LAW*

By P. B. CARTER[1]

IT is now more than three years since the Privy Council delivered its divided opinion in *Bankers Trust International Ltd.* v. *Todd Shipyards Corporation*,[2] more conveniently and economically referred to as *The Halcyon Isle*. This is an important case concerned with a notoriously intractable type of private inter-national law problem, namely the problem of priority as between conflicting claims, upon which authoritative guidance was previously (and perhaps in significant measure still is) lacking; and it is a case in which two of the five members of the Judicial Committee were constrained to take the course—still relatively unusual in the Privy Council—of delivering a dissenting judgment. It is, however, a case which has provoked remarkably little comment in law journals. This may be indicative of a measure of prudence amongst reputable commentators with which the present writer is not endowed.

The facts of *The Halcyon Isle* were not complicated. Mortgagees, an English bank, held a mortgage dated 27 April 1973 on a British ship, *Halcyon Isle*. In March of the following year American ship-repairers carried out repairs to the ship in New York. Under United States law they were entitled to a maritime lien for the price of these repairs. The ship subsequently left New York. In August 1974 the mortgagees and the ship-repairer both commenced admiralty actions *in rem* against the ship in the High Court of Singapore. The following month the ship was arrested in Singapore in the mortgagees' action, and in March 1975 she was sold by order of the court. The proceeds of this sale were not sufficient to satisfy all the claims made by the owner's creditors. The New York ship-repairers then applied to the High Court for a declara-tion that they were entitled to a maritime lien for the price of the repairs. The English mortgagees applied for a determination of priority of payments from the proceeds of the sale. The Singapore High Court held that, as the ship-repairers were not entitled to a lien under the law of Singapore, the mortgagees' claim was entitled to priority over any such claim made by the ship-repairers. The Singapore Court of Appeal reversed this decision. The Privy Council (Lord Salmon and Lord Scarman dissenting) allowed the mortgagees' further appeal.

The Privy Council was, of course, dealing with the law of Singapore, but Lord Diplock, who delivered the judgment of the majority,[3] expressly pointed out that, as regards the issues involved, '. . . in matters of practice and procedure

---

* © P. B. Carter, 1984.
[1] Barrister and Honorary Bencher of the Middle Temple; Fellow of Wadham College, Oxford.
[2] [1981] A.C. 221; [1980] 3 All E.R. 197; [1980] 2 Lloyd's Rep. 325.
[3] Lord Diplock, Lord Elwyn-Jones and Lord Lane.

as well as the substantive law which it administers there is no relevant difference between the law of Singapore and the law of England'.[4]

The majority decision was summarized by Lord Diplock in the following words:

Their Lordships are accordingly of opinion that in principle, in accordance with long-established English authorities and consistently with international comity . . . the question whether or not in the instant case the necessaries men [i.e. the ship-repairers] are entitled to priority over the mortgagees in the proceeds of sale of the *Halcyon Isle* depends upon whether or not if the repairs to the ship had been done in Singapore the repairers would have been entitled under the law of Singapore to a maritime lien on the *Halcyon Isle* for the price of them. The answer to that question is that they are not. The mortgagees are entitled to priority.[5]

Lord Salmon and Lord Scarman, however, saw the matter rather differently. They said:

The question is—does English law, in circumstances such as these, recognise the maritime lien created by the law of the United States of America, i.e. the lex loci contractus where no such lien exists by its own internal law? In our view the balance of authorities, the comity of nations, private international law and natural justice all answer this question in the affirmative. If this be correct then English law (the lex fori) gives the maritime lien created by the lex loci contractus precedence over the mortgagees' mortgage. If it were otherwise, injustice would prevail.[6]

It will be seen that, although reaching opposing conclusions, the majority and the minority both apparently saw the issue falling to be determined as being, or at least as involving, an issue of priority or precedence, and as being, as such, an issue to be determined by reference to the *lex fori*.

It is the present writer's contention that the widely accepted and deceptively simple doctrine that normally questions of priority are to be regarded as procedural and are accordingly determinable by reference to the *lex fori* cannot be accepted at face value. Investigation of the validity and indeed the meaning of this doctrine must focus first upon precisely what is meant by a 'question of priority', and secondly upon what is involved in determination of such a question by reference to the law of the *forum*. The results of this investigation, in the present writer's view, may suggest that the judgment of the minority in *The Halcyon Isle* is to be preferred to that of the majority.

It would appear to be self-evident that no problem, that can usefully be described as being one of priority, can arise unless it has first been established that there are at least two valid but mutually inconsistent claims. Unfortunately in the past courts have sometimes failed to distinguish between a question as to the validity of a particular claim and a question of its priority (if valid) *vis-à-vis* another valid claim.[7] The validity of each claim must be determined by reference to the law which, in accordance with the rules of private international law

---

[4] [1981] A.C. 221, 229. See, too, the joint judgment of the dissentients at p. 242: 'The issue has arisen in Singapore but, so far as this appeal is concerned, the law of Singapore is substantially the same as the law of England.'

[5] Ibid. 241.

[6] Ibid. 246.

[7] An extreme example of this is provided by the statement of Bankes L.J. in *Republica de Guatemala* v. *Nunez*, [1927] 1 K.B. 669, at p. 684, that the issue there was one of priorities, although in fact neither claim was held to be valid.

obtaining at the *forum*, is deemed to be its governing law. Thus, in *The Halcyon Isle* the validity of the ship-repairer's claim ought properly to be seen, in a Singapore (or English) *forum*, as being the exclusive concern of United States law. Similarly, had it been disputed, the validity of the mortgagees' claim would presumably have been the exclusive concern of English law.

Of course, in a case in which more than one claim is being put forward, and in which, therefore, more than one choice of law rule may be involved, a question of characterization could arise when considering the scope of any of these choice of law rules, in exactly the same way as such a question may arise when considering the scope of a choice of law rule where only one such rule is involved. Characterization of a legal issue, or its allocation to a particular juridical category (this representing a decision as to which choice of law is most apt for its resolution) is achieved by reference to criteria of the *forum*. Indeed characterization forms an integral part of the creative formulation by a *forum* of its choice of law rule. However, as has been emphasized many times, these criteria are criteria uniquely evolved for the sole purpose of delineating the scope of operation of the *forum*'s various choice of law rules. They are criteria which may, or may not, happen to reflect the criteria to which resort is had when characterizing or classifying for the purposes of the domestic law of the *forum*. Thus in *The Halcyon Isle* the circumstance that the right accorded to the ship-repairer under United States law was of a type that would be classified by a Singapore or English court in a domestic context as a maritime lien should not have been seen as being *in itself* a crucial consideration. Ultimate focus should have been upon the legal nature and legal incidents, *per se*, of the ship-repairer's claim under United States law. The only relevance of the characteristics of a maritime lien in Singapore or English domestic law derived from the fact that under United States law his claim happened to have these characteristics. The law governing the validity of the New York transaction was United States law. Once this is accepted, a live problem of characterization (in a conflict of laws sense) could only have arisen if it were to be contended that the question of recognizing a particular but important legal incident of the New York transaction, namely that it conferred upon the ship-repairer the apparently exact equivalent of an English maritime lien, should be separately characterized so as to be taken out of the ambit of the law governing the validity of that transaction. There would, of course, be no purely logical objection to this; but it would be difficult to justify on policy grounds. The dissentient Lords Salmon and Scarman referred apparently approvingly to the ship-repairer's submission that '. . . it is as absurd, in characterising a claim to which the law attaches the security of a maritime lien, to ignore the existence of the lien as it would be to characterise a mortgagee's claim as merely one for the repayment of money lent. In each the security is part of the nature of the claim.'[8] It is accordingly submitted that, in the absence of any compelling countervailing policy factor, in *The Halcyon Isle* not only the validity, but also the legal nature and legal incidents of the New York transaction should clearly have fallen to be determined in accordance with United States law. By the same token, had they been disputed, the nature and incidents, as well as the validity, of the English mortgage transaction would have been matters for the English *lex causae*.

However, the majority of their Lordships recoiled from giving this broad and rational scope to the role of United States law. Analysis of their treatment of the

---

[8] [1981] A.C. 221, 245.

New York transaction is not free from difficulty. Validity in a general sense is acknowledged, but an important feature of the transaction, namely the creation of what would be described in the domestic law of the *forum* as a maritime lien, is discarded. It seems that the majority would have denied recognition to the ship-repairer's lien even if no question of priority *vis-à-vis* another claimant had arisen. They saw a maritime lien as intrinsically procedural or remedial. It is true that Lord Diplock did say at the beginning of the majority judgment that the 'question of law directly involved in this appeal is whether in the distribution of the proceeds of sale the claim of the mortgagees should take priority over the claim of the necessaries men [the ship-repairers] or vice versa'.[9] But the reason why the claim to a lien advanced by the ship-repairer was denied 'priority' was that it was not recognized at all. It was, therefore, only in a broad (or, some might be tempted to say, confusingly loose) sense that the majority decision is as to the priority of claims: only one claim, that of the mortgagees, was regarded as effective.

The legal vacuum resulting from the refusal of the majority to recognize the ship-repairer's lien is filled by resort to the domestic law of the *forum*. However, the nature of this resort is itself not altogether clear: it is expressed partly in terms of according respect to a limitation upon the jurisdiction of the *forum* which would be operative in a domestic case, but also partly in terms of the determination of priorities which the *forum* would make in such a case. Lord Diplock, delivering the opinion of that majority, said:

> Their Lordships therefore conclude that, in principle, the question as to the right to proceed *in rem* against a ship as well as priorities in the distribution between competing claimants of the proceeds of her sale in an action *in rem* in the High Court of Singapore falls to be determined by the lex fori, as if the events that gave rise to the claim had occurred in Singapore.[10]

Later his Lordship, referring to the earlier Court of Appeal case of *The Colorado*,[11] said:

> The reasoning of all three judgments is consistent only with the characterization of a maritime lien in English law as involving rights that are procedural or remedial only, and accordingly the question whether a particular class of claim gives rise to a maritime lien or not as being one to be determined by English law as the lex fori.[12]

To be contrasted with the views of the majority is the conclusion of Lord Salmon and Lord Scarman in their joint judgment that

> If the Admiralty court has, as in the present case, jurisdiction to entertain the claim, it will not disregard the lien. A maritime lien validly conferred by the lex loci is as much part of the claim as is a mortgage similarly valid by the lex loci. Each is a limited right of property securing the claim.[13]

If one accepts this dissenting proposition, as in the present writer's respectful view one should, the court in *The Halcyon Isle* can be seen as being faced with two competing claims each valid by its proper law. Even so no true question of priority would have arisen but for the fact that it was impossible for the court to give full effect (as defined by the relevant *lex causae*) to both claims. For example, had it been shown that under New York law the rights of a ship-repairer would be

---

[9] [1981] A.C. 221, 229.   [10] Ibid. 235.   [11] [1923] P. 102.   [12] [1981] A.C. 221, 238.
[13] Ibid. 250.

subject to the rights of an earlier mortgagee the dilemma, which is presented by a true question of priority, would have been avoided.[14]

The dilemma posed by a true question of priority, such as (at least upon the minority's appreciation) did arise in *The Halcyon Isle*, is to be resolved by reference to the *lex fori*—but not in the same sense that, nor for the same reasons that, questions of procedure generally are determined by the *lex fori*. Considerations of practical convenience dictate that the *forum* should apply its own ground rules when dealing with procedural questions generally. This must obviously mean that the *forum* then has resort to its own domestic law.[15] The practical convenience policy, however, does not reach out to an issue of priority such as that which arose in *The Halcyon Isle*. There no unacceptable inconvenience to the court would have been involved in a decision either way, and indeed the lower courts had reached differing conclusions. Of course, convenience did require that the court decide one way or another, but it did not require that this decision should be in conformity with any pattern of its own domestic law.

Faced with two (or more) valid and competing claims a *forum* has itself to intervene authoritatively. There is no a priori reason for it to apply the law determining the validity and effects of one claim rather than the law covering the validity and effects of another claim.

In some particular contexts policy considerations may indicate that this authoritative intervention should take the form of propounding a separate choice of law rule for the resolution of questions of priority. Thus it is fairly well established that the priority of competing assignments of a debt is determined by the proper law of the original debt.[16] The debtor has an overriding interest in knowing whom he must pay in order to discharge his obligation, and it is reasonable that he should be able to ascertain this by reference to the law governing the only transaction to which in the normal case he has been a party. Similarly there is authority which suggests that the priority of claims against foreign land is to be determined by the *lex situs*.[17] The courts and administrative agencies of the *situs* have effective, exclusively effective and permanently effective control, and it is therefore only reasonable that the priority of claims should be adjudged in accordance with the way in which it would be adjudged in the courts of the *situs*.

More generally, however, the authoritative intervention on the part of the *forum* for the purpose of resolving an issue of priority will take the form of resort to standards of its own rather than to the formulation of a choice of law rule. It is in this sense, and for this reason, that questions of priority can be said to be governed by the *lex fori*—but this obviously in no way implies that a *forum* must apply its own domestic criteria.[18] No consideration of practical convenience requires this, and

---

[14] It is to be observed that on this precise definition of an issue of priority, no such issue will arise if all claims are subject to the same *lex causae*, it then *ex hypothesi* being possible to give full effect to all claims in accordance with that law. But cf. Dicey and Morris, *The Conflict of Laws* (10th edn., 1980), p. 1193.

[15] See ibid., Rule 209: 'All matters of procedure are governed by the domestic law of the country to which the court wherein any legal proceedings are taken belongs (*lex fori*) . . .'; and Comment thereon at p. 1177: 'The primary object of this Rule is to obviate the inconvenience of conducting the trial of a case containing foreign elements in a manner with which the court is unfamiliar.'

[16] See ibid., Rule 83, and *Le Feuvre* v. *Sullivan* (1855), 10 Moo. P.C. 1.

[17] See *Norton* v. *Florence Land and Public Works Co.* (1877), 7 Ch. D. 332.

[18] It is submitted that it should not be regarded as decisive that under the domestic *lex fori*,

indeed for a *forum* automatically to apply its own domestic rules could only be explained in terms of the unwarranted fiction[19] that the fact situation contained no significant foreign elements. What a *forum* is rationally called upon to do is very different and much more difficult. It is to evolve a separate pattern of rules appropriate for the determination of priorities between valid foreign claims of varying sorts. The establishment of such a pattern will involve policy-based creative law-making. It is a task which English conflict of laws jurisprudence has scarcely begun to identify, let alone accomplish.

Categories of claims may themselves differ greatly in their nature, in their legal incidents and in their economic and other consequences. Moreover, the policies that justify according priority to one particular category of claim over another particular category of claim are liable to display great variation in purpose, in direction and in strength. Accordingly the evolving pattern of *forum* rules for the determination of priorities, if it is to reflect these often fundamental diversities, must unavoidably be a pattern of considerable complexity and/or sophistication. Generalization and concomitant arbitrariness is to be eschewed. Focus should in each type of context be upon the appropriate way of dealing with a particular priority dilemma. In *The Halcyon Isle* (assuming, of course, that the validity of the ship-repairer's lien was to be recognized at all) the particular dilemma with which the Privy Council was faced was as to priority between the claim of a ship-repairer and the claim of prior mortgagees of the ship. The present writer respectfully inclines to the view, which is clearly implicit in the joint dissenting judgment of Lord Salmon and Lord Scarman, that the balance of policy arguments favours the claim of the ship-repairer. However, be that as it may, what is important is that the problem be seen as being a problem of a specific type and as a problem to be authoritatively solved by the *forum* in the light of positively and specifically relevant policy considerations. When operating in a transnational context a *forum* ought not to allow itself to be deflected from its task by mechanical misapplication of the verbal formula that matters of procedure are to be determined by reference to the precepts of the *domestic* law of the *forum*. Nor should a *forum* be blinkered by the constraints of locally applicable rules of Admiralty jurisdiction concerning maritime liens. A maritime lien is itself a domestic law concept—a concept to be found in many systems of domestic law, but still a domestic law concept. Stripped of any mystique much of Admiralty law is simply a part of the domestic law of a national *forum*: it has no prerogative in the context of private international law. 'In the climate of a dominating domestic law', said Lord Salmon and Lord Scarman, 'the concepts and principles of the law of the sea wilt and die'.[20]

---

although a ship-repairer does not acquire a lien, a claimant who does acquire a lien under that law does have priority over a mortgagee. It is possible to perceive policy grounds, particularly in the context of the law of the sea (or even of international carriage generally), for a *forum* preferring the claim of a foreign ship-repairer over that of a mortgagee, even if a domestic claimant possessed of a lien on some other ground would not be accorded such priority. Although Lords Salmon and Scarman did mention (pp. 243–4) that 'under the law of Singapore, as of England . . . a claimant who has a maritime lien recognised by the law has priority over a mortgagee', they do not appear to have regarded this as crucial. To do so would be to reintroduce partial reference to the domestic *lex fori*.

[19] The majority of their Lordships in *The Halcyon Isle* seemingly had no qualms about embracing this fiction.

[20] [1981] A.C. 221, 243.

THE *AMINOIL* ARBITRATION*

By F. A. MANN[1]

SHORTLY before his death the late Sir Gerald Fitzmaurice wrote to the present writer that he had just finished an arbitration which led to a 'remarkable' award, and that he hoped at an early date to have a discussion about it. Unfortunately, his untimely death rendered such a discussion impossible. In the absence of the advice or at least the comments of a dear and greatly respected friend the present writer must try to unravel the intricacies of this clearly 'remarkable', but also difficult and far from compellingly reasoned award in the case of the *State of Kuwait* v. *The American Independent Oil Company* (Aminoil).[2] It was rendered by Professor Paul Reuter as President, Professor Hamed Sultan appointed by Kuwait and Sir Gerald appointed by Aminoil. It consists of lxx paragraphs summarizing the facts and 179 paragraphs of reasons together with what Sir Gerald described as a separate opinion of 30 paragraphs, which as to the grounds of decision, though not as to the result, is in effect a dissenting opinion of considerable persuasive force; in memory of a great lawyer characterized by his intellectual integrity as well as his judicial qualities it is permissible to quote in full the last paragraph of his opinion which is likely also to be the last words ever written by him:

> In consequence, and while I naturally hesitate to differ from a view so skilfully constructed and persuasive as that contained in the Award, good faith and my professional conscience compel me to conclude that although the nationalisation of Aminoil's undertaking may otherwise have been perfectly lawful, considered simply in its aspect of an act of the State, it was nevertheless irreconcilable with the stabilisation clauses of a Concession that was still in force at the moment of the take-over.

That in these circumstances the arbitrators agreed on the result is indeed remarkable when the figures are considered: Kuwait claimed some $225m., Aminoil claimed $2.5 billion, alternatively $185m., plus in either case some $450m. Both parties claimed interest. The arbitrators awarded to the Government $123m., to Aminoil $206m., i.e. a net sum of $83m. which with interest and an inflation factor came to a total sum of about $179m.

The principal reason why the award merits analysis lies in these figures, for it is one of the relatively few modern documents which deals with the liability for and the quantum of compensation payable in the event of expropriation. In view of the fact that there exist innumerable treaties and contracts which provide for or may lead to a liability to pay compensation for expropriation, the reasoning adopted by a tribunal such as the arbitrators in the *Aminoil* case is entitled to close attention, though it may be open to doubt whether it is also entitled to be treated as a precedent or is rather a very special case. The general impression conveyed

---

* © Dr. F. A. Mann, 1984.

[1] C.B.E., F.B.A.; Honorary Professor of Law in the University of Bonn; Solicitor of the Supreme Court in London; Member of the Institut de Droit International.

[2] *International Legal Materials*, 21 (1982), p. 976.

by the award is that, as so often in arbitrations, strictly legal considerations may
have been allowed to be pushed aside for the sake of achieving unanimity among
the arbitrators and giving something to both parties.

I. THE FACTS

On 28 June 1948 the Ruler of Kuwait granted to Aminoil for a period of sixty
years a concession for the extraction of petroleum and natural gas. The Ruler was
to be paid certain sums of U.S. dollars (with the benefit of a gold clause). At the
end of the concession in 2008 all Aminoil's property in Kuwait was to vest in the
Ruler. Article 17 was a 'stabilization clause':

> The Shaikh shall not by general or special legislation or by administrative measures
> or by any other act whatever annul this Agreement except as provided in Article 11.
> No alteration shall be made in the terms of this Agreement by either the Shaikh or
> the Company except in the event of the Shaikh and the Company jointly agreeing that
> it is desirable in the interest of both parties to make certain alterations, deletions or
> additions to this Agreement.

Article 18 was an arbitration clause. After Kuwait had become fully independent
a supplemental agreement of 1961 affirmed the concession of 1948 subject to
certain amendments; these included an Article 9 according to which

> If, as a result of changes in the terms of concessions now in existence or as a result of the
> terms of concessions granted hereafter, an increase in benefits to Governments in the
> Middle East should come generally to be received by them, the Company shall consult with
> the Ruler whether in the light of all relevant circumstances, including the conditions in
> which operations are carried out, and taking into account all payments made, any
> alterations in the terms of the agreements between the Ruler and the Company would be
> equitable to the parties.

A further draft agreement was prepared in 1973. It abolished the gold clause,
included a new arbitration clause, provided for the enactment of a tax law,
suggested that in future 'the Company should not be denied a reasonable
opportunity of earning a reasonable rate of return (having regard to the risks
involved) on the total capital employed in its business attributable to Kuwait', and
included the following provision about the applicable law:[3]

> The parties base their relations with regard to the agreements between them on the
> principle of goodwill and good faith. Taking account of the different nationalities of the
> parties, the agreements between them shall be given effect, and must be interpreted and
> applied, in conformity with principles common to the laws of Kuwait and of the State of
> New York, U.S.A., and in the absence of such common principles, then in conformity with
> the principles of law normally recognized by civilized states in general, including those
> which have been applied by international tribunals.

The Company, as the arbitrators held, accepted this draft agreement in December 1973. During the following years many further changes took place either as
a result of negotiation or by the Government's unilateral action. Still further
changes were under discussion, when on 19 September 1977 Kuwait issued
decree No. 124 whereby the concession of 1948 was terminated, all the Com-

---

[3] One learns with some surprise from para. 6 of the award that the parties made no reference to this
clause. On this point see below under the heading 'The Proper Law'.

pany's property in Kuwait was to 'revert' to the State and a compensation committee was to be established to assess the compensation due to the Company and its outstanding obligations to the State.

In light of this only too familiar action by Kuwait the Company started arbitration proceedings in London as envisaged by the arbitration clauses in the contracts between the parties. But these proceedings were discontinued after the parties had concluded in July 1979 a special arbitration agreement which provided for arbitration in Paris; the reasons for this change do not appear from the award.

II. THE LAW OF THE ARBITRATION

The special agreement which the parties concluded in 1979 provided for 'transnational arbitration' and thus introduced into the case a most unfortunate, confusing and misleading conception. Nobody has as yet been able to explain what 'transnational' means, with the result that the term is used when parties or their advisors do not know or do not wish or care to know what they want; one can only agree with Sir John Donaldson M.R. who recently said that he found 'the concept of a supernational or transnational body of law difficult to accept. It seems to me that all private law has a nationality, although I fully accept that laws of different nationalities may be identical, whether by design, by common social pressures leading to common solutions or by common origin.'[4] In the present case, however, the term 'transnational' was continuously being used, although its legal connotation remained unexplained.

The arbitration agreement includes many provisions of a very special character. That the President was to be appointed by the President of the International Court of Justice is by no means unusual and is in law without any significance. On the other hand, the agreement also provided that unless otherwise agreed by the parties and subject to any mandatory provisions of the law of the place in which the arbitration is held, i.e. France, 'the Tribunal shall prescribe the procedure applicable to the arbitration on the basis of natural justice and of such principles of transnational arbitration procedure as it may find applicable'. This obsession with 'transnational' principles enabled the Tribunal to hold that in principle 'the Parties have chosen the French legal system' in regard to any mandatory provisions of the procedural law—an obvious conclusion, for in the absence of a truly international arbitration (which would presuppose the consent of France) it is impossible to imagine an arbitration held in Paris which would proceed according to non-French procedural law except to the extent permitted by French law. The arbitrators in fact settled appropriate Rules of Procedure which contain nothing that a French court could object to. Nevertheless the arbitrators felt unable to part from this aspect of the case without again emphasizing that 'having regard to the way in which the Tribunal has been constituted its international or rather transnational character is apparent' (paragraph 5). The point of this remark which seems to state the obvious is not readily discernible.

III. THE PROPER LAW

If the law governing the relations between the parties had exclusively been that defined by the above Article in the 1973 agreement its identity ought not to have

---

[4] *Amin Rasheed Shipping Corporation* v. *Kuwait Insurance Co.*, [1983] 1 W.L.R. 229, at p. 237.

caused much difficulty. If one analyses this verbose and imprecise Article it is plain that the first sentence can be ignored and that the first and the second part of the second sentence is comprised in the third part, for the instruction to give effect to the agreement between the parties and to apply principles common to Kuwait and New York must mean that both are included in the 'principles of law normally recognized by civilized states in general'. In other words, there cannot be principles common to Kuwait and New York which do not form part of generally recognized principles of law. If one then asks which is the *legal system* to which such verbiage refers, it can only be public international law of which the generally recognized principles of law are a constituent part. That contracts between a State and a private person can be submitted to public international law and that a reference to the generally recognized principles is tantamount to a reference to public international law was by 1973 well known[5] to both theory and practice. This is what, on a true construction of the clause, the parties must have meant. The arbitrators seem to agree, for they state in terms (paragraph 7): 'Clearly, it must have been the general principles of law that were chiefly present to the minds of the Government of Kuwait and its associates.' It must only be added that those general principles are not, but are a source of, a legal system.

Curiously enough, however, one learns from the award (paragraph 6) that 'the Parties did not, in the course of the present arbitration proceedings, make any reference to' the text of 1973. The reason no doubt was that the arbitration agreement of 1979 instructed the arbitrators to 'decide according to law' and defined that law as follows (Article III):

> The law governing the substantive issues between the Parties shall be determined by the Tribunal, having regard to the quality of the Parties, the transnational character of their relations and the principles of law and practice prevailing in the modern world.

The meaning of this clause, as the arbitrators seem to have recognized (in paragraph 8), is ambiguous. Does it mean that the Tribunal was to determine the proper law? Or does it mean that the Tribunal was to interpret the proper law as fixed by the parties by taking certain matters, including (once again) 'the transnational character of their relations', into account? The Tribunal did not in clear terms decide this conflict or express its views on the proper law to be applied by it; it used some elegant phrases to gloss over the issue (paragraphs 6 to 10), so that it is impossible to say with precision what rules it applied. There is only one fact that stands out: the Tribunal does not anywhere refer to academic material, but such decisions as are cited are all decisions of international tribunals, particularly the International Court of Justice, and there are also references to Article 38 of the Statute of the International Court (paragraph 6) and to the Vienna Convention on the Law of Treaties (paragraph 32). Does this mean that the Tribunal in fact applied public international law as, it is submitted, the agreement of 1973 required it to do?

---

[5] The power to 'internationalize' State contracts was first suggested in this *Year Book*, 21 (1944), p. 11 at p. 19, and further developed in this *Year Book*, 35 (1959), p. 34, where at p. 51 it was also suggested that a reference to the application of general principles implies a reference to public international law as the proper law. Since then the literature on the subject has grown enormously. The latest publication (including a bibliography) is by Jutta Stoll, *Vereinbarungen zwischen Staat und ausländischem Investor* (1982).

IV. The Issues

The issues in the arbitration were defined by Article III of the arbitration agreement. The parties recognized 'that the restoration of the Parties to their respective positions prior to 20 September 1977 and/or the resumption of operations under the 28 June 1948 Agreement (as amended) would be impracticable in any event, and the Company will therefore seek monetary damages instead'. The Tribunal was thus given the task of deciding 'the amount of compensation, if any, payable by the Government to the Company in respect of the assets acquired by the Government under Article 2 of Decree Law No. 124'; the amount of damages, if any, in respect of the termination of the 1948 agreement by Decree No. 124; the amount payable by or to the Government in respect of royalties, taxes or other obligations; and interest.

It appears, therefore, that the principle of liability was in no way admitted, and the Tribunal was under a duty in the first place to establish whether and on what basis either party was liable to make any payment.

On the first two issues Sir Gerald Fitzmaurice's argument is simple. In his view the stabilization clauses, one of which is quoted above, rendered the nationalization or expropriation wrongful. The reasons given in paragraphs 19–30 of his opinion are, it is submitted, convincing and, indeed, irresistible—a characterization which, unfortunately, does not fit the majority's reasoning. Its conclusion was (paragraph 102) that 'the take-over of Aminoil's enterprise was not in 1977 inconsistent with the contract of concession, provided always that the nationalisation did not possess any confiscatory character'. The inconsistency was lacking on account of the fact that 'no doubt contractual limitations on the State's right to nationalise are juridically possible, but what that would involve would be a particularly serious undertaking which would have to be *expressly* stipulated for. . . . In the present case, however, the existence of such a stipulation would have to be presumed as being covered by the general language of the stabilisation clauses.' At the same time 'these provisions are far from having lost all their value and efficacity on that account, since, by *impliedly* requiring that nationalisation shall not have any confiscatory character, they reinforce the necessity for a proper indemnification as a condition of it' (paragraphs 95 and 96). The prohibition of 1948 and 1961 'not by general or special legislation or administrative measures or by any other act whatever' to annul the concession has little or no meaning except that it implies something nowhere mentioned, viz. the duty to pay proper compensation for that which most readers would hold to be specifically prohibited.

We have long known, of course, that there is nothing for which lawyers cannot find words, but there can be few instances of a more blatant distortion of plain language. One can understand, though one is bound to reject, the argument that the stabilization clauses do not specifically prohibit nationalization, expropriation or confiscation. Yet in an international document it would have been difficult to employ more suitable words to comprise such 'acts' than those in fact used; if, as the Tribunal held, notwithstanding their terms, the stabilization clauses rendered a nationalization lawful, one cannot easily answer the question what affirmative meaning and effect may be attributed to these clauses. But there are no rules of interpretation in any system of law, certainly not in international law (cf. Article 31 of the Vienna Convention) which would permit or require the implication of a duty to pay appropriate compensation into the terms of the stabilization clauses.

There are very many points which arise from the majority's discussion of the question of liability. In truth, however, they relate to quantum, though in view of the odd scheme adopted by the majority for the structure of its award, they are presented as problems of liability. One[6] of them concerns the meaning and effect of Article 9 of the 1961 agreement, which calls for a few words of comment.

Article 9 imposes a duty to consult in the event of a change of certain circumstances. The Tribunal treats this as a duty to negotiate (paragraphs 18 and 20). The latter, as we know, has in the course of the last fifteen years or so in public international law become a legally enforceable or at any rate material and effective duty. That similar principles apply to a duty to consult has, it is believed, nowhere been laid down. Yet we now learn that the duty to consult contemplates 'agreement by mutual consent' (paragraph 24). The interesting and important question which frequently arises in arbitration proceedings concerned with long-term contracts clearly embedded in a municipal system of law is whether an arbitrator has the power to impose the agreement which the parties were unable to reach. (An arbitration tribunal consisting of Mr. Mark Littman Q.C. as Chairman, the Hon. Mr. Ogilvie Thompson, the former Chief Justice of South Africa, and the present writer, which a few years ago sat in Paris and had to apply South African and/or English law, answered the question in the negative, the present writer dissenting.)[7] The arbitrators in *Aminoil* had 'no doubt that, speaking generally, a tribunal cannot substitute itself for the parties in order to make good a missing segment of their contractual relations—or to modify a contract—unless that right is conferred upon it by law or by the express consent of the Parties' (paragraph 74). Since this is a point of great and general practical importance, the *ratio decidendi* should be quoted in full:

It is not open to doubt that an arbitral tribunal—constituted on the basis of a 'compromissory' clause contained in relevant agreements between the parties to the case, and seized in the matter unilaterally by one of the parties only—could not, by way of modifying or completing a contract, prescribe how a provision such as the Abu Dhabi formula must be applied. For that, the consent of both parties would be necessary.

---

[6] Another interesting but elementary discussion rejects Aminoil's argument that its consent to the 1973 agreement was vitiated by duress (paras. 40 to 46). The argument was indeed untenable and does not require discussion in the present context.

[7] The so-called fairness clause read as follows: 'If for any reason or reasons beyond the control of either . . . or . . . (be it by reason of legislation or other unforeseeable events and circumstances including but not limited to a change in parity of currencies other than the U.S. Dollar) the basic premises of this contract or the economic circumstances change in such a way that the execution of this contract or any particular term or terms thereof would cause undue hardship to one of the partners or unduly favour one party to the detriment of the other, the parties shall consult together with the aim of finding a mutually acceptable solution for the removal of such hardship.' The award is dated 17 May 1976 and bears the reference no. 2756 of the International Chamber of Commerce. Both parties were agreed that South African courts would have regard to English law. Hence English law was freely referred to, in particular *Sykes* v. *Fine Fare Ltd.*, [1967] 1 Ll.L.R. 53. It is not to be doubted that normally a judge or arbitrator cannot make or modify a contract for the parties. The question in such cases is whether on its true construction the clause, *combined with the arbitration clause*, exceptionally confers such powers. This can only be so where an objective standard such as reasonableness is set and it is a specific and narrow point such as a price which on the basis of evidence can be judicially decided. See the text.

The argument on the one hand is that, of course, no tribunal can rewrite a contract: this would far exceed the judicial function. On the other hand, where it is merely a question of, say, adjusting a price according to objective standards of reasonableness, there is, it is submitted, no reason why judges or arbitrators should not be empowered or able to do so. A limited function in this sense is inherent in the arbitration clause: it authorizes arbitrators to decide disputes which come within the scope of the judicial function. The point thus becomes a matter of degree. It ought not to be disposed of by urging some generalities about rewriting contracts. The real question is whether in a given case the specific task which the arbitrators are required to perform falls within the judicial function which they are authorized to exercise.

It may be that, notwithstanding its initial doubts about its own jurisdiction, the *Aminoil* Tribunal is not wholly opposed to the approach which has just been outlined, for the Tribunal concluded (paragraph 79) that within the framework of a general settlement it had jurisdiction to determine the amount due, including some amount owing by Aminoil to the Government under Article 9 and the Abu Dhabi[8] formula. The reason given for this conclusion was (paragraph 75) that the Tribunal was 'not expected to devise new provisions that will govern the contractual relations of the Parties for the future, but to liquidate the various consequences of their past conduct and of the contractual clauses that once bound them but are now at an end'. One need only add that if it is within the jurisdiction of arbitrators to ascertain amounts due in the past, there is no reason why their judicial function should preclude them from assessing the amounts payable in future.

V. COMPENSATION

The crucial section of the award dealing with the quantum of compensation payable by Kuwait for taking a business with a life limited to thirty years and producing so volatile a commodity as oil (paragraphs 137 to 178) makes it clear that the Tribunal was supplied with much evidence by accountants and other experts on the various methods of valuation and calculation, on the facts to be taken into account, and on a variety of figures relating to numerous aspects. The award deals with the whole of this material in a somewhat cursory fashion, so that its significance as a precedent for the process of actual valuation is limited. On the other hand, much was said on the principles which in law should guide that process.

The Tribunal took as its starting-point 'the most general formulation of the rules applicable for a lawful nationalisation', viz. the United Nations General Assembly Resolution 1803 (XVII) of 1962, according to which in the event of nationalization 'the owner shall be paid appropriate compensation, in accordance with the rules in force in the State taking such measures in the exercise of its sovereignty and in accordance with international law'[9] (paragraph 143). This

---

[8] This formula, developed by the Gulf States in the heyday of their economic power in November 1974, meant the imposition of a royalty rate of 20 per cent of posted prices and a tax rate of 85 per cent in respect of oil income. See para. 53 of the award.

[9] The reference to the rules applicable in the expropriating State is of course the most unfortunate feature of this Resolution. In the present case the point was not material because the Tribunal held that the law of Kuwait had adopted and included the rules of international law: para. 6.

means 'that in the case of the present dispute there is no room for rules of compensation that would make nonsense of foreign investment' (paragraph 146). Accordingly compensation 'must be calculated on a basis such as to warrant the upkeep of a flow of investment in the future' (paragraph 147). The legitimate expectations of the parties refer to the contractual equilibrium and 'cannot be neglected,—neither when it is a question of proceeding to necessary adaptations during the course of the contract nor when it is a question of awarding compensation' (paragraphs 148 and 149). There are several methods of valuation, but the conception which 'must guide the Tribunal' is that adopted by the parties 'in the course of their relations and negotiations,—namely that of the reasonable rate of return' (paragraph 154). Kuwait's contention based on 'precedents resulting from a series of transnational negotiations and agreements about compensation' in the oil industry and allowing 'only the net book value of the redeemable assets' could not be accepted (paragraphs 155 and 156). In particular as a matter of law there was no *opinio juris* such as required by the *North Sea Continental Shelf* cases[10] in support of such a contention; where States or companies had accepted net book value, 'economic pressures . . . lay at the root of' such precedents that 'had nothing to do with law, and do not enable them to be regarded as components of the formation of a general legal rule' (paragraph 157). On the other hand, while 'attitudes taken up by a party over the long course of a negotiation that eventually breaks down cannot be made the basis of an arbitral or judicial decision', the fact is 'that over the years Aminoil had come to accept the principle of a moderate estimate of profits and that it was this that constituted its legitimate expectation' (paragraph 161).

In assessing compensation inflation must be taken into account. Hence 'in calculating the value of depreciating assets it would be unfair to settle it on the basis of a superannuated cost consisting of the original purchase price, when that price has no relation to the actual present cost' (paragraph 166). Indeed 'if it were thought necessary to arrive at the total figure of the capital invested by Aminoil in its undertaking it would be appropriate to do so without holding the dollars of 1977[11] to be equivalent to those of 1948' (paragraph 169).

When, finally, the Tribunal comes to deal with actual figures, it states in a single, almost hidden, sentence in paragraph 176 that 'a balanced appraisal of the circumstances leads the Tribunal to fix $10 million as a reasonable rate of return for Aminoil'.[12] How this figure was arrived at is in no way explained except that the Tribunal refers to the fact 'that the important works which were to have been carried out by the Company in the near future, and financed, at least partly out of the profit of the undertaking, ceased to be a charge on it'. Whether the $10m. is high or low and how it is related to relevant circumstances such as value of assets, price of oil, costs of production and so forth or what proportion of a total sum it represents, all this is not vouchsafed. The lack of guidance is a matter for regret. The Tribunal then proceeds to assess the values both of the various components

---

[10] *I.C.J. Reports*, 1969, p. 45, para. 77.

[11] The reference to 1977, the year of the taking, is surprising. Precedent would appear to point in the direction of taking the date of assessment as a basis: see Mann, *The Legal Aspect of Money* (4th edn., 1982), pp. 131–3. The Tribunal could have avoided much of the discussion about the element of inflation if it had based itself on the values in 1982. It is submitted that this should have been done, particularly if the taking had been held to be wrongful so as to entitle Aminoil to damages. In accordance with principle future inflation had to be disregarded.

[12] This was an annual figure which was increased by an inflation factor of 10 per cent.

of the undertaking separately considered and of the undertaking itself. As regards the different concrete components a joint report of accountants 'furnishes acceptable indications concerning the assets other than fixed assets'. However, no figure is mentioned. As regards the fixed assets 'it is a depreciated replacement value that seems appropriate'. Again no figure is mentioned. Instead the Tribunal states 'the conclusion that, at the date of 19 September 1977 a sum estimated at $206,041,000 represented the reasonably appraised value of what constituted the object of the takeover' (paragraph 178). Deducting liabilities and allowing for inflation the Tribunal arrived at the final figures mentioned above.

In other words, unless the writer is guilty of a grave misunderstanding, the Tribunal allowed nothing for loss of profit during the remaining thirty years of the concession. If this conclusion is correct it would have been welcome to have it expressed and to read about such support as it has in international (or if the Tribunal should prefer it: transnational) practice, in academic literature and in comparative material, i.e. in the sources which Article 38 of the Statute of the International Court of Justice enumerates.

VI. CONCLUSION

A French author who extended an enthusiastic welcome to the decision describes it as its great merit that 'les éléments les plus juridiques *du nouvel ordre international* ont reçu en quelque sorte leur reconnaissance'.[13] He mentions in the first place 'l'interprétation hardie des clauses de stabilisation qui rappelle . . . que l'on ne peut assimiler complètement un Etat contractant à un contractant privé'. If, as seems likely, the Tribunal applied public international law, then on the very point mentioned by Professor Kahn it left a gap by its failure to refer to the principle underlying Article 26 of the Vienna Convention on the Law of Treaties[14] according to which treaties and, indeed, all agreements governed by international law are binding upon the parties and must be performed by them in good faith. From this point of view the stabilization clauses, as Sir Gerald Fitzmaurice emphasized, cannot be ignored or distorted in the manner adopted by the majority and it was not possible to speak of a lawful nationalization. Rather the taking became illegal. This is the central problem raised by the award, but it is by no means the only one. Looking at the award[15] as a whole one should hesitate long before attributing persuasive force to it. In fact this award once again raises well-known doubts about the wisdom and, sometimes, the legality of publishing awards which are rendered in arbitrations between parties other than States and, therefore, are not strictly international in character.

[13] Philippe Kahn, *Clunet*, 1982, p. 844 at p. 868. Italics supplied.
[14] Cmnd. 7964.
[15] It includes many points which were not discussed in the present Note. They appeared to be of minor importance, but it could be well understood if on this aspect opinions differed.

THE ANGLO-BRAZILIAN DISPUTE OVER
THE ISLAND OF TRINDADE, 1895-6*

By GEOFFREY MARSTON[1]

I N the Atlantic Ocean about six hundred miles from the coast of Brazil, in latitude 20° 30′ south, longitude 29° 20′ west, lies the Ilha da Trindade,[2] a rugged mass of volcanic rock some four miles long and two miles wide which is now undisputably under Brazilian sovereignty.[3] Twenty-six miles east of Trindade lies a group of four rocks known collectively as the Ilhas Martin Vaz, also undisputably Brazilian. The purpose of this paper is to bring from obscurity the facts of a long-forgotten quarrel between Britain and Brazil over title to Trindade and the Ilhas Martin Vaz.

I. The Relevant History Prior to 1895

The early history of Trindade and Martin Vaz is sketchy. The islands were probably discovered by Portuguese navigators in the early sixteenth century but no further activity on the ground seems to have been authenticated until the English astronomer Halley sighted the islands in April 1700. Halley landed on Trindade, recording in his journal: '. . . I took possession of the island in His Majesty's name, as knowing it to be granted by the King's Letters Patents, leaving the Union flag flying.'[4] Halley had been commissioned master and commander of His Majesty's ship the *Paramour* in August 1698 and in October of that year the Admiralty instructed him to sail southward of the equator to observe variations of the compass. His intructions continued:

You are likewise to make the like observations at as many of the islands in the Seas between the aforesaid coasts [i.e. those of South America and Africa] as you can (without too much deviation) bring into your course: and if the Season of the Yeare permit, you are to stand soe farr into the South, till you discover the Coast of the Terra Incognita, supposed to lye between Magelan's Streights and the Cape of Good Hope, which Coast you are carefully to lay downe in its true position.[5]

© Dr. Geoffrey Marston, 1984.

[1] LL.M., Ph.D. (Lond.); Lecturer in Law, University of Cambridge; Fellow of Sidney Sussex College.

[2] The Portuguese spelling has been used but in the documents relating to the dispute the island's name is spelled variously as 'Trinidad', 'Trinité' or 'Trinidada'. The island must not be confused with the former British island of Trinidad, now part of the independent State of Trinidad and Tobago.

[3] Neither Trindade nor Martin Vaz had any indigenous inhabitants. In 1971 it was reported that Trindade was occupied by a detachment of Brazilian marines (*South America Pilot* (11th edn., 1975), vol. 1, pp. 25–6). Its strategic importance today may be assessed by observing its location relative to the direct line of communication between Ascension Island and the Falkland Islands. For a Brazilian summary of the island's history, see *Grande Enciclopédia Portuguesa e Brasileira*, vol. 32, pp. 866–7.

[4] Alexander Dalrymple, *A Collection of Voyages, chiefly in the Southern Atlantick Ocean* (1775) (entry for 17 April 1700). This work reproduced Halley's journal of the voyage.

[5] Reproduced in E. F. MacPike (ed.), *Correspondence and Papers of Edmond Halley* (1932), p. 243 (Appendix XI).

There is no evidence available to show that Halley was expressly authorized to annex territory in the name of the Crown, nor is there any evidence that the Crown expressly ratified Halley's purported annexation in its name.

By an order dated 22 February 1724,[6] the King of Portugal, who was at that time the sovereign of Brazil, instructed the Governor of Rio de Janeiro to fortify Trindade to prevent its use as a staging post by English slaving entrepreneurs who were reported to have formed a settlement thereon. It does not appear what, if any, steps were taken to implement this order; at all events no permanent settlement was established at this time by either Britain or Portugal.

The next relevant event did not occur until 1781.[7] In January of that year Captain George Johnstone, commodore of a squadron about to leave for the Cape of Good Hope, was directed to obey instructions from the Principal Secretary of State for the Southern Department. Acting presumably on instructions so received, in August 1781 Johnstone dispatched a vessel from St. Helena to land a body of troops on Trindade. The reason for this measure remains unclear: it could have been a temporary strategic step in the war then being waged against France and Spain, or on the other hand it might have been to give the island a function similar to that performed by the East India Company on St. Helena, i.e. a refitting and revictualling station. British intentions for the long-term future of the island were probably still undetermined when on 30 May 1782 the Portuguese Minister in London, the Chevalier de Pinto, complained to Charles Fox, who the previous month had been appointed the first holder of the office of Principal Secretary of State for Foreign Affairs, about the continued presence of British troops on Trindade. He asserted that there was no doubt that the island, and those of Martin Vaz, were discovered by the Portuguese, who had formed settlements thereon from time to time, and that they were dependencies of the Principality of Brazil. He protested about the 'mysterious and clandestine' British occupation without the consent of the Viceroy of Brazil and claimed that it was contrary to the treaties between Britain and Portugal for Britain to occupy the island in order to attack the vessels of States with which Portugal was at peace. He called for Trindade to be evacuated immediately 'comme faisant partie des domaines de Sa Majesté Très-Fidèle'.

The Lords Commissioners of the Admiralty, to whom Fox had sent the Portuguese note, denied all responsibility for the incident and referred Fox to the other Principal Secretary of State, the Earl of Shelburne. On 19 July 1782 Lord Grantham, who had succeeded Fox, instructed the Lords Commissioners 'that you do give immediate orders for evacuating the said island and for putting a stop to the cruizes from thence, of which M. le Chevalier de Pinto complains in the Memorial which he presented by order of his Court'.

On 22 August 1782 the Lords Commissioners of the Admiralty sent an order to the commanding officer of the British garrison on Trindade directing him to evacuate the island and embark on the vessel carrying the order.[8] In December 1782, the Viceroy of Brazil, acting on the instructions of the Portuguese Government which had communicated to him a copy of the Admiralty order obtained

---

[6] Reproduced in Foreign Office Confidential Print (hereinafter abbreviated to F.O.C.P.) 6794, p. 61.

[7] The relevant documents for the events of 1781 and 1782 are printed, unless otherwise indicated, in F.O.C.P. 6794, pp. 29–33.

[8] F.O.C.P. 6794, pp. 58–9; see also *Foreign Relations of the United States*, 1895, pt. i, p. 69.

through the Portuguese Minister in London, sent a task force to Trindade primarily to establish a presence there but also to cause the speedy evacuation of the British troops. The Viceroy's instructions to the commander of the task force contained the following passage:

> As it might happen, however, that the aforesaid English Commander may, for some reason unknown to us, hesitate to proceed promptly and loyally to the evacuation of the said island, the present expedition is furnished with instructions from Her Majesty which have been communicated to you, and in view of which you shall effect by force the ends which cannot be obtained by the persuasion of reason and justice.[9]

When the Portuguese force arrived at Trindade, however, the British troops had already departed. A Portuguese garrison was established which remained until some time in 1795 when it was withdrawn.

In August 1822, a declaration of independence was issued in Brazil without specific mention of Trindade and Martin Vaz as forming part of the territory.[10] On 30 August 1823, however, in a project for the constitution of the 'United Kingdom of Portugal, Brazil and the Algarves' issued in Rio de Janeiro, the territory was stated to comprise certain provinces together with 'the islands of Fernando Noronha, and Trindade, and others adjacent'.[11] The definitive Brazilian Constitution, promulgated in 1826, did not list separately the provinces or refer to any island.[12]

Following Brazilian independence and before the events described in full below, Trindade was visited from time to time by the naval vessels of both Britain and Brazil although there were no further attempts to form a settlement thereon. Its visitors of longest sojourn were groups of adventurers seeking the lost treasure of Lima, reputed to have been buried on the island.[13] The very existence of Trindade and Martin Vaz had probably faded from the collective memory of the British Foreign Office when there arrived a communication addressed to the Foreign Secretary, Lord Rosebery, dated 18 September 1893, in which the writer, one Harden Hickey of New York, announced his intention of setting up a Principality on Trindade. In the course of this communication, which was sent to a number of States, Hickey wrote:

> D'après le Droit de Gens, les territoires relais—*derelict*—appartiennent à qui veut se les approprier; et l'île de Trinidad, délaissée depuis des années, rentre certainement dans la catégorie sous-nommée.[14]

The Admiralty, which had been asked by the Foreign Office to advise it on the matter, reported of Trindade that '[i]ts possession is of no value to England, as it is not in any line of route, and it has no harbour. I am to add that there is no Record in this Office of its annexation by Brazil or by any other Power.'[15] No reply was sent to Hickey, since in the words of Sir T. V. Lister, Assistant Under-

---

[9] F.O.C.P. 6794, p. 60.

[10] *British and Foreign State Papers*, vol. 9, p. 736.

[11] Ibid., vol. 10, p. 1009.

[12] Ibid., vol. 13, p. 936.

[13] See, e.g., E. F. Knight, *The Cruise of the 'Falcon'*, vol. 2 (1884), pp. 202–43; *The Cruise of the 'Alerte'* (1890). A concession to explore for and to extract natural products on Trindade was granted to an individual by the Brazilian Department of Agriculture on 29 November 1884 (F.O.C.P. 6878, p. 5).

[14] Public Record Office reference F.O. 13/754, f. 2.

[15] Ibid., ff. 8–9.

Secretary of State at the Foreign Office, '[a]n acknowledgement would be a sort of admission of his claim'.[16] By a communication, equally unacknowledged by Britain, dated 5 January 1894, Hickey notified Lord Rosebery that the island would henceforth be called the Principality of Trinidad, with himself as Prince thereof—'lequel m'a déjà été reconnues par plusieurs puissances'.[17]

II. THE BRITISH ANNEXATION OF 1895

The source of the dispute which was soon to break out between Britain and Brazil lay in a letter dated 27 November 1894 addressed to the British Foreign Secretary, Lord Kimberley, by Admiral Richards, Chairman of the Telegraph Construction and Maintenance Company of London.[18] He pointed out that the Brazilian Government had presented a Bill to Congress to enable it to purchase cables laid along the Brazilian coast, the cables being the property of English companies; should this occur, the continuity of British telegraph communications with the River Plate would be broken and traffic would have to pass over Brazilian- or American-owned lines. Richards was of the view that a cable laid between Ascension Island and Buenos Aires would be too long for commercial success but that if such a cable could be routed by way of Trindade Island it could be expediently broken into two sections. Having mentioned Halley's act of possession of 1700 and the failed 'English settlement' of 1781, he continued:

> If there is any doubt whether this country has the power to grant the landing rights, I would venture to suggest that (if it is not considered British territory) Her Majesty's Government, looking to the great interests involved, might be pleased to resume formal possession of the island, and to grant us permission to land a cable, and establish a station there if found necessary.

Within the Foreign Office, a clerk, F. H. C. Streatfeild, minuted on 5 December 1894 that should it be considered advisable for Britain to take possession of the

---

[16] Ibid., f. 9ᵛ.

[17] Ibid., f. 15ʳ and ᵛ. In a prospectus to potential settlers, Hickey (who later took the name of 'James I of Trinidad') stated: 'Aucune nation n'a soulevé la moindre objection, et plusieurs ont d'ores et déjà reconnu le nouveau petit Etat: la "Principauté de Trinidad". Aucun gouvernement n'avait du reste le droit de jouer le rôle du chien dans la mangeoire; le baron Harden Hickey, avant de s'embarquer dans cette entreprise, avait eu soin de bien se renseigner auprès des autorités en matière de droit international, qui lui apprirent qu'il pouvait marcher sans crainte' (F.O. 13/755, ff. 216–17). The 'Principality' applied unsuccessfully to the Swiss Government for membership of the Universal Postal Union; see *Revue générale de droit international public*, 1 (1894), p. 179.

[18] F.O.C.P. 6794, pp. 1–2. The original official documents concerning the dispute are bound together in four Foreign Office case volumes (F.O. 13/754–6 and 782). Some, but not all, of these documents are printed in two Foreign Office Confidential Prints, Nos. 6794 and 6878 (P.R.O. references F.O. 881/6794 and 6878), with the titles 'Correspondence as to the Title to the Island of Trinidad (South Atlantic)'. In addition, there are many documents relating to the dispute in the private papers of the 3rd Marquess of Salisbury at Hatfield House. Inspection of these documents and the publication of extracts therefrom have been kindly permitted by the present Marquess of Salisbury.

The diplomatic correspondence and other documents up to 11 January 1896 were published by the Brazilian Ministry of Foreign Affairs (*Correspondencia e documentos diplomaticos sobre a occupação da Ilha da Trindade*, Rio de Janeiro, 1896: Supplement to Annexe No. 1 of the *Relatorio*, 1896). This does not add substantially to the story gleaned from the British archives. The author is indebted to Ambassador G. E. do Nascimento e Silva for bringing this document to his attention. See also H. Accioly, *Tratado de direito internacional publico*, vol. 2 (1934), pp. 176–7, and *Foreign Relations of the United States*, 1895, pt. i, pp. 63–70.

island this could be effected either (1) by formally annexing it; (2) by proclaiming a British protectorate over it; or (3) by granting a lease of it to the telegraph company.[19] Although Lord Kimberley favoured the lease possibility, the Colonial Office advised that it favoured outright annexation, since it considered Britain to have been upstaged by France in 1878 over the Chesterfield Islands by virtue of France taking formal possession before British lessees had completed their title by occupation.[20] Lord Kimberley thereupon instructed that immediate steps be taken by the Admiralty to take possession of Trindade. Accordingly, on 11 January 1895, the Admiralty sent the following signal to the senior British naval officer on the south-east coast of South America:

As Trinidad Island may be required for a telegraph station, you are to send a ship of war there, and, if no record of ownership by any foreign Power exists, Trinidad and Martin Vaz are to be annexed to the British Crown as uninhabited, and not belonging to any foreign Power. Flag is to be hoisted; Proclamation, in accordance with draft p. 62 of the Station Orders, is to be read, and a record is to be left on Trinidad Island. Treat this as Confidential, and acknowledge receipt.[21]

Commander Foley of the *Barracouta* was dispatched from Montevideo and carried out the above instructions on 24 and 25 January 1895. In reporting on 4 February 1895, Foley advised his senior officer of the text of the proclamation he had read and left on Trindade:

Whereas I have it in command from Her Majesty Queen Victoria, through her Principal Secretary of State for the Colonies, to assert the sovereign rights of Her Majesty over the Island of Trinidad and the adjacent rocks of Martin Vaz, the same having been taken possession of by Her Majesty as being uninhabited and not belonging to any Power.

Now, therefore, I, Francis John Foley, Esq., Commander in Her Majesty's Royal Navy, at present commanding Her Majesty's ship 'Barracouta', do hereby proclaim and declare to all men that from and after the date of these presents, the full sovereignty of the Island of Trinidad and the adjacent rocks of Martin Vaz, situated between 20° 25′ south, and 20° 35′ south of the Equator, and 28° 50′ west and 29° 30′ west of Greenwich, vests together with their dependencies, in Her Majesty Queen Victoria, her heirs and successors, for ever.[22]

III. The Brazilian Protest

Although the British annexation had been carried out in a confidential manner, news of it leaked to the London press and through this to the press in Rio de Janeiro. On 20 July 1895 the Brazilian Minister in London, A. de Souza Corrêa, called at the Foreign Office to enquire about the situation. The Assistant Under-Secretary of State, Francis Bertie, told him that as long ago as 1700 Britain had taken possession of Trindade and that 'there could be no question of Brazilian sovereignty'.[23] Corrêa replied that his Government would protest and that material injury would be caused to Brazil since telegraphic communication from the River Plate to Europe would no longer pass over Brazilian-owned lines. In his memorandum of the conversation, Bertie concluded: 'Of course, no heed must be given to the Brazilian claim; it is merely an attempt to establish a telegraphic monopoly.'[24]

---

[19] F.O.C.P. 6794, p. 2.
[20] Ibid., p. 4. The Law Officers' opinion on this subject, dated 11 November 1878, is printed in McNair (ed.), *International Law Opinions*, vol. 1, pp. 320–1.
[21] F.O.C.P. 6794, p. 7.   [22] Ibid., p. 14.   [23] Ibid., p. 19.   [24] Ibid.

On the same day in Brazil, the Minister for Foreign Affairs, Carlos de Carvalho, asked the British Minister resident in Rio de Janeiro, E. C. H. Phipps, for the background to the press reports. He told Phipps that Brazil had inherited the island from Portugal and that Brazilian rights must be defended.[25] The Marquess of Salisbury, who was now the British Prime Minister and Secretary of State for Foreign Affairs, cabled Phipps on 21 July 1895 that British title stemmed from the 1700 act of possession and that no protest was then made by Portugal. He concluded:

Her Majesty's Government cannot consent to waive their rights to the island, which is required as a telegraph cable station, and you should, in friendly terms, warn the Brazilian Government that they trust the latter will not send a ship to assert a right of sovereignty, as they could only regard it as a deliberately unfriendly act on the part of Brazil.[26]

From Rio de Janeiro, where 3,000 people had assembled to express popular indignation against the British act, Phipps cabled Salisbury on 23 July 1895 that '[t]he whole question is rather one of susceptibility; and I think that his Excellency [Carvalho] would be glad to grant us, for a nominal rent, a perpetual lease of the island with full control'.[27]

The Brazilians, however, were carrying out research which confirmed them in their legal position. In notes addressed to Phipps, dated 22 and 23 July 1895, Carvalho set out the Brazilian case for sovereignty over Trindade and Martin Vaz.[28] In particular, he asserted that prior to Brazil's independence Trindade was a possession of Portugal and ceased to be so on independence; thereafter Brazilian warships paid official visits to the island and a decree of the Brazilian Government in 1884 expressly recited that it was part of the Province of Espiritu Santo. Carvalho relied also on the Portuguese order of 1724 setting out measures to be taken against English slaving entrepreneurs on the island, an act which was 'no doubt, a solemn protest against the act practised in 1700 by Captain Halley'. Above all, the Brazilian Minister relied on the British Admiralty order of 22 August 1782 for the evacuation of the island; in his words, 'the best title of right that Brazil possesses over the Island of Trinidad is the solemn, positive, and practical acknowledgment of that right by the English Admiralty, who in 1782 sent decisive orders to the English officer in command on the Island of Trinidad to evacuate it without delay, and to hand it over to the Portuguese Government as a possession of the Kingdom of Portugal in South America, belonging to the Vice-Regency of Brazil'.[29]

Much of the note of 22 July 1895 was taken up with refuting an argument that Trindade was *res nullius* as abandoned territory. Carvalho remarked *inter alia*:

Abandonment . . . depends on the intention to renounce and on the cessation of physical power over the thing possessed, and must not be confounded with mere neglect to use or withdrawal. The possessor may leave the thing possessed unoccupied or in neglect and, nevertheless, preserve dominion over it. . . .

Abandonment can ensue only on an express manifestation of the will, inasmuch as the *animus* is the possibility of the reproduction of the first act of will by which the possession

---

[25] Ibid., p. 20.   [26] Ibid.   [27] Ibid., p. 21.

[28] Ibid., pp. 55-7 (note of 22 July); pp. 57-8 (note of 23 July). The notes were written in the Portuguese language; the translations of these and other notes from the Brazilian and Portuguese Governments are those found in the Foreign Office files.

[29] Ibid., pp. 57-8.

was acquired. . . . In order that abandonment may take place it is necessary that a fresh act of will should be exerted in a sense opposed to that of the first act—*animus in contrarium actus.* . . .

If Brazil has not manifested by an express act its desire to abandon the island which was adjudicated to the Brazilian continent by the fact of its political independence, if . . . there does not exist such a state of affairs as prevents it from disposing of the island and utilizing it at any time and in any manner it thinks fit, then with the rest of its dominion it has preserved full possession of the island, and as the latter is not a *res pro derelicta* its occupation in the name of the English Government does not form a legal title for its acquisition.[30]

By a note dated 27 July 1895, the Brazilian Minister in London, Corrêa, formally protested to Salisbury. Having referred to the events of 1782 and to various concessions granted to individuals by the Brazilian Government in respect of the island, he wrote:

Le Brésil a donc toujours maintenu les droits dont il avait hérité du Portugal, et la prise de possession de l'Ile de Trinidade par une nation étrangère constitue une violation du territoire national. Il importe donc d'affirmer ces droits dans toute leur intégrité et le Gouvernement de la République des Etats-Unis du Brésil me charge à cet effet de protester solennellement contre l'occupation faite au nom de sa Majesté Britannique.[31]

By a note of the same day, the 'Secretary of State for Foreign Affairs' of the 'Principality of Trinidad' sent to Salisbury and to other States a copy of a note he had sent to the Secretary of State of the United States of America asking the latter 'de reconnaître la Principauté de Trinidad comme Etat indépendant et de s'entendre avec les autres Puissances Américaines pour garantir sa *neutralité*'.[32] This, he continued, would be in the true spirit of the Monroe doctrine.

IV. The Arguments Harden

On receipt of Phipps's cable relating the outline of Carvalho's notes, the Foreign Office commissioned work at the Public Record Office into the events of 1782. The Admiralty order of 22 August 1782 could not be found, however, the excuse given by the Admiralty being that the papers had been 'weeded'.[33] The rediscovery of the papers of 1782 by the Brazilian Government must have come as an unhappy surprise to the British officials. In particular, Bertie must have been embarrassed to learn that the British force had been ordered to evacuate Trindade following protest by Portugal, whereas as late as 23 July 1895 he had told Corrêa that the force was 'only withdrawn because the island was found to be useless for colonizing purposes'.[34] Some of this embarrassment can be seen permeating a telegram sent by Salisbury to Phipps on 30 July 1895. In part this read:

In order to carry on the controversy, it would be necessary to refer to incomplete, and in some respects inconclusive, documents, to clear up which long research would be required, and from which endless discussion might ensue.

Her Majesty's Government are therefore prepared, as an act of friendship, and in preference to leaving the matter in a state of suspense, which is most unsatisfactory, to take a lease of the island from the Brazilian Government for use as a telegraphic station.

The duration of the lease should be unlimited as long as the cable is kept up, and the

---

[30] F.O.C.P. 6794, pp. 56–7.   [31] Ibid., pp. 26–7.   [32] Ibid., pp. 45–6 (original emphasis).
[33] F.O. 13/755, f. 45. The Brazilian Government, however, had available to it the copy forwarded to Rio by the Portuguese Government in 1782.
[34] F.O.C.P. 6794, p. 20A.

rent merely nominal. Her Majesty's Government would give an engagement not to fortify the island or use it as a naval or military post, and they would make it a condition that the station should be free from interference and taxation by Brazil.[35]

By a note dated 8 August 1895, Corrêa presented to Salisbury a memorandum of 'informations et faits relatifs à l'Ile de Trindade' which set out details of Portuguese and Brazilian activity in respect of the disputed islands. The memorandum went on:

L'île, quoique déserte depuis 1798, ne peut être considérée comme ayant été abandonnée ni par le Portugal, qui ne l'avait pas évacué alors *sine spe redeundi*, ni par le Brésil, qui a toujours affirmé les droits qu'il tient de son ancienne mère patrie, et, par des actes réitérés et publics, l'intention d'employer utilement et d'exploiter ses possessions de l'Archipel de Trindade.

Encore en 1893 le Gouvernement de la République fit connaître qu'il s'opposerait à la tentative du Baron Harden Hickey, citoyen des Etats-Unis de l'Amérique du Nord, qui avait distribué des prospectus pour engager des aventuriers à le suivre à l'Ile de Trindade, qu'il voulait occuper en y fondant une Principauté. . . .

Le Brésil a donc toujours maintenu, *animo et facto*, les droits dont il avait hérité du Portugal et ses droits ne sauraient être invalidés par l'occupation initiée en janvier 1895, au nom de Sa Majesté Britannique.[36]

Although Phipps initially cabled that the 'lease-back' arrangement was favourably received by the Brazilian Government,[37] he later reported that the latter considered that its contract of 1893 with the Western and Brazilian Telegraph Company 'absolutely precluded' it from granting a lease to the British Government since the Brazilian Government had therein bound itself not to concede any other cable 'between any part of the territory of the United States of Brazil' and any part of the territory of Uruguay or of Argentina.[38] Phipps, who regarded this information as a rejection of the 'lease-back' proposal, asked Carvalho if another solution could be suggested. Apart from a faint hint that compensation might be given to Brazil on the boundary with British Guiana, a possibility ruled out by Phipps, Carvalho could see no solution other than the satisfaction of Brazil's claim to the island.[39]

More work, meanwhile, was being carried out in the Foreign Office on the history of Trindade and on the international law relating to sovereignty over territory, in particular title by discovery. In an internal memorandum dated 5 August 1895 Bertie reviewed the history in the light of the Brazilian arguments to date and continued:

The flaw in our title is our evacuation of the island in 1782 at the request of Portugal, who claimed it as part of the Principality of Brazil, but it is not a matter of course that it passed to Brazil in 1822 when the independence of that country was established, even if our evacuation in 1782 should be held to be a full acknowledgment of Portuguese sovereignty. It might be argued that on the abandonment of the island by the Portuguese garrison in 1797 [sic] the British title revived. . . .

The independence of Brazil was recognized by Portugal by a Treaty dated the 29th August 1825. The Brazilian Constitution was promulgated in 1826, but it did not specifically mention Trinidad. We have no official record of Brazil having ever garrisoned or occupied the island, and certainly no traces of such occupation have been discovered by Her Majesty's ships who have visited it. It may, therefore, be considered to have been derelict, and consequently open to any Power that might choose to take possession of it. . . .

In view, however, of the correspondence of 1782 with Portugal, we have not a good case. On the other hand the title of Brazil is not unassailable.[40]

In Brazil, there were rumours of impending legislative action against British firms and, furthermore, Phipps reported that the Brazilian Government's attitude towards certain claims on it by British subjects was hardening. In a dispatch dated 1 September 1895 Phipps reported of a meeting he had had with Carvalho as follows:

His Excellency said that until the Trinidad question was settled it would be difficult, or even impossible, for him to press on the settlement of any of the pending British claims. Since he had shown me the correspondence which would be found in the British Foreign Office archives of the year 1782, he could not conceive any arguments which could possibly be brought forward by Her Majesty's Government shaking the profound conviction which he entertained that the island was a Brazilian possession, and that it could only be by the existence of 'le droit du plus fort' that Her Majesty's Government could possibly think of retaining it.[41]

Phipps went on to report that Carvalho acknowledged that, as a young nation, Brazil had perhaps 'childish susceptibilities', but he had to take these into consideration and 'humour the people with whom he had to deal'.

V. The Law Officers are Consulted

On 2 October 1895 the Foreign Office consulted the Law Officers of the Crown, Sir Richard Webster, Attorney-General, and Sir Robert Finlay, Solicitor-General. The consultation consisted in submitting to them the papers on the dispute, including therein the 1782 correspondence, and in asking them to approve a draft dispatch to Phipps. In the covering memorandum, Bertie asked the Law Officers 'whether the doctrine and arguments contained in the draft despatch are tenable according to international law, or, if not, to what extent and in what respects you consider that they may advantageously be modified'.[42]

The Law Officers replied on 24 October 1895 approving the draft dispatch with certain suggested modifications. They were of opinion that the British case depended on the fact that the island was unoccupied, and a *terra nullius*, when it was annexed in 1895; it could not be based on the fact of British occupation in the eighteenth century in view of the Portuguese protest in 1782 and consequent British evacuation. They continued:

The strength of the British case . . . rests, firstly, on the fact that there never has been any occupation of any sort of the island by Brazil, and that there is nothing to show that any title which Portugal had, passed to Brazil; and secondly, that the absence of any occupation by either Portugal or Brazil since 1795 is sufficient to show an abandonment of any territorial rights which existed before that date.[43]

The Law Officers considered that the case of St. Lucia was very much in point, and that the occasional visits by Brazilian warships counted for nothing. They concluded:

[40] F.O.C.P. 6794, pp. 42–3.   [41] Ibid., p. 88.   [42] Ibid., p. 90.
[43] Ibid., pp. 92, 92B–C. The opinion and the draft dispatch are printed in McNair, op. cit. above (p. 226 n. 20), pp. 302–3.

The question is not, in our opinion, merely whether the Portuguese or Brazilian Government expressly formed the intention of abandoning the island, but whether their conduct was not such that abandonment must be presumed to have taken place so as to confer a title on the British Government by occupation.[44]

In the private papers of Lord Salisbury there is a memorandum, dated 11 November 1895, written by the Lord Chancellor, Lord Halsbury. The circumstances in which this document was prepared cannot be deduced and it is uncertain, in particular, whether he had before him the draft dispatch as amended by the Law Officers, or, alternatively, the draft dispatch as submitted to the Law Officers. Lord Halsbury wrote:

I am unable to concur in those parts of the proposed despatch which treat of the title to the island. It lays down in terms I think far too broad the doctrine of continuity of actual corporeal possession as being essential to the continuance of the dominion of the island which is according to undisputed facts admitted to have once belonged to Portugal and if so to have passed to Brazil.

As to this it is clear that the island having been occupied by a British force in May 1782, that this was immediately resisted by a protest from the Portuguese Government and that protest was based upon the proprietary right of the Portuguese Crown [reference to page deleted]. On the 19th of July following the British Government ordered an evacuation of the island, that after that, actual occupation of the island was continued by the Portuguese for fifteen years. It would, I think, be impossible to maintain in the face of these facts that Portugal has not established a complete title at all events as against Great Britain by real occupation and possession under it. To this may be added a very instructive discussion by Bynkershoek—1st Chapter *De origine dominii* of his longer treatise *de dominio maris* page 124 of the edition of 1767—where the distinction I was insisting on is discussed at length and the principle I think proved though Bynkershoek is an author who strenuously combats the notion of mere paper claims.

Of course what acts are necessary to continue the title and negative what Mr. Hall speaks of as definite abandonment must differ infinitely according both to circumstances and the nature of the territory sought to be kept. These considerations dispose of most of the international authorities quoted.

Those authorities are dealing with the original acquisition of unoccupied territories and lay down what would hardly be disputed, that a mere paper claim is ineffectual to effect a title to unoccupied territory.

But once it is assumed that the islands became Portuguese territory a very different question arises.[45]

Lord Halsbury went on to consider that the evidence presented by Brazil based on the history of the island 'was very difficult to reply to' and he concluded:

I think the question of the original discovery is under the circumstances irrelevant and I have therefore not discussed it.

The final version of the dispatch was sent to Phipps on 18 November 1895 'for your guidance in any further conversations'.[46] After setting out in brief the history of the dispute and of the island, including the events of 1782, Salisbury disclaimed any British title founded upon Halley's activity in 1700 and placed the root of British title squarely on the occupation of a *terra nullius* in 1895. He asserted that '[t]he language of jurists is clear that a mere paper occupation, devoid of all

[44] F.O.C.P. 6794, p. 92.   [45] Hatfield House MSS. 3M/A/90/1.
[46] F.O.C.P. 6794, pp. 92D–E; McNair, op. cit. above (p. 226 n. 20), pp. 302–5.

effective character, will not preserve a claim to sovereignty over an indefinite number of years, and modern writers speak more emphatically in that sense than their predecessors'. After referring to the instance of St. Lucia and relying on a passage from W. E. Hall, the dispatch concluded on this point:

It is impossible to contend that there was any ground for presuming an intention to return [on the part of Portugal]; and the period of a century which has elapsed since the Portuguese garrison was entirely withdrawn, and with it all the inhabitants of the island, must be taken to exceed 'a reasonable time'.[47]

Having mentioned the 'effective government' provision of the Treaty of Berlin in 1885 as 'evidence of the tendency of international opinion', Salisbury turned from 'broad considerations of general law' to what he described as 'a very special feature'; Trindade could not support any considerable community nor could it be of utility for military or naval purposes, but it was the only spot on earth capable of being used as a landing-place for the proposed cable without the enterprise being financially and technically impracticable. He then formulated the British con-clusion from this as follows:

Where, by natural conditions, the commodity and interests of vast populations depend upon a spot of the earth's surface being put to the use for which it has a special and singular aptitude, it is straining the right of sovereignty very far to say that the owners of this spot of earth shall have the right to declare that, under no conditions, shall it be put to that use, and to withdraw it from the service of mankind.[48]

Salisbury concluded his dispatch by indicating that Britain was willing to submit the question of title to arbitration, if the two Governments could agree upon a satisfactory arbitrator.

When the dispatch arrived in Rio de Janeiro, Phipps sent a private telegram to Lord Salisbury advising him that the paragraph in it referring to Trindade as 'a very special feature' would certainly cause irritation in Brazil.[49] On 16 Decem-ber 1895 Salisbury replied by cable:

I cannot omit that paragraph. It constitutes the defence of the action of the late and present government.[50]

On 18 December 1895 Phipps cabled Eric Barrington, Lord Salisbury's private secretary, to the effect that the dispatch had been left as it was[51] and in a private letter to Barrington, dated 8 January 1896, Phipps wrote that he 'was ashamed to worry Lord Salisbury with private telegrams about the suppressing of a para-graph in his despatch'. He continued:

I of course quite understood the impossibility under the circumstances of omitting it, but I felt sure they would take hold of it as they have done.[52]

VI. The Brazilian Response

Although Phipps reported that the Brazilian Government initially favoured the suggestion of arbitration, both political and public opinion in Brazil hardened against it even before the transmission to Carvalho on 16 December 1895 of the

[47] F.O.C.P. 6794, p. 92E; McNair, op. cit. above (p. 226 n. 20), p. 304.
[48] F.O.C.P. 6794, p. 92E; McNair, op. cit. above (p. 226 n. 20), p. 305.
[49] Hatfield House MSS. 3M/A/130/40.
[50] Ibid. 3M/A/130/42 verso.   [51] Ibid. 3M/A/130/44.   [52] Ibid. 3M/A/130/46.

text of Salisbury's above dispatch. Phipps described the view of one influential politician towards arbitration as being 'only acceptable in a case of doubtful right or of a litigious interest, and not in one in which Brazilian rights are clear and patent and interests legitimate and fundamental'.[53] Phipps reported on 23 November 1895, however, that Carvalho took a better view of mediation.[54]

On 7 January 1896 Carvalho gave Phipps his formal reply to Salisbury's dispatch of 18 November 1895.[55] He set out to refute all the British arguments, maintaining that the island was not ownerless in 1895, that in law it had continued to belong to Brazil after independence, and that the fact that 'through local unfitness, whether permanent or temporary, it is unoccupied and ungoverned does not imply abandonment, nor does it give to any other Power the right to take possession of the territory as if it were a *res nullius*'. The Brazilian note went on to assert that the evacuation of the British troops in 1782 amounted to recognition of the right of Portugal to the island and was not merely a compliance by Britain with a treaty provision prohibiting a particular use of Trindade; since independence, Brazil had performed a series of acts evidencing its intention of maintaining its rights, including the concession of 1884 for the working of minerals. Carvalho claimed that Lord Salisbury 'confounds the *jus possedendi*, right derived from dominion, and the *jus possessionis*, right derived from simple fact. It is sought by this confusion to appeal to a species of international prescription, entirely arbitrary if not violent, with a refusal to recognize the affirmed and repeated intention of Brazil not to abandon her rights.' The Brazilian note went on to reject the suggestion of arbitration, since acceptance of it 'would be contributing to cast doubt upon absolute principles of right, and would be sanctioning discussion upon a thesis which, incidentally put forward, constitutes a serious menace to the sovereignty of such nations as may have an extended territory and restricted means of utilizing it'.

Carvalho then turned to Salisbury's argument that the right of sovereignty was strained in withdrawing such a spot as Trindade from the service of mankind. He described this as an 'alarming assumption' and continued:

This reflection of Lord Salisbury sufficed to dissipate all doubt as to the possibility of accepting the proposal. In this postulate is embodied the abstract theory of *dominio eminente de civilisação* over any portion of the earth, dominion which would be excusable [sc. exercised (Portuguese *exercido*: F.O. 13/782, f. 27)] by the nation which, regarding itself as the patron of humanity, encounters on the part of the owners of such spot of the earth sufficient weakness to submit to such act of disappropriation *à titre gratuit*, viz., conquest.[56]

He concluded the note by expressing the hope that what Britain did in 1782 she might do again now.

The scene then moved briefly to the British House of Commons where on 13 February 1896 the Parliamentary Under-Secretary of State for Foreign Affairs, G. N. Curzon, stated in reply to a question:

The Island of Trinidad was occupied by Great Britain in 1781, and was evacuated in

---

[53] F.O.C.P. 6794, p. 102.
[54] Ibid. Carvalho mentioned as a precedent the mediation by the Pope between Germany and Spain over the Caroline Islands.
[55] F.O.C.P. 6878, pp. 12–17.
[56] Ibid., p. 16.

1782 upon representations made, not by the Government of Brazil, which had not at that time an independent existence, but by the Government of Portugal.

The records of the transaction are in the archives of the Public Departments.

The island was occupied by the late Government, not on the ground of its previous occupation by Great Britain in 1781, but on the ground that, having been abandoned for a century, it belonged to no one. Her Majesty's Government have proposed arbitration to the Brazilian Government as, in their opinion, the best solution of the difficulty.[57]

A supplementary question was then asked, whether the sovereignty of Portugal was recognized by Britain in 1782. Curzon replied:

That is an inference which may be drawn from the action of the Government of 1782, but I cannot say what their motives were.[58]

On 9 March 1896, Phipps, who had been subject to virulent abuse in the Brazilian press over his actions in the Trindade affair, took leave of the President of Brazil.[59] At the leave-taking interview, the President, Prudente de Moraes, told Phipps that it was not the mere assumption of possession of Trindade which had so painfully affected public opinion in Brazil as 'rather the want of consideration to Brazilian feelings which had been evidenced by the clandestine character of the occupation, effected, as it were, without notification of any description'. He added that he was an advocate of arbitration in principle, but only in cases of doubtful right; in the present case, the rights of Brazil were 'patent and beyond dispute'; he personally did not admit the Monroe doctrine to the extent set out in President Cleveland's Message to Congress, since he regarded South America as being for the South Americans and not for the North Americans, though subject to such just claims as European Powers might have in South America.[60]

VII. THE INTERVENTION OF PORTUGAL

(a) The Unofficial Correspondence

The affair continued to simmer without indication that Brazil was willing to accept anything other than a withdrawal by Britain of its claim to the islands; and Brazil in particular was not disposed to admit United States intervention as one means of settlement. Then, in a private letter dated 14 April 1896 from the British Minister in Lisbon, Sir H. MacDonell, to Lord Salisbury, came news of a new initiative. MacDonell reported that he had recently had a confidential conversation with Luis de Soveral, the Portuguese Minister for Foreign Affairs, in which the latter had first impressed on MacDonell the need for observing the utmost secrecy 'as he wished to shield the dignity and *amour propre* of all parties

[57] Hansard, *Parliamentary Debates*, 4th series, vol. 37, cols. 228–9.
[58] Ibid., col. 229.
[59] F.O.C.P. 6878, p. 26.
[60] It is relevant to note here that the dispute came in a period of significance for the settlement of disputes. Britain and the United States of America had entered into negotiations for a general treaty of arbitration. On 2 December 1895 President Cleveland gave his annual Message to Congress in which he called upon Britain to submit its boundary dispute with Venezuela to impartial arbitration (*Foreign Relations of the United States*, 1895, pt. i, pp. xxviii–xxix); dissatisfied with the British reply, Cleveland issued another message to Congress, dated 17 December 1895, in which he based the Monroe doctrine on principles of international law (ibid., pp. 542–5). Furthermore, it was on 20 August 1896 that the Lord Chief Justice of England, Lord Russell of Killowen, delivered his famous Saratoga Springs address on the subject of international arbitration.

concerned'. Soveral's proposal, which he said was known only to his Prime Minister and himself, involved the acceptance by Britain and Brazil of the 'good offices' of Portugal in the following manner:

It appears that in the Act of Cession, or rather in the Act by which Portugal recognized the independence of Brazil, the Island of Trindade—which was intended to form part of the territory ceded—was by some accident omitted to be specified or named. Technically therefore, it might be in the power of Portugal to advance just such an ostensible claim to it as might justify its surrender to Portugal by Brazil, it being previously and privately understood that the island should be immediately afterwards retroceded to the Republic, with the condition that the right of England should be recognized—if necessary in perpetuity—to land a cable and establish thereon a telegraphic station.[61]

Soveral denied MacDonell's surmise that the Brazilian Government had prompted the overture and, in reporting the news to Salisbury, MacDonell doubted whether Brazil would indeed agree 'to surrender for a composition the concrete right which they at present assert to the Island'.

In a private telegram dated 28 April 1896, Salisbury replied to MacDonell:

Express my sincere acknowledgments to the Minister for Foreign Affairs for his friendly action in the matter of Trinidad.
We shall accept very willingly the mediation of Portugal if it is first accepted by, or proposed by, Brazil.[62]

On 4 May 1896 MacDonell notified Salisbury by private telegram that Soveral had told him of Brazil's willingness to accept the 'good offices' of Portugal.[63] The discussion then turned to the mechanism for achieving a result satisfactory to all parties concerned. On 10 June 1896 MacDonell sent a private telegram to Salisbury stating that he feared Brazil might raise some objection to the landing of a cable on Trindade. He proposed that Soveral address a note to Salisbury giving the reasons why the island belonged to Brazil and stating that it would be desirable to all if Salisbury would recognize Brazilian sovereignty; Soveral, on his part, would undertake to obtain from Brazil a formal promise to the effect that its Government would sanction the establishment of a cable in perpetuity.[64] Salisbury replied to MacDonell on 11 June 1896 as follows:

We are ready to leave to Portugal the decision whether the island shall belong to Great Britain or to Brazil. I will accept thankfully the assistance of Portugal in obtaining from Brazil as a condition of our recognition the sanction of the establishment of a cable and cable station there.[65]

In a private telegram to Salisbury dated 27 June 1896, MacDonell passed on the following message at Soveral's request:

Portuguese Minister for Foreign Affairs proposes that he should address an official note to Your Lordship through Portuguese Minister in London, asking Her Majesty's Government to recognize sovereignty of Brazil over island of Trinidad, setting forth grounds upon which he recommends the recognition. No reference will be made in the note to any previous understanding with regard to landing of the British cable. With the sanction of

---

[61] Hatfield House MSS. 3M/A/128/6.   [62] Ibid. 3M/A/128/38.   [63] Ibid. 3M/A/128/8.
[64] Ibid. 3M/A/128/12. On 13 May 1896, MacDonell had informed Lord Salisbury's private secretary, Barrington, that he felt 'somewhat suspicious lest these gentlemen [Soveral and his Minister in London] make a cat's-paw of us to curry favour with the Brazilians' (ibid. 3M/A/128/10).
[65] Ibid. 3M/A/128/12.

Her Majesty's Government, he proposes to make this recognition public. The recognition to be immediately followed by request addressed by Her Majesty's Government to Brazil through the Portuguese Government, asking permission to land cable and establish station for permanent use on the island, it being secretly understood with Brazil that this permission shall at once be granted.[66]

Salisbury cabled MacDonell on 29 June 1896 in reply:

In view of what has happened I do not think I can make the simple recognition asked for by Portugal. But I am quite ready to refer the matter either to the arbitration or mediation of Portugal.[67]

In the light of this reply, MacDonell went back to Soveral and in a private telegram dated 16 July 1896 he set out Soveral's new suggested method of proceeding:

Portuguese Representative at Rio has at the instance of Portugal's Minister for Foreign Affairs received the written assurance of Brazilian Government that they are prepared to sanction landing of British cable and the establishment of a telegraph station on the island. Consequently if Your Lordship will now authorize Portuguese Minister for Foreign Affairs to inform Brazilian Government that Her Majesty's Government are willing, on his recommendation, to recognize Brazilian sovereignty over island he will then obtain from the Brazilian Government formal declaration sanctioning the landing of cable, in exchange for which he would wish to be formally authorized by Her Majesty's Government to guarantee recognition by Her Majesty's Government of the sovereignty of Brazilian Government.[68]

Salisbury's reaction to this proposed procedure was set out in a private telegram sent to MacDonell the next day, 17 July 1896. In it, he stated:

I am very anxious to do what Monsieur de Soveral wishes: but he does not see my difficulty. If Portugal, acting as mediator, pronounces that the island really belongs to Brazil, I will accept that decision. But I cannot, spontaneously, retract the assertion of title made by my predecessor and myself: nor can I give the island away gratuitously. It seems to me therefore it is for Portugal first to accept from the two powers the office of mediator.[69]

MacDonell telegraphed Salisbury on 18 July 1896 that as Brazil objected to the use of the word 'mediator' Soveral proposed to solve the question by the offer of his 'good offices'.[70] MacDonell summarized the state of play in the course of a private letter to Salisbury dated 20 July 1896:

. . . Brazil having accepted the good offices of Portugal has secretly sanctioned the landing of the cable. This sanction will be formally recognized when Monsieur de Soveral officially makes known his views on the merits of the case.

On Your Lordship's acceptance of his 'good offices', Monsieur de Soveral will declare his opinion by addressing a note to the Portuguese Legation (copy of which I enclose) stating the grounds upon which he considers the sovereignty of the Island to belong to Brazil. Simultaneously he will demand of Brazil the official sanction referred to.[71]

Also in the private archives of the Marquess of Salisbury is a minute from Sir T. H. Sanderson, Permanent Under-Secretary of State at the Foreign Office, suggesting certain amendments to the proposed Portuguese note. Sanderson concluded:

[66] Hatfield House MSS. 3M/A/128/13.   [67] Ibid.   [68] Ibid. 3M/A/128/15.
[69] Ibid. 3M/A/128/42.   [70] Ibid. 3M/A/128/16.   [71] Ibid. 3M/A/128/17.

I understand that Monsieur de Soveral promises simultaneously to demand from the Brazilian Government an official assurance that the landing of a telegraph cable shall be sanctioned, but we ought to be sure that the answer will be favourable.[72]

The Salisbury archives then contain the draft by Sanderson of a cable to MacDonell of the same date, accepting Soveral's proposed note with some suggested modifications.[73] The last paragraph of the draft cable was in terms of the conclusion to Sanderson's minute above but was crossed through, it appears by Salisbury himself, who initialled the draft before dispatch.

(b) *The Official Correspondence*

None of the above private correspondence found its way into either the Confidential Print or the Foreign Office files. The first piece of official correspondence relating to Soveral's intervention was a note from him to MacDonell dated 20 July 1896. This note, the text of which was already known to MacDonell and Salisbury, read as follows:

It has come to the knowledge of His Majesty's Government that between the Government of Her Britannic Majesty and that of the Republic of the United States of Brazil a serious disagreement has recently arisen with respect to the occupation of the Island of Trinidad.

The island was discovered in the 16th century by Portuguese navigators, and remained notoriously under the dominion of Portugal without any interruption until the end of the first quarter of this century.

His Majesty's Government find themselves, therefore, in a position which enables them to form an impartial judgment as to the justice of the case in dispute.

They are consequently willing, inspired by feelings of cordial esteem and friendship which closely unite Portugal to the two High Contending Parties, to offer their good offices for a more prompt and friendly settlement of the incident, in the event of Her Britannic Majesty's Government being animated by the same kindly feelings and deeming it expedient to accept their offer.[74]

Having advised the Brazilian Minister in London, Corrêa, that Britain was willing to accept Portuguese good offices, mediation or arbitration, Salisbury informed MacDonell in an official dispatch dated 29 July 1896 that Britain accepted the good offices of the Portuguese Government.[75] This news was officially communicated to Soveral by MacDonell on 3 August 1896.[76]

Brazil having also accepted the Portuguese offer, matters now moved rapidly. *The Times* in its issue of 6 August 1896 reported that on the previous day the Portuguese Government had issued a press statement to the effect that it had decided in favour of Brazil and that Britain had accepted the decision. A cautionary footnote added that 'Reuter's Agency states that it learns on trustworthy authority that the announcement of the recognition by the British Government of the sovereignty of Brazil over the island of Trinidad is premature, although a solution in favour of the sovereignty of Brazil over the islet is not impossible'. Indeed on 5 August 1896 the Brazilian Legation in Lisbon cabled to Brazil the text of a message signed by Soveral stating an opinion in favour of Brazilian sovereignty and announcing that the British Government 'has already

[72] Ibid. 3M/A/128/45.   [73] Ibid. 3M/A/128/44.
[74] F.O.C.P. 6878, p. 28. The original document, in Portuguese, is in F.O. 179/327, ff. 229–30.
[75] F.O.C.P. 6878, p. 29.   [76] Ibid., p. 27.

nobly declared that it recognizes the sovereignty of Brazil over the Island of Trinidad'.[77] This news was greeted with public rejoicing in Rio de Janeiro when the news broke there on 6 August 1896.

It was not until 7 August 1896 that the Portuguese chargé d'affaires in London, A. de Castro, formally communicated to the Foreign Office the note the text of which had been substantially agreed between Salisbury and Soveral a week earlier. The note set out briefly the history of Portuguese sovereignty and the recognition of it by Britain in 1782. It then continued:

> When, under the Treaty of Rio de Janeiro of the 29th August, 1825, Portugal proclaimed the independence of its ancient Colony, the Island of Trinidad was transferred to Brazil, together with the group to which it belongs, for formal possession by the new Empire. There could be no doubt in the mind of His Majesty's Government on that point, although no special mention of this transfer is made in the Treaty referred to, the island being, as it was annexed for administrative purposes to the Province of Espiritu Santo, a dependency of the Captaincy Major of Rio de Janeiro.
>
> It is certain that every effort to cultivate and people the island having failed, including what was done after the above-mentioned temporary occupation, the island remained up to our time uncultivated and uninhabited, and therefore apparently abandoned.
>
> It was this apparent abandonment which led to the recent and inexact supposition that the island had been definitely and really abandoned. The correspondence exchanged in 1782, and the consequent recognition of Portuguese sovereignty by the British Government having been, not unnaturally, forgotten; but this transitory abandonment of the island being caused by its peculiar condition, and the Brazilian Government never having failed to assert by its actions its intention of possessing it, this state of things was sufficient fully to explain, and does fully explain, the error which occurred, but could not, in the opinion of His Majesty's Government, justify or legitimize the occupation and taking possession carried out in consequence of this error.
>
> In view of these facts, and in view of the sincere conviction now set forth by His Majesty's Government as to the rights claimed by the Brazilian Government, they trust that the Government of Her Britannic Majesty will be prepared to recognize the full sovereignty of Brazil over the island in question.[78]

By a cable dated 7 August 1896, Salisbury instructed MacDonell:

> You are authorized to inform the Minister for Foreign Affairs that Her Majesty's Government are prepared to accept the opinion thus expressed, and in deference thereto, to withdraw their claim to the possession of Trinidad.[79]

VIII. The Closing Stages

The House of Commons, and by this means the nation, was informed of the outcome of the dispute through a Parliamentary answer from the Under-Secretary of State for Foreign Affairs on 13 August 1896.[80] The flagstaff and other insignia of sovereignty left on Trindade were removed by the *Barracouta* on 28 August 1896.[81] There is no indication in the British public records or in the private archives of Lord Salisbury that the 'written assurance' by the Brazilian

---

[77] F.O.C.P. 6878, pp. 40–1.   [78] Ibid., pp. 31–2.

[79] Ibid., p. 32. It was observed in France that '[i]ntervention du Portugal semble, d'ailleurs, avoir été motivée surtout par le désir de fournir l'Angleterre une porte honorable de sortie . . .': *Revue générale de droit international public*, 4 (1897), p. 148.

[80] Hansard, *Parliamentary Debates*, 4th series, vol. 44, cols. 744–5.

[81] F.O.C.P. 6878, pp. 43–5.

Government permitting the landing of a British cable was ever officially given. The formal correspondence between Soveral and the two Governments in dispute was published in the official Portuguese journal *Diario do Governo* after Salisbury had agreed without demur to a request by Soveral that the dates of the official dispatches to and from Britain be altered 'in view of their coinciding better with the correspondence on the subject with Brazil'.[82] Much to his delight, and without great cost to the British Treasury, Soveral was appointed an honorary member of the Order of the Knights Grand Cross of St. Michael and St. George.[83] As for the fate of Baron Harden Hickey—'King James I of Trinidad'—the final Foreign Office case volume on the dispute carries as its ultimate folio a cutting from the *Pall Mall Gazette* of 11 February 1898 recording the death from self-administered poison in a hotel in El Paso, Texas, of the 'soi-disant Prince of Trinidad'.[84]

---

[82] *Diario do Governo*, 25 August 1896 (F.O. 13/782, f. 345). Thus Soveral's official note dated 20 July 1896 was printed as being dated 1 May 1896; the date of the Portuguese Government's official conclusion was printed as 20 July 1896 instead of 7 August 1896. The *Revue générale* (see p. 238 n. 79 above) used the falsified dates.

[83] *London Gazette*, 1897, p. 185; see also Hatfield House MSS. 3M/A/128/24.

[84] F.O. 13/782, f. 378.

REVIEWS OF BOOKS

Encyclopedia of Public International Law. Volume 3: *Use of Force, War and Neutrality, Peace Treaties* (*A–M*); Volume 4: *Use of Force, War and Neutrality, Peace Treaties* (*N–Z*); Volume 5: *International Organizations in General, Universal International Organizations and Cooperation.* Published under the auspices of the Max Planck Institute, under the direction of RUDOLPH BERNHARDT. Amsterdam: North Holland Publishing Company, 1981–2. Volume 3, 299 pp. Volume 4, 375 pp. Volume 5, 427 pp.

These three volumes maintain the very high standard set by the first volume in this comprehensive and highly ambitious venture. The entries vary enormously in their scope. In the two volumes devoted to the use of force, one finds entries on major topics such as aggression, civil war, intervention, land warfare, neutrality and self-defence, and much smaller entries on topics which are either very precise (e.g. *Graf Spee*, Martens Clause, Mines) or are in the nature of case-notes on actual cases or incidents.

The need to cross-reference is accepted by the editors and is liberally done. Thus a somewhat inadequate treatment of self-defence in three pages (Brun-Otto Bryde) is supplemented by a far more thorough entry on the use of force in nine pages (Albrecht Randelzhofer). Indeed, in the nature of things a certain degree of overlap is inevitable. For example, there are separate entries for Guerrilla Forces (Otto Kimminich), Mercenaries (Antonio Cassese), Liberation Movements (Konrad Ginther) and Wars of National Liberation (Henn-Juri Uibopuu); and obviously there is duplication. Yet there is no obvious answer, for to embrace all categories in a more general heading of 'Combatants' (and that, too, is a separate heading) would simply mean that the work would cease to be an encyclopedia with the advantages of separate, specific entries.

It is to be expected that, in a work of so large a compass, views will be expressed which are controversial. For example, this reviewer would not share the conclusions of Randelzhofer (Use of Force) or Beyerlin (Humanitarian Intervention) that force used in the protection of nationals abroad is unlawful. The latter's treatment of the sources of law is not without interest. Having reviewed the various illustrations from State practice supporting the view that such force is lawful, Beyerlin notes that the issues were highly disputed in the Security Council—which, of course, cuts both ways—and then points to a widespread view in the literature condemning such action. What is implied, therefore, is that literature is a more persuasive source or evidence of customary law than State practice.

Yet in some ways it is more satisfying to see the author reach a view, even if one disagrees with it, than to see no view expressed. The article on Nuclear Tests (Herbert von Arx) is disappointing in this respect. He rightly draws attention to the various rules governing the legality of nuclear testing, but offers no real conclusion on their effect. In certain cases a view is expressed, but it lacks conviction simply because it is not a *reasoned* view. Erik Suy (United Nations Peace-keeping System) tells us, categorically, that host State consent is necessary for *all* peace-keeping operations. Why should this be so if the operation is decided upon by a mandatory resolution of the Security Council under Chapter Seven of the United Nations Charter? Ludwig Weber (Cuban Quarantine) accepts the permissibility of the argument of anticipatory self-defence (incidentally, this is not a view consistently held by other contributors) but fails to explain why the imminent possession of medium range ballistic missiles by Cuba was an unlawful act.

Volume 5, on Universal Organizations, will in due course be followed by Volume 6 on Regional Organizations. It is certainly comprehensive, and entries appear on Inmarsat, Intelsat, Interpol, and even the United Nations University. Perhaps the most interesting entries are not so much those devoted to particular organizations—although these are all valuable—but rather those dealing with the more general, theoretical problems. There are excellent entries on Resolutions (Henry G. Schermers), Treaty-Making Power (Karl Zemanek), Voting (Schermers) and the Veto (Fritz Munch), and International Legislation (Skubiszewski). The quality of this volume will, if matched by the forthcoming volume on Regional Organizations, be such as to make it an acceptable source-book in any general postgraduate course on the law of international organizations.   D. W. Bowett

*Völkerrecht als Rechtsordnung, Internationale Gerichtsbarkeit, Menschen-
rechte. Festschrift für Hermann Mosler.* Edited by Rudolf Bernhardt,
Wilhelm Karl Geck, Günther Jaenicke and Helmut Steinberger.
Berlin, Heidelberg, New York: Springer-Verlag, 1983. xiv + 1057 pp.

There is, possibly, only one thing worse than not being either the devotee of, or contributor to, a truly monumental Festschrift such as the present one, and that is being a reviewer, a kind of 'scientific groupie'. Naturally, Professor Mosler's eminence called for a special celebratory effort: 52 essays (27 in German, 13 in English, 9 in French and 3 in Spanish) by as many celebrities in the field of public and international law. Rich birthday cakes, though, may cause indigestion and if the present review appears somewhat muted it is due to the exhausting effort of absorbing some thousand pages of a formidable *chef d'œuvre*. One of the oldest and least controversial German proverbs says: 'allzuviel ist ungesund'. The editor's choice of the threefold title indicates Mosler's main scientific interest. There is unfortunately no corresponding classification of essays under these headings so as to achieve some thematic cohesion of contributions, ostensibly, because several essays might not have fitted any of the chosen themes. However, instead of selecting some other more comprehensively fitting categories for the sake of presentation, the editors 'arranged' all essays merely in alphabetical order of their authors. Nevertheless, the sheer richness of the material presents an agonizing dilemma to a reviewer. Leaving aside essays about historical (Truyol Serra, A.; Verosta, S.) or mainly domestic constitutional subjects (Bayer, H.-W.; Doehring, K.; Fromont, M.; Partsch, K. J.; Puente Egido, J.; Rudolf, W.; Schlochauer, H.-J.; Schneider, H.; Schweisfurth, T.; Steinberger, H.; Tsatsos, D. Th.), one may group the remaining articles into those dealing with various aspects of human rights (Bastid, S.; Bernhardt, R.; Evrigenis, D.; Fitzmaurice, Sir Gerald; Ganshof Van Der Meersch, W. J.; Hailbronner, K.; Matscher, F.; Miyazaki, S.; Ress, G.; Suy, E.; Tomuschat, C.); those relating to issues involving structural elements of an international legal order such as: sources (Ballreich, H.; Bleckmann, A.; Frowein, J. A.; Lachs, M.; Monaco, R.; Munch, F.; Reuter, P.; Rosenne, S.), legal personality (Barberis, J. A.) and the relationship between international law, E.E.C. law and municipal law respectively (Bothe, M.; Evrigenis, D.; Hilf, M.; Mann, F. A.; Pescatore, P.). Other groups comprise subjects related to international organizations (Klein, F.; Schermers, H. G.; Seidl-Hohenveldern, I.; Skubiszewski, K.; Sperduti, G.), international tribunals (Elias, T. O.; Gros, A.; Jiménez De Aréchaga, E. V.; Mangoldt, H.; McWhinney, E.; Oda, S.; Schachter, O.) and the law of the sea (Geck, W. K.; Jaenicke, G.). The above subdivision is, of course, rough and necessarily arbitrary and several articles straddle various fields of public international law. There are also substantive overlaps: for example, there are three essays on intervention in the International Court of Justice.

Ballreich investigates 'Wesen und Wirkung' of consensus in international law, affirming at the outset that this novel technique of law-making has become indispensable and requires elucidation. This, however, he does not do by means of a review of pertinent practice, and one's faint foreboding that 'Wesen' heralds theoretical excursions soon comes true. Interestingly, he traces the functional characteristics of 'consensus' in municipal civil and public law and distinguishes it from informal consent which some scholars think is the basis both of international law and international obligation (cf. Parry, *Sources and Evidences of Inter-*

national Law, p. 2). However, no comparable analysis is made with respect to State practice beyond the correct but rather bland statement that international organizations and in particular the United Nations proceed pragmatically only, as if this were tantamount to sin itself. However, if a definition is to be considered the kernel of a theoretical groundwork, one could have mentioned the legal opinion of the Secretary-General of the United Nations on the use of the term 'consensus' in United Nations practice (*United Nations Juridical Yearbook*, 1974, p. 163) which shows an 'increasing tendency to formulate and even to adopt treaties by consensus' (Review of the Multilateral Treaty Making Process, Report of the Secretary-General, AE/35/312 (27 August 1980), paragraph 58). Ballreich doubts the benefits if not the wisdom of proceeding by 'consensus': firstly, because the old conviction that static law must be made dynamic has been overcome and, secondly, because the benefit of the acceleration of proceedings in plenary session tends to be obliterated by time-consuming attention to the minutiae of drafting in smaller groups. This point might have best been illustrated by reference to the proceedings at UNCLOS III.

It is particularly that experience which underlies Rosenne's examination of the meaning of 'authentic text' in modern treaty law, a complex subject rarely covered by writers. His aim is an assessment of the scope of the juridical content, if any, of the word 'authentic' with respect to multilingual instruments in the light of Articles 10 and 33 of the Vienna Convention on the Law of Treaties. A review of a small selection of international tribunals (International Court of Justice, Arbitral Tribunal and Mixed Commission for the Agreement on German Debts, Court of Justice of the European Communities, European Court of Human Rights) serves to demonstrate that judicial interpretation exhibits little concern for the principle of the interpretation of the single treaty in accordance with its authentic language versions, and in particular by reference to the Vienna Convention. This relative disinterest is paralleled by that of participants in international conferences after San Francisco and prior to the sophisticated machinery for achieving linguistic concordance set up by UNCLOS III. The term 'authentic' in Article 33 is not accompanied by instructions for use. But then, Rosenne argues, formal linguistic concordance apart, 'perhaps the ultimate aim is to reach something more elusive—conceptual concordance in all cases' (p. 784). Commendable though such profundity must be it can hardly be expected to expedite the cumbersome and empirically developing process of international conference law-making, or to resolve all questions of judicial interpretation.

Lachs searches for the 'threshold of law-making'. Consent expressed in treaties remains the principal instrument governing inter-State relations, but their increased complexity has led to the evolution of new treaty and law-making procedures by international organizations. Why, one must ask, do some scholars never tire of demanding precision in distinguishing formal and other 'imperfect' sources of law? Is it for reasons of rigorous systematic cohesion amongst the sources of law, or because they prefer sheep to be distinguished from goats, or vice versa? Of course, Lachs concludes his survey of law-making processes with the recognition that 'recent developments have undoubtedly contributed to widening the possibility of passing the threshold' (p. 500). It appears that the threshold he has in mind is that of legality. This metaphor, though, does not appear to be a happy one: firstly, there is no single threshold because there is a growing variety and flexibility of tests which determine whether binding force has been attained, as the author himself points out. Secondly, it wrongly suggests some mechanical barrier or dam separating a legal 'panta rei' as it were from an orderly stream. However, such props are no more necessary to the concept of order in law than is the date of Columbus's arrival in America to the concept of the 'modern age'. Whether one adopts the term 'authority' with its different shades of stringency or some other expression of 'continuum' is immaterial. What matters is that there is an increasing need for regulation for which established formal procedures are inadequate.

Monaco's contribution is a striking example of unyielding procrustean formalism in response to the challenge of atypical sources in international law: it would seem that preoccupation with their assimilation into the hierarchical order of traditional categories of sources has now been abandoned by most international lawyers.

Bleckmann analyses the practice of customary international law as consecutive law-making (*konsekutive Rechtsetzung*) and dismisses the dominant view of the doctrine according to which mere factual conduct followed by *opinio juris* creates customary international law. He is emphatic that practice does not merely consist of factual conduct but also consists of legal acts by which it is sought to determine or shape a legal problem in either the domestic or international legal order. Practice therefore simply means asserting an abstract legal rule as one of customary international law *uno actu*. However, the dominant doctrinal view seems no longer attached to the view of separate steps and to attack it on that ground means shooting at clay pigeons instead of at real ones. Indeed it has been observed that conduct of collectivities of rational beings is hardly ever mindless (Parry, op. cit., p. 61). Conversely, *opinio juris* as a distinct endowment of conduct was described as 'mere fiction' (Judge Lachs, dissenting opinion in the *North Sea Continental Shelf* cases, *I.C.J. Reports*, 1969, p. 231).

Bleckmann also castigates dominant opinion for what he perceives as lack of dogmatic orientation and methodologically feeble pragmatism. He says that the content of State practice itself, not pronouncements by the Permanent Court of International Justice and the International Court of Justice, should be analysed to elicit the conditions for the emergence of customary international law. Criticism of reliance on such pronouncements is, of course, justified. The Court tends to think in terms of rights and obligations between the parties before it. Sometimes, State practice is not actually investigated at all, yet inferences as to its content may be made (cf. the clear implication of the invalidity of Iceland's claim to exclusive fisheries jurisdiction beyond twelve miles without a direct ruling on this United Kingdom submission, *Fisheries Jurisdiction* case, 1974). One has become accustomed to being enriched by the acuity and complexity of argument displayed in the works of this author. Bleckmann contends that where a State begins to adopt a new practice this must be analysed as assertion of a legal rule (*Behauptung eines Rechtssatzes*)—*contra legem*—rather than as erroneous cognition and interpretation of the existing rule of law (*Rechtserkenntnis*), as practice based on 'error' would none the less be obligatory. Use of the term and concept of a 'claim' would perhaps help to avoid unnecessary conceptual tangles such as these. A single claim does not give rise to a rule of customary international law, but concordant accumulation of claims may have this effect.

Frowein and Münch address the concepts of 'obligations *erga omnes*' and '*jus cogens*' respectively, both taking some critical inspiration from Mosler's 'The International Society as a Legal Community' (*Recueil des cours*, 140 (1974-IV), p. 1). Distrust of the unifying potential of such notions as the 'international community' in the face of a conflict-torn and crisis-ridden international legal order underlies their examination of these supporting pillars of 'international society'.

Münch points out that the idea of *jus cogens* has spread into all the books and concentrates therefore on two more neglected aspects: the relationship of *jus cogens* to equivalent and related phenomena in municipal law; and on a tentative catalogue of norms having the effect of *jus cogens*. His brief perusal of municipal private law reveals little more than that, in the absence of statutory definitions, it is left to interpretation to ascertain the peremptory character of substantive as well as procedural norms, sometimes without any reference to an overriding *ordre public*. By contrast Münch suggests that constitutional law and, in particular, the formulation of a new substantive '*contrat social*' after a revolution offers a better model to emulate. The compilation of a catalogue is necessary since Article 53 of the Vienna Convention on the Law of Treaties deals only with the effect of *jus cogens* without providing either a definition or a list of its manifestations. Unavoidably, there is the danger of some subjectivity in selecting legal values for special protection, a problem which the emergence of a majority opinion must remedy.

Frowein reflects on the question of the enforceability *erga omnes* of obligations, the protection of which constitutes a legal interest of the community of States as a whole. Conceptually, the well-known distinction made by the Court of Justice in the *Barcelona Traction* case is widely accepted today. On the other hand, Frowein's examples of sanctions by way of reprisal by third States cannot be considered as clear-cut evidence of relevant State practice. One notable exception is the formal sanctions adopted by the foreign ministers of the European Community against Iran for a gross violation of the rules of international law governing diplomatic immunity. Furthermore, as Frowein points out, apart from the abortive claim by Liberia and Ethiopia in the *South West Africa* cases (*Second Phase*, I.C.J. Reports, 1966, p. 4), no State has as yet attempted to enforce *erga omnes* obligations without a special interest of its own.

Everling asks whether the member States of the European Community are still 'masters of the treaty' and summarizes practice tending to show that the sheer volume of Community regulation and its significance for the life of individuals have loosened the grip of the member States of the European Community. Hitherto, the question of the relationship between the European Economic Community and international law has been examined with excessive conceptual 'determinism'. This writer asks pragmatically, if somewhat defensively, whether international law is still needed to supplement the Community legal order. The provisions of a number of treaties as well as the numerous areas in which harmonization has been carried out and the gradual acquisition of additional competences by the Community may be advanced as arguments supporting the contention that an autonomous and self-sufficient legal order has emerged and developed beyond 'the point of return' quite apart from those considerations based upon political, economic and social interdependence.

Recognition of a fast-growing practice of the European Communities of entering into bilateral and multilateral treaties as well as participation in other international organizations prompted Hilf to embark on an interesting and comprehensive survey of the European Communities and mechanisms for international dispute settlement. Earlier reticence to accept judicial dispute settlement is ascribed to the fact that the bulk of E.E.C. treaties had been concluded in pursuance of a common commercial policy where negotiations achieve a better balance of interests than adjudication. However, both the commitment of member States to the tradition of adjudication in support of the rule of law and a consolidation of external competences militate in favour of increased use of *ad hoc* dispute settlement procedures without institutionalized encumbrances.

This volume contains many thoroughly searching essays on human rights. Without disrespect to any of them, only that of the late Sir Gerald Fitzmaurice will be mentioned here. Having drafted but not delivered a dissenting minority judgment in *The Sunday Times* case, he contributed 'Some Reflections on the European Convention on Human Rights—and on Human Rights'. In his view both the manner in which the European Convention is drafted and modes of interpretation adopted by the Commission and the Court have lead to the blurring of distinctions between different acts violating human rights. Consequently, he insists on redrawing the lines between serious matters (in his view only human rights *stricto sensu* with immanence in the notion of man) and civic rights, mere matters of socio-economics, as he puts it. He makes a spirited attack on the tendency to equate those human rights which are rooted in the law of nature with 'those that are man-made'. To support his contention that such an approach involves legal and historical impropriety, Fitzmaurice refers to the drafting history of the United Nations Covenants, as well as to a range of terms which denoted man's entitlement to certain rights *iure naturale* (self-evident, self-existent, inalienable, inherent, ordained by man, by nature, absolute, immemorial, founded in nature and reason), to be preserved from all (State) infringement. With his emphasis on the need to afford the 'most fundamental of human rights and freedoms' (Articles 2–6 and 9 of the European Convention) superior protection—strict interpretation, no derogations—he joins Münch's idea of *jus cogens* in all but name. In the *Barcelona Traction* case the International Court of Justice used the phrase 'basic rights of the human person' which, being 'the concern of all states' gave rise to obligations *erga omnes*, the term 'basic' marking the distinction which the Court made between such rights and the fundamental human rights enshrined in international human rights treaties. It will be recalled that when Sir Gerald Fitzmaurice was acting as one of the majority judges in the *South West Africa* cases (*Second Phase, I.C.J. Reports*, 1966, p. 4) he rejected the concept of *actio popularis* in international law. It would seem that this state of affairs has been left largely unaltered by the *Barcelona Traction* case or the joint dissenting opinion in the *Nuclear Test* cases (*I.C.J. Reports*, 1974, p. 370). However, given the naturalist position adopted by Sir Gerald Fitzmaurice, one wonders whether he might now be prepared to accept an *actio popularis* as a procedural complement to safeguard fundamental human rights against serious breaches in the absence of enforcement machinery such as that available under the European Convention.

Essays on 'international organizations' comprise 'Remarks on the Interpretation of the United Nations Charter' by Skubiszewski; a stimulating analysis of issues of litispendence and *res judicata* in connection with questions of the parallel competences of the Security Council and the International Court of Justice with respect to disputes likely to endanger international peace and security by Klein; an account of questions arising from the E.E.C. membership of other international organizations by Schermers; thoughts on the capacity of third States to invoke the international responsibility of the member States of an international organization despite the latter's independent international legal personality by Seidl-Hohenveldern; and comments on the question of the accession by the European Communities to the Convention on Human Rights and Fundamental Freedoms by Sperduti.

By far the longest individual contribution is by Geck, one of the editors, who discusses the freedom of navigation for warships after UNCLOS III and who concludes that such freedom has on the whole been reduced, particularly because the space of the high seas in which it could be exercised has been restricted by special zones beneficial to coastal States. Geck's faith in the deterrent effect of the global presence of naval forces in all parts of the seas upon further extension of national jurisdiction into the high seas echoes O'Connell's view that freedom of navigation of naval forces is essentially a historical corollary of that of merchant ships which they protected.

This Festschrift features many other interesting essays, a proper review of which would require a monograph of its own. However, space allotted to book reviews is notoriously limited. A list of contributors and of Mosler's main publications completes this most valuable volume, practical use of which might have been enhanced by a touch of greater editorial stringency and, above all, an index. This is a book of impressive scholarship and many ideas. It will stimulate many others.

                                                                    FRIEDL WEISS

New Rules for Victims of Armed Conflicts. By MICHAEL BOTHE, KARL JOSEF PARTSCH and WALDEMAR A. SOLF. The Hague: Martinus Nijhoff, 1982. xxii + 744 pp. ƒ 340.00.

Documents on the Laws of War. Edited by ADAM ROBERTS and RICHARD GUELFF. Oxford: Clarendon Press, 1982. xii + 498 pp. £18·50 hard cover, £10·95 paper cover.

The publication of these two volumes is further evidence of the revival of academic interest in the laws of armed conflict. Both are welcome additions to the literature on the subject and will prove extremely useful to anyone interested in this area of international law.

New Rules for Victims of Armed Conflicts is the latest of the spate of books about the two 1977 Protocols additional to the Geneva Conventions of 1949. The work is a detailed commentary on the text of the Protocols written by three authors who were all involved in the Diplomatic Conference which drew up the new agreements—Professors Bothe and Partsch were members of the delegation of the Federal Republic of Germany, while Mr. Solf was a member of the United States delegation. Their book is intended primarily as a work of reference. The text of each article of the Protocols is given in full. This is followed by a guide to the history of the provision, containing references to the pre-Conference work (such as the reports of the Conference of Government Experts and the Conference of Red Cross experts and reference to the corresponding provisions of the I.C.R.C. draft Protocols) and the Conference drafting history. There are also references to any declarations or reservations concerning the provision and to the pre-existing law (if any) from which the article in question is derived. The latter is a particularly valuable feature of the book. The authors do not confine themselves to citing the more obvious provisions of the 1949 Geneva Conventions or the Hague Conventions of 1907 but include references to provisions in earlier agreements which may be said to reflect a trend which was later taken up and developed in the Protocols. Thus, for example, the notes to Article 47 of the First Protocol, which provides that mercenaries have no right to be treated as prisoners of war, contains references to the prohibition on the formation of corps on the territory of neutral States (Hague Convention No. V of 1907) as well as to the definitions of lawful combatants in the 1907 and 1949 Conventions.

The commentaries which follow the text of each article are the work of the author who was most closely involved in the drafting of that provision (the Table of Contents indicates who was responsible for each section). The principal emphasis is on the drafting history and the light which this sheds on the meaning of each part of the text. The commentaries are thus a valuable source of information on the intricate pattern of understandings about the meaning of certain provisions and the relationship between the different sections of the Protocols which did not find its way into the text, especially in the case of those provisions which were the product of frequently uneasy compromises between the different groups at the Conference. Much of this information can, of course, be gleaned from other sources but the advantages of having it available in so accessible a form are obvious. Moreover, because the book was published some five years after the conclusion of the Conference, the commentaries also review much of the other literature on the Protocols. This feature of the volume is particularly evident in the commentaries on some of the more controversial provisions of the Protocols, such as Article 1 (4) of the First Protocol. This article confers upon 'armed conflicts in which peoples are fighting against colonial domination and alien occupation and against racist regimes in the exercise of their right of self-determination' the status of international conflicts. The commentary on this provision is a careful analysis of the scope of the concept of self-determination and concludes, as have several other writers, that outside Palestine and South Africa this provision was not intended to have any real significance.

The value of this book as a work of reference is also enhanced by a detailed index and a 'Guide to Documentation' which assists the reader in ascertaining the fate of the various provisions of the I.C.R.C. draft protocols and explains how to follow up the references to the original conference documents (the source quoted throughout this book) in the seventeen-volume *Official Records* (the source more commonly available).

Documents on the Laws of War is a collection of the basic texts needed by anyone studying the laws of armed conflict: twenty-nine documents ranging from the 1856 Paris Declaration respecting Maritime Law to the 1981 United Nations Convention on Conventional Weapons. The bulk of the documents included are treaties but the volume also includes a few other texts considered to be particularly influential, such as the 1971 Resolution of the Institut de Droit International on the application of the laws of armed conflict to hostilities involving United Nations forces. The documents are set out in a particularly convenient form. Each treaty is accompanied by a table listing the States which have become parties and giving details of reservations and interpretative declarations. A brief note gives details of the dates of adoption and entry into force of each agreement, the authentic languages and references to the series in which the treaty is reproduced. In the case of treaties for which there is no authentic English text the source of the translation is also given.

While this collection of documents is nowhere near as comprehensive as D. Schindler and J. Toman, *The Law of Armed Conflicts: A Collection of Conventions, Resolutions and Other Documents* (2nd edn., 1981), its much lower price will make it available to a far wider audience. Students are particularly likely to find it helpful and this reviewer can testify how much easier it is to lecture on the laws of armed conflict to a class which has ready access to all the main documents. On the whole, the selection of documents is a good one, the editors stating in their Introduction that they confined their choice to documents of contemporary relevance and relating to the *ius in bello* rather than the *ius ad bellum* (pp. 16–18). It is regrettable, however, that this latter principle of selection is used to justify the exclusion of Hague Convention No. III Relative to the Opening of Hostilities, 1907. This agreement is surely relevant to *ius in bello*, not least because it lays down the circumstances in which a neutral State will be bound by the law of neutrality in the absence of a formal notification of a state of war. The omission of the resolutions adopted at the final meeting of the Geneva Diplomatic Conference of 1949 (which are appended to the text of the 1949 Geneva Conventions in the British *Manual of Military Law*) is also a pity. The book is, however, so useful that it is to be hoped that there will be many future editions in which these documents might be included.

CHRISTOPHER GREENWOOD

Derecho Internacional Público: Principios Fundamentales. By ANTONIO ROMERO BROTONS. Madrid: Editorial Tecnos, S.A., 1982. 342 pp.

This book provides a critical analysis of certain leading areas and principles of international law in the light of the changes and developments that have occurred in recent decades. The author, a Professor of International Law at the Universidad Autónoma de Madrid, has chosen to concentrate on what he perceives to be the 'palpitant questions' today: sovereignty of the State and non-intervention (chapter 3); the right of self-determination (chapters 4 and 5); the use of force and maintenance of international peace and security (chapters 6 and 7); peaceful settlement of disputes (chapter 8); and international co-operation and development (chapters 9 and 10). The author indicates that in subsequent volumes he will examine, *inter alia*, the formation and application of international law, international personality and the regimes of land, marine and air spaces.

The volume under review follows an orderly and rational plan. The primary emphasis is on the context in which international law operates, that is to say, the contemporary community of nations. Thus, before taking on specific issues, in chapter 1 the author discusses the changes that have occurred in the international community, particularly since 1945, and the manner in which those changes have transformed international law. While the author refers to changes deriving from several sources he believes that decolonization constitutes the single most important historical event since 1945. He criticizes traditional international law as being the product of a 'eurocentric' society and asserts that 'Recourse to force, to war, was a means to achieve the accord that ultimately made it possible to transform the ambitions of the more powerful [nations] into juridical norms' (p. 30). By contrast, when commenting on the law of contemporary international society, the author observes that the new international law is the product of a heterogeneous and universal society and has been shaped by ideological and political confrontations between the capitalist and marxist-leninist blocs and by the struggle between the rich industrialized countries and the poor countries to gain control over natural resources, markets and development (pp. 35–6).

In chapter 2, the author discusses the nature and the process of identification of peremptory norms of international law or *'jus cogens'*. In dealing with this issue he examines the doctrine and practice of the Soviet Union and of the new independent States regarding international law in general and concludes that 'it is normal that the new and the revolutionary States should seek to alter the *status quo* and change the content of a body of law that does not reflect their interests and goals adequately' (p. 52).

Having laid the groundwork in chapters 1 and 2, he then goes on to analyse the principal issues in the remaining chapters. Chapter 3, on sovereignty and non-intervention, reiterates some of the ideas and views on 'spheres of influence' expressed by the author in a previous book.[1] The discussion of the principle of self-determination in chapters 4 and 5 is commendable on two counts: it is both perceptive and up to date. There is an interesting and—one could say—novel analysis of the Malvinas (Falklands) conflict (pp. 145–8), though this reviewer was not persuaded by the argument to the effect that, under the existing circumstances, the invasion of the islands by the armed forces of Argentina was not inconsistent with Article 2 (4) of the United Nations Charter. The analysis of the question of Gibraltar is thorough and objective.

The 'prohibition of the use of force' is the title of chapters 6 and 7, although the latter focuses exclusively on disarmament. Chapter 6 focuses primarily on the prohibition of the use of force and it logically includes a section on collective measures for the maintenance of peace and security and a lucid discussion of the competence of regional arrangements vis-à-vis the competence of the United Nations in the settlement of regional disputes and with regard to 'enforcement action'. Chapter 8 deals with the peaceful settlement of disputes, and finally chapters 9 and 10 are devoted to the law applicable to international co-operation for development and to the new international economic order.

Although reference to other authors is frequent, the volume contains no citations and there is not one footnote in the entire text. Quite often, the reader will find it difficult to determine whether the author is referring to his own or to someone else's ideas. Although there is a lengthy and valuable bibliography at the end of each chapter, one can still detect some shortcomings in this regard. For example, the reference to Professor B. V. A. Röling appears in the bibliography at the end of chapter 2, when in fact most of the issues discussed by the author in chapter 1 were already amply discussed by Professor Röling in his book *International Law in an Expanded World*, published in 1960.

The book is written clearly and constitutes a valuable contribution to the study of certain key questions of contemporary international law.　　　　DOMINGO E. ACEVEDO

International Law: Teaching and Practice. Edited by BIN CHENG. London: Stevens & Sons, 1982. xxix + 287 pp. £23.

Surprisingly, because a collection of essays on *International Law: Teaching and Practice* is not calculated to inspire an enthusiastic response in a reviewer, this is an interesting and readable book. The editor, Bin Cheng, explains that it is not intended as a response to the doubts that are frequently expressed as to the practical significance and legal status of international law—though it serves as an effective attack on these: 'It is rather an attempt by those engaged in the teaching and practice of international law to review what they are doing and to examine together some of the many problems with which they are faced.'

The first section deals with the identification and identity of international law. On these fundamental questions there is today little agreement. Developments this century, particularly since the Second World War, have threatened traditional conceptions of the sources of international law. Jennings's brief and stimulating paper accordingly challenges international lawyers to acknowledge these changes and to develop new categories to describe the law-making processes and tests of validity of international law. This theme is also taken up in Bin Cheng's epilogue and in his appendix on 'instant' international customary law. The papers of MacGibbon and Higgins neatly illustrate the vast gulf that can divide international lawyers in this area; the former in his discussion of General Assembly resolutions strongly reaffirms the traditional approach whereas the latter expounds (considerably more clearly than its originator) her version of the McDougal policy-oriented approach to international law. In the last paper in this section Butler discusses regional and sectional diversities.

[1] *La Hegemonía Norteamericana, Factor de Crisis en la OEA* (1972).

The second section, 'International Law and Contemporary Problems', also concerns the demands that new developments are making on international law: how is it to deal with the problem of political world order (a wildly idiosyncratic piece by Schwarzenberger), with the call for a new international economic order (Simmonds), with the impact of E.E.C. law (White) and of technology (Fawcett). Appropriately the section is completed by a trenchant warning from Brownlie as to the dangers involved in overspecialization in these and other areas.

The third section provides a comprehensive survey of the different aspects of the practice of international law: Bathurst contributes a straightforward guide for the intending practitioner; Elias discusses the problems facing the International Court of Justice. The history of the legal advisers in the Foreign Office and their wide-ranging role today is authoritatively dealt with by Sinclair, and Mensah writes well on the important question of the development of international law in international organizations, using illustrations from his experience in I.M.C.O. In the final section, on the teaching of international law, Brown and de la Rochère give an overview of the situation in the United Kingdom and France respectively. Inevitably this will be of interest mainly to those who are themselves involved in teaching.

Taken as a whole this collection of essays largely satisfies the editor's aim of showing the major problems and challenges facing international law, and it will perhaps be especially useful in giving students a picture of the functioning of the international legal system.

CHRISTINE GRAY

Interim Protection: a Functional Approach. By JEROME B. ELKIND. The Hague, Boston and London: Martinus Nijhoff, 1981. xxiv + 287 pp. ƒ140.

Article 41 of the Statute of the International Court of Justice empowers the Court to indicate provisional measures (or interim measures, as they are usually called) in order to preserve the respective rights of the parties to cases before it. In the past, this provision was rarely invoked, but seven applications were made in the 1970s including, most recently, that in the *Case Concerning United States Diplomatic and Consular Staff in Tehran*. These cases prompted a revival of interest amongst writers, but this is the first comprehensive treatise in the English language on the subject since the pioneering work of Dumbauld (*Interim Measures of Protection in International Controversies* (1932)).[1]

The author has adopted a rather ambitious theoretical basis for his work—what he calls the 'functional approach'. This is to some extent based on Cheng's approach to 'general principles of law': Dr. Elkind thinks that general principles of municipal law are sources of international law if and in so far as they exemplify or embody a principle of law implicit in any legal system. If international law aims to protect the same interests as municipal law in a given field, these general principles will apply in the former field too, the laws of particular municipal systems being of merely evidential value. As a general methodology, this functional approach seems somewhat open to question. In particular, the interests to be protected may be only superficially similar (e.g. are sovereignty and private property as analogous as the author seems to suggest at p. 18?), and the structural characteristics of international law are different from those of municipal law—a point which is particularly relevant to any consideration of the judicial process. One may also wonder whether interim protection is a 'principle' of law at all; is it not, rather, a piece of judicial machinery? This is not to say that the author's comparisons with interlocutory injunctions and the like in domestic systems, following in the footsteps of Dumbauld and others, are without value; but their value seems to this reviewer to lie more in the fact that they exemplify problems which may arise, and embody solutions which have commended themselves to other

[1] Another work, *Interim Measures in the Hague Court* by Jerzy Sztucki, was published in 1983, too late to be considered in this review.

decision-makers. In this connection, it is a little curious and somewhat unfortunate that the author has not dealt with the case law of other international tribunals.

A brief chapter on the history of interim protection is followed by a detailed account of the evolution of the Rules of Court on this subject, and another summarizes the cases in which interim protection has been sought from the Permanent Court of International Justice and the International Court of Justice.

There are a number of substantive problems connected with interim protection, and these are dealt with competently and fairly by the author. He discusses the circumstances which justify the indication of interim measures and the problem of the non-appearing respondent. In considering whether interim measures are binding, Dr. Elkind reviews the judicial and academic authorities before coming to the conclusion that 'insofar as we have shown interim protection to be an essential part of the peace-keeping process of the United Nations, a functional or teleological approach would seem to be called for', and concludes that interim measures are binding (p. 163). With respect, the premiss seems open to question.

A substantial chapter is devoted to the much-debated question whether the Court is entitled to indicate interim measures before it has determined whether it has jurisdiction over the merits and, if so, how confident it has to be that it will ultimately determine that it does have jurisdiction over the merits. The author correctly identifies the basis of the jurisdiction in Article 41 of the Statute as being Article 93 of the United Nations Charter and Article 35 of the Statute. However, he goes on to submit that, this being so, the Court is entitled to indicate interim measures of protection even if the probability of an ultimate finding that it has jurisdiction is relatively small (p. 192). This conclusion does not inevitably follow from the earlier one, if only because judicial propriety could warrant a more cautious approach, and too cavalier an attitude towards the subject of substantive jurisdiction may unfairly prejudice the respondent. Dr. Elkind's test is out of line with the trend of decision in the World Court and in international arbitral tribunals. The author is kind enough to devote substantial attention to the present reviewer's article on 'Interim Measures of Protection in Cases of Contested Jurisdiction'[2] and in particular to the suggestion that, in place of a 'cut-off point' on a scale of likelihood of substantive jurisdiction, a flexible test would be more appropriate: if the case is so urgent as prima facie to justify the imposition of interim measures, the Court should then take into account not only the degree of likelihood of its ultimately finding that it has jurisdiction over the merits, but also the likelihood of the applicant's succeeding on the merits and all other factors bearing on the possible prejudice to the parties, including the degree of urgency and of seriousness of the anticipated harm. In cases where there is an imminent prospect of extremely serious damage, and the case looks reasonably convincing on merits, the Court might justifiably be somewhat less stringent (though it should never be cavalier) about the jurisdictional factor than in cases where the other factors are less strongly in the applicant's favour. The author's principal objection to this approach seems to be that it is too discretionary. With respect, this seems to ignore the fact that, within certain limits, the remedy is in any case and necessarily discretionary, though the discretion does of course have to be exercised in a principled manner. It is submitted that the author has not shown that a flexible approach which seeks to preserve the rights of both parties to the dispute is less satisfactory than an inflexible rule which in some cases might tip the scales too much in favour of the applicant for interim relief, and in others too much in favour of the respondent.

There are some misprints and errors (e.g. the last sentence on p. 96), but on the whole the treatment of the material is thoroughgoing and competent. Interim measures are likely to continue to be applied for from time to time, and Dr. Elkind has performed a very useful service to scholars and practitioners by bringing the literature up to date.

MAURICE MENDELSON

[2] See this *Year Book*, 46 (1972–3), p. 259.

The Foundations of European Community Law. By T. C. HARTLEY. Oxford: Clarendon Press, 1981. xxxiv + 546 + (index) 5 pp. £20·00 hard cover, £13·95 paper cover.

This book successfully blends the qualities of a monograph with those of a case book and learned commentary; it combines crisp analysis with a narrative of almost bucolic serenity.

The Community law discussed in it was not created as 'foundations' in the sense of a *'Grundnorm'* or hierarchically superior set of principles. However, the title is well chosen in as much as it refers to a body of fundamental rules and the mechanisms, and techniques, for their creation, interpretation and development by Community institutions and particularly the Court of Justice. It is this focus on the structural and procedural elements of the Community constitutional legal order which, one can safely predict, will secure for the book a measure of longevity not so readily possessed by other books on Community law.

The book is divided into five parts. Part I describes the Community institutions. Hartley's account of the political institutions—particularly that of the Commission, is tellingly curt (a necessary but tiresome exercise for a common lawyer?). This is merely underlined by a rather listless use of the well-worn clichés about the 'supranational bureaucracy'. On the other hand, there is the perceptive forecast that the Community will either 'go forward to become a federation or [it] will regress and eventually break up' (p. 6). Given this insight, it is surprising that extensive discussions of reform of the Commission as the pivotal driving force of European integration, which are the subject of four major Reports (Vedel, Tindemans, Spierenburg, Three Wise Men), are not even mentioned in passing. As was observed in Editorial Comments: 'To have a "Europe des Rapports" is not necessarily a bad thing. To file and forget good reports *is*, however' (*Common Market Law Review*, 17 (1980), p. 6).

By contrast all aspects of the work of the European Court are thoroughly discussed, sometimes in extravagant detail (application served on the defendant, 'usually by registered post'). Two useful sections on 'the form of Judgment' and on 'precedent' will dispel many a student's anxiety about unaccustomed judicial style and function.

Part II on the Community legal system comprises sections on 'Acts of the Member States', 'Community Acts', 'General Principles of Law' and 'Agreements with Third States'. This traditional classification of acts of the Community legal system is convenient. It is also deceptively simple and probably incomplete. From the outset, the typology of the treaties themselves (Article 14 E.C.S.C., 189 E.E.C.; 161 EURATOM) was difficult to operate: only the effects of regulations, directives and decisions are defined in positive terms. However, the Community treaties also provide for other forms of acts without defining their legal effects (particularly the 'programmes', see Article 46 (3) sub-paragraph 3 E.C.S.C.; Article 54 E.E.C.). Practice, moreover, has added a whole range of Community 'utterances' whose classification as 'sources' of Community law in a wider sense is not clear (e.g. E.E.C. Declaration on an Environmental Programme; the Joint Declaration on Fundamental Rights; Summit Resolutions). Furthermore certain overlaps may occur: thus, as Hartley previously observed (p. 15), the European Council may, according to the subject-matter under consideration, assume the functions of the Council of the European Communities, or those of a separate political conference or indeed, one might add, that of the COREPER; it may at any rate only be a matter of time until the European Council will assume legislative powers under Article 189 E.E.C. All this merely illustrates the fact that a restriction of the scope of sources to that set up by the treaties and a relegation of these other instances of Community practice to the political sphere of the Communities can no longer be considered a sufficient statement of the sources of the Community legal order. Classification under expressly stated heads of sources is unimportant. What matters is whether conduct is in fact determined by these 'political' acts, in a way reminiscent of normative prescriptions.

Hartley, of course, does not contrive to accommodate such practice under established heads of jurisdiction. He does not on the other hand go so far as to acknowledge their capacity to create normative expectations. For example, this capacity would seem to be recognized implicitly in Article 3 (3) of the 1972 Act of Accession. The issues involved are familiar ones elsewhere. Thus constitutional reality or practice may depart appreciably from the text of a written constitution. Constitutional conventions under the 'Constitution' of the United Kingdom may also be mentioned here. International lawyers too have abandoned attempts to subsume 'inchoate' sources under Article 38 of the Statute of the International Court of Justice. In international law concepts such as 'soft law' or 'subsequent practice' reflect awareness that there may be degrees of legal authority beyond the dichotomy 'binding/not binding'. Admittedly, such analogies are of limited utility. After all the Communities have established 'a new legal order'. Transformation of extra constitutional practice (not subsequently the subject of enacted E.E.C. law)—*praeter legem*—into some kind of 'customary' Community law may, in the case of the Communities, be a sign of faltering vigour. What is considered dynamic in ordinary international organizations may well have to be seen as a retrograde drift from 'supranationalism' in the case of the Communities.

Part III is entitled 'Community Law and the Member States' and discusses the key concepts of direct effect and supremacy of Community law as well as the relationship and interplay of the Community legal order with the various systems of municipal law.

Part IV on judicial review is central among the 'foundations': the rule of law in operation. The importance of this part is self-evident. The annual work-load of the Court has increased steadily over the years (1982: 345 new cases, 185 judgments; 1981: 323 and 128). It is in this section that Hartley's analytical skills are most enjoyable, and instructive. It is a comprehensive account of the Court's contribution to safeguarding the Community constitutional and administrative rule of law, except for some minor heads of jurisdiction *sui generis* which are either mentioned elsewhere in the book (legal proceedings under Article 228 E.E.C., pursuant to an arbitration clause agreed to by the Community: Article 181 E.E.C.; interim measures: 186 E.E.C., 158 EURATOM, 39 E.C.S.C.) or omitted altogether (suspension of the application of a contested act: 185 E.E.C.; compulsory retirement of a Commission member: Article 13 Merger Treaty).

Part V on Community liability covers a subject which the author's previous publications have done much to elucidate. Hartley's conclusion is that the chances of succeeding in an action in tort against the Community are at present very slim. The difficulty is that all the conditions of Article 215 (2) must be fulfilled by an applicant (so held again in Case 26/81 of 29 September 1982), proof of damage, causation and fault being the major obstacles. However, as anticipated by Hartley, the first awards of damages have been made now (Cases 261/78 and 262/78, 6 October 1982). Tables of Community treaties, of United Kingdom statutes and of cases and an index complete this volume.

This monograph easily tops the league of English language texts within the range of subjects covered. It is not an ambitious book, either as to its scope or as to the breadth of the material used. Its excellence does not lie in some dazzling display of the mastery of European E.E.C.-literature, for in fact only a very small amount of relevant literature is digested or referred to for further reading at the end of each section. The book might also disappoint those who believe that the probing and testing of theories and conceptual refinements must accompany empirical analysis of 'the law'. This book's most outstanding quality is its in-depth analysis of the sources of Community law itself. This is done in straightforward simple language, occasionally interspersed with lecture-like rhetorical questions. Clarity of disposition and expression make it an eminently readable book. Its modest price makes it an attractive purchase. Students of E.E.C. law are bound to select this book as their preferred companion. FRIEDL WEISS

Die Organisationsstruktur der Europäischen Gemeinschaften (Max Planck Institut für ausländisches öffentliches Recht und Völkerrecht: *Beiträge zum ausländischen öffentlichen Recht und Völkerrecht*, Volume 79). By MEINHARD HILF. Berlin, Heidelberg, New York: Springer-Verlag, 1982. xviii + 442 pp.

The fact that the author undertook this research work as someone who knows the internal structure of the Community from his own professional experience gives special interest to this study, which was accepted as a 'Habilitation' by the University of Heidelberg. Based upon the text of the Treaties of Rome, which contain only incomplete organizational provisions, the author looks at the organizational structure as it has been developed since the foundation of the Community.

In the first part, Dr. Hilf describes the rapid growth of the Community. More interesting is the second part which analyses organizational reality. A number of organizational units within the Community seem to have formed an independent, individual life. One of the great merits of this chapter is that it attempts an institutional and legal characterization of these units. The author differentiates between the various organizational levels and identifies a 'tertiary level of Community organization' (p. 109). This tertiary level is studied in a lucid way and adds a good deal to the understanding and rethinking of European institutional law. The same can be said about the presentation of the organizational periphery, to which belong private agencies instituted by the Community. The third part of the study points out the ways in which organizational structures could become important for the future development of the Community's organizational law. In order to show the different possibilities, the author undertakes a horizontal comparison with the organizational structures of other international organizations (pp. 224–52). The conclusion is that the 'limitless, reproductive capacity' of international organizations has resulted in uncontrollable developments giving rise to an 'anarchical overlapping of powers' (p. 254). The result of the 'vertical comparison', i.e. the comparison with the organizational law of the member States, is to disclose that all members of the Community possess organizational units of the central administration with and without legal capacity, and organizational units set up under private law. The author should not be reproached because the result of the comparative analysis is not very startling. The initial question of how other international organizations and member States of the Community deal with somewhat independent administrative units is not without interest.

In the last part, the study concentrates on fundamental principles of European organizational law. In spite of the complexity and organizational diversification, these principles should ideally present a systematic, organizational clarity, and reflect the observance of the legal limits laid down by the treaties. In fact, the Community has developed a conglomerate of organizational structures, with and without legal capacity, which is difficult to systematize. The relationship with the primary institutions ranges from nearly complete independence to complete control. The author reveals that in this complexity of organizational structures, some unsystematical features exist which should be eliminated in the future. He leaves no doubt that this complexity of organizational structure is necessary and useful for such an organization, provided central planning is assured and overlapping powers are avoided. Although the first steps toward global planning are now being made by the Commission and Parliament, it is too early to speak about 'the organization of the organization'. Dr. Hilf points out that established structures, even if they have been proved ineffective, can hardly be reformed. It is doubtful whether the Community could find the internal capacity for self-correction to ensure a more effective control amongst the different institutions and units. This analysis of the present state of affairs is already a contribution to the planning of future policy. Therefore, this study should be of interest to academics as well as those who are politically responsible for the future of the European Community.

HANS-JOACHIM MENGEL

Thesaurus Acroasium of the Institute of Public International Law and International Relations of Thessaloniki. Volume VIII: *The Law of the European Communities and Greece.* Thessaloniki: Institute of Public International Law and International Relations, 1979. xv + 668 pp.

The Institute of Public International Law and International Relations of Thessaloniki was founded by legislative decree in 1966. It is subsidized by the Greek State, and has organized annually sessions of lectures and seminars on contemporary problems of international law and international relations. The volume under consideration contains lectures and papers delivered at the Fifth Annual Session of the Institute.

Part I of the Volume contains the texts of fifteen lectures, eight being in French and seven in English. Subjects include 'Le Marché Commun dans le cadre de l'économie internationale' (by Angelos Angelopoulos, Governor of the National Bank of Greece); 'The Renovating Role of the European Court' (by Alexander Chloros, then Director of the Centre of European Law at King's College, London, who was sadly to enjoy such a short term of office as a Judge of the European Court of Justice); and 'Effets internationaux des décisions civiles et commerciales dans la Communauté Economique Européenne' (by Octavian Capatina, Professor at Bucharest). A useful balance is maintained between the internal aspects of Community law (e.g. Professor Kovar's lecture on 'Les Rapports entre le droit Communautaire et le droit des états membres') and the relationship between the Community and third countries (e.g. 'The External Relations of the European Communities', by Professor Frans A. M. Alting von Geusau, and 'Yugoslavia and the European Economic Community', by Professor Ljubisa Adamovic).

Part II of the Volume, 'Travaux Pratiques', contains seminar papers on four topics: the social law of the Communities, the relationship between Community law and the law of the member States, Community institutions, and the external relations of the Communities. Most of the papers are in French. Under the heading of social law, there are discussions of equal pay in national law and Community law, and of the public policy proviso to the principle of the free movement of workers. The relationship between Community law and national law is explained by papers on Case 6/64, *Costa* v. *E.N.E.L.*, [1964] E.C.R. 585, on fundamental rights, on the German Constitutional Court's judgment of 29 May 1974 in the *Internationale Handelsgesellschaft* case, [1974] 2 C.M.L.R. 545, and on Community law and the penal law of the member States. The section on Community institutions includes essays on the Commission, on direct elections to the Parliament, as well as on structural comparison between European economic integration and economic integration in Africa, and an examination of the impact on Greek public administration of the E.E.C. The final section contains nine papers on the external relations of the Communities, including essays on the relationship between general international law and Community law, the division of powers between the organs of the Community in the conclusion of treaties, and the relations between the Communities and the countries in the Mediterranean area.

This eighth volume of the *Thesaurus Acroasium* (translateable as *Collected Courses* or *Recueil des cours*) contains a useful and comprehensive collection of essays on the law of the European Communities and Greece, from the perspective of Community law, international law and national law. The objects of the Institute which produced it include the study of international problems of particular interest to Greece, and of international organizations, including the E.E.C. It cannot be denied that these objects are ably pursued in the work in question.   DERRICK WYATT

The Teacher in International Law. By MANFRED LACHS. The Hague, Boston, London: Martinus Nijhoff, 1982. 236 pp.

This book is an expanded version of the lectures which Judge Lachs delivered at the Hague Academy of International Law in 1976.

A large part of the book consists of a brief historical survey of the leading writers on international law, from earliest times to the present day (although writers who are still living are omitted from the survey). The twentieth century is dealt with at greater length than any previous century. On the whole, however, the survey is too brief to add very much to books such as Nussbaum's *A Concise History of the Law of Nations*, apart from dealing with some writers who were too recent to be mentioned by Nussbaum and some Polish and Russian writers who are little known in the West.

The following chapter of the book, in which Judge Lachs examines the way in which international law is (or should be) taught, is more successful. He suggests that international law should be a compulsory part of every law course, and that students of international law should have a thorough knowledge of other aspects of international relations and a basic knowledge of the natural sciences and technology. These are counsels of perfection indeed! On a more realistic note, the author suggests ways of overcoming students' scepticism about international law (pp. 155–7) and emphasizes the need for teachers of international law to explain it to the general public (pp. 162–6).

Finally, the author examines the impact of teachers and teachings on the development of international law. In addition to influencing international law through the careers of their pupils, teachers are often cited in judgments, diplomatic correspondence and Parliamentary debates, and many teachers have also served as advocates, judges, diplomats or legal advisers to their governments. Of particular interest are the passages in which Judge Lachs (presumably drawing on his own experience as a judge on the International Court of Justice and as a former member of the International Law Commission) discusses the new outlook on international law which a teacher acquires when he becomes a judge (pp. 184–7), and the problems of codifying international law (pp. 187–99)—a task in which teachers of international law have a particularly important role to play.

MICHAEL AKEHURST

International Claims: Contemporary European Practice (*Procedural Aspects of International Law Series*, Volume 15). Edited by RICHARD B. LILLICH and BURNS H. WESTON. Charlottesville: University Press of Virginia, 1982. x + 204 pp. (including index). $25.

This volume provides a valuable supplement to earlier volumes in this series by Professors Lillich and Weston, with other collaborators. It is in effect a companion volume to *International Claims: Their Preparation and Presentation* (1962), by Lillich and Christenson (reviewed in this *Year Book*, 38 (1962), p. 515); *International Claims: Postwar British Practice* (1967), by Lillich (reviewed in this *Year Book*, 42 (1967), p. 345); *International Claims: Postwar French Practice* (1971), by Weston (reviewed in this *Year Book*, 45 (1971), p. 490); and *International Claims: Their Settlement by Lump Sum Agreements* (1975) (2 parts), by Lillich and Weston.

The latest work consists of a short introduction by the editors, followed by four substantial studies of State practice: Austrian practice by Ignaz Seidl-Hohenveldern, Belgian practice by George T. Yates III and Thomas E. Carbonneau, Italian practice by Andrea Giardina and Swiss practice by Lucius Caflisch. All four States have had interesting experience in claims and distribution practice. The material is presented well and the studies contain many items of interest, particularly relating to the claims of shareholders, the nationality of corporations and the substance of the formula 'property, rights and interests'.

By and large the contributors eschew extensive commentary on the material and it is a quality of this series that the practice is presented in a straightforward way and not used to decorate a thesis of some kind. The piece by Seidl-Hohenveldern is a model of deft and incisive analysis of a mass of evidence. A number of the studies include material concerning problems of State responsibility (an element not very clearly indicated in the index).

Caflisch includes some fairly extensive comment on the *Barcelona Traction* case. Giardina makes some tentative remarks on the problem of how to evaluate the practice concerning lump sum settlements. As this writer points out (pp. 97–8), it is necessary to go beyond the general affirmation that such agreements count as evidence of customary law.

It would be a fine thing if the generality of recent publications were as useful and as well-produced as this book.   IAN BROWNLIE

International Law in Contemporary Perspective. By MYRES S. MCDOUGAL and W. MICHAEL REISMAN. Mineola, New York: Foundation Press Inc., 1981. lxviii + 1584 pp.

International Law Essays. By MYRES S. MCDOUGAL and W. MICHAEL REISMAN. Mineola, New York: Foundation Press Inc., 1981. vii + 638 pp.

Myres McDougal and his various associates have written numerous important monographs and articles on various aspects of international law, but *International Law in Contemporary Perspective* is their first attempt at a general account of the subject and their first book designed specially for students. Its form is that of a 'casebook': more specifically, it contains extracts from cases, treaties and other instruments, as well as selections from previously published writings (mainly by McDougal and his associates), all linked together by short, specially written passages of exposition and questions for the student. Rightly conscious, however, that those who are instructed purely by this method are in danger of 'losing sight of the forest for the trees', the authors have attempted to provide something more narrative, jurisprudential and general in the shape of *International Law Essays*. As its title indicates, this is not a treatise as such, but a collection of eleven articles of a theoretical character by McDougal and his associates. Since all of this material has been previously published in journals and elsewhere between 1959 and 1980, it is not proposed to review the companion volume separately here. Suffice it to say that it is very convenient to have these essays together under one cover, but that there are substantial overlaps between them, an index would have been useful, and there are quite a few misprints.

Viewed purely as a volume of 'cases and materials', the larger volume has significant virtues and some defects. One weakness of the generality of international law casebooks is that the extracts are too short: the student may obtain an imprecise or even false impression of the meaning of a judicial (or academic) pronouncement by reading it out of its context, and fails to develop an ability to read between the lines or a sense of the way in which the typical dispute raises a plurality of issues from different branches of the subject. Here the extracts are generous and on the whole well chosen. Another virtue is that the authors have not kept to the beaten track: a number of familiar authorities are used in novel ways, and a number of unfamiliar ones cited with telling effect. Few, if any, even amongst the 'most highly qualified publicists' would not learn something new and valuable from a careful perusal of this volume.

There are, however, deficiencies. The book is too long for a student text: although the authors say (p. xvii) that they are conscious of the limitations imposed by a fourteen-week American law school course, they concede that teachers will have to be selective (p. xix)— which is something of an understatement. There is far too much repetition and overlap between the two volumes: for instance, pp. 84–6 contain an extract from an article in *Yale Studies in World Public Order* which is reproduced in full (save for one passage, presumably omitted in error) in the *Essays* volume. On the other hand, there is a reference at p. 90 to another article, without mentioning that it, too, is reproduced in the companion volume. The absence of a documents supplement is something of an inconvenience. Non-American readers will probably feel that too much attention is paid to purely domestic questions. One can also quibble about the choice of material in particular instances. Even with the addition of some pertinent questions at p. 46, one may wonder whether the interim measures order and the judgment of the International Court of Justice in the *Nuclear Tests* cases, especially without the pleadings, are the best introduction to the making and application of international law. The section on State responsibility is thin and not particularly well expounded, the treatment of the New International Economic Order and remedies for expropriation (pp. 46–76 and 950–2) inadequate. The book is not organized under traditional headings, but in accordance with the McDougal system; the reader who is unfamiliar with this, or the teacher who does not subscribe to the methodology, will have difficulty in finding his way around. A good index would have helped, but the fourteen pages provided are somewhat inadequate: for instance, one searches it in vain for pirate broadcasting (discussed at p. 1371) or for the Shaba Province intervention (pp. 875–6).

The book is, then, principally of value as an introduction to, and exposition of, the policy-oriented approach to international law emanating from the Yale Law School— an approach which is somewhat too little criticized in the U.S.A., and somewhat too readily dismissed here. It would need at least an article, and probably a book, to do full justice to the theory; for present purposes a few, necessarily summary, points must suffice.

The authors' insistence on taking into account all contextual factors is often said to blur the distinction between *lex lata* and *lex ferenda*, between law and politics, etc. However, a purely black-letter approach lacks realism, particularly when one bears in mind the relatively undeveloped state of the system's secondary rules of recognition, adjudication, change and enforcement. McDougal's emphasis (mirroring the teachings of Llewellyn and others) on the multiplicity of decision-makers and the decentralized character of the international legal process is one of the most valuable insights we have been given, and one which is still insufficiently appreciated by those who adopt an excessively court-oriented approach to what the law prescribes. It may also be observed that the authors regard the making of recommendations *de lege ferenda* as an integral part of their task, and there can be no doubt that, for this purpose, a proper contextual analysis is likely to produce better solutions. On the other hand, so far as the *lex lata* is concerned, it would seem that the Yale approach rather exaggerates the open texture of norms; in particular, there is a difference between a proposition being arguable, and its being arguable *in good faith* or *reasonably*, let alone *correctly*.

Professor McDougal and his collaborators open the texture of the law considerably wider by their insistence on adopting a policy-oriented approach by which ambiguities (or alleged ambiguities) are to be resolved in the manner most conducive to 'human dignity'— a state of affairs, roughly speaking, in which the largest number of people possess the largest amount of the 'values' of 'health, safety, comfort, affection, respect, skill, enlightenment, rectitude, wealth and power'. As used to be said of Motherhood in the old days, few would confess to being against these things; the problem is that views will differ widely as to the weight to be given to these values in relation to each other in a given situation, and also as to the best means of promoting them. The comment has sometimes been made that McDougal's elaborate system tends to result in the conclusion that what is good for the United States is good for human dignity. This is too crude a caricature: it is noteworthy that Professor Falk, for example, has applied somewhat similar techniques and come up with diametrically opposite solutions. However, there is no denying that a staunch patriotism and hostility to communism pervades much of McDougal's writing (see, for example, his piece on the Cuban missile quarantine, reproduced at pp. 983 ff.); and the fact that the application of his technique can produce a great diversity of solutions does not reassure us as to its utility or—despite the 'scientific' language—objectivity. Furthermore, one may wonder whether this emphasis on the goal of 'human dignity' is not a little over-ambitious, and possibly even dangerous, in a world which is unable at present even to ensure order and in which there is a serious risk of a cataclysm which will sweep away every trace of the human race, let alone its dignity. This tension between the demands of justice and of order is not new; it is exemplified in Reisman's piece on 'Private Armies' (*Essays*,

p. 142); with respect, neither the solution he proffers to the particular problem, nor the technique which produces it, are wholly convincing.

Finally, there is the question of the medium. The authors' aim is to educate and inform students and decision-makers, but unfortunately the size and style of the book deter all but the most dedicated. One reason for the great length of this and most works emanating from the Yale school of international lawyers is their insistence, in the name of scientific thoroughness, on working their way through and permutating an elaborate matrix of 'participants, perspectives, situations, power bases, strategies, outcomes and effects', each with its own subdivisions and further ramifications. The technique is sometimes criticized on the grounds that the best international lawyers do this sort of thing instinctively; but it has to be recognized that lesser mortals might find a check-list useful, and even Homer nods. Nevertheless, it is one thing to ensure that one has covered all of the material from all points of view before putting pen to paper; it is another to insist on inflicting it all on the reader, for it must be said that the application of the McDougal technique results in a good deal of repetition and statement of the obvious or trivial. Another problem is the language. An author of a scientific work cannot be criticized for inventing new words, or specially defining existing ones, if everyday language is inadequate for his purposes. But the present authors do not always respect this important proviso and, even when they are not deploying their special terminology, their prose is often over-elaborate, stilted or hard to follow. This is puzzling, because both McDougal and Reisman have shown that they are capable of clarity and elegance; but they seem to lose the facility when they start to be 'scientific'. Or perhaps really firm editing is incompatible with so prodigious an output. Either way, the outcome is such expressions—to name but four—as 'past decisions are repositories of latent data with which to confirm or disconfirm theoretical models of the interdetermination among relevant interacting factors', 'should this development transpire', 'obsolesced', and 'an intellectual armory for bringing into focus the global process of effective power'.

The authors are very interested in communications theory, and it is unfortunate that these deficiencies in its practice will repel many of the book's potential readers. Those who persist will find the exercise rewarding.   MAURICE MENDELSON

The Legal Aspect of Money. By F. A. MANN. 4th edition. Oxford: Oxford University Press, 1982. 580 pp. + tables and index. £35.

It is more than a decade since the appearance of the last edition of this superb work, a decade which has seen sweeping changes in the international monetary system and in methods of arranging international finance. The withdrawal by the United States of its undertaking to the International Monetary Fund to exchange gold for dollars led to the collapse of the par value system and the displacement of gold by the Special Drawing Right as the principal reserve asset and the I.M.F. unit of account. The E.E.C. developed its own system, the E.M.S., based on the European Currency Unit. These changes in monetary systems were accompanied in the private sector by the explosive growth of multinational companies and of international banking and finance. The 1970s saw the emergence of increasingly sophisticated methods of raising capital through syndicated Eurocurrency loans, international bond issues and negotiable certificates of deposit. Severe political upheavals made lenders acutely conscious of the problem of sovereign risk, whilst frequent fluctuations in exchange rates brought about a re-examination of rules of law and procedure relating to foreign money obligations, with a dramatic abandonment of the breach-date rule by the House of Lords in *Miliangos* v. *George Frank (Textiles) Ltd.*, [1976] A.C. 443.

Dr. Mann has therefore had to undertake a formidable task in researching for this new edition, a task made all the harder by the wide range of his book, which covers both private law and public international law. He has achieved the rewriting with singular success.

Few significant developments have escaped the author's notice. Particularly valuable is his exposition of case law, both English and foreign, on exchange control under the I.M.F. agreement, to which a full chapter is devoted. Dr. Mann takes issue with the English courts on their narrow interpretation of 'exchange contract', contrasting their very literal approach with the broader interpretation adopted by courts in France and Germany. At the same time, he has a refreshing willingness to admit to error, as where, for example, he now concedes that Article VIII (2) of the Bretton-Woods Agreement is a rule of substantive law, not a conflict rule. Dr. Mann gives an interesting, if brief, analysis of the legal nature of the Eurodollar, a question that would no doubt have been settled so far as English law is concerned but for the settlement of the United States–Iran litigation. In that connection, it is disappointing that Dr. Mann has not given us the benefit of his views on the legal nature of clearing-house funds and the implications of an 'unwind' rendered necessary by the default of a participating bank.

There are a few minor production errors. On p. 25, the report reference for *R. v. Behm* is omitted, whilst *R. v. Thompson*, referred to on p. 24, is not included in the table of cases. But in general the standard of production is high, particularly in view of the substantial number of foreign language references; and for sheer breadth and depth of scholarship this work remains in a class of its own.

R. M. GOODE

The Dynamics of Development in the European Human Rights Convention System. By CLOVIS C. MORRISSON. The Hague: Martinus Nijhoff, 1981. xii + 174 pp. $39.50, ƒ100.

The aim of this short book is to examine the extent to which the principles of the European Convention have been developed by the Judges of the Court and the members of the Commission and to consider the general issue of their approach to the Convention.

Part One is entitled 'Attitudes of the Commissioners and Judges' and the two chapters which deal with this question are by far the most interesting part of the work. Here Professor Morrisson, whose earlier writing on the Convention will be familiar to many readers of this *Year Book*, reviews the rival philosophies of activism and self-restraint in the work of the Commission and Court and the extent to which agreement and disagreement are manifest in their actual practice. With the aid of an elaborate statistical analysis, detailed in two appendices and various tables and diagrams, the author provides an admirable demonstration of the breadth of opinion to be found in both bodies and significant differences in their approach to key issues. The author necessarily paints with a broad brush and many of his insights could usefully be developed in a more detailed study. In general, however, the reader is left in no doubt as to the significance of the inarticulate (and sometimes articulate) major premiss in the decisions of judges and commissioners, and chapter 1 at least should be required reading for all students of the Convention.

The second part consists of a review of the interpretation and application by the Court and the Commission of four representative articles of the Convention: Article 3, which prohibits torture and inhuman or degrading treatment or punishment; Article 6 (1), guaranteeing the right to a fair trial; Article 10, which provides for the right to freedom of expression; and Article 27 (2), requiring the Commission to reject any application regarded as an abuse of the right of petition. As an introduction to the kinds of issues which arise at Strasbourg these chapters will be useful to anyone unfamiliar with the Convention. The author's approach, however, is descriptive rather than analytical and this, together with a brevity which omits, for example, any discussion of the points of principle raised by Sir Gerald Fitzmaurice in the *Irish* and *Tyrer* cases, will leave the knowledgeable reader dissatisfied. Had a number of tantalizing references to the judicial approach to similar problems in the United States been fully developed, these chapters would be much more interesting.

In addition to the material already mentioned the appendix includes the full text of the

Convention and its protocols. There is no index but the book has been well produced with only one or two minor misprints. 'Court of Appeals' (p. 106) is a small stylistic solecism and, to those not conversant with the World Series, 'a real round house curve' (p. 108) may need translation.   J. G. MERRILLS

The United Nations and the Control of International Violence: a Legal and Political Analysis. By JOHN F. MURPHY. Manchester: Manchester University Press, 1983. xii + 212 pp. £22·50.

As the subtitle of this book implies, the author has combined the approaches of the international lawyer and of the political scientist; he is as much concerned with the effectiveness of legal rules as with their interpretation. Most of the book is concerned with what the author calls 'traditional international violence', and includes chapters dealing with the attitudes adopted by the Security Council, the General Assembly, the Secretary-General and the International Court of Justice. But there is also a valuable discussion of 'non-traditional international violence' (assistance given by one State to liberation movements, insurgents, assassins or terrorists in another State). Professor Murphy concludes that the United Nations has been less successful in controlling non-traditional international violence than in controlling traditional international violence, partly because the rules of the United Nations Charter were drafted with traditional international violence in mind.

The author examines a large number of legal issues and a large number of international disputes. His summaries of these issues and disputes are usually very fair and beautifully clear (e.g. the excellent summary of the arguments for and against humanitarian intervention on pp. 18-19). However, at times the author's desire for brevity produces distortions; for instance, when discussing Israel's raid on Entebbe airport in 1976, he mentions on pp. 188-9 that Israel and the United States argued that international law allows a State in certain circumstances to use force to protect its nationals abroad, but he fails to mention that many States replied that international law never permits the use of force for that purpose (cf. your reviewer's discussion of the same incident in *International Relations*, 5 (1977), pp. 3, 19-23). One cannot help wishing that the author had written a longer book, in which he could have investigated some of the issues at greater length. In particular, it is surprising that there is no mention of the Security Council debate on Israel's bombing of Iraq's nuclear reactor in 1981, in which many States said that international law never permits the use of force in *anticipatory* self-defence (see *International Legal Materials*, 20 (1981), pp. 965-97, and *United Nations Chronicle*, 1981, no. 8, pp. 5-9 and 61-74).

The book contains a considerable number of misprints. Errors of substance are fewer, but occasionally appear, particularly in the author's discussion of the Falkland Islands conflict. The author says on p. 71 that the United Kingdom once proposed to refer the question of sovereignty over the Falkland Islands to the International Court of Justice; in fact, the United Kingdom offered to submit the question of sovereignty over the Falkland Islands *Dependencies* to the International Court of Justice, but has never made a similar offer in respect of the Falkland Islands themselves (Argentina offered to refer the dispute over the Falkland Islands to arbitration in 1884, but the United Kingdom refused). The author makes little attempt to discuss the question of title to the Falkland Islands, and states baldly that 'Britain virtually acknowledged the legitimacy of the Argentine claim in 1980 when it offered to turn the islands over to Argentina in return for a long lease' (p. 67). But an offer to settle a dispute by a compromise has never been treated as an implied recognition that one's opponent's case is well founded, and it is most undesirable that it should be so interpreted.

On the whole, however, this book is accurate and perceptive, and deserves to be read by everyone interested in the role played by international law in controlling international violence.   MICHAEL AKEHURST

The International Law of the Sea. Volume I. By D. P. O'CONNELL, edited by I. A. SHEARER. Oxford: Oxford University Press, 1982. xxxiii + 634 pp. £40.

The premature death of O'Connell in 1979 deprived international law of one of its ablest and most productive exponents. The publication of this massive work, eventually to comprise a second volume, is due to the good offices of Professor Shearer of Sydney University, who has edited and updated the chapters which had been completed in draft by O'Connell at the time of his death.

The volume begins with a historical chapter, fully reflecting O'Connell's keen historical interest. Reflecting also his long connection with the Royal Australian Navy, it emphasizes how the development of the law was controlled by 'the philosophy of effective power'. Traditionally this meant naval power. The two brief sections on the 1958/60 Geneva Conventions and the Third Law of the Sea Conference, which conclude this chapter, are to some extent disappointing in their failure to recognize that the philosophy of effective power no longer controls the law (or, if it does, it is not simply naval power but a far more complex notion of political power).

The second chapter is, in many ways, the most interesting in the volume. Entitled 'The General Principles of the Law of the Sea', it in fact ranges over the whole gamut of factors controlling legal change: unilateral action, custom, acquiescence, protest, codifying conventions. There is some discussion of the normative effect of the law of the sea conventions (pp. 44–9), but the comments on the effect of the 1982 Convention are disappointing. 'It is a matter for analysis in each instance to what extent the draft Caracas Convention does embody new law' (p. 49). That is true. Yet we are really given no hint as to the legal position with regard to the international sea-bed area, given that a significant number of States have refused to ratify and contemplate sea-bed mining activities outside the Convention regime. Doubtless, had he survived, O'Connell would have tackled this difficult question.

Chapter 3 is a predominantly historical approach to the question of the juridical nature of the territorial sea followed by an equally historical approach in chapter 4 to the question of the extent of the territorial sea. There are contexts in which this approach is invaluable; for example, in deciding nice questions of whether 'property' exists, or whether jurisdictional competence extends to the territorial sea. Yet it must be accepted that, for the many new States which now claim a territorial sea, these are highly academic questions: for them sovereignty is the clear answer. As to the question of limits, O'Connell is more tentative than one would expect. It would seem difficult, in 1983, to question the validity of a 12-mile limit, and equally difficult to claim more.

Chapter 5 on 'Measurement of the Territorial Sea' is a very welcome, and rather technical, treatment of what is, after all, a technical problem. It deals with choice of tide level, location of the low-water datum, reefs, atolls, artificial islands, pack ice, straight baselines and the marked relaxation in State practice of the rather rigid requirements for the use of straight baselines contained in Article 4 of the 1958 Convention. Chapter 6 on 'Archipelagos' will be familiar to readers of the *Year Book*, although updated to some extent by reference to the new Convention.

Rather curiously, the treatment of bays, ports and straits does not immediately follow (although very much concerned with the same questions of measurement), but, instead, we have an excellent chapter on innocent passage. O'Connell suggests (at pp. 273–4) that the formulation in the 1982 Convention may have the effect of shifting the burden of proof so that the vessel now has to prove its innocence, rather than the coastal State proving non-innocence. Perhaps, but international tribunals are not keen on deciding disputes on the basis of the burden of proof. His conclusion that a submerged submarine in the territorial sea will find it difficult to prove innocence is no doubt correct, and he does not rule out the legality of direct attack against such a submarine as a last resort, pointing out that the

U.S.S.R. itself threatened such measures against foreign submarines in 1961 (and so can hardly protest against Swedish and Norwegian measures of like kind).

The treatment of bays in chapters 9 and 10 is perhaps as good as any in the currently available literature. Its heavily historical emphasis is relieved by an excellent discussion of the decisions of the United States Supreme Court in the 1969 *Louisiana* case and the 1964 *California* case. Yet many problems remain unresolved and reference might also be made to the current litigation involving Long Island Sound and Mississippi Sound. The discussion on historic waters in chapter 11 includes the very perceptive comment that '. . . it is likely that the category of historic waters will change its fundamental character, so that history will play a less prominent role than one would reasonably expect, and strategic and economic factors a much greater one' (p. 425). One has to think only of China's claims to Pohai Bay or Libya's to the Gulf of Sirte to see the force of this observation.

The discussion of the legal regime of the sea-bed in chapter 12 is clear evidence that O'Connell was prepared to grapple with the contributions which earth sciences might make to an understanding of the shelf, the concept of 'natural prolongation', the distinction between continental and oceanic crusts, and so forth. Unhappily, the 1982 judgment in the *Tunisia/Libya* case came too late to be included. Similarly, with regard to the area beyond national jurisdiction, apart from noting the United States vote against the 1982 Convention and the resolution on 'pioneer investors', it was not possible to anticipate some of the very difficult problems which will now arise between parties and non-parties over the competing claims to these resources.

The final three chapters on the continental shelf, fishery zones and the E.E.Z. are detailed and valuable. They omit all discussion of maritime boundaries, for these are to be the subject of the first chapter of Volume II, when it appears.

It is quite clear that, when the two volumes are published, the entire work will be a *tour de force*. One suspects that O'Connell will become, to this generation, what Gidel was to the last. If one needed to be reminded how great a loss we suffered with O'Connell's early death, this work is certainly such a reminder. D. W. BOWETT

Les Voies de recours ouvertes aux fonctionnaires internationaux. By ALAIN PELLET. Paris: Éditions A. Pedone, 1982. 201 pp. 70 F.fr.

This book, a reprint of an article published in the *Revue générale de droit international public* in 1981, is a detailed and competent study of international administrative tribunals. The author devotes special attention to current proposals for reforming the O.E.C.D. Appeals Board. However, he deals only with international administrative tribunals, and not at all with the substantive law which they apply (apart from a very brief mention of the question of discretionary powers on pp. 142–6), and this is likely to restrict considerably the number of people who will want to read his book. MICHAEL AKEHURST

International Law governing Communications and Information. By EDWARD W. PLOMAN. London: Frances Pinter Ltd., 1982. xvi + 367 pp. £25.

The purpose of this collection of documents is to assemble under one cover the major legal instruments concerned with communications and information at the international level, together with resolutions, declarations, draft conventions and other material of a quasi-legal character, the importance of which, where policy not infrequently has yet to be translated into law, is obvious.

The editor, who has had extensive experience with the European Broadcasting Union and a number of other institutions, has organized his somewhat amorphous material into an intelligible form by dividing it into ten parts. The titles of these: telecommunications law; postal law; space law; intellectual property rights; information law (including protection of privacy); trade and customs regulation; culture and education; and national security and law enforcement, give an idea of the breadth of materials included, which range from familiar items like the European Convention on Human Rights to such specialized items as the 'Points for possible inclusion in draft international standards for the protection of the rights of the individual against threats arising from the use of computerized personal data systems' from a report by the United Nations Secretary-General in 1976.

The sections vary in length from over a hundred pages to no more than two, a reflection of both differing states of legal development and the editor's decision to omit the numerous bilateral agreements to be found in the field of communications and information and certain other material, in order to concentrate on the relevant multilateral conventions, including the constituent instruments of international organizations and the major regional agreements. Subject to this limitation, no significant omissions were noted. The documents are well laid out and, thanks to concise introductions at the beginning of each section, a good table of contents and an index, particularly easy to use.

A book dealing with such highly charged and changeable matters as satellite broadcasting, the protection of computer programs and the New World Information Order is bound to be overtaken by events almost as soon as it is printed. Nevertheless, a collection such as this, which brings together for the first time basic reference materials in a new and important field, is a worthwhile acquisition for any law library.   J. G. MERRILLS

Self-Determination in Law and Practice. By MICHLA POMERANCE. The Hague, Boston, London: Martinus Nijhoff, 1982. xii + 154 pp.

The title of this book is rather a misnomer, because one of its themes is that the practice of the United Nations has *not* created a new law of self-determination, because resolution 1514 and subsequent resolutions go far beyond the terms of the United Nations Charter (chapter 2) and because United Nations resolutions cannot create law (chapter 9). The author also points out that some of the resolutions, dealing with wars of national liberation, conflict with the law against the use of force (chapter 8).

Most of the book is devoted to exposing inconsistencies in the practice of the United Nations. The author argues that these inconsistencies are partly the result of the inherent imprecision of the concept of self-determination and partly the result of political bias against colonialism and neo-colonialism. It is difficult to pass an objective judgment on such charges; one man's inconsistency is another man's flexibility, and one man's bias is another man's principle. But it would be hard to deny that there is some element of uncertainty and inconsistency in United Nations practice, especially as regards the applicability or non-applicability of self-determination outside the 'colonial' context (there are several references to this problem throughout the book, although, in view of the problem's importance, it might have been better if these references had been grouped together and expanded).

Even in the context of decolonization, there are inconsistencies, particularly the controversial denial of separate self-determination to 'colonial enclaves' such as Gibraltar. But one cannot help feeling that the author spoils a good case by overstating it. Some of the inconsistencies are more apparent than real, or are caused by disagreement about the facts, not about the law (for instance, everyone agreed that the people of West Irian were entitled to self-determination, but disagreed about the genuineness of the vote for union with Indonesia). Other apparent inconsistencies are caused by attempts (often clumsy or unsuccessful, but not always unprincipled) to reconcile self-determination with other principles. For instance, when the General Assembly reluctantly approved the partition of the Belgian trust territory of Ruanda Urundi into the separate States of Rwanda and Burundi, it was departing from its normal practice of treating each trust territory or colony as a single unit for the purposes of self-determination, but this inconsistency was caused, not by bias, but by an attempt to prevent hostilities between the tribes inhabiting Ruanda Urundi; in other words, the General Assembly was trying to reconcile the principles of self-determination and territorial integrity with the principle of preserving peace.

This is a controversial book, but even those who disagree with the author's conclusions will learn much from reading it. Some of the wider issues, such as the relationship between United Nations resolutions and the sources of international law, are dealt with too briefly, but the author has carried out thorough and well-documented research into United Nations practice on decolonization; the book has a good index and will provide a mine of factual information for all subsequent writers on the subject.   MICHAEL AKEHURST

The International Law of Human Rights. By PAUL SIEGHART. Oxford: Clarendon Press, 1983. xxiv + 569 pp. £45.

This book is intended as a 'plain handbook' of the modern international law on human rights which a practitioner or student can use as a primary work of reference to discover the extent to which a particular right is recognized and protected by the principal international agreements on human rights and whether the relevant provisions of those agreements are binding on the State with which he is concerned. To that end, the author concentrates on providing an 'annotated code' of the five principal agreements currently in force: the International Covenants on Civil and Political and Economic and Social Rights (1966), the European Convention on Human Rights (1950), the European Social Charter (1961), and the American Convention on Human Rights (1969). The book also covers the African Charter on Human and Peoples' Rights (1981), which the author anticipates will enter into force during the lifetime of the book, and the Universal Declaration on Human Rights (1948) and the American Declaration of the Rights and Duties of Man (1948) which, the author argues, have come to impose legally binding obligations, at least on members of the United Nations and the Organization of American States respectively. Reference is also made, though in less detail, to a number of other agreements and instruments.

The method of presentation is systematic and well conceived. Each of the major areas of human rights is dealt with in turn. The relevant provisions of the eight principal texts are set out (or the absence of any relevant provisions noted). These texts are followed by cross-references which make it possible to discover very quickly whether there are any provisions for derogation from the right in question, any relevant savings clauses or reservations and any subsidiary instruments. There is then a detailed analysis of the principal features of the right in question with reference to the jurisprudence of the international human rights courts and tribunals, as well as selected decisions of national courts applying either one of the international agreements or a similar provision in a national Bill of Rights. Other chapters describe the machinery for international interpretation, enforcement and supervision of the agreements and analyse the clauses of general application, such as those on derogation and territorial scope. Finally, an appendix lists the parties to each of the agreements and sets out the texts of all reservations and interpretative declarations. The book is up to date to 1 January 1982.

As a work of reference, this book is a considerable success. The convenience of having all the major texts set out in this systematic fashion will be obvious to anyone interested in human rights and should assist many British students to widen their horizons beyond the provisions of the European Convention on Human Rights. The wealth of references to case law is also enormously valuable. The jurisprudence of the United Nations Human Rights Committee, the European Court of Human Rights and the European Commission of Human Rights is reviewed in considerable detail, as are the reports of the Inter-American Commission on Human Rights. The method of presentation adopted in the book has the added value that it is likely to encourage a measure of cross-fertilization between these different bodies of case law. The references to national decisions are less comprehensive but are none the less useful. The opinions of the Privy Council are of particular interest since they constitute a body of case law developed by one court interpreting several different national laws for the protection of human rights.

Two omissions do, however, require comment. The first is the general omission of references to interpretations of the human rights agreements by political organs such as committees of ministers (p. xxi). This is understandable given the aims of the book and the desire to keep its length to a manageable size but it is none the less a pity in view of the importance of declarations made by some of the political institutions. The second is the omission of almost any reference to the case law of the Court of Justice of the European Communities, only one of whose decisions (Case 36/75, *Rutili*, [1975] E.C.R. 1219) is mentioned and then only in passing (p. 182 n. 15). This omission is regrettable for two reasons. First, the Court has delivered several interesting judgments concerning individual human rights, particularly the right to property and restrictions thereon (see, e.g., Case 4/73, *Nold* (2), [1974] E.C.R. 491). Secondly, the status of the human rights agreements in Community law may have important implications for the domestic effect of those agreements in the United Kingdom.

The question of domestic effect of the agreements is considered in the first part of the volume, in which the author seeks to provide an introduction to the law of human rights. This is the least successful part of the work. While some introduction to the subject was clearly necessary, the discussion of the nature of law, with which the book begins, is rather too abstract. In addition, the chapter on the important topic of domestic effect is somewhat oversimplified. The whole issue is presented in terms of whether or not there is a conflict between domestic law and international human rights law and no consideration is given to the way in which human rights provisions may be used as an aid to interpretation of domestic laws. Nevertheless, these are minor criticisms. Taken as a whole the book is an immensely valuable work of reference which deserves the widest possible readership.

CHRISTOPHER GREENWOOD

Vereinbarungen zwischen Staat und ausländischem Investor (Max Planck Institut für ausländisches öffentliches Recht und Völkerrecht: Beitrage zum ausländischen öffentlichen Recht und Völkerrecht, Volume 80). By JUTTA STOLL. Berlin, Heidelberg, New York: Springer-Verlag, 1982. xi + 166 pp.

In Volume 80 of the prestigious series of the Max Planck Institut, Dr. Stoll asks how the protection of a foreign investment contract between a State and a private investor can be guaranteed by international law. In the first part, she underlines the importance of the problem by giving examples. In the second part, she analyses the international jurisprudence and concludes that there is no common opinion of the arbitration tribunals in judging conflicts between the host State and a foreign private investor (p. 22). The next chapters (pp. 23–93) present the different possibilities for protecting private investments and conclude that 'the relationship between the investor and home State' is not taken enough into consideration (p. 92).

The author concentrates on protection by the home State. This protection should be guaranteed where the host State has made some unilateral binding declaration in favour of the home State by agreeing to so-called 'stabilization' or 'protective' clauses in the contract with the private investor. In these clauses, normally, the host State guarantees not to act unilaterally to the disadvantage of the private investor. This solution seems rather doubtful. There are fundamental problems in finding out whether the home State has really been the addressee. It is not convincing to see in such stabilization clauses a unilateral declaration in favour of a third State. There is a considerable difference between the wish of the host State to guarantee, in a contract with a private investor, that it will not take any unilateral measures which would prejudice the contract, and the renunciation by this State of its sovereign rights in favour of another State. This would be such an important step for the host State to take that it cannot be implied, and more is needed than interpretation of a contract with a private investor. The difficulty of interpreting such stabilization clauses was shown in the award in *Kuwait* v. *Aminoil*.

The proposed solution also neglects the private character of the investment contract, even if we could admit that these contracts 'have moved more into the international law arena'. The study is an interesting, but not fundamental, contribution to the discussion of this problem.

HANS-JOACHIM MENGEL

L'Interprétation en droit international public (Bibliothèque de droit international, Volume 75). By SERGE SUR. Paris: Librairie générale de droit et de jurisprudence, 1974. x + 449 pp.

The first virtue of this monograph is its comprehensiveness. The book covers the whole of interpretation in international law and thus bridges a gap in the literature. In fact, to most writers interpretation is synonymous with *treaty* interpretation, and much has been published on this matter. Dr. Sur did well by moving beyond the familiar and perhaps overwritten treaty context. The book presents a full picture of interpretation in all the ramifications of our discipline. Obviously, the space devoted to the interpretation of treaties has had to be considerable, yet the author's interest is wider. The notion, function and modalities of interpretation in international law at large dominate this carefully researched work.

Needless to say, such a broad subject was not easy to handle. More often than not it becomes elusive as it tends to melt away in an array of theoretical problems. Indeed, the questions of natural law and positivism, sources, hierarchy of norms, sovereignty, domestic jurisdiction and application of law are all present in the book and are often debated at length. The author, however, successfully manages to stay within the confines of interpretation proper. He divided his large material into two parts, the criterion being the role of interpretation in maintaining or otherwise the coherence of the international legal order.

The book starts with a discourse on the relationship between international law and politics. Interpretation is a means whereby politics penetrate into law, and the interplay between the two is the prevailing factor in the author's definition of interpretation. So it is in his entire analysis.

Dr. Sur is far from rejecting the philological sense of the word, but he concludes that 'to interpret a text, a given behaviour of States or organs competent to act in international order is to transform a will, an activity, or a situation of political origin into a juridical behaviour and, *vice versa*, to derive, from juridical elements, the possibility, or the framework of a political action which in turn reintegrates itself into the juridical order by a new transposition' (p. 85). Thus interpretation is a hinge (*charnière*) linking law to politics. This is the key thesis of the book, though the author does not blur the distinction between the two. On the contrary, he insists on a careful separation of law and fact and he emphasizes the difference between the existence of law and its application.

The less centralized the legal system, the greater the role of interpretation. Co-existence of conflicting interpretations results from concurrent competences of the interpreting organs and entities. Unilateral interpretations destroy the coherence of the legal order. On the other hand, concerted interpretation, according to Dr. Sur, can have two aspects. It can still exercise a weakening influence on the law by softening it and by revealing what he describes as the tension between treaty law, which tends to a certain formalism, and customary law. However, concerted as opposed to unilateral interpretation normally favours the coherence of the legal order. In its second part the book deals extensively with the latter hypothesis.

The formula itself is rather broad, for it embodies any interpretation obtained through the co-operation of the interested States or organizations. To increase and reinforce the positive impact of concerted interpretation the author supports a greater measure of its regulation. The codification of the methods of interpretation tends to limit the political freedom of the interpreters. While the relevant provisions of the Vienna Convention of 1969 partly implement this postulate with regard to treaties, in the area of customary law the imprecision of methods of interpretation contributes to the political freedom in fulfilling the task of the determination of law. That freedom is still greater when the aim is to establish the circumstances which are relevant to the application of law.

In any case, co-ordination of unilateral and conflicting interpretations is not to be brought about through the decisions of the International Court of Justice. The I.C.J. Statute imposes certain limits on the Court's interpretative function, and further restrictions follow from the diversified nature of the society of sovereign States. Their divisions become visible whenever the Court makes attempts at clothing its political interpretations in judicial pronouncements. States reject a 'government of judges' in international law, and the Court has clearly failed as an organ of centralized interpretation. Dr. Sur criticizes the assimilation of contentious and advisory procedures and suggests a reform of the latter. In particular, the Court could submit more than one answer whenever various interpretations are possible and leave the choice to the competent organ. The individual or dissenting opinions would thus disappear, for they would be integrated into the decision.

First of all, however, the author is a partisan of codification and development of law in a way that would decrease the role of custom. In his view written law facilitates concerted interpretation by fixing its framework and supplying its basis.

Dr. Sur shows a fine grasp of theoretical problems and a remarkable erudition. The book is an important contribution to the study and understanding of international law. The richness of the contents would make an index welcome. The repeated mistakes in the spelling of some well-known names are to be regretted.   K. Skubiszewski

The Application of the Rule of Exhaustion of Local Remedies in International Law. By A. A. Cançado Trindade. Cambridge: Cambridge University Press, 1983. xi + 443 pp. £30.

This book is welcome not least because it is evidence of the revival of the series of Cambridge Studies in International and Comparative Law. Its author is a Brazilian scholar and it is important to note that, whilst he has a good deal to say about the rule of exhaustion of local remedies in international law, his particular emphasis is on the rule in the domain of international protection of human rights. And in this domain it is the practice of the Commission and the Court under the European Convention on Human Rights which provides the bulk of the material on which the author relies.

The book examines successively the rationale for the rule, the conditions for its application, the burden of proof relating to the rule, the extent of application of the rule, the 'time-factor' in its application and, finally, certain special problems arising from the issue of admissibility of petitions, claims for compensation, declaratory judgments and certain procedural issues. It is well written and well researched, and many of Dr. Trindade's conclusions are applicable quite outside the context of human rights claims. He rightly challenges the view—expressed by classical writers like Borchard and Eagleton—that exhaustion of local remedies must be pursued to the point where a denial of justice occurs: and that then, and only then, may an international claim be presented. The basis of the international claim must certainly be an international wrong: but it does not have to be the wrong of denial of justice in addition to the original wrong complained of.

So, too, in chapter 3, the author has an excellent, general discussion of the burden of proof. He notes the detailed discussion of this in the *Norwegian Loans* case, and Lauterpacht's attempt to advance rules to deal with the distribution of this burden between the parties: but, of course, the Court's judgment did not proceed on these grounds. Indeed, none of the judicial or arbitral awards is truly dispositive of these issues. The author's conclusions are, perhaps unfortunately, confined to human rights claims, but they are essentially that the claimant must make out a prima facie case to show remedies were exhausted, but that the respondent State must show such remedies did exist and were adequate and effective (p. 170). Yet it is here that the danger of extrapolating from human right claims to general international law becomes apparent. For, as the author subsequently argues in his concluding chapter, there may well be a duty on the State to provide local remedies for violations of human rights: this is certainly the view adopted by the European Commission. It is doubtful, however, that this can be extended to a more general proposition that a State is under a legal duty to provide local remedies for any breach of international law in relation to an alien.

To state the problem is not, however, to criticize the author for failing to provide the solution. The law is not yet sufficiently developed to allow a solution to be expounded as established law. The issues have been raised by Dr. Trindade in his highly intelligent book, and for that we owe him a debt of gratitude.   D. W. BOWETT

People Matter. Views on International Human Rights Policy. By THEO VAN BOVEN. Amsterdam: Meulenhoff, 1982. 186 pp. *f* 34.50.

This is a collection of statements and addresses by the man who was Director of the United Nations Division of Human Rights in Geneva from 1977 to 1982. The termination of the author's appointment was the result of policy differences with the Secretary-General who, we are told, considered him too outspoken. If this was so, it is a sad reflection of the pressures to which modern international civil servants are subjected, since in all cases the murders and other officially inspired atrocities condemned by the author were already well documented.

In addition to the above, apparently controversial, material the author's observations range over the whole field of human rights and include comments on racism, social justice, the rights of women and children, and the demand for a new world economic order. Interesting issues which are touched on include the role of the Commission on Human Rights and relations between the Human Rights Committee and the Specialized Agencies. The inspirational tone, entirely appropriate for speeches on human rights, results in a level of analysis which will disappoint the reader in search of a detailed discussion of particular problems. The importance of human rights as a United Nations objective will bear repetition, however, while Dr. van Boven's call for both resources and personal commitment to further the cause draws attention to the vital relation between the moral and the material in all such efforts to promote human welfare.   J. G. MERRILLS

DECISIONS OF BRITISH COURTS DURING 1983 INVOLVING QUESTIONS OF PUBLIC OR PRIVATE INTERNATIONAL LAW

A. PUBLIC INTERNATIONAL LAW*

Jurisdiction—continental shelf—foreign employer's duty to collect United Kingdom income tax in respect of employment on installation on United Kingdom continental shelf

Case No. 1. Clark (*Inspector of Taxes*) v. *Oceanic Contractors Inc.*, [1983] 2 A.C. 130, [1983] 1 All E.R. 133, [1983] 2 W.L.R. 94, H.L., reversing [1982] 1 W.L.R. 222, C.A., reversing [1981] 1 W.L.R. 59, Dillon J. The decision of Dillon J. in this case was noted briefly in an earlier volume of this *Year Book*.[1] The successive reversals by the Court of Appeal of Dillon J.'s judgment, and (by a narrow majority and for different reasons) by the House of Lords of the Court of Appeal, illustrate the unwisdom of courts' attempting to supply the deficiencies of taxation legislation with respect to extraterritorial activities. As Lord Lowry commented, once the 'worldwide' argument, based on a straightforwardly literal interpretation of the relevant provisions, was rejected it was difficult indeed to find any 'half-way house, or a safe anchorage, in the North Sea'.[2] So the Court of Appeal concluded; but three members of the House of Lords were able to discern two or perhaps three such anchorages, where they severally, and rather uneasily, rested.

The respondents, a foreign company, not locally resident for tax purposes, installed and maintained oiling platforms and pipelines in the North Sea, operating from bases in Brussels and Antwerp. Some of their activities were conducted in the British sector of the North Sea, a 'designated area' under the Continental Shelf Act 1964. The company itself, and its employees, were clearly liable to United Kingdom tax in respect of profits and salaries arising from activities in the British sector. But it was disputed whether the company was required to operate the P.A.Y.E. system of tax deductions for those employees. The Finance Act 1970 section 204, which imposed the obligations to make P.A.Y.E. deductions, was stated to extend to 'any payment of, or on account of, any income assessable to income tax' under Schedule E, which includes both foreigners working in part in the United Kingdom or in a designated area under the Continental Shelf Act 1964, and United Kingdom residents engaged in part of their employment abroad. For the Crown it was argued that section 204 required no territorial limitation at all, since it was machinery incidental to the underlying liability to tax which *was* territorially limited. The difficulty with this was that it failed to distinguish between the obligation to pay tax and the obligation to withhold it under the P.A.Y.E. scheme. A foreign employer with no connection at all with the United Kingdom could therefore be affected solely because his

---

* © Professor James Crawford, 1984.

[1] This *Year Book*, 52 (1981), pp. 313–14.

[2] [1983] 2 A.C. 130 at p. 158.

employee was a United Kingdom resident, and it was no answer that in many such cases the legislation would be practically unenforceable. It did not add to the attractiveness of an over-broad interpretation of section 204 that it could only be enforced in an essentially arbitrary way (that is, only in those cases where the employer happened to come to or have assets in the United Kingdom).[3] For these reasons the 'literal' interpretation of section 204 was unanimously rejected, although surprisingly it retained a lingering attraction for Lords Wilberforce and Roskill.[4] But Dillon J. had managed to discover a distinction between local employment (including employment in a designated area) and foreign employment, which avoided the worst of these difficulties:[5] the question on appeal was whether this, or some alternative distinction, could be safely constructed. The Court of Appeal, rejecting Dillon J.'s view, thought not, as did a minority in the House of Lords.[6] But a majority in the House of Lords, while rejecting Dillon J.'s reasoning, in substance agreed with his conclusion. Lord Scarman laid down a requirement of the employer's 'tax presence' in the United Kingdom (a requirement the respondent clearly satisfied).[7] Lord Wilberforce extracted from section 38 (4) of the Finance Act 1973 a similar, but rather more precise, requirement, that the person carry on trade 'through a branch or agency in the United Kingdom'.[8] Lord Roskill agreed with both.[9] Presumably it is necessary that the employer's 'tax presence' or 'trade' be related to the employment in question, although this is one of a number of obscurities in the majority's interpretation of section 204.[10]

Enforcement of foreign legislation—extraterritorial legislation—consistency with international law—protection of cultural property—public policy of the forum

Case No. 2. *Attorney-General of New Zealand* v. *Ortiz and Others*, [1983] 2 Lloyd's Rep. 265, [1983] 2 All E.R. 93, [1983] 2 W.L.R. 809, H.L. The decision of the Court of Appeal in this case included some observations by Lord Denning M.R. on its international law implications: these were noted in the last volume of this *Year Book*.[11] The decision of the Court of Appeal was affirmed by the House of Lords, but without reference to these wider implications.[12]

'Piracy'—theft by armed band from ship anchored in territorial waters—thieves opposing capture by force after detection—whether shipowners entitled to indemnity for loss by piracy under war risks policy

Case No. 3. *Athens Maritime Enterprises Corporation* v. *Hellenic Mutual War Risks Association (Bermuda) Inc.*, [1983] Q.B. 647, [1983] 1 All E.R. 590, [1983] 2 W.L.R. 425, Staughton J. The plaintiff's ship was anchored in the Chittagong

---

[3] Cf. [1982] 1 W.L.R. 222 at pp. 226–8 *per* Lawton L.J., at pp. 231–3 *per* Brightman L.J.

[4] [1983] 2 A.C. 130 at pp. 153–4 *per* Lord Wilberforce; at p. 161 *per* Lord Roskill.

[5] [1981] 1 W.L.R. 59 at p. 66.

[6] [1983] 2 A.C. 130 at pp. 156–7 *per* Lord Edmund-Davies; at pp. 158–60 *per* Lord Lowry.

[7] At pp. 147–8.   [8] At pp. 150–3.   [9] At p. 161.

[10] Cf. at pp. 159–60 *per* Lord Lowry. Another decision on extraterritorial jurisdiction was *Attorney-General's Reference (No. 1 of 1982)*, [1983] 3 W.L.R. 72. There the Court of Appeal firmly declined an invitation to extend the scope of local jurisdiction over foreign conspiracies, based on the effect of the conspiracy on persons within the jurisdiction.

[11] This *Year Book*, 53 (1982), pp. 280–1.

[12] Cf. [1983] 2 Lloyd's Rep. 265 at pp. 270, 272 *per* Lord Brightman.

Roads, within the territorial sea of Bangladesh, when a group of six or seven men armed with knives boarded the ship and stole mooring lines and other equipment. They were detected and threatened members of the crew, but then escaped when officers armed with a pistol and rockets approached. The plaintiff claimed for the loss from the defendant association under a war risks policy which included loss arising from 'piracy'. It was argued for the defendant that piracy could not be committed by stealth but required some overt threat or use of force. This argument succeeded, the trial judge holding the case to be 'one of clandestine theft which was discovered; force or threat of force [being] used by the men to make good their escape'.[13] For present purposes, however, the question of place of commission is of greater interest.

As a matter of international law, it is probable that piracy can only be committed in areas beyond national jurisdiction—and, therefore, not in the territorial sea of a State.[14] It does not follow that the common law, in its definition of piracy, should apply the same jurisdictional limitation—even if in other respects the definition of piracy is drawn from international law.[15] Nor does it follow that the term 'piracy' in an insurance policy need carry the same technical meaning. As Staughton J. said:

there is compelling authority for the view that in public international law piracy can only occur outside the jurisdiction of any State . . . Both the need for a definition of piracy in public international law and the reason why that definition is, in general, confined to acts committed on the high seas, appear from article 19 of the Convention [on the High Seas (1958)] . . . When robbery with violence is committed within the jurisdiction of a State, it is not thought necessary to give every State the right to seize, prosecute and punish offenders. It is by no means self-evident that similar considerations point to the same definition of piracy for domestic purposes, and in particular the interpretation of contracts of insurance. [Counsel] submitted that if I held that there was a loss by piracy in the present case, then every robber on board a houseboat on the Thames will be liable to prosecution in every country in the world. I do not accept that submission. It is not my intention to derogate from the existing rules of public international law on the topic of piracy, even if I have power to do so. But a different rule, for the purpose of interpreting contracts of insurance, will not give rise to the disastrous consequence envisaged by [that] submission. A ship-owner whose property is taken by robbers is not much concerned whether that takes place in or outside territorial waters. Nor should I have thought that the precise location was of much concern to insurers, save to the extent that robbery is a good deal more likely on board a ship in a port or estuary, than it is 12 miles out or more.[16]

What then was the territorial scope of 'piracy' for present purposes? After examining the authorities Staughton J. rejected the submission that it applied to all places within the common law jurisdiction of the Court of Admiralty (the 'high seas' in the Admiralty sense).

But I see no reason to limit piracy to acts outside territorial waters. In the context of an insurance policy, if a ship is, in the ordinary meaning of the phrase, 'at sea' or if the attack upon her can be described as 'a maritime offence' . . . then for the business purposes of a policy of insurance she is, in my judgment, in a place where piracy can be committed.[17]

[13] [1983] Q.B. 647 at p. 660.
[14] Cf. Geneva Convention on the High Seas 1958, Article 19: *United Nations Treaty Series*, vol. 450, p. 11; Brownlie, *Principles of Public International Law* (3rd edn., 1979), pp. 243-5. But cf. Greig, *International Law* (2nd edn., 1976), p. 332, cited by Staughton J. as suggesting a contrary view.
[15] As to which cf. *In re Piracy Jure Gentium*, [1934] A.C. 586.
[16] [1983] Q.B. 647 at pp. 654-5.   [17] At p. 658.

Since there was no doubt that the ship here was 'at sea', or that the offence was a 'maritime' one, in these senses, it was clear that the theft was capable of being classified as 'piracy', had the other attributes of force or overt threat been present.[18]

Municipal law—relation to international convention—interpretation—reference to French text and travaux préparatoires—*Warsaw Convention as amended at the Hague 1955—Carriage by Air Act 1961*

Case No. 4. Goldman v. *Thai Airways International Ltd.*, [1983] 3 All E.R. 693, C.A. In a series of decisions in the 1970s the House of Lords substantially reformed the common law rules for interpretation of treaties and treaty-implementing statutes.[19] These principles are, according to Lord Diplock, 'now too well established to call for citation of authority':[20] it remains for the courts to apply them, a process which will no doubt illuminate both the judges' capacity for dealing with issues of international interpretation, and also the utility (or otherwise) of the interpretative principles themselves.

The facts in the present case were simple. The plaintiff was flying in a Thai Airways DC8 from London to Bangkok. While over Turkey the plane encountered severe clear air turbulence and the plaintiff, whose seatbelt was not fastened, struck the roof, sustaining serious spinal injury. The pilot was aware that turbulence was forecast for the area but did not illuminate the 'fasten seatbelts' sign. Under the Warsaw Convention as amended at the Hague in 1955,[21] Article 22 (1), the damages recoverable were limited to approximately £11,800, unless the plaintiff could show that the pilot had acted 'with intent to cause damage or recklessly and with knowledge that damage would probably result' under Article 25, in which case full damages (in this case, about £41,000) could be awarded. The trial judge held Article 25 applicable; the Court of Appeal unanimously disagreed, so that only the limited amount payable under Article 22 (1) could be claimed. The Court held that the phrase 'recklessly and with knowledge that damage would probably result' in Article 25 should be interpreted literally, and required actual knowledge. Eveleigh L.J., who delivered the leading judgment, found confirmation of this view in the *travaux préparatoires* to the Convention. He said:

> I had thought that I had found support for my reading of art. 25 when I looked at the French text and saw the words 'avec conscience'. I had thought that phrase imported the meaning of awareness. In view of the decision of the French Cour de Cassation I hesitate to use the French text to support my interpretation of art. 25. However, I do see confirmation in the *travaux préparatoires*.

At the ICAO international conference at The Hague in 1955–56 a draft of art. 25

---

[18] On jurisdiction with respect to hijacking see *R.* v. *Moussa Membar*, [1983] *Crim. L.R.* 618 (allegation of aircraft commander's complicity in hijacking consistent with conviction of hijackers). On the determination of a state of war for the purposes of frustration of a charter-party see *Finelevet A.G.* v. *Vinava Shipping Co. Ltd.*, [1982] 2 All E.R. 658 (no rule that a war or declaration of war frustrated a contract; the question is one of fact in each case).

[19] See esp. *James Buchanan & Co. Ltd.* v. *Babco Forwarding & Shipping (U.K.) Ltd.*, [1978] A.C. 141, this *Year Book*, 49 (1978), pp. 276–81; *Fothergill* v. *Monarch Airlines Ltd.*, [1981] A.C. 141, this *Year Book*, 51 (1980), pp. 291–3.

[20] *Garland* v. *British Rail Engineering Ltd.*, [1982] 2 All E.R. 402, 415 *per* Lord Diplock; this *Year Book*, 53 (1982), pp. 291–3.

[21] Cmd. 9824 (1955), given the force of law in the U.K. by the Carriage by Air Act 1961, s. 1 (1).

prepared at Rio de Janiero was considered. This provided for unlimited liability only where there was proved an intent to cause damage. Widely differing opinions were expressed, but there seemed to be a general consensus that some further restriction of liability would be possible if the limits imposed by art. 21 were increased. At the same time it was said that the Rio de Janiero proposal would allow immunity in cases where there clearly was moral turpitude. The Norwegian delegation submitted a proposal that after the words 'done with intent to cause damage' there should be added 'or recklessly by not caring whether or not damage was likely to result'. In discussion reference was made to the question of whether or not actual knowledge of the risk would be required. The record reads:

'Mr Garnault (France) said . . . The text of the Working Group included the idea of "recklessness" as well as the idea of "without caring that damage would probably result". For some delegates, the latter words meant that the author of the fault had knowledge of the damage which would probably result. Therefore, he suggested that the words "without caring", in the text of the Working Group be replaced by the words "with knowledge".'

A vote was taken as to which of the following three phrases should be added to the requirement that an intention should be proved: (a) 'and has acted recklessly': (b) 'and has acted recklessly and knew or should have known that damage would probably result': (c) 'and has acted recklessly and knew that damage would probably result'. It was (c) that received the largest number of votes. If the interpretation adopted by the judge was the one intended, it would be sufficient to stop at the word 'recklessly' as in (a). It seems to me that his interpretation makes unnecessary the reference to knowledge which follows.

I must not be thought to give undue weight to submissions made by the United Kingdom delegation, but it is interesting to read the reference to what Mr Wilberforce (as he then was) said in relation to the Norwegian proposal:

'In the test submitted it was stated "recklessly without caring that damage would probably result", and his delegation understood and hoped that these words had been introduced in order to state that the person concerned did know that the probable consequences of his act would be to produce damage.'

I have looked at these papers, not in order to interpret art. 25, but to check on the interpretation which to me it seems to bear. I think that the papers do indeed do that.[22]

The French text (through its use of the word 'en') was also of assistance in establishing that 'the damage anticipated must be of the same kind of damage as that suffered',[23] though that was not a problem on the facts of this case.[24]

[22] [1983] 3 All E.R. 693 at pp. 699–700. Purchas L.J. agreed 'that this interpretation is supported by the travaux préparatoires and in particular [by] the selection of the particular version which finally found its way into the article in favour of the alternatives which had been debated' (at p. 705). O'Connor L.J. also agreed.   [23] At p. 700 per Eveleigh L.J.

[24] Cf., however, Bingham J. in *Data Card Corporation* v. *Air Express International Corporation*, [1983] 2 Lloyd's Rep. 81, a case involving the interpretation of the original Warsaw Convention 1929, Art. 22 (2). He said (at p. 85):

'While . . . English Courts are now sometimes prepared to consider the travaux préparatoires which precede the adoption of international conventions, reliance may be placed on such materials only where they contain a clear and indisputable indication of a definite legislative intention . . . The present materials are, as it seems to me, an excellent example of materials which may not be relied upon, because far from containing a clear and indisputable indication of a definitive legislative intention, they leave one altogether unclear as to what was to be intended to be the rule on the point at issue. Perusal of these materials in the present case serves only to highlight the wisdom of the Courts' cautious approach to such materials. I do not feel it necessary to make any detailed reference to the documents to which I was referred, interesting though they were, because they did not, in my judgment, begin to offer a solution to this case.'

Other cases during the year involving the interpretation or application of international conventions

*European Convention on Human Rights 1950, Article 11 (1)—freedom of associa-
tion—expulsion of trade unionist in resolution of inter-union dispute—validity of
union rules providing for such expulsion*

Case No. 5. Cheall v. *Association of Professional, Executive, Clerical and
Computer Staff*, [1983] 1 All E.R. 1130, H.L., reversing [1982] 3 All E.R. 855,
C.A. The decision of the Court of Appeal in this case was fully noted in the last
volume of this *Year Book*.[25] One issue was whether the so-called 'Bridlington
principles' regulating inter-union membership disputes were, as applied by the
two unions in this case, contrary to public policy on the basis that they
contravened the plaintiff's freedom of association. Some members of the
European Court of Human Rights in the *Young, James and Webster*[26] case had
suggested that Article 11 (1) of the European Convention, which guarantees
freedom of association, should be interpreted so as to secure the right to join a
trade union, or to choose which of several trade unions to join—apparently
irrespective of the rules of those unions or of whether the existence of a 'closed
shop' rendered union membership practically compulsory. Only Lord Denning
M.R. of the majority in the Court of Appeal was attracted by this argument,
though the other members of the Court (and the judge below) all treated the
European Convention as, in principle, relevant. On appeal the House of Lords
unanimously reversed the majority of the Court of Appeal, holding that the
plaintiff's expulsion from the defendant union involved no violation of natural
justice or of his freedom of association. On the 'public policy' point Lord Diplock
stated, rather curtly:

> Finally it was argued that the Bridlington principles, which have been in operation since
> as long ago as 1939, are contrary to public policy, since they restrict the right of the
> individual to join and to remain a member of a trade union of his choice; and that any
> attempt to give effect to any such restriction would, on application by the individual
> affected by it, be prevented by the courts.
>
> This supposed rule of public policy has, it is claimed, always formed part of the common
> law of England but it has now been reinforced by the accession of the United Kingdom
> to the European Convention for the Protection of Human Rights and Fundamental
> Freedoms ... My Lords, freedom of association can only be mutual; there can be no right
> of an individual to associate with other individuals who are not willing to associate with
> him. The body of the membership of APEX, represented by its executive council and
> whose best interests it was the duty of the executive council to promote, were not willing to
> continue to accept Cheall as a fellow-member. No doubt this was because if they continued
> to accept him, they ran the risk of attracting the sanction of suspension or expulsion of
> APEX from the TUC and all the attendant disadvantages to themselves as members of
> APEX that such suspension or expulsion would entail. But I know of no existing rule
> of public policy that would prevent trade unions from entering into arrangements with one
> another which they consider to be in the interests of their members in promoting order in
> industrial relations and enhancing their members' bargaining power with their employers;

included *American Express Co.* v. *British Airways Board*, [1983] 1 W.L.R. 701 (Lloyd J.) (liability of
carrier of mail and postal packets under Warsaw Convention as amended at The Hague; effect of Post
Office Act 1969, s. 29); *Worldwide Carriers Ltd.* v. *Ardtran International Ltd.*, [1983] 1 Lloyd's Rep. 61
(Parker J.) (limitation of actions under Art. 32 (2), International Convention on the Carriage of Goods
by Road 1956; see at pp. 65, 66 for reference to French and German case law on the point); *The Benarty*,
[1983] 2 Lloyd's Rep. 50 (Sheen J.) (application of the principle in *The Hollandia* (this *Year Book*,
53 (1982), pp. 289–91) to Art. VIII of Hague–Visby Rules: see at pp. 56–7).

[25] This *Year Book*, 53 (1982), pp. 282–5.   [26] Series A, vol. 44 (1981), at p. 28.

nor do I think it a permissible exercise of your Lordships' judicial power to create a new rule of public policy to that effect. If this is to be done at all it must be done by Parliament.

Different considerations might apply if the effect of Cheall's expulsion from APEX were to have put his job in jeopardy, either because of the existence of a closed shop or for some other reason. But this is not the case.[27]

As a matter of the interpretation of Article 11 this is plainly right. Otherwise only minorities would have freedom of association. On the other hand, Lord Diplock's reference to 'the existence of a closed shop or . . . some other reason' suggests that the public policy argument, supported by Article 11 of the European Convention, may still have a role to play in some cases.[28]

Principle of equality and non-discrimination—discrimination on the basis of a person's racial group—whether Sikhs a racial group by reason of 'ethnic or national origins'—Race Relations Act 1976, section 3 (1) (b)—International Convention on the Elimination of All Forms of Racial Discrimination 1966, Article 1 (1)

Case No. 6. Mandla v. *Dowell Lee,* [1983] 2 A.C. 548, [1983] 1 All E.R. 1062, [1983] 2 W.L.R. 620, [1983] I.C.R. 385, H.L. As guarantees of equality before the law and non-discrimination on grounds of race are increasingly adopted in international instruments and in national constitutions or legislation, attention is increasingly focused on the meaning of key concepts such as 'discrimination', 'equality' and 'race'. These concepts have been elaborated and invoked in international law for some considerable time, and the (somewhat different) formulations of them in instruments such as the International Convention on the Elimination of All Forms of Racial Discrimination[29] and the International Covenant on Civil and Political Rights[30] have, therefore, a considerable history behind them.[31] It is not surprising that domestic courts called on to apply principles of equality or racial non-discrimination should have regard to their meaning in international law and in the practice of other jurisdictions. This is especially so when the legislation in question is explicitly based on the relevant international conventions, as is the case in Australia[32] and New Zealand.[33] On the other hand, although these are not terms of art peculiar to particular municipal law systems, their implementation can take a variety of forms, and there are important differences between different instruments on basic issues such as the tolerance of 'special measures' of affirmative action, and even on the definition of 'discrimination' itself. Where, as with the Race Relations Act 1976 (U.K.), the legislation in question does not correspond explicitly or closely with the international instrument, it can not be assumed that the same results would be achieved under both. But that is no reason for declining whatever assistance the international practice can provide.

The respondent, the headmaster of a small private school, refused to allow the second appellant to attend the school if he insisted on wearing a turban. The school rules required a boy's hair to be cut short, which was inconsistent with the

---

[27] [1983] 2 A.C. 180 at pp. 190-1.
[28] And see the note by Simpson, *Modern Law Review,* 46 (1983), p. 635.
[29] *United Kingdom Treaty Series,* No. 77 (1969).   [30] Ibid., No. 6 (1977).
[31] See W. A. McKean, *Equality and Discrimination under International Law* (1983).
[32] Racial Discrimination Act 1975 (Cth). See *Commonwealth* v. *Tasmania* (1983), 46 A.L.R. 625 esp. at pp. 791-3 *per* Brennan J.
[33] Race Relations Act 1971.

beliefs and practices of orthodox Sikhs such as the appellants. The initial question was whether Sikhs are a racial group under section 3 (1) of the Race Relations Act 1976; if so, and if the requirement of wearing short hair was not one with which Sikhs 'can comply' under section 1 (l) (b) (i) of the Act, the further and more difficult question was whether that rule was none the less 'justifiable' under section 1 (1) (b) (ii). The House of Lords unanimously held that Sikhs are a racial group by virtue of their ethnic origins, that the appellants could not, in the relevant sense, comply with the requirement, and that the requirement was not 'justifiable'.[34]

Given the much more elaborate definition of discrimination in the 1976 Act compared with the Racial Discrimination Convention, little guidance was to be obtained from the latter on the question of justifiability. On the other hand, the first question, whether Sikhs were a racial group by virtue of their 'ethnic or national origins', was in substance common to the two instruments, given their similarity of language. It is probable that an international court would have little or no difficulty in identifying Sikhs as such as a group, and a similarly broad interpretation has been adopted by courts in other Commonwealth countries. In the event their Lordships reached this conclusion without referring to the Racial Discrimination Convention. But they did rely on a New Zealand decision where the Convention had been relevant.[35] The inevitability of this form of cross-reference, or cross-fertilization, was acknowledged by Lord Fraser. Referring to the New Zealand case, he said:

> There is only one respect in which that decision rests on a basis that is not fully applicable to the instant appeal. That appears from the long title of the New Zealand Act which is as follows:
>
> 'An Act to affirm and promote racial equality in New Zealand and to implement the International Convention on the Elimination of All Forms of Racial Discrimination.'
>
> Neither the 1976 Act nor its predecessors in the United Kingdom, the Race Relations Acts 1965 and 1968, refer to the International Convention on the Elimination of All Forms of Racial Discrimination. The Convention was adopted on 7 March 1966, and was signed by the United Kingdom on 11 October 1966, subject to reservations which are not now material. It was not ratified by the United Kingdom until 7 March 1969 . . . Under the Convention the States parties undertook, inter alia, to prohibit racial discrimination in all its forms, and to guarantee the rights of everyone 'without distinction as to race, colour, or national or ethnic origin' to equality before the law, notably in certain rights which were specified including education (art. 5 (e) (v)). The words which I have quoted are very close to the words found in the 1976 Act and in its predecessors in this country, and they are certainly quite consistent with these United Kingdom Acts having been passed in implementation of the obligation imposed by the Convention. But it is unnecessary to rely in this case on any special rules of construction applicable to legislation which gives effect to international conventions because, for the reasons already explained, a strict or legalistic construction of the words would not, in any event, be appropriate.[36]

Adopting this broad construction, Lord Fraser concluded that:

> For a group to constitute an ethnic group in the sense of the 1976 Act, it must, in my opinion, regard itself, and be regarded by others, as a distinct community by virtue of certain characteristics. Some of these characteristics are essential; others are not essential

---

[34] Reversing the Court of Appeal, [1982] 3 All E.R. 1108.

[35] *King-Ansell* v. *Police*, [1979] 2 N.Z.L.R. 531.

[36] [1983] 1 All E.R. 1062 at pp. 1068-9.

but one or more of them will commonly be found and will help to distinguish the group from the surrounding community. The conditions which appear to me to be essential are these: (1) a long shared history, of which the group is conscious as distinguishing it from other groups, and the memory of which it keeps alive; (2) a cultural tradition of its own, including family and social customs and manners, often but not necessarily associated with religious observance. In addition to those two essential characteristics the following characteristics are, in my opinion, relevant: (3) either a common geographical origin, or descent from a small number of common ancestors; (4) a common language, not necessarily peculiar to the group; (5) a common literature peculiar to the group; (6) a common religion different from that of neighbouring groups or from the general community surrounding it; (7) being a minority or being an oppressed or a dominant group within a larger community, for example a conquered people (say, the inhabitants of England shortly after the Norman conquest) and their conquerors might both be ethnic groups.

A group defined by reference to enough of these characteristics would be capable of including converts, for example, persons who marry into the group, and of excluding apostates. Provided a person who joins the group feels himself or herself to be a member of it, and is accepted by other members, then he is, for the purpose of the 1976 Act, a member.[37]

Foreign State immunity—contract of employment—Indian national employed with Indian High Commission—claim for unfair dismissal—'retrospectivity' of State Immunity Act 1978—position at common law

Case No. 7. Sengupta v. *Republic of India,* [1983] I.C.R. 221, E.A.T. (Browne-Wilkinson J.). The short space of time between the common law's rejection of the doctrine of general foreign State immunity and its replacement, in most of the important common law jurisdictions, by comprehensive legislation has meant that the rules of restrictive immunity at common law have remained rather general and undeveloped. In particular the approach the courts would have taken to such questions as contracts of employment, or local torts causing physical injury or damage to tangible property, has remained unclear. This case, dealing as it does with the former problem as a matter of common law, is accordingly of considerable interest, although in the result it tended to conflate the common law and statutory approaches.

The applicant was an Indian national who came to the United Kingdom in 1966 to work as a teacher and was subsequently employed by the Indian High Commission in London 'in a low clerical grade where he enjoyed very limited diplomatic privileges'.[38] He resigned in 1974 but was re-engaged in 1975 on a similar basis (but without diplomatic privileges of any kind). He was promoted to senior grade in 1979 but was eventually dismissed in February 1981 (after the State Immunity Act 1978 had come into force). Had that Act applied to the case it is clear that the Republic of India would have been immune from the jurisdiction since the employee was, when the proceedings were brought, 'a national of the State concerned' (section 4 (2) (a)), and the High Commission was not an 'establishment maintained by the State in the United Kingdom for commercial purposes' (section 4 (3)).[39] However, the Act does not apply to

---

[37] At pp. 1066-7.   [38] [1983] I.C.R. 221 at p. 223.

[39] Section 16 (1) (a) further excludes from local jurisdiction 'proceedings concerning the employment of the members of a mission within the meaning of the [Vienna] Convention' on Diplomatic Relations of 1961: see Art. 1. Given the extensive definition of this term in the Convention, it is clear that the Republic of India would have been doubly immune under the Act: see [1983] I.C.R. 221 at p. 225 *per* Browne-Wilkinson J.

'proceedings in respect of matters that occurred' before it came into force, and in particular it does not apply to contracts entered into before then (section 23 (3) (b)). This excluded the operation of section 4, but the question was apparently raised whether it also excluded section 1 (the basic statement of immunity from jurisdiction). This extraordinary argument was, not very summarily, rejected:

> In our judgment, where proceedings are based on a contract made before 1978, the proceedings are 'in respect of matters that occurred' before 1978 even if the breach of that contract occurred after 1978. If this were not the case, the Act of 1978 would have a blatantly and illogical retrospective effect. The blanket immunity conferred by section 1 would apply to claims based on pre-1978 contracts (if breached after 1978) yet none of the exceptions to immunity relating to commercial contracts (section 3), contracts of employment (section 4) or arbitration agreements (section 9) would apply because those sections would in those circumstances be expressly excluded by section 23 (3) (b). Therefore in relation to pre-1978 contracts the effect of the Act of 1978 would be to confer absolute immunity on States in relation to all their contractual engagements, an immunity which under the common law operating immediately before the Act of 1978 came into force they did not enjoy. There is neither logic nor justice in construing the Act of 1978 in this way.[40]

It followed that the matter was governed by the common law rather than the 1978 Act, and it was strongly arguable that, under a broad distinction between *acta jure imperii* and *acta jure gestionis*, the appellant's employment was of a routine or 'private' character, notwithstanding that it was employment in a High Commission. The question was whether, in applying the broad common law test, it was sufficient to look at the character of the employee's work or the nature of his particular claim, as distinct from the employer's overall operations. As Browne-Wilkinson J., delivering the judgment of the Employment Appeal Tribunal, noted:

> Although the existence of the distinction between public and private acts is now established, the application of the distinction to individual contracts or types of contracts has not been worked out. For the future, the matter will normally fall to be decided in accordance with the Act of 1978. Unfortunately we have to decide for the first time in England whether claims arising out of a contract of employment at an embassy or High Commission entered into, and breached, by a State fall to be categorised as claims arising from public or private acts of that State. Nearly all the authorities on the point are concerned with commercial transactions entered into by foreign State and not with any other type of contract.[41]

Clearly the Tribunal was uncomfortable with the analogy of 'commercial transactions' or contracts, with its emphasis on 'nature' rather than 'purpose' and on the character of the contract rather than the reasons for its (alleged) breach.[42] Indeed in rejecting that analogy Browne-Wilkinson J. relied on a passage from Lord Wilberforce's speech in *I Congreso del Partido*[43] which, leading as it did to a dissent on the *Marble Islands* claims, was by no means representative of

---

[40] At pp. 224-5.   [41] At p. 226.

[42] The claim, however, was for unfair dismissal contrary to statute, which is not the same thing as an ordinary contractual claim. Although the 1978 Act does not make the distinction (s. 4 (6)) it could have been argued that at common law a foreign State was immune from proceedings in respect of such statutory claims, but not from contractual claims as such.

[43] [1983] A.C. 244 at p. 263, cited at [1983] I.C.R. 221 at pp. 227-8.

the views of the majority in that case. In any event the Appeal Tribunal concluded that:

in seeking to decide whether the claim in this case is excluded by the doctrine of sovereign immunity, we must ask the following questions: (a) Was the contract of a kind which a private individual could enter into? (b) Did the performance of the contract involve the participation of both parties in the public functions of the foreign State, or was it purely collateral to such functions? (d) Will the investigation of the claim by the tribunal involve an investigation into the public or sovereign acts of the foreign State?

If we have asked ourselves the right questions, then in our judgment the necessary result must be that there is no jurisdiction to entertain the applicant's claim. It is true that any private individual can employ another, i.e. can enter into a contract of employment. Therefore in that sense the entry into a contract of employment is a private act. But when one looks to see what is involved in the performance of the applicant's contract, it is clear that the performance of the contract is part of the discharge by the foreign State of its sovereign functions in which the applicant himself, at however lowly a level, is under the terms of his contract of employment necessarily engaged. One of the classic forms of sovereign acts by a foreign State is the representation of that State in a receiving State. From the doctrine of sovereign immunity were derived the concepts that the embassy premises were part of the soil of the foreign sovereign State, and that diplomatic staff are personally immune from local jurisdiction. A contract to work at a diplomatic mission in the work of that mission is a contract to participate in the public acts of the foreign sovereign. The dismissal of the applicant was an act done in pursuance of that public function, i.e. the running of the mission. As a consequence, the fairness of any dismissal from such employment is very likely to involve an investigation by the industrial tribunal into the internal management of the diplomatic representation in the United Kingdom of the Republic of India, an investigation wholly inconsistent with the dignity of the foreign State and an interference with its sovereign functions.[44]

This did not, however, mean that no jurisdiction could ever be asserted at common law over employment in an embassy:

We do not exclude the possibility that, apart from the Act of 1978, employees who are solely concerned with providing the physical environment in which the diplomatic mission operates might be able to claim: that question will have to be decided if and when it arises. But we do not consider that there can be jurisdiction over claims by those engaged in carrying out the work of the mission in however humble a role. The factors which have led us to reach our conclusion on the general principle apply to all such employees. They are engaged in carrying out the public functions of the foreign State: an investigation of their claim might well require an investigation by the tribunal into the conduct of the diplomatic mission. Therefore, in our judgment, at common law a State is immune from claims for unfair dismissal brought by employees at a diplomatic mission who are engaged in carrying on the work of that mission.[45]

It follows that there can be no local jurisdiction to allow a locally recruited embassy typist (as distinct, perhaps, from a window cleaner) to recover wages alleged to be due. The contrast with the situation of an independent contractor is a stark one.

The Appeal Tribunal drew support for this general conclusion from a useful review of the case law in other jurisdictions:

In *De Decker* v. *United States of America* (1956) 23 I.L.R. 209, the Belgian Court of Appeal upheld a claim for State immunity from proceedings brought by an official of the United States Foreign Service. In *Luna* v. *Republic of Rumania* (unreported) an Italian

[44] At pp. 228-9.   [45] At p. 229.

court upheld a claim for immunity from proceedings brought by the employee of a commercial agency which the court held to be 'simply an office of the Rumanian embassy': the employee was employed at a very low grade. In *Conrades v. United Kingdom* (unreported) March 1981, a labour court at Hanover upheld the claim by the United Kingdom Government for immunity from a claim brought by a German national who had been employed for over 30 years as a receptionist and non-confidential clerical worker at the consulate at Hanover. There is no case where immunity has been refused on the grounds that the claimant was not a member of the diplomatic staff. Those cases are to be contrasted with claims brought by employees at institutions run by foreign States but not as part of their diplomatic mission. Thus immunity has been refused by the Italian court in relation to claims by employees at the Hungarian Academy in Rome, at a hospital run by the Vatican in Rome, and at a lycée run by the French Government. In each of these cases the fact that the institution at which the claimant was employed was not discharging a sovereign function of the foreign State was a material consideration.[46]

But the overseas immunity legislation is by no means as categorical in excluding embassy employment disputes. The Canadian Act (in this respect following the United States one) contains no special employment provision: whether the Canadian courts would regard the dispute as arising from 'commercial activity' as defined is unclear. More significantly, perhaps, there is no general exclusion of embassy-related employment in the European Convention on State Immunity of 1972,[47] a point rather glossed over by the Tribunal:

although the European Convention on State Immunity (1972) (in pursuance of which the Act of 1978 was enacted) does not in itself provide any reliable guide to what was the rule of public international law apart from the Act, we think it is material that under the Act of 1978 complete immunity is afforded against any claim relating to employment by a member of the staff of the mission of whatever grade, although total immunity is not granted in relation to other types of employment by a foreign State.[48]

In fact Article 5 of the Convention would only have excluded local jurisdiction in a case such as this on the basis of the appellant's Indian nationality at the time the action was brought. The very general exclusion, in Article 32, of 'privileges and immunities relating to the exercise of the functions of diplomatic missions and consular posts and of persons connected with them' would not have helped the employer here; nothing in the Vienna Convention on Diplomatic Relations prevents the assertion of jurisdiction in a case such as this.[49] In the absence of specific provision in the Vienna Convention it is by no means clear that a total exclusion of local jurisdiction over embassy employment is justified, in particular where the employee was locally recruited. Jurisdiction over unfair dismissal raises more difficult questions, but the broad terms in which this claim was rejected make such distinctions difficult to maintain.[50] On the other hand, it is not surprising that the courts were not prepared to be bolder than the legislature was in enacting the 1978 Act, with its categorical exclusion of embassy employment. Section 23 notwithstanding, the Act seems to be having its own indirect form of retrospective effect.

[46] At pp. 229–30.

[47] Cmnd. 7742; *United Kingdom Treaty Series*, No. 74 (1979).

[48] [1983] I.C.R. 221 at p. 230.

[49] The protection in Art. 24 of the Vienna Convention of the 'archives and documents of the mission' may well have made it difficult to establish a case of unfair dismissal on the merits, but that is another question.

[50] Cf. above, n. 42.

Diplomatic privileges and immunities—diplomatic agent's private residence—dispute over access for purpose of repairing dry rot—whether a 'real action'—whether premises held 'on behalf of the sending State for the purposes of the mission'—Vienna Convention on Diplomatic Relations, Article 31 (1) (a). Foreign State immunity—action for damages for breach of covenant in lease—whether property 'used for the purposes of a diplomatic mission'—State Immunity Act 1978, section 16 (1) (b)

Case No. 8. Intpro Properties (U.K.) Ltd. v. Sauvel, [1983] Q.B. 1019, [1983] 2 All E.R. 495, [1983] 2 W.L.R. 908, C.A., reversing [1983] Q.B. 1019, [1983] 1 All E.R. 658, [1983] 2 W.L.R. 1, Bristow J. In 1979 the plaintiff let to the French Government a furnished house for occupation by the first defendant, financial counsellor to the French embassy in London, and his family. During the currency of the lease dry rot appeared in part of the house; eventually the first defendant refused access to the builders contracted by the plaintiff to repair the damage. This was an apparent breach of the covenant in the lease to allow reasonable access to the premises for such purposes. The plaintiff commenced proceedings against the first defendant, who sought to have the proceedings set aside on the grounds of diplomatic immunity. Leave was obtained to serve the French Government, which entered an appearance but declined to appear to argue the case (maintaining what seems to be a growing and regrettable practice in municipal as in international litigation). Issues of diplomatic and State immunity thus arose with respect to the same transaction.

On the question of diplomatic immunity, the argument for the first defendant[51] was based on Article 31 (1) (a) of the Vienna Convention on Diplomatic Relations of 1961.[52] That Article confers immunity on diplomatic agents in civil proceedings, 'except in the case of a real action relating to private immovable property situated in the territory of the receiving state, unless he holds it on behalf of the sending State for the purposes of the mission'. For the plaintiff to succeed, therefore, the action had to be a 'real action' and the property had to be held otherwise than 'on behalf of the sending State for the purposes of the mission'. Bristow J. held that the plaintiff failed on both points. On the meaning of 'real action' he said:

> A 'real action' is a creature unknown to English law since the Middle Ages. The term in the 1964 Act is a literal translation of 'une action réelle' in the French master text of the treaty. There is no evidence before me from an expert in French law on the nature of an action réelle. If Intpro wishes to rely on this action being a 'real action' it is for it to show me what action réelle means in the terms of the concepts known to English law . . .
>
> In my judgment, Intpro's action does not in any way fit the concept of 'action réelle' as reflected in the commentaries. It is a normal action in personam to enforce by injunction the obligations arising from a lease, and for damages. If the Sauvels are properly joined as defendants, they are in my judgment protected from suit by art. 31 because the action against them is not a real action.[53]

In any event he would have held that the first defendant did not 'hold' the

---

[51] Maintained by counsel previously briefed by M. Sauvel, who appeared as *amicus curiae* at first instance only.

[52] *United Kingdom Treaty Series,* No. 19 (1975), relevant articles of which were given the force of law by the Diplomatic Privileges Act 1964.

[53] [1983] 1 All E.R. 658 at p. 661. The reference to the 'French master text' of the Vienna Convention is, however, confusing: under Art. 53 five texts (including English) are equally authentic.

property at all, since it was the French Government which was the lessee.[54] The result was that the action failed as against the first defendant, a result not disturbed on appeal.[55]

In the meantime, however, the French Government had itself been served and the question was whether it was immune from the jurisdiction—a question of State immunity, though certain State immunities are established by the Vienna Convention and merely preserved by the State Immunity Act 1978.[56] On this question Bristow J. held shortly that the French Government was immune:

By s. 16 (1) (b), s. 6 (1) does not apply to proceedings concerning a State's title to or its possession of property used for the purposes of a diplomatic mission. Note that what is here in play is simply title or possession, and not use as in s. 6 (1). In my judgment this action is an action relating to rights and obligations which arise from the State's possession of [the premises] under its contract of tenancy and so is not simply an action relating to its use of the premises. In my judgment, however, the property, in relation to the State's possession of which this action is brought, is property used by the State for the purposes of a diplomatic mission. It is used to house the financial counsellor of the embassy of London in his capacity as such, plus his family, in circumstances appropriate to his official situation.[57]

The plaintiff company appealed, and Bristow J.'s decision on this point was reversed by a two-judge Court of Appeal. The Court did not, as it might well have done, decide the case on the basis that the obligation to allow access was 'an obligation of the State which by virtue of a contract (whether a commercial transaction or not) falls to be performed wholly or partly in the United Kingdom' within section 3 (1) (b). As May L.J. (with whom Watkins L.J. agreed) said:

[counsel] recognised that as the 1978 Act contains both ss. 3 and 6 it may well be that on its proper construction s. 3 (1) (b) only applies to contracts properly and solely so called, whereas a lease, although in one sense a contract, nevertheless was concerned more particularly with the respective rights of the parties to it to immovable property, that is to say land, in the United Kingdom and consequently fell more appropriately to be dealt with under s. 6 of the 1978 Act. In the light of counsel's approach, I express no concluded opinion on this point.[58]

In fact the assumption so far has been that the various exceptions to immunity enumerated in the 1978 Act are (except where the Act otherwise provides)[59] cumulative rather than alternative, and that each exception is to be fairly construed in its own right, without straining to avoid overlaps between them. In view of counsel's concession here it remains to be seen whether this view will prevail.

The appellant therefore based its case primarily on section 6 (1) (b), and the question was whether the action (which otherwise was plainly covered by section 6 (1) (b)) was excluded by section 16 (1) (b) as 'proceedings concerning a State's . . . possession of property used for the purposes of a diplomatic mission'. May L.J. said:

I think that on its proper construction this phrase contemplates that the premises should be used for the professional diplomatic purposes of such a mission. It is not enough, in my opinion, that the premises are used as a private residence by a diplomatic agent, even though incidentally that diplomatic agent has certain understandable social obligations

---

[54] At pp. 661–2.   [55] [1983] 2 All E.R. 495 at p. 502.   [56] Section 16 (1).
[57] [1983] 1 All E.R. 658 at p. 662.   [58] [1983] 2 All E.R. 495 at p. 500.
[59] As it does with respect to contracts of employment (excluded by s. 3 from the operation of that section) and Admiralty claims (s. 10 (1) (b)).

which he and his wife carry out on the premises . . . I think that one can obtain substantial assistance about the construction of the whole of s. 16 (1) (b) of the 1978 Act from a consideration of arts. 1 and 31 of the Vienna Convention on Diplomatic Relations . . . The 1964 Act and 1961 convention dealt with the immunities of diplomats; the 1978 Act and 1972 convention dealt with the immunities of the sovereign States which those diplomats represent. At least in so far as civil proceedings in respect of land in the United Kingdom is concerned, I would expect the immunities of the foreign State on the one hand and its diplomats on the other to be at least consistent, if not identical.[60]

Having cited the definition of 'premises of the mission' in Article 1 of the Convention, he continued:

In her book *Diplomatic Law: Commentary on the Vienna Convention on Diplomatic Relations* (1976) . . . Denza expressed the view that the specific mention of the residence of the head of the mission in this definition made it clear that residences of other members of the mission cannot form part of the premises of the mission. For my part, I respectfully agree. I think that it follows that, if the premises with which we are concerned . . . were not part of the premises of the mission for the purposes of the 1964 Act, then had M. Sauvel been the tenant and not the French government it could not have been said that he held those premises 'for the purpose of the mission' within art. 31 (1) (a) . . . If this would be a correct approach if the provisions of the 1964 Act were in issue, then, when we are in fact concerned with the 1978 Act, because the actual tenant of the premises was the French government, I think that almost the same words in s. 16 (1) (b) of the 1978 Act should be similarly construed and not be held to reintroduce the immunity to civil proceedings . . . which the earlier s. 6 (1) (b) had excluded.

In addition . . . when one looks for assistance on the construction of the phrase 'proceedings concerning a State's title to or its possession of property' in s. 16 (1) (b) of the 1978 Act from within the Act itself, one sees that s. 6 (1) deals with a State's interest in, or its possession or use of, immovable property in the United Kingdom. There is no corresponding reference to the 'use' of such property in s. 16 (1) (b). Consequently . . . the proceedings to which by s. 16 (1) (b) of the 1978 Act s. 6 (1) of the same Act is not to apply are limited to those in which a State's title to or right to possession of, in the strict sense, is in question. In this respect also, therefore, consistency between the respective 1964 and 1978 provisions is retained.[61]

Although this conclusion can be accepted, it does not with respect follow from the fact that a residence is not part of the 'premises of the mission' under the Vienna Convention that it is not held 'for the purposes of the mission' within Article 31 (1) (a) of that Convention. The point is rather that, if all 'mere' residences of diplomatic agents are so held, then there is no difference, from the point of view of immunity from civil proceedings, between the residence of the head of mission and that of any other diplomatic agent. Yet the Convention deals with these in different terms, thus implying the more restrictive meaning of 'purposes of the mission' that the Court in fact adopted.

Foreign State immunity from execution—embassy bank account—whether used for 'commercial purposes'—State Immunity Act 1978, sections 3 (1) (3), 13 (4), 17 (1)

Case No. 9. Alcom Ltd. v. *Republic of Colombia*, [1984] 1 All E.R. 1, [1983] W.L.R. 906, C.A. One of the peculiarities of the British and Commonwealth case law on foreign State immunity is the almost complete absence of discussion of what has been elsewhere a major area of difficulty—that is, the execution or

---

[60] [1983] 2 All E.R. 495 at pp. 500-1.   [61] At pp. 501-2.

enforcement of judgments.[62] Now that the field is substantially covered by legislation such questions may seem less likely to arise. But as this case amply demonstrates, the legislative provisions are by no means free from difficulty, and the way the courts deal with such difficulties says much about their underlying attitudes to the enforcement of judgments against foreign State property.

The plaintiff obained a default judgment for goods sold and delivered against the Republic of Colombia. Garnishee orders nisi were then granted attaching credits in a bank account in the defendant's name. The Colombian ambassador certified that the funds in the account were exclusively for use in the maintenance of the diplomatic mission. Hobhouse J. at first instance set aside the garnishee orders on the basis that a bank account used for an embassy was to be presumed non-commercial and thus immune from execution. The plaintiff appealed, successfully, and the Court of Appeal restored the garnishee orders. Since leave to appeal to the House of Lords was given, the case will be only briefly noted here, with more detailed comment reserved for the next volume of this *Year Book*.

Under the State Immunity Act 1978, section 13, State property is in general immune from execution unless it is 'for the time being in use or intended for use for commercial purposes'.[63] The head of the State's diplomatic mission can under section 13 (5) certify that property is not in use or intended for use for commercial purposes: that certificate is 'sufficient evidence of that fact unless the contrary is proved'. Had the matter stopped there, it might well have been that the certificate would have been accepted, since the running of an embassy is, in general, as Browne-Wilkinson J. said in *Sengupta* v. *Republic of India*, 'one of the classic forms of sovereign acts by a foreign State'.[64] However, section 17 (1) of the Act defines 'commercial purposes' by linking it to the Act's (stipulative) definition of 'commercial transactions':

'commercial purposes' means purposes of such transactions or activities as are mentioned in section 3 (3) above.

It appears to follow that funds held for the purpose of purchasing goods or services or meeting financial obligations are automatically held for commercial purposes, no matter what the character of those obligations or the purpose of those purchases. Since money or bank credits[65] are almost always going to be 'intended for use' for such purposes it seems to follow that they will almost always be liable to seizure to enforce judgments against the foreign State under the Act.

The respondent sought to avoid this conclusion in two ways. First, it was argued that the phrase 'into which the State enters or in which it engages otherwise then in the exercise of sovereign authority' applies to all three sub-paragraphs of the definition of 'commercial transaction' in section 3 (3) of the Act. This argument might have been supported by reference to the European Convention on State Immunity which appears to guarantee 'the immunity from jurisdiction which foreign States enjoy in respect of acts performed in the exercise of sovereign authority' (Article 24 (1)), but it was, not surprisingly in view of the

---

[62] See Crawford, *American Journal of International Law*, 75 (1981), pp. 847-50.
[63] Section 13 (2), (4).   [64] Above, n. 44.
[65] Which clearly, as Sir John Donaldson M.R. held, constitute 'property' for the purposes of s. 13: [1983] 3 W.L.R. 906 at p. 910.

terms and layout of section 3 (3), firmly rejected. Sir John Donaldson M.R. (with whom May and Dillon L.JJ. agreed) said:

I am quite unable to accept that construction. Had Parliament so intended, it would have cast the section in such a way as to remove the words 'into which a State enters or in which it engages otherwise than in the exercise of sovereign authority' from paragraph (c) and put them in the same position as the words 'but neither paragraph of subsection (1) above applies to a contract of employment between a State and an individual' so as to make it clear that they governed all three paragraphs. There would also have been other ways no doubt of achieving the same result as a matter of drafting, but that is the obvious way of doing it. Indeed, at one stage I did seriously wonder whether, acting without authority, Her Majesty the Queen's printer had wholly altered the sense of the Act by misplacing the words, but there has been no suggestion that that is the case and, indeed, it is an extremely unlikely hypothesis. I fear that we have to construe the section in the way in which it is printed.[66]

Secondly, it was argued that—as Hobhouse J. had held—the Act had to be construed 'against the general background of general principles of international law', and that as a matter of international law funds used to maintain an embassy are used for public or non-commercial purposes. Indeed, the argument might have been taken further: in the light of the decision of the West German Federal Constitutional Court in the *Philippines Embassy* case,[67] it could be argued that a State is entitled to immunity with respect to its 'embassy accounts' as a matter of international law. The *Philippines Embassy* decision was not in fact cited, and the weaker argument from international law was rejected in favour of a literal interpretation of the 1978 Act. Sir John Donaldson M.R. said:

I agree that if the 1978 Act is ambiguous, a court is entitled to have regard to the general principles of international law and to resolve that ambiguity in the way most consistent with those principles. However, those principles appear to require a court to have regard to the transactions under scrutiny rather than to the reasons why the transactions were undertaken . . . In any event, I can detect no ambiguity in the 1978 Act.

[Hobhouse J.'s] view that regard must be had to the primary purpose of running the embassy rather than the secondary purpose of paying for goods and services seems to me . . . to be devoid of justification in fact or on the wording of the Act. The purpose of money in a bank account can never be 'to run an embassy'. It can only be to pay for goods and services or to enter into other transactions which enable the embassy to be run . . .

There remains the alternative basis of [Hobhouse J.'s] judgment, namely that a garnishee order attaches to the whole of any credit balance and that the court accordingly needs to be satisfied that the whole balance is intended for use for commercial purposes. This seems to me to be correct in principle. Accordingly, all three members of the court pressed [counsel] to give examples of expenditure incurred in the day to day running of the embassy which did not fall within the very wide definition of 'commercial transactions' contained in section 3 (3).

The examples given by [Hobhouse J.] do not seem to me to bear out his thesis. The payment of the salary of the ambassador or other embassy officials might indeed be outside the definition, although I can see an argument to the contrary, but it is conceded that they are not in fact paid out of these accounts. His other example, expenditure designed to help stranded citizens, would be incurred for the purpose of a commercial transaction, as defined, being either expenditure for the purpose of a contract for the supply of services,

[66] Ibid.
[67] 46 *BVerfGE* 342 (1977); partly translated in United Nations Legislative Series, *Materials on Jurisdictional Immunities of State and their Property* (1982), pp. 297-321.

for example an air ticket, or a loan or, if a gift or grant to the person concerned, a transaction or activity otherwise than in the exercise of sovereign authority.[68]

The Court accordingly rejected the ambassador's certificate, not on the basis of any bad faith or deception but because it involved a misconception of the meaning of 'commercial purposes' under the Act.[69]

Apparently the consequences of the garnishee orders were drastic, in that they severely affected the functioning of the embassy. The court was, in Sir John Donaldson's words:

told that the telex can no longer be used, because the ambassador cannot be sure when he will be able to pay for the service. Indeed, short of financing the embassy out of his own pocket or persuading the Government of Colombia to remit further funds to this country, I can quite see that the embassy may be brought to a standstill. This is a very remarkable result and one which may well not have been intended by Parliament. Unfortunately we are bound to give effect to parliamentary intentions as expressed in the statute . . .[70]

On the other hand, elsewhere in his judgment the Master of the Rolls had seemed much less perturbed at the result. Commenting on the argument that no embassy funds would, on this view, ever be immune, he said:

I think that there are two answers to this comment. The first is that a mission could have drawing powers on a London account which was not that of the State, but of its central bank. That account would then have the protection of section 14 (4). The second is that the real protection for missions lies in the jurisdictional provisions of section 3 (1). If the State is amenable to the jurisdiction of the English courts in accordance with that subsection, there seems no logical reason why its money should not be attachable in satisfaction of a judgment. Protected property, such as the mission's buildings, is obviously in a different category, but such buildings are not used for commercial purposes.[71]

This is, with respect, not entirely convincing. It is not very satisfactory to allow a State to rely on a device to avoid seizure of its funds in order to justify another provision which is said to go too far, and, moreover, the blanket immunity for central bank funds has itself been cogently criticized.[72] Nor was it much to the point to rely on the State's (limited) jurisdictional immunity as its principal protection when the Act was apparently based on the notion that foreign States have at least some distinct entitlement to immunity from execution. The effect of *Alcom* v. *Republic of Colombia*, if the decision survives on appeal, is that (for States ill-advised enough not to keep their funds in central bank accounts) protection will be almost entirely illusory, so far as liquid assets are concerned. States which choose to keep their money in central bank accounts, on the other hand, will, on Sir John Donaldson's view of the Act, be fully protected. It is hard to resist the conclusion that the execution provisions of the 1978 Act are already in need of review.

Act of foreign State—whether justiciable before English courts—decision of Cuban Government to sever commercial relations with Chile—consequential conversion of Chilean-owned sugar aboard Cuban ships outside Cuba—liability of separate State trading entity responsible for supply of sugar—relation between defence of act of State and foreign State immunity—recognition of Cuban law establishing economic sanctions against Chile—the public policy of the forum

[68] [1983] 3 W.L.R. 906 at pp. 911–12.
[69] At pp. 912–13.
[70] At p. 913. May L.J. also expressed concern: ibid.
[71] At p. 912.
[72] Cf. F. A. Mann, 'The State Immunity Act 1978', this *Year Book*, 50 (1979), p. 43 at pp. 61–2.

Case No. 10. Empresa Exportadora de Azucar v. *Industria Azucarera Nacional S.A.*, [1983] 2 Lloyd's Rep. 171, C.A., affirming Mustill J., unreported, 29 February 1980.[73] This was a further instalment in the lengthy litigation arising out of the rupture of diplomatic and trading relations between Chile and Cuba in 1973 after the overthrow of President Allende. The facts in the present case were the same as those in *I Congreso del Partido*, except that that case was an Admiralty action *in rem* against Cuba itself in respect of its liability as owner of the two ships in which sugar was being carried.[73a] The present case arose out of an arbitration under the rules of the Sugar Association of London, between the Chilean importer and owner of the sugar (IANSA) and the Cuban exporter (Cubazucar). Cubazucar was a separate State trading agency of Cuba but (it was accepted) was not to be identified with the Government of Cuba for the purposes of foreign State immunity. No question of State immunity could therefore arise, but one of a number of defences relied on was that of act of State, and the case accordingly sheds light on the relationship between the two 'defences'.

The arbitrators found that the decision to cancel the sugar contract, to divert the *Marble Islands* (which was on its way to Chile) and to withdraw the partly unloaded *Playa Larga* from its Chilean port, were all taken 'at a high level in the Cuban Government and that Cubazucar . . . were party to such decisions'. They held that the contract was thereby frustrated, but that Cubazucar was liable to IANSA for the value of the sugar in the two ships (which was owned and had been paid for by IANSA under a letter of credit).[74] The contract was held to be frustrated, if not earlier then because further performance of it was made illegal by Cuban Law No. 1256, enacted some sixteen days after the beginning of the coup but retrospective in effect to that date.[75] Cubazucar was therefore not liable for the non-shipment of the balance of sugar outstanding under the contract.

The Council of the Sugar Association then stated a case for the opinion of the High Court. Mustill J. upheld the arbitrators on all points except one: the exception was his holding that, having refused Cubazucar's documentation with respect to the *Marble Islands* cargo, IANSA could not then (on the facts found) claim damages for the loss of the sugar. Both parties appealed, but the Court of Appeal rejected both the appeal and cross-appeal, thus upholding Mustill J.'s judgment in full. The case raised a large number of private law issues, but for present purposes two issues are of significance. On both of them Mustill J.'s very careful judgment was substantially adopted by the Court of Appeal.

1. *Recognition of Cuban Law No. 1256: economic sanctions and local public policy*

Cubazucar argued that the contract, if not frustrated as a result of the coup itself, was frustrated by Cuban Law No. 1256 which made performance illegal. Cubazucar was accordingly not liable for further shipments under the contract.

---

[73] See also the note on the private international law aspects of this case at p. 297, below.

[73a] [1983] A.C. 244; this *Year Book*, 52 (1981), pp. 314–19; ibid., 50 (1979), pp. 225–7; ibid., 49 (1978), pp. 262–7. In the case of one of the ships, the *Marble Islands*, Cuba only became owner after the diversion, but the House of Lords held (by a majority) that the subsequent disposal of the cargo constituted an act for which Cuba could be liable and with respect to which it was not immune from the jurisdiction.

[74] Payment for the sugar in the *Playa Larga* had been made before the coup. On the day of the coup Cubazucar claimed against the letter of credit in respect of the sugar in the *Marble Islands*, knowing that the cargo would not reach Chile.

[75] It was not contended that Cubazucar connived in or procured the enactment of this law.

IANSA argued that the Law was 'penal and discriminatory' and should not, therefore, be recognized by the court as giving rise to illegality or as frustrating the contract. Emphasizing the various meanings of 'recognition' in this context, Mustill J. held that the law was not so repugnant that it should not be recognized. He said:

There is, in my view, no general principle to the effect that confiscatory or discriminatory legislation should be ignored. Instead, each case should be treated on its merits, setting the legislation in the political context in which it was enacted, and examining the impact which it had on the matters in dispute in order to see whether (in the words of Lord Salmon in *Oppenheimer* v. *Cattermole*) the Law was 'so great an offence against human rights that [the English courts] would have nothing to do with it'. The determination of this question may sometimes raise very difficult issues of public policy, but I do not find any such difficulty in the present case. Whatever may have been the position in the days when *Wolff* v. *Oxholm* was decided, it would now be quite impossible to say that economic sanctions taken for political purposes are necessarily contrary to the law of nations. Indeed, the imposition of sanctions may on occasion represent a conformity with, not a contravention of, the principles of international law. Opinions may differ as to the propriety and wisdom of the Cuban legislation. I express no view at all about this. All that need be said is that in my view the legislation was not so repugnant to British ideas of international and personal morality as to require the English Court to ignore the fact that it existed and that it made further performance of the contract impossible.[76]

Ackner L.J., who delivered the judgment of the Court of Appeal, agreed:

The law was directed essentially against Chilean official and semi-official agencies. The seizure was intended in part as a means of achieving compensation for Cuban property damaged as a result of the coup, in which a government strongly hostile to Chile had come into power by military force, and whose existence Chile, rightly or wrongly, clearly considered to be strongly inimical to its political and economic interests. We agree with the view of the learned Judge, which by inference must have been that of the arbitrators, that the legislation was not so repugnant to British ideas of international and personal morality as to require the English Courts to ignore its existence.[77]

In the particular context of the case, this can be accepted: the Law was relevant as much as part of a general situation of mutual economic and political hostility as it was as a juridical act. Moreover, it was, as Ackner L.J. hinted, a continuation of a pattern of trade which was as much politically as economically inspired. To single out—for the purposes of cancelling out—particular acts on one side of the relationship would require particularly strong justification.

2. *Cubazucar's defence based on act of State*

More interesting for present purposes was Cubazucar's general defence based on the 'foreign act of State' doctrine. This had not been relied on before the arbitrators, because Cubazucar's principal line of argument there was that it had *not* been involved in the various Cuban decisions at the time, and could therefore rely on frustration or *force majeure*.[78] However, the arbitrators found that the

---

[76] Judgment of 29 February 1980, transcript, pp. 61–2, citing *Oppenheimer* v. *Cattermole*, [1976] A.C. 249 at p. 283; *Wolff* v. *Oxholm* (1817), 6 M. & S. 92.

[77] [1983] 2 Lloyd's Rep. 171 at p. 190.

[78] Of course a party cannot rely on self-induced frustration: *Maritime National Fish Ltd.*, v. *Ocean Trawlers Ltd.*, [1935] A.C. 524. Nor, under Rule 120 of the contract, could Cubazucar rely on 'Government intervention . . . or any cause of Force Majeure' unless this was 'beyond the Seller's control'.

decisions with respect to the two ships 'were decisions taken at a high level in the Cuban Government and that Cubazucar through their managing director or other representative, were party to such decisions'. On the special case stated, Cubazucar sought to rely on this finding—adverse to it—as establishing a defence of act of State with respect to both cargoes. IANSA argued before Mustill J. both that act of State could not be raised at that stage, or had been waived as a defence, and that in any event it did not exonerate Cubazucar. Mustill J.'s decision was given before the decisions of the House of Lords in *I Congreso del Partido*[79] (holding that Cuba's acts with respect to both ships were not immune from the jurisdiction) and *Buttes Gas and Oil Co.* v. *Hammer (Nos. 2 and 3)*[80] (holding that the court will not 'adjudicate upon the transactions of foreign sovereign states'). He was therefore able to deal with the issue unperplexed by the need to reconcile the two cases, and his careful treatment of the problem is still of considerable interest. He held that the defence was inadmissible and that it would not, in any event, have succeeded. The Court of Appeal, whose decision was given *after* the two House of Lords decisions, in substance agreed.

(a) *Validity of the act of State plea.* After a consideration of the English and United States cases Mustill J. concluded that:

English law does recognise a doctrine of foreign act of state; that the doctrine requires the English Court not to sit in judgment on the acts of foreign sovereigns, done in their capacity as sovereigns, within their own territory; that the doctrine is one of public policy; and that it applies not only where the sovereign is a party to the litigation, but also where the validity of the act is put in issue as part of a dispute between private citizens.[81]

However, the plea did not excuse Cubazucar, for three distinct reasons. First, it only applies where the validity of an act of foreign State performed in the exercise of public powers is an essential ingredient of the case. It is no obstacle that the court's decision may indirectly reflect upon or concern such acts. In Mustill J.'s words, the doctrine

is relevant only where a challenge to the legal validity of the act of a foreign sovereign is an essential part of the case made by one party in respect of a particular issue, so that the Court cannot rule on that issue and hence cannot decide the dispute without investigating and ruling upon the challenge. I use the word 'validity' to denote the characteristic of the act which is under attack: sometimes it is the effectiveness of the act to confer or divest title; sometimes the status of the act as rightful by the local law; and no doubt the doctrine can arise in many other ways. But it is the legal, not the moral, status of the act which must be in dispute, and it must be put directly in issue in the action. Thus, it is not, in my opinion, enough to show that a person reading a narrative which describes the sovereign's act might be led to form an unfavourable view of his conduct, if the expression of an opinion on the point is not necessary to a ruling by the Court. Nor is it sufficient to say that the logic of the decision on the point actually in dispute appears to involve, if carried through to a conclusion, a proposition as to the validity of the foreign sovereign's act. Still less is it a sound objection that the trial of the action will require an investigation of and a finding upon that which the sovereign actually did, as part of establishing the facts on which the cause of action or substantive defence to it is based . . . The doctrine applies only where the status of the sovereign's act lies at the heart of the dispute . . .

---

[79] Above, n. 73.
[80] [1982] A.C. 888; this *Year Book*, 53 (1982), pp. 259–68.
[81] Transcript at p. 77.

Looking now at the facts of the present case in the light of that principle one must ask whether a decision on the questions of law involves the Court, or did involve the arbitrators, in sitting in judgment on the validity of the acts done by the Cuban Government. Those acts are the taking of the decision of the 11th September, 1983, and its carrying into effect by the diversion of the vessels and their cargoes. Even if the cause of action alleged had been conspiracy, *Buttes* v. *Hammer* would have been authority for the view that no such sitting in judgment would be involved. But conspiracy is not alleged, although the arbitrators have, as it happens, included facts from which a conspiracy could be inferred. This is not just a question of pleading: the causes of action relied upon are quite different. To the causes of action actually alleged the activities of the Cuban government are material only because they were the link between the wrongful act of Cubazucar and the damage suffered by IANSA. In order to make good their claim IANSA have to prove that the acts happened and something about why they happened. But there was no need for the arbitrators to investigate or rule upon their character: nor did they do so anywhere in their Award, which nonetheless contains all the facts necessary for a decision upon liability. Nor does the Court need to investigate or rule upon the quality of the government's acts. It need only take the facts found and use them as the foundation for a conclusion of law. Thus, even if the events in question did amount to an act or acts of state, this furnishes no defence to the claim against Cubazucar.[82]

Not surprisingly, Mustill J. found support for his view in what he described as the 'strong case' of *Buttes Gas and Oil Co.* v. *Hammer*,[83] where the Court of Appeal allowed both a foreign conspiracy and a local defamation claim involving a foreign State to proceed. But that decision was reversed by the House of Lords six years later, in terms that (because they included both claims) seem to allow no such distinction between cases 'directly' and 'indirectly' affecting the validity of foreign State acts to be drawn. It was argued in the last volume of this *Year Book* that such a distinction is both necessary and desirable if the coherence of the common law in relation to foreign States is to be preserved.[84] It is perhaps significant therefore that in the first decision after a general non-justiciability rule was established for foreign acts of State, the Court of Appeal found it possible to approve a more refined version of the doctrine. In response to the question whether the court was being asked 'to sit in judgment on the acts of the Cuban government done in its sovereign or governmental capacity' Ackner L.J. said:

We think there are two answers to this question. Firstly, to establish the claim, IANSA did not have to prove anything against the Cuban government. IANSA relied entirely upon Cubazucar having acted in a certain manner. Cubazucar's defence was: We did not so act. Cubazucar was not believed. The facts, as found by the arbitrators, that the decisions implemented by Cubazucar were joint decisions of Cubazucar and the Cuban government do not involve the English Courts sitting in judgment on the Cuban government. IANSA never impugned the validity of any of the Cuban government's acts—except Law 1256, said to be confiscatory and discriminatory—and accordingly the Court was not in a judicial no-man's land . . .

The second answer is that if the Courts were being asked to sit in judgment on the conduct of the Cuban government, then that conduct was not immune from the jurisdiction of the English Courts since its activity was a trading rather than a governmental activity. What the Cuban government did was to induce breaches of contract by Cubazucar. It is the nature of the act that matters, not the motive behind it. That motive cannot alter the nature of the act . . .

Alfred Dunhill of London Inc. v. *The Republic of Cuba* was a case on the United States' doctrine of Act of State. The view of four of the five Judges, who held that no Act of State

---

[82] At pp. 78, 80.   [83] [1975] Q.B. 557.   [84] This *Year Book*, 53 (1982), pp. 264–8.

had occurred, was approved by Lord Wilberforce in his speech in the *I Congreso* case, and had been quoted on a number of previous occasions in the Court of Appeal . . . The Court decided that immunity should be granted only with respect to causes of action arising out of foreign state's public or governmental action and not with respect to those arising out of its commercial or private action. This 'restrictive theory' to the principle of immunity is dealt with in detail by Lord Wilberforce in the *I Congreso* case.

Thus, the nature of the conflict, if contrary to our view it brought into question the legislative or international transactions of the Cuban government, involved an act of a private law character such as a private citizen might have entered into.[85]

In the context of this case it is suggested that the first argument is the better one. The Cuban Government's acts here were plainly performed with respect to particular commercial transactions. They should not be treated as depriving the courts of power to determine the obligations of other parties under those transactions (or indeed of the State itself if it is a party to them).[86] But the Court of Appeal's decision on the point is also of interest in its clear acceptance of a 'commercial transactions exception' to the act of State doctrine, as a correlative to the foreign State immunity rule.

The act of State defence was also rejected for two other, although subsidiary, reasons, both re-emphasizing the court's tendency to confine and restrain that doctrine. The first was the familiar argument that the plea was only available for acts performed within the territory of the foreign State. Mustill J. agreed:

Assuming . . . that the topic is free from direct authority, one may ask: do the rules of public policy which require the English court to abstain from ruling upon the actions of a foreign sovereign within his own territory equally apply to actions which he takes abroad? It seems to me that they do not. One can recognise the force of the argument that the Court should not, as a general rule, permit itself to tackle head-on the legitimacy of acts done by the foreign sovereign within the territory where he himself makes the law, for this might be regarded as a meddling in matters which are no concern of the Court. But when the sovereign leaves his own domain, why should the Court be so reticent? There may be areas of the law where expediency requires a special rule for sovereigns or their followers, even when abroad: e.g., their personal immunity from suit (now circumscribed) and that of persons engaged as belligerents. But I see no such ground of expediency here, and in my view the doctrine of foreign act of state should be confined to the area where it belongs, namely the territory of the sovereign whose act is called in question.[87]

The Court of Appeal also agreed, although their treatment of the House of Lords decision in *Buttes* was ingenious rather than persuasive:

We consider the view he expressed was right and finds support in the speech of Lord Wilberforce in *Buttes Gas and Oil Co. v. Hammer* . . . The point did not have to be decided in *Buttes*' case, which had much of the character of a boundary dispute between States. To attack the decree of 1969/70 extending the Arab Emirate of Sharjah's territorial waters upon the ground that the decree was extra-territorial, would have been to beg the question.

[85] [1983] 2 Lloyd's Rep. 171 at pp. 194–5.

[86] As with the *Playa Larga* bill of lading in *I Congreso del Partido*: see this *Year Book*, 52 (1981), pp. 317–19.

[87] Transcript, at p. 82. He rejected also an extension of the 'territoriality' principle to cover ships:

'One further point must be mentioned in this connection. It was argued for Cubazucar that even if the doctrine has a limited territorial effect, it can properly be applied to the "Marble Island" claim, since the vessel was on the high seas at the time. I do not agree. I am not prepared to apply the doctrine in this limited sense . . . And in any event the vessel did not belong to Mambisa or the government, so that even the fiction of territoriality does not apply' (ibid.).

Where, however, it is clear that the acts relied on were carried out outside the sovereign's own territory, there seems no compelling reason for judicial restraint or abstention. In this case, although the plan may have been made in Cuba, it was carried into effect outside. Accordingly the defence of Act of State would not apply.[88]

Secondly, both courts held that Cubazucar had not discharged the burden of establishing a 'genuine' act of State—a conclusion which had some forensic point since the arbitrators had not been asked to decide the issue. In Mustill J.'s words:

A party who wishes the Court to dismiss a claim which has been established as meritorious in fact and law, on the ground that it involves the investigation of an act of state, should, in my view, be required to establish with conviction that an act of state is indeed involved. Fortuitously, the findings in the Special Case come within reach of this, but I have nevertheless been persuaded that they are insufficient for Cubazucar's purpose . . . If the point had been taken before the arbitrators it would have been necessary to investigate matters such as the following: were the persons who took the decision government officials (and, if so, at what level of authority), or were Ministers also involved; if so, which Ministers, and in particular did the Foreign Minister participate; was authority obtained from the Council of Ministers, or even the Head of State; was the plan a spontaneous reaction to an urgent political crisis, aimed at the specific problems raised by the two cargoes, or did it reflect a broader economic policy already in the course of formulation; did the persons concerned consider whether the actions which they took were justified under (a) Cuban law, and (b) under the provisions of the contract, and, if so, did they take legal advice; what factors led to the decision to claim the price before tendering the shipping documents and what part did the National Bank of Cuba play in the discussion. It is impossible to say what answers would have been given if these questions and similar had been posed at the hearing. What can be said is that a defence of act of state would in practice have been a difficult line to pursue, even if in theory it was not inconsistent with a defence on the merits. On the question of cessation, Cubazucar's evidence was that they had played no part in the diversion of the ships, and that the intervention of the state had been prompted by considerations of safety. This evidence was not believed, and once their primary case had gone, it is hard to envisage Cubazucar putting forward with conviction an entirely different version of events. This being so, I do not consider that the Court would be justified in reading into [the award] a finding which the arbitrators were never asked to make on an issue which had never been mentioned.[89]

It is a remarkable non-justiciability rule which requires such detailed examination of the non-justiciable act—but the Court of Appeal, in very similar language, agreed.[90]

(b) *Waiver of the act of State plea.* Apart from the merits of the plea, both Mustill J. and the Court of Appeal concluded that it was too late for Cubazucar to raise it. Mustill J. put this on several distinct grounds: first, that the arbitrators had already (if Cubazucar's argument were accepted) 'sat in judgment' on the Cuban Government's acts and that it was too late to repair the damage; secondly, that the plea had been in effect waived by Cubazucar's (and Cuba's) actions in permitting the arbitration to proceed to an award without protest; and thirdly, that the argument could not be relied on in the absence of 'sufficient findings of fact to enable the point to be fairly decided'.[91] The Court of Appeal limited themselves to the second point, that of waiver:

We agree with the learned Judge that the plea is capable of waiver and that there was

---

[88] [1983] 2 Lloyd's Rep. 171 at p. 194.   [89] Transcript, at pp. 83–4.
[90] [1983] 2 Lloyd's Rep. 171 at p. 193.   [91] Transcript, at pp. 84–6.

waiver by Cubazucar in permitting the arbitration to proceed to an award without protest and by the government, who undoubtedly had notice of the issues raised in the arbitration, in failing to take any steps either to invoke whatever procedure was appropriate to raise it or to ensure that Cubazucar took the point in the arbitration.[92]

Of the three reasons given by Mustill J., only the third is particularly convincing. To hold that the 'act of state' or non-justiciability plea ceases to be valid because the arbitrator (or a lower court) disregards it seems remarkable, and even more so if the principle is, as Lord Wilberforce has said, 'inherent in the very nature of the judicial process'.[93] A rather similar objection applies to the waiver argument: if the principle is an 'inherent' or jurisdictional one it is hard to see how it can be waived even by the foreign State, and *a fortiori* by an entity which all agreed was distinct from and not to be identified with the State.[94] And the objection could hardly be avoided by claiming the Cuban Government's concurrence: it is too much to imply a waiver from the non-objection of a foreign State to proceedings to which it was not a party and by which it was not bound. Only the third reason (which was not referred to by the Court of Appeal) carries much weight. Clearly it must be possible in an adversary system for a party to conduct itself in such a way that it is precluded from proving facts which would or might raise a plea to the jurisdiction or to the justiciability of the claim. Only this form of 'evidentiary waiver' could plausibly be relied on to avoid the act of State doctrine in this case.

Extradition—relation to deportation—'disguised extradition'—questions of evidence and procedure

Case No. 11. R. v. Bow Street Magistrates, ex parte Mackeson, (1981) 75 Cr. App. R. 24, D.C. *Case No. 12. R. v. Guildford Magistrates' Court, ex parte Healy,* [1983] 1 W.L.R. 108, D.C. The principle, enunciated in *Soblen*'s case,[95] that deportation may not be used as a means of evading restrictions upon the extradition of fugitive offenders, is now an accepted one.[96] But there have been few instances in which courts have been persuaded that a 'disguised extradition' had occurred or was being attempted—a reluctance perhaps increased by the fact that *Soblen* was itself, despite its special facts, a plain case of 'disguised extradition'.[97] These two cases, in one of which the deportee was successful, usefully reaffirm the *Soblen* principle. But they also underline the evidentiary difficulties.

The Divisional Court in *R. v. Bow Street Magistrates, ex parte Mackeson* had no difficulty in concluding that Mackeson's deportation from Zimbabwe/Rhodesia had been in reality a form of extradition. Indeed, this had been candidly admitted by the relevant (Southern Rhodesian) Minister, and was the conclusion as a matter of fact arrived at by the local (Southern Rhodesian) courts.[98] Moreover,

---

[92] [1983] 2 Lloyd's Rep. 171 at pp. 193–4.

[93] *Buttes Gas & Oil Co.* v. *Hammer,* [1982] A.C. 888 at p. 932.

[94] Cf. [1983] 2 Lloyd's Rep. 171 at pp. 191–2, applying *C. Czarnikow Ltd.* v. *Centrala Handlu Zagranicznego Rolimpex,* [1979] A.C. 351.

[95] [1963] 2 Q.B. 243.

[96] Cf. *Barton* v. *Commonwealth* (1974), 131 C.L.R. 477 at pp. 483–6 *per* Barwick C.J., at p. 504 *per* Mason J. (a case of attempted extradition without treaty under the prerogative); *R.* v. *Hartley,* [1978] 2 N.Z.L.R. 199 (a plain case of unlawful and improper extradition in the guise of deportation).

[97] Cf. Professor Bowett's comment in this *Year Book,* 38 (1962), p. 479 at p. 483.

[98] *Mackeson* v. *Minister of Information, Immigration and Tourism,* [1980] 1 S.A. 747, reversed on appeal on other grounds than the question of fact: [1980] 2 S.A. 747.

when the initial request was made by the Metropolitan Police for Mackeson to be returned to the United Kingdom to face trial there on charges of fraud, no machinery for extradition existed between the two countries. As Lord Lane C.J. pointed out:

The circumstances in this case were somewhat complicated by the position which existed by reason of the Unilateral Declaration of Independence. Until 1967 the Fugitive Offenders Act 1881 held good. That was, so to speak, a Commonwealth statute. It applied equally, and affected equally, all the countries in the Commonwealth. But in 1967 that situation changed, because then each country became, for this purpose . . . a separate entity and . . . nearly every country passed its own Act. This could not happen in Zimbabwe-Rhodesia, because of the illegal regime. Consequently no extradition could take place because of the illegal nature of the de facto government. On April 20, 1979, direct rule started, and in those circumstances, technically at least, the 1881 Act started once again to apply in Zimbabwe-Rhodesia, and would have been available had anyone seen fit to use it in order properly to extradite this applicant to the United Kingdom . . . [A]s I have already said, that was not done.[99]

The Court accordingly granted the applicant an order of prohibition to prevent the hearing of committal proceedings in respect of the charges of fraud against him.

The case can be contrasted with *ex parte Healy* where the applicant was deported from the United States to the United Kingdom in a manner which ensured that he would be detained in the United Kingdom to face pending charges there.[100] It was clear that there had been close collaboration between police in the two countries, but the court declined to hold that this was improper or that it was evidence of collusion to evade the extradition procedures. On the other hand, the applicant was offered a choice of deportation to Spain or the United Kingdom. Spain declined to receive him (but it is not clear from the report why that particular choice was given). While accepting the *Soblen* principle, the Divisional Court had no hesitation in holding that it did not apply on the facts. Griffiths L.J. said:

if a criminal wanted in this country is being deported by the United States' authorities of their own motion and for their own purposes, there is no reason whatever why the authorities in the United States should not report to the authorities in this country that they are deporting him and inform this country of the aircraft upon which he will be arriving so that he can be arrested as soon as he arrives here and brought to justice in this country. It is in the interest of the law abiding community that there should be international co-operation to bring wanted criminals to justice: there is no reason whatever to assume because that is done that there is a collusive agreement between the two countries to use the deportation process as a short cut to extradition.[101]

This is no doubt true, but the fact remains that the primary machinery devised by the 'law abiding community' for 'international co-operation to bring wanted criminals to justice' is extradition. In the absence of unusual frankness on the part of the deporting official (as in *Mackeson*'s case) or local bungling or illegality (as in

---

[99] (1981) 75 Cr. App. R. 24 at p. 33.

[100] The report does not specify the charges nor does it state whether the applicant could have been extradited to the U.K. in respect of them.

[101] [1983] 1 W.L.R. 108 at p. 113. The Court added that the appropriate procedure in such cases was to challenge the committal proceedings by an application for judicial review, rather than by asking the committing justice or magistrate to rule on it: at p. 113 *per* Griffiths L.J., at p. 114 *per* McCullough J.

Hartley's case),[102] it seems that the courts will be most reluctant to go behind the formal classification of 'deportation', where a fugitive criminal is effectively compelled to return to his own country.[103]

JAMES CRAWFORD

Note. The important decision of the Court of Appeal in *British Airways Board* v. *Laker Airways Ltd.* is reported at [1983] 3 All E.R. 375. Leave to appeal to the House of Lords having been given (see [1983] 1 W.L.R. 1293) the case will be noted in the next volume of the *Year Book.*

B. PRIVATE INTERNATIONAL LAW*

Penal laws and public policy

Case No. 1. An English court will not enforce either directly or indirectly a foreign penal law. Moreover, and more generally, 'English courts will not enforce or recognize a right, power, capacity, disability or legal relationship arising under the law of a foreign country, if the enforcement or recognition of such right, power, capacity, disability or legal relationship would be inconsistent with the fundamental policy of English law'.[1] These two inhibiting propositions are well-established, but there are (perhaps unavoidable) uncertainties as to their scope and as to their interaction. This is one of the several areas of law which fell to be considered by the Court of Appeal in the recent case of *Empresa Exportadora de Azucar* v. *Industria Azucarera Nacional S.A.* (*The Playa Larga*).[2] The facts of that case were as follows. A dispute arose out of the political action of the Cuban

---

[102] Above, n. 96.

[103] Other decisions on extradition and related problems during the period under review include *Government of the United States of America* v. *Jennings,* [1982] 3 W.L.R. 450 (H.L.), reversing the Divisional Court (see this *Year Book,* 53 (1982), p. 295 n. 168) (causing death by reckless driving properly 'described' as manslaughter in English law); *Dowse* v. *Government of Sweden,* [1983] 2 A.C. 464 (H.L.), affirming the Divisional Court *sub nom. R.* v. *Governor of Pentonville Prison, ex parte Passingham,* [1983] 1 Q.B. 254 (whether statements not made under oath admissible as an 'affirmation'; term 'affirmation' in treaty given its 'primary and natural meaning'); *R.* v. *Chief Metropolitan Magistrate, ex parte Government of Denmark, The Times* 17 May 1983, p. 15 (Divisional Court) (held: the existence of a 'political offence' apart, the Magistrate's only role under the Extradition Acts was to consider relevant English law and the evidence; questions of foreign law and compliance with the treaty a matter for the Divisional Court). On the character of the Extradition Treaty under the Act as peremptory and not waivable by an extradited person cf. *R.* v. *Davies* (1983), 76 Cr. App. R. 120. D was extradited from the U.S.A. on charge of theft. At the trial D agreed to the replacement of those charges by a count of fraudulent trading contrary to Companies Act 1948, s. 332 (3) (which was not an extraditable offence): he was convicted and given a suspended sentence. On a Home Office Reference on the validity of the additional count, the Court of Appeal held that an extradited person had no capacity to consent to or waive violations of the Extradition Act 1870 or the Treaty as implemented under that Act (here s. 19 and Art. 12 respectively). The conviction was accordingly quashed. The decision is a highly technical one in that s. 19 requires only that the accused person have 'been restored or had an opportunity of returning to such foreign State': it would presumably be possible to construct such an opportunity in order for the accused to reject it. The decision reinforces the predominantly formal character of extradition procedures, demonstrated by the two cases noted in the text.

[1] Dicey and Morris, *The Conflict of Laws* (10th edn., 1980), Rule 2.

[2] [1983] 2 Lloyd's Rep. 171; [1983] Com. L.R. 58. See also the note on the public international law aspects of this case at p. 288, above.

Government in breaking off an agreement to sell sugar to Chile when President Allende, with whose regime the agreement had originally been made, was overthrown by a coup in 1973 and replaced by a regime hostile to the Government of Cuba. At the time of the coup one ship involved in the carriage of the sugar was already in a Chilean port with her cargo partly discharged, but she managed to escape on the orders of the Cuban Government. A second ship which was to have carried part of the sugar to Chile was on the high seas and it was diverted. A third ship was still in a Cuban port and never set sail for Chile. The sugar was eventually disposed of in countries friendly to the Cuban Government. The arbitration proceedings and litigation which ensued involved a multiplicity of diverse legal issues. This present commentary is concerned only with aspects of the private international law doctrines referred to above.

The seller of the sugar, Cubazucar, was a Cuban State trading enterprise with a separate juridical personality, and it was common ground that it was not a department of the Cuban State. The buyer, Iansa, was a Chilean private company, the majority of whose shares were held by a Chilean State trading organization. Cubazucar failed to deliver any part of the unshipped balance of the sugar. Iansa claimed in arbitration for damages in respect of this failure. The arbitrators accepted Cubazucar's defence that the contract had been frustrated. This finding was upheld by Mustill J. in the Commercial Court. A further appeal against it to the Court of Appeal was dismissed.

The frustrating event upon which Cubazucar was allowed to rely took the form of the enactment by Cuba, twelve days after the coup in Chile, of Law 1256. This law purported to freeze all property wholly or partly owned, demandable or claimable by Chilean official and semi-official agencies, or by juridical persons in which the Chilean State had a direct or indirect interest. The property was to remain frozen until the establishment of a government 'whose legitimacy may be acknowledged and accepted by the Revolutionary Government of Cuba'. As Ackner L.J., who delivered the judgment of the Court of Appeal, observed, 'The seizure appears, from the wording of the law, to have been intended at least in part as a kind of security for claims by Cuba in respect of loss and damage suffered by Cuban property as a result of the coup'.[3] The arbitrators found that under Cuban law the effect of Law 1256 was to render further performance of the contract illegal. This finding was not challenged before Mustill J. or in the Court of Appeal; but Iansa, the Chilean buyer, contended that nevertheless the enactment of the law could not for several reasons be relied upon as frustrating the contract. Amongst those reasons was the contention that Law 1256 was penal and discriminatory and should accordingly be disregarded in an English *forum*. The arbitrators and Mustill J. accepted that the law was indeed penal and discriminatory, but had held that this did not warrant disregarding it totally. It could constitute a frustrating event. Ackner L.J., delivering the judgment of the Court of Appeal, although affirming this conclusion, seems to have assessed Law 1256 in the wider context of public policy rather than by reference to the rule that precludes the enforcement of foreign penal laws. This approach, it is respectfully submitted, would seem to be correct. The essence of a penal law is that it is designed to punish at the instance of, or on behalf of, the State. The penal law *par excellence* is the rule of criminal law. The mere fact that the operation of a law causes harm or suffering to persons who disregard it or who behave in a particular

---

[3] [1983] 2 Lloyd's Rep. 171, 189.

way does not necessarily render it penal. The *purpose* of the law must be to punish and to punish at the instance of the State. For example, in 1978 Lord Denning M.R. in *S.A. Textiles* v. *Sun and Sand Agencies Ltd.*[4] opined that an award of exemplary damages should not be regarded as penal.[5] In *The Playa Larga* Law 1256 did impose harm or suffering upon persons affected by it, and this could be seen as being at the instance of the Cuban State, but punishment was not its purpose. As Ackner L.J. re-emphasized: 'The seizure was intended in part as a means of achieving compensation for Cuban property damaged as a result of the coup, in which a government strongly hostile to [Cuba][6] had come into power by military force, and whose existence [Cuba],[6] rightly or wrongly, clearly considered to be strongly inimical to its political and economic interests.'[7]

Even if Law 1256 were to be regarded as penal, there would still be doubt as to whether, in seeking to rely upon its enactment as a frustrating event, Cubazucar was infringing the rule that a *forum* will not enforce foreign penal laws. Such a law will not be enforced even indirectly, but this does not mean that a *forum* will never take any account of such a law. Whereas in *Banco de Viscaya* v. *Don Alfonso*[8] Lawrence J. refused to enforce what in form was a contractual right on the grounds that to do so would in substance involve the enforcement of a Spanish penal law, a court will not ignore the vitiating effect of an illegality under the proper law of a contract simply because of the penal nature of that illegality. As Lord Simmonds said in *Regazzoni* v. *Sethia (K.C.)*,[9] '. . . an English court will not enforce a penal law at the suit of a foreign state, yet it would be surprising if it would enforce a contract which required the commission of a crime in that state'. The line between the indirect enforcement of a foreign penal law and mere taking account of it is perhaps not always easy to draw. But if, as is the case, account is taken of a foreign penal law when considering the validity of a contract, it is hard to see why no account should be taken of it when, as in *The Playa Larga*, a court is considering the discharge of a contract by way of frustration.

In *The Playa Larga* Ackner L.J., treating the Cuban Law 1256 in the wider framework of public policy, concluded that 'the legislation was not so repugnant to British ideas of international and personal morality as to require the English courts to ignore its existence'.[10]

The temptation to resort to public policy is often insidious in private international law and it is to be vigilantly guarded against. Two formal patterns of the permitted operation of the doctrine are discernible in the cases. First, the doctrine may be invoked if the nature or content of a foreign rule is so intrinsically repugnant that it will never be applied in England, nor will its application elsewhere ever be recognized in England. As Lord Cross (with whom Lords Hailsham, Hodson and Salmon agreed) said in *Oppenheimer* v. *Cattermole*[11] of a German law depriving German Jews living abroad of their nationality and of their property without compensation, '. . . a law of this sort constitutes so grave an infringement of human rights that the courts of this country ought to refuse to

---

[4] [1978] 1 Q.B. 279.

[5] Ibid., 300. See, too, the famous judgment of Mr. Justice Cardozo in the New York Court of Appeals in *Loucks* v. *Standard Oil Co. of New York* (1918), 120 N.E. Reporter 198.

[6] The word 'Chile' in Lloyd's Law Reports is presumably a misprint for 'Cuba'.

[7] [1983] 2 Lloyd's Rep. 171, 190.   [8] [1935] 1 K.B. 140.   [9] [1958] A.C. 301, 322.

[10] [1983] 2 Lloyd's Rep. 171, 190.

[11] [1976] A.C. 249.

recognise it as a law at all'.[12] Secondly, the protection of the United Kingdom's public, national or international interests may require that a British court should not act in a particular way. Here the focus is not so much upon the content of a foreign law but rather upon the policy implications of its enforcement or recognition by a British court. For example, a court will accordingly be unwilling to enforce a contract involving contravention of a foreign law which prohibits the export of goods to certain countries, particularly if such a law has political overtones, because for a British court to be seen to be enforcing such a contract (albeit entirely valid by its proper law) would be liable to jeopardize at the international political level good relations between the United Kingdom and the country in question.[13] However, in recent decades there have been some disturbing signs of a judicial willingness to see the role of public policy in private international law as extending in a seemingly somewhat free-wheeling way beyond these two established patterns. For example, in the recent House of Lords case of *Vervaeke* v. *Smith*[14] three of their Lordships, in an alternative *ratio*, felt compelled by considerations of public policy to deny recognition to a nullity decree pronounced, on the ground that the marriage was a palpably sham marriage, by a jurisdictionally competent Belgian court. Their Lordships were unanimous in holding that there was in any event another ground for withholding recognition.[15] The invocation of public policy by Lord Hailsham of St Maryle-bone L.C., Lord Simon of Glaisdale and Lord Brandon of Oakbrook was, there-fore, in a sense gratuitous. Viewed from the standpoint of established patterns of resort to public policy, it is obviously difficult to see that a foreign rule invalidating sham marriages is intrinsically repugnant, or why national interests require the withholding of recognition of a decree of a jurisdictionally competent Belgian court. In *Vervaeke* v. *Smith* public policy would appear in fact to have served as little more than a threadbare cloak for the exercise of a discretion deriving from considerations of unfairness having regard to the particular circumstances of the case. A not dissimilar manifestation of the enlarged scope of public policy is to be seen in several cases concerned with the interpretation of section 8 (2) (b) of the Recognition of Divorces and Legal Separations Act 1971, which provides that recognition of a foreign divorce or legal separation may be denied if 'recognition would manifestly be contrary to public policy' (see, e.g., *Kendall* v. *Kendall*[16] and *Joyce* v. *Joyce and O'Hare*[17]).

It is true that most but not all[18] of the illustrations of this relatively recent tendency to inflate the role of public policy, and to see it as sometimes no more than a vehicle for the exercise of an ill-defined, or undefined, discretion, have been in the area of family law. The spectre of insular palm-tree justice is, however, to be

[12] [1976] A.C. 249, 278.

[13] See *Regazzoni* v. *Sethia K.C.*, [1958] A.C. 301.

[14] [1983] 1 A.C. 145.

[15] Moreover, it could be contended that even if the decree had been accorded recognition this should not have had retroactive effect: in this event the actual outcome of the English proceedings would have been the same. See Jaffey, *International and Comparative Law Quarterly*, 32 (1983), p. 500.

[16] [1977] Fam. 208.

[17] [1979] Fam. 93. See, too, the earlier common law case of *Gray (orse. Formosa)* v. *Formosa*, [1963] P. 259, where the terminology of public policy was eschewed, but a nullity decree of a Maltese court, regarded by a majority of the Court of Appeal as jurisdictionally competent, was denied recognition on the ground that it would involve a denial of 'substantial justice'.

[18] See, e.g., some observations of Slade J. in *Winkworth* v. *Christie Manson and Woods*, [1980] Ch. 496, a case concerned with the *inter vivos* transfer of movables.

viewed with alarm in any branch of private international law. The approach taken by Ackner L.J., speaking for the Court of Appeal in *The Playa Larga*, is, therefore, most welcome. His Lordship, after referring to the decision of Upjohn J. in *Re Claim by Helbert Wagg & Co. Ltd.*[19] and to exchange control legislation generally, expressed the view that the statement in *Dicey and Morris* that 'An English court ignores foreign legislation which deprives a contract of effectiveness if the legislation to which the contract is opposed is regarded by English law as discriminatory'[20] seems to go further than the authority warrants. His Lordship then continued:

> The Court must look at all the circumstances, and then consider whether the law is so far-reaching in its scope and effect as *really* to offend against public policy. A Judge should, of course, be *very* slow to refuse to give effect to legislation of a foreign state in any sphere in which, according to the accepted principles of international law, the foreign state has jurisdiction. He may well have an inadequate understanding of the circumstances in which the legislation was passed . . .[21]

That *The Playa Larga* asserts the need for, and demonstrates the exercise of, judicial restraint in invoking public policy in private international law is one of several reasons why it is a matter for regret that the case has not been reported more widely.

Tort: choice of law and contractual limitation of liability

Case No. 2. The judgment of Hodgson J., the trial judge, and that of Robert Goff L.J. (with whom Oliver and Waller L.JJ. agreed) in the Court of Appeal in *Coupland* v. *Arabian Gulf Oil*[22] are somewhat obliquely interesting in several ways. These relate both to the general issue of choice of law in tort in the aftermath of the decision of the House of Lords in *Boys* v. *Chaplin*,[23] and to the supposedly intractable problem of the extent to which it is possible in a private international law context to exclude or limit by the terms of a contract tortious liability which might otherwise arise in the course of its performance.

The facts giving rise to the litigation in *Coupland* v. *Arabian Gulf Oil* were these. The plaintiff, while working in Libya for the defendant oil company, suffered an accident as a result of which he lost the lower part of a leg. As a consequence of this he received payments under Libyan social security and labour laws and under an insurance policy taken out by his employers under the contract of employment. The plaintiff subsequently instituted proceedings against the defendants in England claiming damages for negligence and for breach of contract in causing the accident. On preliminary issues Hodgson J. held that Libyan law was the proper law of the contract, but that in the circumstances of the case this was not material in so far as the plaintiff's claim was in tort. He further held that, as the alleged tort was actionable both under English domestic law and under the Libyan law, Libya being the *locus delicti*, the action in tort should continue.

The learned judge devoted a large part of his judgment to the problem of choice of law in tort. He first drew attention to the scantily reported Court of Appeal case

---

[19] [1956] Ch. 323.
[20] Dicey and Morris, *The Conflict of Laws* (10th edn., 1980), p. 804.
[21] [1983] 2 Lloyd's Rep. 171, 190. Italics supplied.
[22] [1983] 1 W.L.R. 1136.   [23] [1971] A.C. 356.

of *Church of Scientology of California* v. *Commissioner of Police of the Metropolis*.[24] He saw the judgments in that case as making his 'task in approaching *Boys* v. *Chaplin* [1971] A.C. 356 very much easier'.[25] In the *Church of Scientology* case the plaintiffs had claimed damages in respect of a report made by the Metropolitan Police to the West German Federal Police, alleging that the report was defamatory. The Court of Appeal held that their action should not be struck out because it was by no means clear that an action for defamation would fail in Germany, and that, as the matter was most closely connected with England, the plaintiffs might in any event be able to rely upon an exception to the general rule that a tort, if committed abroad, must be actionable both in the *forum* and in the *locus delicti*. In *Coupland* v. *Arabian Gulf Oil* Hodgson J., referring to the *Church of Scientology* case, said: '. . . the importance of the case is that the Court of Appeal came firmly down, with the consent of both counsel, in favour of the *ratio decidendi* in *Boys* v. *Chaplin* [1971] A.C. 356 contained in the speech of Lord Wilberforce, thus, so far as I am concerned, putting an end to the controversy.'[26] His Lordship then quoted from the judgment of Bridge L.J., who in his turn was quoting from the speech of Lord Wilberforce, as follows: 'I would, therefore, restate the basic rule of English law with regard to foreign torts as requiring actionability as a tort according to English law, subject to the condition that civil liability in respect of the relevant claim exists as between the actual parties under the law of the foreign country where the act was done.'[27] Bridge L.J. had then referred to the acceptance by 'the majority of their Lordships' in *Boys* v. *Chaplin* of a 'limited exception to that general rule'.[28] Of that exception, Hodgson J. noted, Bridge L.J. had said: 'The exception to the general rule of double actionability is one newly enunciated by their Lordships in *Boys* v. *Chaplin*. Its true limits will no doubt become clearer as more cases are decided in the courts.'[29] Hodgson J. then concluded that the judgment in the *Church of Scientology* case allowed him 'to go, and go alone, to the speech of Lord Wilberforce with which, in these respects, Lord Hodson concurred, and with which Lord Pearson concurred also'.[30] Hodgson J. proceeded to quote from the speech of Lord Wilberforce at length before reaching the crucial delineation of the exception to the double actionability rule as follows:

the necessary flexibility can be obtained . . . through segregation of the relevant issue and consideration whether, in relation to that issue, the relevant foreign rule ought, as a matter of policy . . . to be applied. For this purpose it is necessary to identify the policy of the rule, to inquire to what situations, with what contacts, it was intended to apply; whether not to apply it, in the circumstances of the instant case, would serve any interest which the rule was devised to meet. This technique appears well adapted to meet cases where the lex delicti either limits or excludes damage for personal injury: it appears even necessary and inevitable.[31]

But, Lord Wilberforce emphasized, this exception

will not be invoked in every case [of such limitation or exclusion of damages] or even, probably, in many cases. The general rule [i.e. the rule of double actionability] must apply unless clear and satisfying grounds are shown why it should be departed from and what solution, derived from what other rule, should be preferred.[32]

[24] *Solicitors' Journal*, 120 (1976), p. 690. See, too, Collins, *International and Comparative Law Quarterly*, 26 (1977), p. 480.   [25] [1983] 1 W.L.R. 1136, 1145.
[26] Ibid., 1145–6.   [27] Ibid., 1146.   [28] Ibid.   [29] Ibid.   [30] Ibid.
[31] Hodgson J., ibid., 1148, citing Lord Wilberforce, [1971] A.C. 391. Italics supplied.
[32] [1983] 1 W.L.R. 1136, 1148.

There then occurs a passage in Hodgson J.'s judgment which is not altogether easy to follow, containing as it does the statement that 'it is clear that the ordinary rule in tort is that the law of the place where the action is being brought—the lex fori—is the law to be applied.[33] However, after finding that the plaintiff's claim was governed by English law, his Lordship further held that 'the defendant cannot succeed on the second part of the rule in *Phillips* v. *Eyre*, . . . were the plaintiff to bring a claim against the defendant in Libya on these facts, that claim would be actionable.'[34] Hodgson J. would appear, therefore, to be in fact applying the double actionability rule and to be doing so without treating as material any exception to it. Any implication from the way in which the matter was put that the burden of proof in respect of the second part of the rule in *Phillips* v. *Eyre* is upon the defendants would, it is respectfully submitted by the present writer, involve a possibly misleading over simplification. Of course, any party who seeks to rely upon foreign law has the burden of proving it. It was, therefore, for the defendant, if he wished to rely upon the second arm of the double actionability rule, to prove the content of Libyan law; but it was for the plaintiff to prove that the defendant had in fact behaved in such a way as to give rise to liability under that law as proved.[35] Robert Goff L.J. in the Court of Appeal proceeded simply on the basis that 'Applying the principles stated by the House of Lords in *Boys* v. *Chaplin* . . . he [Hodgson J.] came to the conclusion that the plaintiff could succeed in an action in tort if he could show that the claim was actionable by the lex fori, which is the law of this country, and the lex delicti, which is the law of Libya'.[36]

In regard to choice of law in tort, *Coupland* v. *Arabian Gulf Oil* represents an affirmation of the general rule of double actionability. It is to be noted that in the Court of Appeal no reference was made to what was said in *Church of Scientology of California* v. *Commissioner of Police of the Metropolis*, nothing was said about the limits of the exception to the rule of double actionability, nor was any reference made to the trial judge's view that in assessing the significance of *Boys* v. *Chaplin* pre-eminence should be accorded to the judgment of Lord Wilberforce. Any allusions to these matters would have been by way of *obiter dicta* as, indeed, was Hodgson J.'s consideration of them. The fact that Hodgson J.'s judgement has been reported along with the report of the case in the Court of Appeal is, however, welcome—particularly in so far as it throws some light upon the ratio of *Boys* v. *Chaplin*, and most particularly in that it serves to focus attention upon Lord Wilberforce's formulation of the exception to the now firmly established test of double actionability. Lord Wilberforce emphasized the need first to segregate the issue. There is implicit in this the rejection of any automatic supposition that the mere fact that an issue arises in the context of a tort claim implies that it is an issue within the ambit of the rule in *Phillips* v. *Eyre*.[37] Once the issue has been segregated one must then have regard to the particular facts of the case and consider whether in the light of any peculiarity of those facts justice demands

---

[33] Ibid., 1149.   [34] Ibid., 1150.

[35] The contrary view probably derives historically from the use of the negative 'not justifiable' in *Phillips* v. *Eyre*, (1870) L.R.6 Q.B.1, 29; but that was explicable on other grounds having regard to a particular fact in the case—namely, that Governor Eyre was relying upon a retroactive Act of Indemnity. By 'the act must not have been justifiable' Willes J. seems to have meant that it must have been civilly wrong and not subsequently justified.

[36] [1983] 1 W.L.R. 1136, 1152.

[37] (1870) L.R. 6 Q.B. 1.

exceptional departure from the double actionability test. It is perhaps not unreasonable to hope that the passage which the present writer has italicized in the passage from Lord Wilberforce set out above will be accorded a degree of authority comparable with that which has been accorded to the oft-cited words of Wilkes J. in *Phillips* v. *Eyre*. However, two supplementary comments may be made.

In *Coupland* v. *Arabian Gulf Oil* Hodgson J. took the view that in *Boys* v. *Chaplin*, Lord Hodson had concurred with Lord Wilberforce in the relevant respects.[38] There is certainly room for the view that the speeches of Lord Hodson and Lord Wilberforce in that case are the most illuminating. However, they differ in emphasis in that Lord Hodson seems to place rather less stress on the need to segregate the issue than does Lord Wilberforce. Indeed Lord Hodson would in effect appear to be willing to apply the 'proper law of the tort' quite widely in non-typical fact situations. The fact situation in *Boys* v. *Chaplin* was non-typical in that all its components were English apart from the solitary circumstance that the tort had been committed in Malta. Perhaps, therefore, Lord Hodson would have been willing to resort exclusively to English law even if the issue had not been simply as to the extent of compensation but had been as to liability. Lord Wilberforce would presumably have applied the double actionability test in relation to that latter issue. One may perhaps be permitted to conjecture further as to other ways in which circumstances may be sufficiently non-typical so as to warrant departure from that test. Would it, in Lord Hodson's view, have been warranted if in *Boys* v. *Chaplin* the plaintiff had been domiciled and resident in a third country and the defendant in a fourth country, but the content of the relevant laws of these two countries had been the same as the corresponding laws of the English *forum*? Again, would the circumstance that the *locus delicti* is palpably fortuitous (as when an alleged defamation is uttered in an airport transit lounge) or the fact that it is unknown (as when an alleged tort is committed on a transcontinental train journey) justify departure from the double actionability rule? The scope of the exception to that rule has not yet been fully worked out, but perhaps its availability will not *always* depend upon the nature of the particular issue—some fact situations may warrant more general departure from it.

Secondly, and conversely, there are some issues which can arise in the context of a tort claim which should be segregated and not subsumed under the double actionability rule quite regardless of any peculiarity of the particular fact situation. For example, whether spouses are barred from suing each other should probably always depend upon the proper law of the spousal relationship. So, too, questions of survival of the right to sue in tort should perhaps fall to be determined by reference to the *lex successionis* in relation to intangible movables.

In *Coupland* v. *Arabian Gulf Oil* the trial judge reached the conclusion that the proper law of the contract was the law of Libya, but that this had no relevance to the claim in tort. Counsel sought to challenge this latter conclusion in the Court of Appeal contending that the claims in tort and contract were interlinked. This submission was decisively rejected by the Court of Appeal. The mere fact that a plaintiff is free to advance a claim either in contract or in tort does not render the proper law of the contract material to the determination of the tort claim. Nor,

---

[38] The learned judge took the view that Lord Pearson, too, concurred with Lord Wilberforce; but this assessment may be regarded as questionable.

presumably, does it render the rule in *Phillips* v. *Eyre*, as interpreted in *Boys* v. *Chaplin*, relevant to the contract claim. What is particularly interesting, however, is that Robert Goff L.J. went on to say:

> In my judgment, on ordinary principles the contract is only relevant to the claim in tort in so far as it does, on its true construction in accordance with the proper law of the contract, have the effect of excluding or restricting the tortious claim. However, this is not a case where an exclusion clause, or anything of that kind, is relied upon by the defence. There is in the contract no clause which limits or restricts the plaintiff's right to claim damages in tort; and so that line of defence is not open to the defendants.[39]

The clear implication of this is that the extent to which it is possible to exclude or limit by the terms of a contract tortious liability, which might otherwise arise in the course of its performance, is to be determined by reference to the proper law of the contract. This is in perfect accord with the approach taken by two members of the Court of Appeal (Stamp and Salmon L.JJ.) in *Sayers* v. *International Drilling Co. N.V.*,[40] but it is inconsistent with the reasoning of Lord Denning M.R. in that case. Stamp and Salmon L.JJ. held that the defendants were able to limit liability because they were allowed to do so under the Dutch proper law. Lord Denning M.R., on the other hand, rested the applicability of Dutch law on his opinion that tort liability is governed by the 'proper law of the tort' coupled with his finding on the facts that that law was Dutch law.[41] It is to be hoped that Robert Goff L.J.'s words will help to dispel doubts as to the correctness of the approach of the majority of the Court of Appeal in *Sayers* v. *International Drilling Co. N.V.* Those doubts have been in part provoked by the Scots case of *Brodin* v. *A/R Seljan*.[42] There a Norwegian seaman on board a Norwegian ship was injured while the ship was docking in Scotland. He sued the owners alleging negligence on the part of the ship's officers. The proper law of the contract of employment appears to have been Norwegian law, but Lord Kissen, sitting in the Outer House of the Court of Session, applied Scots law, and more particularly the Law Reform (Personal Injuries) Act 1948 (section 1 of which abolishes the defence of common employment and by subsection 3 prohibits contracting out). What is not clear is whether this judge sitting at first instance was applying Scots law *qua* law governing tort liability or *qua lex fori*. In other words it is not clear whether exclusive reference would have been to Scots law if the *locus delicti* had been a third country. The better view would seem to be that Scots law was applied *qua lex fori*, a statutory provision of the *forum*, section 1 of the Law Reform (Personal Injuries) Act 1948, being construed as not simply embodying a rule of Scots domestic law but as having conflictual effect so as to override the proper law of a foreign contract—at least in a case in which the *locus delicti* and the *forum* coincide. On this analysis whether the statute will be given wider conflictual effect so as to be applied in a case in which not only the proper law of the contract but

---

[39] [1983] 1 W.L.R. 1136, 1153.

[40] [1971] 1 W.L.R. 1176.

[41] See this *Year Book*, 45 (1971), pp. 404–6.

[42] [1973] S.L.T. 198. See, too, *Canadian Pacific Rail Co.* v. *Parent*, [1917] A.C. 195. There the Privy Council (as a Quebec *forum*) appears to have looked first to the *lex loci delicti* (the law of Ontario) under which recovery would have been precluded having regard to a clause in a Manitoba contract which exempted the defendants. In so far as reference was not directly to the law of Manitoba, as the proper law of the contract, the case may be seen as being at variance with the approach of Stamp and Salmon L.JJ. in *Sayers* v. *International Drilling Co.* and with that of the Court of Appeal in *Coupland* v. *Arabian Gulf Oil*.

also the *locus delicti* is foreign would, of course, raise a further question of statutory interpretation.

Although the balance of authority now seems to point clearly to exclusive reference to the proper law of the contract in order to determine the extent to which it is possible for parties to exclude or limit tortious liability which might otherwise arise in the course of its performance, legitimate reservations may be entertained about unqualified acceptance of such a rule. Suppose a case in which the law of a particular country is the proper law solely by virtue of choice by parties—perhaps having been deliberately chosen for the express purpose of circumventing victim-protecting rules not only of the *lex loci delicti* but also of what would have been the proper law of the contract if objectively determined. To apply the chosen law to the issue under consideration in such circumstances might be regarded as giving unwarranted scope to the philosophy of the autonomy of the parties. Sometimes such a case will be caught by section 27 of the Unfair Contract Terms Act 1977. That section provides that the protection of the Act shall be available 'notwithstanding any contract term which applies or purports to apply the law of some country outside the United Kingdom, where . . . (a) the term appears to the court, or arbitrator or abiter to have been imposed wholly or mainly for the purpose of enabling the party imposing it to evade the operation of this Act . . .'. Although this particular statutory provision will not itself cover all cases, its import perhaps points the way to a more general choice of law rule—namely, that the proper law of a contract in the context under consideration should mean the objectively determined proper law. It would then be possible to conclude that the extent to which parties may by a term in their contract limit or exclude liability in tort, which might otherwise arise in the course of performance of the contract, is to be governed by the proper law objectively determined, the circumstance of the parties' choice being but one factor to be taken into account in that determination. This choice of law rule would, of course, be without prejudice to the way in which the proper law of a contract is to be determined for other purposes. It is a choice of law rule which would be consistent with, and a refinement of, the approach of Stamp and Salmon L.JJ. in *Sayers* v. *International Drilling Co. N.V.* and with the clear implications of what was said by Robert Goff L.J. in *Coupland* v. *Arabian Gulf Oil*.

The proper law of a contract

Case No. 3. The principal, but by no means the only, interest of the recent House of Lords case of *Amin Rasheed Corporation* v. *Kuwait Insurance Co.*[43] lies not so much in the decision as in the observations of Lord Diplock and of Lord Wilberforce concerning the way in which the proper law of a commercial contract is to be identified.

The facts of the case were these. The plaintiffs were a Liberian corporation who owned a cargo vessel, which they insured against war and marine risks with the defendants, a Kuwaiti insurance company. The form of the policy was based upon the Lloyd's standard form of marine policy with various modifications. It gave Kuwait as the place of issue and provided for claims to be payable there. It did not contain a choice of law clause. The vessel was detained by the Saudi Arabian authorities, and the master and crew were imprisoned for several months,

[43] [1983] 3 W.L.R. 241.

seemingly in connection with a claim (which was denied by the plaintiffs) that the vessel had been involved in an attempt to smuggle oil.

The plaintiffs then claimed for total constructive loss of the ship under the Institute War and Strike Clauses which formed part of the policy and they sought leave to serve notice of the writ upon the defendants in Kuwait. In this they relied upon R.S.C. Ord. 11, r. 1 (1) (f), which grounds a discretion to grant leave 'if the action begun by the writ is brought against a defendant not domiciled or ordinarily resident in Scotland to enforce . . . a contract . . . being . . . a contract which . . . (iii) is, by its terms or by implication, governed by English law; . . .'. Bingham J. set aside leave which had been granted under this sub-paragraph, holding that the contract was governed by Kuwaiti law and that accordingly there was no jurisdiction to allow service on the absent defendants. The learned judge further held that even if, contrary to his view, the plaintiffs' claim did fall within R.S.C. Ord. 11, he would exercise his discretion against allowing service. The plaintiffs' appeal was dismissed by a divided Court of Appeal, and they further appealed to the House of Lords. The House unanimously agreed, but for differing reasons, that the proper law of the contract was the law not of Kuwait but of England. However, the House dismissed the plaintiffs' appeal holding that the court's discretion under R.S.C. Ord. 11, r. 1, should be exercised in the same way as had been indicated by Bingham J., namely in favour of the defendants: the plaintiffs had not discharged the burden placed upon them under R.S.C. Ord. 11, r. 4 (2), to show that the case was 'a proper one for service out of the jurisdiction'. Four of their Lordships (Lord Diplock with whom Lord Roskill, Lord Brandon of Oakbrook and Lord Brightman agreed) held the proper law to be English law because, in the words of Lord Diplock, the provisions of the contract 'taken as a whole' point 'by necessary implication . . . ineluctably to the conclusion that the intention of the parties was that their mutual rights and obligations under it should be determined in accordance with the English law of marine insurance'.[44] On the other hand, the fifth Law Lord, Lord Wilberforce, said: 'I can find no basis for inferring, as between the parties to this contract, an intention that the contract should be governed either by English law or by the law of Kuwait.'[45] His Lordship therefore held that 'What has to be done is to look carefully at all those factors normally regarded as relevant when the proper law is being searched for, including of course the nature of the policy itself, and to form a judgment as to the system of law with which that policy in the circumstances has the closest and most real connection.' Lord Wilberforce then 'With no great confidence . . . reached the conclusion that English law is the proper law of this particular contract'.[46]

Although the consideration given by Lord Diplock and Lord Wilberforce to the methodology to be utilized when identifying the proper law of a contract is central to the importance of the case, there are at least four other features of the judgments that merit mention. They are:

1. Leaving aside the discretion point the anterior and specific issue before their Lordships' House was as to whether the contract was 'by its terms, or by implication, governed by English law' within R.S.C. Ord. 11, r. 1 (1) (f) (iii), so as to permit service out of the jurisdiction. However, Lord Wilberforce expressly confirmed 'that the formula used in paragraph (f) (iii) above is equivalent to a requirement that the proper law of the contract should be English law'.[47]

---

[44] Ibid., 247.   [45] Ibid., 253.   [46] Ibid., 256.   [47] Ibid., 253.

Notwithstanding the context of the decision, therefore, the case has a direct relevance to the problem of choice of law.

2. Had the parties expressly chosen either English law or Kuwaiti law as the proper law, there is no reason to suppose that any of their Lordships would have been unwilling to give effect to that choice. Lord Diplock cited with approval the words of Lord Atkin in R. v. *International Trustee for the Protection of Bondholders Aktiengesellschaft*:

> The legal principles which are to guide an English court on the question of the proper law of a contract are now well settled. It is the law which the parties intended to apply. Their intention will be ascertained by the intention expressed in the contract if any, which will be conclusive. If no intention be expressed the intention will be presumed by the court from the terms of the contract and the relevant surrounding circumstances.[48]

Lord Diplock went on to state that if the parties' intention is clear, 'their intention will prevail and the . . . question as to the system of law with which, in the view of the court, the transaction to which the contract relates would, but for such intention of the parties, have had the closest and most real connection, does not arise.'[49] It is a matter for remark that other formulations of the autonomist principle have usually been less starkly absolute and unqualified. Even Lord Wright in the *Vita Food* case, often regarded as the high-water mark of judicial acceptance of this principle, after referring to Lord Atkin's words, conceded that the expressed intention must be '*bona fide* and legal'.[50] More recently Lord Reid in *Whitworth Street Estates Ltd.* v. *Miller* referred to the general entitlement of the parties to choose the governing law as being 'subject it may be to some limitations'.[51] Lord Diplock himself, when in the Court of Appeal in *Mackender* v. *Feldia A.G.*,[52] described the parties' freedom to choose as representing the 'prima facie' rule of the English conflict of laws.[53] One cannot resist the conjecture that, had the parties in *Amin Rasheed Corporation* v. *Kuwait Insurance Co.* expressly chosen the law of some third country, the application of which would have involved contravention of mandatory rules of both English and Kuwaiti law, an escape route from strict application of the principle of autonomy would have been found.[54]

3. Lord Diplock said of the proper law: 'It is the substantive law of the country which the parties have chosen as that by which their mutual legally enforceable rights are to be ascertained, but excluding any *renvoi*, whether of remission or transmission, that the courts of that country might themselves apply if the matter were litigated before them.'[55] This blanket rejection of *renvoi* contrasts with the curious and isolated *dictum* of Lord Wright in the *Vita Food* case: 'There is, in their Lordships' opinion, no ground for refusing to give effect to the express selection of English law as the proper law in the bills of lading. Hence English rules relating to the conflict of laws must be applied to determine how the bills of lading are affected by failure to comply with s. 3 of the Act.'[56] This utterance of

---

[48] [1937] A.C. 500, 529, cited by Lord Diplock, [1983] 3 W.L.R. 241, 246.
[49] [1983] 3 W.L.R. 241, 246.
[50] *Vita Food Products Inc.* v. *Unus Shipping Co. Ltd.*, [1939] A.C. 277, 290.
[51] [1970] A.C. 583, 603.   [52] [1967] 2 Q.B. 590.   [53] At p. 602.
[54] See *The Torni*, [1932] P. 78. Contrast *Vita Food Products Inc.* v. *Unus Shipping Co. Ltd.*, [1939] A.C. 277, where the actual outcome was not significantly affected by the application of the chosen English law rather than an objectively determined law of Newfoundland.
[55] [1983] 3 W.L.R. 241, 246.   [56] [1939] A.C. 277, 292.

Lord Wright has long been regarded as inexplicable,[57] but Lord Diplock's *a priori* and unqualified rejection of *renvoi* seems to go to the other extreme. It may usually, of course, be confidently presumed that, when parties expressly or implicitly choose a governing law, what they have in mind is a system of domestic law. However, there could be a case in which the parties clearly intended otherwise—namely, that their contract should be governed by the law which would be applied in the courts of the indicated country. Such a case is admittedly likely to be rare, but it is hard to see why, if it were to occur, effect should not be given to the parties' intention. Indeed, the general position would appear to be appropriately put in *Dicey and Morris*: '*In the absence of strong evidence to the contrary*, the parties must be deemed to have intended to refer to the domestic rules and not to the conflict rules of their chosen law, and connection with a given legal system is a connection with substantive legal principles, and not with conflict of laws rules.'[58]

4. The concept of what has been called elsewhere the 'delocalized', 'internationalized' or 'transnational' contract is rejected. Lord Diplock said:

My Lords, contracts are incapable of existing in a legal vacuum. They are mere pieces of paper devoid of all legal effect unless they were made by reference to some system of private law which defines the obligations assumed by the parties to the contract by their use of particular forms of words and prescribes the remedies enforceable in a court of justice for failure to perform any of those obligations; and this must be so however widespread geographically the use of a contract employing a particular form of words to express the obligations assumed by the parties may be.[59]

These are, it is respectfully submitted, salutary words.[60] The proper law of a contract, however determined, must be an actual system of contract law, not some impressionistic transnational system, nor even an amalgam of existing systems. At the same time it must be remembered that, as Lord Wilberforce pointed out,

There is nothing unusual in a situation where, under the proper law of the contract, resort is had to some other system of law for purposes of interpretation. In that case, that other system becomes a source of the law upon which the proper law may draw . . . the proper law is not applying a 'conflicts' rule (there may, in fact, be no foreign element in the case) but merely importing a foreign product for domestic use.[61]

Later Lord Wilberforce said:

. . . the Lloyd's S.G. form of policy is taken into a great number of legal systems, sometimes by statute, as in Australia, sometimes as a matter of commercial practice, as in Belgium or Germany, or in the Arabian Gulf, and . . . in such cases, though their legal systems may, and on the evidence do, resort to English law in order to interpret its terms, the contract may be regarded as an Australian, Belgian, German etc. contract.[62]

This particular contrast (even if seen as being one only of emphasis) between the judgment of Lord Diplock and that of Lord Wilberforce, has perhaps more general import. It seems to be indicative of an apparent divergence of attitude to the relationship between problems of validity and problems of interpretation or

---

[57] Falconbridge famously castigated it as a *lapsus calami*: *Selected Essays on the Conflict of Laws* (2nd edn., 1954), p. 404.
[58] *The Conflict of Laws* (10th edn., 1980), p. 750. Italics supplied.
[59] [1983] 3 W.L.R. 241, 249–50.
[60] See Mann, *International and Comparative Law Quarterly*, 33 (1984), p. 193.
[61] [1983] 3 W.L.R. 241, 254.   [62] Ibid., 255.

construction. This divergence, in its turn, may be the key to the explanation of the fundamental discrepancy between the approach of Lord Diplock and that of Lord Wilberforce to the central question of the determination of the proper law of the insurance policy in the instant case.

Lord Diplock defined the proper law as 'the law that governs the interpretation and the validity of the contract . . .',[63] and he emphasized that not only questions of validity but also questions of interpretation are to be determined by direct reference to the proper law. Indeed he said: 'To identify a particular system of law as being that in accordance with which the parties to it intended a contract to be interpreted, identifies that system of law as the "proper law" of the contract'.[64] When searching for the parties' intention it is, on this view, their intention with regard to interpretation that is being sought. On that assumption the words and legal terminology of the contract will clearly be entitled to great weight. Indeed in reaching the conclusion that English law was the proper law of the contract by virtue of the implied choice of the parties Lord Diplock seems to have regarded the use of English form and legal terminology as being virtually conclusive. The only 'surrounding circumstance' of importance was 'that at the time the policy was entered into there was no indigenous law of marine insurance in Kuwait'.[65] His Lordship concluded:

Except by reference to the English statute and the judicial exegesis of the code that it enacts it is not possible to interpret the policy or to determine what those mutual legal rights and obligations are. So applying, as one must in deciding the jurisdiction point, English rules of conflict of laws, the proper law of the contract embodied in the policy is English law.[66]

Lord Wilberforce, as a consequence of emphasizing that the interpretation of a contract may be achieved by reference to the domestic rules of a system of law other than the proper law but incorporated into it, attached less significance to the form and terminology of the contract when investigating the intention of the parties with regard to the proper law. In these circumstances he was unable on the facts of the instant case to discern any intention. He, therefore, had to fall back upon a purely objective test—as he put it, 'the classic process of weighing the factors must be followed, with all the difficulties inherent in the process'.[67] His Lordship did not, of course, deny that the form and terminology of a contract is a factor to be taken into account when searching for the parties' intention as to the governing law;[68] but its significance is obviously much reduced when it is accepted that matters of interpretation are not necessarily determined by

---

[63] [1983] 3 W.L.R. 241, 245. Lord Diplock continued 'and the mode of performance and the consequences of breach of contract'. This would appear to overlook the possibility that some matters pertaining to the mode and manner of performance must be governed by the *lex loci solutionis*: see Dicey and Morris, op. cit. above (p. 309 n. 58), Rule 151 (2) and authorities cited there. His Lordship's reference to the consequences of breach supplies confirmation of the rule that questions of remoteness of damage are governed by the proper law.

[64] [1983] 3 W.L.R. 241, 245.

[65] Lord Diplock attached little weight to the place of contracting or to the place of performance. Of the former he said that having regard to modern methods of communication where international contracts are often negotiated by telex the *locus contractus* is often a mere matter of chance. In the result the *lex loci contractus* has lost much of its significance in determining the proper law of a contract. At the same time the importance of the *lex loci solutionis* must vary with the nature of the contract. In a contract of insurance, especially marine insurance, the law of the place of performance may, as in the instant case, be entitled to little weight in determining the intention of the parties.

[66] [1983] 3 W.L.R. 241, 249.   [67] Ibid., 255.   [68] See ibid., 254.

reference to the proper law's own standards and that the search is for the law governing validity not interpretation *per se*.

One final comment. In the course of his judgment Lord Wilberforce differentiated between cases where the parties' 'mutual intention can be inferred' and cases where 'no such inference being possible, it is necessary to seek the system of law with which the contract has its closest and most real connection', but he noted that 'these situations merge into each other'.[69] It is submitted with respect that, while conceptually they clearly do not merge into each other, the reason why in practice they may appear to do so is at least twofold. First, the determination of the fact of intention (let alone of a commonly held intention) is notoriously difficult. It has to be achieved by assessing the significance of external phenomena, and this is an unavoidably subjective operation, different judges reaching differing conclusions concerning the same facts. The second reason underlying the apparent tendency of these two conceptually different situations to merge in practice is to be found in some uncertainty as to the object of the intention being sought in the former situation, and in some uncertainty as to the object of the connection in the latter situation. The former doubt is resolved if one accepts, as is implicit in Lord Wilberforce's judgment, that in the search for the parties' intention, the focus should be upon their intention in regard to the formation and validity of their contract, and only incidentally (although sometimes importantly) upon questions concerning the interpretation or construction of the words and legal terminology used. The latter source of uncertainty crystallizes into the question as to whether what has to be identified is the closest and most real connection with a legal system or the closest and most real connection with a country (or fact situation). It is suggested that it should be the latter. Investigation of the parties' intention obviously relates to their intention as to a system of governing law. If, however, resort is to be had to a purely objective test only after the search for the parties' intention has been abandoned, it follows *ex hypothesi* that their intention is not available to be taken into account in 'the classic process of weighing the factors'. It would seem to follow that the circumstance that, had there been a discernible intention that intention must have related to a legal system, need no longer be regarded as material. The available factors to be weighed are purely factual. They will only readily relate to a physical phenomenon such as a country, rather than to a conceptual phenomenon such as a putative contract. Even if the issue is framed in terms of an imputed 'intention', and a court purports to enquire as to what law reasonable parties would choose, the answer must be by reference to the country with which the facts, taken as a whole, have the closest and most real connection. That connection is between factual phenomena: between on the one hand the position and activities, actual and contemplated, of the parties, and on the other hand an area of the surface of the globe. It is from that factual connection that an applicable law is derived or, as it may be put, a fictitious reasonable choice is imputed to the parties. Whereas, when the parties' actual intention (express or implied) is available, it directly relates to a system of law, which is then the proper law.

P. B. CARTER

[69] Ibid., 253.

DECISIONS ON THE EUROPEAN CONVENTION ON HUMAN RIGHTS DURING 1983*

Just satisfaction (Article 50)—scope of the Court's powers—causation—costs and expenses

Case No. 1. *Le Compte, Van Leuven and De Meyere* case[1] (Application of Article 50). The Court held unanimously that Belgium was to pay 77,000 Belgian francs to Dr. Le Compte, 63,000 Belgian francs to Dr. Van Leuven and 42,000 Belgian francs to Dr. De Meyere in respect of costs and expenses incurred before the Belgian Court of Cassation and the institutions of the European Convention. A number of other claims for compensation were dismissed.

In its judgment on the merits of the case in 1981 the Court held that there had been a breach of Article 6 (1) of the Convention in that disciplinary proceedings brought against the applicants by the *Ordre des médecins* had not been heard publicly by a tribunal competent to determine all aspects of the matter.[2] The question of just satisfaction under Article 50 was reserved for later consideration.

Article 50 of the Convention provides:

If the Court finds that a decision or a measure taken by a legal authority or any other authority of a High Contracting Party, is completely or partially in conflict with the obligations arising from the present Convention, and if the internal law of the said Party allows only partial reparation to be made for the consequences of this decision or measure, the decision of the Court shall, if necessary, afford just satisfaction to the injured party.

In the present proceedings the applicants sought an undertaking from the Belgian Government that it would take measures to provide partial reparation in the shape of the expunction of the disciplinary and penal sanctions which were the subject of complaint, compensation for pecuniary and non-pecuniary loss, and a reimbursement of fines, costs and legal expenses.

The first of these claims was dismissed. Citing its judgment in the *Marckx* case,[3] the Court observed that under the Convention it was not empowered to direct Belgium to annul the disciplinary sanctions imposed on the three applicants and the sentences passed on Dr. Le Compte in criminal proceedings. It added that although the disciplinary sanctions had been imposed in proceedings which were not in conformity with Article 6 (1) of the Convention, they could not, on that account alone, be regarded as a consequence of the breach, whilst there was 'no connection whatsoever' between the criminal sentences and the breach of the Convention.

* © J. G. Merrills, 1984. I should like to express my gratitude to the Registrar of the Court for his co-operation in the preparation of these notes.
  [1] European Court of Human Rights (E.C.H.R.), judgment of 18 October 1982, Series A, No. 54. French text authentic. The Court consisted of the following Chamber of Judges: Wiarda (President); Thór Vilhjálmsson, Bindschedler-Robert, Liesch, Gölcüklü, Pinheiro Farinha (Judges); Vanwelkenhuyzen (*ad hoc* Judge).
  [2] E.C.H.R., judgment of 23 June 1981, Series A, No. 43. See this *Year Book*, 52 (1981), p. 337.
  [3] E.C.H.R., judgment of 13 June 1979, Series A, No. 31.

Claims for compensation were similarly rejected. The applicants had clearly suffered pecuniary loss when the *Ordre des médecins* had suspended their right to practise. However, the Court held that its finding that the disciplinary proceedings should have been public was not intended to suggest that the facts giving rise to the sanction had not been established, or did not justify the measures taken. There was therefore no causal link between the breach of Article 6 (1) and the disciplinary sanctions to justify an award of compensation. As far as non-pecuniary loss was concerned, the Court held that here, as in a number of previous cases,[4] its finding that the Convention had been violated had already furnished 'just satisfaction' for the purposes of Article 50.

Thus the applicants' claims were upheld only in so far as they related to the reimbursement of costs and expenses and even here several of the claims were disallowed. Of the costs incurred in Belgium, the Court allowed reimbursement of the expenses in the Court of Cassation on the ground that domestic remedies had had to be exhausted before the issue of Article 6 (1) could be brought before the Commission. However, the costs incurred in the Provincial Councils and the Appeals Council of the *Ordre des médecins* were disallowed because the object of these proceedings was neither prevention of the violation of the Convention, nor the obtaining of redress therefor. The fines imposed on Dr. Le Compte when he failed to comply with the order suspending his right to practise were similarly excluded on the ground that the justification for this measure was not affected by the violation of the Convention, while the correctness of the criminal proceedings themselves had not been contested.

As far as the Strasbourg expenses were concerned, the Court accepted that reimbursement was due in principle, but adjudged that in awarding legal costs on an equitable basis it should take into account that the applicants' claims were accepted only in part and that most of their complaints were not simply rejected, but held to be unfounded. Likewise, the Court was prepared to award travel and subsistence expenses to Dr. Le Compte and Dr. Van Leuven on the ground that their presence was potentially valuable, but declined to add anything in respect of their loss of earnings during their four days at Strasbourg.

This was the first of a series of cases on Article 50 decided in the period under review.[5] The decision contains no surprises, but is a straightforward illustration of the principle that the purpose of Article 50 is to provide compensation for a breach of the Convention and nothing more.

Trial within a reasonable time (Article 6 (1))—estoppel—power of the Commission to examine issues ex officio

Case No. 2. Foti and others case.[6] In this case the Court held that Italy had infringed Article 6 (1) of the Convention because the length of the proceedings brought against the four applicants had exceeded a 'reasonable time'.

So far as is relevant for present purposes, the facts were that the four applicants, who were all Italians, had been prosecuted for acts committed in the course of

---

[4] See the *Marckx* case (previous note) and the case of *Engel and others*, Series A, No. 22.

[5] For a review of the Court's earlier jurisprudence on the application of Article 50 see Gray, *Human Rights Review*, 6 (1981), p. 153.

[6] E.C.H.R., judgment of 10 December 1982, Series A, No. 56. French text authentic. The Court consisted of the following Chamber of Judges: Wiarda (President); Bindschedler-Robert, Evrigenis, Pinheiro Farinha, Sir Vincent Evans, Russo, Bernhardt (Judges).

demonstrations in Reggio Calabria between 1970 and 1973. Popular unrest had been triggered off by a decision to move the capital of Calabria from Reggio to Catanzaro and was spread by the economic depression in this part of the region. There were strikes, dynamite bombings and clashes with the police, followed by hundreds of arrests and prosecutions. For reasons of public policy, a number of prosecutions, including three involving Mr. Foti and those involving the other applicants, had been transferred from Reggio to the Potenza Regional Court. Partly on account of the transfer there had been serious delays in hearing the applicants' cases. One of the applicants, Mr. Gullì, complained to the Commission on this ground. Mr. Foti and the other applicants, Mr. Lentini and Mr. Cenerini, invoked Article 6 (1) for other reasons, but the Commission, while rejecting the original complaints, joined these applications with that of Mr. Gullì and decided unanimously that in all four cases the length of the proceedings had exceeded a reasonable time. The Commission then referred the case to the Court.

In applying Article 6 (1) the Court's first step was to determine the length of the proceedings in which each applicant had been involved. For this purpose time usually runs from the moment at which a person is 'charged', that is from 'the official notification given to an individual by the competent authority of an allegation that he has committed a criminal offence'.[7] In the present case the decisions to prosecute the applicants were taken at various times between September 1970 and March 1973. However, Italy did not recognize the right of individual petition until 1 August 1973. The Court agreed with the Commission that in these circumstances that date must be regarded as the beginning of the periods to be considered,[8] but added that in assessing what was a reasonable time thereafter, account must be taken of the state of the proceedings when time began to run. The relevant closing dates were when the various trials had ended and were not a matter of contention. In the light of this the Court decided that the length of time to be reviewed for compatibility with Article 6 (1) ranged from three years and five months in the case of Mr. Lentini to five years and ten months as regards the second set of proceedings against Mr. Foti.

To decide whether the proceedings in question had exceeded a reasonable time the Court made the familiar point that its task is to examine the particular circumstances having regard, amongst other factors, to the complexity of the case, the conduct of the applicants and the conduct of the judicial authorities.[9] The Court agreed with the applicants that the prosecutions were both substantively and procedurally uncomplicated. It also agreed that any delays in the conduct of the proceedings were not imputable to the applicants. However, with regard to the conduct of the Italian authorities, the Court held that the troubles in Reggio Calabria between 1970 and 1973 had important implications for the case. First, 'they engendered an unusual political and social climate, and one in which the courts could legitimately fear, in the event of precipitate convictions or severe sentences, a recrudescence of tension and even a recurrence of the disorders'.[10]

---

[7] Judgment, para. 52; see also the *Eckle* case, Series A, No. 51, para. 73, and this *Year Book*, 53 (1982), p. 317.

[8] The Court noted 'in particular' that the terms of the declaration made by Italy covered only acts, decisions, facts or events occurring after 31 July 1973.

[9] For an earlier statement of this principle see the judgment in the *Eckle* case (above).

[10] Judgment, para. 61.

Secondly, they created an exceptional backlog of business in both the Reggio Regional Court and the courts in Potenza.

Examining the present applications in the light of the above considerations, the Court held that in the first proceedings involving Mr. Foti the delay of three years and ten months between the suspension of a preliminary investigation and his committal for trial was unreasonable in view of the lack of complexity of his case. On the other hand, the delay of a year between the transfer of his case to Potenza and his summons to appear could not be criticized in view of the backlog of pending business. The delay of four years and two months between the appeal by the prosecuting authorities in the second proceedings and the dismissal of the appeal was similarly excessive, but a delay of seven months in holding the hearing at Potenza was not, since the latter court was under a duty to satisfy itself as to the sufficiency of the preliminary investigation. On Mr. Foti's third and final claim the Court held that the period of two years and eleven months between the original charge and the request to have the proceedings remitted to another court was again excessive.

In the case of Mr. Lentini a period of twenty-two months passed between his committal for trial and the request by the prosecutor for a transfer of the proceedings. The Court held that this exceeded any period of respite required by the circumstances, but held that as in the case of Mr. Foti, the exceptional backlog of business at Potenza meant that the subsequent delay in holding the transferred hearing did not amount to a further breach of the Convention.

In the case of Mr. Cenerini a delay of more than nineteen months following the applicant's committal was held to be a breach of Article 6 (1) on grounds similar to the previous application. A second period of about fifteen months between the order to transfer Mr. Cenerini's case and the forwarding of his case-file to Potenza was likewise held to be unjustifiable. However, the extended proceedings before the Potenza Regional Court were held to be justifiable in the circumstances on the ground that successive adjournments of the hearings were required by the absence of key witnesses and other legitimate reasons.

In the case of Mr. Gullì a delay of more than twenty months after committal was held to be unjustifiable. And delays of a year and twenty months respectively at two later stages of his case were similarly condemned.

Thus the Court concluded that in respect of all six sets of proceedings there had been delays incompatible with Article 6 (1). In view of this the Court, like the Commission, decided that it was unnecessary for it to consider any other issues[11] and reserved the question of Article 50 for later consideration.[12]

In the earlier part of its judgment the Court had considered and rejected a number of preliminary objections raised by the Italian Government. A request that the Court should deal more fully with a number of complaints declared inadmissible by the Commission was rejected on the ground that these fell outside the compass of the case referred to the Court. An objection that the applicants had failed to exhaust local remedies, as required by Article 26, was held to be barred by estoppel, the Government having raised the objection too late.

Finally, an objection that as regards three of the applicants the Commission had taken into consideration the issue of reasonable time on its own initiative was

---

[11] It had been suggested at one stage that Article 13 of the Convention might be relevant, but the matter had not been pursued.

[12] For the Court's application of Article 50 see Case No. 15, below.

rejected on the ground that since the information supplied by the applicants showed that their cases had been pending for several years, the Commission had in no way exceeded its jurisdiction by raising Article 6 (1) *ex officio*. Commenting on the scope for initiatives of this kind, the Court said:

The international system of protection established by the Convention functions on the basis of applications, be they governmental or individual, alleging violations (see Articles 24 and 25). It does not enable the Commission and the Court either to take up a matter irrespective of the manner in which it came to their knowledge or even, in the context of pending proceedings, to seize on facts that have not been adduced by the applicant—be it a State or an individual—and to examine those facts for compatibility with the Convention.

The institutions set up under the Convention nonetheless do have jurisdiction to review in the light of the entirety of the Convention's requirements circumstances complained of by an applicant. In the performance of their task, the Convention institutions are, notably, free to attribute to the facts of the case, as found to be established on the evidence before them, a characterisation in law different from that given by the applicant or, if need be, to view the facts in a different manner; furthermore, they have to take account not only of the original application but also of the additional documents intended to complete the latter by eliminating initial omissions or obscurities . . .[13]

This was the only issue on which the Court was not unanimous.[14] The line between legitimate assistance to the applicant and what has been termed 'a roving commission over the facts of a case'[15] is hardly clear cut. So although this is not the first time the Court has had to consider the *ultra petita* rule and its bearing on the work of the Commission, it is unlikely to be the last.

Trial within a reasonable time (Article 6 (1))—estoppel—the meaning of a 'victim' in Article 25—just satisfaction (Article 50)

Case No. 3. Corigliano case.[16] The Court held unanimously that Italy had infringed Article 6 (1) of the Convention because the length of the proceedings brought against the applicant had exceeded a 'reasonable time'. The applicant was awarded 2,200,000 lire in respect of his travel and subsistence expenses under Article 50, other claims for just satisfaction being rejected or held inadmissible.

Like Case No. 2, the present application was concerned with delays in bringing the applicant to trial, following the disturbances in Reggio Calabria. The background, however, was somewhat unusual. In March 1973, during demonstrations in Reggio, the police arrested a Mr. Amodeo in a shop belonging to Mr. Corigliano and in the latter's presence. Mr. Amodeo was tried in the same month and the applicant gave evidence which contradicted that of the arresting officers. However, the police evidence was upheld. Mr. Corigliano thereupon lodged a complaint with the Reggio public prosecutor's office, accusing the President of the Court and the assistant public prosecutor of acting out of personal interest. This in turn led the public prosecutor to begin proceedings against Mr. Corigliano for aggravated slander. After numerous investigations, appeals and a

---

[13] Judgment, para. 44. The point was the subject of further comment in the separate opinion of Judge Pinheiro Farinha.

[14] The decision on this point was by a majority of six votes to one.

[15] The late Sir Gerald Fitzmaurice, dissenting opinion in the *Guzzardi* case, Series A, No. 39, p. 50, and see this *Year Book*, 53 (1982), p. 129.

[16] E.C.H.R., judgment of 10 December 1982, Series A, No. 57. French text authentic. This case was decided by the Chamber constituted to hear the case of *Foti and others* (Case No. 2).

transfer of the case to Messina, the case, which had begun in 1973, was terminated by Mr. Corigliano's acquittal on appeal in 1980.

While the proceedings against him were under way Mr. Corigliano, who was a lawyer, lodged three applications with the Commission. His first and second applications were dismissed, but the third, in which he invoked Article 6 (1), was more successful and in its report of 16 March 1981 the Commission expressed the unanimous opinion that the proceedings against Mr. Corigliano had exceeded a reasonable time. The Commission then referred the case to the Court.

As in the *Foti* case, the Court began its examination of the merits by establishing the period to be considered. The public prosecutor had decided to begin proceedings against Mr. Corigliano in April 1973. However, the applicant had not been informed of the decision until December. In accordance with the general principle that for the purposes of Article 6 (1) a person is 'charged' when he is notified of the allegation, the Court decided that time only began to run in December. The end of the period to be taken into account was clearly February 1980, when the applicant was finally acquitted. Thus the proceedings had lasted for more than six years.

The next step was to consider the reasonableness of this period in the particular circumstances, having regard to the complexity of the case, the conduct of the applicant and the conduct of the judicial authorities. As in *Foti*, the Court held that the legal issues were relatively simple, although the transfer of the case to Messina had added an element of complication. The Government maintained that the applicant had abused his right to appeal and prolonged the proceedings by refusing to appoint a defence lawyer. The Court had no sympathy with these arguments, however, pointing out that the appeals had not in fact caused significant delays and repeating its ruling in the *Eckle* case[17] that 'Article 6 does not require the person concerned actively to co-operate with the judicial authorities'.[18]

The nub of the case was the conduct of the judicial authorities. A detailed review of the handling of the applicant's case before the Messina Regional Court and the Messina Court of Appeal satisfied the Court that these stages, of seven and eleven months respectively, had not been unduly prolonged. However, with regard to the preliminary investigation, which had occupied four years and seven months, the Court concluded that there had been undue delay. Delays occasioned by the transfer of the case to Messina were in themselves excusable,[19] but for two periods of thirteen and fourteen months there appeared to have been no investigations in progress at all. The conclusion was therefore inescapable that at the stage of the preliminary investigation at Messina the proceedings brought against Mr. Corigliano were subject to delays incompatible with Article 6 (1).

Before considering the merits of the case the Court had had to rule on three preliminary objections raised by the Italian Government. The first objection was that the present application was 'substantially the same' as Mr. Corigliano's two previous applications and contained no 'relevant new information' as required by Article 27 (1) (b) of the Convention. The second objection was that the applicant had failed to exhaust local remedies as required by Article 26. Like

[17] E.C.H.R., judgment of 15 July 1982, Series A, No. 51.
[18] Judgment, para. 42.
[19] Presumably for the reason given in *Foti* that the troubles in Reggio Calabria had created a situation in which transfers were necessary, and the courts had a backlog of business.

the Court's treatment of the local remedies point in *Foti*, both objections were held to be barred by estoppel, the Government having raised them out of time.

The third objection was rather different. It was that the applicant could not be regarded as a 'victim' within the meaning of Article 25 (1) because his aim in invoking the Convention was not to speed the course of the prosecution but simply to avoid conviction. In support of this submission the Government cited the fact that following his acquittal in 1980 the applicant had sought to withdraw his application on the ground that the object of the dispute had disappeared, and had changed his mind only when further proceedings (not relevant to the present application) had been instituted against him. The Court decided that although this objection had been raised timeously, it could not be accepted. Explaining that according to its previous decisions 'the word "victim" in Article 25 denotes the person directly affected by the act or omission in issue, the existence of a violation being conceivable even in the absence of prejudice',[20] the Court held that since the duration of the proceedings against Mr. Corigliano directly affected him, it was irrelevant that this was not his major concern.

The final part of the judgment was concerned with the issue of just satisfaction. Like the other issues in the case, this was essentially a matter of applying well-established principles to the facts. Having found that the question of Article 50 was ready for decision, the Court had no difficulty in responding to the applicant's first claim: that the Court should recommend the Italian Government to make the article of the Penal Code concerned with aggravated slander inapplicable to 'political and/or social trials'. Since this claim fell completely outside the scope of the application, it was summarily rejected. Mr. Corigliano's second claim was for damages for breach of the Convention. Here, however, the Court found that material loss was unproven, while any non-pecuniary loss had been sufficiently repaired by the decision on the merits.[21] This claim was therefore also disallowed. The last claim was for costs and expenses. The amount recoverable here was limited by the fact that Mr. Corigliano had incurred no legal costs in pursuing his Convention claim in Italy, and had argued his case before the Commission and Court in person. The award under this head was therefore confined to his travel and subsistence expenses at Strasbourg, a somewhat limited success in the circumstances, which makes an interesting comparison with the final result in *Foti* (Case No. 15).

Meaning of 'contestation' *and of* 'civil rights and obligations' *in Article 6 (1)—right to a* 'fair' *trial by an* 'impartial' *tribunal (Article 6 (1))—right to a public hearing and to a judgment pronounced publicly (Article 6 (1))—freedom from inhuman or degrading punishment (Article 3)—right to freedom of association (Article 11 (1))*

Case No. 4. Albert and Le Compte case.[22] The Court held by a majority of 16 votes to 4 that Belgium had infringed Article 6 (1) of the Convention because the Appeals Council of the *Ordre des médecins* had not heard the applicants' cases

---

[20] Judgment, para. 31.

[21] Evidence that the 'reasonable time' requirement was not one of the applicant's primary concerns, which the Court held to be irrelevant for the purposes of Article 25, weighed against the applicant on the issue of damages.

[22] E.C.H.R., judgment of 10 February 1983, Series A, No. 58. French text authentic. The case was decided by the plenary Court.

publicly and had not pronounced its judgment publicly. A number of other claims were dismissed unanimously.

The applicants were Belgian medical practitioners who had been disciplined by their professional organization, the *Ordre des médecins*. In June 1974 a Provincial Council of the *Ordre* suspended Dr. Albert's right to practise for two years for having issued certificates of unfitness for work without proper examination. This sanction was upheld in November by the Appeals Council of the *Ordre* and in June 1975 the Belgian Court of Cassation dismissed an appeal on a point of law challenging the decision. In March 1974 a different Provincial Council suspended Dr. Le Compte's right to practise for 'improper publicity' and 'contempt of the *Ordre*'. In October the Appeals Council ordered his name to be struck from the Register and in November 1975 his appeal on a point of law was rejected by the Court of Cassation.

Following the dismissal of their appeals both doctors lodged applications with the Commission in which they alleged that their treatment had violated a number of articles of the Convention, notably the guarantees of a fair trial set out in Article 6. The disciplinary procedures of the *Ordre des médecins* had already been the subject of investigation in *Le Compte, Van Leuven and De Meyere*[23] and in the present case, where one of the parties and most of the issues were identical, both the Court and the Commission made extensive use of the earlier ruling.

Article 6 (1) of the Convention, which was the focal point of the present proceedings, provides:

> In the determination of his civil rights and obligations or of any criminal charge against him, everyone is entitled to a fair and public hearing within a reasonable time by an independent and impartial tribunal established by law. Judgment shall be pronounced publicly but the press and public may be excluded from all or part of the trial in the interest of morals, public order or national security in a democratic society, where the interests of juveniles or the protection of the private life of the parties so require, or to the extent strictly necessary in the opinion of the court in special circumstances where publicity would prejudice the interests of justice.

The first question was whether Article 6 (1) was applicable to the type of proceedings here in issue. This depended on whether the disciplinary action against Dr. Albert and Dr. Le Compte gave rise to '*contestations*' (disputes) over their 'civil rights and obligations'. In *Le Compte, Van Leuven and De Meyere* the Court had answered the question affirmatively and the Court in the present case saw no reason to depart from this ruling. Explaining that the disciplinary proceedings were concerned with allegations which the applicants denied, the Court stated that there was no doubt that there was a *contestation*. Was it related to 'civil rights and obligations'? The Court held that as in its previous decision and the earlier case of *König*,[24] the right in issue was the right to continue to exercise the medical profession. In the particular circumstances this was a private right, and thus a civil right, because 'it is by means of private relationships with their clients and patients that doctors in private practice, such as the applicants, avail themselves of the right to continue to practise'.[25] In the Court's view the right to practise was directly in issue before the Appeals Council and the Court of

---

[23] E.C.H.R., judgment of 23 June 1981, Series A, No. 43. See this *Year Book*, 52 (1981), p. 337. The Court's application of Article 50 in this case is Case No. 1 above.

[24] E.C.H.R., judgment of 27 February 1980, Series A, No. 27. See this *Year Book*, 49 (1978), p. 317.

[25] Judgment, para. 28.

Cassation. Thus the requirement that the right in question must be the object, or one of the objects, of the *contestation* was also fulfilled. The conclusion was therefore that Article 6 (1) was applicable to the case.

The next question was how Article 6 (1) applied to disciplinary proceedings. The Court noted that the duty of adjudicating on disciplinary offences is commonly entrusted to the organs of professional associations and observed that such arrangements are not in themselves an infringement of the Convention. However, where the proceedings are subject to Article 6 (1) either the organs themselves must comply with the requirements of the Article, or, if they do not, they must be subject to control by a judicial body with full jurisdiction which does provide such guarantees. In the present case the applicants were dealt with at three levels. Since the Court held that the Provincial Councils need not be examined, the question was whether the Appeals Council, or failing that the Court of Cassation, fulfilled the requirements of Article 6 (1).

The crucial issues were impartiality and publicity. The impartiality of the Court of Cassation was not in doubt and the Court agreed with the Commission that the Appeals Council was equally acceptable. Explaining that 'the personal impartiality of the members of a "tribunal" must be presumed until there is proof to the contrary',[26] the Court observed that neither here, nor on the matter of organizational impartiality, was there any evidence to cause concern.

As far as publicity was concerned, the Court noted that the proceedings before the Court of Cassation were public, but held that since its jurisdiction was confined to appeals on points of law, the requirements of Article 6 (1) could only be satisfied by the procedure in the Appeals Council. Here, however, there had clearly been a breach of the Convention, for under a Royal Decree of 1970 all publicity before the Appeals Council was excluded. It was true that Article 6 (1) contained various exceptions, but none of these could apply to Dr. Le Compte's case, and while Dr. Albert's case was more arguable, none of them applied in fact. Similarly, the rule requiring a public hearing could be waived, but Dr. Le Compte had actively sought a public hearing and there was no evidence that Dr. Albert had intended to waive the right. The Court therefore concluded that the absence of a public hearing had entailed a breach of Article 6 (1).

In addition to their claims under Article 6 (1) both applicants invoked other articles of the Convention. Dr. Albert claimed that he had not received the benefit of the guarantees set out in Article 6 (2) and three sub-paragraphs of Article 6 (3). Dr. Le Compte, for his part, claimed that he had been the victim of violations of Articles 3 and 11.

The various articles invoked by Dr. Albert are all concerned with persons 'charged with a criminal offence'. The Commission decided that there had been no criminal charge and so did not deal with his claims under this head. The Court took a different approach. Holding that it was unnecessary to resolve the issue of characterization, the Court decided that because Article 6 (1) guarantees a 'fair trial' the principles set out in Article 6 (2) and the relevant parts of Article 6 (3) 'are applicable, *mutatis mutandis*, to disciplinary proceedings subject to paragraph 1 in the same way as in the case of a person charged with a criminal offence'.[27]

As regards observance of the presumption of innocence (Article 6 (2)), Dr. Albert claimed that the Provincial Council which heard his case allowed itself to be influenced by his previous criminal record, based its decision on insufficient

---

[26] Ibid., para. 32.   [27] Ibid., para. 39.

evidence and declined to hear evidence in rebuttal. The first claim was rejected on the ground that the Council had only taken the applicant's record into account in order to decide upon an appropriate penalty, and the remaining allegations were rejected on the facts. The applicant's other claims were that he had not been informed of the accusations (Article 6 (3) (a)); that he had not had time to prepare his defence (Article 6 (3) (b)); and that he had been deprived of essential witnesses (Article 6 (3) (d)). These claims also were all rejected on the facts.

Dr. Le Compte claimed that striking him off the medical register violated Article 3 because it constituted a degrading, if not an inhuman, punishment both in its nature and in its effects on his private, professional and family life. This claim, which is typical of the more extravagant interpretations of Article 3,[28] was summarily dismissed. Dr. Le Compte also claimed that the obligation to join the *Ordre des médecins* inhibited freedom of association and so violated Article 11. This argument had been rejected in *Le Compte, Van Leuven and De Meyere*, where the Court held that the *Ordre* could not be regarded as an association within the meaning of Article 11 and that the existence of the *Ordre* and the resultant obligations on practitioners had neither the object nor the effect of limiting the right protected by Article 11 (1). This approach enabled the Court in the earlier case to avoid the question of justification under Article 11 (2), and the more difficult issue of whether the Convention recognizes the freedom not to associate. In the present case the Court confined itself to repeating its earlier conclusions and while rejecting the claim under Article 11, left the other matters unresolved.

The question of just satisfaction for the infringement of the applicants' rights under Article 6 (1) was reserved because the matter was not yet ready for decision.[29]

On all points except the vital matter of the scope and application of Article 6 (1) the Court was unanimous. On the latter—effectively the core of the case—four judges opposed the majority's decision.[30] All four delivered dissenting opinions and repeated the views they had expressed earlier in *Le Compte, Van Leuven and De Meyere*. Their common theme was that the Court was wrong to hold that a case of the present kind involved a *contestation* over civil rights and obligations. The fullest treatment of the issue is to be found in the opinion of Judge Matscher, who made the persuasive point that despite the Court's attempt to confine its decision to the rights of a doctor in private practice, the clear implication of the judgment is that Article 6 (1) protects the right to practise any profession. This would certainly be a radical interpretation of the Convention which the Court may hesitate to endorse. Be that as it may, *Albert and Le Compte*, though in large measure the recapitulation of an earlier decision, shows that the scope of Article 6 (1) is in important respects still a highly controversial question.

Just satisfaction (Article 50)—scope of the Court's powers—whether financial compensation required on the facts—recoverability of costs settled by third party

Case No. 5. *Dudgeon* case (Application of Article 50).[31] The Court held

---

[28] For example, the *Marckx* case, Series A, No. 31. For a comprehensive review of the Court's jurisprudence on Article 3 see Duffy, *International and Comparative Law Quarterly*, 32 (1983), p. 316.

[29] For the Court's application of Article 50 see Case No. 14, below.

[30] The four members of the Court who delivered dissenting opinions were Judges Liesch, Matscher, Pinheiro Farinha and Sir Vincent Evans. In addition Judges Cremona and Bindschedler-Robert delivered a short joint concurring opinion and Judge Thór Vilhjálmsson made a declaration.

[31] E.C.H.R., judgment of 24 February 1983, Series A, No. 59. English text authentic. The Court

unanimously that the United Kingdom was to pay the applicant £3,315 in respect of costs and expenses incurred, but rejected or declared inadmissible certain other claims.

In its judgment on the merits of the case in 1981 the Court held *inter alia* that the applicant had been a victim of a breach of Article 8 of the Convention by reason of the existence in Northern Ireland of laws which had the effect of criminalizing certain homosexual acts committed between consenting adult males in private.[32] The question of 'just satisfaction' under Article 50 was reserved for later consideration.

In the present proceedings the applicant claimed financial compensation for the damage allegedly caused to him by the existence of the impugned legislation, together with a declaration from the British Government that if he were to apply for Civil Service employment in Northern Ireland he would not be discriminated against either on account of his homosexuality or for having petitioned the Commission. He also claimed financial compensation for the distress allegedly caused to him by a police investigation in 1976. His final claim was for legal and other expenses incurred in the proceedings before the Commission and the Court.

The case for awarding compensation for the effect of the legislation was challenged by the United Kingdom on various grounds. The Court accepted that the laws in question had caused the applicant at least some degree of fear and psychological distress, but agreed with the Government's main submission that its earlier judgment constituted 'just satisfaction' for the purposes of Article 50 without the necessity for financial compensation. In reaching this conclusion the Court attached weight to two considerations. Looking to the past, it agreed with the Government that the inference to be drawn from the Court's treatment of the merits was that the laws in question had not always been in breach of the Convention, but rather 'became out of step with changing standards of respect for private life under Article 8'.[33] Turning to the present, the Court noted that following the earlier judgment an Order in Council had been made bringing the law of Northern Ireland into line with that of the rest of the United Kingdom. Thus the applicant had succeeded in his aim of securing a change in the law relating to homosexuality in Northern Ireland.

The request for a declaration from the Government relating to the applicant's employment was rejected on the ground already noted, that the Court has no power to grant relief of this kind. (See Case No. 1 above.) The claim for compensation for the police investigation was treated by the Court in a similar way. While it was not prepared to accept that in agreeing to visit the police station the applicant's position was analogous to that of a person wrongfully detained, the Court agreed that the questioning of the applicant, the seizure of his private papers and the prospect of a criminal prosecution had caused him some degree of distress, suffering, anxiety and inconvenience. Pointing out, however, that the police investigation was no more than an implementation of the laws then in force, the Court held that since these had now been amended, the additional element of prejudice suffered as a result of the police investigation was not such as to call for further compensation.

consisted of the following Chamber of Judges: Ryssdal (President); Cremona, Evrigenis, Matscher, Pinheiro Farinha, Walsh, Sir Vincent Evans (Judges).

[32] E.C.H.R., judgment of 22 October 1981, Series A, No. 45. See this *Year Book*, 52 (1981), p. 343.
[33] Judgment, para. 12.

The Court's rejection of the applicant's various claims for compensation for non-pecuniary loss confirm the impression that unless an applicant can make out a very strong case, the Court is likely to hold that a favourable decision on the merits is enough to satisfy the requirements of Article 50. Compensation for costs and expenses cannot, of course, be approached in the same way and here the present case broke new ground.

Certain items of the applicant's costs were settled by the Northern Ireland Gay Rights Association. According to the British Government this meant that they were not recoverable in proceedings under Article 50 because they were not incurred by the applicant himself. In an important ruling the Court categorically rejected this line of argument. Agreeing with the applicant that 'the legal costs of his case were incurred by him in the sense that he, as client, made himself legally liable to pay his lawyers on an agreed basis',[34] the Court held that 'the wholly private arrangements he made to cover his financial obligations to his lawyers' were not material for the purposes of Article 50. Referring to its earlier judgment in the case of *Luedicke, Belkacem and Koç*,[35] the Court explained that such arrangements were 'to be distinguished from the situation where, the lawyer having accepted to act on the basis of receiving only the fees granted by the Commission under its legal aid scheme, the applicant in question never was under any liability to pay any or any additional fees'.[36] Since nothing of this kind was involved in the present case, the applicant was in principle entitled to recover his costs and expenses.[37]

The Court's decision on this last point is of great importance. The Court and the Commission rely on the willingness of applicants to bring cases forward. Consequently, enabling sponsored litigants like Mr. Dudgeon to recover their costs is a major step in enhancing the effectiveness of the Convention.

Just satisfaction (Article 50)—scope of the Court's powers—whether financial compensation required on the facts—moral damage—costs and expenses

Case No. 6. Campbell and Cosans case (Application of Article 50).[38] The Court held unanimously that the United Kingdom was to pay £940 to Mrs. Campbell and £8,846·60 less 2,300 French francs to Mrs. Cosans, in respect of legal costs and expenses, and £3,000 to Jeffrey Cosans in respect of pecuniary and non-pecuniary loss. A number of other claims were rejected or declared inadmissible.

In its judgment on the merits of the case in 1982 the Court held that the existence of corporal punishment in the schools attended by the applicants' sons did not constitute, as regards those children, a violation of Article 3 of the Convention, but did constitute, as regards their parents, a breach of Article 2 of Protocol 1 to the Convention.[39] It also held that the suspension of Mrs. Cosans's son Jeffrey, following his refusal to accept corporal punishment, was likewise

---

[34] Judgment, para. 21.

[35] E.C.H.R., judgment of 10 March 1980, Series A, No. 36.   [36] Judgment, para. 21.

[37] On its examination of the claim in detail the Court held that with the exception of £1,290 payable on a contingency basis and a sum of £50 for the travel and accommodation expenses of an expert whose presence was not essential, the applicant was entitled to the legal and other costs claimed.

[38] E.C.H.R., judgment of 22 March 1983, Series A, No. 60. English text authentic. The Court consisted of the following Chamber of Judges: Ryssdal (President); Thór Vilhjálmsson, Leisch, Gölcüklü, Walsh, Sir Vincent Evans, Macdonald (Judges).

[39] E.C.H.R., judgment of 25 February 1982, Series A, No. 48. See this *Year Book*, 53 (1982), p. 307.

a breach of Article 2. The question of just satisfaction under Article 50 was reserved.

In the present proceedings Mrs. Campbell claimed £3,000 in respect of her personal expenses and 'due compensation'. This claim was rejected by the Court on the ground that the applicant had produced no evidence that she incurred expenses over and above those covered by the Commission's legal aid payments and because the finding of a violation of the Convention in the earlier judgment was itself sufficient to provide just satisfaction. Mrs. Campbell also submitted a supplementary, but unquantified, claim in respect of the cost of obtaining private education for her children. However, since the applicant had declined to provide the name of the school involved and had not denied a newspaper report that her son Gordon was attending an independent school which used corporal punishment, this claim too was rejected for lack of evidence.

Mrs. Campbell also sought an undertaking from the Government that her children would not be subject to any form of corporal punishment at schools within the United Kingdom's jurisdiction. As already noted, claims in this form are always rejected by the Court and the present case was no exception. Explaining that 'the Court's judgments leave to the Contracting State concerned the choice of the means to be utilised in its domestic legal system for performance of its obligation under Article 53',[40] the Court held that it was not empowered to direct the United Kingdom to give the undertaking requested.

Mrs. Cosans's main claim was £5,000 for 'moral damage'. This sum contained an element of material damage, since it included the cost of medical treatment. However, the applicant had not produced a medical report and in view of this the Court agreed with the Commission that this aspect of the claim must be rejected for lack of evidence. As regards the remainder of the claim the United Kingdom argued that, as with Mrs. Campbell, the earlier judgment should be regarded as adequate satisfaction. The Commission was unsympathetic to this argument, but the Court, though prepared to acknowledge that Mrs. Cosans had suffered some distress as a result of her son's suspension, agreed with the Government that no financial compensation was required.

Jeffrey Cosans's claim was for £25,000 for 'moral damage' on the ground that his suspension from school had prevented the completion of his education and affected his employment prospects. This claim was contested by the Government on the ground that there was no evidence to link his unemployment with his incomplete schooling, and also challenged on a number of points of detail.

After reviewing the facts, so far as they could be established on the evidence available, the Court agreed with the Commission's delegates that the applicant must be regarded as having suffered some non-pecuniary loss in the form of mental anxiety, feelings of disadvantage and the loss of the opportunity to develop his intellectual potential. The Court similarly agreed that the suspension might well have contributed to the applicant's difficulty in finding employment and thus have occasioned material loss. On this point, however, the Court found that even without the suspension, the applicant would probably have obtained only limited qualifications. In view of this, the fact that the applicant did not appear to have explored the possibilities open to him, and the uncertain prospects of employment generally, the Court held that the applicant's suspension could not be regarded as

[40] Judgment, para. 16.

the principal cause of his material difficulties. Taking the above factors into account, together with the applicant's entitlement to social security benefits, and recognizing the considerable element of uncertainty in its assessment, the Court decided that the sum of £3,000 would provide an equitable satisfaction of the claim.

In addition to the claims for pecuniary and non-pecuniary loss already considered, Mrs. Campbell and Mrs. Cosans both claimed various sums by way of legal costs and expenses. For costs and expenses to be recoverable it must be shown that they were actually incurred, necessarily incurred and reasonable as to quantum. The present case, in which a number of the applicants' claims were disallowed, is a good illustration of how strictly the Court applies these principles. Mrs. Campbell, for instance, claimed £700 for certain expenses of the solicitor who represented her at Strasbourg and almost £8,500 in respect of the services of her adviser before the Commission. Both claims were disallowed: the first on the ground that the applicant had not established that she had paid, or was liable to pay, any sums over and above the amount received by way of legal aid, and the second on the ground that the cost of an adviser was not 'necessarily' incurred, bearing in mind that Mrs. Campbell already had the services of a barrister and a solicitor. Similarly, Mrs. Campbell's claim for £1,700 in respect of the fees and travel expenses of counsel was reduced by the sum she had already received by way of legal aid, namely £60, and, more significantly, by £700 on the ground that she had not established that it was necessary to employ counsel who had to travel from America. Mrs. Cosans's claim was likewise reduced. As well as a deduction of the 2,300 French francs which she had already received by way of legal aid, the Court held that the claim of more than £9,000 for the fees of Mrs. Cosans's counsel was not reasonable as to quantum and, in accordance with a formula suggested by the Government, reduced this item by more than a third.

Right of access to the courts (Article 6 (1))—right to respect for correspondence (Article 8)—the meaning of 'in accordance with the law' and 'necessary in a democratic society' in Article 8 (2)—right to an effective remedy before a national authority (Article 13)

Case No. 7. Silver and others case.[41] The Court held unanimously that the censorship of the applicants' mail by the prison authorities in the United Kingdom had given rise to violations of Articles 8 and 13 of the Convention. The Court also held unanimously that the refusal of a petition by Mr. Silver for permission to seek legal advice constituted a violation of Article 6 (1).

This case originated in seven applications lodged with the European Commission at various dates between November 1972 and July 1975. At issue was the action of the authorities in stopping sixty-two letters written by the applicants, six of whom were serving prison sentences in the United Kingdom. In addition, one applicant complained of delay in posting one of his letters and one of the withholding of one of his incoming letters. In the case of the applicant who was not in prison, Mrs. Colne, the letters in question were examples of correspondence which she was prevented from continuing with the imprisoned brother of a friend.

[41] E.C.H.R., judgment of 25 March 1983, Series A, No. 61. English text authentic. The Court consisted of the following Chamber of Judges: Wiarda (President); Thór Vilhjálmsson, Gölcüklü, Matscher, Pettiti, Sir Vincent Evans, Russo (Judges).

In the case of the other applicants the letters were addressed to, or sent by, various people, including relatives, solicitors, M.P.s and journalists. The correspondence dealt with many subjects including prison conditions, legal proceedings, business transactions and personal matters. In addition, in November 1972 one of the applicants, Mr. Silver, had petitioned the Home Secretary for permission to seek legal advice concerning allegedly negligent treatment in prison, but in April 1973 leave had been refused.

In its report of 11 October 1980 the Commission expressed the opinion that the refusal of Mr. Silver's petition constituted a denial of his right of access to the courts, contrary to Article 6 (1); that save in respect of six letters, the censorship of the applicants' mail constituted an unjustified interference with the right to respect for correspondence guaranteed by Article 8; that there was no effective domestic remedy for these violations as required by Article 13; and finally that it was unnecessary to examine the applicants' claims under Article 10.

An unusual feature of the proceedings in the Court was that many of the Commission's findings were not contested by the Government, which sought instead to emphasize the changes which had been made in the control of prisoners' correspondence by new arrangements introduced in 1981.[42] The Court, however, held that it was not concerned to review the new regime and directed its attention to the applicants' claims in respect of earlier events.

Mr. Silver's claim under Article 6 (1) caused the Court no problems. In its judgment in the *Golder* case[43] in 1975 the Court held that a right of access to the courts is implicit in the right to a fair and public hearing, and the Home Secretary's refusal to grant Mr. Silver permission to seek legal advice was on any view a clear contravention of this principle. The Government conceded as much by not contesting the Commission's finding on this point, but arguing instead that the Court should decline to rule on the matter in the light of the changes in law and practice since the *Golder* ruling. The Court rejected the Government's plea on the ground that the changes in question could not restore a right which had been violated in 1972 and which was now the basis of a claim for just satisfaction. It therefore concluded that since there was no material difference between the facts of the present case and those of *Golder*, there had been a violation of Article 6 (1).

The claims under Article 8 were more complex. That article reads as follows:

1. Everyone has the right to respect for his private and family life, his home and his correspondence.
2. There shall be no interference by a public authority with the exercise of this right except such as is in accordance with the law and is necessary in a democratic society in the interests of national security, public safety or the economic well-being of the country, for the prevention of disorder or crime, for the protection of health or morals, or for the protection of the rights and freedoms of others.

There was no doubt that in the present case there had been 'interferences by a public authority' with the exercise of the applicants' right to respect for their correspondence which is guaranteed by paragraph 1. The question was therefore whether the actions in question fell within any of the exceptions in paragraph 2.

---

[42] For details of the new practice see paragraphs 25 to 56 of the judgment. Although not in issue in the present proceedings, the changes were noted with satisfaction by the Court (para. 79) and played some part in the proceedings concerned with Article 50 (see Case No. 13).

[43] E.C.H.R., judgment of 21 February 1975, Series A, No. 18. See this *Year Book*, 47 (1973–4), p. 391.

The first question was whether the interference was 'in accordance with the law'. The expression 'prescribed by law', which is to be found in the qualifying provision of Article 10, was thoroughly considered by the Court in the *Sunday Times* case[44] and it was agreed that the explanation of the phrase to be found in that judgment was directly relevant to the present proceedings. The first principle that emerges from the earlier case is that the interference in question must have some basis in domestic law. It was common ground that a basis for the prison authorities' action was to be found not in the Home Secretary's Orders and Instructions, which lack the force of law, but in the Prison Act 1964 and the Rules made thereunder. A second principle is that the law must be adequately accessible. Clearly the Prison Act and Rules met this criterion but the Orders and Instructions, which were (and in some respects still are) unpublished, did not. A third principle is that the law must be sufficiently precise to enable the citizen to foresee, as far as is reasonable in the circumstances, the consequences of his conduct. However, the interpretation and application of many laws are questions of practice and in the present case, which concerned the screening of approximately ten million items of correspondence each year, the Court recognized that a significant element of discretion was unavoidable. Since the purpose of the Home Secretary's Orders and Instructions was to regulate that discretion, the Court considered that to the limited extent that the applicants had been made aware of their contents, they could be taken into account in deciding whether the foreseeability criterion had been satisfied in the application of the Rules.

A final point made by the Court was that any interference with the individual's rights must be subject to effective control, a matter of particular importance where, as in the present case, the executive enjoys wide discretionary powers. However, the Court did not accept the applicants' argument that safeguards must always be incorporated in the actual text authorizing the interference. The question of safeguards being closely linked with that of effective remedies, the Court addressed this issue later, when it considered Article 13.

Applying the above principles to the facts of the case, the Court noted that in a number of cases the Commission had concluded that correspondence had been stopped on grounds that were not foreseeable and that this finding had not been contested by the Government. The prohibitions in question, which included representations connected with a prisoner's trial, conviction or sentence, and material intended for publication, as well as the use of grossly improper language, covered the majority of the letters involved in the case. In respect of these items the Court found no reason to differ from the Commission's view that because the grounds of interference were not foreseeable, the interference in question was not 'in accordance with the law'.

In a further twenty-six cases the Commission's finding was contested. These were equally divided between those in which a finding that the Convention had been broken was challenged by the Government and those in which the opposite conclusion was challenged by the applicants. All the Government's claims were upheld on the ground that the basis of the interference had been specified as precisely as the circumstances permitted. On the other hand, all the applicants' challenges were disallowed on the ground that there is no requirement that the

---

[44] E.C.H.R., judgment of 26 April 1979, Series A, No. 30. See this *Year Book*, 50 (1979), p. 257.

directions set out in the Orders and Instructions must be contained in the substantive law.

The second question in applying Article 8 (2) is whether an interference with correspondence has a legitimate aim. In the present case the applicants did not allege that the restrictions in issue were designed or applied for a purpose other than those listed in Article 8 (2) and in the proceedings before the Commission the Government pleaded that the aims pursued were 'the prevention of disorder', 'the prevention of crime', 'the protection of morals', and/or 'the protection of the rights and freedoms of others'. The matter was not discussed before the Court which consequently concluded that each interference had an aim that was legitimate under Article 8.

The third and final question was whether the interferences were 'necessary in a democratic society'. This was more contentious and so before examining the facts, the Court again set out the principles to be found in its earlier jurisprudence, which it summarized as follows:

(a) the adjective 'necessary' is not synonymous with 'indispensable', neither has it the flexibility of such expressions as 'admissible', 'ordinary', 'useful', 'reasonable', or 'desirable'.

(b) the Contracting States enjoy a certain but not unlimited margin of appreciation in the matter of the imposition of restrictions, but it is for the Court to give the final ruling on whether they are compatible with the Convention.

(c) the phrase 'necessary in a democratic society' means that, to be compatible with the Convention, the interference must, *inter alia*, correspond to a 'pressing social need' and be 'proportionate to the legitimate aim pursued'.

(d) those paragraphs of Articles of the Convention which provide for an exception to a right guaranteed are to be narrowly interpreted.[45]

To these the Court added the consideration that when dealing with the correspondence of prisoners 'regard has to be paid to the ordinary and reasonable requirements of imprisonment' because 'some measure of control over prisoners' correspondence is called for and is not itself incompatible with the Convention'.[46]

The Commission had expressed the opinion that in a large number of cases the applicants' letters had been stopped on a ground that could not be regarded as 'necessary in a democratic society'. Most of these findings were not contested by the Government and were endorsed by the Court. It is unnecessary to give details here, although it should be noted that the prohibited correspondence concerned a variety of matters which the Government claimed would now be permitted. The contested items were various letters on which either the Government or the applicants took issue with Commission's view as to whether a particular interference had been shown to be necessary. Again it is unnecessary to go into details except to note that in the one instance where it challenged the Commission the Government was upheld, while the six challenges mounted by the applicants were all unsuccessful. In the last-mentioned cases the interferences with correspondence were held to be both 'in accordance with the law' and 'necessary in a democratic society' and therefore justifiable. In the remaining fifty-seven cases the Court's conclusion was that there had been a violation of Article 8.

Whether the stopping of the applicants' letters also violated their rights under

[45] Judgment, para. 97. Principles (a), (b) and (c) were put forward in the *Handyside* case, Series A, No. 24; and principle (d) in the *Klass* case, Series A, No. 28.

[46] Judgment, para. 98. This point had already been made in the *Golder* case.

Article 10 was an issue which the Commission had found it unnecessary to consider. The basis for its opinion was that in the context of correspondence the right to freedom of expression is guaranteed by Article 8. This conclusion was not disputed by either the applicants or the Government, and so the Court held that this claim need not be considered further.

Article 13 of the Convention provides as follows:

> Everyone whose rights and freedoms as set forth in this Convention are violated shall have an effective remedy before a national authority notwithstanding that the violation has been committed by persons acting in an official capacity.

The Court agreed with the Commission that it was unnecessary to consider this article in relation to either Article 6 (1) or Article 10, but decided that it must be examined in relation to Article 8, in order to deal with the issue of safeguards. The Commission, having considered the various possible channels of complaint, concluded that there was no effective domestic remedy and consequently a breach of Article 13. The Court, as before, began its examination of the issue by stating the relevant principles. The principles to emerge from the case law on Article 13, said the Court, include the following:

(a) where an individual has an arguable claim to be a victim of a violation of the rights set forth in the Convention, he should have a remedy before a national authority in order both to have his claim decided and, if appropriate, to obtain redress;

(b) the authority referred to in Article 13 may not necessarily be a judicial authority but, if it is not, its powers and the guarantees which it affords are relevant in determining whether the remedy before it is effective;

(c) although no single remedy may itself entirely satisfy the requirements of Article 13, the aggregate of remedies provided for under domestic law may do so;

(d) neither Article 13 nor the Convention in general lays down for the Contracting States any given manner for ensuring within their internal law the effective implementation of any of the provisions of the Convention—for example, by incorporating the Convention into domestic law.[47]

On the facts there were four channels of complaint available. Of these, two, an application to the Board of Visitors and an application to the Parliamentary Commissioner for Administration, could be quickly dismissed. The Board of Visitors could not enforce its conclusions or entertain applications from non-prisoners, while the Parliamentary Commissioner had no power to render a binding decision granting redress. Neither could therefore be regarded as providing an effective remedy. The remaining possibilities were a petition to the Home Secretary and the institution of proceedings in the English courts. But these too were less than adequate. If there were a complaint to the Home Secretary as to the validity of an Order or Instruction concerning the control of correspondence, he would in effect be a judge in his own cause. The courts, on the other hand, had a supervisory jurisdiction which was limited to determining whether powers had been exercised arbitrarily, in bad faith, from an improper motive or in an *ultra vires* manner. As a result, when, as here, interferences with correspondence were in accordance with English law, there could be no question of judicial redress.

---

[47] Judgment, para. 113. Principles (a) and (b) were put forward in the *Klass* case, Series A, No. 28; principle (c) in the *Van Droogenbroeck* case, Series A, No. 50; and principle (d) in the *Swedish Engine Drivers' Union* case, Series A, No. 20.

The Court therefore concluded that, to the extent that the applicable regulations were incompatible with the Convention, the channels of complaint available did not provide an effective remedy. To the extent, however, that those regulations were compatible with Article 8, it decided that the aggregate of these remedies satisfied the requirements of Article 13 in cases where they were available. Accordingly, the Court held unanimously that in all the instances where it had found a violation of Article 8 and in one other case,[48] there had been a violation of Article 13.

The Court's decision on just satisfaction under Article 50 was reserved and, as Case No. 13, is described below.

This was by far the most important case involving the United Kingdom in the period under review.[49] It is largely an application of existing law, but apart from its significance for the particular applicants, is a useful example of how the statements of principle so characteristic of the Court's jurisprudence generate solutions for concrete and subtly variable situations. Given the nature of the issue, it is not inconceivable that more cases concerning prisoners' correspondence will come before the Court. However, if the revised arrangements have indeed brought British practice into line with the Convention, it is possible that future disputes will be resolved at a very much earlier stage.

The field of application of Article 6 (2) as regards subject-matter and time—the presumption of innocence (Article 6 (2))—just satisfaction (Article 50)

Case No. 8 Minelli case.[50] In this case, which concerned Switzerland, the Court held unanimously that the applicant had been the victim of a breach of Article 6 (2) which incorporates the principle of the presumption of innocence. Switzerland was ordered to pay the applicant 8668·65 Swiss francs in respect of his costs and expenses.

The applicant was a Swiss journalist who published an article in a daily newspaper making accusations of fraud against a company and its director. In 1972 the company and its director instituted a prosecution for defamation through the press against the applicant. In 1974 the proceedings were adjourned, pending the outcome of a case against another journalist, Mr. Fust, who had written a similar article. In 1976 the Chamber of the Canton of Zürich Assize Court decided that it could not hear the complaint against the applicant because the limitation period had expired. However, in view of the fact that Mr. Fust had been convicted, the Court concluded that without the time-bar Mr. Minelli would 'in all probability' have been convicted. It therefore directed him to pay two-thirds of the investigation and trial costs and to compensate the private prosecutors for their expenses. The applicant's appeal against this decision to the Federal Court was dismissed in May 1979. In the following month Mr. Minelli lodged an application with the European Commission, alleging that the decision at first instance had

---

[48] A letter written by Mr. Silver was stopped on grounds which were justifiable under Article 8, but there was no opportunity to challenge this by means of a petition to the Home Secretary because Mr. Silver already had another petition pending.

[49] The other cases were all concerned only with the application of Article 50: see Cases No. 5, 6, and 13.

[50] E.C.H.R., judgment of 25 March 1983, Series A, No. 62. French text authentic. The case was decided by the following Chamber of Judges: Wiarda (President); Bindschedler-Robert, Lagergren, Gölcüklü, Matscher, Macdonald, Russo (Judges).

violated Article 6 (2) of the Convention. In its report of 16 May 1981 the Commission upheld this submission unanimously. In October of the same year the case was referred to the Court by the Commission and the Swiss Government.

Article 6 (2) of the Convention provides:

> Everyone charged with a criminal offence shall be presumed innocent until proved guilty according to law.

The Government's main plea was that the case fell outside the ambit of this provision both *ratione materiae* and *ratione temporis*. On the first point the Government accepted that Mr. Minelli was 'charged with a criminal offence', but argued that he had not had to answer a 'criminal charge against him', as provided in Article 6 (1). Since Article 6 (2) was concerned only with the requirements of a fair criminal trial, the present proceedings, which were basically civil in character, fell outside it.

The Court had no difficulty in identifying the error in the Swiss argument. Pointing out that 'the infringement of an individual's "civil" right sometimes also constitutes a criminal offence',[51] the Court explained that to determine whether there is a 'criminal charge' calls for a consideration of the accused's situation in the light of the fact that the object of Article 6 is the protection of the rights of the defence. In Switzerland defamation is punishable under the Federal Criminal Code and prosecution, though set in motion by a complaint, is governed by the Cantonal Codes of Criminal Procedure, while penalties become part of an individual's criminal record. In such circumstances the Court had no doubt as to the criminal nature of the proceedings brought against Mr. Minelli.

An alternative argument concerning the subject-matter of the case was that when ruling on the question of costs, the Swiss Court was exercising a purely administrative function to which the presumption of innocence was quite irrelevant. This argument, which had been raised and rejected in the *Adolf* case,[52] was likewise rejected here. Holding that Article 6 (2) 'governs criminal proceedings in their entirety, irrespective of the outcome of the prosecution, and not solely the examination of the merits of the charge',[53] the Court observed that since the Chamber of the Assize Court had established that the statutory limitation period had expired and made its ruling as to costs simultaneously, this was a particularly straightforward case.

The Government's attempt to limit the scope of Article 6 (2) *ratione temporis* was equally unconvincing. Here the argument was that the presumption of innocence only applied until the expiry of the limitation period and had no bearing on the subsequent proceedings. Rightly the Court had little time for this submission. It explained that whilst limitation extinguished the criminal action, an official procedural act of the Chamber of the Assize Court was required to establish the fact. At this final stage of the proceedings it was clear from the decision complained of that the applicant continued to be regarded as 'charged with a criminal offence'. He was thus still entitled to the protection of Article 6.

Having held that Article 6 (2) was applicable, the Court's next task was to consider whether it had been complied with. The Government submitted that the Chamber of the Assize Court had taken the applicant's conduct into account

---

[51] Judgment, para. 28.
[52] E.C.H.R., judgment of 26 March 1982, Series A, No. 49. See this *Year Book*, 53 (1982), p. 312.
[53] Judgment, para. 30.

only as a hypothesis for the purpose of apportioning costs, which was different, so it was argued, from a finding of guilt. The Court, however, agreed with the Commission that this distinction was not important. The test was not what the Court found, but the opinion reflected in its judgment. In the Court's words:

. . . the presumption of innocence will be violated if, without the accused's having previously been proved guilty according to law and, notably, without his having had the opportunity of exercising his rights of defence, a judicial decision concerning him reflects an opinion that he is guilty. This may be so even in the absence of any formal finding; it suffices that there is some reasoning suggesting that the court regards the accused as guilty.[54]

In view of the Assize Court's finding that Mr. Minelli would 'very probably' have been convicted, the Court concluded that its decision was incompatible with respect for the presumption of innocence.

The decision at first instance had to be read in the light of the Federal Court's judgment of 1979. But the Court held that this had done nothing to alter matters. The Federal Court had merely clarified the reasons for the original decision without altering their meaning or scope. By rejecting the appeal it had confirmed the decision in law and approved the substance of the decision in law. There had therefore been a violation of Article 6 (2).

There remained the issue of just satisfaction under Article 50 which the Court found was ready for decision. The Court acknowledged that Mr. Minelli might have suffered some degree of non-pecuniary loss as a result of the infringement of his rights, but held that since his press article lay at the root of the case, adequate compensation had already been furnished by the ruling on the merits. In respect of the cost of the Swiss proceedings the Court held that the applicant was entitled to recover the sums he was required to pay as a result of the decision of the Assize Court, the costs of his appeal and a proportion of his other expenses. His costs and expenses at Strasbourg were allowed in full.

There have been relatively few cases dealing with the presumption of innocence[55] and the present case, though a straightforward application of the principle, is a useful addition. The finding that the way the proceedings against Mr. Minelli were terminated violated Article 6 (2) provides an interesting contrast with the Court's decision in *Adolf*, where the facts were such as to raise this issue but no violation was found to have occurred. It was suggested in argument that the present case raised the question of whether, as a matter of principle, it is consonant with the presumption of innocence to direct a person to pay costs where he has been acquitted, or proceedings have terminated without a conviction in some other way. The Court declined to address this question, but its reasoning suggests that it is how such a system is operated, rather than the system itself, that may infringe the Convention. On a more general note, the case, like those on other aspects of Article 6, shows how practices which have been taken for granted in the domestic legal process for many years may, when subjected to challenge, fail to measure up to the standards prescribed by the European Convention.

[54] Ibid., para. 37.
[55] In addition to the *Adolf* case (above) see *Albert and Le Compte* (Case No. 4) and *Engel and others*, Series A, No. 22. See also this *Year Book*, 48 (1976–7), p. 386.

Just satisfaction (Article 50)—causation—non-pecuniary loss—standing to claim fees and expenses

Case No. 9. Van Droogenbroeck case (Application of Article 50).[56] The Court held unanimously that Belgium was to pay to the applicant 20,000 Belgian francs in respect of non-pecuniary loss and rejected the remainder of the claim for just satisfaction.

In its judgment on the merits of the case in 1982 the plenary Court held that when Mr. Van Droogenbroeck was detained by the Belgian authorities pursuant to section 25 of the Social Protection Act of 1964 he had not been able to take proceedings to challenge the lawfulness of his detention as required by Article 5 (4) of the Convention.[57] The Court reserved the question of just satisfaction under Article 50 and referred it to the Chamber initially constituted to examine the case.

In the present proceedings the applicant (in person) claimed more than 11,000,000 Belgian francs, with interest, as compensation for the period of more than five years during which he claimed he had been detained in conditions contrary to Article 5 (4). He also asserted that he was suffering from a 20 per cent incapacity for work, attributable to 'nervous disorder', said to have been caused by his detention, and sought the appointment of a medical expert and the payment of a provisional sum of 100,000 Belgian francs, again with interest.

To the extent that the applicant was seeking compensation for pecuniary loss, his claim encountered what in the Court's view were fatal objections. Apart from the fact that the earlier judgment related only to periods of detention totalling less than four years, the Court had there concluded that the applicant's detention was compatible with Article 5 (1) and that there was nothing to suggest that if Mr. Van Droogenbroeck had had the benefit of Article 5 (4) he would have been released earlier. Thus no compensation was required for loss caused by the applicant's detention, since in itself this had not been contrary to the Convention.

The Court agreed, however, that the absence of the guarantees provided by Article 5 (4) could be said to have caused the applicant some non-pecuniary loss and that for this its earlier judgment alone could not be said to provide just satisfaction. Having regard to Article 5 (5), the Court decided that the applicant was entitled to 20,000 Belgian francs under this head.

The decision to reject the claim for compensation for pecuniary loss is a straightforward application of the principle, already seen in Case No. 1, that the purpose of proceedings under Article 50 is not to pay the applicant for losses that are merely associated in some way with a breach of the Convention, but to provide compensation only for losses which the breach in question has caused. The decision to award compensation for non-pecuniary loss, on the other hand, and the remark that Article 5 (5) is 'a rule of substance to be taken into account in the exercise of the competence conferred by Article 50'[58] reflect the view that arrest or detention in contravention of any provision of Article 5 cannot be regarded lightly and is in line with earlier jurisprudence.[59]

---

[56] E.C.H.R., judgment of 25 April 1983, Series A, No. 63. French text authentic. The Court consisted of the following Chamber of Judges: Wiarda (President); Cremona, Ganshof van der Meersch, Gölcüklü, Pinheiro Farinha, Walsh, Russo (Judges).

[57] E.C.H.R., judgment of 24 June 1982, Series A, No. 50. See this *Year Book*, 53 (1982), p. 314.

[58] Judgment, para. 13.

[59] See the *Neumeister* case (Application of Article 50), Series A, No. 17, and this *Year Book*, 47 (1974-5), p. 388.

An unusual feature of the present case was that in addition to the claim for compensation by the applicant, the Court was also presented with a claim for fees and expenses drawn up by a Mr. Van Damme, the lawyer who had represented Mr. Van Droogenbroeck in Belgium and at Strasbourg, but whose right to act for him the applicant now denied. Not surprisingly this claim, which amounted to some 381,750 Belgian francs, was disputed by the Government on the ground that it was not made by the applicant, who alone has the status of an injured party for the purposes of Article 50. Moreover, as the Court pointed out, it was apparent that the applicant did not have to meet any legal expenses in connection with his applications for release from detention, and as far as the proceedings in Strasbourg were concerned, had received free legal aid and had not sought to show that he had a claim to the reimbursement of any additional fees or expenses. In these circumstances the Court had no hesitation in concluding that the claims set out by Mr. Van Damme must be rejected in their entirety.

The decision is clearly correct but highlights the difficulties which may arise when an applicant dismisses his legal representative prior to proceedings under Article 50 and the importance of the decision in *Dudgeon* (Case No. 5) which permits costs which are met by a third party to be included in an applicant's claim.

The right to legal assistance in criminal cases (Article 6 (3) (c))—proof of lack of means—the interests of justice—relationship between the three rights guaranteed— just satisfaction (Article 50)

Case No. 10. Pakelli case.[60] The Court held unanimously that the Federal Republic of Germany had infringed Article 6 (3) (c) of the Convention when the Federal Court refused the applicant's request to appoint official defence counsel for hearings in a criminal appeal on points of law. The respondent State was ordered to pay the applicant 668·96 German marks in respect of his legal costs and expenses.

In 1976 the applicant, a Turkish citizen resident in the Federal Republic of Germany, was convicted of the illegal importation of cannabis and tax evasion and sentenced to a term of imprisonment. After various proceedings which need not be described, the case came before the Federal Court which received a memorial prepared by the applicant's lawyer R., setting out the grounds of appeal, and decided to hold an oral hearing. An application by R. to be officially appointed as the applicant's lawyer for the oral proceedings was refused on the grounds *inter alia* that neither the facts of the case, nor the legal issues it raised, justified such an appointment. In November 1977, after a hearing in the presence of a Federal public prosecutor at which neither the applicant nor R. was present, the applicant's appeal was dismissed. An attempt to take a further appeal to the Federal Constitutional Court in 1978 was unsuccessful.

Towards the end of 1978 Mr. Pakelli lodged an application with the Commission, alleging that the Federal Court's refusal to appoint an official defence counsel had violated Articles 6 (1) and 6 (3) (c) of the Convention. In its report of 12 December 1981 the Commission was of the unanimous opinion that there had been a violation of the latter provision and with one dissent held that it was not

---

[60] E.C.H.R., judgment of 25 April 1983, Series A, No. 64. French text authentic. The Court consisted of the following Chamber of Judges: Wiarda (President); Ryssdal, Liesch, Pettiti, Walsh, Bernhardt, Gersing (Judges).

required to examine Article 6 (1). In May 1982 the case was referred to the Court by the Commission and Federal Government.

Article 6 (3) (c) reads as follows:

Everyone charged with a criminal offence has the following minimum rights:

. . .

 (c) to defend himself in person or through legal assistance of his own choosing or, if he has not sufficient means to pay for legal assistance, to be given it free when the interests of justice so require.

Since it was not disputed that this provision was applicable, the main issue in the present case was whether Mr. Pakelli had satisfied the conditions for free legal assistance laid down by this provision.

The first condition was that he had insufficient means to pay for legal assistance at the relevant time. Here the Government argued that there was nothing to substantiate the applicant's assertion and a certain amount of contrary evidence. The Court held that the Government was entitled to take this point, but noted that the Federal Court had refused the applicant's offer to supply a certificate of indigence. It noted also that in 1979 he had satisfied the Commission that he qualified for legal aid in respect of his Strasbourg application. Thus while Mr. Pakelli's financial position in 1977 was necessarily a matter of speculation, the Court was prepared to hold that in the circumstances he had satisfied the first condition.

The second condition was that 'the interests of justice' required the provision of legal assistance. Here the Government pointed out that the hearing on appeal was limited to points of law, that the issues were not complicated and that the applicant could have appeared in person. Finally, and here perhaps was the heart of the respondent's case, the Government argued that in appeals on points of law the role of the Federal public prosecutor was to examine the case from a completely independent standpoint. He was thus similar to the *Procureur général* in the Belgian Court of Cassation, whose role the Court had considered and approved more than ten years earlier in the *Delcourt* case.[61]

The Court, like the Commission, found these submissions unconvincing. It began by noting that the fact that the Federal Court had departed from its usual practice and decided that a hearing was necessary indicated that the oral proceedings were potentially important to the decision. From this it followed that to provide a fair trial it was necessary to ensure that both parties were present. Although the scope of the appellate proceedings was limited in certain respects, nineteen different points had been raised and 'Mr. Pakelli would have been able, had his lawyer appeared before the court, to explain his complaints, to supply further particulars thereof if need be and to develop his written arguments'.[62] There were, moreover, important legal issues concerning the interpretation of the Code of Criminal Procedure which fell to be considered and it was clear that here, and on the other matters relating to his appeal, the personal appearance of the appellant could not have compensated for the absence of his lawyer.

The final and decisive consideration was that at the oral stage the proceedings before the Federal Court had not been conducted with the participation of both parties. If there had been no hearing the Federal public prosecutor's office would

---

[61] E.C.H.R., judgment of 17 January 1970, Series A, No. 11. For a critical review see Nadelmann, *American Journal of International Law*, 66 (1972), p. 509.

[62] Judgment, para. 37.

have filed its submissions in writing and communicated them to the applicant, who would have been entitled to reply. This opportunity should therefore have been made available at the hearings. It followed that the precise role of the Federal public prosecutor's office was not important. For, 'By refusing to provide him with a defence counsel, the Federal Court deprived him, during the oral stage of the proceedings, of the opportunity of influencing the outcome of the case, a possibility that he would have retained had the proceedings been conducted entirely in writing.'[63] In these circumstances the Court, like the Commission, considered that the interests of justice required the applicant to be granted legal assistance for the hearings before the Federal Court and concluded that as a result there had been a breach of Article 6 (3) (c).

The Court prefaced its consideration of the above issues by deciding an important point of interpretation. Under German law Mr. Pakelli would have been allowed to argue his case in person before the Federal Court. The Government, relying on the fact that in the English text the three rights set out in Article 6 (3) (c) are linked by the disjunctive 'or', suggested that where a right of audience exists, there is never a right to free legal assistance. Not surprisingly this interpretation, which would limit the right to legal assistance very significantly, was rejected. Pointing out that in the French text the second and third rights are linked by 'et' not 'ou', the Court held that:

Having regard to the object and purpose of this paragraph, which is designed to ensure effective protection of the rights of the defence . . . the French text here provides the more reliable guidance . . . Accordingly, a 'person charged with a criminal offence' who does not wish to defend himself in person must be able to have recourse to legal assistance of his own choosing; if he does not have sufficient means to pay for such assistance, he is entitled under the Convention to be given it free when the interests of justice so require.[64]

The applicant, it will be recalled, had also invoked Article 6 (1), arguing that the refusal to grant him legal assistance had prejudiced his right to a fair trial. The Court pointed out that the provisions of Article 6 (3) (c) 'represent specific applications of the principle of a fair trial',[65] and held that any breach of Article 6 (1) was absorbed by its earlier finding. It therefore agreed with the Commission that there was no call to consider this point further.

The last issue in the case was the question of just satisfaction for the applicant under Article 50. Having decided that the question was ready for decision, the Court rejected a request that it annul the Federal Court's judgment and direct the Government to repudiate certain passages therein, on the ground that the measures requested were beyond its powers. A claim for damages for non-pecuniary loss was likewise dismissed on the ground that such loss had not been proved and because the judgment itself provided sufficient satisfaction. The applicant's claim for his costs and expenses in seeking to have the breach of Article 6 (3) (c) rectified by the Federal Constitutional Court was disputed by the Government,[66] but allowed to stand.

It was established in the *Artico* case[67] that Article 6 (3) (c) is fully applicable to

[63] Ibid., para. 39.   [64] Ibid., para. 31.   [65] Ibid., para. 42.

[66] In response to the Government's argument that because the applicant's lawyer had not pressed for payment he must be taken to have waived his rights, the Court observed that 'in a human rights case a lawyer will be acting in the general interest if he agrees to represent or assist a litigant even if the latter is not in a position to pay him immediately': judgment, para. 47.

[67] E.C.H.R., judgment of 13 May 1980, Series A, No. 37. See this *Year Book*, 51 (1980), p. 332.

appeal proceedings in so far as such proceedings are provided for. Except for the argument about the significance of the right of personal appearance, the present case therefore turned largely on the facts. By giving the applicant the benefit of the doubt on the issue of indigence, the Court took an approach which was clearly sensible in the circumstances and by deciding that 'the interests of justice' required the provision of legal assistance, underlined the fundamental importance of the principle of equality of arms. Neither in *Artico* nor in the present case was the Court prepared to accept the argument that the issues were so straightforward as to make representation unnecessary. This is as it should be. While there are certainly cases where that argument can succeed,[68] criminal appeals on points of law are surely the type of case in which legal representation at hearings, from public funds if necessary, should be regarded as the norm.

Just satisfaction (Article 50)—causation—non-pecuniary damage—costs and expenses

Case No. *11.* Eckle case (Application of Article 50).[69] The Court held unanimously that the Federal Republic of Germany should pay each applicant 9,641·10 German marks in respect of costs and expenses. The rest of the claims for just satisfaction were rejected.

In its judgment on the merits in 1982 the Court found that the length of two sets of criminal proceedings brought against Mr. and Mrs. Eckle had exceeded a 'reasonable time', contrary to Article 6 (1) of the Convention.[70] The question of just satisfaction under Article 50 was reserved.

In the present proceedings both applicants claimed substantial sums as compensation for material loss on the ground that if the national authorities had complied with Article 6 (1), they would have been able to continue their business and professional activities.[71] This was very much like the argument put forward in Le Compte, Van Leuven and De Meyere (Case No. 1), where a different aspect of Article 6 (1) was in issue, and subsequently in Van Droogenbroeck (Case No. 9), which involved Article 5 (4). In those cases, as we have seen, the Court held that in the absence of a causal link between the breach of the Convention and the applicant's loss, there can be no question of compensation. Mr. and Mrs. Eckle's claim was rejected for the same reason. Pointing out that its earlier judgment 'did not in any manner hold, or carry the implication, that their prosecution, conviction and imprisonment were also in breach of the Convention',[72] the Court held that the applicants' financial losses were not attributable to the length of the proceedings against them, but resulted 'from the very existence and outcome of the prosecutions brought against them'.[73] As such they were clearly irrecoverable.

Both applicants also sought considerable sums as compensation for non-pecuniary loss. The basis of their claim here was that the proceedings against them could have been conducted more expeditiously. This was denied by the Govern-

---

[68] See *Engel and others* case, Series A, No. 22, and this *Year Book*, 48 (1976–7), p. 386.

[69] E.C.H.R., judgment of 21 June 1983, Series A, No. 65. French text authentic. The Court consisted of the following Chamber of Judges: Ryssdal (President); Thór Vilhjálmsson, Ganshof van der Meersch, Liesch, Pinheiro Farinha, Pettiti, Bernhardt (Judges).

[70] E.C.H.R., judgment of 15 July 1982, Series A, No. 51. See this *Year Book*, 53 (1982), p. 317.

[71] A request that the Court defer its application of Article 50 until the outcome of certain domestic legal proceedings was rejected.   [72] Judgment, para. 20.   [73] Ibid.

ment, which submitted that the claims were in any case grossly excessive. The Court decided that the failure to conclude the proceedings within a reasonable time had caused the applicants disadvantage and inconvenience. It pointed out, however, that the Trier Regional Court took account of the time-factor by mitigating the applicants' sentences, and that other proceedings in Cologne were discontinued. Moreover, it was relevant that the crimes with which the applicants were charged were serious and the outcome heavy sentences of imprisonment. Taking all the elements into account, the Court concluded that the case was like *Corigliano* (Case No. 3), in that any claim for non-pecuniary loss had been sufficiently satisfied by the judgment on the merits.

There remained the claim for legal costs and expenses. Here at least the applicants had some success, though in accordance with its previous practice the Court subjected the claim to detailed scrutiny and all but a handful of items were disallowed. As in *Le Compte, Van Leuven and De Meyere* (Case No. 1) a number of claims for legal fees were refused on the ground that the expenditures in question were unconnected with the violation. Similarly, as in *Campbell and Cosans* (Case No. 6), the Court held that certain expenditures were unnecessary and others unreasonable as to quantum. In respect of some of the expenses incurred in the Federal Republic the Court awarded only a proportion of the claim on the ground that the litigation in question was not concerned solely with the length of the proceedings.

It is unnecessary to examine this aspect of the case further except to note that in the course of its item-by-item review of the applicants' claims the Court made two points of general significance. In response to the Government's argument that the claims for lawyers' fees and disbursements did not correspond to the Federal Scale, the Court explained that in this respect it is not bound by domestic scales or standards. Although this point has been made before[74] and any fee must, of course, be reasonable as to quantum, the fact that the Court makes its own assessment is clearly of some importance.

The second point is that in seeking to persuade the Court to award the applicants only a proportion of the costs of the Strasbourg proceedings, the Government relied on the fact that a number of their complaints had been rejected by the Commission. In *Le Compte, Van Leuven and De Meyere*, it will be recalled, an argument of this kind was accepted. Here, however, it was rejected on the ground that the complaints in question had failed at the admissibility stage, and not on the ground that they were manifestly ill-founded, but because they were out of time or domestic remedies had not been exhausted. The Court's decision that the examination of these questions was not of such complexity that its outcome warranted a deduction from the applicants' Strasbourg costs is a useful indication of the scope of the earlier decision.

Trial within a reasonable time (Article 6 (1))—just satisfaction (Article 50)

Case No. 12. Zimmermann and Steiner case.[75] The Court held unanimously that Switzerland had infringed Article 6 (1) of the Convention because the length of

---

[74] See the *König* case, Series A, No. 36, the *Sunday Times* case, Series A, No. 38, and para. 35 of the present judgment.

[75] E.C.H.R., judgment of 13 July 1983, Series A, No. 66. French text authentic. The Court consisted of the following Chamber of Judges: Wiarda (President); Bindschedler-Robert, Evrigenis, Matscher, Pinheiro Farinha, Pettiti, Macdonald (Judges).

the proceedings with respect to the applicants' administrative law appeal to the Federal Court had exceeded a 'reasonable time'. The applicants were also awarded 2,460 Swiss francs in respect of their costs and expenses.

The applicants in this case were Swiss nationals who were tenants of flats near Zürich airport. In 1974 they sought compensation from the Canton of Zürich for the damage caused by noise and air pollution from the airport. Their case was referred to the local Federal Assessment Commission which rejected their claims. This decision was served on the applicants in March 1977 and in the following month they lodged an administrative law appeal with the Federal Court. Owing to its excessive work load, the Federal Court was unable to deal with the case promptly and its decision dismissing their appeal was not handed down until October 1980. The delay in obtaining this decision was the basis of the applicants' complaint to the Commission, which in its report of 9 March 1982 expressed the unanimous opinion that there had been a violation of Article 6 (1). The case was then referred to the Court by the Commission and the Swiss Government.

Unlike the cases on length of proceedings examined earlier, the present case concerned administrative and not criminal proceedings. It was agreed, however, that the 'rights' claimed by Mr. Zimmermann and Mr. Steiner before the Federal Court—being personal or property rights—were private and therefore 'civil' within the meaning of Article 6 (1). It was equally clear that the sole subject of complaint, and therefore the only matter in issue, was the length of the proceedings before the Federal Court. Thus the period to be taken into consideration ran from April 1977, when the applicants lodged their appeal, to October 1980, when the Court gave its judgment.

Noting that for a case dealt with at a single jurisdictional level a delay of almost three and a half years 'calls for close scrutiny',[76] the Court referred to the established principle that the reasonableness of the length of proceedings depends on all the circumstances, having regard to the complexity of the case and the conduct of the applicants and the competent authorities, adding that what was at stake for the applicants is also relevant and that 'only delays attributable to the State'[77] can justify a finding of a failure to comply with the Convention.

In the present case it was clear that the legal and factual issues were not complex and that no blame for the delays could be attributed to the applicants. Everything therefore depended on the Court's assessment of the conduct of the Swiss authorities and in particular on whether the backlog of pending business could be regarded as excusing the delay. Statistical evidence demonstrated that the Federal Court had experienced an enormous growth in its work-load in recent years. The Government argued that this meant that cases had to be dealt with according to their urgency and importance and that of necessity some cases, like those of the applicants, would be subject to considerable delay. The Court, however, decided that this was no answer to the claim. It was prepared to agree that 'a temporary backlog of business does not involve liability on the part of the Contracting States provided that they take, with the requisite promptness, remedial action to deal with an exceptional situation of this kind'.[78] But it emphasized that the fundamental principle remains the duty of States to organize their legal systems so as to allow their courts to comply with the Convention. Thus although creating priority categories may be acceptable as a provisional expedient, 'if a state of affairs of this kind is prolonged and becomes a matter of structural organisation,

---

[76] Judgment, para. 23.   [77] Ibid., para. 24.   [78] Ibid., para. 29.

such methods are no longer sufficient and the State will not be able to postpone further the adoption of effective measures'.[79]

The Court had no doubt that in the present case the evidence revealed a situation which could only be dealt with by structural reorganization. The Swiss authorities had shown a willingness to tackle the problem, but the minor structural improvements which had been made were clearly an inadequate response. Thus the lapse of nearly three and a half years in dealing with the applicants' case could not be attributable to temporary difficulties and the backlog of business could not deprive them of their right to a hearing within a reasonable time. There had therefore been a violation of Article 6 (1).

The only other issue in the case was the question of just satisfaction under Article 50. In accordance with the reluctance to award compensation for non-pecuniary loss already noted, the Court held that any prejudice to the applicants was adequately compensated by its ruling on the merits. On the matter of costs and expenses, reimbursement was ordered in respect of their lawyer's fee for attempting to expedite the Swiss proceedings, and a claim for the cost of the Strasbourg proceedings (which was not contested) was allowed in full.

The Court's decision that there had been a breach of Article 6 (1) in this case may be compared with its decision in 1981 in *Buchholz*.[80] In that case, which concerned the Federal Republic of Germany, there was a delay of almost five years before the domestic decision was rendered, but the Court held that the proceedings had not been unduly prolonged. Unlike the present case, however, the claim had passed through several stages, and while a backlog of business was again a factor, the Court was satisfied that steps had been taken to alleviate the problem. There is no doubt that a rise in the volume of litigation has recently caused difficulties for several parties to the Convention. In *Buchholz*, *Foti* (Case No. 2) and the present case, the Court has indicated that it is aware of the situation and willing to make allowances for it. What it is not prepared to do is to permit the legal systems of Contracting States to live in a permanent state of emergency instead of getting to the root of the problem. In making this clear in *Zimmermann and Steiner* the Court is to be commended for recognizing one of the primary purposes of the Convention.

Just satisfaction (Article 50)—'general' and 'special' damages—costs and expenses

Case No. 13. Silver and others case (Application of Article 50).[81] The Court held unanimously that the United Kingdom was to pay the applicants the sum of £31,661·57 less 34,692 French francs in respect of their costs and expenses in proceedings before the Commission and the Court. The remainder of the claims were rejected.

The Court's judgment on the merits (Case No. 7 above) held that the stopping of the applicants' mail by the prison authorities constituted violations of Articles 8 and 13 of the Convention. It also held that the refusal of a petition by Mr. Silver for permission to seek legal advice constituted a breach of Article 6 (1). The question of just satisfaction under Article 50 was reserved.

---

[79] Ibid.

[80] E.C.H.R., judgment of 6 May 1981, Series A, No. 42. See also this *Year Book*, 52 (1981), p. 335.

[81] E.C.H.R., judgment of 24 October 1983, Series A, No. 67. English text authentic. The Court consisted of the following Chamber of Judges: Wiarda (President); Thór Vilhjálmsson, Gölcüklü, Matscher, Pettiti, Sir Vincent Evans, Russo (Judges).

The first claim examined by the Court in the present proceedings was a claim by all the applicants for general damages for the violation of their Convention rights. Claiming that they had been caused very great distress, they emphasized the scale of the breaches and the absence of any effective domestic remedy, a point which was underlined by the fact that complaints about censorship had themselves been censored. The Government's main plea was that an award of general damages was neither necessary nor appropriate. The Court, in considering what was 'equitable in all the circumstances of the case', was prepared to accept that the applicants might have experienced annoyance and frustration as a result of the restriction of their correspondence, but decided that this was not of such intensity as to justify an award of compensation for non-pecuniary loss. Agreeing with the Government that it was important that only a small proportion of the applicants' mail had been stopped, the Court held that it could also take into account the substantial improvement in the arrangements for controlling prisoners' correspondence which had been introduced as a result of the present applications.[82] In the circumstances therefore the Court decided that its earlier judgment was sufficient to provide just satisfaction for this aspect of the claim.

Claims for special damages on behalf of three of the applicants were also rejected and can be dealt with quite briefly. On behalf of Mr. Silver, who had died while his case was pending before the Commission, it was argued that the stopping of correspondence concerning medical treatment and diet had caused him great distress and adversely affected his health. The claim was rejected on the ground that the injury alleged 'was of a purely personal nature, involved no element of material damage and did not affect his estate'.[83] Mr. McMahon, whose sentence had been remitted following the publication of a book concerning his case and a campaign to establish his innocence, claimed that the restriction of his correspondence might have delayed the reconsideration of his case and sought damages for wrongful imprisonment. The Court, however, regarded this possibility as unproven and therefore rejected this claim on the facts. Lastly Mr. Carne, who had been punished for sending clandestine letters, sought compensation on the ground that if his legitimate correspondence had been permitted, he would have avoided any penalty. Though the Court agreed that the limitations on the applicant's correspondence might have been one reason for his subterfuge, it pointed out that the latter was a transgression of prison regulations, and held that in all the circumstances there was no necessity to award compensation on this score.

The Court's rejection of these claims echoes its earlier judgments and demonstrates its reluctance to regard damages for non-pecuniary loss as other than an exceptional remedy. Of the various claims for special damages only the last appears to have had much substance, while the treatment of the claims for general damages confirms the impression of *Dudgeon* and other cases that when steps have been taken to remedy a deficiency in the law revealed by an application, the Court will tend to regard its judgment on the merits as a sufficient satisfaction of the claim.

The last issue to be considered was the applicants' claim for costs and expenses. Here the Court rejected arguments by the Government that in a number of

---

[82] It should be noted, however, that the conformity of the new arrangements with the Convention was not in issue in the earlier proceedings.

[83] Judgment, para. 12.

instances the amounts claimed were unreasonable as to quantum, but accepted that the brief fees of counsel for appearance before the Court should be reduced. On this point the Court developed its observations in *Eckle* (Case No. 11) by explaining that, though it is not bound by domestic practice in respect of allowable costs, such parallels can be of assistance. At the forefront of the Court's approach to the issue of quantum is the consideration that the 'high costs of litigation may themselves constitute a serious impediment to the effective protection of human rights'[84] which calls for a careful scrutiny of claims for costs and expenses. It should be noted, however, that a claim by the Government that the cost of employing counsel for the friendly settlement negotiations should be disallowed was not accepted. As the Court explained, the Government was very fully represented at the negotiations, which involved far-reaching modifications to the system of control of correspondence. In deciding that in these circumstances 'the participation of counsel with experience in the matter was of great importance'[85] the Court was rightly recognizing that in its application of Article 50 the minimization of cost is only one among several policy considerations that may be relevant.

Just satisfaction (Article 50)—scope of the Court's powers—non-pecuniary damage—causation—nominal damages—costs and expenses

Case No. 14. Albert and Le Compte case (Application of Article 50).[86] The Court held unanimously that Belgium was to pay Dr. Le Compte 77,000 Belgian francs in respect of costs and expenses. The remainder of the claims for just satisfaction were rejected.

The judgment of the plenary Court on the merits (Case No. 4 above) held that there had been a breach of Article 6 (1) of the Convention because the Appeals Council of the *Ordre des médecins* had not heard the applicants' cases publicly and had not pronounced its judgment publicly. The Court reserved the question of just satisfaction under Article 50 and referred it to the Chamber initially constituted to examine the case.

In the present proceedings Dr. Le Compte sought the adoption by the Government of measures providing partial reparation in the form of the expunction of all the sanctions imposed on him both disciplinary and penal, together with the withdrawal of a circular issued by the Minister of Justice, prohibiting all dispensing chemists in Belgium from making up the applicant's prescriptions. It will be recalled that in *Le Compte, Van Leuven and De Meyere* (Case No. 1) a very similar claim by Dr. Le Compte had been rejected on the ground that the Court has no power to grant reparation in this form, and the present claim was dismissed in identical terms.

Dr. Le Compte's claim for financial compensation was equally unsuccessful. As in the earlier case, the Court held that its finding that the applicants' case should have been heard publicly in no way cast doubt on the outcome of the proceedings.

---

[84] The quotation is from the case of *James, Young and Webster* (Application of Article 50), Series A, No. 55, para. 15, and is repeated in paragraph 18 of the present judgment. See also this *Year Book*, 53 (1982), p. 322.

[85] Judgment, para. 20 (f).

[86] E.C.H.R., judgment of 24 October 1983, Series A, No. 68. French text authentic. The Court consisted of the following Chamber of Judges: Wiarda (President); Cremona, Ganshof van der Meersch, Evrigenis, Pinheiro Farinha, Sir Vincent Evans, Macdonald (Judges).

There was therefore no causal link between the withdrawal of Dr. Le Compte's right to practise and the Court's decision that the Convention had been violated, and consequently no case for awarding compensation. Similarly, Dr. Albert's only claim in the present proceedings, a request for a token award of one Belgian franc for non-pecuniary damage, was rejected on the ground that the Court's judgment on the merits was enough to provide just satisfaction.

On the matter of costs and expenses Dr. Le Compte sought a sum identical to that awarded in *Le Compte, Van Leuven and De Meyere*. Since this was not disputed by the Government, the whole sum requested was granted by the Court.

Just satisfaction (Article 50)—friendly settlement—assessment of compensation— costs and expenses

Case No. 15. Foti and others case (Application of Article 50).[87] The Court unanimously decided to strike the case from its list as regards Mr. Foti and Mr. Lentini and took formal note of the partial settlement reached in the case of Mr. Gullì. It also held that Italy was to pay 1,000,000 lire to Mr. Gullì in respect of legal fees and expenses and 10,000,000 lire to Mr. Cenerini as compensation for damage suffered. The remainder of the claims were rejected.

The Court's judgment on the merits (Case No. 2 above) held that there had been a breach of Article 6 (1) of the Convention because the applicants' cases had not been heard within a reasonable time. The question of just compensation under Article 50 was reserved.

Of all the cases involving Article 50 in the period under review, this was the only one in which applicants whose cases the Court had upheld on the merits succeeded in negotiating a friendly settlement with the Government concerned. As a result, the final stage of the proceedings required the Court to verify the equitable nature of the agreed settlements and then to deal with certain outstanding issues.

Under the settlements with Mr. Foti and Mr. Lentini the Government was to pay each applicant 6,000,000 lire, part of which was to go to their lawyers. This arrangement was to constitute a full settlement of their claims and was not objected to by the Commission's delegate. In these circumstances the Court had no hesitation in striking the cases of these applicants from its list.

In the case of Mr. Gullì the proposed settlement consisted of the offer of a job by the municipality of Reggio Calabria, but the applicant's claim for fees and expenses amounting to 15,000,000 lire was still outstanding. In the absence of any objection by the Commission's delegate the Court approved the partial agreement, and turned its attention to the issue still in dispute. Bearing in mind that the applicant had received legal aid, the Government argued that his claim for fees and expenses was excessive. The Court agreed and, emphasizing that the applicant had supplied little in the way of evidence to justify his claim, reduced the award to the sum of 1,000,000 lire.

The fourth applicant, Mr. Cenerini, had not succeeded in negotiating a friendly settlement and claimed 100,000,000 lire as compensation for loss of his employment. As with the previous applicant, the Court noted that Mr. Cenerini had failed

---

[87] E.C.H.R., judgment of 21 November 1983, Series A, No. 69. French text authentic. The Court consisted of the following Chamber of Judges: Wiarda (President); Ryssdal, Ganshof van der Meersch, Bindschedler-Robert, Pinheiro Farinha, Russo, Bernhardt (Judges).

to support his claim with evidence, but none the less decided that some compensation was due. Taking into account the Government's view that the claim was excessive and the opinion of the Commission's delegate that the applicant's position was only partly attributable to the length of the criminal proceedings against him, the Court decided that an award of one tenth of the sum claimed would constitute just satisfaction.

Why are friendly settlements of the type approved in *Foti* so rare? As far as compensation is concerned, it would appear from the cases considered earlier that applicants currently have little incentive to moderate their claims. Governments, on the other hand, have no reason to accept claims that are extravagant, or *a fortiori* to promise action beyond their legal powers. On the question of fees and expenses, applicants are bound to ask for reimbursement of their actual expenditure, while Governments, knowing that it is the policy of the Court to limit the cost of litigation, can be expected to urge reductions wherever possible. In any case, as domestic practice in areas such as negligence demonstrates, the application of general principles will always produce litigation and it must also be borne in mind that only recently has the number of successful applications begun to generate a significant jurisprudence on Article 50, so the Court is still in the process of establishing the appropriate standards. The cases decided in the period under review may be seen therefore as a reflection of the Court's present stage of development, as well as the consequence of its increasing scale of activity.

J. G. MERRILLS

DECISIONS OF THE COURT OF JUSTICE OF THE EUROPEAN COMMUNITIES DURING 1982*

When do treaties between the E.E.C. and a non-member State create rights for individuals?

Case No. 1. Hauptzollamt Mainz v. Kupferberg.[1] There was a dispute between the parties about the amount of tax payable on port wine imported from Portugal into Germany. The defendants contended that German tax law violated the first paragraph of Article 21 of the free trade agreement between the E.E.C. and Portugal, which provides:

The Contracting Parties shall refrain from any measure or practice of an internal fiscal nature establishing, whether directly or indirectly, discrimination between the products of one Contracting Party and like products originating in the territory of the other Contracting Party.

The German court hearing the case asked the Court of Justice of the European Communities to give a preliminary ruling under Article 177 of the E.E.C. Treaty on the interpretation of Article 21.

The first question was whether Article 21 created rights for individuals. The Court of Justice of the European Communities held that this question must be decided in accordance with Community law, and not in accordance with the municipal law of the national court hearing the case. Treaties concluded with non-member States formed part of Community law; if national courts applied their own rules of municipal law to answer the question whether such a treaty created rights for individuals, the question would be answered in different ways in different member States, which would be contrary to the basic principle of Community law that Community law must be applied uniformly in all member States.

The Court pointed out that the E.E.C. and the non-member State in question were at liberty to insert an express provision in the treaty about its effects or lack of effects on the rights of individuals. However, in the absence of such an express provision, the question whether the treaty created rights for individuals had to be decided 'by the courts having jurisdiction in the matter, and in particular by the Court of Justice' of the European Communities. In deciding that question, the Court would not necessarily follow decisions by the courts of the other contracting party; the question whether the treaty created rights for individuals was not normally subject to any requirement of reciprocity.

According to the general rules of international law there must be *bona fide* performance of every agreement. Although each contracting party is responsible for executing fully the commitments which it has undertaken it is nevertheless free to determine the legal means appropriate for attaining that end in its legal system unless the agreement, interpreted in

---

* © Dr. Michael Akehurst, 1984.

[1] [1982] E.C.R. 3641. For a comparison between this case and earlier cases, see Bebr, *Common Market Law Review*, 20 (1983), p. 35.

the light of its subject-matter and purpose, itself specifies those means. Subject to that reservation, the fact that the courts of one of the parties consider that certain of the stipulations in the agreement are of direct application [i.e. create rights for individuals] whereas the courts of the other party do not recognize such direct application is not in itself such as to constitute a lack of reciprocity in the implementation of the agreement.

The Court held that the test to be applied to determine whether a provision of a treaty with a non-member State created rights for individuals was whether that provision was precise and unconditional. This is, of course, the test which the Court applies to determine whether a provision of the E.E.C. Treaty creates rights for individuals. But the Court added that it was also necessary to consider the nature, structure, object and purpose of the treaty. It seems, therefore, that the fact that a provision of the E.E.C. Treaty has been held to create rights for individuals does not necessarily mean that a similarly worded provision of a treaty with a non-member State will also be held to create rights for individuals.[2]

The British, Danish, French and German governments, which intervened in the proceedings before the Court, argued that provisions of free trade agreements between the E.E.C. and non-member States could not create rights for individuals because of 'the institutional framework established by such agreements in order to settle differences between the contracting parties and safeguard clauses allowing the parties to derogate from such agreements'. The Court rejected that argument in the following words:

As the [four intervening] governments have emphasized, the free trade agreements provide for joint committees responsible for the administration of the agreements and for their proper implementation. To that end they may make recommendations and, in the cases expressly provided for by the agreement in question, take decisions.

The mere fact that the contracting parties have established a special institutional framework for consultations and negotiations *inter se* in relation to the implementation of the agreement is not in itself sufficient to exclude all judicial application of that agreement. The fact that a court of one of the parties applies to a specific case before it a provision of the agreement involving an unconditional and precise obligation and therefore not requiring any prior intervention on the part of the joint committee does not adversely affect the powers that the agreement confers on that committee.

As regards the safeguard clauses which enable the parties to derogate from certain provisions of the agreement, it should be observed that they apply only in specific circumstances and as a general rule after consideration within the joint committee in the presence of both parties. Apart from specific situations which may involve their application, the existence of such clauses, which, moreover, do not affect the provisions prohibiting tax discrimination, is not sufficient in itself to affect the direct applicability which may attach to certain stipulations in the agreement.

It follows from all the foregoing considerations that neither the nature nor the structure of the Agreement concluded with Portugal may prevent a trader from relying on the provisions of the said Agreement before a court in the Community.

However, there is a clear implication in these remarks by the Court that a treaty with a non-member State would not be regarded as sufficiently precise and unconditional to create rights for individuals if it contained loosely worded escape clauses or if it left the manner of the treaty's implementation to be decided by subsequent negotiations between the contracting parties or by decisions of organs created by the treaty. Indeed, the Court of Justice of the European Communities

[2] Plender, *Yearbook of European Law*, 2 (1982), pp. 57, 89-92; id., *Cambridge Law Journal*, 42 (1983), pp. 279, 288-92. See also below, p. 350.

has held, for these (or very similar) reasons, that the General Agreement on Tariffs and Trade does not create rights for individuals.[3]

The Court went on to say that the question whether a particular provision of a treaty with a non-member State is sufficiently precise and unconditional to have direct effect (i.e. to create rights for individuals) must be considered in the context of the treaty of which it forms part. (It is, of course, possible for one provision of a treaty to create rights for individuals even though other provisions of the same treaty do not create rights for individuals.)

In order to reply to the question on the direct effect of the first paragraph of Article 21 of the Agreement between the Community and Portugal it is necessary to analyse the provision in the light of both the object and purpose of the Agreement and of its context.

After analysing the important contribution made by the first paragraph of Article 21 to the fulfilment of the purposes of the free trade agreement as a whole, the Court concluded that

the first paragraph of Article 21 of the Agreement imposes on the Contracting Parties an unconditional rule against discrimination in matters of taxation, which is dependent only on a finding that the products affected by a particular system of taxation are of like nature. . . . As such this provision may be applied by a court and thus produce direct effects throughout the Community.

Finally, the Court interpreted the content of the non-discrimination principle laid down by Article 21, and held, in effect,[4] that German tax law did not violate Article 21. Most of the points made by the Court in this context are of more interest to tax lawyers than to international lawyers, and will therefore not be discussed in the present case note. However, the Court did make one point of more general interest, concerning the relationship between the first paragraph of Article 21 of the free trade agreement with Portugal and the first paragraph of Article 95 of the E.E.C. Treaty, which provides:

No member State shall impose, directly or indirectly, on the products of other member States any internal taxation of any kind in excess of that imposed directly or indirectly on similar domestic products.

The defendants argued that the interpretations which the Court had placed on Article 95 in earlier cases should be applied to Article 21.[5] The Court rejected that argument in the following words:

. . . although Article 21 of the Agreement [with Portugal] and Article 95 of the E.E.C.

[3] *International Fruit Company N.V.* v. *Produktschap voor Groenten en Fruit*, [1972] E.C.R. 1219 (this *Year Book*, 46 (1972–3), p. 445); *Carl Schlüter* v. *Hauptzollamt Lörrach*, [1973] E.C.R. 1135; Petersmann, *Common Market Law Review*, 20 (1983), pp. 397, 411–15. Cf. the criticism of these cases by Petersmann, ibid., pp. 415–37, and Mastellone, ibid., pp. 559, 568–80. On the competence of the Court of Justice of the European Communities to interpret G.A.T.T. under Article 177 of the E.E.C. Treaty, see Petersmann, ibid., pp. 397–404.

[4] A preliminary ruling under Article 177 deals only with the interpretation or validity of rules of Community law; the case then goes back to the national court, which must apply the preliminary ruling to the facts of the case and decide (where relevant) whether national law violates Community law. But in practice the Court of Justice of the European Communities often, as in this case, phrases its interpretation of Community law in such a way as to imply clearly whether or not national law is in conformity with Community law.

[5] It is not easy to see how this argument, even if it had succeeded, would have helped the defendants, because, as the Advocate General showed, the interpretations which the Court had previously placed on Article 95 did not support the interpretations which the defendants sought to place on Article 21: [1982] E.C.R. 3678–9.

Treaty have the same object inasmuch as they aim at the elimination of tax discrimination, both provisions, which are moreover worded differently, must however be considered and interpreted in their own context.

... [T]he E.E.C. Treaty and the Agreement on free trade pursue different objectives. It follows that the interpretations given to Article 95 of the Treaty cannot be applied by way of simple analogy to the Agreement on free trade.[6]

The Court is an enthusiastic supporter of teleological interpretation. When different treaties pursue different ends, it is understandable that the Court will interpret them differently. A free trade agreement is intended to produce free trade, and nothing more. The E.E.C. Treaty is intended to produce a much greater degree of economic integration. Since the aims of a free trade agreement are much narrower than the aims of the E.E.C. Treaty, it is not surprising that the Court sometimes interprets provisions of free trade agreements more narrowly than similarly worded provisions of the E.E.C. Treaty.[7]

Exclusive fishing zones—'exclusive' means 'exclusive'

Case No. 2. Directeur des affaires maritimes du littoral du sud-ouest v. *Marticorena-Otazo.*[8] On 3 November 1976 the Council of Ministers of the European Communities adopted a resolution which provided that the member States would by concerted action extend as from 1 January 1977 their fishing zones to 200 nautical miles off their North Sea and Atlantic coasts. Vessels from non-member States would be permitted to fish in the fishing zones of member States only if they were covered by treaties between the E.E.C. and the non-member State in question or (pending the conclusion of such treaties) by licences issued by the Commission of the European Communities.

A reciprocal fishing Agreement between the E.E.C. and Spain was signed on 15 April 1980; following ratification, it came into force on 22 May 1981, although it was provisionally applied by the contracting parties as from the date of signature. Even before the signature of this Agreement, however, Spain had co-operated with the Commission of the European Communities in implementing E.E.C. regulations which prohibited fishing by Spanish vessels in the fishing zones of E.E.C. member States unless those vessels held licences issued by the

---

[6] [1982] E.C.R. 3666.

[7] The outstanding example is *Polydor* v. *Harlequin*, [1982] E.C.R. 329, where the Court held that the doctrine of the exhaustion of industrial and commercial property rights, which the Court had deduced from Articles 30 and 36 of the E.E.C. Treaty, did not apply to trade between the E.E.C. and Portugal, despite the fact that the wording of Articles 14 (2) and 23 of the free trade agreement between the E.E.C. and Portugal was virtually the same as the wording of Articles 30 and 36 of the E.E.C. Treaty. The Court said (ibid., p. 349):

'The considerations which led to that interpretation of Articles 30 and 36 of the [E.E.C.] Treaty do not apply in the context of the relations between the Community and Portugal as defined by the [free trade] agreement. It is apparent from an examination of the Agreement that . . . it does not have the same purpose as the E.E.C. Treaty. . . .

'It follows that in the context of the [free trade] Agreement restrictions on trade in goods may be considered to be justified on the ground of the protection of industrial and commercial property in a situation in which their justification would not be possible within the Community.'

See also *Procureur de la République* v. *Bouhelier*, [1979] E.C.R. 3151, 3160, 3164; Plender, *Yearbook of European Law*, 2 (1982), pp. 57, 80–2 and 87–92; id., *Cambridge Law Journal*, 42 (1983), pp. 279, 288–92.

[8] [1982] E.C.R. 3819.

Commission; for instance, the Spanish government had distributed the Commission licences among Spanish fishing vessels.

In 1981 the Court of Justice of the European Communities decided two cases involving Spanish fishermen who had been prosecuted for fishing in France's fishing zone without E.E.C. licences. The fishermen pleaded that the relevant E.E.C. regulations were contrary to the London Fisheries Convention of 1964 and the Geneva Convention on Fishing and Conservation of the Living Resources of the High Seas of 1958, but the Court held that 'the relations established between the Community and Spain' (which included the informal relations established before the signature of the Agreement of 15 April 1980) had 'replaced' or had been 'substituted for' the rules which had previously governed fishing within 200 nautical miles of the coasts of member States. The Court therefore concluded that 'Spanish fishermen may not rely on prior international agreements between France and Spain in order to prevent the application of the . . . regulations adopted by the Community in the event of any incompatibility between the two categories of provisions'.[9]

Four similar cases came before the Court of Justice of the European Communities in 1982, and the Court repeated the rulings which it had given in 1981.[10] But some of the cases involved new points. For instance, an additional charge against the defendant in *Directeur des affaires maritimes du littoral du sud-ouest* v. *Marticorena-Otazo* was that he had violated E.E.C. regulations about the minimum mesh-size of fishing nets. On this point the Court said:

> The validity of those regulations, which apply without distinction to all persons fishing in certain maritime waters under the sovereignty or jurisdiction of the member States, has not been contested by the parties to the proceedings and the Court has not found any factor of such a kind as to affect the validity of those regulations.[11]

A more difficult point in the *Marticorena-Otazo* case arose from the fact that the defendant had been prosecuted for fishing in France's fishing zone on 2 February 1981, at a time when there was no E.E.C. regulation in force concerning the licensing of Spanish fishing vessels; Regulation 3305/80 expired on 31 January 1981, and Regulation 554/81 reintroduced the system of licences only with effect from 4 March 1981. He argued that during the intervening period Spanish fishermen could fish freely and without licences in the fishing zones of E.E.C. member States. The Court of Justice refused to discuss this argument because the French court, which had referred the case to the Court of Justice of the European Communities under Article 177 of the E.E.C. Treaty, had requested the Court of Justice of the European Communities to give a ruling only on the validity of the E.E.C. regulations, and not on the legal effect of the absence of such regulations.[12] However, Mr. Advocate General Capotorti did deal with this argument in his opinion.[13]

On 2 February 1981 the Agreement of 15 April 1980 between the Community and Spain was being provisionally applied, and the defendant argued that this

[9] *Crujeiras Tome* v. *Procureur de la République*, [1981] E.C.R. 2997; *Procureur général* v. *Arbelaiz-Emazabel*, [1981] E.C.R. 2961. See this *Year Book*, 53 (1982), pp. 325–31.

[10] *Directeur des affaires maritimes du littoral du sud-ouest* v. *Marticorena-Otazo*, [1982] E.C.R. 3819; *Directeur des affaires maritimes du littoral du sud-ouest* v. *Campandeguy Sagarzazu*, [1982] E.C.R. 3847; *Arantzamendi-Osa* v. *Procureur de la République*, [1982] E.C.R. 3927; *Administrateur des affaires maritimes, Bayonne* v. *Dorca Marina*, [1982] E.C.R. 3949.

[11] [1982] E.C.R. 3835.   [12] Ibid., pp. 3834–5.   [13] Ibid., pp. 3839–45.

Agreement entitled Spanish fishermen to fish in the fishing zones of E.E.C. member States during the periods when no Community regulation established a system of licences for them. This interpretation of the Agreement of 15 April 1980 was rejected by the Advocate General, who pointed out that Article 3 of the Agreement provided that each party should annually allot a share of the total allowable catch to the fishing vessels of the other party 'after appropriate reciprocal consultations' which were to take place each year; and the reason why no licences were issued to Spanish vessels between 31 January 1981 and 4 March 1981 was that the appropriate consultations between the Community and Spain had not been completed. The Advocate General concluded that the Agreement of 15 April 1980 gave Spanish fishermen no right to fish in the fishing zones of member States 'until there is a positive outcome of the "appropriate reciprocal consultations"' referred to in Article 3.

He added that his interpretation of the Agreement of 15 April 1980 was also supported by 'arguments based on general international law'.

As the Court is aware, the Agreement was concluded after the extension to 200 nautical miles of the fishery zone of the member States in the waters of the Atlantic and in the North Sea (on 1 January 1977) and the similar extension of the Spanish economic zone (with effect from 15 March 1978). The Court is further aware that the Community and Spanish decisions were in accordance with the general trend in the new law of the sea which developed in the 1970s and became clearly apparent when the Third United Nations Conference on the Law of the Sea was held, during which recognition of the economic zone of 200 miles was one of the points on which the States taking part agreed. The preamble to the Agreement between the . . . Community and Spain states that it took into account the work of the conference and affirms that the extension by coastal States of the areas of biological resources falling within their jurisdiction should 'be conducted pursuant to and in accordance with the principles of international law'. The individual clauses of the Agreement must accordingly be interpreted within the framework of those principles.

There is no doubt that the fact that the belt of sea between 12 and 200 miles from the coast falls under the 'jurisdiction' of the coastal State with regard to the exploitation of economic resources, in particular fishing, means that that State is entitled to exclude the fishermen of other countries, and this is incompatible with the alleged right of the latter to obtain access to that belt of sea in the absence of an international agreement authorizing them to do so or of specific permission from the authorities of the coastal State. In substance the rules which have always been applied in the territorial waters of the States today also cover the economic zone (which is properly described as 'exclusive') although solely with regard to the exploitation of the resources of such waters. The Agreement between the Community and Spain accordingly establishes the rules governing fishing in the 'fishing zones falling under the jurisdiction of each party' without drawing a distinction between the territorial waters and the economic zone; and the preamble refers to the exercise of 'sovereign rights for the purpose of exploring, exploiting, conserving and managing' the resources falling within the area 200 miles from the coast and at no point distinguishes between the two belts of sea into which these 200 miles are legally divided.

It is true that the . . . Convention on the Law of the Sea, which resulted from the Third United Nations Conference . . ., does provide that each coastal State must give other States access to the catch exceeding its own harvesting capacity within the limits necessary for the conservation of fishing resources (Article 62 (2)). The same provision however shows that the determination of the total allowable catch and of the harvesting capacity of the coastal State is a matter for that State itself (in this case for the Community) and that in any event access for the fishermen of . . . [other] countries requires an agreement. Furthermore, in the part concerning the procedure for resolving disputes . . . the Convention . . . emphasizes (in Article 297 (3)) the sovereign nature of the rights to the living resources of the economic zone and the consequent discretionary powers of the coastal State for determining the volume of catches, its own harvesting capacity and the allocation of surpluses amongst other States. . . .

The state of general international law ultimately leads to the same conclusion as that which resulted from my analysis of the Agreement on Fisheries between the . . . Community and Spain: in the absence of arrangements for authorizations by the Community foreign fishermen are prohibited from entering [sc. fishing in] the zone which extends 200 miles from the Atlantic coast of the member States. . . .

It is also in the light of general international law and of the Agreement on Fisheries between the Community and Spain that it is necessary to reject the idea of the continued existence of 'historical rights' of Spanish fishermen or of their revival during the periods when there were no Community rules [about licences]. Under the present system of the law of the sea there does not seem to be any possibility of according a special status to persons habitually frequenting certain fishing zones. . . .[14]

This frank recognition of the exclusive character of the fishing zones claimed by the member States of the E.E.C. is to be preferred to the unconvincing attempts by the Court in some other cases[15] to argue that the system of licences for fishing vessels from non-member States was merely a non-discriminatory arrangement for the conservation of fisheries.

Exclusive fishing zones—human rights

Case No. 3. Administrateur des affaires maritimes, Bayonne v. *Dorca Marina and others.*[16] This case, like the previous one, concerned Spanish fishermen who were prosecuted in a French court for fishing in France's fishing zone without an E.E.C. licence. Their main defence was that the E.E.C. regulations forbidding Spanish fishermen to fish in the fishing zones of E.E.C. member States without an E.E.C. licence were contrary to the Geneva Convention of 1958 on Fishing and Conservation of the Living Resources of the High Seas and to the London Fisheries Convention of 1964. This was an argument which the Court of Justice of the European Communities had rejected in 1981,[17] and in the present case the Court rejected it again by simply referring to its 1981 judgment.

But the defendants also submitted new arguments in support of their contention that the relevant E.E.C. regulations were invalid.

They claim first of all that the provisions of those regulations, in so far as they prescribe that Spanish fishermen must hold a fishing licence and do not impose the same requirement for fishing by fishermen of the member States, are contrary to the principles of non-discrimination set out in the various conventions on the protection of human rights, and in particular in Article 14 of the European Convention for the Protection of Human Rights and Fundamental Freedoms.

The Court of Justice of the European Communities rejected this argument in the following words:

Even if it is supposed that such provisions, which guarantee non-discrimination in the enjoyment of the rights and freedoms set out in the convention in which they appear, are applicable to economic activities such as fishing, it is impossible to classify as

---

[14] [1982] E.C.R. 3842–4. See also ibid., pp. 3945–6.

[15] See this *Year Book*, 53 (1982), pp. 325–6 and 329–31, especially p. 330. See also below, pp. 353–4.

[16] [1982] E.C.R. 3949.

[17] *Crujeiras Tome* v. *Procureur de la République*, [1981] E.C.R. 3014; this *Year Book*, 53 (1982), p. 325.

discriminatory a situation in which both Spanish fishermen and fishermen of member States must comply with a system of catch quotas even though the manner of verifying catches is different. Verification by the use of a licensing system is intended to ensure that the catch quotas laid down for the fishing vessels of non-member countries are complied with, since, in the case of such vessels, no checks can be carried out in the adjacent coastal ports as those vessels normally return to their ports of origin to land their catches.[18]

With respect, the Court's approach is unconvincing, since there have been occasions on which Spanish fishing vessels have been totally prohibited from fishing in the fishing zones of member States, without any similar prohibition being placed on fishing vessels from member States.[19] Mr. Advocate General Capotorti dealt with the issue of discrimination more thoroughly in the following words:

Both the provisions of Article 14 of the European Convention on Human Rights and the corresponding provisions of the two . . . [international] covenants on human rights (Article 2 (1) of the Covenant on Civil and Political Rights and Article 2 (2) of the Covenant on Economic, Social and Cultural Rights) require non-discrimination in the enjoyment of the rights recognized by each of these international legal instruments. But no right to fish in the economic zone of any country is recognized by the European Convention or by the covenants.[20] With regard to the principle that all persons are equal before the law and to the right to the equal protection of the law (Article 26 of the . . . [International] Covenant on Civil and Political Rights), it is indeed the case that they guarantee the formal equality of persons with regard to each legal order considered as a whole, but only in order to preclude the legislature from introducing arbitrary discrimination or differences in treatment without any objective justification whatever.

In particular, the prohibition of all discrimination based on national origin does not in any way prevent legislation from creating a large number of differences in the treatment of nationals and foreigners, above all in the field of public law, provided that the basis of rules of that nature is reasonable (as is unquestionably the case as regards the requirement of fishing licences within the framework of the measures for the conservation of the resources of the sea and of the related system of fishing quotas).[21]

A further argument by the defendants was summarized by the Court as follows:

The defendants . . . claim that Article 13 of Regulation 1569/81, which provides for the penalties of withdrawal of fishing licences and the postponement of the granting of new licences which the Commission may impose for failure to comply with the Community rules on fishing, is invalid. That article is said to constitute a breach of the *audi alteram partem* principle since no provision is made for the right of the fishermen in question to be heard before a penalty is imposed.[22] In addition it is contended that the penalties provided for are excessive since they may be extended to all the vessels of a ship-owner who is found to have contravened the rules.

---

[18] [1982] E.C.R. 3959.   [19] See above, pp. 352–3.

[20] Mr. Advocate General Capotorti pointed out later that the relevant E.E.C. regulations did not infringe the right to work or the freedom to engage in economic activity, because they did not prevent the defendants from earning their living by fishing; at the most, the regulations merely restricted the areas in which they might fish: [1982] E.C.R. 3944.

[21] [1982] E.C.R. 3943.

[22] The facts of the case are not stated fully in the report, but the brief summary of the defendants' arguments says that the defendants complained 'that they did not have the opportunity to make known their point of view when the penalties of withdrawal and non-renewal of their licences, which are provided for by Article 13 of Regulation 1569/81, were imposed': [1982] E.C.R. 3956.

Article 13 of Regulation 1569/81 (*Official Journal*, 1981, L 154/1) provides for the withdrawal and non-renewal of licences 'for vessels which have not complied with the obligations provided for in this Regulation'. It says nothing about the *audi alteram partem* principle.

The defendants also argued that Regulation 1569/81 was invalid because it was retroactive. The Court refused to consider these arguments because they 'concern the validity of Regulation 1569/81 in relation to superior principles of law recognized within the Community legal order, a problem which does not come within the context of the preliminary question submitted to the Court'.[23] (The French court, which had referred the case to the Court of Justice of the European Communities under Article 177 of the E.E.C. Treaty, had asked the Court of Justice of the European Communities to rule only on the question of the validity of the relevant regulations 'having regard to prior international obligations'.) Yet the Court's refusal to consider the defendants' arguments was over-hasty, because part of the defendants' arguments was that Article 13 of Regulation 1569/81 violated Articles 6 and 7 of the European Convention on Human Rights, which was certainly a prior international obligation for the member States of the E.E.C. (although probably not for the Community, as distinct from its member States);[24] since the Court had just considered the defendants' argument about Article 14 of the European Convention on Human Rights, it was inconsistent to refuse to consider their arguments about Articles 6 and 7.

Unlike the Court, the Advocate General did consider the defendants' arguments on their merits. He distinguished Article 6 of the European Convention on Human Rights on the grounds that it required a hearing only in judicial proceedings, not in administrative proceedings, and he distinguished the non-retroactivity rule in Article 7 on the grounds that it applied only to criminal law.[25]

On the other hand, it is possible that Article 13 of Regulation 1569/81 violated three principles of *Community* law—*audi alteram partem* (in Community law, this principle applies to administrative proceedings as well as to judicial proceedings), non-retroactivity (in Community law, this principle is not limited to criminal law) and proportionality (which prohibits, among other things, excessive penalties).[26] Astonishingly, Mr. Advocate General Capotorti said nothing at all about the principles of non-retroactivity and proportionality. As regards the *audi alteram partem* principle, he said that it should not be applied in the present context because the Community needed to act swiftly against people guilty of overfishing. This argument may have some merit, but unfortunately he also suggested other, more objectionable, reasons for not applying the *audi alteram partem* principle.[27] For instance, he said that that principle 'is valid in relationships between an administration and its officials but . . . may not be transposed automatically to any relationship between the administration and individuals'[28]—a statement which overlooks the fact that the Court has applied the principle in many cases involving individuals who were not officials.[29] He also said that the individuals upon whom the Commission had imposed penalties could ask the Court to annul those penalties under Article 173 of the E.E.C. Treaty; they would then have a chance to state their case to the Court, and he implied that this made it unnecessary for them to have a right to state their case to the Commission before the Commission

---

[23] [1982] E.C.R. 3959.
[24] This *Year Book*, 52 (1981), p. 42.   [25] [1982] E.C.R. 3943-5.
[26] On these three principles, see Schermers, *Judicial Protection in the European Communities* (3rd edn., 1983), pp. 39-42, 51-7 and 65-7.
[27] [1982] E.C.R. 3943-4.   [28] Ibid., p. 3944.
[29] *Transocean Marine Paint Association* v. *Commission*, [1974] E.C.R. 1063, 1079-80, 1088-9; *Hoffmann-La Roche* v. *Commission*, [1979] E.C.R. 461, 511, 512; Schermers, op. cit. above (n. 26), pp. 39-42.

imposed the penalties. This approach is open to serious objections, which were ably stated by Mr. Advocate General Warner in the *Distillers* case;[30] but Mr. Advocate General Capotorti did not mention the opinion given by Mr. Warner in the *Distillers* case.

Conservation of fisheries—fishing quotas—discrimination on grounds of nationality

Case No. 4. *Anklagemyndigheden* v. *Kerr*.[31] Mr. Kerr, a British fisherman, was prosecuted in a Danish court for catching shrimps off the coast of Greenland in 1978. Denmark permitted shrimps to be caught in the relevant area by fishing vessels from the Faeroe Islands,[32] Greenland,[33] Denmark and France, but not by fishing vessels from other member States of the E.E.C. Mr. Kerr argued that Denmark had violated European Community law by discriminating on grounds of nationality, and the Danish court asked the Court of Justice of the European Communities to give a preliminary ruling under Article 177 of the E.E.C. Treaty on the relevant rules of Community law.

Article 7 of the E.E.C. Treaty provides: 'Within the scope of application of this Treaty, and without prejudice to any special provisions contained therein, any discrimination on grounds of nationality shall be prohibited. . . .'[34] Article 2 (1) of Regulation 101/76 provides:

Rules applied by each member State in respect of fishing in the maritime waters coming under its sovereignty or within its jurisdiction shall not lead to differences in treatment of other member States.

Member States shall ensure in particular equal conditions of access to and use of the fishing grounds situated in the waters referred to in the preceding sub-paragraph for all fishing vessels flying the flag of a member State and registered in Community territory.[35]

The E.E.C. Council of Ministers adopted resolutions in 1976 and 1978 which provided that, if the Council of Ministers could not agree on measures for the conservation of fisheries, member States would be entitled to adopt such measures, subject to certain conditions, one of which was that conservation measures had to be non-discriminatory.

Nobody disputed the competence of the Danish government to fix a total allowable catch for shrimps in waters adjacent to the coast of Greenland, but Mr.

---

[30] [1980] E.C.R. 2229, 2297–8; this *Year Book*, 52 (1981), pp. 359–60.

[31] [1982] E.C.R. 4053.

[32] The Faeroe Islands are under Danish sovereignty, but enjoy extensive self-government and do not form part of the E.E.C.

[33] Greenland is under Danish sovereignty and forms part of the E.E.C. In 1982 Greenland applied to leave the E.E.C.; negotiations arising out of this application are still taking place. See Harhoff, *Common Market Law Review*, 20 (1983), p. 13.

[34] Article 7 is usually applied in conjunction with other provisions of the E.E.C. Treaty, or (as in this case) in conjunction with implementing regulations. But it seems that Article 7 is sufficient, on its own, to create rights for an individual against a member State (*Wilhelm* v. *Bundeskartellamt*, [1969] E.C.R. 1, 15–16; *Sacchi*, [1974] E.C.R. 409, 431; *Boussac* v. *Gerstenmaier*, [1980] E.C.R. 3427; *Oebel*, [1981] E.C.R. 1993, 2007). On the other hand, it is possible that Article 7 does not create rights for one individual against another (this *Year Book*, 47 (1974–5), pp. 432–3), except in the case of an individual who enjoys monopoly powers conferred by the *State* and who discriminates against other individuals on grounds of nationality (*Sacchi*, [1974] E.C.R. 409, 431).

[35] In other words, member States have a right to fish in one another's waters. This rule is subject to certain exceptions laid down by Articles 100, 101 and 103 of the Act of Accession, 1972, but those exceptions are not relevant to the present case.

Kerr (supported by the British government, which intervened in the proceedings) argued that Denmark had acted unlawfully by allocating quotas on a discriminatory basis. The Court of Justice of the European Communities rejected that argument in the following words:

As regards the allocation of the total allowable catch, it must in the first place be borne in mind that the catch quota allocated to the Faeroe Islands was . . . the result of a framework agreement on fisheries signed by the Community on the one hand and by the government of Denmark and the local administration of the Faeroe Islands on the other. . . .

The advantages accorded to the fishermen of the Faeroe Islands were granted in return for the right which was conferred on Community fishermen to catch other species of fish in the maritime waters within the jurisdiction of those islands; the resultant quotas were allocated by the Council amongst certain member States [including the United Kingdom] under the common fisheries policy, in particular to compensate for the loss of catch potential in the waters of non-member countries. . . .

The quantity of shrimps available which was included in the recommended catch-quota was not, after deduction of the share reserved for the Faeroe Islands, sufficient to permit the allocation to each of the member States concerned[36] of a quota capable of being exploited on a profitable basis. In those circumstances, Denmark decided to divide the quota available between only two member States. Accordingly, it allocated the highest quota (15,245 tonnes) to Greenland, where the local population is particularly dependent on fishing in the waters in question, and divided the rest between France (692 tonnes) and Denmark (2,900 tonnes). It complied with the proposed allocation for 1978 which the Commission of the European Communities had submitted to the Council in October 1977. Denmark thus allocated a catch-quota only to member States which had fished for shrimps in the area in question before the end of 1976.

. . .

. . . [T]he Danish government was confronted with the need to adopt a protective measure, which was both effective and workable, in a limited zone of its maritime waters within its direct jurisdiction. In determining that measure, it took account of the proposals made at the time by the Commission for all waters within the jurisdiction of the member States and based on the maintenance of a comprehensive balance between the interests of all the fishermen of all the member States. . . .

Examination of the method applied demonstrates that the Danish authorities allocated the quotas in accordance with objective criteria, taking into account, in the first place, the needs of the coastal population, and secondly, the need to maintain a situation temporarily created in the region in question, even though the fishing zone in question had only recently been discovered and exploited.

In those circumstances, . . . the division of the fishing quota under the measure adopted by the Danish authority cannot be regarded as amounting to discrimination on grounds of nationality contrary to Article 7 of the [E.E.C.] Treaty and to the provisions . . . of Regulation 101/76.

The *dispositif* of the Court's ruling reads as follows:

As long as the Community had not exercised its power to take measures for the conservation of the biological resources of the sea, a management and conservation measure adopted by a member State . . ., which had as its purpose to fix a total catch-quota, allocating it amongst certain member States, cannot be regarded as contrary to the principle prohibiting discrimination, embodied in Article 7 of the E.E.C. Treaty and in . . . Regulation 101/76, if . . . the measure was justified by objective considerations relating to

---

[36] The meaning of 'member States concerned' is unclear, but presumably this term included the United Kingdom, which, although it had never fished for shrimps in the area in question, had applied unsuccessfully for a shrimp quota in 1977.

the protection of the needs of the coastal population concerned and to the maintenance of a situation temporarily created in the area in question.

The fact that the *dispositif* does not mention certain points which were mentioned earlier in the judgment raises some doubts about the exact scope of the Court's ruling.

First, the *dispositif* says nothing about the agreement with the Faeroe Islands. This is understandable when one remembers that the Community rule against discrimination on grounds of nationality applies only between nationals of member States; discrimination in favour of nationals of a non-member State[37] may sometimes violate other rules of Community law,[38] but it can never violate the Community rule against discrimination on grounds of nationality. Since the Danish court had asked the Court of Justice of the European Communities to interpret only the latter rule, it is not surprising that the *dispositif* of the Court's ruling said nothing about a situation which was obviously not covered by the rule in question.

Secondly, the *dispositif* does not mention the fact that the total allowable catch was too small 'to permit the allocation to each of the member States concerned of a quota capable of being exploited on a profitable basis'. This raises the question whether it is always permissible to grant preferential treatment to local fishermen who are dependent on local fisheries, and to other member States which have fished there in the past, or whether such preferential treatment is permissible only if the total allowable catch is too small 'to permit the allocation to each of the member States concerned of a quota capable of being exploited on a profitable basis'. The fact that the *dispositif* does not mention the smallness of the total allowable catch indicates that such preferential treatment is always permissible. It is possible, however, that the *extent* to which such preferential treatment may be granted will vary according to the size of the total allowable catch;[39] this is a point which the judgment does not make clear.

Thirdly, the *dispositif* does not mention the fact that Denmark was acting in accordance with proposals made by the Commission. Does this mean that that fact was not crucial to an appraisal of the legality of Denmark's behaviour? The answer is probably yes, because it is hard to see how unlawful discrimination can become lawful simply because it has been proposed by the Commission.[40] The Court's

---

[37] The Faeroe Islands are not an independent State, but, since they are not part of the E.E.C., their inhabitants can be equated with nationals of a non-member State for the purposes of the present argument.

[38] Under the Hague Resolution adopted by the E.E.C. Council of Ministers in 1976, vessels from non-member States may fish in the fishing zones of member States only if they are covered by treaties between the E.E.C. and the non-member State in question or by licences issued by the Commission of the European Communities. Denmark would thus have been violating the Hague Resolution if she had granted a catch-quota to the Faeroe Islands in the absence of a treaty between the Faeroe Islands and the E.E.C., or in the absence of licences issued by the Commission of the European Communities.

[39] If the total allowable catch had been larger, would Denmark have been under an obligation to make *slight* reductions in the *large* quotas granted to Greenland, Denmark and France, in order to grant *small* quotas to other member States such as the United Kingdom?

[40] The Commission's proposals (which were not adopted by the Council of Ministers, because of dissension among the member States) were concerned with *all* fishing zones in the Community. It was therefore possible for the Commission to balance losses by one member State in one area against gains by that member State in another area, thus achieving a fair balance. But a decision by one member State to apply the Commission's proposals in only one area will not necessarily produce a fair balance; there is no guarantee that application by one member State in one area will be accompanied by

reference, earlier in the judgment, to the fact that Denmark was acting in accordance with proposals made by the Commission should therefore be treated as an *obiter dictum*, not as part of the *ratio decidendi*.

The facts of the case occurred in 1978, i.e. at a time when competence over conservation of fisheries was shared between the Community and its member States. This point was emphasized several times in the Court's judgment. Under Article 102 of the Act of Accession,[41] the Community was supposed to have exclusive competence over the conservation of fisheries after the end of 1978, which might suggest at first sight that the principles laid down in the *Kerr* case are no longer applicable. However, the Council of Ministers was unable to agree on measures for the conservation of fisheries by the deadline fixed in Article 102, and the Court of Justice of the European Communities held that in these circumstances national measures adopted before the end of 1978 remained in force after the end of 1978; after 1978, national authorities had no power to adopt new rules on conservation, but they did have a power to make limited amendments (with the approval of the Commission) to existing national rules on conservation, in order to adapt them to changing needs.[42] It seems, therefore, that the principles laid down in the *Kerr* case continued to apply after the end of 1978.

In 1983 the E.E.C. adopted comprehensive rules for the conservation of fisheries, which replaced pre-existing national measures. However, Article 18 (2) of Regulation 171/83 provides: 'Where the conservation of certain species or fishing grounds is seriously threatened and where any delay would result in damage which would be difficult to repair, the coastal State may take appropriate *non-discriminatory* conservation measures in respect of the waters under its jurisdiction' (such national measures may be subsequently cancelled or amended by the Commission or the Council).[43] It seems reasonable to conclude that the principles laid down in the *Kerr* case will apply to national measures adopted under Article 18 (2) of the Regulation 171/83.

MICHAEL AKEHURST

application by other member States in other areas (although in fact all the member States except the United Kingdom were applying the Commission's proposals in 1978).

[41] As interpreted in *Firma J. van Dam en Zonen*, [1979] E.C.R. 2345. The Act of Accession is annexed to the Treaty of Accession, whereby the United Kingdom, Denmark and Ireland joined the Communities in 1973.

[42] *Commission of the European Communities* v. *United Kingdom*, [1981] E.C.R. 1045; this *Year Book*, 53 (1982), p. 331.

[43] *Official Journal*, 1983, L 24/14 (italics added).

UNITED KINGDOM MATERIALS ON INTERNATIONAL LAW 1983*

Edited by GEOFFREY MARSTON[1]

[*Editorial note*: The Editor has noted that discrepancies exist between the column references to some items from Parliamentary Debates given in the previous issues of UKMIL and the column references given to the same items in the bound volumes of the Parliamentary Debates. This is likely to have occurred in particular with items appearing in the Written Answers part of the volumes of House of Commons Debates. UKMIL is necessarily prepared from the daily and weekly editions of the Parliamentary Debates and it appears that the printers, largely for technical reasons, have a practice of revising the layout when preparing the text for the bound volumes, which are issued up to nine months later. This leads in some volumes to a renumbering of the columns. In the present issue of UKMIL it has been possible to cite the column numbers in the bound, definitive, volumes of the Parliamentary Debates.]

INDEX[2]

  * Editorial arrangement and comments © Geoffrey Marston, 1984. Copyright in the materials cited is in the original copyright holders.
  [1] LL.M., Ph.D. (Lond.): Lecturer in Law, University of Cambridge; Fellow of Sidney Sussex College. The assistance of Mr. A. D. Watts, Deputy Legal Adviser, and Mr. C. A. Whomersley, Assistant Legal Adviser, Foreign and Commonwealth Office, is gratefully acknowledged.
  [2] Based on the *Model Plan for the Classification of Documents concerning State Practice in the field of Public International Law* adopted by the Committee of Ministers of the Council of Europe in Resolution (68) 17 of 28 June 1968.

Abbreviations

H.C. Debs.	*Hansard*, House of Commons Debates (6th series)
H.L. Debs.	*Hansard*, House of Lords Debates
Cmnd.	Command Paper (5th series)
UKMIL	*United Kingdom Materials on International Law*

Part One: II. A. *International law in general—relationship between international law and municipal law—in general*

In the course of a speech to the Security Council of the United Nations on the subject of the destruction by the Soviet Union of a Korean commercial aircraft, the United Kingdom Permanent Representative, Sir John Thomson, stated on 12 September 1983:

> . . . the Soviet defence has been of a narrow and legalistic kind, based upon the provisions of Soviet internal legislation and on claims that that legislation is in accordance with international regulations. The provisions of the Soviet internal legislation in question have not been quoted to us. Whatever their content may be, there is a basic principle of international law that a State may not invoke the provisions of its internal law in order to evade or avoid its international obligations, least of all international obligations of as fundamental a character as have been an issue in the present debate.

(S/PV. 2476, p. 57; a statement along similar lines was made by the United Kingdom representative to the Council of the International Civil Aviation Authority on 15 September 1983.)

Part One: II. C. *International law in general—relationship between international law and municipal law—municipal remedies for violations of international law*

(See Part Four: VI. and Part Eight: II. D., below (Nuclear Materials (Offences) Bill).)

In reply to the question whether Her Majesty's Government will consider limiting the scope of the European Convention on Human Rights, the Parliamentary Under-Secretary of State, Home Office, wrote:

> The European Convention on Human Rights is a multilateral treaty ratified by the United Kingdom and other member states of the Council of Europe. The Government have no plans to seek any renegotiation of its terms. The convention, as such, forms no part of our domestic law; our acceptance of its obligations reflects our conviction that our law already guarantees the fundamental rights and freedoms which are the subject of the convention. We can see no ground for limiting the scope of those in any way.

(H.C. Debs., vol. 42, Written Answers, cols. *297–8*: 11 May 1983.)

In moving the Second Reading in the House of Lords of the Repatriation of Prisoners Bill, the Parliamentary Under-Secretary of State, Home Office, Lord Elton, referred to the Council of Europe Convention on the Transfer of Sentenced Persons. He continued:

> On 29th July this year my right honourable friend the Home Secretary announced the United Kingdom Government's intention to sign the Council of Europe Convention in August and to introduce general enabling legislation as soon as possible. The convention was accordingly signed on behalf of the United Kingdom on 25th August and the present Bill was duly introduced in your

Lordships' House on 24th November. The convention has now been signed by 14 of the 21 Council of Europe states in addition to Canada and the United States of America, but no state has yet ratified it. It will come into force three months after it has been ratified by three Council of Europe states.

Those are the antecedents of the Bill. Before I turn to its provisions I think I should explain our general approach to this legislation. First, the Bill does not in itself have the effect of implementing the Council of Europe Convention. It provides general enabling powers, so that the Government will be able in due course not only to ratify this convention, but also to conclude such other agreements as may be necessary to effect the transfer of prisoners. Secondly, it follows from this that we have had to strike a balance between the requirements we have judged necessary to put on the face of the Bill and those which we think are best left to the discretion of the Secretary of State in dealing with the circumstances of the particular case. This is a difficult balance to strike, and I hope your Lordships will feel that we have got it about right.

In considering that issue, I hope your Lordships will realise that the Bill is designed not only to enable us to accede to the convention. It will also provide the provisions under which we shall be able to come to terms with individual states which do not wish to accede to the convention and whose laws and traditions may be very different from ours but from whose prisons we wish nevertheless to retrieve a British citizen to serve his term in the United Kingdom.

(H.L. Debs, vol. 446, col. 752: 21 December 1983.)

Part Two: I. *Sources of international law—treaties*

(See also Part Two: X., Part Two: XI. and Part Six: II. B., below.)

In reply to the question what United Kingdom obligations exist under the Nootka Sound convention in relation to former Spanish colonies, the Minister of State, Foreign and Commonwealth Office, wrote:

Under article 6 of the Nootka Sound convention 1790, Britain and Spain agreed not to make any settlement on the eastern or western coasts of South America, or on the adjacent islands to the south, already held by Spain. However, the convention was terminated in 1795 as a result of the war between Britain and Spain. In 1811 Spain evacuated the Falkland Islands and abandoned them, so that, although the convention was revived in 1814, it could not then be taken to apply to the Falkland Islands.

(H.C. Debs., vol. 235, Written Answers, col. 275: 7 February 1983.)

In the course of a debate on the subject of sporting links with South Africa, the Parliamentary Under-Secretary of State for the Environment, Mr. Neil Macfarlane, stated of the so-called 'Gleneagles Agreement':

The paper which has prompted this debate is called the 1977 Commonwealth Statement on Apartheid in Sport. As hon. Members know, its popular name derives from the fact that it was drafted by Commonwealth Heads of Government during their weekend retreat at a Scottish hotel and golf complex in 1977. . . .

The statement is not a formal agreement. There are no signatories and it is not legally binding. It is a policy statement agreed by Commonwealth leaders giving expression to the deep abhorrence of apartheid, particularly in sport, shared by the Commonwealth . . .

(H.C. Debs., vol. 36, col. 1119: 9 February 1983; see also H.C. Debs., vol. 37, col. 927: 23 February 1983.)

In reply to the question whether Her Majesty's Government recognizes any residual obligations to the Kurds or Armenians as a signatory of the treaty of Sevres in 1920, the Minister of State, Foreign and Commonwealth Office, wrote:

The treaty of Sevres of 1920 never entered into force.

(H.C. Debs., vol. 37, Written Answers, col. *277*: 18 February 1983.)

In reply to a question, the Minister of State, Foreign and Commonwealth Office, wrote:

No treaties have been signed since 1970 between the Soviet Union and the Western Alliance as such. There is cause for concern over the Soviet Union's fulfilment of certain clauses of the Helsinki Final Act, which was signed in 1975 by 35 countries, including the Soviet Union and all NATO members. However, this is not a treaty and is not legally binding.

(H.L. Debs., vol. 439, col. 1130: 1 March 1983.)

Part Two: II. *Sources of international law—custom*

(See Part Three: I. D. 2. (statement of 7 April 1983), below.)

Part Two: VIII. *Sources of international law—restatement by formal processes of codification and progressive development*

(See Part Three: I. D. 2. (statement of 7 April 1983), Part Five: VIII. A. (statement of 15 November 1983) and Part Five: VIII. B. (statement of 17 November 1982), below.)

Part Two X. *Sources of international law—acquisition and loss of rights*

(See also Part Eight: II. A. (material on Falkland Islands), below.)

The Foreign and Commonwealth Office submitted to the Foreign Affairs Committee of the House of Commons a memorandum, dated 17 December 1982, on the subject of the Falkland Islands. The memorandum, which took the form of replies to questions posed by the Committee, read in part as follows:

Question 15

When was the argument of prescription first advanced?

Prescription is a well-recognised concept in international law, deriving initially from principles of Roman law. There has been no occasion, comparable to that of the making of the unilateral Application to the ICJ concerning the Dependencies, when this or other detailed legal arguments have been formally advanced by HMG in relation to the Falkland Islands.

Question 16

What distinction in international law is there between prescription and acquisitive prescription?

'Prescription' in international law is a means of acquiring title to territory, other than territory which is *terra nullius*, by means of long continued possession. Writers on international law tend to draw a distinction between 'acquisitive prescription' and 'extinctive prescription'. Title by 'acquisitive prescription' arises out of long-continued possession where no original source of title can be shown to exist or where possession in the first instance is in the face of an adverse title and the legitimate proprietor has taken no measures to assert his right or has been unable to do so. 'Extinctive prescription' has really little to do with title; it is a concept analogous to that of limitation in domestic law and connotes essentially that failure to present a claim within a reasonable time may result in the loss of competence to enforce it.

(*Parliamentary Papers*, 1982–3, House of Commons, Paper 31–vi, pp. 149–50.)

In the course of his evidence to the Committee on 17 January 1983, Sir Ian Sinclair, Legal Adviser, Foreign and Commonwealth Office, was asked the following question:

Much of the British case seems to be based on the rights of prescription. It seems to be a well established principle of international law that full rights of prescription are only achieved with the acquiescence of the other claimants. Now according to your own answer to question No. 11 in your memorandum [see below, p. 465] you admit that the Argentine Government made seven formal protests in the last century starting way back in 1833 and then repeatedly this century have also made protests. It seems therefore that Argentina has demonstrated a distinct lack of acquiescence. Does that not weaken Britain's case?

Sir Ian Sinclair replied:

Could I take that in two parts? First of all, as a matter of general principle, I do not think we would entirely accept that prescription cannot be operative unless there is acquiescence by the other party to the dispute. In the response which we gave to question 16 posed by the Committee, we said—and here in fact we quoted from [*Note by Witness*: 'Relied upon' would be more accurate than 'quoted from'. The actual passage is taken almost verbatim from Hall, *A Treatise on International Law*, 8th edn. (1924), p. 143, which is cited with approval by Jennings.] a book entitled 'The Acquisition of Territory in International Law' by Sir Robert Jennings, who is now the British judge in the International Court: 'Title by acquisitive prescription arises out of long continued possession where no original source of title can be shown to exist or where possession in the first instance is in the face of an adverse title and the legitimate proprietor has taken no measures to assert his right or has been unable to do so.' You may say the latter part of that has some relevance to the question of acquiescence, and I do not dispute that, but what I would point out (and here again I refer to the response we gave to question 11 [see below, p. 465] is that there were two periods, one of 35 years between 1849 and 1884, and another of 20 years between 1888 and 1908, when Argentina did not protest our presence on the Falkland Islands. Also I would recall that Professor Fawcett pointed out in earlier evidence that mere protest in itself may not be sufficient to prevent the accrual of title by prescription.

(Ibid., pp. 164–5.)

Earlier in his evidence, Sir Ian Sinclair was asked why the United Kingdom, which had recognized the United Provinces as a sovereign, independent entity in 1823, had not thereby recognized its legal right to perform state activities in the Falkland Islands at that time. He replied:

. . . one must recall that any evidence of Buenos Aires activity in relation to the Falklands prior to 1823 is extremely sketchy. There was, of course, and this must be conceded, the visit by Col Jewett in 1820. You must remember the historical circumstances of the time. At that time we had no diplomatic representation in Buenos Aires because we did not recognise the newly-emergent administration there, so the fact that Col Jewett visited was certainly not, as far as we are aware, known to us at the time. So, the question as to why we did not protest is explicable on the basis that we simply had no knowledge of that. Oddly enough, as I think we have said in the written responses we have given to the Committee, Col Jewett's ship eventually went to the United States and was condemned as a pirate ship. Certainly prior to 1826 there was little or no activity in relation to the Islands on the part of the Buenos Aires administration at the time, nothing that we would regard as being anything in the form of state activity. The treaty of friendship which we concluded in 1825 does not contain any reference to the Falkland Islands but again that is perfectly explicable. It was a general treaty of friendship and, I think, commerce.

(Ibid., pp. 162–3.)

Sir Ian later observed that he knew of no treaty concluded with Spain whereby the United Kingdom acknowledged title to the Falkland Islands. (Ibid., p. 166.)

In reply to the suggestion that the present situation was not a case of acquisitive prescription since there was a good source of title prior to 1833 in the title of Spain and the United Provinces, Sir Ian Sinclair stated:

I would certainly dispute both. I dispute the title of Spain on the grounds that even if one concedes what is internationally called effective occupation of the Islands between 1774 and 1811, certainly without question they abandoned the Islands in 1811 and they were then uninhabited and unoccupied except for occasional visits from whalers and sealers for a considerable period until the mid-1820s.

(Ibid., pp. 165–6.)

Sir Ian Sinclair was then asked how long a territory has to be abandoned before another State can claim it. He replied:

I do not think there is any particular rule of thumb one can lay down in relation to abandonment of territory. It will depend on an analysis of all the relevant circumstances—whether there is an intention to abandon and whether even if there is no intention to abandon there is abandonment for a certain period of time. One cannot really quantify what the period of time might be.

(Ibid.)

A member of the Committee put the following question to Sir Ian Sinclair:

The second point you made is where possession in the first instance is 'in the face of an adverse title and the legitimate proprietor has taken no measures to assert his right or has been unable to do so'. As I understand it, looking at your memorandum, in Section 2, the United Provinces had taken steps to assert their right. They sent soldiers, a schooner of war and a Commander—does this not constitute a step to assert that right?

He replied:

Of course there is what is, and will no doubt continue to be, a disputed question, the extent to which there has been state activity by and on behalf of the United Provinces during the period between 1820 and 1831, 1832 and 1833. The facts are in dispute. We, for our part, take the view that the extent of activity by the United Provinces in relation to the Falkland Islands was insufficient to confer title. You will recall that in 1829 we did vigorously protest as soon as the Government in Buenos Aires issued a decree purporting to appoint a civil and political governor in the Islands. We repeated that protest in 1832.

(Ibid., p. 166.)

The member then asked:

But if it is insufficient to secure a title for the United Provinces to send soldiers, a naval vessel and a naval commander, if it is insufficient for them to establish their title, how is it sufficient for the British by doing a similar thing to establish their title?

Sir Ian replied:

We have been there for 150 years. Certainly that is a consideration which would have to be taken into account in trying to assess the relative weights of the claims.

(Ibid.)

Another member of the Committee took up the last answer:

Just going back to your reply . . . Sir Ian, about the 150 years being the basis of our claim, in your interesting answer to our question 9 [see below, p. 464] you make it clear (and I do not think there is any doubt about it) that the United Provinces forces on the Falklands commanded by Senor Dineda did not resist and that he was, as you say, severely admonished when he got back to Buenos Aires. I take it from what you said that even if he had done so, in the way in which our Marines did recently, or even in some token form or semi-token form by firing or whatever, that would make no difference whatsoever to our case for tenure and it does not rest on the fact that they went quietly?

In reply, Sir Ian Sinclair stated:

No, it does not rest on that fact. That fact reinforces the argument we would produce no doubt at the time, but the point remains, as Professor Fawcett pointed out in the evidence which he gave, that there is the principle of intertemporal law which states that a juridical fact must be appreciated in the light of the law contemporary with it. That is an exact quotation from the judgment of Judge Huber in the Island of Palmas Arbitration in 1928.

(Ibid., p. 167.)

In the course of a debate on the subject of dependent territories, the Minister of State, Foreign and Commonwealth Office, Mr. Cranley Onslow, referred to Gibraltar. He went on to state:

On Wednesday the House was informed by my right hon. Friend the Member for Mid-Oxon (Mr. Hurd) that it is 'quite normal' for ships participating in an exercise such as Springtrain—which is an annual exercise—to visit Gibraltar. Her Majesty's ambassador in Madrid has made that clear to the Spanish Foreign Ministry, and the Spanish Ministry of Defence was informed of the visit before-hand as a matter of courtesy. Given that the Spanish protest was in the form of a statement issued to the public rather than being addressed to us, there was no need, as some hon. Members have suggested, for us to respond.

(H.C. Debs., vol. 40, col. 1100: 15 April 1983.)

Part Two: XI. *Sources of international law*—jus cogens

(See also Part Three: I. A. 2. (statement of 18 October 1983) and Part Eleven: II. A. 1. (statement of 17 November 1982), below.)

In the course of a statement made on 7 April 1983 to the Conference on the Succession of States in respect of State Property, Archives and Debt, held in Vienna, the representative of the United Kingdom, Mr. J. R. Freeland, remarked in respect of the draft Convention on this subject before the Conference:

. . . my delegation cannot accept the references in Articles 14, 26, 28, 29 and 36 of the draft text to the 'principle of permanent sovereignty over wealth and natural resources' and to certain other so-called 'rights'. My delegation does not accept that these 'principles' and 'rights', as so described, have the force of *ius cogens*. Further, we believe that to suggest that bilateral agreements might be in-validated by virtue of these vaguely formed 'principles' and 'rights' would be a very dangerous path to follow, because it could lead to the undermining of stability in international relations and even to the undermining of the rule '*pacta sunt servanda*'.

(Text provided by the Foreign and Commonwealth Office.)

Part Three: I. A. 1. *Subjects of international law—States—international status—sovereignty and independence*

(See also Parts Three: I. A. 2. (statement of 18 October 1983), Three: I. C. 4. (material on Brunei and St. Kitts/Nevis) and Eleven:

II. A. 1. (Convention on Long-Range Transboundary Air Pollution), below.)

In the course of a debate in the House of Lords on the subject of Grenada, the Minister of State, Foreign and Commonwealth Office, Baroness Young, stated:

The House will wish me also to say something about the position of Her Majesty The Queen in relation to Grenada and about the constitutional position of the Governor General. Grenada is a fully independent realm within the Commonwealth and the Queen is Queen of Grenada and as such the Head of State. The Governor General, Sir Paul Scoon, is her representative. I should emphasise that he is neither British himself nor is he in any sense the representative of the British Government. The Governor General would normally act on the advice of Her Majesty's Ministers in Grenada. Although the constitution under which Grenada came to independence in 1973 was suspended at the time of the revolution in 1979, the Queen remained Head of State and the Governor General's position as her representative also remained.

Early last month the People's Revolutionary Government was deposed by the Revolutionary Military Council, which, as far as we are aware, enacted no legislation concerning the Governor General's functions. This left him in office as Her Majesty's representative but, in the absence of the source of advice stipulated by the existing law, in effect in a vacuum. With the disappearance of the Military Council, this vacuum remained. In that situation, the Governor General had to decide what steps it was appropriate for him to take to ensure that Her Majesty's government in Grenada was carried on.

We now know that the Governor General is calling together a group of responsible citizens as an advisory council to assist him in governing the country until such time as it can be restored to normal conditions, and we understand that he is basing this action on Section 57 of the 1973 constitution. We would see no reason to dissent from the Governor General's view that this is a legally proper course for him to take. Indeed, we see this as a responsible action entirely consistent with the authority delegated to him by the Crown.

(H.L. Debs., vol. 444, cols. 440–1: 1 November 1983.)

In the course of a debate held on 2 November 1983 in the Second Committee of the General Assembly on the report of the Economic and Social Council, the United Kingdom representative, Mr. Dun, referred to a statement made to the Committee by the Cuban representative. Mr. Dun went on:

He had tried to make the United Kingdom Government responsible for the safety of Cubans in Grenada, but that showed a complete and perhaps deliberate lack of understanding of the position. Since Grenada's accession to independence, the United Kingdom Government had no responsibility for its internal or external affairs. Moreover, the Governor-General was a Grenadian national and any questions regarding his constitutional status and powers or his authority were internal affairs of Grenada and had nothing whatever to do with the United Kingdom Government. He [i.e. Mr. Dun] also wished to point out that his

Government was represented in Grenada by a diplomatic mission which, like the Cuban ambassador, was accredited to the Governor-General.

(A/C. 2/38/SR. 26, p. 16.)

Part Three: I. A. 2. *Subjects of international law—States—international status—non-intervention and non-use of force*

(See also Part Twelve: II. I. 1., below.)

In reply to a question on the subject of persons sentenced to death in South Africa, the Minister of State, Foreign and Commonwealth Office, wrote in part:

These cases involve South African citizens who were convicted under South African law and we therefore have no formal standing in the matter.

(H.C. Debs., vol. 35, Written Answers, col. *381*: 25 January 1983.)

In reply to a question on the subject of the Political Affairs Committee of the European Assembly, the Prime Minister wrote:

Her Majesty's Government have ensured that our partners are fully aware of our view that the European Parliament has no business to discuss the internal political affairs of a member state.

(H.C. Debs., vol. 38, Written Answers, col. *459*: 10 March 1983.)

In reply to the question whether Her Majesty's Government will make representations to the Indian Government about the arrest of Dr. Jack Prager, due to appear before the courts in West Bengal, the Parliamentary Under-Secretary of State, Foreign and Commonwealth Office, wrote:

No. Such representations would constitute an interference in the judicial proceedings of another state.

(H.C. Debs., vol. 39, Written Answers, col. *43*: 14 March 1983.)

In reply to a question, the Prime Minister wrote:

The United Kingdom has no responsibilities under the Lancaster House agreement in relation to the internal affairs of Zimbabwe, which is of course an independent country. However, as a co-signatory of the Lancaster House agreement we maintain a close interest in developments in Zimbabwe.

(H.C. Debs., vol. 39, Written Answers, col. *280*: 18 March 1983.)

In the course of a debate on the subject of dependent territories, the Minister of State, Foreign and Commonwealth Office, Mr. Cranley Onslow, stated:

The Spanish Government—which is a member of NATO—have consistently ruled out the use of force in connection with their claim to Gibraltar. Furthermore, Spain, as a party to the North Atlantic treaty, is bound by article 1 of the treaty, in which the parties undertake to refrain from the threat or use of force in their international relations.

(H.C. Debs., vol. 40, col. *1100*: 15 April 1983.)

In reply to a question, the Minister of State, Foreign and Commonwealth Office, wrote:

The United Kingdom has not signed any bilateral non-aggression treaties since signing the United Nations charter in 1945. The principle of non-aggression is one of the fundamental principles of the United Nations charter. All members of the United Nations are under an obligation to settle international disputes by peaceful means and to refrain from acts of aggression.

(H.C. Debs., vol. 42, Written Answers, col. *30*: 3 May 1983.)

In reply to a question, the Secretary of State for Foreign and Commonwealth Affairs, Mr. Francis Pym, stated orally:

The United Kingdom itself gave an assurance in [1978] that we would not use nuclear weapons against non-nuclear weapon states which are parties to the non-proliferation treaty or a similar international agreement except if they attack us, our forces, our dependent territories or our allies in association or alliance with a nuclear weapon state.

Mr. Pym later observed:

I remind the hon. Gentleman of the clear declaration that was made by NATO, and reaffirmed as recently as last summer, that the Alliance would not use any weapons, nuclear or conventional, unless attacked. That is the most forthcoming statement of its kind that has been made.

(H.C. Debs., vol. 42, cols. 777-8: 11 May 1983.)

In reply to a question about the detention in Turkey of two British subjects on charges of photography in a military zone, the Minister of State, Foreign and Commonwealth Office, wrote in part:

From first being notified of the arrest of Mr. Albrecht and Mr. Buisson both the Embassy in Ankara and the Consulate-General in Istanbul have done everything possible to expedite the legal proceedings and in the meantime to ensure the comfort of the two men. However, Her Majesty's Government cannot intervene in the legal proceedings of another sovereign state.

(H.L. Debs., vol. 443, col. 968: 14 July 1983; see also H.C. Debs., vol. 46, Written Answers, col. *172*: 20 July 1983.)

In reply to a question, the Secretary of State for Foreign and Commonwealth Affairs, Sir Geoffrey Howe, stated:

We shall continue to take suitable opportunities to remind members of the United Nations, including Argentina, that the threat or use of force to settle international disputes is forbidden under the United Nations charter.

(H.C. Debs., vol. 46, col. 368: 20 July 1983.)

In a statement delivered on 18 October 1983 to the Sixth Committee of the General Assembly in discussing the report of the United Nations Special Committee on enhancing the effectiveness of the principle of non-use of force in international relations, the United Kingdom representative, Mr. F. Berman, observed:

The prohibition on the threat or use of force established by the United Nations Charter is a principle of fundamental importance in international law and in our present system of international relations. It is of such fundamental importance as to justify re-stating yet again what the status of this principle is, what it means and the dangers of undermining it.

In the first place, the prevention and removal of threats to the peace and the suppression of acts of aggression or other breaches of the peace is established at the very head of the Charter, in paragraph 1 of Article 1, as one of the basic purposes of the United Nations. Quite understandably, within the context of the same paragraph, it is bracketed together with the peaceful adjustment or settlement of international disputes or situations in conformity with the principles of justice and international law. The essential complement to that statement of the purposes of the Organisation is to be found in Article 2. Article 2 obliges both the Organisation and its members, in pursuit of the purposes stated in Article 1, to act in accordance with a series of principles. Having enunciated the principle of sovereign equality, Article 2 goes on immediately to lay down the principle of the good-faith fulfilment of Charter obligations. In other words, the Charter goes beyond the normal and inevitable rule of international law that obligations assumed under a Treaty must be performed in good faith—*pacta sunt servanda*. It elevates the fulfilment in good faith of Charter obligations into a fundamental principle of the functioning of the Organisation. The Charter is of course replete with obligations undertaken by the Member States on entry into membership. But the succeeding paragraphs of Article 2 elevate certain of them into a status of their own, as Principles of the United Nations. It is surely not without significance that the prior place is given, in paragraph 3 of Article 2, to the obligation laid on all members to 'settle their international disputes by peaceful means in such a manner that international peace and security, and justice, are not endangered'. Immediately following that is paragraph 4 according to which all members 'shall refrain in their international relations from the threat or use of force against the territorial integrity or political independence of any State or in any other manner inconsistent with the purposes of the United Nations'. That is the system created, with deliberate care, by Articles 1 and 2 of the Charter. The capstone to this system is provided by Article 103, which lays down that, in the event of a conflict between the obligations of members under the Charter and their obligations under any other international agreement, their Charter obligations shall prevail. If that last provision applies (as on its wording it clearly does) to *all* obligations under the Charter, how strongly must it apply to obligations which are enunciated as being 'Principles of the United Nations'? This is the basis on which many commentators have stated that the Charter prohibition on the threat or use of force is a rule of *ius cogens*. Clearly, it would qualify to be treated as such for the purposes of Article 53 of the Vienna Convention on the Law of Treaties. In other words, any Treaty arrangement which purported to permit or to provide for the use of force incompatible with the Charter would be void.

At the end of that recital, there can be no doubt of any kind as to the status of the principle of the non-use of force. Given the crystal clarity of the words of the Charter, is there any doubt about its meaning? My delegation's answer would be 'no'. For States which are genuinely seeking to fulfil in good faith their Charter obligations, there should be no difficulty in understanding what the Charter prohibition means or how they should set about applying it in particular cases. There is, however, the argument, which was eloquently advanced by the distinguished Representative of Yugoslavia amongst others, that the United Nations has benefited greatly by the elaboration, in declarations of one kind or another, of basic Charter principles. That may well be true in cases where Charter obligations are phrased in a manner that might be obscure or where circumstances in international society have changed to such an extent since the Charter was drafted that it becomes necessary to make an effort to reinterpret or clarify existing Charter obligations in such a way as to facilitate their application in concrete cases. Is anything of the sort necessary in the case of the non-use of force principle? In that regard, the world has not changed. The increase in the number of States and the membership of this Organisation has not altered in any way the importance of preserving their independence and territorial integrity or the right of their peoples to determine their own political, social and economic systems free from outside interference. The threat or use of force remains what it has always been since the founding of our Organisation.

It is of course to be noted that the Declaration on Principles of International Law Concerning Friendly Relations and Cooperation among States in accordance with the Charter of the United Nations contains a principle dealing with the obligation to refrain from the threat or use of force. Its 13 paragraphs set out to interpret existing Charter obligations and to draw some conclusions from them. That of course was a document whose status was carefully negotiated and it was drafted and eventually adopted by the General Assembly by consensus. It is often cited as having considerable authority in the practice of our Organisation. Do we need anything more? There is an onus on those who say that the principle of the non-use of force requires further elaboration, to show that we do need something more. This onus has not been discharged.

Mr. Berman later stated:

The danger of undermining the Charter prohibition on the threat or use of force is two-fold. Both aspects have been dealt with by numerous previous speakers in the debate but I would like to touch on them again myself, because of their real importance. In the first place, the very suggestion that there is a need for a new 'world treaty' necessarily carries the implication that there is something unsatisfactory or inadequate about the UN Charter. However ingenious the arguments the proponents of the 'world Treaty' may advance, they cannot get round this fundamental point. Why do we need a new treaty prohibition if the Charter itself imposes a fundamental prohibition on the threat or use of force, and if we are all prepared to recognise and respect this in our international conduct? Of course we have heard the argument that elaboration of Charter principles has taken place before and that treaties have been concluded which base themselves on Charter provisions. The international Covenants on Human Rights are a good example. Such a case goes back to Charter provisions which specifically require that the Organisation should develop programmes of action in this area. But is there any case in which we have set out to re-negotiate by treaty one of the basic principles of the Organisation laid down in Article 2? I say flatly that there cannot be any warrant for doing that now or in the future, and that there is no comparable case in the practice of the Organisation in the past.

To make this point is not to make a purely formalistic argument or a debating point. What stares us in the face is that, as soon as we begin to negotiate a new treaty on this basic Charter principle, we shall find ourselves grappling, not with re-enacting the existing prohibition on the threat or use of force, but with a whole series of exceptions or alleged exceptions or claimed exceptions to that prohibition. This danger should be our main preoccupation. In this context, we cannot ignore the fact that the proposal for a 'world treaty' was and remains the initiative of the Soviet Union. It continues to be the Soviet Union and its military allies who urge the idea of a world treaty, although this idea is clearly not supported by a majority of the membership. We cannot afford to ignore in this context that the Soviet Union has been guilty of numerous uses of force both before the present initiative was launched in 1977 and since. The Soviet Union's attempts to advance the doctrine of limited sovereignty, which would authorise intervention by armed force in the affairs of its neighbours, is well known. Equally well known is the persistent attempt to gain international respectability for that pernicious doctrine. We are all of us too well aware of the use made of the doctrine in practice, both in terms of the actual deployment of Soviet armed forces to other countries and in terms of the maintenance of the threat to do so as a means of coercing the policies of the Soviet Union's neighbours. We continue to be painfully aware of the effective extension of this doctrine even to a Non-Aligned country, Afghanistan, which has been roundly condemned by the United Nations, but with apparently no effect on the policies of the Soviet Union. Now, how are we to reconcile this Soviet behaviour with the proposal for a new world treaty? Are we to assume that the Soviet Union would like to change its ways, but needs the cover of a new treaty, over and above the UN Charter, in order to do so? This seems hardly credible from a State which has been and continues to be an outright opponent of Charter amendment. Perhaps we should conclude therefore that the Soviet Union would treat the negotiation of a new world treaty as a golden opportunity to introduce escape clauses so as to validate retrospectively Soviet intervention in Afghanistan and elsewhere. Or are we simply to assume that the Soviet Union would ignore the provisions of any future document if it conflicted with the Brezhnev doctrine? There are many questions here which need an answer but the answer can only come from the Soviet Union.

(Text provided by the Foreign and Commonwealth Office; see also A/C. 6/38/SR. 18, pp. 4–6.)

In the course of a debate in the General Assembly on the subject of the Falkland Islands, the United Kingdom Permanent Representative, Sir John Thomson, stated on 15 November 1983:

. . . I cannot complete my speech without some reference to those parts of the Charter on which we had to rely when the Falkland Islands were invaded only 18 months ago. That invasion took place in flagrant violation of Article 2, subparagraphs 3 and 4, of the Charter. While we were trying to settle the dispute by peaceful means the other side not only threatened but used force in a manner inconsistent with the Purposes of the United Nations. We cannot forget that surprise attack, nor that it proceeded in defiance of a mandatory Security Council resolution passed under Chapter VII.

(A/38/PV. 57, p. 58.)

In reply to a question on the subject of cruelty to dogs killed for human consumption in Korea, the Minister of State, Foreign and Commonwealth Office, wrote:

This is a matter that falls within the Korean Government's domestic jurisdiction. However, the Korean Government can be in no doubt about the feeling of many people in this country on this question.

(H.C. Debs., vol. 49, Written Answers, col. *108*; 22 November 1983.)

In reply to a question, the Minister of State, Foreign and Commonwealth Office, wrote:

Our policy on South Africa's relations with its neighbours is consistently expressed wherever appropriate, namely that relations between states should be conducted on the basis of non-violence, non-interference in internal affairs, respect for borders and acceptance of the responsibilities of statehood.

(Ibid., Written Answers, col. *375*: 28 November 1983.)

In reply to a question about certain Turkish nationals imprisoned in Turkey, Mr. Raymond Whitney, Parliamentary Under-Secretary of State, Foreign and Commonwealth Office, said:

. . . appeals have been lodged in these cases and, therefore, they are sub judice. The Government have consistently made clear to the Turkish authorities our concern, and that of the British people, about continuing allegations of violations of human rights. However, it is not normal practice for the Government formally to intervene with the Government of another country on behalf of that country's citizens.

(Ibid., vol. 50, col. 311: 7 December 1983.)

Part Three: I. B. 1. *Subjects of international law—States—recognition—recognition of States*

In reply to a question, the Prime Minister wrote:

We continue to recognise only one Cypriot state: the Republic of Cyprus under the Government of President Kyprianou. Any contacts with the Turkish Cypriot authorities would be on the basis that they do not constitute a legitimate Government.

(Ibid., Written Answers, col. *219*: 8 December 1983.)

Part Three: I. B. 2. *Subjects of international law—States—recognition—recognition of governments*

In reply to the question on what criteria Her Majesty's Government have supported the Democratic Kampuchean Coalition as the United

Nations representative of Kampuchea, the Minister of State, Foreign and Commonwealth Office, wrote:

At last year's General Assembly of the United Nations, the credentials committee, which examines the credentials of all representatives at the General Assembly, recommended acceptance of the credentials of the delegation of the Coalition Government of Democratic Kampuchea. We supported the committee's recommendations, which are made on the basis of technical considerations. In our view the maintenance of the existing representation of Cambodia at the United Nations is in line with our overall objective, which we share with the ASEAN countries and the majority of United Nations members, of bringing about the implementation of the recommendations of the International Conference of Kampuchea-Cambodia. These call for the withdrawal of Vietnamese forces, the establishment of a neutral and independent state and the holding of free elections.

(Ibid., vol. 46, Written Answers, col. *493*: 27 July 1983.)

In the course of a debate on 24 October 1983 on the credentials of representatives to the thirty-eighth session of the General Assembly, the United Kingdom representative, Mr. Margetson, stated in that body:

With regard to the adoption of the report of the Credentials Committee, I should emphasize that the fact that my delegation has raised no formal challenge to the credentials of the delegation of Afghanistan should in no way be taken to imply that the Government of the United Kingdom regards the present régime in Kabul as being a government.

(A/38/PV. 34, p. 63.)

Part Three: I. B. 5. *Subjects of international law—States—recognition— non-recognition*

In reply to a question on the subject of recognition of the Democratic People's Republic of Korea, the Minister of State, Foreign and Commonwealth Office, wrote:

. . . our policy on the recognition of North Korea remained unchanged. That policy is that recognition is inappropriate while the exceptional circumstances in the Korean peninsula persist.

(H.C. Debs., vol. 35, Written Answers, col. *18*: 17 January 1983; see also ibid., cols. *202–3*: 20 January 1983.)

In reply to a question, the Parliamentary Under-Secretary of State, Foreign and Commonwealth Office, wrote:

Successive British Governments have recognised *de facto* the incorporation of Latvia, Estonia and Lithuania into the Soviet Union, but have not recognised this incorporation *de jure*. There has been no change in this policy.

(Ibid., vol. 38, Written Answers, col. *434*: 9 March 1983; see also ibid., vol. 47, Written Answers, col. *85*: 25 October 1983.)

In reply to a question, the Parliamentary Under-Secretary of State, Department of the Environment, Mr. Neil Macfarlane, stated in part:

The visit by the Transkei rugby team was not a visit of a representative team. It could not be because Her Majesty's Government do not recognise Transkei, or any of the South African so-called homelands, as independent.

(Ibid., vol. 39, col. *852*: 23 March 1983.)

In reply to a question, the Minister of State, Foreign and Commonwealth Office, wrote:

In 1940 Her Majesty's Government ceased to recognise any authorities as constituting the Governments of the Baltic states and they still take a similar position. Thus there is no authority which can appoint diplomatic representatives for Latvia, Estonia and Lithuania. Therefore, no persons who did not hold diplomatic rank in the legations of those countries in 1940 can be accorded diplomatic courtesies. But the Government have no intention of recognising *de jure* the incorporation of the Baltic states into the Soviet Union.

(H.L. Debs., vol. 440, col. 1449: 28 March 1983.)

In reply to a question, the Parliamentary Under-Secretary of State, Foreign and Commonwealth Office, wrote:

We do not recognise the 'Turkish Federated State of Cyprus' and therefore have no formal relations with its authorities. The British high commission in Nicosia, nevertheless, has such informal dealings as are necessary with those authorities to try to protect the interests of British nationals, and is continuing to press for outstanding compensation claims to be dealt with expeditiously.

(H.C. Debs., vol. 46, Written Answers, col. *246*: 22 July 1983.)

In reply to the question whether Her Majesty's Government will list those sovereign States whose incorporation into other States has been recognized by it *de facto* but not *de jure*, the Minister of State, Foreign and Commonwealth Office, wrote:

The Government have recognised that the Baltic states of Estonia, Latvia and Lithuania have been incorporated de facto into the Soviet Union, but they have not recognised this de jure. No other examples of the situation to which my hon. Friend refers have occurred at least since the second world war.

(Ibid., vol. 47, Written Answers, col. *384*: 2 November 1983.)

In the course of a debate on the subject of Cyprus, the Government spokesman in the House of Lords, Lord Trefgarne, stated:

. . . after the United Nations debate Mr. Denktash began to threaten to declare an independent Turkish Cypriot state in Northern Cyprus. The British Government took these threats very seriously both in the summer and when they were renewed in the last few weeks. We made it very clear to Mr. Denktash, and to the Turkish Government, that we were opposed to any such move. We believed that it would make a solution to the Cyprus problem more difficult to find. We told Mr. Denktash that a declaration of independence was in the interests neither of

Cyprus as a whole nor of his own community. We told him, and the Turkish Government, quite unequivocally that we would not recognise a purported new state and that a declaration of independence would amount to secession, which would be incompatible with the 1960 treaty arrangements. Most of our major allies agreed with our views and made similar representations.

. . .

The Government have made it clear that we deplore this action by the Turkish Cypriot community, particularly as it came at a time when the Secretary General, at Mr. Denktash's suggestion, was preparing the ground for a summit meeting between the two communities. We will not recognise the new state which they claim to have established.

(H.L. Debs., vol. 444, col. 1314: 16 November 1983.)

Speaking in the Security Council, the United Kingdom Permanent Representative, Sir John Thomson, stated on 18 November 1983:

My Foreign Secretary has said in Parliament that the British Government deplores this action by the Turkish Cypriot community. We recognize only one Cypriot State, the Republic of Cyprus under the Government of President Kyprianou. The Turkish Cypriot action is incompatible with the state of affairs brought about by the Treaties governing the establishment of the Republic of Cyprus. My Government has treaty obligations in this respect which we share with the Governments of Greece and Turkey.

(S/PV. 2500, p. 38.)

In reply to a question, the Parliamentary Under-Secretary of State, Foreign and Commonwealth Office, wrote:

It will remain our practice not to recognise travel documents issued by the Turkish Cypriot authorities, nor to endorse them with entry clearances. When a Turkish Cypriot is granted an entry clearance for admission to the United Kingdom it will continue to be endorsed on a separate declaration of identity issued by the appropriate British representative.

(H.C. Debs., vol. 49, Written Answers, col. 257: 24 November 1983.)

Reporting to the House of Commons on the Commonwealth Heads of Government Meeting in Delhi in November 1983, the Prime Minister, Mrs. Margaret Thatcher, stated:

With regard to Cyprus, Commonwealth leaders fully endorsed United Nations Security Council resolution 541 which deplored the Turkish Cypriot declaration of secession as legally invalid, requested the United Nations Secretary-General to pursue his mission of good offices and called upon the parties to co-operate fully.

(Ibid., vol. 49, col. 989: 1 December 1983.)

In reply to a question, the Minister of State, Foreign and Commonwealth Office, Mr. Richard Luce, stated:

It remains our view that there are no authorities in Cambodia with which we can deal as a Government.

... in 1979 we withdrew recognition from the Pol Pot Government and accepted the recommendations of the United Nations Credentials Committee that it should give credentials to the three main component parts of the resistance coalition. The Government face two alternatives, neither of which is perfect. The alternative to supporting the resistance coalition is supporting the occupation of Cambodia by 150,000 Vietnamese troops. That would be wholly wrong.

(Ibid., vol. 50, col. 305: 7 December 1983.)

In reply to the further question whether Her Majesty's Government normally recognizes Governments which are in *de facto* control, the Minister said:

One criterion that we must take into account is whether a Government have effective control over all the territory of a country. Another factor at the moment, however, is that if the 150,000 Vietnamese troops were not in Cambodia that Government would have virtually no control. I cannot believe that it is right to support the existence of Vietnamese troops in Cambodia.

(Ibid.)

In response to news that a number of British citizens had been charged with theft from the casino at Sun City, Bophuthatswana, a Foreign and Commonwealth Office spokesman in London is reported to have said on 13 December 1983 that the ability of the British consular authorities in Johannesburg to provide protection would be 'severely limited'. The report of his remarks went on:

The United Kingdom, like all other foreign governments except South Africa, does not recognize Bophuthatswana as an independent sovereign state. British officials therefore do not have any dealings with anyone who purports to represent the so-called Government.

(*The Times*, 14 December 1983.)

Part Three: I. C. 4. *Subjects of international law—States—types of States—dependent States and territories*

(See also Part Eight: II. A., Part Nine: IX. (Reciprocal Fisheries Agreement), Part Eleven: II. A. 2., and Part Thirteen: I. D. (item of 1 November 1983), below.)

The Foreign and Commonwealth Office submitted to the Foreign Affairs Committee of the House of Commons a memorandum, dated 17 December 1982, on the subject of the Falkland Islands. The memorandum, which took the form of answers to questions posed by the Committee, read in part as follows:

Question 19

What are the main statutory and other provisions governing the constitution and government of the Falklands?

The main instruments governing the constitution and government of the Falkland Islands are:

The Falkland Islands Letters Patent, 1948–62;

The instructions passed under the Royal Sign Manual and Signet to the Governor and Commander-in-chief of the Colony and Dependencies of 13 December 1948, as amended ('the Royal Instructions');

The Falkland Islands (Legislative Council) Orders in Council, 1948–77;

The Falkland Islands and Dependencies (Interim Administration) Order 1982.

. . .

Question 20

What recent constitutional developments have there been on the Falklands? What has been the history of the franchise there? What are the present franchise qualifications for elections to the Legislative Council?

1. The Falkland Islands and Dependencies (Interim Administration) Order 1982 made provision for the interim administration of the Falkland Islands and Dependencies by the establishment of a Civil Commissioner and a Military Commissioner. Under the Order the Military Commissioner has responsibility for the defence and internal security (with the exception of the police) of the Colony and the Dependencies. The Civil Commissioner is required to consult the Military Commissioner on any matter which falls within the responsibility of the Military Commissioner and accept any advice on such matters tendered by the Military Commissioner. The Order also suspended the office of Governor and Commander-in-Chief and vested the functions of that office in the Civil Commissioner.

2. In 1843, the British Parliament passed an Act establishing a civil government in the Falkland Islands. The first Executive and Legislative Councils were set up in 1845. Members of the Executive Council and Legislative Council were appointed by the Governor until 1949. In 1949 the system was introduced under which four members of the 12-strong Legislative Council could be elected by universal adult suffrage. In 1964, the size of the Council was reduced to eight, half of the members being elected. The present form of the Islands Councils dates from 21 November 1977 when the Falkland Islands (Legislative Council) (Amendment) Order 1977 came into force. The Governor (now the Civil Commissioner) is assisted in government administration by an Executive Council composed of two elected and two *ex officio* members of the Legislative Council and two nominated members. The Legislative Council, composed of two *ex officio* and six elected members, has the power to 'make laws for the peace, order and good government of the territory'. Any member of the Council may introduce a Bill or propose a motion. Legislation is passed by a simple majority. Elections are by universal adult suffrage, Port Stanley being represented by three elected members, East and West Falkland by one each, and one further member representing all country districts. General elections were held in 1981. In 1977 the voting age was lowered from 21 to 18 years.

3. Under the Falklands Islands Legislative Council (Elections) Ordinance 1948, as amended, the franchise is open to British subjects over the age of 18 years who have resided in the relevant electoral area during the 'qualifying period'. This

is defined as 12 months in the case of a person born in the Colony and three years in the case of a person not born there.

. . .

Question 23

What limits are placed and by whom on the Falklands Legislative Council? What powers of taxation have they?

The functions, composition and powers of the Legislative Council are set out in the constitutional instruments referred to above, in particular the Falkland Islands (Legislative Council) Orders in Council, 1948 to 1977. Under those instruments the Civil Commissioner has a general power, with the advice and consent of the Legislative Council, to make laws for the peace, order and good government of the Falkland Islands. This includes power to make laws to raise revenue through taxation. The Secretary of State does have power to disallow any law to which the Civil Commissioner has given his consent but this power is rarely exercised. Furthermore, there is a limited class of laws to which, except in case of urgency the Civil Commissioner may not assent without first obtaining the approval of the Secretary of State. These are set out in Article 16 of the Royal Instructions.

Question 24

Does this structure differ in any way from other dependencies, e.g. Turks and Caicos?

Apart from the Falkland Islands and Dependencies (Interim Administration) Order 1982, described in the answer to Question 20 above, the basic constitutional structure is similar to that of other dependent territories. What differences there are reflect essentially the degree of self-government of the dependent territory concerned.

(*Parliamentary Papers*, 1982–3, House of Commons, Paper 31-vi, pp. 150–2.)

In the course of a further memorandum to the Committee, dated 18 January 1983, the Foreign and Commonwealth Office replied to the question what is the status of the Falklands in relation to the E.E.C. and the Lomé Convention.

The Falkland Islands and Dependencies are associated with the European Community under Part IV of the EEC Treaty which governs relations between the Community and certain dependent territories of Member States. The purpose of association is 'to promote the economic and social development of the countries and territories and to establish close economic relations between them and the Community as a whole'. The association arrangements are currently to be found in an EC Council Decision of 16 December 1980 (known as the OCT Decision) which provides for access for exports from the dependent territories and develop-ment aid from the European Development Fund. The arrangements are very similar to those in the Lomé Convention. However the Falkland Islands are not eligible to accede to the Lomé Convention itself since that is a treaty between sovereign states to which dependent territories cannot be party.

(Ibid., p. 155.)

In reply to a question, the Minister of State, Foreign and Commonwealth Office, wrote:

In accordance with article (4) of the 1966 exchange of notes concerning the availability for defence purposes of the British Indian Ocean Territory (Cmnd. 3231), no charge is made to the United States Government for the use of sites on Diego Garcia.

. . .

No land in Diego Garcia is leased to the United States Government. Immovable structures, installations and buildings for the United States Navy support facility on Diego Garcia may, after consultation with the appropriate administrative authorities of the United Kingdom, be constructed within the specific area shown in the plan in the annex to the 1976 exchange of notes concerning a United States support facility on Diego Garcia (Cmnd. 6413).

(HC. Debs., vol. 40, Written Answers, col. 45: 28 March 1983.)

In reply to a question, the Minister of State, Foreign and Commonwealth Office, wrote:

The remaining British dependent territories are as follows:

Anguilla
Bermuda
British Antarctic Territory
British Virgin Islands
Cayman Islands
Falkland Islands
Falkland Islands Dependencies
Gibraltar
Hong Kong
Montserrat
Pitcairn Group of Islands
St. Helena and Dependencies (Ascension and Tristan da Cunha are
    dependencies of St. Helena)
Turks and Caicos Islands

(Ibid., Written Answers, col. 431: 14 April 1983.)

In the course of a debate on the subject of dependent territories, the Minister of State, Foreign and Commonwealth Office, Mr. Cranley Onslow, said:

. . . the Government are fully committed to the policy followed by successive Governments since 1945 of giving every help and encouragement to those dependent territories that wish to become independent, while not forcing independence on those which do not wish it. . . . The Government's policy is fully in accord with our obligations under the United Nations charter, especially article 73, and wherever independence is feasible we shall continue to try to create the conditions that will make it a realistic and desirable objective.

The converse of that is that, wherever independence appears not to be feasible, or where local governments make it clear that they do not wish their territories to become independent, we are willing to continue to bear the full duties and responsibilities that accompany sovereignty. However, ultimately, the Government of the day and Parliament must be responsible for taking decisions on our dependent territories. We cannot allow the United Nations to impose a certain international status on people who do not wish it. We have sometimes had to dissociate ourselves from views expressed by the United Nations special decolonisation committee or the General Assembly, but we have no reason to be defensive about the way in which successive Governments have carried out their responsibilities, and about one third of the member states of the United Nations have reached independence as a result of the way in which Britain has discharged its obligations. That should be put on record today, just as I am glad to put it on record that we shall continue, wherever possible, to act in the same spirit towards our remaining territories, assisting them in a manner appropriate to their circumstances.

(Ibid., cols. 1098–9: 15 April 1983.)

Mr. Onslow then remarked:

The motion and speech of my hon. Friend suggested that in some cases dependent territories might be integrated into the United Kingdom. The idea is not new, and was considered in the 1950s in relation to Malta and, since then, in relation to the Seychelles and Gibraltar. However, every time that it is considered, it has been found impractical. It involves permanent assimilation into the metropolitan power, representation in the metropolitan legislature, and equalisation of legislation, social services and taxation, which would raise serious problems for any or all of our territories even if it proved to be consistent with our responsibilities under the United Nations charter. We prefer to retain the straight choice between continued dependence or full independence, but we are willing to consider on their merits any proposals for alternative arrangements.

My hon. Friend . . . mentioned the French model. That is a peculiarly French system that has evolved over a long time, and it could not be transplanted to Britain any more easily than many other French institutions which my hon. Friend does not find congenial to British soil.

(Ibid., col. 1099.)

Later in his speech, Mr. Onslow stated:

Under the treaty of friendship and co-operation with Brunei, which was entered into by the previous Government on 1 January 1979, Brunei will resume full international responsibility as a sovereign independent state on 31 December this year. The sultanate has enjoyed full internal self-government since 1971. My noble Friend Lord Belstead is at present in Brunei to discuss various aspects of the United Kingdom's defence relationship with that country after it resumes full international responsibility on 31 December. From that date the United Kingdom will relinquish the consultative commitment for the defence of Brunei, which was undertaken in the 1971 agreement.

(Ibid., col. 1101.)

In moving the approval of the draft Saint Christopher and Nevis

Termination of Association Order 1983, the Minister of State, Foreign and Commonwealth Office, Mr. Cranley Onslow, stated:

The order, which terminates the status of association between the United Kingdom and St. Kitts and Nevis, will be made under section 10(2) of the West Indies Act 1967. Any order made under that section is required to be laid in draft before Parliament and to be approved by resolution of each House of Parliament.

. . .

It is proposed that the order should come into effect on 19 September 1983. Thereupon the islands of St. Christopher and Nevis will become a fully independent sovereign federal democratic State which should be described as the Federation of Saint Christopher and Nevis, or simply Saint Christopher and Nevis, or St. Kitts and Nevis for short. Her Majesty the Queen will be head of the independent State.

The Federation of Saint Christopher and Nevis is the sixth and last of the Associated States in the eastern Caribbean to move to full independence, following Grenada in 1974, Dominica in 1978, St. Lucia and St. Vincent in 1979, and Antigua and Barbuda in 1981.

In view of the importance of this occasion both to us and to the peoples of St. Kitts and Nevis, the House will expect me to comment briefly on the geography and history of these islands. They lie in the northern part of the Leeward group of the Lesser Antilles in the eastern Caribbean. They were united by the federal Act 1882, together with Anguilla, which was formally detached in 1980, and became a state in association with the United Kingdom on 27 February 1967. The two islands, which are very attractive, are separated by a channel some two miles in width. St. Kitts has an area of 65 square miles and Nevis of 36 square miles. The population of the two islands is about 45,000: St. Kitts has a population of 35,000, and Nevis a population of 10,000.

St. Kitts was discovered by Colombus on his second voyage in 1493, and was the first island in the West Indies to be colonised by the English when Sir Thomas Warner took settlers there in 1623. It became known as the 'Mother Colony of the West Indies'. Intermittent warfare between the English and the French during the 17th century ravaged the economy of the island. It was, however, ceded to Britain by the treaty of Utrecht in 1713. The last fighting on the island took place in 1782 when the French captured Brimstone Hill after a memorable siege and once more took possession. The island was finally restored to Britain by the treaty of Versailles in 1783.

Nevis, also sighted by Colombus on his second voyage, was settled by the English in 1628 and soon became one of the most prosperous of the Antilles. Although it suffered from French and Spanish attacks in the 17th and 18th centuries, it maintained a sound economic position until the middle of the 19th century. Indeed, it became a popular and fashionable resort. As readers of David Waldor's book will know, Lord Nelson was married to Frances Nisbett in Nevis in 1787, when he was stationed in the West Indies. Britain therefore has a historic and prolonged connection with the islands.

The West Indies Act 1967 created the concept of associated statehood. This enabled certain small territories in the eastern Caribbean, which were not then ready to move to full independence, to be given full internal self government. The United Kingdom retained responsibility only for defence and external affairs, although certain of the latter responsibilities were also delegated to the Associated States' Governments. As I have already indicated there has been a steady movement on the part of these states, over the past nine years, towards full independence.

Under the 1967 Act there are two ways in which independence can be achieved. The first is under section 10(1) whereby a two thirds majority in the legislative council and a two thirds majority of those who vote in a referendum can give an associated state the right to opt for independence, irrespective of the views of this House. Secondly, there is the alternative under section 10(2) whereby Her Majesty may by Order in Council terminate the status of association. As is usual under this alternative, the House of Assembly of St. Christopher and Nevis have by way of resolution requested termination and there is no reason not to accede to that request. This is the same method as has been followed in the transition to independence of the other five Associated States.

British policy on the application of section 10(2) of the West Indies Act has been consistent under successive Governments. Provided that two particular criteria are met, we are prepared to move the necessary order. These criteria are, that it is demonstrated to our satisfaction that independence is the wish of the majority of the people in the state, and, secondly, that the independence constitution properly protects the rights and freedoms of these people. I am satisfied that both criteria have been met in this case. A constitutional conference was held at Lancaster House in December last year under my chairmanship. The coalition Government of St. Kitts and Nevis led by Premier Dr. Simmonds and an Opposition delegation led by Mr. Moore participated. The draft before the conference had been prepared by the State Government and embodied proposals which were published in July 1982, subsequently discussed fully in the Associated State and approved by the State's House of Assembly in October. I visited the islands later in October to meet the political leaders and to familiarise myself with the issues. I was entirely satisfied that all the political parties there were agreed on the principle of independence and that this was the wish of the majority of the people.

The constitutional conference produced a report which was a thoroughly considered basis for a constitution. Regrettably the Opposition delegation felt that the proposals they put before the conference were not adequately discussed and they participated intermittently, not taking part in the signing ceremony. I am satisfied however that their criticisms of the manner in which the conference was conducted were unjustified.

When the St. Kitts and Nevis Government delegation were presented with reasoned, careful and constructive criticisms of their draft constitution they showed that they were prepared to go a considerable way towards meeting the Opposition's point of view. The Opposition had full opportunity to present their own proposals as well as to comment in detail on the draft constitution before the conference. The final version of the constitution which incorporated amendments made in the light of conference decisions was debated over a period of three days in the St. Christopher and Nevis House of Assembly. The constitution was then approved by a resolution of St. Kitts and Nevis House of Assembly, a copy of which I have had placed in the Library of the House.

The proposed constitution is similar to those under which the other associated states became independent. It does, however, contain some novel features in that it contains provisions for the autonomy of Nevis within the federation, and for secession of Nevis from the federation. The provisions for Nevis to secede would require the introduction and the pasage of a Bill in the Nevis Assembly supported by a two thirds majority of the elected members. This would subsequently need to be approved by a referendum in Nevis by not less than two thirds of the votes cast by persons registered on the parliamentary electoral roll there. Further provisions would ensure that adequate notification of the proposals for separation, including the proposals for its future constitution, would be given to enable proper discussion and explanation to take place. Arrangements would be made for independent and impartial observers appointed by an independent international body to observe the procedures involved in the referendum and to report publicly on the manner in which it had been carried out. The provisions for the Nevis Legislature and Administration, the financial provisions and the right of secession will be entrenched in the constitution. For this reason we are confident that the interests of the people of Nevis have been safeguarded.

. . .

As it is the wish of the majority of the people of St. Kitts and Nevis for independence, it is incumbent upon us to respond now to that wish. With full independence the state of St. Kitts and Nevis can further develop its co-operation with neighbouring states, especially within the Organisation of Eastern Caribbean States, in the activities of which an independent St. Kitts and Nevis can play a full part. That will be an important contribution to the stability of the region.

(Ibid., vol. 42, cols. 518–521: 5 May 1983; for Government statements in the House of Lords, see H.L. Debs., vol. 442, cols. 357–60 and 369: 9 May 1983.)

In reply to a question, the Parliamentary Under-Secretary of State, Foreign and Commonwealth Office, wrote:

The United Kingdom signed the Convention on International Trade in Endangered Species of Wild Fauna and Flora on 3 March 1973. The signature was deemed to have included all the territories for whose foreign relations Her Majesty's Government was responsible. Hong Kong was included in Her Majesty's Government's ratification of the Convention on 2 August 1976.

(H.C. Debs., vol. 42, Written Answers, col. *436*: 12 May 1983.)

In its *amicus curiae* Brief filed in November 1983 in litigation concerning the Bank of Nova Scotia's branch in the Cayman Islands (for a summary of the facts of this litigation, see below, p. 515), the United Kingdom Government wrote:

Cayman is a dependent territory of the United Kingdom. Under the Cayman Islands (Constitution) Order 1972, questions concerning Cayman's external affairs, police and internal security are reserved to the Governor of Cayman as instructed from time to time by the Secretary of State for Foreign and Commonwealth Affairs of the United Kingdom on behalf of Her Majesty the Queen. Otherwise the Cayman Government is largely responsible for Cayman's internal affairs as provided by the Cayman Constitution. The issues raised in this case are matters concerning the external affairs, police and internal security of Cayman.

(Amicus curiae Brief of the United Kingdom, pp. 2–3 (footnotes deleted): United States Court of Appeals for the Eleventh Circuit: *In re Grand Jury Proceedings the Bank of Nova Scotia; United States of America* v. *The Bank of Nova Scotia*.)

In a footnote to the last sentence of the above passage, it was stated in part:

The undersigned counsel desires that this Court and the parties understand that the proposition in the text constitutes the official position of the United Kingdom, and is concurred in by Cayman, as a matter of British and Caymanian constitutional law.

(Ibid., p. 3.)

Part Three: I. D. 2. *Subjects of international law—States—formation, continuity and succession of States—identity, continuity and succession*

(See also Part Three: I. E. (Written Answer of 12 December 1983) and Part Six: II. B., below.)

In reply to a question on the subject of the Guatemala—Belize territorial dispute, the Minister of State, Foreign and Commonwealth Office, Mr. Cranley Onslow, stated:

Britain is no longer a principal in the dispute, because Belize is an independent sovereign state.

(H.C. Debs., vol. 36, col. 985: 9 February 1983; see also ibid., vol. 37, Written Answers, col. 277: 18 February 1983 and H.L. Debs, vol. 446, col. 713: 20 December 1983.)

In reply to the question why a payment by the Foreign and Commonwealth Office to 'Palestine' was listed in the Appropriation Accounts for 1981–2, the Minister of State, Foreign and Commonwealth Office, Mr. Douglas Hurd, stated:

When the mandate for Palestine terminated in 1948 certain liabilities of the former Palestine Government remained outstanding to be met by Her Majesty's Government.

The payment of £341 listed under subhead 'B4: Palestine' in the 1981–82 Appropriation Accounts was for a new artificial leg for Mr. M. A. Issa, who used to work for the former Palestine Government.

(H.C. Debs., vol. 36, col. 986: 9 February 1983.)

In the course of a statement made on 7 April 1983 to the Conference on the Succession of States in respect of State Property, Archives and Debt, held in Vienna, the United Kingdom representative, Mr. J. R. Freeland, remarked with regard to the draft Convention before the Conference:

I am sorry to have to say that my delegation cannot regard the text before us as representing either a codification of existing international law or emerging rules of customary international law. It will have no legal force except as between any eventual parties to it.

Accordingly . . . my delegation could not support the adoption of the text before us and found itself obliged to vote against the adoption of that text. I say this with great regret, the more so in view of my country's support for the process of codification and for the work of the International Law Commission. We hope that this is an experience that will not be repeated.

(Text provided by the Foreign and Commonwealth Office.)

On 18 April 1983, the Permanent Representative of the United Kingdom to the United Nations in New York, Sir John Thomson, addressed the following note to the Secretary-General:

With reference to Your Excellency's Note No. LE 222 Dominica of 2 March 1983 with which was transmitted a communication from the Government of the Commonwealth of Dominica, I have the honour, on the direction of the Government of the United Kingdom, to make the following declaration.

The Government of the United Kingdom hereby declare that, when the Commonwealth of Dominica became an independent sovereign state on 3 November 1978, the Government of the United Kingdom ceased to have the obligations and rights they formerly had, as the authority responsible for the administration of the Commonwealth of Dominica, by virtue of any international instrument applying to the Commonwealth of Dominica.

I request that this statement should be circulated to all members of the United Nations and United Nations agencies.

(Text provided by the Foreign and Commonwealth Office.)

By a note to the Secretary-General of the United Nations dated 27 January 1983, the Permanent Representative of Guatemala wrote:

On instructions from the Government of Guatemala, I have the honour to refer to circular note LE 222 Belize dated 17 December 1982, which was received by the Mission of Guatemala on 10 January 1983 and in which the United Kingdom Mission to the United Nations declares that the United Kingdom Government has ceased to have the obligations and rights it formerly had in relation to the administration of Belize, by virtue of any international instrument applying to Belize [see UKMIL 1982, p. 366]. As you are aware, and as we affirm through this note, the granting of independence to Belize by the United Kingdom is a unilateral act which is not recognized by Guatemala since this is not a case of a colony which is being granted independence but of a territory which is the subject of a dispute not yet resolved. The United Kingdom cannot disregard its territorial dispute with Guatemala, or its legal liability for the damage caused to Guatemala and for its failure to fulfil various obligations it has had with respect to Guatemala in connection with Belize.

Guatemala will continue to press its claim to the entire territory of Belize in accordance with the principles of international law and will demand that the United Kingdom fulfil its obligations and make reparation for the damage and injury it has done to Guatemala.

In reply, the Permanent Representative of the United Kingdom, Sir John Thomson, wrote on 4 May 1983 to the Secretary-General as follows:

I have the honour, with reference to the Note dated 27 January 1983 from the

Permanent Representative of Guatemala to the United Nations, to state the following on instructions from the Government of the United Kingdom:

From the time of Belize's independence and admission to the United Nations in September 1981, the Government of the United Kingdom has not had a territorial dispute with Guatemala. The Government of the United Kingdom was and is under no legal liability or obligations to make reparation to Guatemala.

(Texts provided by the Foreign and Commonwealth Office.)

Part Three: I. E. *Subjects of international law—States—self-determination*

(See also Part Three: III. D., and Part Eight: II. A. (written answer of 4 May 1983), below.)

In a letter dated 28 April 1982 addressed to the President of the Security Council, the United Kingdom Permanent Representative to the United Nations in New York, Sir Anthony Parsons, wrote in part:

With regard to the question of self-determination, I wish to draw Your Excellency's attention to the following points. Self-determination is usually referred to these days in the United Nations not as a principle, but rather as an 'inalienable right': in other words, it is a right which cannot be taken away. This right derives principally from the Charter and the Covenants on Human Rights. Article 1(2) of the Charter refers to self-determination of 'peoples' and article 73 recognises 'that the interests of the inhabitants' of territories such as the Falkland Islands are paramount. Article 1 of the two International Covenants on Human Rights contains the following provision:

1. *All* peoples have the right to self-determination. By virtue of that right they freely determine their political status and freely pursue their economic, social and cultural development. (emphasis added)

Paragraph 3 of the same article establishes that the duty to promote the realisation of this right is imposed upon all states parties and not only upon those administering territories.

The Falkland Islanders are a people. The United Kingdom ratified both the Human Rights Covenants on their behalf. They are a permanent population. Over half of the people can trace back their roots on the Island to 1850. They have no other home. They have as is well known expressed their wishes regarding their political status in free and fair elections, the last having been held as recently as October 1981. The consistent practice of the United Nations shows that there is no minimum figure for a population to qualify for the right to self-determination: it suffices to cite the case of St Helena, another South Atlantic island with about 4000 people whose right to self-determination has been consistently upheld. The United Kingdom cannot accept that the right of self-determination as enshrined in the Charter and the Human Rights Covenants is subject to a special exception in the case of the Falkland Islands. This conclusion is confirmed by the Friendly Relations Declaration, adopted by consensus in 1970.

(S/15007.)

In a statement made on 29 September 1982 in the course of a general debate before the General Assembly, the Secretary of State for Foreign and Commonwealth Affairs, Mr. Francis Pym, observed:

Another of the basic principles [of the United Nations] is self-determination. It is a principle whose implementation has preoccupied this Organization and informed its proceedings ever since its inception. The right of all peoples to self-determination is enshrined in the two Covenants on human rights and underlined in such important United Nations documents as the Declaration on Friendly Relations. Indeed, the United Nations has long since come to regard self-determination as not just a principle but an inalienable right.

Self-determination is therefore fundamental to British foreign policy. Thanks to our recognition of this right in regard to our own dependencies, nearly 50 Members of this Assembly have taken their places here.

(A/37/PV. 9, p. 63.)

In the course of replying to a letter which had raised certain points on the history of the Falkland Islands, the Secretary of State for Foreign and Commonwealth Affairs, Mr. Francis Pym, having discussed the concept of prescription, wrote in July 1982:

The current principle of self-determination is of more recent origin. But there is no reason why we should not refer to it in support of our legal arguments as a whole, since the population of the Falkland Islands have been established there for so long a period. It is widely regarded as relevant to decisions on legal rights.

(Text provided by the Foreign and Commonwealth Office.)

In the course of replying to a letter on a similar subject, the Minister of State, Foreign and Commonwealth Office, Mr. Cranley Onslow, wrote in September 1982:

With a subject as complicated as the history of the Falklands and the conclusions that may be drawn from that history for sovereignty, it is inevitable that there will be differing and, in some cases, conflicting views. We naturally acknowledge the scholarship and research that went into the book by Julius Goebel, but that does not mean we give it any more weight than other documents on the same subject.

It would be misleading to attach any particular significance to what might appear to be shifts in the factors which at any particular time carried most weight in the Government's thinking. Our case is based on *all* the facts and circumstances, both before and after 1833. For example, the right of self-determination, which is now such an important part of our case, has emerged only relatively recently as a principle of international law.

(Text provided by the Foreign and Commonwealth Office.)

In the course of a letter dated 8 October 1982, addressed to the President of the Security Council, the United Kingdom Permanent Representative, Sir John Thomson, wrote:

The United Kingdom stands firmly by its obligations towards the population accepted 'as a sacred trust' under Article 73 of the Charter of the United Nations and by the right of self-determination, endorsed in the Charter itself, in General Assembly resolution 1514 (XV), in the Declaration on Principles of International

Law concerning Friendly Relations and Co-operation among States in Accordance with the Charter of the United Nations, as well as in the International Covenants on Civil and Political Rights and on Economic and Social Rights, to which the United Kingdom is a party and which have been extended to the Falkland Islands. Until Argentina, too, is prepared to give an unequivocal commitment to the applicable provisions of the Charter, including the right of self-determination, the United Kingdom rejects any Argentine pretension to speak about the interests of the Falkland Islanders.

(S/15452.)

In a letter dated 28 October 1982 addressed to the Secretary-General of the United Nations, the United Kingdom Permanent Representative, Sir John Thomson, wrote in part:

I should like to emphasize one point in particular. The annex to the letter from the Permanent Representative of Argentina [A/37/553], under the heading 'Background', claims in three places that the General Assembly has 'ruled out the applicability of the right of self-determination to this particular special case'. The decisions in question are the Committee of 24's conclusions and recommendations of 13 November 1964 and the General Assembly's resolutions 2065 (XX) of 16 December 1965 and 3160 (XXVIII) of 14 December 1973. However, it will be seen from the texts themselves (reprinted in annex II to the Argentine document) that none of them contains anything to support the Argentine allegation. In fact, all three decisions draw their inspiration from resolution 1514 (XV), which declares in its operative paragraph 2 that: 'All peoples have the right to self-determination; by virtue of that right they freely determine their political status and freely pursue their economic, social and cultural development'. The same part of the Argentine document refers also to the Declarations of the Movement of Non-Aligned Countries. Significantly, however, it fails to draw attention to the fact that the most recent communiqué of the meeting of the Ministers for Foreign Affairs and heads of delegation of the non-aligned countries, held in New York earlier this month, made specific mention in the context of the Falkland Islands dispute of the principles of the non-aligned movement: as everyone knows, the non-aligned principles include the non-use of force, the settlement of disputes exclusively by peaceful means, and self-determination.

These are no doubt the reasons why the Argentine document seeks to obscure the essential facts by insisting that the dispute is exclusively about sovereignty and that there are only two parties to it, the Islanders being excluded. The position of the United Kingdom does not depend on sophistry of this kind, but on basic Charter principles, notably the United Kingdom's clear obligation under Article 73 to recognize the interests of the inhabitants of the Falkland Islanders as paramount.

(A/37/582.)

[*Editorial note*: The above items should be read in conjunction with the material under this heading in UKMIL 1982.]

In the course of his evidence to the Foreign Affairs Committee of the House of Commons on 17 January 1983, Sir Ian Sinclair, Legal Adviser, Foreign and Commonwealth Office, was asked to what extent does the

British claim to sovereignty over the Falkland Islands rest upon self-determination, as distinct from other grounds. He replied:

The principle of self-determination as it developed basically since 1919 is primarily significant in the context of our responsibilities towards the Islanders, but that principle and, of course, the consistently expressed wishes of the Islanders are features which we would clearly wish to draw upon as part of our case on the title. It is not frankly possible to quantify the extent to which our title rests on that particular element as opposed to others.

(*Parliamentary Papers*, 1982–3, House of Commons, Paper 31-vi, pp. 163–4.)

Sir Ian Sinclair was later asked whether the small number of Falkland Islands residents affected the concept of self-determination. He replied:

. . . that is certainly not true so far as the practice of the United Nations in applying the provisions of Article 73 of the Charter is concerned. Under Article 73(e) of the Charter there is an obligation on administering powers to report on all territories which have not yet reached self-government and so far as the United Nations is concerned, the principle of self-determination always applies. We do certainly furnish information under Article 73(e) of the Charter in relation to such territories as Pitcairn Island, which has only 63 inhabitants, St. Helena and the two dependencies of St Helena, Tristan da Cunha and Ascension Island. So I think it is very difficult to say that so far as practice in the United Nations is concerned the principle of self-determination stops short at any particular figure of population. I could perhaps add to that of course that there may be certain political and economic factors which make the option of independence as one of the elements of the principle of self-determination perhaps not entirely viable— where the population is extremely exiguous, although even there I would point out that we granted independence to Tuvalu a few years ago, and Tuvalu has a population, I believe, of under 6,000. I could perhaps also mention as a further example of United Nations practice, the case of the Island of Niue. This is an island which is linked with New Zealand. There was a General Assembly Resolution, 3285 (XXIX) of 1974, which took note that the people of Niue had voted by a substantial majority for self-government and free association with New Zealand and considered that in so doing the people of Niue had freely expressed their wishes and had exercised their right to self-determination in accordance with the principles of the Charter of the United Nations and the Declaration on the granting of independence to colonial countries and peoples. Now the latest figure I have for the population of Niue is 3,954.

(Ibid., p.164.)

Asked what was meant by 'peoples' in Article 1 of the United Nations Charter, Sir Ian Sinclair replied:

This is a very difficult question, Mr Chairman. I have to say of course that there is no internationally accepted definition of the term 'peoples'. What one needs to consider are the circumstances of each particular case in which the principle may be invoked. Amongst the considerations to which we for our part attach importance in considering whether the principle of self-determination is applicable, is whether the people in a particular territory constitute a settled and self-sustaining community with its own institutions and civil administration built up over many years. That seems to us a kind of practical working definition of what we believe the concept to mean. But I must confess that that is not necessarily an internationally accepted definition. I have simply given you our own working definition or rule of thumb.

(Ibid.)

In reply to the question whether the problem of citizenship for the Falkland Islanders would have consequences for their self-determination, Sir Ian Sinclair stated:

... it does not seem to me that it has necessarily any consequences so far as the applications of the principle of self-determination is concerned. The question of whether and in what circumstances British citizenship should be conferred on the Falkland Islanders is a matter for Ministers to respond to rather than for ourselves. I wanted to make the general point that, at any rate so far as I can seek to make any judgment, the question whether the Falkland Islanders are accorded British citizenship would not necessarily have any impact on their claim to be a people having a right of self-determination. As I said earlier, there is no internationally accepted definition of the term and there have been claims made in the past on the principle of self-determination that certain ethnic or tribal groups even within a recognised state are entitled to the right of self-determination. It is more of a political than a legal principle. This is the problem.

(Ibid., p. 165.)

Sir Ian Sinclair was then asked whether the United Kingdom has ever contemplated making the Falkland Islands independent or, alternatively, part of metropolitan United Kingdom on the French model. He replied:

... I think that is perhaps a matter you should put to ministers rather than to myself. Simply on the general issue arising out of the two questions you put to me, perhaps I could quote from Resolution 2625 of the General Assembly of the United Nations which relates to the principle of self-determination and which says, 'The establishment of a sovereign and independent state, the free association or integration with an independent state or the emergence into any other political status freely determined by a people constitute modes of implementing the right of self-determination by that people. So inevitably, I think, in the light of that either the option of independence or integration would be regarded as being a mode of implementing the principle of self-determination.

(Ibid, p. 167.)

During the course of a debate in the House of Lords on the subject of Spanish restrictions on access to Gibraltar, the Minister of State, Foreign and Commonwealth Office, stated:

... our commitment to honour the wishes of the people of Gibraltar is totally clear and is set out in the 1969 Gibraltar Constitution, and it is specifically referred to in the Lisbon Agreement.

(H.L. Debs., vol. 438, col. 367: 27 January 1983; see also H.C. Debs., vol. 38, Written Answers, col. *427*: 9 March 1983.)

In the course of a letter dated 19 May 1983 addressed to the Secretary-General of the United Nations, the Permanent Representative of the United Kingdom, Sir John Thomson, replied to an earlier Argentine letter which had referred to the Franks Report. Sir John Thomson wrote:

. . . The report demonstrates in the clearest fashion the consistent adherence of successive British Governments to the principle of self-determination and respect for the freely expressed wishes of the Falkland Islanders. This is indeed a fundamental aspect of the dispute, but one which has been consistently evaded by the Argentine authorities.

The Argentine letter refers to Security Council resolution 505 (1982), but makes no mention at all of resolution 502 (1982): these resolutions of the Security Council were rendered nugatory by Argentina's own refusal to comply with the basic principles of resolution 502 (1982). There is no indication in this or in the rest of the letter that the Argentine Government had abandoned its attitude that, for it, negotiations about the Falkland Islands can have only one outcome—the transfer of sovereignty to Argentina, irrespective of the wishes of the Falkland Islanders. Nor is there any indication that Argentina has abandoned its attitude of rejecting the application of the universal principle of self-determination which is enshrined in the Charter of the United Nations, in United Nations declarations and resolutions and in the consistent practice of the Organization in relation to Dependent Territories. In short, there is no sign of the fundamental change of heart by Argentina which is necessary for the settlement of United Kingdom/Argentine differences.

(S/15774, p. 2.)

In the course of a debate on the subject of dependent territories, the Minister of State, Foreign and Commonwealth Office, Mr. Cranley Onslow, stated:

Independence for Gibraltar . . . is governed by article 10 of the Treaty of Utrecht of 1713 which . . . states:

'And in case it shall thereafter seem meet to the Crown of Great Britain to grant, sell or by any means to alienate therefrom the propriety of the said town of Gibraltar, it is hereby agreed and concluded, that the Preference of having the same shall always be given to the Crown of Spain before any others.'

If my hon. Friend subscribes, as the United Kingdom does, to the terms of that treaty, he has to pay attention to what it says. But equally . . . the people of Gibraltar have shown themselves repeatedly and massively to be against any change in the present status. The last voting figures were 12,000 to 44.

The people of Gibraltar clearly wish to retain their links with Britain and we stand firmly by the assurances about the future status of Gibraltar which are enshrined in the preamble to the territory's constitution.

(H.C. Debs., vol. 40, col. 1100: 15 April 1983. For the text of the preamble to Gibraltar's constitution, see Gibraltar Constitution Order 1969 (*Statutory Instruments*, 1969, vol. II, p. 3602) and UKMIL 1982, p. 373.)

In the course of a debate on the subject of human rights violations, the Government Minister in the House of Lords, Lord Trefgarne, stated:

In excess of 100,000 Soviet troops continue to prop up a puppet regime, depriving the Afghan people of the fundamental human right of self-determination.

(H.L. Debs., vol. 443, col. 1238: 20 July 1983.)

In a letter dated 25 August 1983 addressed to the Secretary-General of the United Nations, the Permanent Representative of the United Kingdom to the United Nations in New York, Sir John Thomson, referred to two letters sent to the Secretary-General by the Argentine Permanent Representative. He wrote in part:

The United Kingdom's attitude towards General Assembly resolution 37/9 is well known. This resolution failed to give express recognition to the right of the people of the Falkland Islands to self-determination and appeared to suggest that the status of the Islands should be changed irrespective of the manifest wishes of the Islanders. The references in the Argentine letter of 28 June (A/38/287-S/15849) to the preservation of the way of life and traditions of the Falkland Islanders and the effective protection of their interests are no substitute for recognition of the fundamental right of self-determination. The offensive references in the Argentine letter to 'illegal colonial presence' overlook the fact that the present arrangement remains the form of government preferred by the inhabitants who have recently experienced the Argentine alternative. The United Kingdom, for its part, will continue to promote the rights and interests of the Falkland Islanders, in accordance with their freely and clearly expressed wishes.

(S/15938, p. 2.)

In the course of a debate on 2 September 1983 in the General Assembly's Special Committee on the Situation with regard to the Implementation of the Declaration of the Granting of Independence to Colonial Countries and Peoples, the United Kingdom delegate, Mr. Mortimer, stated:

. . . the representative of Czechoslovakia has just made some extremely inappropriate remarks about an island that is a dependency of the United Kingdom, namely, Ascension Island, alleging that the presence of military facilities on that island constituted an impediment to self-determination.

May I just say, as my colleagues and I have pointed out in the Sub-Committee on Small Territories, that Ascension Island has no indigenous population. It cannot therefore be described as a Non-Self-Governing Territory as laid down in Article 73 of the United Nations Charter. It therefore falls outside the remit of the Committee of 24.

May I also remind the Committee that the item that is being discussed here concerns military activities and arrangements by colonial Powers in Territories under their administration which might be impeding the implementation of the Declaration on the Granting of Independence to Colonial Countries and Peoples.

If there is no population whose right to self-determination can be impeded, what right has the representative of Czechoslovakia to raise this question here?

(A/AC. 109/PV. 1238, p. 51.)

Speaking later in the same debate, the United Kingdom Permanent Representative, Sir John Thomson, remarked:

In the Committee of 24, it is above all appropriate to speak of obligations, particularly the obligations placed by the Charter on the United Kingdom as the administering Power for the Falkland Islands. Those are responsibilities I hope no one in this Committee would seek to question. In the Charter provisions on self-determination, as well as in Article 73, we find chapter and verse showing that the British Government's responsibilities towards the people of the Falkland Islands and their Charter obligations mutually support and reinforce one another. Our policies have firm Charter backing and we will continue to pursue them.

The principal concern of this Committee is the economic and political well-being of non-self-governing peoples and, in particular, their right to self-determination. I have no doubt that Committee members know Article 73, resolution 1514 (XV) and the Friendly Relations Declarations by heart, but I hope they will bear with me if I quote from them today.

The first part of Article 73 is particularly significant:

'Members of the United Nations which have or assume responsibilities for the administration of territories whose peoples have not yet attained a full measure of self-government recognize the principle that the interests of the inhabitants of those territories are paramount'.

These are profound words; they are strong words. If we as the administering Power accept that the interests of the inhabitants of the Falkland Islands are paramount, how can we negotiate with another Government about transferring sovereignty when that is manifestly contrary to what the people of the Islands see as their interests? The administering Power cannot move in direct contradiction to the wishes of the people of the Territories concerned. How can we say that their interests and their wishes stand in direct opposition to one another? Administering Powers accept 'as a sacred trust the obligation to promote to the utmost [their] well-being'. In particular, they undertake

'to ensure, with due respect for the culture of the peoples concerned, their political, economic, social and educational advancement, their just treatment, and their protection against abuses'.

May I add, in parentheses, Sir, that an invasion by 10,000 troops is an abuse indeed.

And it is the obligation of this Committee to support us in so doing. May I repeat—it is the obligation of this Committee to support us in carrying out our responsibilities as administering Power to ensure, with due respect for the culture of the people concerned, their political, economic, social and educational advancement, their just treatment and their protection against abuses. The abuses come from one direction only.

Some, though I would hope not members of this Committee, which has always maintained that factors such as the size of the population and geographical isolation should not militate against any people's right to self-determination in accordance with the Charter, may argue that Article 73 allows the interests of the inhabitants to be overridden. But it is surely not for one country to lay down where another people's interests lie. The inhabitants of a settled and largely self-governing Territory like the Falklands must surely be the best judge of that.

Suggestions to the contrary can only encourage interference in the internal affairs of other States and the unprincipled use of force. It is of course the classic argument used by those who wish to further their territorial ambitions. But for the United Kingdom as administering Power to accept that argument would be to acquiesce in handing over a people to alien and unwanted rule. It is not the sort of argument which the Committee of 24 by its very nature could accept. For it runs directly counter to the Declaration on the Granting of Independence to Colonial Countries and Peoples, which states that:

> 'The subjection of peoples to alien subjugation, domination and exploitation constitutes a denial of fundamental human rights, is contrary to the Charter of the United Nations and is an impediment to the promotion of world peace and co-operation.' (*resolution 1514 (XV)*)

That seems to me a fairly comprehensive statement which applies directly to the Falklands.

I have dwelt at some length on the responsibilities placed on us by the Charter because it leads to the heart of the matter. It is the origin of my Government's co-operation with this Committee. The Committee has repeatedly declared its belief in the inalienable right of self-determination. 'Inalienable is a very strong word. It means birthright: it means you cannot get rid of it; it means that the Falklanders have a right of self-determination which no one can take from them. The United Kingdom shares that view. In the process of decolonization, which this year will see a further two dependent Territories, Saint Kitts-Nevis and Brunei, achieve independence, we have held fast to that principle. There is no reason if, for example, the people of Tokelau, the Cocos Islands and Pitcairn can enjoy the right to self-determination, the people of the Falkland Islands cannot. This right is the right recognized in General Assembly resolution 1514 (XV), the Declaration on the Granting of Independence to Colonial Countries and Peoples, which lies at the origin of this Committee. Forgive me, Sir, if I repeat what must already be so familiar to members of the Committee, but the second operative paragraph of the Declaration is particularly relevant:

> 'All peoples have the right to self-determination; by virtue of that right they freely determine their political status and freely pursue their economic, social and cultural development.' (*ibid.*)

This is another very clear statement.

These words have been taken up into the International Covenants on Civil and Political Rights and on Economic and Social Rights, both of which have been ratified by the United Kingdom and extend to the Falkland Islands. They admirably and succinctly summarize what we stand for in the case of the Falkland Islanders. Moreover, the General Assembly itself has repeatedly asserted that self-determination is an inalienable right, of equal standing to other fundamental human rights. The General Assembly continues to assert that right on behalf of the remaining dependent Territories and also on behalf of certain other peoples. The right of self-determination, as propounded by the international community, offers many small and powerless peoples a moral and legal safeguard against being overwhelmed, assimilated or conquered by ambitious and unscrupulous neighbours. Like other human rights, self-determination is a concept which can be convenient to certain Governments on some occasions and inconvenient when it runs counter to their untramelled exercise of arbitrary power. This is not, however, a reason to set it aside; on the contrary, such situations require that the principle be asserted with great conviction. It would not be reasonable to believe that members of a Committee seriously concerned with the future of the people of the remaining Non-Self-Governing Territories are willing to be selective in their application of this inalienable right.

(A/AC. 109/PV. 1238.)

In a statement made on 28 September 1983 during a general debate before the General Assembly, the Secretary of State for Foreign and Commonwealth Affairs, Sir Geoffrey Howe, observed:

We will continue to defend the right—the inalienable right—of the people of the Falkland Islands to self-determination, a right to which they are no less entitled than other small island peoples . . .

(A/38/PV. 10, p. 72.)

In the course of a speech to the General Assembly on 19 October 1983, the United Kingdom representative, Mr. Margetson, having referred to events in East Timor, stated:

This relates to the right—the inalienable right—of self-determination, which most of us regard as one of the fundamental principles on which this Organization is based.

(Ibid. 33, p. 102.)

In the course of answering a question about the Baltic States, the Minister of State, Foreign and Commonwealth Office, wrote:

We support the right of all peoples to self-determination and deplore any infringement of national sovereignty.

(H.C. Debs., vol. 47, Written Answers, col. 85: 25 October 1983.)

In the course of a speech on 28 October 1983 to the Security Council on the situation in Grenada, the United Kingdom Permanent Representative, Sir John Thomson, stated:

I suggest that in accordance with the vast majority of the speeches we have heard and on the basis of the Charter our common aim should be the emergence of a constitutional Grenadian Government freely elected by the Grenadian people. I am talking, of course, about a real democratic Government based on the exercise of self-determination by the Grenadian people.

(S/PV. 2491, pp. 93–5.)

Later in his speech, Sir John Thomson observed:

It is not for us to tell the Grenadian people how to run their affairs. But I believe we can legitimately give encouragement to the forces of constitutionality and to the right of self-determination. That is the message which my delegation would like to see go out from this debate.

(Ibid., p. 98.)

In the course of a debate in the General Assembly on 15 November 1983 on the subject of the Falkland Islands, Sir John Thomson stated:

It ... closely touches on basic international principles. It is a question on which the United Kingdom has specific obligations towards the United Nations under Article 73 of the Charter. I wish to stress that the main importance in this forum of the Falklands question is that it deals with the rights of people—admittedly a small number of people, but people are people and rights are rights. The Charter of the United Nations does not prescribe that the rights it lays down are to be enjoyed only by populations of 5 million or 10 million or 20 million, or any other number.

. . .

I suppose that every single day during the General Assembly one speaker or another in this chamber has used the hallowed phrase 'the inalienable right of self-determination'. It has been used frequently in recent days about the small population of Grenada. In the Falklands the population is smaller though the land is larger than Grenada. The population of Grenada would fit into a large football stadium, the population of the Falklands into a small football stadium, but is the size of the football stadium to be the determinant of whether or not a people has the right of self-determination? The answer is obvious. As I have already said, right are rights.

There is a simple reason why the draft resolution before us makes no reference to the inalienable right of self-determination. The Foreign Minister of Argentina told us plainly last year that it was an essential part of his case that self-determination did not apply to the Falkland Islanders. That was repeated during the general debate at this year's session and the Argentine Foreign Minister repeated it again in his speech yesterday. In the Fourth Committee yesterday afternoon the Argentine representative went so far as to say that the General Assembly had specifically taken away the Falkland Islanders' right of self-determination. This, he said, was a special and unique exception to an otherwise universal rule. When I pointed out that the essence of an 'inalienable' right was that it could not be taken away, the Argentine representative said that it was in fact the United Kingdom which was responsible for taking that inalienable right away from the Falkland Islanders.

These are very strange and bizarre propositions. Does anyone seriously hold that the process of decolonization involves a denial of the inalienable principle of self-determination? What the Argentine representative seems to have been referring to was a statement by the United Kingdom representative in the Committee of 24 in 1964 in which he warned his fellow representatives that the use of incautious phraseology in their draft resolution would not be reconcilable with the right of self-determination which the Falkland Islanders undoubtedly possess. I repeat that warning today. I do so specifically in relation to the draft resolution before us.

I am even more strengthened in doing so by the fact that the Argentine delegation has put down in writing the interpretation which it will seek to place upon the votes of delegations who support their draft resolution. Members of the Assembly will see this in section I, page 2, of document A/38/563 where Argentina puts delegations on notice that, if they vote for the present resolution, Argentina will interpret their vote as rejecting the application of the right of self-determination in what they call 'this special individual case'. The words of the Argentine delegation are even underlined, so there can be no doubt of its intentions. Members of the Assembly have been warned.

The whole notion of there being this single and unique exception in the case of the Falkland Islanders to a principle that is recognized as being universal is so strange that the Assembly will want to consider it further.

I have already welcomed the fact that Argentina, even if somewhat belatedly, now accepts that the Falkland Islands are properly in the list of Territories covered by Article 73 of the Charter. The Argentine Foreign Minister drew the correct conclusion yesterday that this also made resolution 1514 (XV) applicable to the Falkland Islands. I am sure that this is a conclusion with which this Assembly as a whole will also agree. But it seems that the Argentine Foreign Minister wanted to perform a conjuring trick: by invoking resolution 1514 (XV) he wanted to make it disappear. He did this by claiming that paragraph 6 of the resolution was overriding and prevailed over anything else in the resolution. The flaws in his reasoning are obvious. First, the history of resolution 1514 (XV) shows that paragraph 6 was intended to deal with something quite different; secondly, by invoking the mirage of territorial integrity the Foreign Minister begs the whole question. No doubt it fits in with his way of thinking to presuppose or assume that Argentine sovereignty over the Territory is established and British sovereignty non-existent, but that is hardly an approach calculated to convince my Government or the world at large. Finally, he cannot show any shred of an indication in the wording of resolution 1514 (XV) that the fundamental principles laid down there in its paragraphs 1–5 and 7, especially that of the inalienable right to self-determination, were subject to any form of limitation, let alone what is now claimed to be a 'special and individual exception' for one particular case.

Self-determination is a principle of the United Nations, and as such has general application. I must also draw the Assembly's attention to Article 73 of the United Nations Charter which, though of narrow application, is precisely relevant to the case of the Falklands. It is specifically in accordance with this Article that for some 30 odd years my Government has been reporting to the United Nations on a long list of British colonies. Most of the colonies on the original list have now been removed from it. They have exercised the right of self-determination and they are now either sitting here in this Assembly as sovereign and equal countries, or they have chosen, by their own free will, to join up with neighbouring States. What has been right for the majority of countries on the list is surely right for the others. The Falkland Islanders are as well able to exercise self-determination as other islanders, in the Caribbean or the Pacific or elsewhere.

The reference in the draft resolution before us to the interests of the islanders is no substitute for the essential principle of self-determination. Argentina is willing to accept references to their interests, while reserving to itself the judgement of where those interests lie. But this is quite inconsistent with the clear words of the Charter. Article 73 says plainly that the interests of the islanders are 'paramount' and also obliges the United Kingdom, as the administering Power, to promote their well-being to the upmost and to develop their self-government. These are plain words. I deployed this argument last year, but it has had no real answer. Indeed, there is no answer to it. It would obviously be contrary to the Charter for the interests of the islanders to be left to Argentina to decide. It is the islanders themselves who must be allowed to decide what their interests really are and it is accordingly by their wishes, not by any one else's assessments of their interests, that we must be guided.

May I refer in parenthesis to the second preambular paragraph of the draft resolution, which claims that the continuation of colonial situations is incompatible with the United Nations ideal of universal peace? This is another distortion of resolution 1514 (XV). Resolution 1514 (XV) says that the continued existence of 'colonialism' impedes the social, cultural and economic development of dependent peoples and militates against the United Nations ideal of universal peace. The United Kingdom of course was not the author of that resolution, so perhaps it is not for me to say what the authors meant. But they cannot possibly have meant that the maintenance of a form of government that is in accordance with the clear and firmly expressed wishes of the people concerned threatens international peace; nor could they possibly have meant that the progressive development of self-government in the Falklands impedes the social, cultural and economic development of the Falkland Islanders. Resolution 1514 (XV) is, of course, one of the hallowed texts on the right of self-determination. The friendly relations Declaration is another. So are the two International Covenants on Human Rights. The second preambular paragraph of the draft resolution is therefore nonsense. The Charter, after all, is aimed at securing international peace, and simultaneously provides for bringing colonies peacefully to self-government through self-determination. So there is no inconsistency between the two. What is inconsistent with the United Nations idea of universal peace is any attempt to deny self-government, to suppress self-determination or to hand people over to foreign rule against their will. If any delegations doubt this, I would ask them to think carefully and dispassionately. I would also ask them to read the whole Charter carefully, not least Article 73, to study the whole of resolution 1514 (XV), the whole of the friendly relations Declaration and the Human Rights Covenants. That will leave them in no doubt as to the central place in this question of the inalienable right of self-determination.

(A/38/PV. 57, pp. 43–52, *passim*.)

Speaking in explanation of vote at the close of the same debate on 16 November 1983, Sir John Thomson observed:

. . . the Argentine draft resolution is intended, as the Argentine Foreign Minister has himself made clear, to prejudge the outcome of the dispute. The Foreign Minister has made it clear that for him the only possible result is for Britain to hand over to Argentina sovereignty over the islands together with the people who inhabit them. He has explicitly said that the only possible outcome of decolonization in the case of the Falklands is a transfer of sovereignty. That is why the draft resolution insists upon talking about a sovereignty dispute and only a sovereignty dispute. That is inconsistent with both the doctrine and the practice of the United Nations. Resolution 1514 (XV) for example makes it clear that decolonization must take place in accordance with the 'freely expressed will and desire' of the people. That is, the Falklanders must choose.

Furthermore the Argentine delegation has made it absolutely clear that it interprets its draft resolution as meaning that the General Assembly thereby removes the inalienable right of self-determination from the Falklanders. By what authority could the General Assembly do this? How could it possibly do this if the right of self-determination is indeed inalienable? Let me repeat, people are people and rights are rights. As I said yesterday, let no one come to me after this debate and say that they support both this draft resolution as interpreted by Argentina and the right of self-determination.

I have already said that what this draft resolution omits is even more important than what it contains. It omits the basic principles of the Charter which apply to this case. First and foremost it omits the principle of self-determination. Next it omits a recognition that my Government has obligations to the Falklanders and to the United Nations under Article 73 of the Charter. Indeed, it does worse than omit this crucial point. It falsifies the meaning of Article 73. It refers to the 'interests' of the population of the Falkland Islands, and the word 'interests' appears in Article 73, but it neglects to quote that Article accurately. It should have said that 'the interests of the inhabitants of these territories are paramount'. Surely it is not for the invaders to decide what are the interests of the people they are trying to subjugate? It is evidence that the Charter intends that these paramount interests shall be expressed through the exercise of the right of self-determination.

(Ibid. 59, pp. 51–2.)

In reply to the question

Whether, in view of our debt of honour and moral obligation to the Somalis arising from arrangements with Ethiopia (Abyssinia) between 1897 and 1954, they will instruct our Permanent Representative at the United Nations to raise the question of self-determination for Somalis in Ethiopia as a right to which they are entitled under the Charter (and numerous subsequent resolutions),

the Minister of State, Foreign and Commonwealth Office, wrote:

No. Our position is one of support for the Organisation of African Unity policy of accepting the colonial boundaries inherited by the newly-independent African states: indeed, it has been widely accepted at the United Nations that the right of self-determination does not give every distinct group or territorial sub-division within a state the right to secede from it and thereby dismember the territorial integrity or political unity of sovereign independent states.

(H.L. Debs., vol. 446, cols. 93–4: 12 December 1983.)

Part Three: II. A. 1. (c). *Subjects of international law—international organizations—in general—legal status—privileges and immunities*

(See also Part Five: VIII. A (statements of 10 December 1982 and 15 November 1983, and answer of 12 December 1983), below.)

The joint Committee on Statutory Instruments took evidence from the Foreign and Commonwealth Office on the subject of the draft Commonwealth Foundation (Immunities and Privileges) Order 1983, and the draft

Commonwealth Telecommunications Organization (Immunities and Privileges) Order 1983. In particular, the Committee wished to know whether the International Organizations Act 1968 gave all the authority needed to promulgate the above draft Orders, particularly in respect of the inviolability of official papers. At the request of the Joint Committee, the Foreign and Commonwealth Office presented a memorandum, dated 31 January 1983, which read as follows:

. . . the Foreign and Commonwealth Office submit this memorandum to the Committee concerning the power to grant inviolability for official papers and instruments to representatives to the above organisations.

The FCO confirm that in their view the immunity from suit and legal process accorded by Part II, paragraph 9 of Schedule 1 to the International Organisations Act 1968 covers inviolability for official papers and documents. In their view, the expression 'immunity from suit and legal process' is a comprehensive one. It includes personal inviolability, immunity from civil and criminal proceedings, from execution of judgments and from giving evidence as a witness, and inviolability of residence and personal property, including papers and documents.

. . . it is accepted that the FCO reading makes paragraph 2 of Part I of Schedule 1 strictly redundant. However, this provision identifies separately an immunity which is commonly of critical concern to the organisation, and the FCO would consider that the ability to demonstrate the grant of inviolability with clarity was a sufficient justification for this paragraph.

. . . the FCO consider that the expression 'immunity from jurisdiction' in Article 10(1)(a) of the Commonwealth Foundation Agreement and Article 13(1)(a) of the CTO Agreement may be construed more narrowly than 'immunity from suit and legal process' in that the former would apply only to legal proceedings issued against a representative. The identification of inviolability of papers by these Agreements is indeed one reason why they are identified separately in the Orders.

. . . the FCO would again maintain that the distinction made in Schedule 1 to the 1964 Act between immunity from jurisdiction (Article 31) and the inviolability of papers and documents (Article 30.2) can be explained by the narrower meaning which may be attached to the expression 'immunity from jurisdiction' as compared with 'immunity from suit and legal process'.

. . . the FCO accept that inviolability of residence is covered by immunity from suit and legal process and that its separate treatment under Part II, paragraph 9 of Schedule 1 to the 1968 Act is not strictly necessary. But in the FCO's view, its separate treatment is justified because inviolability of residence is commonly identified separately in the relevant international instruments, including the Vienna Convention on Diplomatic Relations which is scheduled to the 1964 Act and the Commonwealth Foundation and CTO agreements to which the Committee refer. This in turn reflects not only the importance attached to inviolability of residence by the international instruments concerned, but also the fact that the term 'immunity from jurisdiction' is a narrower one than 'immunity from suit and legal process' employed by Schedule 1 to the 1968 Act.

The FCO have reconsidered the Ninth Report of the Committee for the 1975–6 Session and the minutes of evidence before the Committee on that occasion. However, they do not consider that there is sufficient uncertainty about the scope of Part II, paragraph 9 of Schedule 1 to the 1968 Act to cast doubt upon the *vires* of the two Orders presently before the Committee. This is particularly so in view of the very long practice in according separate inviolability of papers under the 1968 Act, both before and after 1975 and also under the International Organisations (Immunities and Privileges) Act 1950 whose Schedule was in similar terms: see for example the Western European Union (Privileges and Immunities) Order 1955 SI 1955/1209, Articles 14 and 15.

For these reasons, the FCO did not consider it necessary to clarify the point in the International Organisations Act, 1981.

(Text provided by the Foreign and Commonwealth Office.)

Giving evidence to the Joint Committee on 1 February 1983, Mr. I. K. Mathers, Assistant Legal Adviser, Foreign and Commonwealth Office, stated:

I think if this question had come to me at first blush I would have said I was not very happy with the position as it has arisen. It is clear that the schedule to the 1968 Act enables us by Order in Council to grant immunity from suit and legal process and inviolability of residence for the benefit of representatives of other States to organisations. The question which, essentially, you have raised is, 'Well it does not say anything about inviolability of official papers and yet here you are in these two Orders purporting to accord inviolability for personal papers'. This same question was raised by your Committee in 1975 on the occasion of the draft International Cocoa Organisation (Privileges and Immunities) Order and the answer which my predecessors gave to your Committee and subsequently to both Houses, was that although, certainly, the Act does not refer specifically to inviolability for personal papers, we have always regarded that as being covered by a more general term, 'immunity from suit and legal process'. We have not had, since you raised the question again, the opportunity to examine it in much greater depth, but we have found out that the provision made here had been made in previous Orders as long ago as 1955, as is mentioned in our memorandum, and indeed goes further back to 1948, because the International Organisations Act took over the wording of its predecessor the International Organisations (Immunities and Privileges) Act of 1950, which in turn took over the precise wording of its predecessor, the Diplomatic Privileges (Extension) Act of 1944. Many orders made under those Acts contained exactly the same provision. Indeed it has become what you might almost call a '*clause de style*'. It has come down now for over 30 years.

(*Parliamentary Papers*, 1982–3, House of Commons, Paper 29–xiii, p. 1.)

In reply to the question why nothing was done to clarify the point in the International Organizations Act 1981, Mr. Mathers replied:

I am not sure whether any full consideration was given to that possibility. What I have found, and I have gone into the papers, is that a number of questions were raised as possible candidates for an amended Act and this did not feature among them, although other points which had been raised at more or less a similar time had been taken up and instructions were given to counsel. So it is my assumption that the Foreign and Commonwealth Office considered that over the years, as the practice had developed, there was not sufficient doubt to warrant any change.

. . .

Could I just add to my previous remarks that assuming the possibility of legislation about this was considered in some depth in 1981, I have no doubt that my colleagues who would have been responsible would have had in mind the fact that ten orders have been made since 1975 with exactly the same provision and no comment has been raised in this Committee about it or in either House. Just seen in that very narrow time span, I think this is worth commenting on.

(Ibid., p. 2.)

In the House of Commons Sixth Standing Committee on Statutory Instruments, etc., the Minister of State, Foreign and Commonwealth Office, Mr. Cranley Onslow, introduced discussion of the draft Commonwealth Foundation (Immunities and Privileges) Order 1983, African Development Bank (Immunities and Privileges) Order 1983, and Commonwealth Telecommunications (Immunities and Privileges) Order 1983. Commencing with the first draft Order, he stated:

The immunities and privileges which are granted by the order are usual for an organisation of this kind, and are limited to what is needed to enable the foundation to carry out its functions. It will have a degree of protection from certain administrative and judicial measures taken against its property, but will not enjoy any wider immunity from jurisdiction. It will also have exemption from income and capital gains tax, and from important duties and certain other indirect taxes. These exemptions will be subject to the usual restrictions to protect the Revenue.

The chairman and governors will have immunity from jurisdiction only while carrying out their duties on behalf of the foundation. They will have certain other facilities to enable them to perform their functions as the representatives of member states.

The director of the foundation will enjoy broadly similar privileges to those enjoyed by a diplomatic agent, unless he is a national of, or permanently resident in, this country. He will not, however, have immunity in respect of motor accidents or traffic offences.

Other staff members of the foundation will have immunity from jurisdiction in respect of their official acts, and will enjoy exemption from customs duty on their personal and household effects if coming from overseas to take up appointments here. When the foundation has established its own internal tax system, the proceeds of which will be applied for the benefit of the foundation, the staff members will be exempted from the payment of United Kingdom income tax on their salaries.

I now turn to the draft Commonwealth Telecommunications order. Like the foundation, the Commonwealth Telecommunications Organisation has been in existence for some time. Indeed, it has its origins in the laying of a submarine cable across the Pacific in 1902. Since then, the machinery for Commonwealth co-operation has been through various incarnations culminating in the present organisation which was set up in 1969 with its headquarters here in London. Its purpose is to promote Commonwealth co-operation in all aspects of external telecommunications and to encourage the efficient development and exploitation of the Commonwealth telecommunications system. The cost-sharing provisions of its financial arrangements give valuable support to its members in both the development and operation of external telecommunications.

The 1977 Commonwealth telecommunications conference invited the United Kingdom Government to examine the possibility of granting the organisation a status similar to that enjoyed by international organisations. This formal request was one of the reasons for the subsequent passing of the International Organisations Act 1981 ... Since then, a draft headquarters agreement has been negotiated with the organisation, and this order gives effect to that agreement.

The immunities and privileges proposed are those which are functionally necessary. The organisation will have a limited immunity from suit and legal process, exemption from taxes on income and capital gains, and exemption from import duties and certain other direct taxes. These taxation exemptions are subject to the normal restrictions to protect the Revenue.

Representatives will have immunity from jurisdiction while performing their official duties, and other customary facilities. Staff members will have immunity in respect of their official acts and customs duty privileges on their personal effects if coming from overseas to take up their appointments. On the establishment of an internal income tax scheme by the organisation, staff members will be exempted from the payment of United Kingdom income tax on salaries paid by the organisation. None of the staff, or representatives, will enjoy any immunity for road traffic accidents or offences.

Finally, I turn to the African Development Bank order, which extends to the bank those immunities and privileges we have agreed to provide on our joining this organisation.

. . .

In 1978, the bank opened an office in London, and the African Development Bank (Privileges) Order was made to grant that office legal personality and exemption from income tax and capital gains tax.

. . .

The order now before the Committee replaces the 1978 Privileges Order, re-providing the legal personality and the exemption from taxes contained in that order. The bank, which has only a staff of two in London, will in addition receive similar privileges and immunities to the two Commonwealth organisations.

(H.C. Debs., 1982–3, Sixth Standing Committee on Statutory Instruments, 2 February 1983, cols. 4–5.)

Moving the approval in the House of Lords of the Commonwealth Foundation (Immunities and Privileges) Order 1983, the Commonwealth Telecommunications Organisation (Immunities and Privileges) Order 1983, and the African Development Bank (Immunities and Privileges) Order 1983, the Government spokeman, Lord Skelmersdale, stated:

These three organisations will, generally speaking, enjoy the same privileges and immunities as other organisations of a comparable kind. The most notable distinction is between the two Commonwealth organisations, on the one hand, and the African Development Bank, on the other. The former have their headquarters in London, and accordingly we need to provide a wider range of facilities for them to function here. These are to cover not only the organisations and their staffs but the representatives of the member states when they come here to deal with the organisation's affairs.

In this regard, your Lordships may like to know that a special feature of the Commonwealth Foundation Order is that it provides for the chairman of the foundation, who is appointed direct by the Commonwealth Heads of Government, to enjoy privileges and immunities identical to those enjoyed by the governors, as the member states' representatives are known. As the African Development Bank has its headquarters in Abidjan, it is not necessary for the bank's small office here to enjoy quite the same range of immunities. This being said, we do not consider that the bank will in any way be inhibited from carrying out its functions here.

Knowing your Lordships' concern over such matters, I hope I can reassure the House by saying that none of the orders would allow the organisations or people connected with them to flout our traffic laws or to escape responsibility for any motor accidents in which they may unfortunately be involved. Further, I feel I can also assure your Lordships that these organisations will continue to conduct their affairs in a wholly responsible fashion.

I am sure that your Lordships will agree that these three important and useful organisations deserve our support. The immunities and privileges to be accorded by these orders will demonstrate our wish to work for their continuing success. I beg to move.

(H.L. Debs., vol. 438, col. 953: 2 February 1983.)

Replying to the debate on the subject, Lord Skelmersdale stated:

No one in this Chamber, or indeed in another place, would pay scant regard to the opinions of such an august body as the Select Committee on Statutory Instruments, and I certainly will not do so. The noble Lord, Lord Oram, referred to the 10th Report, which, as he said, is not yet printed. As he also said, the committee considers that there appears to be doubt as to whether these Commonwealth orders are *intra vires*. I understand that the report explains that doubt arises over whether, under the provisions of the International Organisations Act 1968, inviolability can be accorded to the official papers of a representative. The committee fully recognises that this should be done and, indeed, it is required to be done to comply with the two headquarters agreements governing the legal status of the organisations in question. The committee's concern is whether this can be achieved in the manner provided by the two orders which are before your Lordships this evening.

In this regard, the committee also raised the question as to why the point was not clarified by the International Organisations Act 1981, which, as we know, was before this House two years ago and which made certain changes to the original 1968 Act. This is no defence, but this is not a new issue. It was last raised in 1975 by the Joint Committee on Statutory Instruments, in connection with a similar order then before the committee concerning the International Cocoa Organisation. It is clear that, in giving approval to that draft order, the House showed that it accepted the Government's views and did not share the Joint Committee's concern. In the interim, 10 other orders containing similar provisions have received the House's approval, thereby demonstrating, I believe, that the view we continue to hold has all along been valid.

In our opinion, the arguments now advanced by the Joint Committee do not overturn this view. However, any report of the Joint Committee must, as I said at the beginning of this passage in my speech, be taken very seriously indeed, and, lest this latest report should give rise to any doubt, I should like to assure your Lordships that it will, of course, be given the most careful consideration with a view to taking any action which may be necessary to clarify the position.

(Ibid., cols., 955-6.)

In reply to the question how many International Immunities and Privileges Orders under the International Organisations Act 1968 are currently in force, the Government spokesman in the House of Lords, Lord Skelmersdale, stated:

. . . there are 54 such orders.

. . .

. . . each organisation, when it is decided to have members here or to grant immunities in this country to that organisation, is discussed with Her Majesty's Government on its merits. . . . There are two things to which they certainly do not apply: one is car tax and the other is parking fines.

(Ibid., vol. 439, col. 449: 18 February 1983.)

In moving the approval of the International Jute Organization (Immunities and Privileges) Order 1983, the Government Minister in the House of Lords, Lord Lyell, stated in part:

. . . the international Agreement on Jute and Jute Products, a copy of which was laid before the House on 22nd March 1983 [Cmnd. 8825], was opened for signature on 3rd January this year. It was signed on behalf of the United Kingdom on 6th June. The main element in the agreement is the establishment of an International Jute Organisation. The purpose of the draft order before your Lordships is to accord the organisation legal personality. Once this is done, we can proceed to early ratification of the agreement.

The organisation will propose, approve and seek finance for projects in the fields of research and development, cost reduction, market promotion, competitiveness (particularly in relation to synthetic products) and, above all, dissemination of information. The agreement does not provide for market stabilisation measures, although it does envisage that further consideration may be given to the possibility of stabilisation of prices and supplies.

The headquarters of the organisation is situated in Dhaka in Bangladesh. The Government of Bangladesh will conclude a headquarters agreement with the organisation to accord it such privileges and immunities as will be considered necessary for the organisation's efficient funding in Bangladesh. However, we must meet our obligations under the jute agreement by according the organisation legal personality. This means that the organisation will be able, where necessary, to conclude contracts, buy and sell property and to institute and defend legal proceedings in those states. The order does no more than that. It grants no privileges and no immunities to the organisation.

(Ibid., vol. 443, col. 1019: 18 July 1983.)

In moving the approval in the House of Lords of the Eurocontrol (Immunities and Privileges) (Amendment) Order 1983, the Government Minister, Lord Lyell, stated in part:

. . . it gives effect in United Kingdom law to the requirements of a Protocol which amends the 1960 Convention that created the European Organisation for the Safety of Air Navigation, more normally known as Eurocontrol. The protocol was signed on 12th February 1981, and laid before the House in October 1982.

The purpose of this draft Order is to implement Articles 22(7), 23 and 24 of the amended Convention by providing for immunity from suit and legal process for the Director General of the organisation, inviolability for the official papers and documents of representatives of the contracting parties, and by exempting from our social security scheme those members of Eurocontrol's staff who are neither British citizens nor permanent residents of this country. Currently Eurocontrol has no premises or property here: the Director General and all of his staff work outside the United Kingdom, and we have no reason to believe that this situation will change in the near future. The grant of these privileges and immunities is not, therefore, expected to have any significant effect here. However, all contracting parties are obliged to provide for them under the terms of the amended Convention, and they may be required should Eurocontrol hold a meeting here.

(Ibid., vol. 446, col. 784: 21 December 1983.)

Part Three: II. A. 2. (b). *Subjects of international law—international organizations—in general—participation of States in international organizations—suspension, withdrawal and expulsion*

In explanation of his vote on 13 October 1983 against a draft resolution dealing with South Africa's nuclear capabilities presented to the General Conference of the International Atomic Energy Agency, the United Kingdom representative, Mr. Henderson, referred to a paragraph of the draft resolution requesting the Agency to prevent South Africa from participating in its technical groups. He continued:

. . . we think that the suspension of rights and privileges which the Board is asked to consider by operative paragraph 4 could only be made under Article 19 of the Statute, following persistent violation of the Statute. We consider that South Africa has not so violated the Statute; and therefore that the Board does not need to discuss this question.

(Text provided by the Foreign and Commonwealth Office.)

Part Three: II. A. 3. *Subjects of international law—international organizations—in general—legal effects of acts of international organizations*

(See also Part Three: III. D. (statement of 7 April 1983) and Part Nine: VII. A. 5. (written answer of 14 April 1983), below.)

In reply to a question, the Parliamentary Under-Secretary of State, Department of the Environment, wrote in part:

. . . in February the United Kingdom took the initiative in obtaining a further scrutiny of the scientific evidence within the London dumping convention. Although a resolution was subsequently passed by the LDC consultative meeting calling for suspension of dumping pending the outcome of this scrutiny, that resolution does not have any legal force and was not based on scientific evidence.

(H.C. Debs., vol. 46, Written Answers, col. 552: 28 July 1983.)

In the course of a speech to the General Conference of the International Atomic Energy Agency on 12 October 1983, the United Kingdom representative, Mr. Henderson, referred to a resolution taken at the London Dumping Convention meeting in February 1983 to suspend sea disposal operations pending the outcome of a scientific review of the factors for and against sea disposal. He continued:

. . . it was recognised by the delegates to the 1983 London Dumping Convention meeting that the resolution on suspension was not binding on members.

(Text provided by the Foreign and Commonwealth Office.)

In explanation of his country's vote against a draft resolution dealing with South Africa's capacities presented to the same Conference, Mr. Henderson stated on 13 October 1983:

Preambular paragraph (b) and operative paragraph 1 both refer to General Assembly resolutions 37/74 and 37/69. The United Kingdom voted against both these resolutions, and we maintain our opposition. I also note that there is no obligation upon this Agency to implement resolutions of the General Assembly.

(Text provided by the Foreign and Commonwealth Office.)

On 11 November 1983, the General Assembly considered a draft resolution dealing with the policies of apartheid of the Government of South Africa and in particular the constitutional proposals approved by the South African electorate. The draft resolution contained as its second preambular paragraph the statement 'Reaffirming that apartheid is a crime against humanity and a threat to international peace and security', and as its operative paragraph 1 'Declares that the so-called 'constitutional proposals' are contrary to the principles of the Charter of the United Nations . . .'. Speaking in the debate on the draft resolution, the United Kingdom representative, Mr. Barrington, stated in part:

My delegation must reserve its position on certain specific aspects of the resolution, including the second preambular paragraph and operative paragraph 1, which contain assertions that in our view go beyond the competence of this Assembly under the Charter.

(A/38/PV. 56, p. 52.)

Part Three: II. B. 3. *Subjects of international law—international organizations—particular types of organizations—organizations constituting integrated communities*

In reply to a question, the Attorney-General wrote:

There is no right of appeal to the European Court of Justice against a conviction imposed by a United Kingdom court. But where a case which is before a United Kingdom court necessarily turns on a question of the interpretation of Community law, the domestic court may—and in certain circumstances must—obtain a preliminary ruling on that question from the European Court of Justice before determining the case.

(H.C. Debs., vol. 35, Written Answers, col. *17*: 17 January 1983.)

In reply to the question 'whether it is the case that if six members of the European Community sign the UNLOSC Convention text, the convention will be binding on all members of the Community, and if so what are the Government's intentions given that France, Holland, Ireland, Greece and Denmark are ready to sign while Britain, Germany, Belgium and Italy are not and Luxembourg alone remains undecided', the Minister of State, Foreign and Commonwealth Office, wrote:

The present position is that Denmark, France, Greece, Ireland and the Netherlands signed the convention on 10th December 1982. If six of the member states have signed, the convention allows signature by the Community itself; but before the Community could sign, the Council would have to come to a decision to that effect. Signature alone would not commit the Community since a further procedure of formal confirmation, again calling for a decision by the Council, would be required for this purpose.

(H.L. Debs., vol. 438, col. 1417: 10 February 1983.)

In reply to the question whether Government Departments should describe the Assembly of the European Community as such and not as the Parliament, the Prime Minister wrote:

The term 'Assembly' appears in the treaties, but the institution has described itself since 1962 as the 'European Parliament' and this term is generally in use throughout the Community. We accepted this usage on taking office. Whatever terminology is used, the nature of the institution is not in doubt. We will continue to use the term 'Assembly' in legal texts or where it is necessary to distinguish that institution from Parliament in Westminster.

(H.C. Debs., vol. 37, Written Answers, col. *380*: 22 February 1983.)

In reply to a question, the Prime Minister wrote:

The United Kingdom has been the defendant in the following proceedings before the European Court of Justice:

Case 31/77R *Commission v. United Kingdom* (1977) ECR 921—the United Kingdom's pigmeat subsidy—interim decision given against the defendant.

Case 128/78, *Commission v. United Kingdom* (1979) ECR 419—tachographs—judgment against the defendant.

Case 141/78, *France v. United Kingdom* (1979) ECR 2923—Agriculture (fisheries)—judgment against the defendant.

Case 231/78, *Commission v. United Kingdom* (1979) ECR 1447—Agriculture (restrictions on import of potatoes)—judgment against the defendant.

Case 170/78, *Commission v. United Kingdom* (1980) ECR 417—Tax on wine—parties ordered to re-examine the subject of the dispute.

Case 32/79, *Commission v. United Kingdom* (1980) ECR 2403—Agriculture (fisheries)—judgment against the defendant.

Case 804/79, *Commission v. United Kingdom* (1981) ECR 1045—Agriculture (fisheries)—judgment against the defendant.

Case 61/81, *Commission v. United Kingdom* (not yet reported)—Equal pay for men and women—judgment against the defendant.

Case 40/82, *Commission v. United Kingdom* (not yet reported)—Agriculture (Newcastle disease in poultry)—judgment against the defendant.

Case 124/81, *Commission v. United Kingdom* (not yet reported)—Agriculture (Import of UHT milk)—judgment against the defendant.

Case 165/82, *Commission v. United Kingdom* (not yet reported)—Equal treatment for men and women as regards access to employment, vocational training and promotion—case still pending.

(Ibid., vol. 38, Written Answers, cols. *250–1*: 4 March 1983.)

In reply to questions on the subject of the Convention for Trade in Endangered Species and the European Community's possible accession to it, the Government Minister in the House of Lords wrote in part:

It is appropriate for the convention to apply to the organisations responsible for the trade with which it is concerned.

. . .

The European Community's accession to the convention is being negotiated in accordance with a decision by the Council of Ministers on 14th March 1977. Parliament scrutinised the proposed decision in the usual way and environmental organisations were aware of it.

(H.L. Debs., vol. 441, col. 470: 18 April 1983.)

In reply to a question, the Parliamentary Under-Secretary of State, Department of Trade, wrote:

The European Community has a wide range of preferential trade agreements with a number of countries.

There are association agreements, properly so called, only with Cyprus, Malta and Turkey. These agreements are distinguished by involving a commitment to eventual customs union. There are, however, also agreements with each of the member states of the European Free Trade Association—EFTA—providing, inter alia, for free trade in industrial products; an agreement with Spain providing for mutually preferential trade; co-operation agreements—which provide for non-reciprocal preferential access to Community markets, and for financial aid—with most other Mediterranean countries and with Jordan; an agreement with 63 African, Caribbean and Pacific developing countries—the Lomé convention—which provides, besides trade preference, for co-operation in the fields of general economic, industrial, agricultural and technological development; and the Community's generalised scheme of preferences—GSP—which offers reduced-duty or duty-free access for imports of some 1,700 items of processed agricultural and industrial products originating in developing countries. Fuller descriptions of the terms of most of the above agreements can be found in 'British Business in Europe', June 1981, a copy of which is in the Library.

In contracting any agreement with any third country, due account is always taken of all relevant considerations.

(H.C. Debs., vol. 41, Written Answers, cols. 58–9: 19 April 1983.)

Part Three: III. D. *Subjects of international law—subjects of international law other than States and organizations—mandated and trust territories, Namibia*

In reply to a question, the Minister of State, Foreign and Commonwealth Office, wrote:

The Government remain committed to achieving an internationally acceptable settlement in Namibia in accordance with Security Council resolution 435, which provides for United Nations-supervised elections. Further internal elections would not be helpful in our efforts to achieve that goal.

(Ibid., vol. 35, Written Answers, col. 147: 19 January 1983.)

In reply to a question on the possible application by the United Nations Organization of a form of trusteeship to communities subject to conflicting claims of sovereignty, the Minister of State, Foreign and Commonwealth Office, Lord Belstead, stated:

The system of trusteeship does not apply of course to independent states, members of the United Nations, but to dependencies. The Charter provides in Article 77c that the latter may be voluntarily placed in trusteeship, and that I have no doubt is what is in the noble Lord's mind. So far as I know, this has never been put into effect ever since 1945. I have no reason particularly to believe that it should be put into effect now.

(H.L. Debs., vol. 439, col. 447: 18 February 1983.)

The Vienna Conference on Succession of States in respect of State Property, Archives and Debts adopted a resolution, proposed by the Group of 77, which read in part as follows:

. . . that the relevant articles of the Vienna Convention on Succession of States in respect of State Property, Archives and Debts shall be interpreted, in the case of Namibia, in conformity with United Nations resolutions on the question of Namibia.

In explanation of vote, the United Kingdom representative stated on 7 April 1983:

I should like to make a brief statement on behalf of the delegations of Canada, the Federal Republic of Germany, France and the United States, as well as my own delegation.

As in the case of the comparable resolution which was adopted at the 1978 Conference, our five delegations take the view that the resolution . . . is one which is not within the competence of this Conference to adopt. As its terms of reference make clear, the concerns of the Conference should properly be not with individual cases of succession but with the drafting of a Convention on the question generally. We shall consequently abstain.

(Text provided by the Foreign and Commonwealth Office.)

In a speech to the Security Council, on 23 May 1983, the United Kingdom representative, Sir John Thomson, stated:

. . . we have constantly been aware of the deep feelings aroused by the unlawful occupation of Namibia . . .

(S/PV. 2439, p. 21.)

Later in his speech he said:

We do not accept South Africa's occupation of Namibia as lawful.

(Ibid., p. 33.)

Sir John Thomson then remarked:

The right to self-determination is recognized by all.

(Ibid., p. 36.)

In reply to a question, the Parliamentary Under-Secretary of State, Foreign and Commonwealth Office, wrote in part:

We and our partners in the Five have regular contact with representatives of Namibian political parties through our embassies in South Africa and elsewhere. We continue to take account of their views and concerns in our efforts to achieve an internationally acceptable settlement in Namibia in accordance with Security Council resolution 435.

(H.C. Debs., vol. 44, Written Answers, col. *167*: 1 July 1983.)

In the course of a debate on the subject of the Falkland Islands, the Minister of State, Foreign and Commonwealth Office, Baroness Young, stated:

The other suggestion related to a United Nations trusteeship. The United Nations accepts that Britain is the sole administering authority for the Falklands. As such, and in fulfilment of our responsibilities under Article 73 of the charter, we have made it clear that we shall not allow any constitutional arrangements to be imposed on the islanders against their wishes.

(H.L. Debs., vol. 445, col. 1060: 6 December 1983.)

Part Three: III. F. *Subjects of international law—subjects of international law other than States and organizations—miscellaneous*

(See Part Five: VIII. A. (statement of 15 November 1983 with reference to national liberation movements), below.)

Part Four: I. *The individual (including the corporation) in international law—nationality*

The Foreign and Commonwealth Office submitted to the Foreign

Relations Committee of the House of Commons a memorandum, dated 17 December 1982, on the subject of the Falkland Islands. The memorandum, which took the form of replies to questions posed by the Committee, read in part as follows:

Question 21

What is the legal definition of a Falkland Islander?

There is no legal definition of a Falkland Islander. The nearest equivalent is the definition of a 'permanent resident' contained in the Falkland Islands Immigration Ordinance 1965, as amended. This definition comprises—

(a) persons born in the Colony or Dependencies, or of parents who at the time of their birth were ordinarily resident there, or
(b) a person ordinarily resident in the Colony or Dependencies and who has been so resident there for seven years and since completion of such residence, has not been ordinarily resident for a continuous period of seven years or more in any other country, or
(c) a dependent of a person referred to in (a) or (b), or
(d) a person who has obtained the status of British subject by reason of a grant by the Governor of a certificate of naturalisation.

(*Parliamentary Papers*, 1982–3, House of Commons, Paper 31-vi, p. 151.)

The following Note, dated 31 December 1982, was sent by Her Majesty's Ambassador at Rome to the Minister for Foreign Affairs of Italy:

On instructions from Her Majesty's Principal Secretary of State for Foreign and Commonwealth Affairs, I have the honour to refer to the Treaty between the Member States of the European Communities and the Kingdom of Denmark, Ireland, the Kingdom of Norway and the United Kingdom of Great Britain and Northern Ireland concerning the accession of the latter States to the European Economic Community and to the European Atomic Energy Community, done at Brussels on 22 January 1972([1]).

When the United Kingdom joined the European Communities in 1973 there was annexed to the Treaty of Accession a formal Declaration([2]) by the United Kingdom defining the term 'national' in relation to the United Kingdom for the purposes of the Treaties and Community legislation. A precise definition was necessary to identify in terms of United Kingdom legislation those persons who by virtue of their close connection with the United Kingdom itself or with Gibraltar would be entitled to the rights conferred by the Treaties, particularly in regard to free movement and the right of establishment.

Last year the United Kingdom Parliament revised British nationality law in terms of the British Nationality Act 1981. The entry into force of this Act on 1 January 1983 will mean that the United Kingdom Declaration no longer corresponds exactly with United Kingdom legislation. I am to inform you therefore that the Declaration is no longer valid and to communicate the following Declaration on behalf of the Government of the United Kingdom of Great Britain and Northern Ireland to replace it:

'In view of the entry into force of the British Nationality Act 1981, the

Government of the United Kingdom of Great Britain and Northern Ireland makes the following Declaration, which will replace, as from 1 January 1983, that made at the time of signature of the Treaty of Accession by the United Kingdom to the European Communities:

"As to the United Kingdom of Great Britain and Northern Ireland the terms 'nationals', 'nationals of Member States' or 'nationals of Member States and overseas countries and territories' wherever used in the Treaty establishing the European Economic Community([3]), the Treaty establishing the European Atomic Energy Community([4]) or the Treaty establishing the European Coal and Steel Community([5]) or in any of the Community acts deriving from those Treaties, are to be understood to refer to:

(a) British citizens;
(b) Persons who are British subjects by virtue of Part IV of the British Nationality Act 1981 and who have the right of abode in the United Kingdom and are therefore exempt from United Kingdom immigration control;
(c) British Dependent Territories citizens who acquire their citizenship from a connection with Gibraltar.

The reference in Article 6 of the third Protocol([6]) to the Act of Accession of 22 January 1972, on the Channel Islands and the Isle of Man to 'any citizen of the United Kingdom and Colonies' is to be understood as referring to 'any British citizen'."

[1] Treaty Series No. 18 (1979), Cmnd. 7463.
[2] Treaty Series No. 18 (1979), Cmnd. 7463, p. 272.
[3] Treaty Series No. 15 (1979), Cmnd. 7460.
[4] Treaty Series No. 17 (1979), Cmnd. 7462.
[5] Treaty Series No. 16 (1979), Cmnd. 7461.
[6] Treaty Series No. 18 (1979), Cmnd. 7463, p. 244.

(*United Kingdom Treaty Series*, No. 67 (1983) (Cmnd. 9062).)

In reply to a question on the subject of proposals by the Government of Zimbabwe to abolish dual nationality and to remove British passports from those Zimbabwean citizens entitled to carry them, the Parliamentary Under-Secretary of State, Home Office, Lord Elton, stated:

Her Majesty's Government are aware of the legislation now awaiting presidential assent in Harare. This does constitute an amendment to the constitution agreed at Lancaster House but it was passed by both Houses in accordance with the provisions of the Lancaster House agreement for amendments to the constitution. I can, however, confirm that the right to British citizenship, once properly acquired, cannot be removed from any individual without his expressed consent. This is fully understood by the Government of Zimbabwe.

(H.L. Debs., vol. 441, col. 183: 13 April 1983.)

In reply to the further question whether British passports confiscated by another State would be replaced automatically on application to the nearest British consulate, Lord Elton stated:

. . . under the provisions of the British Nationality Act 1981 a person who has renounced British citizenship is entitled to re-acquire that citizenship by registration if he is aged 18 or more and is of sound mind, and provided that the renunciation was necessary to enable him to retain or acquire some other citizenship or nationality. This provision may be taken advantage of only once. I suspect that I have perhaps taken the noble Lord's question further than he intended. If he is concerned only with the re-acquisition of a passport, as opposed to nationality, I can say that while it is true that in certain exceptional circumstances—for example, where a British national has voluntarily surrendered his passport as a condition of bail—it may be appropriate to withhold replacement of a passport held by the authorities of another country, I can nevertheless assure him that, as a general rule, any British passport impounded by those authorities would be replaced, on application, by a British consular official, subject to the applicant's satisfactorily establishing his identity and his claim to citizenship.

(Ibid., col. 184.)

In reply to the question which countries do not permit British citizens to have dual nationality, the Parliamentary Under-Secretary of State, Foreign and Commonwealth Office, wrote:

Although our posts overseas keep us informed about the nationality laws of their host countries, we could not justify the research necessary to produce a definitive list of countries which do not permit dual nationality.

There are various forms of restrictions on dual nationality. Where it is necessary for Her Majesty's Government to establish the precise position of British nationals under the nationality law of another country, the Foreign and Commonwealth Office seek specific information from the authorities concerned.

(H.C. Debs., vol. 40, Written Answers, col. 437: 14 April 1983.)

In moving the approval of the draft Saint Christopher and Nevis Termination of Association Order 1983, the Minister of State, Foreign and Commonwealth Office, Mr. Cranley Onslow, stated:

The two subsections refer to citizenship of the new state, which will be the first of our remaining territories to become independent after the entry into force of the British Nationality Act 1981 on 1 January 1983.

It has been agreed that any person who was born in St. Kitts and Nevis and is a British Dependent Territories citizen immediately before independence will become a St. Kitts and Nevis citizen automatically on independence. So too will certain other British dependent territories citizens, including those who are such by virtue of a parental or grandparental connection with St. Kitts and Nevis. Provision is also made for certain persons to become citizens, who were born or otherwise had a connection with Anguilla before 19 December 1980, the date of separation of Anguilla from St. Kitts and Nevis, and who have been resident in St. Kitts and Nevis. Further provision is made for persons to become citizens after independence by virtue of birth or registration.

Those who were formerly citizens of the United Kingdom and Colonies by virtue of a connection with St. Kitts and Nevis became British dependent territories citizens under the 1981 Act. They will become citizens of Saint Christopher and Nevis on independence day, when they will lose their British dependent territories citizenship unless they qualify for retention of that citizenship by virtue of a connection with a remaining dependency. I emphasise that no one will lose British citizenship as a result of the independence of St. Kitts and Nevis. Dual citizenship will be permitted.

(Ibid., vol. 42, col. 517: 5 May 1983.)

In reply to the question whether refugees from Vietnam, landed in Hong Kong, will in due course be able to claim entry into the United Kingdom as Hong Kong citizens, the Minister of State, Home Office, wrote:

The dependencies do not have separate citizenships. The acquisition of British dependent territories citizenship in a dependency is a matter for the authorities of that country. Entry to the United Kingdom for those subject to control under the Immigration Act 1971 is governed by the published immigration rules—House of Commons Paper 169.

(H.C. Debs., vol. 40, Written Answers, col. *372*: 12 May 1983.)

Part Four: V. *The individual (including the corporation) in international law—statelessness, refugees*

In reply to a question, the Minister of State, Home Office, wrote:

Ghanaians expelled from Nigeria can return to their own country and are not refugees within the definition of the 1951 convention relating to the status of refugees and its 1967 protocol; any application for settlement in the United Kingdom would be considered under the relevant immigration rules.

(Ibid., vol. 36, Written Answers, col. *235*: 7 February 1983)

In reply to a question on the subject of the persecution of Baha'is in Iran, the Government spokesman in the House of Lords, Lord Skelmersdale, stated:

. . . an Iranian who is a member of the Baha'i faith would qualify for recognition as a refugee in this country and would therefore be protected from return to Iran.

(H.L. Debs., vol. 440, col. 80: 8 March 1983.)

In reply to a question, the Parliamentary Under-Secretary of State, Foreign and Commonwealth Office, wrote:

The United Nations High Commissioner for Refugees is normally responsible for the resettlement of Vietnamese refugees. He takes into account a number of factors including the preferences of the refugees, historical and cultural ties and language, and family connections as well as the readiness of recipient countries to admit refugees for resettlement. Their distribution throughout Europe is therefore unlikely to be equal though there have been significant and welcome contributions by many countries to the sharing of this international responsibility.

(H.C. Debs., vol. 39, Written Answers, col. *1176*: 25 March 1983.)

In the course of a debate in the House of Lords on the subject of the deportation to Romania of Mr. Stancu Papusoiu, the Government spokesman, Lord Elton, stated:

... the United Nations Convention on Refugees, implemented for this country, in our Immigration Rules, makes it quite clear ... that the criterion for the status of refugees is a well-founded fear of being persecuted for reasons of race, religion, nationality, or membership of a particular social group or holding particular political opinions. The United Nations High Commissioner for Refugees himself distinguishes emphatically between refugees and economic migrants. To abandon that distinction would undermine the convention and reduce our ability to accept genuine refugees.

(H.L. Debs., vol. 440, col. 1543: 29 March 1983.)

Later in the debate, Lord Elton stated:

In today's *Times* my noble friend suggested—and he repeated it this evening—that the anti-emigration laws in Romania are in breach of Article 13 of the Universal Declaration on Human Rights, and Article 12 of the International Convention on Civil and Political Rights. He argues from that that if Mr. Papusoiu is subsequently punished for having broken those laws, he will be subject to political persecution. But if we follow that line of reasoning, it is to arrive at a *reductio ad absurdum*, for it would inevitably give a claim to asylum in this country to the entire population of every country—and there are many—in which such laws existed. That is why the United Nations High Commission for Refugees' *Handbook on Procedures for Refugee Recognition* lays down that considerations of punishment for illegal immigration, or overstaying abroad, are relevant only if a person qualifies on other grounds as a refugee. Those other grounds are the grounds for which, all along, we have been looking, in vain.

(Ibid., cols. 1546–7.)

In the course of replying to a question on the subject of political refugees, the Minister of State, Home Office, Mr. David Waddington, stated:

We try our best to apply sympathetically and fairly the criteria laid down in the United Nations convention for the treatment of refugees. There would be grave risks if we ignored those criteria in a commendable wish to help others. The whole process of political asylum could be devalued.

We simply cannot proceed on the assumption that anybody who comes to this country from eastern Europe has the right to asylum here just because if he returned to his own country he might suffer penalties. If we followed that policy we would give a contingent right of asylum to every citizen from every country behind the iron curtain.

(H.C. Debs., vol. 40, cols. 459–60: 31 March 1983.)

In reply to a question, the Parliamentary Under-Secretary of State, Foreign and Commonwealth Office, Mr. Malcolm Rifkind, stated:

The principal international obligations of the United Kingdom towards refugees are those arising under the United Nations convention relating to the status of refugees of 1951, as modified by the protocol of 1967. The convention defines a refugee and gives guidance on international standards for the treatment of refugees.

(Ibid., col. 788: 13 April 1983.)

Part Four: VI. *The individual (including the corporation) in international law—immigration and emigration, extradition, expulsion and asylum*

(See also Part Eight: II. D. (debate on Nuclear Material (Offences) Bill), below.)

The Foreign and Commonwealth Office submitted to the Foreign Relations Committee of the House of Commons a memorandum, dated 17 December 1982, on the subject of the Falkland Islands. The memorandum, which took the form of replies to questions posed by the Committee, contained the following item:

Question 22

What is the legal position relating to the control of immigration into the Islands, and what are the respective responsibilities of the UK Government and the FIG?

The control of immigration into the Falkland Islands is a matter which falls within the responsibility of the Falkland Islands Government and is governed by the Falkland Islands Immigration Ordinance 1965, as amended.

(*Parliamentary Papers*, 1982–3, House of Commons, Paper 31-vi, p. 151; see also H.C. Debs, vol. 440, cols. 1340–1: 28 March 1983.)

In reply to a question on the subject of the United Kingdom–United States treaty of extradition, the Parliamentary Under-Secretary of State, Foreign and Commonwealth Office, wrote:

The problem of securing the extradition of fugitives who claim their offences are political is regularly reviewed between our respective officials. The possibility of amending the treaty is related to the progress of amendments to the United States Extradition Act which were introduced in the last Congress but not adopted.

(H.C. Debs., vol. 36, Written Answers, col. *388*: 9 February 1983.)

In reply to a question, the Minister of State, Foreign and Commonwealth Office, wrote in part:

The Nigerian Government have acted to expel aliens living illegally in their country, irrespective of nationality. None of the neighbouring states principally concerned has questioned the legitimacy of this action. Nor have Her Majesty's Government done so. We have, however, through normal channels, made the Nigerian authorities aware of the concern felt in this country at the manner in which the decision was carried out.

(Ibid., col. *449*: 10 February 1983; see also H.L. Debs., vol. 439, col. 506: 21 February 1983.)

In moving the second reading in the House of Commons of the Nuclear Material (Offences) Bill, implementing the United Nations Convention on the Physical Protection of Nuclear Material, 1980, the Minister of State, Home Office, Mr David Waddington, stated:

The convention requires that the offences should be extraditable between contracting states, and clause 5 makes the necessary provisions. I should emphasise that the traditional safeguards governing the return of fugitive offenders will still apply and the Bill does not change in any respect the procedures in our courts and their attendant safeguards. We are not binding ourselves to return a person to a state merely because that state asks for extradition in any circumstances.

(Ibid., col. 946: 8 February 1983.)

In moving the second reading of the same Bill in the House of Lords, the Government spokesman, Lord Elton, stated:

Article 7 obliges a state to ensure that certain acts are punishable offences, and Articles 8 to 12 require the establishment of jurisdiction over such offences wherever they occur; and in the event of such cases a state must either submit the case for prosecution in its courts or extradite the alleged offender. The objective is to ensure, as far as possible, that the perpetrator of such an offence does not find a safe haven in another country. We would regard extradition as the most practicable and appropriate course where the offence had occurred abroad. . . .

Subsection (2) provides for the Extradition Act to be applied to states which are party to the convention but with which we have no extradition treaty. A request for extradition will be considered in accordance with the usual procedures and the traditional safeguards will still apply. Subsection (3) would allow extradition to be granted under the provisions of the Extradition Act 1870 for offences committed outside the territory of the requesting state in circumstances where that state claims jurisdiction similar in scope to that provided for in Clause 1. A similar provision in relation to the Fugitive Offenders Act 1967 is not needed because under that Act a fugitive may be returned for an offence committed in a third state.

(H.L. Debs., vol. 440, cols. 982–4 *passim*: 21 March 1983.)

In reply to a question on the subject of the possible extradition of Walther Rauff from Chile, the Minister of State, Foreign and Commonwealth Office, wrote:

In 1955 the Government of the Federal Republic of Germany assumed responsibility for the prosecution of all Nazi war criminals, with the exception of those major criminals such as Martin Bormann, arraigned at Nuremberg. It is for the Federal Republic of Germany, not Her Majesty's Government, to take the initiative in co-ordinating representations to states known to be, or suspected of, harbouring other Nazi war criminals.

In the case of Walter Rauff, a request by the Federal Republic of Germany for his extradition was rejected in 1963 by the Chilean supreme court. Subsequent

German requests to Presidents Allende and Pinochet for Rauff's extradition also failed.

The extradition treaty between Chile and the United Kingdom cannot be invoked because it applies only to offences committed in the territory of one of the parties.

(H.C. Debs., vol. 38, Written Answers, cols. *430–1* : 9 March 1983.)

In reply to the following question—

To ask Her Majesty's Government whether in the interests of the suppression of international crime they will consider the consolidation of the extradition statutes, and the conclusion of treaties to establish or re-establish effective extradition relations where they have lapsed—

the Parliamentary Under-Secretary of State, Home Office, Lord Elton, stated:

. . . the law and practice of extradition were reviewed by an Inter-Departmental Working Party, whose report was published in May 1982 [see UKMIL 1982, pp. 402–6]. The report was sent for comment to individuals and organisations known to have an interest in the subject, and we are considering their responses before deciding what action to take on the recommendations of the working party. It has not been the practice to negotiate or re-negotiate our extradition treaties while decisions on the review of the Extradition Act are pending.

. . .

Accession to the convention would require more than consolidation of the existing statutes. If the number of designations were to be small enough to make it worth our while to sign, we should at least have to remove the requirement for proof of a *prima facie* case before extradition can be granted. This is a point which was covered in the report and attracted during the period for consultation many comments which are now being considered. The coming into force of new legislation substantively different from the present would mean the renegotiation of all our existing treaties, and that would take a very long time.

(H.L. Debs., vol. 442, cols. 1–2: 3 May 1983.)

In reply to a question on the subject of Guatemala, the Parliamentary Under-Secretary of State, Foreign and Commonwealth Office, wrote:

An extradition treaty was concluded in 1885. There have been no extradition cases from either country since 1923.

(H.C. Debs., vol. 50, Written Answers, col. *421* : 13 December 1983.)

In reply to a question, the Parliamentary Under-Secretary of State, Home Office, wrote:

The following tables give information about the numbers of persons extradited to and from the United Kingdom in the years 1978 to 1982, by country:

TABLE A

Persons extradited to foreign countries under the Extradition Act 1870

	1978	1979	1980	1981	1982
Belgium	—	1	3	—	2
Denmark	1	1	1	—	1
Finland	—	—	—	—	1
France	2	2	1	1	—
Federal Republic of Germany	4	3	—	3	2
Israel	1	—	—	—	1
Italy	1	2	—	2	1
Netherlands	1	1	3	1	3
Norway	—	1	—	1	—
Panama	—	—	1	—	—
Sweden	—	—	—	1	4
Switzerland	2	1	3	2	—
United States of America	2	2	5	2	3
TOTAL	14	14	17	13	18

TABLE B

Persons extradited to Commonwealth countries and Dependent Territories under the Fugitive Offenders Act 1967

	1978	1979	1980	1981	1982
Australia	2	3	3	—	2
Canada	—	2	—	4	2
Cyprus	—	—	—	1	—
Hong Kong	1	1	—	—	—
Malta	—	—	—	1	—
Nauru	—	—	1	—	—
New Zealand	1	—	2	—	—
Singapore	—	1	—	—	—
TOTAL	·4	7	6	6	4

TABLE C

Persons extradited to the United Kingdom from foreign countries

	1978	1979	1980	1981	1982
Belgium	1	—	—	1	—
Denmark	—	—	—	—	1
France	2	4	1	3	2
Federal Republic of Germany	3	2	—	4	—
Israel	—	—	—	—	1
Netherlands	—	1	1	1	—
Norway	1	—	—	—	—
Portugal	—	—	—	—	1
Sweden	—	—	1	—	—
United States of America	1	5	4	5	—
TOTAL	8	12	7	14	5

TABLE D

Persons extradited to the United Kingdom from Commonwealth countries and Dependent Territories

	1978	1979	1980	1981	1982
Australia	1	—	—	1	—
Bermuda	—	—	—	—	1
Barbados	—	1	—	—	—
Guyana	1	—	—	—	—
Gibraltar	—	—	2	1	—
India	1	—	—	—	—
Malta	2	—	—	—	—
Sri Lanka	1	—	—	—	—
TOTAL	6	1	2	2	1

(Ibid., vol. 51, Written Answers, cols. *127–8*: 20 December 1983.)

In reply to the question whether entry visas would be granted to nationals of North Korea, the Minister of State, Home Office, wrote:

Any such applications would be considered in accordance with the immigration rules. Her Majesty's Government do not recognise North Korea as a state and the immigration rules provide that a person who produces a passport or travel document issued by a Government who are not recognised by Her Majesty's Government may be refused entry on that ground alone.

(Ibid., vol. 46, Written Answers, col. *688*: 29 July 1983.)

Part Four: VII. *The individual (including the corporation) in international law—protection of human rights and fundamental freedoms*

In the course of a statement made on 29 September 1982 in a general debate before the General Assembly, the Secretary of State for Foreign and Commonwealth Affairs, Mr. Francis Pym, remarked:

A . . . basic principle of the United Nations is respect for human rights, entrenched since 1948 in the Universal Declaration to which we all subscribe.

(A/37/PV. 9, p. 63.)

In reply to a question, the Minister of State, Foreign and Commonwealth Office, wrote:

The Government continue to make the Turkish authorities aware of our concern over alleged violations of human rights. The Turkish authorities claim that they are making genuine efforts to investigate allegations and, where these allegations are proven, to punish the culprits. We shall continue to watch developments closely.

(H.C. Debs., vol. 35, Written Answers, col. *89*: 18 January 1983.)

In moving the second reading of the Marriage Bill, the Government spokesman in the House of Lords, Lord Elton, stated:

At this point I should remind your Lordships of an international obligation which is relevant to the marriage of detained persons. This is contained in the European Convention on Human Rights. Article 12 of the Convention guarantees to men and women of marriageable age the right to marry. Clearly the mere fact of the imprisonment or detention prevents a detained person from exercising that right fully. The European Commission of Human Rights has recently considered two cases which raise the question of how far the rights guaranteed by Article 12 of the Convention would apply to prisoners. The Commission's opinion was that the right to marry was, in essence, the right to form a legally-binding association between a man and a woman and that this right should not be denied on the grounds that, as one partner was detained, the couple would not be able to live together. The Commission concluded that the imposition of a substantial delay before a prisoner could exercise his right to marry, as would often happen if a prisoner had to wait until the end of his sentence, was a violation of Article 12 of the Convention. I should perhaps make it absolutely clear that this does not mean that prisoners have either the right to live with a spouse or the right to receive conjugal visits.

The Government have accepted the Commission's findings but, as things stand, prisoners are not able at present to marry in a prison established in England and Wales. Consideration had therefore to be given to making arrangements for a prisoner who wishes to marry to go to a convenient church, chapel or register office. Sometimes this is not difficult because the prisoner can be given temporary release for the wedding; but in many cases arrangements have to be made for the prisoner to be escorted by staff both to and from the place where he can marry.

(H.L. Debs., vol. 438, cols. 482–3: 28 January 1983.)

In reply to the question whether the Secretary of State 'will instruct the United Kingdom's representatives at the currently resumed Madrid conference to raise the imprisonment of Anatoly Shcharansky as a breach of the Final Act of the Helsinki Agreement', the Minister of State, Foreign and Commonwealth Office, wrote:

We have raised the Soviet treatment of Mr. Shcharansky many times at the CSCE conference at Madrid and our delegation will do so again when the conference resumes on 8 February.

(H.C. Debs., vol. 36, Written Answers, col. *30*: 31 January 1983; see also H.C. Debs., vol. 36, cols. 989–90: 9 February 1983.)

In the course of a debate on the subject of abducted children, the Minister of State, Foreign and Commonwealth Office, Mr. Douglas Hurd, stated:

. . . international law is an important part of the argument and, perhaps, of our hopes for improving the position of parents in the plight that he described. There are two forthcoming international conventions that could be helpful. There is the European Convention on Recognition and Enforcement of Decisions concerning Custody of Children and on Restoration of Custody of Children 1980. We have signed that, and are considering ratification. We are also considering whether we should sign and ratify a second convention, which is an international convention going wider than the membership of the Council of Europe, that being the Hague Convention on Civil Aspects of International Child Abduction 1980. That convention would deal with the practice of international child abduction by providing procedures to ensure that the right of custody and access under the law of one contracting state are effectively respected in another contracting state.

My right hon. and noble Friend the Lord Chancellor has recently issued a consultation document about the Hague convention. He has set out, at great length, the proposals of the convention and also discussed its relationship with the European convention. He has asked that all interested people should, by 29 April, give his Department their views on whether Britain should sign and ratify the Hague convention and ratify the European convention. . . . it is no good supposing that the international obligation would be only one way. It would not simply be a matter of enabling a British parent with British court orders, in cases covered by the convention, to recover children who had been taken abroad by the other parent. It would also enable parents living overseas to come to Britain with foreign court orders to obtain children presently living here.

I suspect that we might have debates of an opposite nature as parents with children living in Britain found that they might be removed from them because of an order granted in a foreign court. That would be the consequence of Britain adhering to one or both of the conventions.

. . . in the present state of international law, when the two conventions are not in force in respect of Britain, children are under the jurisdiction of the courts in the country in which they happen to live. British court orders, or the fact that the children are wards of a British court, do not automatically mean that the orders are applicable where the children happen to live. We have to deal with the courts and authorities of the country where the child happens to be.

(Ibid., cols. 830–1: 7 February 1983.)

In reporting on the progress by the U.S.S.R. and Eastern European countries on implementing the Helsinki Final Act during the last six months of 1982, the Parliamentary Under-Secretary of State, Foreign and Commonwealth Office, wrote of Poland:

Social organisations suspended under martial law have now been permitted to resume activity. All existing trade unions, however, including the free trade union Solidarity, were outlawed by the new trade union law. Her Majesty's Government have already made it clear that they particularly deplore this action.

(Ibid., Written Answers, col. 380: 9 February 1983.)

In reply to a question, the Minister of State, Foreign and Commonwealth Office, wrote:

The United Kingdom delegation to the United Nations Commission on Human Rights has drawn the attention of the commission to human rights violations by Soviet forces in Afghanistan, including the massacre in Logar province. We are deeply disturbed by the reports of this atrocity.

(Ibid., col. 388: 9 February 1983.)

In reply to the question on what grounds Her Majesty's Government are defending a case before the European Commission on Human Rights relating to the nationalization of the aircraft and shipbuilding industries, the Prime Minister wrote:

Under the Commission's rules of procedure, all proceedings before it, including all pleadings, are confidential. The Government will continue to observe this rule. Broadly, we are contesting the applications made to the Commission because we do not accept that the compensation arrangements under the Aircraft and Shipbuilding Industries Act 1977 involved any breach of the United Kingdom's legal obligations under the human rights convention, however objectionable its terms were on other grounds.

(Ibid., vol. 38, Written Answers, col. 87: 1 March 1983.)

In reply to a question, the Minister of State, Foreign and Commonwealth Office, wrote:

On 3 March our delegation at the United Nations Commission on Human Rights co-sponsored a draft resolution urging the Government of Iran to respect the human rights of all individuals within its jurisdiction. The European Ten have also decided to make a further approach to the Iranian authorities about persecution of the Baha'is.

(Ibid., col. 432: 9 March 1983; see also H.C. Debs, vol. 39, col. 1183: 24 March 1983.)

In the course of a debate on the subject of summary and arbitrary executions, the Parliamentary Under-Secretary of State, Foreign and Commonwealth Office, Mr. Malcolm Rifkind, stated:

The Government have recently made clear their concern about any human rights violations wherever they occur, and human rights violations are not, unfortunately, the prerogative of any one region in the world or any one political system. It has now become generally accepted that human rights are a legitimate matter for international concern. This is a relatively recent development and is not a view that is publicly endorsed by all states yet. Indeed, it is opposed by some. However, successive British Governments together with other Western countries have consistently worked to get this view more widely accepted. The practice of the United Nations, particularly over the past 10 years, has supported our view, and the United Nations has increasingly expressed concern and tried to take action on countries where there are sustained and severe violations of human rights.

The right to life is a fundamental human right. Extrajudicial killing, or murder, by Governments is a particularly flagrant and breathtaking violation of one of man's most basic rights. The question remains how we can best use our influence to persuade Governments to put an end to this terrible practice. We believe that it is best in this case to work through the United Nations, since it is important that the international community as a whole should be involved, that its authority should be invoked, and that it should be seen to act. If the international community acts together, this is more likely to achieve the right result than if the task is left to a few, generally Western, countries to express their concern.

The United Nations is seized of this problem, which it terms summary and arbitrary executions, and has had strong British support in trying to grapple with this question. When the United Nations Secretary-General last year asked Governments for their views on this problem, the British Government stated our views clearly in the following terms:

'United Kingdom believes that summary or arbitrary execution constitutes one of the gravest violations of human rights, and that protection against such violations constitutes a fundamental obligation of States in the field of human rights. The International Covenant on Civil and Political Rights provides for safeguards against summary or arbitrary execution in its Articles 6 and 9 as does Article 2 of the European Convention on Human Rights to which the United Kingdom is also a party.'

The British Government went on to say:

'The United Kingdom also believes that where States fail to live up to this fundamental obligation on human rights, the appropriate United Nations and other bodies should not hesitate to examine and deal with such abuses in accordance with the various relevant international instruments and United Nations Resolutions'.

The United Nations Economic and Social Council therefore last year passed a resolution with United Kingdom support which appointed a special rapporteur to examine the question of summary or arbitrary executions. My hon. Friend referred very eloquently to the rapporteur's conclusions. This report, prepared by Mr. Amos Wako, was discussed at the United Nations Human Rights Commission this year in Geneva. The commission adopted by consensus, a consensus which the British delegation strongly supported, a resolution which expressed its deep concern at the practice of summary executions and which extended the mandate of the special rapporteur for a further year. This grave violation of human rights will therefore continue to receive attention, and we shall have an opportunity at next year's commission meeting to consider what further steps can most usefully be taken within the United Nations machinery.

The practice of summary executions not only cuts across any sense of natural justice, but is also contrary to the Universal Declaration of Human Rights adopted by the United Nations in 1948. It is also contrary to the provisions of the International Covenant on Civil and Political Rights, which I mentioned earlier. This covenant, which the United Kingdom ratified in 1976, is a legally binding instrument. Unfortunately, only about half the membership of the United Nations have ratified this covenant, and some of those countries that have, act in flagrant violation of some of its provisions. We have, therefore, consistently urged more countries to consider ratifying the convention, and we have urged all countries that have ratified to observe its provisions. At the same time, we continue to seek to ensure that the machinery established by the United Nations to monitor the implementation of the covenant is as effective as possible.

United Nations action, particularly in the humanitarian field, can often provide the best results. For example, in 1980, largely as a result of a United Kingdom initiative, a five-man working group was set up to look into the question of 'disappearances' and to examine individual cases. The group is currently chaired by Viscount Colville of Culross who sits in his personal capacity, although he is also the leader of the United Kingdom delegation to the Human Rights Commission. The work of the group has been solely inspired by humanitarian considerations; it aims to provide information for relatives about those who have disappeared and to encourage Governments to put an end to this practice. It has achieved better results than initially expected, and although difficult to quantify it has undoubtedly, by prompt action, also saved some lives. Governments can no longer indulge in this practice in the belief that no one outside the country will notice or care.

We hope that now that the United Nations is seized of the problem of summary executions, and that a report listing countries guilty of this practice has been produced, the Governments concerned will realise that people in the world at large do notice and care.

(Ibid., vol. 39, cols. 1176–8: 25 March 1983; see also ibid., vol. 40, Written Answers, cols. 47–8: 28 March 1983.)

In reply to a question, the Minister of State, Foreign and Commonwealth Office, wrote:

The Foreign and Commonwealth Office has overall responsibility for the conduct of all proceedings in cases concerning the European Convention on Human Rights. When the Commission communicates a case to the United Kingdom and seeks information regarding admissibility and merits, the Foreign and Commonwealth Office acts as the agent, and consults other Government departments as and when necessary. The following departments were consulted with regard to the eight cases in question:

Young, James and Webster Department of Employment

X; Silver and Others; ⎫
Golder; Tyrer   ⎬ Home Office
                        ⎭

Dudgeon; Ireland versus the United Kingdom Home Office and Northern Ireland Office.

In the case of *Campbell and Cosans*, where a breach of the First Protocol to the Convention was found to have occurred, the Scottish Office were consulted.

(H.L. Debs., vol. 441, cols. 90-1: 11 April 1983.)

In reply to a question, the Attorney-General wrote:

Since May 1979 the following judgments of the European Court of Human Rights have been given in which the Court has found the United Kingdom to be in breach of provisions of the European Convention on Human Rights:

The case of Young, James and Webster—breach of Article 11 (freedom of association) arising out of the operation of the closed shop in relation to the applicants.

Campbell and Cosans v. United Kingdom—breach of Article 2 of Protocol No. 1 (right to respect for religious and philosophical convictions in the provision of education) in relation to the refusal to allow the applicants to insist on their children being exempt from corporal punishment.

Dudgeon v. United Kingdom—breach of Article 8 (respect for private life) in relation to the prohibition in Northern Ireland of homosexual conduct carried out in private between consenting adults.

X v. United Kingdom—breach of Article 5(4) (review procedure for lawfulness of detention) in relation to the detention of a mental health patient.

Silver and others v. United Kingdom—breach of Articles 6(1) (right to a hearing in the determination of civil rights), 8 (right to respect for correspondence) and 13 (right to an effective remedy) in relation to the stopping or delaying of certain letters written by prisoners.

In all these cases the court did not find the United Kingdom to be in breach in respect of other matters complained of by the applicants. Findings by the court are made in the context of the particular facts of the cases before it, rather than on assertions of established practices.

(H.C. Debs., vol. 40, Written Answers, cols. *364-5*: 12 April 1983.)

In the course of a debate on the subject of human rights violations, the Government Minister in the House of Lords, Lord Trefgarne, stated:

We have repeatedly made clear our concern about human rights and, like our predecessors and other Western Governments, we have insisted that violations of basic rights are a legitimate matter of international concern, debate and action. Some countries still take the view that any such expression of concern is an unwarranted interference in their internal domestic affairs. But one of the more heartening developments in recent years is that this argument is now widely seen as hollow special pleading when it relates to abuses which clearly contravene the fundamental standards of decency expressed in the Universal Declaration of Human Rights. The practice of the United Nations, particularly over the past 10 years or so, has endorsed this view and the United Nations and its subsidiary bodies, notably the Commission on Human Rights, have increasingly expressed concern and tried to take action where there is evidence of gross violations of human rights. The United Kingdom has been in the forefront of these developments and the international community can be in no doubt of our unequivocal position on these matters.

(H.L. Debs., vol. 443, cols. 1236-7: 20 July 1983.)

In reply to the question how many individual applications have been made against each of the States which have accepted the compulsory jurisdiction of the European Convention on Human Rights for each year 1978 to 1982, the Parliamentary Under-Secretary of State, Foreign and Commonwealth Office, wrote:

I take the question to refer to states which have accepted the right of individual petition under Article 25 of the European Convention for the Protection of Human Rights and Fundamental Freedoms. On this basis the information is as follows:

	1978	1979	1980	1981	1982
Austria	27	23	28	32	30
Belgium	13	32	26	22	27
Denmark	2	8	7	3	7
Federal Republic of Germany	115	120	106	109	98
France*	—	—	—	7	93
Iceland	—	—	1	—	—
Ireland	9	5	4	9	23
Italy	14	21	31	20	15
Luxembourg	2	2	1	—	1
Netherlands	19	22	24	21	24
Norway	2	1	1	3	2
Portugal	—	3	3	3	8
Spain*	—	—	—	4	12
Sweden	4	9	11	8	18
Switzerland	31	32	44	31	42
United Kingdom	97	100	103	132	190
TOTAL	335	378	390	404	590

* France and Spain accepted the right of individual petition in 1981.

(H.C. Debs., vol. 46, Written Answers, cols. 195-6: 21 July 1983.)

In reply to a question on the subject of corporal punishment in schools, the Secretary of State for Education and Science wrote:

As a party to the European Convention on Human Rights since 1951 the Government are bound by the decisions of the European Court of Human Rights in any case under the convention to which they are a party. In the Campbell and Cosans case the court decided that where a parent holds a philosophical conviction against corporal punishment at school this must be respected by the state. My right hon. Friend the Secretary of State for Wales and I intend to give effect to the court's judgment in England and Wales proposing in due course legislation which will grant to parents who hold a conviction against corporal punishment the right to have their children exempted from corporal punishment in maintained schools. We believe that parents will exercise this right responsibly.

(Ibid., col. *545*: 28 July 1983; see also ibid., col. *608*)

In reply to the question whether legislation will be introduced to incorporate Article 6 of the European Convention on Human Rights into United Kingdom law, the Prime Minister wrote:

No. I consider that the existing arrangements satisfy our obligation under Article 6 of the Convention.

(Ibid., vol. 48, Written Answers, col. *522*: 17 November 1983; see also ibid., col. *32*: 7 November 1983.)

Part Five: IV. *Organs of the State—diplomatic agents and missions*

The following Note, dated 24 November 1982, was sent to all diplomatic missions in London:

Her Majesty's Principal Secretary of State for Foreign and Commonwealth Affairs presents his compliments to Their Excellencies the High Commissioners and Ambassadors and the Acting High Commissioners and Chargés d'Affaires in the United Kingdom and has the honour to refer to his Note TXC 182/2 dated January 1982 about the entitlement to the use of VIP suites at London Airport. The present Note concerns searches of persons and baggage in the VIP suites at London Airport.

The Secretary of State would like to take this opportunity to remind Heads of Mission that all passengers departing from United Kingdom Airports may be searched before boarding an aircraft in order to ensure the safety of all air travellers. Sir Denis Greenhill's letter of 13 October 1970 and Foreign and Commonwealth Office Note of 9 August 1973 asked for the co-operation of all airline passengers, however distinguished, in submitting with tolerance and good grace to personal and baggage checks in the interest of their own safety and that of all their fellow passengers. Airlines are fully entitled to refuse to carry any passenger who is unwilling to be searched. In practice, however, airport authorities will not search those important visitors from overseas (as distinct from British citizens) who are entitled to use VIP lounges in their own right. All other departing passengers may, as hitherto, be searched before boarding their aircraft, although a search may not in practice be carried out in every instance. Searches will be undertaken as discreetly as possible by security staff who will check baggage by hand, but will often use a hand-held detector for checks of persons.

The Secretary of State hopes that in the interests of air safety Heads of Mission will encourage the compliance of diplomatic staff appointed in London who may be asked to submit to a search when they are leaving the United Kingdom by air. Missions may wish to report these requirements to their Governments.

The Secretary of State regrets the circumstances which make these security precautions necessary but is confident of Their Excellencies' understanding and co-operation in a matter which concerns the safety of all, and is particularly important in guaranteeing the security of all VIPs.

(Text provided by the Foreign and Commonwealth Office.)

In reply to the question whether Her Majesty's Government 'will provide a translation into English of the expressions *bout de papier* and *aide-mémoire*, frequently used by the Foreign and Commonwealth Office and cited in the Franks Report, and tell the House the difference, if any, between the two', the Minister of State, Foreign and Commonwealth Office, wrote:

When a communication is made orally to the representative of another Government, it is sometimes advisable to hand over a written account of the points made or questions asked. The most formal way is to leave a *note verbale* (third person note). A less formal way is the *aide-mémoire* (also known as a *mémoire* or memorandum). It is written in the third person and is dated, but it has no opening or closing courtesies, address, signature or official stamp. A method suitable for leaving a record of purely factual material is the 'piece of paper' (*bout de papier*), typed on unheaded paper with no courtesies, date, signature or official stamp.

(H.L. Debs., vol. 438, col. 248: 25 January 1983.)

In reply to the question 'what reply has been given to the request of the Government of Malta that there should be no contact between the United Kingdom high commission and the Opposition in Malta', the Minister of State, Foreign and Commonwealth Office, wrote:

We have informed the Maltese authorities that the activities of the British High Commission in Valletta will continue to be guided by the Vienna convention on diplomatic relations. We believe that the matter has now been resolved satisfactorily.

(H.C. Debs., vol. 37, Written Answers, col. *364*: 21 February 1983.)

In reply to a question, the Minister of State, Foreign and Commonwealth Office, wrote:

Her Majesty's Government do not have diplomatic relations with the following States: Albania, Argentina, Cambodia, Comoros, and Guatemala.

(Ibid., vol. 42, Written Answers, col. *146*: 5 May 1983.)

In reply to a question, the Minister of State, Foreign and Commonwealth Office, wrote:

Her Majesty's ambassador in Washington has no direct responsibility for the United Kingdom delegation to the International Monetary Fund. But the head of that delegation, who is the United Kingdom executive director of the

International Monetary Fund, also holds the position of Minister (Economic) on the staff of the ambassador.

(Ibid., col. *518*: 13 May 1983.)

Part Five: V. *Organs of the State—consular agents and consulates*

In reply to a question on the subject of facilities provided by United Kingdom consulates in situations where United Kingdom citizens have died in suspicious circumstances, the Parliamentary Under-Secretary of State, Foreign and Commonwealth Office, wrote:

Our consuls abroad provide whatever practical help and advice they can to relatives and friends of the deceased—for example, by putting them in touch with the police and local authorities. They will also provide a list of local lawyers, names of suitable interpreters, and give advice about local burial, cremation, or repatriation of the remains. It is, however, for the local police to investigate any suspicious circumstances concerning the death.

(Ibid., vol. 40, Written Answers, col. *416*: 13 April 1983.)

Part Five: VII. *Organs of the State—armed forces*

(See also Part Five: VIII. B (agreement with Israel), Part Seven: II. B. and Part Eight: II. C., below.)

In reply to a question, the Minister of State for the Armed Forces wrote:

The United States forces are stationed in the United Kingdom under the general provisions of the North Atlantic Treaty, the Agreement regarding the Status of Forces of Parties to the North Atlantic Treaty (1951) and the Visiting Forces Act 1952. There is also a number of supplementary undertakings and agreements which either amplify these main documents or relate to the use of individual bases or facilities.

More specifically, the use of United States bases in the United Kingdom in an emergency is governed by the agreement reached between Mr. Attlee and President Truman in October 1951 and reaffirmed by Sir Winston Churchill and President Truman in a joint communiqué of January 1952.

Land, including that at Daws Hill, High Wycombe, which is made available under these arrangements is not leased to the United States forces and remains the property of the Ministry of Defence.

(Ibid., vol. 37, Written Answers, col. *36*: 14 February 1983; see also H.L. Debs., vol. 440, col. 924: 17 March 1983)

In the course of replying to a question, the Minister of State for Defence Procurement wrote:

British forces exercise in Kenya under arrangements contained in an exchange of letters signed on 14 July 1967 (Cmnd. 3581).

(H.C. Debs., vol. 51, Written Answers, col. *421*: 22 December 1983.)

Part Five: VIII. A. *Organs of the State—immunity of organs of the State—diplomatic and consular immunity*

(See also Part Five: IV. (Note of 24 November 1982), above.)

In the course of a debate held on 10 December 1982 in the Sixth Committee of the General Assembly on the report of the Committee on Relations with the Host Country, the United Kingdom representative, Mr. F. Berman, stated that:

... normally his country, which was a member of the Committee on Relations with the Host Country, would certainly have joined in a consensus on the draft resolution relating to the Committee's report. At the current session, however, that report (A/37/26) gave rise to an important issue, namely, the extent of the privileges and immunities of permanent observers to the United Nations. That issue had been basic to the statements made at the current meeting by the representative of the Byelorussian SSR and at the preceding meeting by the representative of the Soviet Union, both in support of the statement by the Permanent Observer of the Democratic People's Republic of Korea on the previous day, which had been based almost entirely on incorrect concepts. He was thinking not so much of factual error as of the way in which the statement had dealt with questions relating to international law. Where the statement of the representative of the Soviet Union was concerned, he had been puzzled by the quotation from a statement by the Legal Counsel of the United Nations, the exact source of which had not been indicated. Thinking that it might have been taken from the opinion given by the Legal Counsel on 14 November to the Committee on Relations with the Host Country at the latter's request, he had scrutinized that opinion, in which the Legal Counsel's conclusion seemed to be that permanent observer missions enjoyed functional immunity. He did not entirely agree with that opinion, which went too far in drawing conclusions, by analogy, from Article 105 of the Charter of the United Nations; that article, like the other relevant instruments, made no mention of observers to the United Nations. Such conclusions went beyond the practice followed in London, and certainly further than the agreement concluded by the United Kingdom Government with a specialized agency that had its headquarters there. In any case, the Committee on Relations with the Host Country should proceed with extreme caution, acting on the principle that obligations could not be imposed on the host State without its consent.

... Many of the arguments advanced in the statement made the previous day by the Permanent Observer of the Democratic People's Republic of Korea, and many of the conclusions drawn from them, were unfounded. For instance, on page 13 of that statement it was said that the Convention on the Privileges and Immunities of the United Nations and the Headquarters Agreement applied explicitly to the Permanent Observer Mission of the Democratic People's Republic of Korea; mention was also made of that country's membership in specialized agencies. Neither the Convention nor the Agreement referred to observer missions; only Members of the United Nations were mentioned in them. Nor did they deal with the specialized agencies, which were the subject of a separate Convention concluded at a later date. The statement also said that a permanent observer mission was entitled to privileges and immunities under the

1961 Vienna Convention on Diplomatic Relations. That Convention could not confer privileges and immunities on members of the staff of an observer mission who were not members of the diplomatic staff accredited to the host country. In addition, the statement had invoked considerations of justice and humanity, such considerations could not of course be ignored, but the question of granting privileges and immunities remained essentially a question of law which should be addressed with appropriate legal arguments, and simply asserting that such privileges and immunities existed did not make it so.

(A/C. 6/37/SR. 67, p. 8.)

In the course of a debate in the House of Lords on the subject of the rate arrears on the Soviet trade delegation's premises in London, the Minister of State, Foreign and Commonwealth Office, Lord Belstead, stated in reply to a series of questions:

. . . the rates on the premises used by the Soviet trade delegation in Highgate remain unpaid. I understand that the arrears total over £500,000. The Government are pressing the Soviet authorities in discussion to see whether a negotiated settlement of the problem can be found. We also remain in contact with Camden Council.

. . .

. . . Camden Council have indicated that they may institute legal proceedings, and we in the Foreign Office, for our part, stand ready to provide a certificate to the court as to whether these premises enjoy immunity from rates if Camden Council institutes legal proceedings.

. . .

. . . the argument put forward is that the Soviet Union claims that the services are diplomatic and enjoy all immunities. This, regrettably, ignores an undertaking given by the Soviet Union in 1934 to pay all the rates. So far as what the Soviet trade delegation in these premises is involved in, the 1934 agreement sets out the functions of the Soviet trade delegation in some detail. Those functions include the promotion, facilitation and conduct of trade. So far as the talks are concerned, they are between the British Government and the Soviet Union.

. . .

. . . the commercial section of our embassy in Moscow is an integral part of the embassy and therefore not analogous to the Soviet trade delegation.

(H.L. Debs., vol. 438, cols. 911–12: 3 February 1983)

In reply to the question whether the Secretary of State 'will seek to amend the Diplomatic Privileges Act of 1964 to enable local authorities and other public organisations to recoup loss of rates and payments, where overseas representatives are at present protected by diplomatic privilege', the Minister of State, Foreign and Commonwealth Office, wrote:

No. The Diplomatic Privileges Act 1964, in respect of the premises of the mission and in respect of diplomatic agents, provides for exemption from municipal dues and taxes, except those payable for specific services rendered. Where such exemption has been granted under the 1964 Act, it is the practice for the Treasury to bear the non-beneficial portion of the rates—the part not reflecting specific services rendered—while the mission concerned bears the beneficial portion.

It is the practice of the Foreign and Commonwealth Office to make representations to heads of mission in cases where the mission itself or a member of its staff owes money to any public or private organisation and where diplomatic immunity precludes legal action against the debtor.

(H.C. Debs., vol. 37, Written Answers, col. *450*: 23 February 1983.)

In reply to a question, the Parliamentary Under-Secretary of State, Foreign and Commonwealth Office, wrote:

In accordance with article 5 of the 1934 temporary commercial agreement between the United Kingdom and the Soviet Union, only the Soviet trade representative and his two deputies are accorded diplomatic privileges and immunities. I have no plans at present to change the arrangements set out in the agreement.

(Ibid., vol. 38, Written Answers, col. *248*: 4 March 1983.)

In March 1983 a car belonging to the British Embassy in Warsaw, and occupied by members of the Military Attaché's staff, was fired upon by Polish soldiers outside Warsaw. A protest was made immediately and a prompt apology was received from the Polish Ministry of Foreign Affairs.

In reply to a question, the Minister of State, Foreign and Commonwealth Office, wrote:

In negotiations between British and Soviet delegations held recently in London and Moscow, arrangements were worked out on the question of the rating of the building of the Trade Delegation of the USSR in London at 33 Highgate West Hill. The arrangements provide a mutually satisfactory settlement of this question for the period from 1969 to the present and also for the current rating year. They are without prejudice to legal positions. They provide for a Soviet contribution which corresponds to 60 per cent of the rates. This has been paid by the Soviet Embassy to the British Government. The British Government have made it up to 100 per cent and transmitted the whole sum to Camden Council. In addition there are certain flats to which the usual arrangements as regards rating relief will apply, on the basis that they are occupied by persons personally enjoying diplomatic privileges. These arrangements as a whole apply to the arrears and also to the rating year from 1st April 1983 to 31st March 1984. As regards matters concerning the rating of the above mentioned building in subsequent years, these will be further discussed with a view to reaching a settlement during the current rating year.

(H.L. Debs., vol. 441, col. 180: 12 April 1983; see also H.C. Debs., vol. 40, Written Answers, col. *416*: 13 April 1983.)

In reply to a question about the possibility of serving a repairs notice in respect of the Iranian Embassy in Prince's Gate, London, the Government Minister in the House of Lords, Lord Skelmersdale, said in part:

. . . given the vulnerability of our diplomatic compound in Tehran to which I have already referred, the sensitivity of diplomatic relations and the United Kingdom's counter-claim of damage to the Tehran Embassy, repairs notice action would seem inappropriate and possibly also counter-productive.
. . .

If it were not a diplomatic immunity situation there would be recourse to the courts; but regretfully that avenue is not open to the Government.

(H.L. Debs., vol. 443, cols. 715–16: 12 July 1983.)

In reply to a question, the Parliamentary Under-Secretary of State, Home Office, wrote:

Operational control of the experimental wheel-clamping scheme in force in parts of central London is the responsibility of the Metropolitan Police. I understand that the Commissioner has obtained legal advice which suggests that wheel-clamping contravenes the provisions of the Vienna Convention on Diplomatic Relations; and wheel-clamping of identifiable diplomatic vehicles has accordingly been discontinued. We are, however, examining the situation further.

(Ibid., col. 782: 12 July 1983; see also H.C. Debs., vol. 46, Written Answers, col. 4: 18 July 1983 and H.L. Debs., vol. 443, cols. 1427–9: 26 July 1983.)

In reply to the question whether parking offences would be removed from the protection of diplomatic immunity, the Parliamentary Under-Secretary of State, Foreign and Commonwealth Office, wrote:

No. It is not in our power to do so. Diplomatic agents are obliged under article 41 of the Vienna convention on diplomatic relations to respect the laws and regulations of the United Kingdom; but under article 31 of the convention they are immune from prosecution if they do not do so. We regularly remind diplomatic missions that we expect them to conform to parking regulations, but we cannot oblige them to pay their fixed penalties or fines if they park illegally. Some heads of mission nevertheless require their staff to pay any parking fines which they incur.

(H.C. Debs., vol. 46, Written Answers, col. 44: 18 July 1983.)

In reply to the question whether a review of the Diplomatic Privileges Act 1964 would be undertaken to remedy abuses, the same Minister wrote:

No. The Diplomatic Privileges Act 1964 was enacted to give effect in this country to the provisions of the Vienna Convention on Diplomatic Relations, a multilateral international agreement which the United Kingdom had already signed and has since ratified. We could not significantly amend the Diplomatic Privileges Act without being in breach of our international obligations under the Vienna convention. Moreover the convention provides safeguards for the position of British diplomats serving overseas.

Only a very small minority of the 6,000 or so diplomats in London abuse their privileges or immunity. We keep such abuses under review and make representations to heads of mission whenever we consider it necessary.

(Ibid., col. 174: 20 July 1983.)

Following an attempt by bailiffs sent by the Officers to the Sheriffs of Greater London to seize all goods and chattels at 9–10 Grafton Street, London W.1 in order to satisfy a default judgment against the Republic of Colombia, the Foreign and Commonwealth Office provided to the solicitors acting for the Republic of Colombia the following three certificates in connection with the case of *Alcom Ltd.* v. *Republic of Colombia* (see also [1984] 1 All E.R.1 and [1984] 2 All E.R. 6).

(i) Diplomatic Privileges Act 1964

Certificate

I, Eustace Hubert Beilby Gibbs, Head of Protocol Department of the Foreign and Commonwealth Office, hereby certify that the following premises are regarded by the Foreign and Commonwealth Office as part of the premises of the Colombian Embassy and were so regarded on 27 September 1983:

Embassy: Flat 3A, 3 Hans Crescent, SW1
Consulate: Flat No 10, 140 Park Lane, W1
Coffee Section: 9/10 Grafton Street, W1
Commercial Section: offices 1–5 & 17 (4th floor N Block), 25 Victoria Street, SW1.

20 October 1983

(ii) Diplomatic Privileges Act 1964

Certificate

I, Eustace Hubert Beilby Gibbs, Head of Protocol Department of the Foreign and Commonwealth Office, hereby certify that the following premises are regarded by the Foreign and Commonwealth Office as part of the premises of the Colombian Embassy and were so regarded on 27 September 1983:

Embassy: Flat 3A, 3 Hans Crescent, SW1
Coffee Section: 9/10 Grafton Street, W1
Commercial Section: offices 1–5 & 17 (4th floor N Block), 25 Victoria Street, SW1
Residence: 76 Chester Square, SW1
76 Ebury Mews East, SW1

and that the following premises are regarded by the Foreign and Commonwealth Office as part of the premises of the Colombian Consulates-General in London and Liverpool and were so regarded on 27 September 1983:

Consulate-General: Flat No 10, 140 Park Lane, W1
Consulate-General: Offices 47–49, 3rd Floor
Prudential Buildings, 36 Dale Street, Liverpool 2.

21 October 1983

(iii)

I, Eustace Hubert Beilby Gibbs, Head of Protocol Department of the Foreign and Commonwealth Office, hereby certify that the following premises have been notified to the Foreign and Commonwealth Office as the private residences of the persons named being persons notified as members of the diplomatic or administrative and technical staff of the Colombian Embassy and were so regarded on 27 September 1983 (this list is not exhaustive):—

[List of names and premises omitted]

24 October 1983

(Texts provided by the Foreign and Commonwealth Office.)

In reply to a question, the Parliamentary Under-Secretary of State, Foreign and Commonwealth Office, wrote:

We are precluded by the provisions of article 27 of the Vienna Convention on Diplomatic Relations from opening or detaining diplomatic bags, but diplomatic missions are well aware of the need for strict compliance with our laws concerning firearms. If evidence were to come to light that these laws had been flouted by a person enjoying diplomatic immunity, we should not hesitate to take firm action.

(H.C. Debs., vol. 48, Written Answers, col. 238: 11 November 1983.)

In a statement on 15 November 1983 to the Sixth Committee of the General Assembly during its debate on the annual report of the International Law Commission, the United Kingdom representative, Sir Ian Sinclair, observed in respect of the topic of the diplomatic courier and unaccompanied diplomatic bag:

. . . my delegation have serious reservations about the need for a new international instrument on this matter, given that most of the salient points concerning the status of the diplomatic courier and the unaccompanied diplomatic bag are already covered by existing codification conventions, notably the Vienna Conventions on Diplomatic and Consular Relations.

. . . my delegation are firmly convinced that the work of codification on this topic should be accomplished within a much smaller compass. Attention should be concentrated on filling the few gaps in the existing codification conventions. An elaborate super-structure is not called for. Moreover, care should be taken not to equate the status of the diplomatic courier, a transient and peripatetic figure, with the status of a permanent, semi-permanent or even temporary diplomatic agent. What is required in the way of privileges and immunities for the latter is not necessarily required for the former, because of the very short period of time the courier spends in the receiving State or, indeed, in the transit State.

(Text provided by the Foreign and Commonwealth Office.)

Turning to another aspect of the same topic, Sir Ian Sinclair remarked:

The issue is of course whether the scope of the draft should be expanded to include couriers and bags used for official purposes by international organisations or by other entities such as recognised national liberation movements. My delegation have grave reservations about expanding the scope of the draft in this way. To do so would, as is suggested in paragraph 148 of the Commission's Report, seriously limit the possible acceptability of the draft to many States. It would also result in considerable delay in completing the project. Substantial modifications would have to be made to the draft articles to accommodate the special features of international organisations and national liberation movements. At the very least, we think that the Commission should complete its first reading of the draft as a whole on the basis of the scope indicated in Article 1. The Commission and the Sixth Committee could then review the position, so that a final decision can be reached.

(Text provided by the Foreign and Commonwealth Office.)

In reply to the question whether Her Majesty's Government will seek to renegotiate the relevant treaties relating to diplomatic immunity so that all diplomats may no longer avoid prosecution for infringements of motoring legislation, such as illegal parking, the Parliamentary Under-Secretary of State, Foreign and Commonwealth Office, wrote:

This would represent a significant departure from established international law and practice. There is no realistic prospect of securing general agreement to it.

(H.C. Debs., vol. 50, Written Answers, col. *171*: 7 December 1983.)

In reply to a question, the Parliamentary Under-Secretary of State, Home Office, Lord Elton, stated:

We have now completed a detailed review of the wheel clamping of diplomatic vehicles. This review has confirmed that wheelclamping of diplomatic vehicles would be in breach of the Vienna Convention on Diplomatic Relations, and that it is therefore not legally possible to apply wheelclamps to such vehicles. Instead we propose to tackle the wider problem arising from the numbers of diplomatic vehicles in London. The Government are introducing the following new arrangements to reduce their numbers.

The first new measure arises from the distinction which exists between different types of diplomatic immunity. Representatives of certain international organisations, such as the United Nations and NATO and certain consular staff, are not entitled to full immunity, but only to immunity in connection with acts arising from their official duties. These representatives are at present issued with category 'X' registration plates, which are also issued to certain staff entitled to full immunity. In future, 'X' category registration plates will be reserved for vehicles whose users are only entitled to immunity arising from their official acts. I am advised that as soon as the necessary re-plating has been carried out, 'X' category vehicles, of which there will then be some 400, will be eligible for wheel clamping.

Secondly, we are placing a firm limit on the number of vehicles for which 'D' registration plates will be issued. These are plates issued for vehicles used by persons entitled to full diplomatic immunity. In future, issue of 'D' plates for official vehicles will be limited to a maximum of one set per notified diplomat per mission.

Thirdly, issue of 'D' plates for private vehicles will be limited to a maximum of two sets per diplomatic household. These measures should result in significant reduction in the number of vehicles exempt from wheel clamping.

(H.L. Debs., vol. 446, cols. 3–4: 12 December 1983.)

In reply to a further question on the same topic, Lord Elton observed:

. . . there are 5,718 cars used by members of foreign and Commonwealth missions entitled to diplomatic immunity. A provisional total of 74,674 fixed penalty notices were cancelled on grounds of diplomatic immunity in the first nine months of this year.

. . .

When a person who is entitled to immunity is alleged to have committed a criminal offence the police report the facts of the case to the Home Office and the Home Office then recommends to the Foreign and Commonwealth Office such further action as is considered appropriate.

As to parking offences, the procedure is to produce a list of the places and times of the offences and the registration marks of the vehicles, from which the heads of mission can deduce who is to blame.

. . .

. . . clamping is only resorted to by 11 countries in the world. Of those, five do not grant automatic diplomatic immunity; in only two instances have members of British missions been clamped and on each occasion they paid the fine, I am assured.

(Ibid., cols. 7–8.)

Part Five: VIII. B. *Organs of the State—immunity of organs of the State— immunity other than diplomatic and consular*

(See also Part Eight: II. C. (debate on Visiting Forces Act 1952), below.)

Speaking on 17 November 1982 in the Sixth Committee of the General Assembly during a debate on the annual report of the International Law Commission, the United Kingdom representative, Mr. F. Berman, stated:

His delegation had on previous occasions emphasized that the topic of jurisdictional immunities of States and their property was ripe for codification and that the rules of international law applicable in the field required fundamental reappraisal and restatement. It was therefore gratified by the progress which had been made on the topic during the Commission's thirty-fourth session. It was not surprising that the consideration of new draft articles 11 and 12 should have given rise to further references to the fundamental law contained in draft article 6. Given that article's central position in the scheme of the topic, it was bound to provoke differences of view, and his own delegation would continue to reserve judgment on it until it was possible to reach agreement on the areas to which State immunity did not apply and on whether the pertinent provisions were worded with sufficient flexibility to accommodate possible future developments.

(A/C.6/37/SR.48.)

On 30 September 1982 there came into force an Exchange of Notes between the United Kingdom and Israeli Governments concerning a Supplementary Arrangement in respect of the Immunities of British Military Members of the Multinational Force and Observers (MFO) while on leave in Israel. The Exchange of Notes was supplementary to the

Agreement between the United Kingdom and Israeli Governments (*United Kingdom Treaty Series*, No. 37 (1982) (Cmnd. 8646)) which itself was made pursuant to a Protocol of 3 August 1981 (ibid.) related to the Treaty of Peace of 26 March 1979 between the Governments of Israel and Egypt.

In brief outline the Exchange of Notes provides that the United Kingdom Government waives the immunity of vacationing British members of the MFO who are reasonably suspected of having committed, while on leave in Israel, certain acts contrary to Israeli law, in order to permit the Israeli authorities to detain such persons for the purpose of carrying out investigations, in accordance with applicable legal procedures. Furthermore, the United Kingdom agreed to waive the immunities of vacationing members of the MFO whom the Israeli Government intends to bring to trial for weapons offences and drugs felonies committed while on leave in Israel.

(*United Kingdom Treaty Series*, No. 24 (1982) (Cmnd. 8871).)

An exchange of Notes between the United Kingdom and Lebanese Governments was concluded on 31 January 1983, concerning the deployment of a British contingent for the multinational force in Lebanon. The Lebanese Note stated in part:

> ... the members of the British Force shall enjoy the privileges and immunities accorded the technical and administrative staff of the British Embassy in Beirut, and shall be exempt from Immigration and Customs requirements and restrictions on entering or departing from Lebanon. The appropriate British authorities may exercise jurisdiction over the British Force in accordance with British Service Law. Personnel, property and equipment of the British Force introduced into Lebanon shall be exempt from any form of tax, duty, charge or levy.

(Ibid., No. 9 (1983) (Cmnd. 8823); see also ibid. No. 75 (1983) (Cmnd. 9081).)

In a statement on 10 November 1983 to the Sixth Committee of the General Assembly during its debate on the annual report of the International Law Commission, the United Kingdom representative, Sir Ian Sinclair, observed in respect of the Commission's discussion of jurisdictional immunities:

> Another . . . doctrinal problem stems from the fundamental difference of opinion between two schools of thought, both of which are represented in the Commission. According to one school of thought, the principle of State immunity admits of no exceptions save those deriving from the express or implied consent of the State entitled to assert immunity. According to the other school of thought, the principle of State immunity applies only so far as to ensure that the courts of one State do not pronounce upon the validity of acts performed by another State in the exercise of its sovereign authority. The question is whether one starts from the assumption that exceptions from a prior and overriding principle of State immunity have to be justified on a case by case basis; or from the opposite assumption that, because the principle of immunity itself operates by way of

exception to the dominating principle of territorial jurisdiction, it requires to be justified by reference to the functional need to protect the sovereign rights of foreign States operating or present in the territory of the forum State. The Commission has to navigate carefully between the rocks of these two opposed schools of thought.

(Text provided by the Foreign and Commonwealth Office.)

Turning to Article 12 of the Commission's draft articles on jurisdictional immunity, Sir Ian Sinclair went on:

We all know that the courts of those States which have for many years applied the so-called restrictive theory of immunity have encountered particular difficulty in assessing whether, and if so, to what extent, that theory should be applied in the case of State contracts which, at one and the same time, are *prima facie* commercial in nature and yet serve a typically State purpose. This has led to conflicting decisions of national courts on whether the principle of immunity does or does not apply in relation to contracts for defence equipment of varying kinds. If the *nature* of such a contract alone is considered, it may be deemed to be commercial; but, if the *purpose* of the contract is also taken into account, the conclusion may be different. The Commission have sought to reconcile these opposing viewpoints by adopting an interpretative provision which permits reference being made to the purpose of the contract where, in the practice of the foreign state concerned, that purpose is relevant to determining the non-commercial character of the contract. This is a most significant qualification of the basic rule set out in Article 12, and it is a qualification which my government will wish to study carefully. In practice, and leaving aside theoretical or doctrinal differences, it appears to set the point of balance at about midway between those States which (like my own) favour the restrictive theory of immunity and those which still adhere to the so-called absolute theory of immunity.

(Text provided by the Foreign and Commonwealth Office.)

Part Six: I. B. *Treaties—conclusion and entry into force—reservations and declarations to multilateral treaties*

(See also Part Eight: II. A. (Note of 19 October 1983), below.)

On 28 October 1982, the Government of the Union of Soviet Socialist Republics transmitted to the Secretary-General, for deposit, its instrument of ratification of the International Convention concerning the Use of Broadcasting in the Cause of Peace 1936. The instrument contained the following reservation and declarations:

[1] The Union of Soviet Socialist Republics does not consider itself bound by the provisions of article 7 of the Convention under which any dispute that may arise regarding the interpretation or application of the Convention which has not been settled by means of negotiations shall be submitted to arbitration or to judicial settlement at the request of one of the Parties, and declares that, for the submission of such a dispute to arbitration or to judicial settlement, the agreement of all Parties to the dispute shall be essential in every separate case;

[2] The Union of Soviet Socialist Republics declares that it retains the right to

take any measures to preserve its interests both in the event of failure by other States to observe the provisions of the Convention and in the event of any other actions that encroach on the interests of the USSR;

[3] The Union of Soviet Socialist Republics declares that the provisions of article 14 of the Convention are obsolete and contradict the Declaration on the Granting of Independence to Colonial Countries and Peoples adopted by the United Nations General Assembly (resolution 1514 (XV) of 14 December 1960).

By a Note dated 5 November 1982, the Secretary-General advised the Contracting Parties as follows:

It is the Secretary-General's understanding that the reservation and declarations made upon ratification by the Government of the USSR supersede the declarations made upon signature, on 23 September 1936, and that the declaration reproduced above under [2] does not purport to modify the legal effect of any provision of the Convention.

The Convention, it will be recalled is one of those in respect of which the Secretary-General exercises, under resolution 24 (I) of the General Assembly, the secretariat functions previously carried out by the Secretary-General of the League of Nations. It will also be recalled that, in that capacity, the Secretary-General adheres to the practice followed by the League of Nations with regard to reservations in cases where the multilateral treaty concerned does not provide for reservations. The procedure has been described in the *Summary of the Practice of the Secretary-General as Depositary of Multilateral* Agreements, doc. ST/LEG/7, paras. 58–59, and in the publication *Multilateral Treaties Deposited with the Secretary-General—Status as at 31 December 1981*, doc. ST/LEG/SER.E/1, p. 648, footnote 5.

In accordance with the practice referred to above, the Secretary-General will consider that he may proceed with the deposit of the instrument of ratification of the Convention by the Government of the Union of SSR with the above-quoted reservation at the expiry of a 90-day period from the date of the present notification unless, within that time, he has been informed of an objection by any Contracting Party (meaning, a State having ratified, or acceded or succeeded to, the Convention). As provided for by article 12, the Convention would then enter into force for the Union of Soviet Socialist Republics sixty days after the date of the deposit.

By a Note dated 7 December 1983, the United Kingdom Permanent Representative to the United Nations in New York informed the Secretary-General as follows:

On instructions from Her Majesty's Principal Secretary of State for Foreign and Commonwealth Affairs, I have to inform you that the Government of the United Kingdom of Great Britain and Northern Ireland wish to place on record the following:

1. They do not accept the reservation to Article 7 of the Convention reproduced under (1) of your Note.

2. They note Your Excellency's understanding that the declaration reproduced under (2) of your Note does not purport to modify the legal effect of any provision of the Convention. If, contrary to this understanding, the declaration were

intended to modify the legal effect of any provision of the Convention, they would consider it incompatible with the object and purpose of the Convention, particularly when taken together with the purported reservation to Article 7.

3. They do not accept the declaration concerning Article 14 reproduced under (3) of your Note.

4. They do not consider any of the foregoing statements as precluding the entry into force of the Convention for the Union of Soviet Socialist Republics.

(Texts provided by the Foreign and Commonwealth Office.)

Part Six: I. C. *Treaties—conclusion and entry into force—entry into force, ratification*

In reply to the question why Her Majesty's Government had not ratified the 1970 U.N.E.S.C.O. Convention on the Means of Prohibiting and Preventing the Illicit Import, Export and Transfer of Cultural Property, the Minister of State, Foreign and Commonwealth Office, Lord Belstead, stated:

Her Majesty's Government have always been in sympathy with the aims of the convention, but ratification poses administrative, legal and financial difficulties and would require legislation. The Government are still studying these difficulties.

(H.L. Debs., vol. 441, cols. 97–8: 12 April 1983.)

Part Six: II. A. *Treaties—observance, application and interpretation—observance*

(See Part Twelve: II. B. (item of 13 July 1983), below.)

Part Six: II. B. *Treaties—observance, application and interpretation—application*

(See also Part Eight: II. A. (Note of 19 October 1983) and Part Fourteen: I. B. 10. (statement of 19 May 1983), below.)

In the course of his evidence to the Foreign Affairs Committee of the House of Commons on the subject of the Falkland Islands, Sir Ian Sinclair, Legal Adviser, Foreign and Commonwealth Office, was asked about the Nootka Sound Convention of 1790 and, in particular, why the United Kingdom did not recognize the United Provinces as the lawful inheritors of Spanish rights under that Convention. He stated:

. . . as to the Nootka Sound Convention, that Convention in terms terminated as between Britain and Spain in 1795 as a result of war between Britain and Spain. It was revived as between Britain and Spain in 1814 but you will recall that in 1811 Spain evacuated the Islands and abandoned them, so that as from 1811 onwards there was no longer any obligation as far as the United Kingdom was concerned in terms of the Nootka Sound Convention not to occupy possessions already occupied by Spain. So I think that disposes of the argument on the Nootka Sound Convention.

In reply to a further question, Sir Ian Sinclair made the following observation:

What I was saying was that the Nootka Sound Convention in effect terminated in 1795 because of the outbreak of war between Britain and Spain. It was revived in 1814 but by 1814 Spain had evacuated and abandoned the Islands. The obligation under the Nootka Sound Convention was, so far as we were concerned, an obligation not to occupy any territories at the time occupied by Spain. Clearly that obligation could no longer apply to territories which were no longer occupied by Spain at the time.

. . . the Nootka Sound Convention during the time in which it was in force contained this obligation on our part, as a counterpart to various other obligations by Spain, not to occupy any territories occupied by Spain. All I am saying is after 1811 that obligation was no longer relevant as far as the Falkland Islands were concerned because Spain no longer occupied the Falkland Islands.

Asked to what territories the Convention would have applied in 1814, Sir Ian stated:

Various other territories on the Latin American continent at that time occupied by Spain to the extent that they were not under the control of former Spanish colonies which had achieved independence from Spain.

(*Parliamentary Papers*, 1982–3, House of Commons, Paper 31-vi, pp. 162–3.)

Part Six: II. D. *Treaties—observance, application and interpretation— treaties and third States*

(See Part Eight: II. C. (material on Berlin) and Part Eight: IV. (statement of 29 November 1983), below.)

Part Six: II. E. *Treaties—observance, application and interpretation— treaty succession*

(See Part Three: I. E. (Written Answer of 12 December 1983) and Part Six: II. B., above.)

Part Six: IV. C. *Treaties—invalidity, termination and suspension of operation—termination, suspension of operation, denunciation*

The United Kingdom provided the following Note, dated 27 June 1983, to the Legal Committee of the International Maritime Organization on the subject of the procedure for co-ordinating denunciation of the 1957 Brussels Limitation Convention with the entry into force of the 1976 London Limitation Convention:

At the recent 50th session of the Legal Committee the United Kingdom delegation informed members that, in consultation with the respective depositories in London and Brussels, the United Kingdom had adopted a special procedure in order to be able to achieve its desired objective of co-ordinating denunciation of the Brussels International Convention relating to the Limitation of the Liability of Owners of Seagoing Ships 1957 (the 1957 Brussels Limitation Convention) with the eventual entry into force of the International Convention on Limitation of Liability for Maritime Claims 1976 (the 1976 London Limitation Convention).

The problem to be overcome arises from the fact that the periods prescribed on the one hand for notice of denunciation of the 1957 Brussels Limitation Convention (Article 13) and on the other hand for entry into force of the 1976 London Limitation Convention (Article 17) once the twelfth state has deposited its instrument of ratification, etc. are approximately the same (twelve months or possibly a few days longer in the latter case). There would therefore be insufficient time to deposit an instrument of denunciation to the 1957 Brussels Limitation Convention *after* the conditions for entry into force of the 1976 London Limitation Convention had been met.

In order to overcome this problem the United Kingdom, with the agreement of the depositories, has deposited an instrument of denunciation of the 1957 Brussels Limitation Convention with the Belgian Government in which the operative date is defined, not in absolute terms, but in terms of the date, at present unknown, when the 1976 London Limitation Convention will enter into force. The United Kingdom Authorities and the two depositories have agreed to inform each other of the actual date as soon as it has been determined by IMO. It is believed this approach may be of interest to some other members who may wish to achieve the same result.

The form of wording used by the United Kingdom is as follows:

'On the instructions of Her Majesty's Principal Secretary of State for Foreign and Commonwealth Affairs, I have the honour to refer to the International Convention relating to the Limitation of the Liability of Owners of Seagoing Ships, done at Brussels on 10 October 1957 and, in accordance with Article 13 thereof, to inform you that the United Kingdom of Great Britain and Northern Ireland hereby denounces the said Convention. It is the wish of the Government of the United Kingdom that the effective date of this denunciation shall be that on which the Convention on Limitation of Liability for Maritime Claims, done at London on 19 November 1976, enters into force in accordance with Article 17, paragraph 1 thereof. The Government of the United Kingdom will ensure that the Government of Belgium is notified of this date as soon as it becomes known.

'I have the honour to request that the contents of this Note are circulated to the other States Parties to the Brussels Convention of 1957 referred to above.'

(IMO reference LEG 51/9.)

Part Six: V. *Treaties—depositaries, notification, correction and registration*

(See Part Six: I. B., above.)

Part Seven: II. B. *Personal jurisdiction—exercise—military jurisdiction*

(See also Part Five: VII. and Part Five: VIII. B. (agreement with Israel), above; Part Eight: II. C., below.)

In reply to the question what is the juridical status of the British forces in Lebanon, the Minister of State for the Armed Forces wrote:

The deployment of British forces in Lebanon as part of the multinational force is in accordance with the terms of a formal exchange of letters concluded between the British and Lebanon Governments. This provides that command authority will be exercised exclusively by the British Government through diplomatic and military channels and that British service personnel in Lebanon will remain under British jurisdiction in accordance with British Service law.

(H.C. Debs., vol. 37, Written Answers, col. *36*: 14 February 1983)

In reply to a question on the subject of British forces in Belize, the Minister of State, Foreign and Commonwealth Office, wrote:

British forces remain in Belize in accordance with the exchange of notes presented to Parliament in April 1982 in Cmnd. 8520. The agreement provides that the forces are under British command and military jurisdiction. The garrison is there at the request of the Belize Government to assist in the defence of Belize against external aggression.

(Ibid., vol. 38, Written Answers, cols. *213–14*: 3 March 1983.)

Part Eight: I. A. *State territory and territorial jurisdiction—parts of territory, delimitation—frontiers*

(See also Part Three: I. E. (Written Answer of 12 December 1983), above and Part Eight: II. A. (letter of 28 April 1982), below.)

Article I (e) (ii) of an Agreement for the Promotion and Protection of Investments, signed by the Governments of the United Kingdom and Costa Rica on 7 September 1982, contains the following definition:

'territory' in respect of the Republic of Costa Rica: that bounded by the Caribbean Sea, the Pacific Ocean, and the Republics of Nicaragua and Panama. The frontiers of the Republic are those determined by the Canas-Jérez Treaty of 15 April 1858, ratified by the Cleveland Award of 22 March 1888, with respect to Nicaragua, and the Echandi Montero-Fernandez Jaén Treaty of 1 May 1941 with respect to Panama. The island of Coco, situated in the Pacific Ocean, forms part of the national territory.

(Cmnd. 8767.)

Part Eight: II. A. *State territory and territorial jurisdiction—territorial jurisdiction—territorial sovereignty*

(See also Part Two: X., above.)

In a letter dated 28 April 1982, addressed to the President of the Security Council, the United Kingdom Permanent Representative to the United Nations in New York, Sir Anthony Parsons, wrote with regard to the Falkland Islands:

Turning to the question of sovereignty, the United Kingdom, whilst fully maintaining its position, acknowledges that its sovereignty has been disputed by Argentina on the basis of certain events in 1833. Attached to this letter is a memorandum setting out the history of settlement of the Falkland Islands. This shows that France has maintained a colony for about 3 years, Spain for at most about 41 years, the United Kingdom 158 years and Buenos Aires about at most 6 years. In particular, the present population of the Falkland Islands has been there, generation after generation, for the last 149 years, maintaining a viable pastoral economy and distinctive way of life. And whereas the French, Spanish and Buenos Ayrean colonies were very small (under 100 people), the only significant permanent population has been that from the mid-19th century to the present day, averaging just under 2000 persons.

Whilst no doubt much time and energy could be spent in reviewing the history of the Falkland Islands between the first settlement in 1764 and 1833, and whilst the United Kingdom is confident about the strength of its legal case over that period, these factors cannot be allowed to override the right of self-determination. In 1833, the age of the railway was just opening in Europe and it hardly seems appropriate to decide issues involving the welfare of people alive in the latter part of the 20th century on the basis of (disputed) events in the early part of the 19th century or even the 18th century. If the international community were to discount 149 years of history, there would hardly be an international boundary which did not immediately become subject to dispute.

(S/15007.)

The memorandum annexed to this letter read in part as follows:

History of the settlement of the Falkland Islands

14 August 1592	The English ship Desire, captained by John Davis, was driven off course in a storm to 'certaine isles never before discovered . . . lying 50 leagues or better from the ashore east and northerly from the (Magellan) Straits'.
27 January 1690	Captain John Strong of the British ship Welfare, made the first recorded landing on the island. He gave the name 'Falkland' to the sound between the two main islands in the group, after Viscount Falkland who was the treasurer of the British Royal Navy. The islands were uninhabited.
1700–1710	The Falkland Islands were visited by French seal hunters, from St Malo (hence the French name of Les Isles Malouines). No settlements were established.
31 January 1764	A Frenchman (Louis Bougainville) established a settlement at the west end of Berkeley Sound (north-west of modern Stanley). The settlement was called Port Louis.
June 1764	A British expedition left to found a settlement.
August 1764	Formal possession of the islands was announced in the name of King Louis XV of France.
January 1765	The British expedition surveyed West Falkland and established a post at Port Egmont. Commodore Byron took formal possession of all the Islands for King George III.
June 1765	Commodore Byron reported that he had 'coasted the

	islands for 70 leagues and saw no evidence of anyone being there'.
January 1766	A second British expedition, led by Captain Macbride completed the settlement at Port Egmont and erected a block house for the defence of the settlement. In December 1766, he discovered the existence of the Bougainville settlement and gave the settlers formal notice to leave British territory.
April 1767	France relinquished its claim to the islands to Spain in return for a financial indemnity. Spain re-named Port Louis as Puerto de la Soledad.
November 1769	The Captain of a British frigate ordered a Spanish ship to move away from Port Egmont. The Governor of the Spanish colony called on the British settlers to leave and the British captain warned the Spaniards to leave within 6 months.
4 June 1770	A Spanish frigate entered Port Egmont and was joined two days later by 4 Spanish ships to expel the British settlers.
10 June 1770	The British settlers capitulated and set sail for the United Kingdom. The United Kingdom protested to the Government of Spain.
22 January 1771	Spain issued a declaration in response to the British protest, agreeing to restore to the United Kingdom the possession of Port Egmont. The Spanish declaration stated that the restoration of Port Egmont to British possession 'cannot nor ought in any wise to affect the question of the prior right of sovereignty to the Malouines Islands, otherwise called Falkland's Islands'. The British accepted this declaration, together with full performance of the Spanish undertakings, as satisfaction for the injury done to the United Kingdom on 10 June 1770.
September 1771	Port Egmont was formally restored to the United Kingdom.
May 1774	The British establishment at Port Egmont was closed for reasons of economy. The British commanding officer left the British flag flying and a plaque declaring the Falkland Islands 'to be the sole right and property' of King George III.
1777	The buildings at Port Egmont were destroyed by the Spanish.
1784	Spanish colony had 82 inhabitants (including 28 convicts).
June 1806	The Spanish settlement at Soledad was abandoned. Islands uninhabited.
9 November 1820	Col. Jewett paid a brief visit and took formal possession of the Falkland Islands on behalf of the newly independent government in Buenos Aires, without

	establishing a settlement. He found many vessels engaged in sealing including several British and US vessels.
1823	An attempt by Don Jorge Pacheco of Buenos Aires to establish a settlement failed.
5 January 1828	The government in Buenos Aires issued a decree establishing a colony at Soledad. Mr Vernet, a Hamburg merchant of French descent, and naturalised citizen of Buenos Aires was given three years to establish a colony and provision was made in case the population should extend to other islands.
10 June 1829	A decree was issued by the government of Buenos Aires asserting sovereignty, as successor to Spain, over the Falkland Islands.
30 August 1829	Mr Vernet established the colony, with only 20 men in whom he had confidence, according to his own account.
19 November 1829	The British Chargé d'Affaires at Buenos Aires delivered a formal protest against the above decree on the grounds that 'an authority has been assumed, incompatible with His Britannic Majesty's rights of sovereignty over the Falkland Islands. These rights founded upon the original discovery and subsequent occupation of the said islands, acquired an additional sanction from the restoration by (Spain) of the British settlement in the year 1771. . . .'
25 November 1829	The Minister of Foreign Relations of Buenos Aires acknowledged receipt of the protest.
1831	Vernet's colony numbered about 100 persons.
July 1831	Three US sealing vessels were seized by Mr Vernet, who subsequently took one of them, the schooner 'Harriet' to Buenos Aires where it was declared a prize by the government.
November 1831	The US consul denied that Mr Vernet had any right to capture and detain US vessels engaged in the fisheries at the Falkland Islands and remonstrating against all measures, including the decree of 10 June 1829, asserting a claim to the Falkland Islands. A formal protest was made in respect of the 'Harriet' and two other vessels, the 'Superior' and the 'Breakwater'.
December 1831	The Minister at Buenos Aires replied that an enquiry was being undertaken, but that the protest could not be admitted because the US consul did not appear to have been specially authorised.
June 1832	The US ship 'Lexington' under Captain Silas Duncan arrived at the Falkland Islands and destroyed the colony set up by Buenos Aires. The colonists fled. Some were captured and taken by the 'Lexington' to

	Montevideo. Duncan declared the islands free of all government.
20 June 1832	The US Chargé d'Affaires in Buenos Aires addressed a Note to the Minister responsible for foreign affairs about the seizure of the three US vessels. On instructions, the Chargé denied 'the existence of any right in this Republic to interrupt, molest, detain or capture any vessels belonging to citizens of the United States . . .'. The US government demanded restitution of all captured property and an indemnity, pointing out 'that the citizens of the United States have enjoyed the rights of free fishery in these regions unmolested . . .'.
September 1832	Governor appointed ad interim by Buenos Ayrean government.
December 1832– 3 January 1833	Captain Onslow of HMS Clio occupied Port Egmont. On reaching Soledad, Captain Onslow found a detachment of 25 Buenos Ayrean soldiers and their schooner 'Sarandi'. A mutiny had previously occurred at Port Louis while the 'Sarandi' was at sea and the mutineers had killed the Governor. The Commander of the Argentine schooner had placed the mutineers in irons aboard a British schooner and they were, at his request, taken to Buenos Aires. Most people elected to be repatriated: 18 were persuaded to stay behind. Not a shot was fired on either side. Captain Onslow re-asserted British sovereignty, by raising the flag.
22 January 1833	The Minister at Buenos Aires protested to the British Chargé d'Affaires.
May 1833	The United Kingdom rejected the protest and affirmed that the Falkland Islands belonged to the Crown.
1833	Buenos Aires presented a claim to the US government in respect of USS Lexington's action. Diplomatic correspondence continued until at least 1886 but the US government rejected the claim for compensation on the grounds that it depended on the question of sovereignty.
1841	British Lieutenant Governor appointed and civil administration organised in Port Louis.
1841–2	Further protests about British settlement rejected.
1844	Capital moved to Stanley.
1845	Governor appointed. Legislative Council and Executive Council set up.
1851	Population estimated at 787 (see below).
1884–88	Further Argentine protests made and rejected.
1949	Elections to the Legislative Council instituted on the basis of universal adult suffrage.

1977   Voting age lowered to 18.
September/October 1981   General elections held for the Legislative Council.

Since the first census in 1851, the population has increased substantially, reaching a peak in the mid-1930s of some 2,400 inhabitants. Censuses have been taken every ten years and full details are in the annex to this account. The community thus established has set up its own social, economic and cultural structures within a framework which evolved in accordance with the wishes of the islanders themselves. They have freedom of expression and all of the basic rights guaranteed to them under the United Nations Charter. The United Kingdom, as administering authority, has submitted comprehensive information on the territory annually under Article 73(e) of the Charter and an up to date account based on this information is readily available in the Committee of 24's most recent working paper on the islands (document A/AC109/670 of 5 August 1981).

(Ibid.)

In response to a letter raising certain points on the history of the Falkland Islands, the Secretary of State for Foreign and Commonwealth affairs, Mr. Francis Pym, replied in July 1982 in part:

Successive governments of the United Kingdom have been advised that the legal title of the UK to the Falkland Islands is fundamentally sound and have always acted on that basis. You refer to a number of comments made in the past at various dates by individual officials in the FCO. I do not think it right to concentrate on a few isolated and selective expressions of doubt. The strength of our case depends on a detailed legal examination of all relevant events and factors. Even leaving aside arguments in our favour based on events before 1833, we have been consistently advised that our title can be soundly based on our possession of the Islands from 1833. Our case rests on the facts, on prescription and on the principle of self-determination. It is not affected by single comments taken out of context made by officials or even an Ambassador in Buenos Aires, especially when they were made many years ago at a time when our continuous possession had lasted much less long and the principle of self-determination was not recognised as it is today.

   . . .

Prescription as a mode of acquiring territory is generally recognised in international law and is referred to in the standard works. It is certainly justifiable for us to rely on it in connection with the Falkland Islands.

   . . .

In all discussions with the Argentine Government the Government have of course taken into account the legal position and the legal advice which has been given to successive governments over the years.

(Text provided by the Foreign and Commonwealth Office.)

[Editorial note: The above items should be read in conjunction with the material under this heading in UKMIL 1982.]

The Foreign and Commonwealth Office submitted to the Foreign Affairs Committee of the House of Commons a memorandum, dated

17 December 1982, on the Falkland Islands. The memorandum, which replied to questions posed by the Committee, read in part as follows:

Question 1

Why has the British claim to 'first discovery' (which was the basis of our claim throughout the nineteenth century) apparently been abandoned?

The UK has not abandoned its claim to 'first discovery' of the Falkland Islands, but we accept that there are conflicting claims and that the historical evidence available at present is obscure and uncertain. Our claim to first discovery has never of itself formed the basis for our claim to sovereignty over the Islands.

Question 2

What status does the recorded landing of Captain Strong in 1690 have in international law?

Captain Strong did not take formal possession of the Islands in the name of the Crown. But his recorded landing in 1690 is evidence of British interest in the Islands at that time.

Question 3

Is the British claim to sovereignty by virtue of early settlement (January 1766–May 1774) comparable with that of Spain (1767–1811)?

1. The British claim to sovereignty over the Falkland Islands by virtue of early settlement is based on formal possession of West Falkland and 'all the neighbouring islands', claimed by Commodore John Byron in the name of HMG in January 1765. An expedition led by Captain McBride established a settlement at Port Egmont on 8 January 1766. Apart from a period between June 1770, when the British were expelled by the Spanish, and January 1771, when Britain and Spain exchanged Declarations to resolve the problem and restore the *status quo*, British occupation continued until 1774. When Britain withdrew from the Falkland Islands in 1774 for reasons of economy, a lead plaque was left behind declaring the Islands to be the 'sole right and property' of George III. There is no record of any written agreement or of any formal commitment by Britain to renounce sovereignty on withdrawal from Port Egmont.

2. Spain's claim to sovereignty (as set out in the Argentine protest of 1833) is based on the formal French occupation of the Falkland Islands in April 1764. The French rights were surrendered to the Spanish Government, in exchange for a financial indemnity, in April 1767. Spanish occupation from 1774 to 1811 was undisturbed by any other power.

3. Britain never accepted the Spanish claim to sovereignty, on the basis of purchase from France, over the Falkland Islands. In particular, the fact that Spain occupied the Islands alone from 1774 to 1811 is not an indication that Britain accepted Spanish sovereignty over them. The Spanish garrison and settlement on the Islands were withdrawn in 1811, after which the Islands remained uninhabited until the early 1820s, apart from fleeting visits by sealers and whalers of various nationalities.

. . .

Question 5

Did the Argentine formal possession of the islands in November 1820 (not 1829) occasion any British protest?

There was no British protest about Colonel Daniel Jewett's action in taking formal possession of the Falkland Islands in November 1820. There was no British diplomatic representation in Buenos Aires at the time and there is no reason to suppose that HMG knew of Jewett's action when it took place. It should, moreover, be noted that the act of possession was made in the name of a government which was not recognised either by Britain or any other foreign power at the time. No act of occupation followed the ceremony of claiming possession. The Islands remained without any effective government and Jewett quickly returned to Buenos Aires, his ship subsequently being condemned in the United States as a pirate.

Question 6

Is it the case that the United Provinces (Argentina) established a settlement in 1824 and re-established it from 1826–1833? Would this amount to 'effective occupation'?

1. The United Provinces did not establish a settlement in 1824. However, in 1826 Louis Vernet, a naturalised citizen of Buenos Aires, undertook a purely private venture to establish a small settlement at Puerto de la Soledad. It was not until January 1828 that the Argentine Government issued a decree giving Vernet three years to establish a colony on East Falkland. On 10 June 1829 the same Government issued a decree setting forth its claimed rights to the Falkland Islands, based on what it regarded as inherited rights from the Spanish Viceroyalty of La Plata. At the same time the Government issued a second decree appointing Vernet as Political and Military Governor of the Falkland Islands. He himself later admitted that the foundation of the colony was entirely his own work, that he received no assistance at any time from his Government and that the Islands paid no taxation.

2. In August 1831, Vernet seized three American sealing ships in an attempt to control fishing in Falkland Islands waters. The US Consul in Buenos Aires promptly denied the Argentine right to regulate seal fishing and in December 1831, Captain Duncan of the USS Lexington landed an armed party at Puerto de la Soledad, destroyed the fort, dispersed the colonists and declared the Islands 'free of all government'. By the time of the arrival of the British in 1833 the Colony was in a sorry state: deserted apart from a small garrison and a few settlers of various nationalities.

3. HMG do not consider that Vernet's actions in the name of the Argentine Government amounted to effective occupation of the Islands sufficient to confer a valid title on Argentina.

Question 7

On what other occasions besides November 1829 did the British protest Argentine actions?

The British Government protested again on 28 September 1832. This British protest repeated the terms of the previous protest sent in November 1829, stating that the Argentine action assumed an authority 'incompatible with His Britannic Majesty's Rights of Sovereignty of the Falkland Islands'.

Question 8

Does the disbandment by force of the Argentine settlement by Captain Duncan of USS Lexington in December 1831 establish *terra nullius* status?

Captain Duncan's action is described in the answer to Question 6. In and of itself, this action would not have been sufficient to establish *terra nullius* status.

Question 9

Were the Islands taken by force in January 1833 against Argentine protests?

1. The Falkland Islands were not taken by force in 1833. The facts are as follows. In December 1832 the British Admiralty's instructions to go to the Falklands to exercise Britain's rights of sovereignty reached Captain Onslow of the warship HMS Clio. Captain Onslow occupied Port Egmont on West Falkland, which was uninhabited. He put up a signal post dated 23 December 1832, stating that the Islands belonged to Great Britain. Captain Onslow arrived at Puerto de la Soledad on 2 January 1833. He informed the settlement that he had come to take possession of the Islands in the name of His Britannic Majesty, and persuaded the Buenos Airean Commander, Pinedo, and the remaining members of his garrison, to leave peacefully. On arrival at Buenos Aires Pinedo was severely admonished for offering no resistance. The settlement at the time of Onslow's arrival was a small one comprising a number of settlers of various nationalities, several ex-convicts from the penal reserve, and a few farmhands ('gauchos').

2. Captain Onslow's own account of taking possession of the Falklands was sent in a despatch to the British Chargé d'Affaires in Buenos Aires on 19 December 1833.

'I have the honour to report H.M. Ship under my command visited Port Egmont, West Falkland, 20th December, 1832, and found on Saunders Island the ruins of our Establishment. I left, on what appeared to me to have been Fort George, a signal staff, with the following inscription:—

"Visited by H.B.M.S. Clio for the purpose of exercising the Rights of Sovereignty, 23rd December, 1832."

'Not finding any inhabitants, or the foreign settlement alluded to in the Commander-in-Chief's instructions, at West Falkland, I sailed to Berkeley Sound, East Falkland, where I arrived on the 2nd January, 1833, and found the Settlement with 25 soldiers, under the Buenos Ayrean Flag; also a Schooner of War (the Sarandi) under the same colours. I waited upon the Commander of the Schooner, and learnt from him that he commanded both by sea and land. He informed me a mutiny had taken place, whilst he was at sea, amongst the soldiers, they had killed their Commander, and were in a state of great insubordination; so much so, that the settlers were afraid to pursue their avocations, and all appeared anarchy and confusion. I had great trouble to persuade twelve of the "Gauchos" to remain on the Settlement; otherwise cattle could not have been caught, and the advantages of refreshments to the shipping must have ceased. I acquainted the Buenos Ayrean Commander, *civilly*, with the object of my Mission to these Islands, and requested him to haul down the Flag on shore, and to embark his Force "he being in a possession belonging to the Crown of Great Britain; that I came to these Islands to exercise the Right of Sovereignty over them." At first, he consented to do so, provided I would state to him in writing, my Mission. I did so, but only observed, what I had before verbally communicated to him, and declined any further correspondence on the subject. He visited me at 5 a.m. the following morning, to request me to allow the Buenos Ayrean Flag to fly on shore, till the 5th instant: when he would sail, and take with him the force, and such of the settlers as were desirous to leave the Island. I told him his request, as far as it related to the Flag, was inadmissible, he then consented to embark the soldiers, and left me for that purpose; but I observed he still kept the Flag flying on shore. I landed immediately, hoisted the British Flag, and sent an Officer to haul down the Foreign Flag, and to deliver it on board the schooner. He sailed the evening 4th instant, taking with him part of the soldiers, with several of the inhabitants, who wished to return to Buenos Ayres. The mutineers he had placed in irons, on board the British schooner Rapid, by the consent of her Master, previous to my arrival, and had freighted for accordingly to take them to Buenos Ayres. She sailed on the 5th instant.'

Question 10

Is it or has it ever been part of the British claim that by 1833 the Islands were *terra nullius*?

The British case has not been put in these terms. However, as indicated in the reply to Question 6, we do not consider that the sporadic acts of occupation and administration by Argentina in the period prior to 1833 were sufficient to confer a valid title on Argentina.

Question 11

On how many occasions between 1833 and 1968 did Argentina protest at Britain's occupation?

The Argentine Government formally protested about the British occupation of the Falkland Islands in 1833, 1834, 1841, 1842, 1849, 1884 and 1888. During this century Argentina has, in official correspondence with HMG and in many other fora, repeatedly placed on record her claim to the Falklands. It is not possible to provide a more precise figure.

Question 12

Is it the case that doubts existed within the Foreign Office over the legality of British actions in this period? (ie 1833–1968)

With a subject as complicated as the history of the Falkland Islands, it is inevitable that individual officials will have differing and in some cases conflicting views. This is natural, but it is also irrelevant. Successive British Governments have made it clear that they have no doubts about our sovereignty over the Falkland Islands.

Question 14

What is the basis of the Argentine claim to the Falkland Islands Dependencies, and the basis of the Argentine and Chilean claims to British Antarctica?

1. *Terminology*

In paragraph 5 of the answer to Question 1 contained in our Memorandum 20/82 [see UKMIL 1982, p. 436] it was explained that prior to 1962 the Falkland Islands Dependencies comprised territories which, since 1962, have been designated as the Falkland Islands Dependencies (South Georgia and the South Sandwich Islands) plus the British Antarctic Territory. In providing an answer to this question the place-name Falkland Islands Dependencies is used only to mean South Georgia and the South Sandwich Islands, unless the sense clearly demands otherwise.

2. *Argentine claim to the Falkland Islands Dependencies*

As was stated in paragraph 9 of the answer to Question 1 in our Memorandum 20/82 [see UKMIL 1982, p. 437], Argentina did not make any claim to South Georgia until 1927 and no specific claim to the South Sandwich Islands was made until 1948 (although a reservation of rights claimed by Argentina was made in 1937 in general terms in relation to what is now known as the Falkland Islands Dependencies and the British Antarctic Territory).

3. Prior to recent events the Dependencies have at no stage in their history been occupied by Argentina, although an illegal scientific station was established on one of the South Sandwich Islands in 1976. This had no implications for sovereignty. As far as is known the Argentine Government has never officially described in detail the basis on which it claims the Falkland Islands Dependencies. It would not be in Her Majesty's Government's interests to speculate as to what that basis might be.

4. The reasons for Her Majesty's Government's rejection of Argentine pretensions to sovereignty over the Falkland Islands Dependencies, and the basis on which the sovereignty of the United Kingdom over those Dependencies rests, are set out in the Application filed by the United Kingdom with the International Court of Justice in May 1955 instituting proceedings against Argentina, especially paragraphs 6–34.

5. *Argentine claim to the British Antarctic Territory*

The Government of Argentina first formulated pretensions in 1925 to the South Orkney Islands, and in 1937 to the remainder of what is now known as British Antarctic Territory (by way of a general reservation of rights claimed by Argentina over all of the Falkland Islands Dependencies as then comprised). Subsequently, Argentina, in a notice of claim deposited on Deception Island (South Shetlands) in January 1942, and in a Note addressed to the United Kingdom Government on 15 February 1943, defined her pretensions in the area south of 60° South as covering all Antarctic lands and Dependencies between longitudes 25° and 68°34′ West. This westerly limit was later extended by a decree of 2 September 1946 to longitude 74° West.

6. As far as is known the Argentine Government has never officially described in detail the basis on which it claims those parts of the British Antarctic Territory lying between 25° and 74° West. Again it would not be in Her Majesty's Government's interests to speculate as to what that basis might be.

7. The reasons for Her Majesty's Government's rejection of Argentine pretensions to sovereignty over what is now the British Antarctic Territory, the ineffectiveness of Argentine encroachments on certain parts of that Territory in

displacing British sovereignty, and the basis on which the sovereignty of the United Kingdom rests, are explained in the Application filed with the International Court of Justice in May 1955 (see paragraph 4 above).

8. *Chilean claim to the British Antarctic Territory*

The Government of the Republic of Chile declared by Presidential Decree of 6 November 1940 that all lands, islands, islets, reefs, glaciers (pack-ice), etc, already known or to be discovered, and their respective territorial waters, in the sector between longitude 53° and 90° West of Greenwich, constitute the Chilean Antarctic or Chilean Antarctic Territory.

9. Unlike the Argentine Government, the Government of Chile has described in detail the basis of its claim to that part of Antarctica subject to the Decree quoted above. On 22 January 1947 the Chilean Minister for External Relations, Señor Raul Juliet, made a speech to the Chilean Senate. An extract from that speech dealing with Chilean claims in Antarctica will be provided separately. The reasons for Her Majesty's Government's rejection of Chilean pretensions to sovereignty over what is now the British Antarctic Territory, the ineffectiveness of Chilean encroachments on certain parts of that Territory in displacing British sovereignty, and the basis on which the sovereignty of the United Kingdom rests, are explained in the Application filed with the International Court of Justice in May 1955 instituting proceedings against Chile, especially paragraphs 6–32.

(*Parliamentary Papers*, 1982–3, House of Commons, Paper 31-vi, pp. 144–9 *passim*.)

In the course of his evidence to the above Committee on 17 January 1983, Sir Ian Sinclair, Legal Adviser, Foreign and Commonwealth Office, stated:

... I for my part am satisfied that our action in 1833 can readily be defended as having been legal, not only by the standards of the time, which ... is the relevant test, but even also by contemporary standards. In that context I would draw attention to the written evidence which we have already submitted in our second memorandum, particularly the response to questions 5, 7, 8 and 9. These contain such factual materials as we have available as to the nature of the circumstances in 1833, and in particular our response to question 9 gives a complete indication of the contents of the report which Captain Onslow made on his taking repossession of the Islands in 1833.

(Ibid., p. 162.)

Later, Sir Ian Sinclair was asked about the Spanish claim to have been the original sovereign of the Falkland Islands. He replied in part:

... it is certainly a claim which in the eighteenth century we did not accept. Of course ... I suppose that part and parcel of the Spanish claim might go back to the old Papal Bulls and the concept that there was a line of division as between Spain and Portugal. So in their case they would no doubt contend that occupation was not necessarily all that relevant. But I do not think this was a concept which was universal—certainly not universally recognised even as early as the eighteenth century. Far from it. Anyway, I think our position in the eighteenth century and subsequently has been that we did not regard Spain as having acquired title to the Falkland Islands, whether by virtue of some kind of transfer from France or otherwise.

(Ibid., p. 165.)

Sir Ian Sinclair was then asked to assess the legal basis of the Argentine argument that the Falkland Islands are in Argentina's geographical area. He replied:

. . . international law knows no principle that title to territory can derive from mere contiguity. If it were otherwise, there would be a whole series of situations around the globe where the title to territories would immediately come into open dispute. I need mention only the Channel Islands, for example.

(Ibid., p. 169.)

In reply to a question on the subject of Diego Garcia, the Minister of State, Foreign and Commonwealth Office, wrote:

The Government of India have indicated to us their opposition to the presence of military forces of non-littoral states in the Indian ocean and their support for Mauritius' claim to the Chagos Archipelago.

The Mauritian claim has not been the subject of a vote by the United Nations ad hoc committee on the Indian ocean.

(H.C. Debs., vol. 37, Written Answers, col. 450: 23 February 1983.)

In reply to a question on the subject of a declaration made at the non-aligned summit in Delhi, the Minister of State, Foreign and Commonwealth Office, wrote in part:

In another section the declaration supports the claim of Mauritius to sovereignty over Diego Garcia, disregarding the fact that the islands of the Chagos archipelago have been under continuous British sovereignty since 1814.

(Ibid., vol. 39, Written Answers, col. 42: 14 March 1983.)

In reply to a question, the Minister of State for the Armed Forces wrote:

On 20 June 1982 HMS Endurance removed Argentine personnel from Southern Thule and raised a Union flag. When HMS Hecate visited Thule on 19 December 1982 she found an Argentine flag flying at the base and the Union flag folded nearby. The Union flag was replaced and the Argentine one removed. We do not know when and how this exchange of flags took place, but we do not view the incident as a serious indication of Argentine intent to re-establish a presence on the dependencies. However, in view of the possibility that Argentina might seek to re-occupy the base on Southern Thule we have destroyed the buildings. The only structures now remaining are two beacons, a flagpole with a Union flag flying and a fully stocked refuge hut.

. . .

The structures destroyed comprised a meteorological station set up illegally by Argentina in 1976. This was done to prevent Argentine re-occupation of the station. We have preserved shelter on Southern Thule in the form of a refuge hut, sealed against the snow and fully stocked with provisions.

(Ibid., col. 250: 17 March 1983.)

In reply to the question 'which States, other than the United Kingdom, currently recognize the legality of the Jordanian annexation of the West Bank in 1952', the Minister of State, Foreign and Commonwealth Office, wrote:

That is for those concerned to say. But as far as we know, no United Nations member state raised objection to the entry of Jordan into the United Nations as a state on both banks of the Jordan in 1955, or has since raised objection.

(Ibid., vol. 42, Written Answers, col. 84: 4 May 1983.)

In reply to the further question 'what is the policy of Her Majesty's Government as to the lawful sovereignty over the West Bank', the same Minister wrote:

We believe that Israel should put an end to the territorial occupation which it has maintained since 1967, and that the future of the territories in question should be determined in negotiations which must place the Palestinian people in a position, by an appropriate process defined within the framework of the comprehensive peace settlement, to exercise fully its right to self-determination.

(Ibid.)

In the course of a letter dated 19 May 1983 addressed to the Secretary-General of the United Nations, the Permanent Representative of the United Kingdom, Sir John Thomson, replied to an earlier letter to the Secretary-General from the Argentine Government. He wrote:

. . . a further word must be said about the Argentine letter's terminology. The use of the circumlocution 'the sovereignty of the territories covered by the "Question of the Malvinas"' is no doubt intended to blur the distinction between the Falkland Islands on the one hand, and South Georgia and the South Sandwich Islands on the other. The United Kingdom rejects this. South Georgia and the South Sandwich Islands were not the subject of last year's General Assembly debate. They are geographically, legally and historically distinct from the Falkland Islands, and the arguments on which Argentina bases her claim to sovereignty over the Falkland Islands have no application to them.

(S/15774, p. 2.)

In reply to the question upon which treaty does the United Kingdom's claim to Gibraltar rest, the Parliamentary Under-Secretary of State, Foreign and Commonwealth Office, wrote:

The treaty upon which the United Kingdom bases its title to Gibraltar is the treaty of peace and friendship between Great Britain and Spain, signed at Utrecht, 2–13 July 1713. The relevant passage [is] Article X. . . .

(H.C. Debs., vol. 45, Written Answers, col. 45: 4 July 1983.)

During a plenary debate in ECOSOC held on 25 July 1983, the United Kingdom representative exercised a right of reply to a statement about the Falkland Islands made by the Argentine representative. He stated:

First I noticed that the Falklands were mentioned in the same breath as South Georgia and the South Sandwich Islands. Before this canard gains ground let me make clear the necessary distinction. For there is a distinction to be made. It is an important one and it will appeal to those who cherish the law.

The question of title to the Falkland Islands and the question of title to the Falkland Island dependencies are totally separate and distinct ones. As good lawyers know, apples and pears do not mix. At no stage prior to recent events have the dependencies been occupied by Argentina. Whatever historical basis Argentina may advance for her claim to the Falkland Islands . . . this could have no application to the Dependencies. They are simply administered by the Falklands for convenience.

(Text provided by the Foreign and Commonwealth Office.)

The following Note, dated 19 October 1983, was delivered to the Secretary-General of the International Maritime Organization:

The Secretary of State for Foreign and Commonwealth Affairs presents his compliments to the Secretary General of the International Maritime Organization and has the honour to refer to the Secretary-General's circular (PAL/Circ. 8) of 15 June 1983 concerning the accession of the Government of Argentina to the Athens Convention relating to the Carriage of Passengers and Their Luggage by Sea of 1974. In its instrument of accession Argentina stated that it rejected the extension of the Convention, and the Protocol to it of 1976, to the Falkland Islands, categorised the designation of the Falkland Islands as incorrect and claimed that it had sovereign rights over the Islands, asserting that they form an integral part of its national territory.

The Government of the United Kingdom of Great Britain and Northern Ireland reject each and every one of these statements and assertions. The United Kingdom has no doubt as to its sovereignty over the Falkland Islands and thus its right to include them within the scope of application of international agreements to which it is a party. The United Kingdom cannot accept that the Government of the Argentine Republic has any rights in this regard. Nor can the United Kingdom accept that the Falkland Islands are incorrectly designated.

(Text provided by the Foreign and Commonwealth Office.)

In the course of a debate in the General Assembly on 15 November 1983 on the subject of the Falkland Islands, the United Kingdom Permanent Representative, Sir John Thomson, stated:

. . . my Government has no doubt that the Falkland Islands, the subject of this debate, are British. The same holds true for the South Sandwich Islands and South Georgia, which are not the subject of the present debate. These latter islands were taken into possession by Captain Cook in 1775 and Argentina never thought to advance a claim to them until well into the present century. As to the

Falklands, the other side must also have some doubts about their sovereignty claim to them since there were no inhabitants in the islands when they were discovered by the British and they have been in continuous British occupation for 150 years. That goes beyond the foundation of many States represented here in the General Assembly. It is also worth recalling that the United States, for example, acquired Texas and California quite some years after the beginning of continuous British settlement in the Falklands. It may be worth adding, in the light of what one speaker said this afternoon, that many of the people of the Falklands have been there for six generations or more; the islanders have no other home than the Falklands.

(A/38/PV. 57, p. 42.)

The Permanent Representative of the United Kingdom to the United Nations, Sir John Thomson, addressed the following letter, dated 17 November 1983, to the President of the General Assembly:

I have the honour to refer to the address made to the General Assembly on 27 September 1983 by His Excellency the Prime Minister of Mauritius in which he referred to his country's 'just and legitimate claim over the Chagos Archipelago'.

I have been instructed to draw to Your Excellency's attention the fact that sovereignty over the Chagos Archipelago is vested in the United Kingdom of Great Britain and Northern Ireland. At no time has Mauritius had sovereignty over the Chagos Islands. In 1968, when Mauritius became an independent sovereign state, the Islands did not form part of the colony which then gained independence. Prior to 1968 the Chagos Islands were legally distinct from Mauritius, although they were for convenience administered by the (British Colonial) Government of Mauritius until they were incorporated in the British Indian Ocean Territory in 1965. Notwithstanding the above, the British Government have undertaken to cede the Islands of the Chagos Archipelago to Mauritius when they are no longer required for defence purposes.

(Text provided by the Foreign and Commonwealth Office.)

In reply to a question, the Minister of State, Foreign and Commonwealth Office, wrote:

For a long time we have recognised Chinese suzerainty over Tibet. This has been on the understanding that Tibet is regarded as autonomous. It was proclaimed an autonomous region in 1965.

(H.C. Debs., vol. 49, Written Answers, col. *109*: 22 November 1983.)

In reply to the question what discussions had been held with the Government of Honduras over sovereignty of the Sapodilla Cays, the Parliamentary Under-Secretary of State, Foreign and Commonwealth Office, wrote:

None. The Sapodilla Cays are part of the territory of Belize which is an independent sovereign state.

(Ibid., vol. 51, Written Answers, col. *196*: 20 December 1983.)

In reply to a later question, the same Minister wrote:

The 1965 Guatemalan constitution, since suspended, asserted Belize to be a part of Guatemala; but the Government of Guatemala have never published the documentary basis for their claim to Belize. Belize is internationally recognised as an independent sovereign nation.

(Ibid., col. *228*: 21 December 1983.)

Part Eight: II. C. *State territory and territorial jurisdiction—territorial jurisdiction—concurrent territorial jurisdiction*

(See also Part Five: VII. and Part Seven: II. B., above.)

Following certain letters sent by the Soviet, German Democratic Republic and Hungarian delegates to the Chairman of the Thirtieth Session of the Commission on Narcotic Drugs, the United States delegate wrote to the Chairman on 16 February 1983 as follows:

With respect to the letter of February 15, 1983, from the Representative of the Union of Soviet Socialist Republics to you concerning the reference to the Federal Health Office of the Federal Republic of Germany in document E/CN.7/1983/INF.2/Rev.1 of the Commission on Narcotic Drugs, I wish to state the following on behalf of the Delegations of France, the United Kingdom, and the United States of America.

The establishment of the Federal Health Office in the western sectors of Berlin was approved by the French, British and American authorities acting on the basis of their supreme authority. These authorities are satisfied that the Federal Health Office does not perform, in the western sectors of Berlin, acts in exercise of direct state authority over the western sectors of Berlin. Neither the location nor the activities of that office in the western sectors of Berlin, therefore, contravenes any of the provisions of the Quadripartite Agreement.

With reference to the statement of February 15, 1983, by the Representative of Hungary and the letter of the Observer of the German Democratic Republic, dated February 14, 1983, I wish to point out that States which are not parties to the Quadripartite Agreement of September 3, 1971, are not competent to comment authoritatively on its provisions.

Furthermore, Annex IV of the Quadripartite Agreement stipulates that, provided matters of security and status are not affected, the Federal Republic of Germany may represent the interests of the western sectors of Berlin in international conferences and that western sectors of Berlin residents may participate jointly with participants from the Federal Republic of Germany in international exchanges. Finally, as a matter of principle, it is for the Federal Republic of Germany alone to decide on the composition of its delegations.

(Text provided by the Foreign and Commonwealth Office.)

In response to a Note sent to the depositary State, Australia, in which the Soviet Union commented on the extension to the Western sectors of Berlin of the Convention on the Conservation of Antarctic Marine Living Resources, the French Embassy in Canberra presented the following Note, dated 22 March 1983, to the Australian Government on behalf of the Governments of France, the United Kingdom and the United States:

—Dans une communication au Gouvernement de l'URSS qui fait partie intégrante (annexe IV A) de l'accord quadripartite du 3 septembre 1971, les Gouvernements de France, du Royaume-Uni et des Etats-Unis ont confirmé que, à condition que les questions de sécurité et de statut ne soient pas affectées et que l'extension soit précisée dans chaque cas, les accords et arrangements internationaux auxquels la République Fédérale d'Allemagne devient partie, peuvent être étendus aux secteurs occidentaux de Berlin conformément aux procédures établies. Pour sa part le Gouvernement de l'URSS dans une communication aux trois Puissances qui fait également partie intégrante (annexe IV B) de l'accord quadripartite du 3 septembre 1971, a affirmé qu'il ne soulèverait pas d'objection contre une telle extension.

— Les procédures établies auxquelles il est fait référence ci-dessus et qui ont été confirmées par l'accord quadripartite, sont destinées inter alia, à donner aux autorités des trois Puissances la possibilité de garantir que les accords et arrangements internationaux auxquels la République Fédérale d'Allemagne devient partie et qui doivent être étendus aux secteurs occidentaux de Berlin le sont de telle manière que les questions de sécurité et de statut ne soient pas affectées.

En autorisant l'extension de la Convention mentionnée ci-dessus aux secteurs occidentaux de Berlin, les autorités des trois Puissances ont pris les dispositions nécessaires pour garantir que les questions de sécurité et de statut ne sont pas affectées. En conséquence, la validité de la déclaration de Berlin faite par la République Fédérale d'Allemagne conformément aux procédures établies n'est pas affectée et la Convention continue de s'appliquer pleinement aux secteurs occidentaux de Berlin et d'y produire tous ses effets.

— La note Soviétique se réfère également à l'extension aux secteurs occidentaux de Berlin du Traité de l'Antarctique. A cet égard, les trois Puissances souhaitent appeler à nouveau l'attention sur la note du Département d'Etat des Etats-Unis du 21 Août 1980 diffusée par le Département d'Etat dans sa note du 12 janvier 1981.[1]

(Text provided by the Foreign and Commonwealth Office.)

In response to a Note sent to the depositary State in which the Soviet Union commented on a statement made by the Federal Republic of Germany in ratifying the International Convention for the Regulation of Whaling, the United States Secretary of State issued the following Note, dated 5 April 1983:

. . . the Secretary of State sets forth below the view of the Governments of France, the United Kingdom of Great Britain and Northern Ireland, and the United States of America.

The Governments of France, the United Kingdom of Great Britain and Northern Ireland, and the United States of America wish to point out that the Soviet note referred to above contains an incomplete and therefore misleading reference to the Quadripartite Agreement of September 3, 1971. The provision of

---

[1] *Editorial note*: The text of this Note, which was sent on behalf also of the United Kingdom and France, is reproduced in *American Journal of International Law*, 75 (1980), p. 944.

the Quadripartite Agreement to which reference is made states that 'the ties between the Western Sectors of Berlin and the Federal Republic of Germany will be maintained and developed, taking into account that these Sectors continue not to be a part of the Federal Republic and not to be governed by it.'

(Text provided by the Foreign and Commonwealth Office.)

In response to letters sent to the President of the Thirty-sixth World Health Assembly by the delegates of the Soviet Union and the German Democratic Republic, the delegate of France, in a letter to the President dated 12 May 1983, wrote:

On behalf of the delegations of France, the United Kingdom of Great Britain and Northern Ireland and the United States of America I wish to state that the letter from the Soviet delegate contains an incomplete and consequently misleading reference to the Quadripartite Agreement of 3 September 1971. The relevant passage of that Agreement to which the Soviet Representative refers provides that the ties between the Western Sectors of Berlin and the Federal Republic of Germany will be maintained and developed, taking into account that the Sectors continue not to be a constituent part of the Federal Republic of Germany and not to be governed by it.

Furthermore, there is nothing in the Quadripartite Agreement which supports the contention that residents of the Western Sectors of Berlin may not be included in the delegation of the Federal Republic of Germany to international Conferences.

In fact, Annex 4 of the Quadripartite Agreement stipulates that, provided matters of security and status are not affected, the Federal Republic of Germany may represent the interests of the Western Sectors of Berlin in international conferences and that Western Sectors of Berlin residents may participate jointly with participants from the Federal Republic of Germany in international meetings. Furthermore, as a matter of principle, it is for the Federal Republic of Germany alone to decide on the composition of its delegations.

We would like to take this opportunity to bring to your attention that States which are not parties to the Quadripartite Agreement are not competent to comment authoritatively on its provisions.

(World Health Organization: A 36/INF.Doc./16.)

The following communication, dated 19 May 1983, was sent to the Secretary-General of the International Maritime Organization by the Governments of the United Kingdom, the United States and France:

In a communication to the Government of the Union of Soviet Socialist Republics, which is an integral part (Annex IVA) of the Quadripartite Agreement of 3 September 1971, the Governments of France, the United Kingdom and the United States, without prejudice to the maintenance of their rights and responsibilities relating to the representation abroad of the interests of the Western Sectors of Berlin, confirmed that, provided that matters of status and security are not affected and provided that the extension is specified in each case, international agreements and arrangements entered into by the Federal Republic of Germany may be extended to the Western Sectors of Berlin in accordance with established procedures. For its part, the Government of the Union of Soviet Socialist Republics, in a communication to the Governments of the Three Powers which is similarly an integral part (Annex IVB) of the Quadripartite Agreement, affirmed that it would raise no objections to such extension.

The established procedures referred to above, which were endorsed in the Quadripartite Agreement, are designed *inter alia* to afford the authorities of the Three Powers the opportunity to ensure that international agreements and arrangements entered into by the Federal Republic of Germany which are to be extended to the Western Sectors of Berlin are extended in such a way that matters of status and security are not affected.

When authorizing the extension of the International Convention for the Prevention of Pollution from Ships, 1973, the Protocol of 1978 relating to the International Convention for the Prevention of Pollution from Ships, 1973, and the International Convention on Maritime Search and Rescue, 1979, to the Western Sectors of Berlin, the authorities of the Three Powers took such steps as were necessary to ensure that matters of security and status were not affected. Accordingly, the validity of the Berlin declaration made by the Federal Republic of Germany in accordance with established procedures is unaffected and the application of the MARPOL Convention and related Protocol and the International Convention on Maritime Search and Rescue to the Western Sectors of Berlin continues in full force and effect.

(I.M.O. document: PMP/Circ. 21; see also MP/Circ. and SAR/Circ. 14 for similar documents.)

In response to a communication sent to the Secretary-General of the International Maritime Organization by the German Democratic Republic on the subject of the application to West Berlin of the International Convention on Standards of Training, Certification and Watchkeeping for Seafarers, 1978, the Secretary of State for Foreign and Commonwealth Affairs wrote to the Secretary-General on 30 August 1983 as follows:

In connection with this communication, the Secretary of State for Foreign and Commonwealth Affairs would like to reaffirm, on behalf of the Governments of the United Kingdom of Great Britain and Northern Ireland, of France and of the United States of America, that States which are not parties to the Quadripartite Agreement are not competent to comment authoritatively on its provisions.

The three Governments do not consider it necessary, nor do they intend, to respond to any further communication on this subject from States which are not parties to the Quadripartite Agreement. This should not be taken to imply any change of the position of the three Governments in this matter.

(Text provided by the Foreign and Commonwealth Office.)

In response to letters sent in October 1983 to the Chairman of the E.C.E. Working Party on Low- and Non-Waste Technology by the delegations of the Soviet Union and the German Democratic Republic, the delegate of the United Kingdom wrote to the Chairman as follows:

On behalf of the Governments of France, the United States of America and the

United Kingdom of Great Britain and Northern Ireland, I should like to address you on the subject raised by the Head of the USSR Delegation in his letter to you of 20 October 1983.

The establishment of the Federal Environmental Agency in the western sectors of Berlin was approved by the French, American and British authorities acting on the basis of their supreme authority. These authorities are satisfied that the Federal Environmental Agency does not perform in the western sectors of Berlin acts in exercise of direct State authority over the western sectors of Berlin. Neither the location nor the activities of that Agency, in the western sectors of Berlin, therefore, contravenes any of the provisions of the Quadripartite Agreement.

We cannot agree that the involvement of institutions such as the Federal Environmental Agency in any way impedes the work of the ECE.

Furthermore, there is nothing in the Quadripartite Agreement which supports the contention that residents in the western sectors of Berlin may not be included in delegations of the Federal Republic of Germany to international conferences; in fact Annex IV of the Quadripartite Agreement stipulates that, provided matters of security and status are not affected, the Federal Republic of Germany may represent the interests of the western sectors of Berlin in international conferences and that western sectors of Berlin residents may participate jointly with participants from the Federal Republic of Germany in international exchanges. Furthermore, as a matter of principle, it is for the Federal Republic of Germany alone to decide on the composition of its delegation.

As far as the letter of the Head of the Delegation of the German Democratic Republic dated 20 October, is concerned, I would like to state that States which are not parties to the Quadripartite Agreement are not competent to comment authoritatively on its provisions.

(E.C.E. document: ENV/WP. 2/9; Annex II, pp. 1–2.)

A letter in similar terms was sent on 9 June 1983 by the French delegation, on behalf also of the United Kingdom and United States delegations, to the Chairman of the Executive Body for the Convention on Long-range Transboundary Air Pollution at its first session (ibid.: EB.AIR/1, Annex V, p. 1).

A letter in similar terms was sent on 10 November 1983 by the United States delegation, on behalf also of the United Kingdom and French delegations, to the Chairman of the *ad hoc* Meeting on Financing of E.M.E.P.

A letter in similar terms was sent on 11 November 1983 by the United States delegation, on behalf also of the United Kingdom and French delegations, to the Chairman of the Steering Body to E.M.E.P.

A letter in similar terms was sent on 1 December 1983 by the United States delegation, on behalf also of the United Kingdom and French delegations, to the Chairman of the Group of Experts on Environmental Impact Assessment.

A letter in similar terms was sent on 1 December 1983 by the French delegation, on behalf also of the United Kingdom and United States delegations, to the Chairman of the Special Working Group of Experts on the Protection of the Marine Environment against Land-based Pollution.

(Texts, not reproduced here, provided by the Foreign and Commonwealth Office.)

In a statement made on 15 November 1983 to the Sixth Committee of the General Assembly during its debate on the annual report of the International Law Commission, the United Kingdom representative, Sir Ian Sinclair, observed in the context of the topic of the non-navigational uses of international watercourses:

The Special Rapporteur has also raised with us the question whether reference should be made in Article 6 of his draft to the concept that, in certain circumstances, the international watercourse system (or, perhaps more accurately, the waters of such a system) constitutes a 'shared natural resource.' Mr Chairman, it is only too well-known that words and phrases may acquire overtones which their ordinary meaning may not necessarily convey. Such appears to be the case with the phrase 'shared natural resource.' *Prima facie*, my delegation have no difficulty with the phrase as such when it is used to designate a resource which, *by its very nature*, cannot be made subject to the sole sovereignty and control of a single State. Such must, in our view, be the case with the waters of an international watercourse system at least, where the use of the waters in one system State affects the use of the waters in another system State. . . . There is no derogation from the principle of permanent sovereignty over natural resources involved in recognition of the notion that the waters of an international watercourse system may, in certain circumscribed conditions, constitute a shared natural resource.

(Text provided by the Foreign and Commonwealth Office.)

In the course of a debate on the subject of the Visiting Forces Act 1952, the Parliamentary Under-Secretary of State, Home Office, Mr. David Mellor, said:

I am sure that a majority of hon. Members realise only too well that American forces have been in the United Kingdom for more than 40 years. Their presence has been beneficial to the United Kingdom both as staunch allies in the war and defenders of peace through the NATO Alliance thereafter. Their presence has also been largely uncontroversial, and rightly so. For over 30 years, the framework of the criminal law within which they operate and other important matters have been covered by the Visiting Forces Act 1952. It is important that we should know something of the history of that Act. It has an impeccably bipartisan pedigree, as I shall show. As I shall also demonstrate, there is no commonsense reason why that bipartisanship should come to an end, although there may be strong political reasons why some hon. Members are keen to ruffle the surface of what have otherwise been, on the whole, relatively calm waters.

The NATO Alliance requires that troops of several Alliance nations are stationed in other Alliance countries. The NATO agreement was concluded in London in 1951 and signed . . . by Herbert Morrison, a representative of the then Labour Government. It was concluded between the NATO states and agreed on by the NATO allies. The 1952 Act of the incoming Conservative Government gave effect to the provisions of that agreement in United Kingdom law and allowed the Government to go to ratify the agreement in 1954. Apart from a modification to deal with hijacking, the Act has been untouched for the past 30 years. It has survived Labour and Conservative Governments alike—rightly so, as I hope to demonstrate.

As has been made clear in other speeches, the important sections of the Act are sections 2 and 3. Section 2 deals with jurisdiction. It enables the courts and authorities of the visiting force to exercise in the United Kingdom the ordinary powers of discipline and administration necessary to preserve the good order of the force. I am sure that there is no dispute over the need for that as it is essential for a military force to be able to maintain discipline if it is to be an effective force. It is clearly sensible for foreign service men visiting a country to serve under their own code of discipline rather than that of the receiving state. We maintain forces abroad as well as being hosts here. The 1951 agreement provides the basis on which we can maintain discipline in our forces serving in other NATO countries. The section does not create jurisdiction but merely enables the courts and authorities of the visiting force to exercise in our territory the jurisdiction that their law gives them over persons subject to their jurisdiction.

Thus, when a visiting service man commits an act that is an offence against the law of his own country, but is not against the law of the country in which he is stationed, the authorities of the visiting force have exclusive jurisdiction. Conversely, if he commits an act that is an offence against the law of the country in which he is stationed, but is not against the law of his own country . . . the authorities of the country in which he is stationed have exclusive jurisdiction. If, however, a visiting service man commits an act that is an offence against the law of both the sending country and the United Kingdom, the jurisdiction of the courts of the visiting force is concurrent—I stress the word concurrent—with that of the United Kingdom courts. Where concurrent jurisdiction arises, the arrangements for determining which court will deal with the case are set out in section 3 of the Act.

Section 3 gives effect to article VII 3(a) of the Status of Forces Agreement 1951 and provides that in most cases United Kingdom courts will have primary rights to deal with offences committed by visiting service men that infringe United Kingdom laws. . . .

The only exceptions to this general rule occur in circumstances where the offence arose out of and in the course of duty, or it was committed solely against persons or property associated with the visiting force. In such cases, the primary jurisdiction is exercised by the authority of the visiting force, but the United Kingdom courts have a secondary right of jurisdiction. They may exercise that right if the authorities of the visiting force decide not to exercise their primary right of jurisdiction and deal with the case under their law.

There has been a suggestion in some quarters that United States service men are above the law and can act irresponsibly and get away with it. That is categorically not the case. In 1982, more than 2,100 United States service men . . . were convicted in United Kingdom courts, about 2,000 of which were for traffic offences. By comparison, in the same year about 1,500 United Kingdom service men were tried in Germany for motoring offences by the German courts. It is instructive to look at the balance of work in the two courts given that there are twice as many British soldiers in Germany as there are United States troops in the United Kingdom. The figures hardly show that the United Kingdom courts are not dealing with offences committed by United States troops. In no sense are United States military personnel above the law.

. . .

Turning to serious crime, which has rightly been raised in the debate, in the past two years there have been 27 instances of serious offences of violence committed by United States military personnel against United Kingdom citizens.

For the avoidance of doubt, most occurred in pub and disco fights. All of these incidents—I stress, all of these—were dealt with by the United Kingdom courts. Five American service men are presently in our prisons.

It has been said that United States service men are immune from appearing before any British court, criminal or civil, if they can claim to be on duty at the time. I wish to clarify what that means, I hope helpfully, especially bearing in mind the comments of my hon. Friend the Member for Newbury. I assure him that there is no question of the United States authorities claiming that their service men are on duty willy nilly regardless of the facts. That is not the case.

I accept that the case raised by the hon. Member for Fife, Central, which took place in August 1965, involving a Mrs. MacDonald, could bear an unfortunate interpretation on that issue. I assure the House that the United States authorities would not now regard, and have not regarded for some considerable time, a service man driving to and from his base in his own car as being on duty and therefore susceptible to their jurisdiction and not ours. We would not stand idly by and not make representations were such a position to arise.

In cases where the alleged offender claims to have been on duty, the primary jurisdiction is exercised by the authorities of the visiting force. The United Kingdom courts have a secondary right of jurisdiction which they may exercise if the authorities of the visiting force decide not to exercise their primary right of jurisdiction. In no sense can someone get away with it without a hearing being held by either the British or American courts. Where it may be thought that the individual concerned is on duty and therefore susceptible to the United States regime and not to ours, the United Kingdom prosecuting authorities are entitled—this is specifically set out in article VII 3(c) of the 1951 agreement—to ask the visiting state to waive its primary right where the issue seems to be of special importance. That deals with the serious matters that have been raised.

I have been dealing in the main with criminal law, but it is crucial that we do not forget civil law. . . . Civil law is vital to an individual and his dependants if he has been injured by the negligence or default of a United States service man. His full civil entitlements are protected.

On the crucial question of compensation, article VIII of the agreement sets out the obligations of the contracting parties. In the United Kingdom, the claims commission deals with any claims made against visiting forces. If the claim is admitted and the damages agreed, the damages are paid by the Secretary of State for Defence as a successor in title to the Secretary of State for War under the authority of section 9 of the Visiting Forces Act 1952.

If the claim is not admitted, a United Kingdom claimant has a right to bring proceedings in the United Kingdom courts against a member of the visiting force concerned, just as he can if he is dissatisfied with the financial arrangements offered to him by the claims commission. Any judgment obtained would be discharged by the Secretary of State for Defence. If a settlement is arrived at without proceeding to trial, payment will also be made by the Secretary of State.

In accordance with paragraph 5 of article VIII, 75 per cent. of any award is recovered from the sending state. The court will deal with the matter as in any similar hearing between two United Kingdom citizens where a tort has been committed, or where there is a dispute that a tort has been committed and the claimant is a citizen of the United Kingdom and the defendant a member of the United Kingdom Armed Forces. I hope that that information is sufficient for the House to be in no doubt about the position.

I want to give the House some facts about how the civil claim arrangements have worked during the past five years. The claims commission has handled about 430 claims a year against United States service men, all of which have involved road traffic accidents. In each year about 15 cases have involved personal injury, but not more than two fatal injuries. The majority of cases are settled amicably out of court.

There has also been an accusation that the United Kingdom is a soft touch, that United States forces in other NATO countries are treated more toughly by the authorities, and that British forces overseas are subject to more vigorous rules than their United States counterparts in Britain. That is absolutely not the case.

The United Kingdom has done nothing that is not fully reciprocated by other states that are party to the 1951 agreement. I have already given the revealing comparison between cases against the United States service men in the United Kingdom and those against United Kingdom service men in the German courts. The 1952 Act is not administered at arm's length between United Kingdom and United States authorities. It is not the case that the Americans might take a view that a service man was on duty and that that was the end of the matter.

The 1952 Act is administered by a continuous and constructive dialogue. I know that my right hon. Friend the Secretary of State for Defence would want to look carefully at any details suggesting that something has gone amiss. If he was persuaded that there was a difficulty, he would raise that with the American authorities.

Generally, if an incident occurs outside a United States base, the police will investigate the matter and inform the United States authorities if they consider it appropriate to institute proceedings. If the United States authorities claim primary jurisdiction, for example, on the grounds that the incident took place during official duties, the police would not normally pursue the matter further, unless—I stress this—they considered the claim of the United States authorities to exercise jurisdiction to be unreasonable. In that event they will report the matter to the Director of Public Prosecutions. If the DPP shares the concern of the police, the action of the United States authorities is likely to be to bring the matter to the notice of the Home Office. It would then be for my right hon. and learned Friend, the Home Secretary, in consultation with the Foreign and Commonwealth Office, to make representations to the United States authorities at diplomatic level.

It is inevitable . . . that over 30 years with hundreds, if not thousands, of cases of one type or another arising each year, there have been some unhappy cases. I accept that, but overall it is clear beyond peradventure that the Act has worked well and can continue to work well. It has done so without widespread acrimony or any of the general unfairness that some hon. Members have sought to contend arises by giving a rather partial account of one or two hard cases.

I am not here to answer for the Ministry of Defence. I am a Home Office Minister, but, inevitably, a great deal has been said about Greenham Common.... Under this Act, we are concerned by and large with motoring and occasionally other offences committed away from the base. During the past 30 years, that is the generality of the cases that have fallen within the ambit of the Act.

I repudiate the suggestion that the Act provides immunity to United States service men who may fire upon civilian demonstrators. The use of firearms by United States service men, just as with United Kingdom service men, is governed by rules of engagement designed to ensure that fire is opened only in accordance with the law of the land and the doctrine of the minimum force that is necessary and reasonable to protect life and vital installations. In case there is any doubt about the circumstances in which that might occur, I confirm that there is no possibility of United States service men opening fire in the vicinity of demonstrators on the fringes of nuclear bases. There are a number of security personnel who can, and will, deal with those demonstrators without armed force.

All our efforts are designed to ensure that demonstrators cannot put themselves into a position where they might face any danger of being in an area where service men would have to consider using firearms. I go so far as to say that if a person has reached the area where that possibility arises, it will be clear that he or she is not in the business of peacefully demonstrating against cruise missiles. If he or she has reached that point, it will be clear that there is an intention to interfere with a nuclear warhead. In that context, I believe that I carry the House with me in saying that firearms should be available for use strictly as a last resort, and I hope that those remarks will be of assistance to those who raised those matters.

I have noted the concern expressed by hon. Members about some aspects of the operation of the Act, and we are in no sense complacent about it. In giving what I believe to be a fair account of its workings, I hope that that has been clear. It is apparent that most of the concern derives from the interpretation which it is feared United States authorities may in some cases place upon the issue of jurisdiction, especially in relation to the question of what may or may not constitute official duty. I shall ensure that the points made by hon. Members are drawn to the attention of the competent United States authorities. In addition, I emphasise that the Government's intention—if any case arises in which the United States authorities appear to be adopting what seems to be an unreasonably extensive interpretation of what constitutes official duty—is to make the most strenuous representations to ensure that the spirit, as well as the letter, of the NATO agreement is fully respected. I hope that my hon. Friend the Member for Newbury will convey that message loud and clear to his constituents as they are entitled to know where we stand on this.

More generally, we shall be prepared to make representations to the United States authorities if other aspects of any case give cause for concern. I believe that in general the 1951 agreement and the 1952 Act have for 30 years provided a workable and satisfactory basis for foreign forces in this country. Nevertheless, we shall keep their operation under close scrutiny and shall not hesistate to act whenever we consider that there are grounds for doing so.

(H.C. Debs., vol. 51, cols. 103–8: 19 December 1983.)

Part Eight: II. D. *State territory and territorial jurisdiction—territorial jurisdiction—extra-territoriality*

In moving the Second Reading in the House of Commons of the Nuclear Material (Offences) Bill, the Minister of State, Home Office, Mr. David Waddington, stated:

The Bill is designed to enable the United Kingdom Government to ratify, without reservation, the United Nations convention on the physical protection of nuclear material.

The convention recognises the need for co-operation between states to ensure adequate protection of nuclear material used for peaceful purposes during transit between states. It also calls upon states to create a common range of criminal offences for which extradition may be granted.

The convention was opened for signature on 3 March 1980 in Vienna and New York and was signed by the United Kingdom on 30 June 1980. It will come into force when 21 states have ratified it. So far, five states have ratified, but 28 others have signed. The convention follows the pattern of other international conventions dealing with specific problems—for example, The Hague convention for the suppression of unlawful seizure of aircraft, usually known as the hijacking convention; the Montreal convention for the suppression of unlawful acts against the safety of civil aviation; the convention on the prevention and punishment of crimes against internationally protected persons; and, more recently, the convention against the taking of hostages.

. . .

Article 7 . . . obliges us to create new offences. Furthermore, each state is required to establish jurisdiction in respect of these offences wherever they occur, and, when an offender is within the jurisdiction, a state must either prosecute or extradite. Usually, where the events have occurred abroad, extradition will be the more practicable and appropriate course. But the aim of the convention is to ensure, as far as possible, that, one way or another, the offender does not find a safe haven in another country. The country to which he flees can either extradite or, if not willing to do so—perhaps because the person is one of its nationals—bring the man to trial.

Similarly, other acts which we are required to penalise correspond to offences under the Offences against the Person Act 1861, the Theft Act 1968 and the Criminal Damage Act 1971, or their Scottish equivalents. All that has been necessary in respect of these offences, therefore, has been to ensure that we have necessary extra-territorial jurisdiction over them when they are committed abroad in relation to, or by means of, nuclear material. This is achieved by clause 1 of the Bill.

. . .

Let me revert for one moment to jurisdiction. The convention requires signatories to ensure that they have jurisdiction over the offences that it covers when they are committed in their territory or on board one of their ships or aircraft, when the alleged offender is one of their nationals, and when the offence has been committed elsewhere but the alleged offender is found in their territory and they do not extradite him.

The law of the United Kingdom is based on the territorial principle.

Historically our courts have jurisdiction over any crime committed here or, with certain exceptions, on our ships and aircraft, but in general they do not have jurisdiction over offences committed abroad, even by United Kingdom nationals, and certainly not over foreign nationals. There is, however, a small number of exceptions of long standing, such as murder, over which our courts have always had jurisdiction, even when committed by 'a subject of Her Majesty' on land abroad.

In addition there is a small but growing number of offences which have arisen out of international conventions and in respect of which the United Kingdom has agreed with other nations that their seriousness in conjunction with their international character merits special measures. Hijacking and the taking of hostages are obvious examples. It is, however, a common feature of international conventions of this sort that signatories are obliged either to extradite offenders or to prosecute them, and the convention on the physical protection of nuclear materials is no exception. It is our normal practice to extradite offenders who have committed offences abroad, and I cannot envisage our having to exercise the extraterritorial jurisdiction created in the Bill except in the most exceptional circumstances.

(Ibid., vol. 36, cols. 944–6: 8 February 1983; see also H.L. Debs., vol. 440, cols. 981–4: 21 March 1983.)

In reply to a question on the subject of the application of United States laws to the subsidiaries in the United Kingdom of United States corporations, in particular in relation to the countering of the Arab trade boycott of Israel, the Minister of State, Department of Trade, wrote:

This is a longstanding problem on which our discussions with the United States Administration have recently been intensified because of the impending review of the United States Export Administration Act. The Act is one of the principal laws which is applied extraterritorially and regulations made under it include those relating to the countering of the Arab trade boycott of Israel. We have made it clear that we regard the application of these laws to companies registered and doing business in the United Kingdom as quite unjustified and contrary to international law.

(H.C. Debs., vol. 37, Written Answers, col. 548: 25 February 1983.)

In reply to a question, the Prime Minister wrote in part:

... reciprocal arrangements [with the Republic of Ireland] already exist, under the Criminal Jurisdiction Act 1975, for extraterritorial jurisdiction in respect of serious crimes of the sort committed by terrorists.

(Ibid., vol. 38, Written Answers, col. 352: 8 March 1983.)

In reply to a question, the Parliamentary Under-Secretary, Department of Trade, wrote:

The Government have in recent years made representations to the United States authorities on a number of occasions about the effects of US legislation on the legitimate trading interests of British companies. A major example last year concerned the US embargo on the supply of equipment for the Siberian pipeline.

More recently, we have made representations to the United States about the Export Administration Act, under which the pipeline measures were introduced, and which is up for renewal this year. We are urging the US authorities to amend this legislation so that it no longer provides for extraterritorial application of the kind to which we object.

We have also made representations about the effects of US anti-trust laws on United Kingdom companies in several industries.

(Ibid., vol. 39, Written Answers, col. *70*: 14 March 1983.)

In reply to a question, the Secretary of State for Foreign and Commonwealth Affairs wrote:

The Government would like the extraterritorial provisions of the United States Export Administration Act to be removed. We have made our views known very clearly to the Americans, and the European Community has also raised the matter with the United States.

The Bill is now under discussion in the Congress. We are taking every opportunity to ensure that our concern is brought to the attention of the United States Administration and Congress.

In reply to a further question, the Secretary of State wrote:

The Export Administration Act, which is due to be reauthorised by Congress by the end of September, is an enabling Act. It is impossible at this stage to quantify its likely effect in practice, but, judging by the effects of the use made of the present Export Administration Act, for example in the case of the Siberian pipeline, it is likely to be damaging to British trading interests.

(Ibid., vol. 42, Written Answers, col. *318*: 11 May 1983.)

On 24 June 1983, the following press notice was issued jointly by the Department of Trade and Industry and the Department of Transport:

Mr Cecil Parkinson, Secretary of State for Trade and Industry, and Mr Tom King, Secretary of State for Transport, today announced that the powers under Sections 1 and 2 of the Protection of Trading Interests Act 1980 have been exercised to safeguard United Kingdom trading interests affected by the application of United States' anti-trust laws.

The British Government has made representations to the US Government about the unilateral application of its anti-trust laws to aviation activities covered by our bilateral treaty—the UK/US Air Services Agreement (Bermuda 2). Mr Tom King now considers that it is necessary to respond to this unilateral application of US law to matters covered by Bermuda 2 by reflecting HM Government's position in instruments made under the 1980 Act. This Act was expressly designed to provide protection from requirements, prohibitions and judgments imposed or given under the laws of countries outside the United Kingdom and affecting the trading or other interests of persons in the United Kingdom. Mr Parkinson, whose Department is generally responsible for UK trading interests, is satisfied that the statutory powers should be exercised in these circumstances and has accordingly made an Order and Direction under the Act.

The Order under Section 1 reflects the Government's view that the present attempts to apply US anti-trust laws to activities of airlines designated under Bermuda 2 by HMG are damaging to or threaten to damage UK trading interests. The associated Direction under Section 1 prohibits any person carrying on business in the UK from complying with requirements imposed pursuant to these US laws. The Direction under Section 2 of the Act has been made to ensure that certain commercial documents and commercial information are not made available for any proceedings in the US without the consent of the Secretary of State for Trade and Industry.

A consent has been given so that the Section 1 Direction shall not apply to US airlines. The Section 2 Direction applies to certain documents and information in the possession of any person in the UK including US airlines.

. . .

Discussions between the two Governments are expected to continue with a view to resolving the underlying dispute and any jurisdictional issues which may arise.

(Text provided by the Foreign and Commonwealth Office.)

The Order referred to above is the Protection of Trading Interests (U.S. Antitrust Measures) Order 1983, Statutory Instruments, 1983, No. 900. The texts of the Directions are as follows:

Protection of Trading Interests Act 1980
General Direction by the Secretary of State (under Section 1)

Whereas the Secretary of State:

(1) has directed . . . that section 1 of the Protection of Trading Interests Act 1980 . . . ('the 1980 Act') shall apply, in the circumstances specified by him, to sections 1 and 2 of the United States' Sherman Act and sections 4 and 4A of the United States' Clayton Act ('the US antitrust measures');

(2) has considered the effect of the US antitrust measures on United Kingdom designated airlines and in particular on their ability freely to participate in discussions or agreements relating to tariffs or other matters relating to the operation of air services authorised pursuant to the Bermuda 2 Agreement;

(3) has considered the effect of the US measures on the trading interests of the United Kingdom;

(4) considers that the following direction is appropriate for avoiding damage to the trading interests of the United Kingdom:

Now, therefore, the Secretary of State, in exercise of his powers under section 1 (3) of the 1980 Act, hereby gives the following Direction:—

1. Except with the consent of the Secretary of State no person in the United Kingdom who carries on business there shall comply, or cause or permit compliance, with any requirement or prohibition imposed on that person pursuant to the US antitrust measures in so far as such requirement or prohibition relates to or arises out of any of the cases described in article 2(2) of the Protection of Trading Interests (US Antitrust Measures) Order 1983.

2. Expressions used in this Direction shall have the meanings assigned to them

by the Protection of Trading Interests (US Antitrust Measures) Order 1983 for the purposes of that Order.

3. This Direction shall come into operation on 27th June 1983.

23rd June 1983.

Minister for Trade
Department of Trade and
Industry

PROTECTION OF TRADING INTERESTS ACT 1980

GENERAL DIRECTION BY THE SECRETARY OF STATE (UNDER SECTION 2)

WHEREAS it appears to the Secretary of State:

(a) that the United States' Department of Justice has begun an investigation into alleged price fixing and other allegations relating to the air transport of passengers over the North Atlantic for possible violations of sections 1 and 2 of the 'Sherman' Act . . .; and that for this purpose a grand jury ('the grand jury') has been empanelled in the District of Columbia in the United States of America;

(b) that a requirement may be imposed on a person or persons in the United Kingdom to produce to the United States' Department of Justice or the grand jury commercial documents which are not within the territorial jurisdiction of the United States or to furnish to the United States' Department of Justice or the grand jury commercial information;

(c) that civil antitrust proceedings of a penal nature are now pending in the United States' District Court for the District of Columbia ('the District Court') relating to similar matters to those which are the subject of the United States' Department of Justice investigation and that commercial documents and commercial information which are produced in the civil antitrust proceedings may be utilised in the Department of Justice investigation or before the grand jury;

(d) that a requirement may be imposed on a person or persons in the United Kingdom to produce to the District Court commercial documents which are not within the territorial jurisdiction of the United States or to furnish to the District Court commercial information;

(e) that any such requirement would be inadmissible within the meaning of section 2 (2) and (3) of the Protection of Trading Interests Act 1980 . . . (the '1980 Act'):

Now, therefore, the Secretary of State, in exercise of his powers under section 2 of the 1980 Act, gives the following directions:

1. Except with the consent of the Secretary of State no person or persons in the United Kingdom shall comply, or cause or permit compliance, whether by themselves, their officers, servants or agents, with any requirement to produce or furnish to the United States' Department of Justice, the grand jury or the District Court any commercial document in the United Kingdom or any commercial information which relates to the said Department of Justice investigation or the grand jury or District Court proceedings.

2. For the purpose of this direction and in relation to any requirement of the United States' Department of Justice, the grand jury or the District Court, the making of a request or demand or requirement to produce or furnish any

document or information to a person specified in the requirement shall be treated as subsection (5) of section 2 of the 1980 Act treats such matters for the purposes of that section.

3. Expressions used in this direction shall have the meanings assigned to them by the 1980 Act for the purposes of that Act.

4. This Direction shall come into operation on 4th July 1983 and shall supersede the General Direction given by the Secretary of State under section 2 on 23rd June 1983.

Minister of State for Industry

Department of Trade and

Industry

1st July 1983.

In the course of his argument before the Court of Appeal on 13 July 1983 in the case of *British Airways Board* v. *Laker Airways Ltd. et al.*, Mr. Peter Scott, Q.C., counsel for the Attorney-General, stated:

In general, substantive jurisdiction in anti-trust matters, in the view of the British Government, should only be taken on the basis either of the territorial principle or the nationality principle. There is nothing in the nature of anti-trust proceedings as such which justifies a wider application of these principles, that is to say, a wider application than is generally accepted in other matters. On the contrary, there is much in the nature of anti-trust which is the reflection of the public economic law of the State which calls for a narrower application of these principles. As your Lordships will appreciate, in inherently international activity, like aviation or shipping, it may be difficult to apply these principles with precision, but the activities can take place in both of the States concerned. In those cases, Her Majesty's Government would expect a State enforcing its regulatory laws to do so with restraint and only after paying due attention and due regard to the interests of the other State concerned, and to its own treaty obligations.

([1983] 3 All E.R. 375, 403–4.)

In reply to a question, the Minister of State, Foreign and Commonwealth Office, wrote:

[The Secretary of State for Foreign and Commonwealth Affairs] made it clear [to the President of the United States of America] that we are totally opposed to unitary taxation, which is contrary to international practice.

(H.C. Debs., vol. 46, Written Answers, col. *377*: 26 July 1983.)

In the course of its *amicus curiae* Brief, filed in November 1983, in respect of the Bank of Nova Scotia (for a summary of the facts of this litigation, see below, p. 515) the United Kingdom Government wrote:

The United Kingdom does not recognize the extra-territorial jurisdiction of the United States in any capacity. As far as the United Kingdom is concerned, this case is not and cannot be a matter involving extraterritoriality at all.

(*Amicus curiae* Brief of the United Kingdom, p. 8, footnote 27 in part: United States Court of Appeals for the Eleventh Circuit: In re *Grand Jury Proceedings the Bank of Nova Scotia: United States of America* v. *The Bank of Nova Scotia*.)

Part Eight: IV. *State territory and territorial jurisdiction—regime under the Antarctic Treaty*

The Foreign and Commonwealth Office submitted to the Foreign Affairs Committee of the House of Commons a memorandum, dated 17 December 1982, on the subject of the Falkland Islands and Dependencies. In the memorandum the following passage appeared:

In December 1959 both Argentina and Chile, together with the United Kingdom and nine other States, concluded the Antarctic Treaty. Since the entry into force of that Treaty in June 1961, the legal position of States with rights of or claims to territorial sovereignty in the area to which it applies has been affected by Article IV of the Treaty . . .

(*Parliamentary Papers*, 1982-3, House of Commons, Paper 31-vi, p. 149.)

In the course of his evidence to the above Committee, given on 17 January 1983, the Legal Adviser, Foreign and Commonwealth Office, Sir Ian Sinclair, was asked to comment on a suggestion that the Falkland Islands be placed under the regime of the Antarctic Treaty. He replied:

I think it presents certain problems, Mr Chairman. It does depend very much upon . . . what you regard as being the principles which it would seek to apply, because certainly there are some principles in the Antarctic Treaty which could not be applied very easily in the case of the Falkland Islands—for instance, the principle that the nations of each party can in effect have equal access to any part of the territory in the Antarctic. This, of course, derives from the fact that the Antarctic is basically uninhabited territory, there is no permanent population there so it is perfectly feasible to consider a situation in which the nationals of any contracting party can visit any part of Antarctica provided you have a sovereignty umbrella that no activity is to be regarded as increasing or decreasing your claim to sovereignty. But where you have a territory such as the Falkland Islands which is inhabited, has a settled population, to apply that principle I think would give rise to very serious difficulties.

(Ibid., p. 169.)

In reply to a question, the Minister of State, Foreign and Commonwealth Office, wrote:

The recent consultations in Wellington about the Antarctic minerals regime were informal and no conclusions were reached. We hope that these discussions can be carried forward to meetings to be held in Canberra in April and in Bonn in July. The United Kingdom delegation will continue to work for international agreement governing the exploitation of oil and minerals in the Antarctic.

(H.C. Debs., vol. 37, Written Answers, col. *362*: 21 February 1983.)

On 21 September 1983, the United Kingdom Permanent Representative to the United Nations in New York, Sir John Thomson, delivered the following statement to the General Committee of the General Assembly:

I have been asked to read out to the General Committee the text of a statement which was agreed by the Consultative Parties to the Antarctic Treaty in August, and the contents of which have been conveyed to the Secretary General. This statement bears upon the request by the delegations of Malaysia and Antigua and Barbuda, which is now before us, for the inscription of the present item on the agenda of the General Assembly.

'The Antarctic Treaty which is open to all countries of the world and is of unlimited duration establishes Antarctica as a region of unparalleled international cooperation in the interests of all mankind.

a) It is based on the United Nations Charter, promotes its purposes and principles and confirms Antarctica as a zone of peace.
b) It excludes Antarctica from the arms race by prohibiting any measures of a military nature such as the establishment of military bases and fortifications, the carrying out of military manoeuvres or the testing of any type of weapons including nuclear weapons.
c) It encourages and facilitates scientific cooperation and the exchange of scientific information beneficial to all States.
d) It protects the natural environment for all mankind.

The Treaty establishes a comprehensive system of on-site inspection by observers to promote the objectives and ensure the observance of the Treaty.

The Treaty serves the international community well and has averted international strife and conflict over Antarctica. It removes the potential for sovereignty disputes between Treaty Parties.

Revision or replacement of the Treaty, which is now being suggested by Malaysia and Antigua, would undermine this system of international law and order in Antarctica with very serious consequences for international peace and cooperation. It is unrealistic to think that in the present state of world affairs a new or better legal regime for Antarctica could be agreed upon. The undermining of the Treaty could open the way to an arms race in the region and might lead to new territorial claims. It would not serve the interest of any country, or group of countries, if Antarctica became an area of international conflict and discord.

The Treaty system has proved to be a remarkably successful, practical and dynamic arrangement. Every effort should be made to preserve and maintain it.

It is for these reasons that the Consultative Parties to the Antarctic Treaty have serious reservations about the initiative by the governments of Malaysia and Antigua and Barbuda and about any attempts to revise or replace the present Treaty system. The present initiative inaccurately represents the Antarctic Treaty of 1959 while implying that there is a need for revision or replacement of the Antarctic Treaty system, something which could only be achieved under international law by the Parties to the Treaty.'

Mr Chairman, I would like to add that the above text, which will be circulated in due course as a document of the General Assembly, fully reflects the views of the United Kingdom, which is one of the original Parties to the Antarctic Treaty and maintains a substantial programme of scientific research in Antarctica. It is the long standing practice of the United Kingdom not to oppose the inscription of new agenda items, provided that they conform to the United Nations Charter.

Having indicated the serious reservations which my delegation fully shares as to whether discussion of Antarctica at the General Assembly is either necessary or useful, my delegation will not seek to oppose its inscription. I would, however, like to express our firm expectation that any discussion of the item by the General Assembly will have as its aim to recognise the great value of the Antarctic Treaty System and to support it as a unique example of international cooperation in the interests of world peace and security to the benefit of all.

(Text provided by the Foreign and Commonwealth Office.)

In reply to a letter from a member of the public, the Foreign and Commonwealth Office wrote in October 1983 in the following terms:

The Government believe that the development of such resources as there may be in Antarctica is best conducted within the framework of agreed international arrangements which adequately take account of the various national and international interests involved: these include particularly environmental and conservation considerations, the position of the States concerned as regards sovereignty, and the need to maintain and strengthen the Antarctic Treaty system.

So far as concerns living resources, such international arrangements exist in the form of the Agreed Measures for the Conservation of Antarctic Fauna and Flora adopted in [1964] under the Antarctic Treaty, the Convention for the Conservation of Antarctic Seals [1972], and the Convention for the Conservation of Antarctic Marine Living Resources 1980. The United Kingdom has approved the Agreed Measures, and is a party to both Conventions: all three instruments are in force and effective.

As you may know, there is no commercial development of Antarctic living resources by British companies or institutions, though we would not seek to prohibit any such activities which were not in contravention of our obligations under the agreements mentioned above or of the Antarctic Treaty Act 1967.

So far as concerns Antarctic mineral resources, no agreed international arrangements yet exist. Very little is known about the existence or extent of any mineral resources in Antarctica. However, if mineral resources are discovered there in quantities which make their development economic and in locations where they are technically and logistically recoverable, then commercial interest in their development is likely to arise. For that reason, we believe that it is highly desirable to reach international agreement before any substantial resources are discovered on general arrangements which would apply in the event of any minerals activity taking place. To this end, we began negotiations with the other Consultative Parties to the Antarctic Treaty and within the framework of the Antarctic Treaty system, in June 1982 to try to elaborate an Antarctic minerals regime. The basis on which those negotiations are being conducted was laid down in recommendation XI-I of the XIth Antarctic Treaty Consultative Meeting in Buenos Aires in 1981. The negotiations are still under way.

(Text provided by the Foreign and Commonwealth Office.)

On 29 November 1983, a statement on the subject of the regime in Antarctica was delivered to the First Committee of the General Assembly by the United Kingdom representative, Dr. J. A. Heap. In the course of this statement, Dr. Heap remarked:

I should like to develop three themes of which any comprehensive factual and objective study of Antarctica must take account. These themes are: firstly, that the Antarctic Treaty itself and the system that has been developed under it is a remarkable exercise in prudent forethought; secondly that the system has shown itself capable of dynamic development; and thirdly, that the essential, and I mean essential, requirement for the development of the system has been, and will be in the future, a willingness on the part of the States involved in Antarctica not to push their legal positions to the limit —in a word the need for political forbearance and accommodation.

I said that the first of my themes was that the Treaty System was an exercise in prudent forethought. I should like to list for you a number of notable 'firsts' that have been achieved by agreement between States within the Treaty system:

The Antarctic Treaty was the first international agreement to:

—demilitarise a whole continent;
—provide for on site inspection of all activities on a continent;
—outlaw nuclear explosions or the dumping of radio-active waste;
—ensure freedom of scientific investigation and require that the results be freely available;
—set aside, in favour of cooperation, conflicting views about the legal basis which should underlie the management of affairs over a whole continent.

In view of the critical state of affairs as it was in Antarctica in 1958, I believe these 'firsts' can only be seen as remarkable and prudent measures. Measures, moreover, which are totally consistent with the Charter of the United Nations.

Since the Antarctic Treaty came into force in 1961 the development of a large number of agreements through its consultative mechanism have given rise to a number of other 'firsts':

—The Agreed Measures for the Conservation of Antarctic Fauna and Flora was the first international agreement to prohibit the killing of any native mammal or native bird in Antarctica without a permit and to arrange for details of the permits issued to be internationally exchanged;

—The Convention for the Conservation of Antarctic Seals was the first and is, I believe, so far the only international agreement to regulate the utilization of a living resource *before* any industry had developed to exploit it;

—The Convention for the Conservation of Antarctic Marine Living Resources is the first international agreement to require that regulation of the utilization of target species shall have regard to the effect that utilization has on the ecosystem as a whole.

—More generally, certain pioneering recommendations of the Treaty's Consultative procedures require that the first consideration to be applied to a new activity in Antarctica is not whether it is profitable or in the interests of one or more governments. Instead, prior consideration has to be given to whether or not it will have adverse effects on the Antarctic environment. This test is, itself, a notable first, unparalleled anywhere else in the world.

I suggest . . . that what I have called this exercise in prudent forethought is unique and is something of which the world at large should take note. I submit that all these firsts, and more especially those measures taken to protect Antarctic marine living resources, are in marked contrast to what happened before the

Treaty system came into being. There are precedents in the achievements of the Consultative Parties which could, with great benefit, be applied elsewhere in the world.

None of these 'firsts' give substantive rights to the parties to the agreements. They all circumscribe the freedom of action of all parties. Overwhelmingly, they consist of obligations and not of rights. This record of achievement should go far to put right the misconception that the Consultative Parties are carving Antarctica up for their own benefit.

This brings me to the second of my themes—that the system has shown itself capable of dynamic development. You may say . . . that it has been easy for the Consultative Parties to the Treaty to achieve these firsts in such a milieu as the Antarctic where activities do not develop all that quickly. I would answer by pointing to the fact that lack of urgency is, most frequently in international affairs, the excuse for inactivity. The record elsewhere shows few examples of prudent international action to preempt the undesirable effects of what can be foreseen. I believe that the record shows that that is not the case in Antarctica. There is, however, a positive reason why the Consultative Parties have acted *before* the need to do so has become acute. It is a political reason. It concerns the irreconcilable nature of their opposing views as to the legal basis on which Antarctic activities can be regulated. If the search for these agreements had been left until strong national interests were engaged on the part of States asserting sovereignty and States not recognising such assertions, there would have been no agreements. It must be one of the choicer international ironies that so much good should come out of an inability to agree about the basis on which that good should be done.

And so I come to the last of the themes I wish to explore—that the essential requirement for maintaining the peace and stability of the Antarctic is that the States involved must act with forbearance. None of them must push its view about the legal basis for Antarctic management to the limit.

Perhaps I can best elaborate this by reference to the potential for the Antarctic to contribute to the supply of minerals. It is this possibility which has done much to awaken the interests of other States, States outside the Treaty System, in the future of the Antarctic. It is widely known that the Consultative Parties of the Antarctic Treaty are engaged in an attempt to hammer out between them a regime for the regulation of mineral activity in the Antarctic.

Let us first recall that no one has yet discovered any minerals, including oil, in Antarctica of a quality or in quantities which would be economically exploitable if they were situated elsewhere in the world. The probability of finding such deposits is remote. Moreover, it is very probable that even if such deposits are found, they will never be economically exploitable.

Let us now look at the opening positions of the two sides in these negotiations. On the one hand, those States asserting sovereignty in Antarctica start from the position that there can be no exploitation of minerals in their areas which is not wholly regulated by them. On the other hand, those States who do not recognise such assertions of sovereignty start from the position that their nationals are free to go to Antarctica to search for and exploit minerals and that no other State has the right to regulate, in any sense, the activities of their nationals. The two positions are diametrically opposed. For all practical purposes, there could be virtually no mineral activity, even prospecting, which would not give rise to the high probability of a dispute.

If, however, anyone were to go prospecting in the Antarctic, the fat would then be in the fire and it would be too late to start looking for a regime. The national interests of States would become strongly engaged and the prospect of achieving a rational and reasonable regime would rapidly recede. I have earlier made the point that the genius of the Treaty system has been to avoid just such situations.

So, there are two conclusions which can be drawn from an appreciation of the starting positions of the two sides in the negotiation. The first is if any State on either side were determined to push its view of the legal basis for managing Antarctic affairs to its logical conclusion there could be no agreement. I shall return to this conclusion. The second conclusion is that it is easier for each side to consider the sort of accommodation they will necessarily be called upon to make before events on the ground give rise to new and difficult situations.

The second conclusion is that the outcome of the negotiations between the Antarctic Treaty Consultative Parties will break entirely new ground. There has never been such a negotiation anywhere else in the world before. These negotiations, which are a demanding exercise in imaginative statesmanship, are likely to come up with new ideas as to how States can rub along together—just as has the Antarctic Treaty itself.

. . . I should now like . . . to address what I see as the central core of the reasoning of those who want to burden the agenda of the United Nations with an agenda item on Antarctica. I say 'burden' because the United Kingdom, as was stated by my Permanent Representative in the General Committee, has serious reservations as to whether a discussion of Antarctica at the General Assembly is either necessary or useful. We do not wish to avoid discussing Antarctica anywhere with anyone. That is not our intention. But the issue is one of priorities. My government finds it strange that with all the problems which the world now faces the General Assembly should take time to address, as if it were a real problem, a matter which, if it is anything, is one of the world's best examples of international cooperation, peace and harmony which actually works.

The core of the concern of those who see shortcomings in the Antarctic Treaty System is not so much the question of whether the concept of the common heritage of mankind is applicable to Antarctica—an application which I should say, in passing, my government would reject. It is rather what they view as the arrogation by a few powers of the management of Antarctica. They want to deny to the Antarctic Treaty Consultative Parties their role in the management of that continent. They couple this with charges of excessive secrecy in the goings on of Consultative Meetings.

It would . . . be wrong for any Consultative Party to brush these arguments aside as of no consequence. They have been sincerely made, and they deserve a serious answer. The appeal of the case put by the distinguished Representative of Antigua and Barbuda based on the waning of colonialism and the rising tide of democratization is immediate and attractive. But it takes little account of the realities of Antarctica. I want, if I can, to explain why.

Dr. Heap then set out instances of scientific research in Antarctica particularly by the United Kingdom and continued:

I believe . . . that since the United Kingdom, amongst others, has the capacity to undertake such research, it also has in a sense a certain obligation to do so. This is a moral, not any sort of legal, obligation.

I also believe . . . that with that presence and the first hand knowledge we have of Antarctica, goes a responsibility to manage what goes on in those icy waters. Here, you will say, is the difficulty, for, it is asserted, the rest of the world, in whose interests we are said to be managing Antarctica, has no say in the management.

But such a charge is misconceived. The Antarctic Treaty Consultative Parties, in managing Antarctica *are denying no one's freedoms in Antarctica other than their own*. The law of treaties requires that no country can be bound by an international agreement to which they are not a party or to which they do not accede. As I have said, the Antarctic Treaty System overwhelmingly consists of obligations and not rights. The Treaty powers can claim, with a considerable measure of justice on their side, that in what they have done in managing Antarctica they have acted in the interests of all mankind. But, . . . and this is the important point, that was not their primary intention. In each case they saw an activity which might go on or which was going on, which, from their knowledge of Antarctica and its history, they appreciated ought to be regulated. The threat driving them on was that of politically more difficult problems for themselves in the future if they failed to act. So they did what they deemed to be necessary as between ourselves. They were binding no one else.

It is not unnatural . . . that having thus restricted their own freedoms to act in Antarctica in accordance with unalloyed national interest, they should seek to ensure that anyone who becomes active in the Antarctic scene should subject himself to the same restrictions.

I challenge those who appear to be dissatisfied with the system to show any obligation which the Treaty Consultative Parties have undertaken which it would not be in the interests of any outsider to undertake if he became active in Antarctica. I challenge them further to show anything which the Antarctic Treaty Consultative Parties have done which is inconsistent with the real interests of an outsider now or with the interests of future generations.

In short . . . the charge that the Antarctic Treaty Consultative Parties are guilty of usurping the prerogatives of other states is false. They have done no more than restrict their own freedoms. This will be as true in the future as it has been in the past. The mineral negotiations will be no exception.

Later in his statement, Dr. Heap made the following observation:

I have suggested that the Treaty System is an exercise in prudent forethought, is dynamic in meeting new challenges and requires political forbearance on the part of the States involved. It is not exclusive in the sense that that word has been used in this debate. And it is not secretive. All these good qualities arise paradoxically, as I have already suggested, from the fact that there is no agreement between those most closely concerned about the underlying legal basis for the management of Antarctic affairs.

The Antarctic Treaty System is therefore, to a very real degree, fragile. The plain truth must be faced that if anyone succeeded in upsetting it, they would have no capacity to pick up the bits and build a new structure. They would need to face exactly the same issues as those faced by the original drafters of the Antarctic Treaty. The Antarctic itself is a place of surpassing beauty which puts under its thrall all those who are fortunate enough to go there. It is plainly different from the rest of the world. It is not surprising therefore that it has given rise to a set of international agreements which, like the Antarctic itself, are *sui generis* in all but their consistency with the Charter of the United Nations.

(Text provided by the Foreign and Commonwealth Office.)

In the course of a debate in the House of Lords on the subject of the Falkland Islands, the Minister of State, Foreign and Commonwealth Office, Baroness Young, stated:

There were a great many suggestions for a multilateral solution to the Falkland Islands. The noble Lord, Lord Kennet, suggested an extension of the Antarctic Treaty area. Whatever the superficial attractions of this solution, it must be borne in mind that the extension of the treaty area to include the Falklands and the Falkland Island dependencies would require the unanimous consent of all 14 consultative parties. It would give not only Argentina but also the Soviet Union and Poland the right to establish scientific stations on sites of their choosing and to man them with military though unarmed personnel. It must also be borne in mind that the Antarctic Treaty is geared to territory where there is no permanent population. Its direct application would not meet the situation of the Falkland Islanders. The treaty was not designed to meet situations such as the Falklands dispute and it would, we believe, be wrong to risk destabilising its regime which has worked so extraordinarily well.

(H.L. Debs., vol. 445, cols. 1059-60: 6 December 1983.)

Part Nine: I. A. *Seas, waterways—territorial Sea—delimitation*

In reply to a question, the Parliamentary Under-Secretary of State, Foreign and Commonwealth Office, wrote:

The territorial sea extends to three nautical miles around the mainland and offshore islands of the United Kingdom, taking into account established baselines.

(H.C. Debs., vol. 36, Written Answers, cols. *277-8*: 7 February 1983.)

In reply to a question, the Minister of State, Foreign and Commonwealth Office, published the following table of territorial seas claimed by States:

TERRITORIAL SEA:

(a) *Less than 12 miles*

Australia	3	Irish Republic	3	São Tomé & Principe	6
Belgium	3	Israel	6	Singapore	3
Belize	3	Jordan	3	Turkey (Aegean)	6
Denmark	3	Kiribati	3	Tuvalu	3
Dominican Republic	6	Lebanon	6	UK	3
Finland	4	Netherlands	3	USA	3
FRG	3	Norway	4	St. Lucia	3
GDR	3	Nicaragua	3	St. Vincent	3
Greece	6	Qatar	3		

(b) 12 miles

Algeria	Honduras	Romania
Antigua	Iceland	Saudi Arabia
Bahrain	India	Seychelles
Bangladesh	Indonesia	Sharjah (UAE)
Barbados	Iran	Solomon Islands
Bulgaria	Iraq	South Africa
Burma	Italy	Spain
Cambodia	Ivory Coast	Sri Lanka
Canada	Jamaica	Sudan
Cape Verde	Japan	Suriname
China	Kenya	Sweden
Colombia	Republic of Korea	Thailand
Comoros	Kuwait	Tonga
Costa Rica	Libya	Trinidad & Tobago
Cuba	Malaysia	Tunisia
Cyprus	Maldives	Turkey (Black Sea and
Djibouti	Malta	Mediterranean outside
Dominica	Mauritius	Aegean)
Egypt	Mexico	USSR
Equatorial Guinea	Monaco	Vanuatu
Ethiopia	Morocco	Venezuela
Fiji	Mozambique	Vietnam
France	Nauru	Western Samoa
Fujairah (UAE)	New Zealand	Yemen Arab Republic
Grenada	Oman	Yemen People's Demo-
Guatemala	Pakistan	cratic Republic
Guinea Bissau	Papua New Guinea	Yugoslavia
Guyana	Poland	Zaire
Haiti	Portugal	

More than 12 miles

Albania	15	El Savador	200	Panama	200
Angola	20	Gabon	100	Peru	200
Argentina	200	Gambia	200	Senegal	150
Benin	200	Ghana	200	Sierra Leone	200
Brazil	200	Guinea	200	Somalia	200
Cameroon	50	Liberia	200	Syria	35
Chile*	200	Madagascar	50	Tanzania	50
Congo	200	Mauritania	70	Togo	30
Ecuador	200	Nigeria	30	Uruguay	200

* 3 miles in Civil Code

(H.L. Debs., vol. 440, cols. 993–4: 21 March 1983.)

In reply to the question which States now recognize no more than a three-mile territorial sea, the Minister of State, Foreign and Commonwealth Office, wrote:

At present, in addition to the United Kingdom and dependent territories, Australia, Belgium, Denmark, Federal Republic of Germany, German Democratic Republic, Irish Republic, Jordan, Kiribati, Netherlands, Nicaragua, Qatar, St. Lucia, St. Vincent, Singapore, Tuvalu and the USA claim no more than a three-mile territorial sea. But Her Majesty's Government are not aware whether these states recognise the claims of other states to wider territorial seas.

(Ibid., col. 995.)

In reply to the question what are the advantages to the United Kingdom of maintaining a three-mile territorial sea, the same Minister of State wrote:

. . . we are now examining the question of the extension of the United Kingdom's territorial sea in the context of the outcome of the United Nations Law of the Sea Conference. While we maintain a three-mile territorial sea we can object on that ground to wider claims by other states which may purport to curtail rights of navigation, particularly in international straits.

(Ibid., col. 996.)

In reply to the question whether Her Majesty's Government will provide maps showing in moderate detail what territorial waters the Soviet Union claims, and what Soviet territorial waters are recognized by Her Majesty's Government, the Minister of State, Foreign and Commonwealth Office, wrote:

The Soviet Union claims a 12 nautical mile territorial sea, but has not made adequate information available on their claims for the purpose of preparing a map showing the information sought . . .

(Ibid., vol. 442, col. 547: 11 May 1983.)

Part Nine: I. B. 1. *Seas, waterways—territorial Sea—legal status—right of innocent passage*

(See Part Nine: XIV. (statement of 4 March 1983), below.)

Part Nine: I. B. 4. *Seas, waterways—territorial sea—legal status— warships*

(See Part Nine: XIV. (statement of 4 March 1983), below.)

Part Nine: III. *Seas, waterways—internal waters, including ports*

By an exchange of notes dated 14 May and 25 May 1979, the United States and United Kingdom Governments concluded an agreement concerning the use of the Louisiana Offshore Oil Port (LOOP) by vessels registered in the United Kingdom, the West Indies Associated States or its other territories or flying the flag of the United Kingdom. The operative part of the exchange of notes is contained in the following extract from the United States letter of 14 May 1979:

I have the honor to refer to the discussions which have taken place between representatives of our two Governments in connection with the establishment of deepwater ports off the coast of the United States and the jurisdictional requirements of the United States Deepwater Port Act of 1974, and to confirm that the two Governments are in agreement that vessels registered in the United Kingdom, the West Indies Associated States or its other territories or flying the flag of the United Kingdom and the personnel on board such vessels utilizing the Louisiana Offshore Oil Port (LOOP, Inc.), a deepwater port facility established under the Deepwater Port Act of 1974, for the purposes stated therein shall, whenever they may be present within the safety zone of such deepwater port, be subject to the jurisdiction of the United States and the United Kingdom on the same basis as when in coastal ports of the United States.

It is the understanding of the Government of the United States and of the Government of the United Kingdom that this agreement shall not apply to vessels registered in the United Kingdom, the West Indies Associated States or its other territories or flying the flag of the United Kingdom merely passing through the safety zone of the Louisiana Offshore Oil Port without calling at or otherwise utilizing the port.

(*United Kingdom Treaty Series*, No. 86 (1979) (Cmnd. 7621): the agreement came into force on 25 May 1979.)

[*Editorial note*: the above item may be read as part of UKMIL 1979.]

In the course of replying to a question about assistance given to the British Merchant Navy, the Parliamentary Under-Secretary of State wrote:

We took a lead in negotiating, and then signed, the Paris memorandum on port state control by which one ship in every four that enters the ports of 14 European nations will be inspected for safety and, if found to be defective, can be detained until the safety deficiencies are put right. This is a major step forward in enforcing international safety requirements and eliminating sub-standard ships.

(H.C. Debs., vol. 37, Written Answers, col. 57: 14 February 1983.)

Part Nine: IV. *Seas, waterways—straits*

(See also Part Nine: I. A. (Written Answer of 21 March 1983 (col. 996)), above.)

In reply to a question, the Minister of State, Foreign and Commonwealth Office, wrote:

We attach importance to the freedom of navigation in the Gulf, including passage through the Straits of Hormuz.

(Ibid., vol. 50, Written Answers, col. *176*: 7 December 1983.)

Part Nine: VI. *Seas, waterways—canals*

On 15 December 1982, the United Kingdom acceded to the Protocol to the Treaty concerning the Permanent Neutrality and Operation of the Panama Canal, concluded between the United States and Panama. The Protocol reads as follows:

Whereas the maintenance of the neutrality of the Panama Canal is important not only to the commerce and security of the United States of America and the

Republic of Panama, but to the peace and security of the Western Hemisphere and to the interests of world commerce as well;

Whereas the regime of neutrality which the United States of America and the Republic of Panama have agreed to maintain will ensure permanent access to the Canal by vessels of all nations on the basis of entire equality;

Whereas the said regime of effective neutrality shall constitute the best protection for the Canal and shall ensure the absence of any hostile act against it;

The Contracting Parties to this Protocol have agreed upon the following:

ARTICLE I

The Contracting Parties hereby acknowledge the regime of permanent neutrality for the Canal established in the Treaty Concerning the Permanent Neutrality and Operation of the Panama Canal and associate themselves with its objectives.

ARTICLE II

The Contracting Parties agree to observe and respect the regime of permanent neutrality of the Canal in time of war as in time of peace, and to ensure that vessels of their registry strictly observe the applicable rules.

ARTICLE III

This Protocol shall be open to accession by all states of the world, and shall enter into force for each State at the time of deposit of its instrument of accession with the Secretary General of the Organization of American States.

(*United Kingdom Treaty Series*, No. 11 (1983) (Cmnd. 8833).)

Part Nine: VII. A. 5. *Seas, waterways—the high seas—freedom of the high seas—other freedoms*

In reply to a question, the Minister of State, Ministry of Agriculture, Fisheries and Food, wrote:

The dumping of radioactive wastes in the Atlantic is subject to the Convention on the Prevention of Marine Pollution by Dumping of Wastes and Other Matter, 1972 (the London Dumping Convention) and to the multilateral consultation and surveillance mechanism for sea dumping of radioactive waste established by the Organisation for Economic Co-operation and Development and administered by the Nuclear Energy Agency.

(H.C. Debs., vol. 37, Written Answers, col. 428: 22 February 1983.)

In reply to the further question why Her Majesty's Government voted against a halt to the dumping of nuclear waste at sea during a recent meeting of the London Dumping Convention, the same Minister wrote:

We did so because the relevant Resolution involved action that was against the policy of Her Majesty's Government and against the spirit of the convention. In particular, it called on member states to act in advance of receiving authoritative scientific advice: to do so would be contrary to the provisions of article XV(2) of the convention.

(Ibid.)

He later added:

It was the policy of Her Majesty's Government that the United Kingdom delegation to the seventh meeting of the London dumping convention should contribute constructively to the work of the convention and should seek to ensure that decisions were in accordance with the terms and spirit of the convention.

(Ibid., cols. 429–30.)

In reply to a further question, the Minister wrote:

The Government have continued the policy adopted by previous Administrations that the dumping at sea of low-level radioactive waste is an acceptable disposal option, provided that such operations are in accord with the internationally agreed rules and, on the basis of expert scientific advice, do not endanger human health or pose a significant risk to the marine environment.

(Ibid., col. 429.)

He gave the amounts of nuclear waste dumped at sea by the United Kingdom as follows:

Year	Gross weight in tonnes*	Radioactivity in curies	
		alpha	beta/gamma
1978	2,080	814	69,307
1979	2,014	1,381	81,080
1980	2,693	1,791	106,079
1981	2,517	2,032	104,709
1982	2,697	1,264	107,512

* Including packaging.

These wastes have all been dumped at one internationally approved site in the North Atlantic which is within 10 nautical miles north and south of 46°N and bounded by 17°30′W and 16°W.

(Ibid.)

In reply to the question what was the attitude of Her Majesty's Government towards the two-year moratorium on the dumping of nuclear waste at sea as adopted by the London Dumping Convention, the Minister of State, Ministry of Agriculture, Fisheries and Food, wrote:

No such moratorium is in force. A resolution passed at the seventh consultative meeting of the London dumping convention called for the voluntary suspension of the dumping of all radioactive wastes. However, this does not in any way alter the convention or its annexes, which continue to provide for the dumping at sea of low-level radioactive wastes.

(Ibid., vol. 40, Written Answers, col. 453: 14 April 1983.)

In the course of a speech on 12 October 1983 to the General Conference of the International Atomic Energy Agency, the United Kingdom representative, Mr. Henderson, referred to the resolution adopted at the London Dumping Convention meeting in February 1983 to suspend sea disposal operations pending the outcome of a scientific review of the factors for and against sea disposal. He went on:

In view of the United Kingdom's prominent role in relation to sea disposal it is appropriate to set out our position clearly. It is the United Kingdom's view that disposal of low level radioactive waste at sea is a safe and environmentally acceptable method, and is consistent with the international standards laid down by the London Dumping Convention and other international bodies including the IAEA. No authoritative scientific evidence has been adduced to suggest that sea disposal in conformity with these guidelines is unsafe. If such evidence were to emerge from the London Dumping Convention review, then the United Kingdom would be prepared to stop sea disposal operations.

(Text provided by the Foreign and Commonwealth Office.)

In reply to a question, the Parliamentary Under-Secretary of State, Department of the Environment, wrote in part:

. . . Disposal at sea of low-level wastes from laboratories, medical uses and other sources is a part of the Government's comprehensive policies for waste management. In international law such disposal is permissible under the London dumping convention if a licence is issued by the national Government. A site in the Atlantic, and detailed procedures, have been recommended by the Organisation for Economic Co-operation and Development, and the OECD nuclear energy agency appoints an observer from another country to accompany such operations.

(H.C. Debs., vol. 46, Written Answers, col. 522: 27 July 1983.)

Part Nine: VII. B. *Seas, waterways—the high seas—nationality of ships*

(See also Part Nine: IX. (debate on British Fishing Boats Bill), below.)

In reply to a question, the Government Minister in the House of Lords wrote:

Facilities for the registration of ships are available in the following British Islands and Dependent Territories in addition to the United Kingdom: Isle of Man, Guernsey, Jersey, Anguilla, Bermuda, the British Virgin Islands, the Cayman Islands, the Falkland Islands, Gibraltar, Hong Kong, Montserrat, St. Helena and the Turks and Caicos Islands.

The qualifications for owning and registering British ships in any of these territories are those set out in Part I of the Merchant Shipping Act 1894, but international conventions relating to the safety of ships, the prevention of pollution, and other shipping matters have been extended only to those territories which have the professional and administrative staff needed to implement them.

This is not a satisfactory situation, and the Government will seek to ensure that all ships entitled to fly the British flag are subject to the same requirements as those on the United Kingdom register. Proposals to that effect were contained in a consultative document issued by the Department of Trade at the end of 1981, and have since been pursued in detailed bilateral talks with the territories concerned, with a view to making suitable provision in forthcoming legislation. The responsibility for shipping and ship registration now rests with the Department of Transport.

(H.L. Debs., vol. 444, cols. 685–6: 3 November 1983.)

In reply to a further question, the Government Minister wrote:

The table below shows the number and tonnage of ships over 500 gross tons registered in the British Islands and Dependent Territories at the end of 1982. Smaller ships have been excluded because most international safety conventions do not apply to them.

	No. of ships	Gross registered tons
Isle of Man	7	21,331
Guernsey	1	527
Jersey	3	2,225
Anguilla	—	—
Bermuda	56	667,016
British Virgin Islands	2	1,417
Cayman Islands	105	272,153
Falkland Islands	2	6,400
Gibraltar	10	18,069
Hong Kong	185	4,008,759
Montserrat	1	711
St. Helena	1	3,150
Turks & Caicos Islands	1	514

Most of the conventions currently in force have been or are being extended to Hong Kong and Bermuda, where suitable arrangements for the survey and control of ships already exist. The detailed bilateral talks with Dependent Territories were designed to secure agreement on satisfactory arrangements in accordance with their needs. They have been made aware of the need to choose between the establishment of the professional maritime administration required to implement relevant international conventions, and restrictions on the size of ships which should in future be accepted on their registers. The implications of these options are being considered and suitable provision will be made in forthcoming legislation to implement the arrangements.

(H.L. Debs., vol. 444, cols. 1442–4: 17 November 1983.)

Part Nine: VII. G. *Seas, waterways—the high seas—pollution*

(See also Part Nine: VII. A. 5., above.)

On 13 September 1983, the United Kingdom, together with seven other western European States and the European Economic Community, signed the Agreement for Co-operation in dealing with Pollution of the North Sea by Oil and other Harmful Substances. The Agreement, which has not yet been ratified by the United Kingdom, applies to the North Sea southwards of 61°N., the Skagerrak and the English Channel and approaches. The area is divided into national zones in respect of which the respective Contracting Parties are obliged to undertake certain responsibilities. Article 8 of the Agreement reads:

(1) The provisions of this Agreement shall not be interpreted as in any way prejudicing the rights and obligations of the Contracting Parties under international law, especially in the field of the prevention and combating of marine pollution.

(2) In no case shall the division into zones referred to in Article 6 of this Agreement be invoked as a precedent or argument in any matter concerning sovereignty or jurisdiction.

(Cmnd. 9104.)

Part Nine: VIII. *Seas, waterways—continental shelf*

(See Part Nine: IX. (statement of 13 October 1982 and letter from Sir Ian Sinclair dated 4 February 1983), below.)

Part Nine: IX. *Seas, waterways—exclusive fishery zone*

The Foreign and Commonwealth Office submitted to the Foreign Affairs Committee of the House of Commons a memorandum, dated 13 October 1982, in answer to questions posed by the Committee. In reply to the question what effect will the United Nations Law of the Sea Convention have on fish and mineral resources in the waters around the Falkland Islands, it was written:

The rights of a coastal State in respect of fisheries and seabed resources under the provisions of the draft United Nations Convention on the Law of the Sea are not greatly different from those generally recognized as existing under current international law and practice.

(*Parliamentary Papers*, 1982-3, H.C., Paper 31-i, p. 7.)

On 4 February 1983, the Legal Adviser to the Foreign and Commonwealth Office, Sir Ian Sinclair, wrote to a correspondent who had referred to a written answer given in the House of Lords on 14 March 1978 by the Minister of State, Foreign and Commonwealth Office, on the subject of the continental shelf and exclusive fishery zone of the Spitsbergen Archipelago (H.L. Debs., vol. 389, col. 1355: UKMIL 1978, pp. 409–10). Sir Ian Sinclair set out the above answer and continued:

The position remains unchanged since 1978 and the United Kingdom still regards the matter, which is one of legal interpretation of certain articles of the Treaty, as unresolved. The Norwegian Government are aware of our reservations on the issues involved. However, the need for conservation of fishery stocks on a strictly non-discriminatory basis is accepted by the United Kingdom and details of the practical measures to give effect to this in the Fisheries Protection Zone are discussed from time to time between Norway and the EEC.

(Text provided by the Foreign and Commonwealth Office.)

On 10 March 1983, the United Kingdom and United States Governments exchanged instruments of ratification of the Reciprocal Fisheries Agreement. The preamble to the Agreement, which was signed on 27 March 1979, reads as follows:

The Government of the United Kingdom of Great Britain and Northern Ireland and the Government of the United States of America;

Seeking to maintain the long-standing and cooperative fisheries relations in adjacent waters which have formed a part of the close ties between the people of the British Virgin Islands and the people of the United States;

Desiring to ensure effective conservation of fishery stocks in the exclusive fishery zones of the British Virgin Islands and the United States;

Taking note of the United States Fishery Conservation and Management Act of 1976, establishing a fishery conservation zone contiguous to the territorial sea of the United States;

Taking note of the Proclamation by the Governor of the British Virgin Islands of 9 March 1977 establishing a fisheries zone contiguous to the territorial sea of the British Virgin Islands;

Recalling that the two Governments have a common approach based on the principle of equidistance regarding the limits of fishery jurisdiction as between the British Virgin Islands and the United States; . . .

(*United Kingdom Treaty Series*, No. 32 (1983) (Cmnd. 8932).)

In moving the Second Reading in the House of Lords of the British Fishing Boats Bill, the Minister of State, Department of Agriculture, Fisheries and Food, Earl Ferrers, observed in part:

This Bill is introduced in order to tackle a growing problem for the United Kingdom fishing industry—that of a large influx of foreign, mainly Spanish, fishing vessels which have re-registered as British. Their motive in re-registering has been in order to circumvent the European Community licensing restrictions. A by-product of their action has been, though, a substantial and adverse effect on the interests of our catchers.

. . .

In brief, the problem is that since May 1980 some 67 ex-Spanish vessels— or British vessels with a Spanish association—have become registered in this country. There are 63 registered at the present time and there are rumours of further potential applicants for registration who are trying to take advantage of the loophole which is provided by the liberal arrangements for registering vessels which, for broader international shipping reasons, we operate.

Their objective is to evade the restrictions on fishing opportunities which are provided for in the Community bilateral agreements between Spain and the Community; and the main activity of these vessels at present is vigorous fishing of the British quota for hake. Valuable non-quota species, such as the angler fish and West Coast sole, are also caught but hake is their main target and the ex-Spanish vessels are fishing against a British national quota which was set up by the efforts of our own catchers. I am sure that your Lordships will agree that this is quite unacceptable. The activities of these vessels not only compete with genuine British catchers, but they make no significant contribution to the fishing economy of this country because most of the catch is landed in Spain, and the bulk of that which is landed here is immediately transported to Spain by lorries direct as soon as it is landed in our ports.

There is the further disagreeable reality that, because of the way in which this is done, catches by these vessels, even when they are landed in the United Kingdom, avoid the levy which is imposed by the Sea Fish Industry Authority, because the fish are not sold here. And not only that but, because of the Spanish connection, the fish so caught benefit from import duty relief and sometimes even access, which is not available to British vessels which wish to land catches in Spain. It is, therefore, to use a colloquialism, a proper mare's nest.

I hope that I have said enough to apprise your Lordships of the nature of the problem and of the reasons for the hostility in many parts of our industry towards the growth of this new 'Spanish armada'. Your Lordships may wonder why we did not decide to tackle the problem through the registration system. Well, we did consider such a course, but we concluded that the solution to what we regard as a short-term problem would not lend itself to this approach because of the need for consistency with our long-term approach to international shipping questions.

. . . The heart of the matter in fact lies in Clause 1. This empowers the fisheries Ministers to make, by order, conditions governing the qualification of British fishing vessels to fish in our waters. The key to this is the crewing of the vessels concerned. At present, apart from the skipper and the first hand (who must, in accordance with other legislation, be British nationals) the crews of the vessels in question are mainly Spanish; and the success of their present operations in fact depends on this. In order to close this loophole, we propose to use the order-making power to ensure that the crew of British fishing vessels must, in future, consist mainly of nationals of the Community.

We have in mind, therefore, to specify in the order a qualification that at least 75 per cent. of the crew of a British fishing boat which is fishing in British waters shall be Community nationals. It is possible, of course, that some of the vessels which will be affected by this change will seek to comply with the new rule by employing more British crew. If that is so, then so be it.

(H.L. Debs., vol. 440, cols. 668-9: 15 March 1983. See also H.C. Debs., vol. 38, cols. 643-7, 673: 7 March 1983.)

In reply to a question on the subject of the exclusive fishery zones of States, the Minister of State, Foreign and Commonwealth Office, produced the following table:

FISHERY LIMITS:

(a) *Less than 200 miles*

Albania	15	Cyprus	12	Iran	50
Algeria	12	Egypt	12	Israel	6
Anguilla	3	Finland	12	Italy	12
Belize	3	Gabon	150	Jordan	3
Bulgaria	12	Greece	6	Republic of Korea	20-200

Lebanon	6	Monaco	12	Tunisia	12
Libya	20	Poland	12	Turkey	12
Madagascar	150	Tanzania	50	UAE	up to 73
Malta	25	Trinidad & Tobago	12	Yugoslavia	12

(b) *200 miles*

Angola
Antigua
Argentina
Australia
Bahamas
Bangladesh
Barbados
Belgium
Benin
Brazil
Burma
Cambodia
Canada
Cape Verde Islands
Chile
Colombia
Comoros
Congo
Costa Rica
Cuba
Denmark
Djibouti
Dominica
Dominican Republic
Ecuador
El Salvador
Fiji
FRG
France (except in
   Mediterranean)
Gambia

Ghana
Grenada
Guatemala
Guinea
Guinea Bissau
Guyana
Haiti
Honduras
Iceland
India
Indonesia
Irish Republic
Ivory Coast
Japan
Kenya
Kiribati
Liberia
Malaysia
Maldives
Mauritania
Mauritius
Mexico
Morocco
Mozambique
Nauru
Netherlands
New Zealand
Nicaragua
Nigeria
Norway
Oman

Pakistan
Panama
Papua New Guinea
Peru
Portugal
São Tomé and Principe
Senegal
Seychelles
Sierra Leone
Solomon Islands
Somalia
South Africa
Spain
Sri Lanka
Suriname
Sweden
Thailand
Togo
Tonga
Tunisia
UK
Uruguay
USA
USSR
Vanuatu
Venezuela
Vietnam
Yemen People's Demo-
   cratic Republic
Zaire

(H.L. Debs., vol. 440, cols. 994–5: 21 March 1983.)

In reply to a question, the Parliamentary Under-Secretary of State, Home Office, wrote:

British fishery limits around the Isle of Man, as around the United Kingdom, were extended to 200 miles (or median lines) under the Fishery Limits Act 1976.

Discussions are being held with the Isle of Man Government on various proposals on fishing, including a suggestion that the island's jurisdiction over fisheries might be extended from the existing 3 mile limit to 12 miles.

(H.C. Debs., vol. 45, Written Answers, col. *216*: 11 July 1983.)

In reply to a question, the Minister of Agriculture, Fisheries and Food wrote:

The Fishery Limits Act 1976 establishes that British fishery limits extend to

200 miles from the baselines from which the breadth of the territorial sea adjacent to the United Kingdom, the Channel Islands and the Isle of Man is measured, or to the median line with other States as appropriate. With other Fisheries Ministers, I exercise general responsibility for questions of fishery protection and conservation throughout British fishery limits in the Irish sea. In addition under the Sea Fisheries Act 1971, the Manx authorities exercise jurisdiction on fisheries matters within the territorial sea round the island.

(Ibid., vol. 46, Written Answers, col. 37: 18 July 1983.)

In reply to a question about the firing at a Peterhead vessel, the *Spes Melior*, by a Norwegian fisheries vessel on 11 December 1983, the Parliamentary Under-Secretary of State, Scottish Office, wrote in part:

All vessels fishing in Norwegian waters, like all vessels fishing in UK waters, must accept and facilitate inspections by the enforcement authorities. According to information supplied by the Norwegian authorities the Spes Melior was in the Norwegian zone of the North Sea in position 58 10° North, 157° East on 11 December, having previously reported to these authorities that fishing operations were being carried out. By the Norwegian account, their coastguard vessel approached to make an inspection but the Spes Melior began to steam away westwards; by radio and signal flares the coastguard repeatedly ordered the Spes Melior to stop for inspection, but the skipper did not comply; shots from handguns were fired across the bow after the crew were warned to clear the deck.

I understand that the Norwegian authorities have informed the owners that the vessel will not be permitted to fish in the Norwegian zone for a period of 8 months from 1 January 1984.

(Ibid., vol. 51, Written Answers, col. 79: 19 December 1983.)

Part Nine: X. *Seas, waterways—exclusive economic zone*

(See also Part Nine: XIV. (statement of 4 March 1983), below.)

In reply to a question on the subject of the exclusive economic zones of States, the Minister of State, Foreign and Commonwealth Office, produced the following table:

States understood to have declared an EEZ of 200 miles:

Antigua	France	Morocco
Bangladesh	Gabon	Mozambique
Barbados	Grenada	Nauru
Burma	Guatemala	New Zealand
Cambodia	Haiti	Norway
Canada	Iceland	Oman
Colombia	India	Pakistan
Comoros	Ivory Coast	Papua New Guinea
Congo	Kenya	Philippines
Costa Rica	Malaysia	Portugal
Cuba	Maldives	Seychelles
Dominican Republic	Mauritius	Solomon Islands
Fiji	Mexico	Spain

Sri Lanka	USA	Western Samoa
Thailand	Vanuatu	Yemen People's Demo-
Tonga	Venezuela	cratic Republic
UAE	Vietnam	

(H.L. Debs., vol. 440, col. 995: 21 March 1983.)

During evidence given on 15 November 1982 to the Foreign Affairs Committee of the House of Commons investigating the Falkland Islands situation, Mr. J. B. Ure, Assistant Under-Secretary of State, Foreign and Commonwealth Office, stated in answer to a question that the United Kingdom has made no formal claim to an economic zone around the Falkland Islands.

(*Parliamentary Papers*, 1982–3, House of Commons, Paper 31-ii, p. 41.)

Part Nine: XI. *Seas, waterways—rivers*

(See Part Eight: II. C. (statement of 15 November 1983), above.)

Part Nine: XII. *Seas, waterways—bed of the sea beyond national jurisdiction*

(See Part Nine: XIV. (statement of 4 March 1983), below.)

In reply to a question on the United Nations Convention on the Law of the Sea, the Minister of State, Foreign and Commonwealth Office, wrote:

Although some provisions of the convention are helpful, those relating to deep seabed mining are not acceptable to us. In order to seek satisfactory improvements in the seabed mining regime, we are participating in the preparatory commission set up to prepare for implementation of parts of the convention.

(H.C. Debs., vol. 50, Written Answers, cols. *173–4*: 7 December 1983.)

Part Nine: XIV. *Seas, waterways—international regime of the sea in general*

(See also Part Three: II. B. 3 (answer of 10 February 1983), above.)

On 4 March 1983, the United Kingdom Mission to the United Nations in New York addressed the following statement to the Secretary-General's Special Representative for the Law of the Sea:

At the final session of the Conference, statements were made regarding the interpretation or application of the Convention [on the Law of the Sea] concerning the rights of a coastal state with regard to the territorial sea, and in particular the innocent passage of warships and other vessels through the territorial sea, the status and regime of the exclusive economic zone, and in particular the rights and obligations of States other than the coastal state concerned within that zone, the delimitation of maritime boundaries of all kinds and the legal status of the deep sea bed beyond national jurisdiction and its resources. A number of statements on these and other matters misinterpret the provisions of the Convention or their effect. The United Kingdom does not accept these statements and wishes to recall the statement made by the leader of the United Kingdom Delegation at the Plenary meeting on 8 December 1982 and to reaffirm its position expressed then and on other occasions during the negotiations.

(Text provided by the Foreign and Commonwealth Office.)

In reply to the question what offshore jurisdictions were recognized by Her Majesty's Government (a) *de jure*, and (b) *de facto*, the Minister of State, Foreign and Commonwealth Office, wrote:

Her Majesty's Government consider that the following zones of offshore national jurisdiction beyond a coastal state's internal and territorial waters are permitted by international law: contiguous zone, fishery zone, exclusive economic zone. In each case, the limits of the zone and the extent of the jurisdiction claimed within it must conform with the rules of international law.

In addition, coastal states exercise sovereign rights over the continental shelf in accordance with international law.

(H.L. Debs., vol. 440, col. 995: 21 March 1983.)

In reply to a question in the House of Lords, the Minister of State, Foreign and Commonwealth Office, wrote that there was no connection between the United Kingdom's purchase of Trident missiles from the United States and the decision not to sign the United Nations Convention on the Law of the Sea.

(Ibid., vol. 446, col. 93: 12 December 1983.)

Part Ten: I. A. *Air space, outer space—sovereignty over air space—extent*

(See also Part Ten: II. A. 2. (debate on Civil Aviation (Eurocontrol) Bill), below.)

In reply to a question, the Government spokesman in the House of Lords, Lord Trefgarne, stated:

. . . we understand that the Soviet state border for their airspace is the line established by the Soviet Law on the Border of the USSR of 24th November 1982.

However, the Soviet authorities are still engaged in defining their claims in the sea area to the north of the Soviet Union and, in answer to recent inquiries, were able to tell us only that they would publish the results of this work when it has been completed. We shall continue to seek this information.

(Ibid., vol. 444, col. 1058: 14 November 1983.)

Part Ten: I. B. *Air space, outer space—sovereignty over air space—limitations*

(See Part Ten: II. A. 2. (debate on Civil Aviation (Eurocontrol) Bill), below.)

Part Ten: II. A. 2. *Air space, outer space—air navigation—civil aviation—treaty regime*

In moving the third reading in the House of Commons of the Civil Aviation (Eurocontrol) Bill, the Parliamentary Under-Secretary of State, Department of Trade, Mr. Ian Sproat, remarked:

The purpose of the Bill . . . is to give effect in United Kingdom law to certain requirements of the protocol amending the 1960 Eurocontrol convention and the multilateral agreement on route charges—both signed on 12 February 1981—and to enable the Government to ratify the protocol and agreement that were presented to Parliament by my right hon. Friend the Secretary of State for Foreign and Commonwealth Affairs last October. Most of the provisions of the protocol and agreement can be implemented under existing legislation, in particular under the Civil Aviation (Eurocontrol) Act 1962 as amended, and now consolidated in the Civil Aviation Act 1982. If enacted, the Bill will amend and add new provisions to the 1982 Act.

The principal change made by the protocol is to transfer back to member states the formal responsibility for the provision of air navigation services above 25,000 ft. It will also enable Eurocontrol to expand and strengthen its role as the focus for co-operation between member states in the future development of air navigation services in addition to continuing with tasks ranging from basic research and development to the training of controllers and engineers.

The transfer of formal responsibility for their upper airspace back to member states should make it easier for states who have held back until now to join the organisation. This will be beneficial both to them and to us. The transfer of responsibility for the whole of national airspace to Eurocontrol would have resulted in an enlarged bureaucracy with supranational powers which would have been costly in manpower and money.

The amending protocol has been signed by the current seven member states—Belgium, the Federal Republic of Germany, France, the Republic of Ireland, Luxembourg, the Netherlands and the United Kingdom, and by Portugal, which will become a full member when the protocol is ratified.

Associated with the amending protocol is a new multilateral agreement on route charges, which has also been signed by Austria, Spain and Switzerland as well as by the eight states which signed the protocol. This replaces the previous agreement, which signified the intention to set up a common charging scheme, and codifies the system for collecting charges for en route navigation facilities and services which resulted.

The main effect of the Bill will be to enable the United Kingdom to play its part in the strengthening of the machinery for the enforcement of claims on behalf of Eurocontrol.

Clause 1 provides for the enforcement and recognition in the United Kingdom of judgments given in foreign courts and determinations by administrative tribunals in respect of route charges for air navigation services.

Clause 2 makes alterations to the existing immunities and privileges of Eurocontrol.

Clause 3 makes a textual amendment to the definition of the Eurocontrol convention to make it clear that it covers all amendments to the convention made with the agreement of the contracting parties.

Clause 4 gives the title, commencement and extent of the powers of the Bill. We are co-operating with the other member states to make Eurocontrol an efficient organisation adapted to the needs of the civil aviation community. The Bill enables us to play a full part in this process and I therefore commend it to the House.

(H.C. Debs., vol. 37, cols. 1116–17: 24 February 1983.)

In reply to questions on the subject of the effect of the United States laws on the operation of British airlines in the United States, the Parliamentary Under-Secretary of State for Trade wrote:

The two Governments are in consultation following notification by the US Government of a contemplated Grand Jury investigation into North Atlantic airline operations.

. . .

The Government consider that United States' law should, in respect of the operation of British airlines in the United States of America, be consistent with the bilateral Air Services Agreement (Bermuda 2), a treaty which regulates and governs airline operations between our two countries.

(Ibid., vol. 39, Written Answers, cols. 70–1: 14 March 1983.)

In reply to a question, the same Minister later wrote:

At consultations held in Washington on 26–27 April the United States delegation did not accept our contention that United States anti-trust laws could not be unilaterally applied within the field bilaterally regulated by the air services agreement. The Government are now considering urgently what further steps to take in order to bring about a resolution of the dispute.

(Ibid., vol. 42, Written Answers, col. 5: 3 May 1983.)

Part Ten: III. *Air space, outer space—outer space*

In answer to the question whether the United Kingdom is a party to any international agreement concerning extraterrestrial bodies, the Parliamentary Under-Secretary of State, Foreign and Commonwealth Office, Mr. Ray Whitney, replied:

The United Kingdom is a party to the Treaty on Principles Governing the Activities of States in the Exploration and Use of Outer Space, including the Moon and Other Celestial Bodies, often called, for short, the Outer Space Treaty 1967.

. . .

. . . the propositions in President Reagan's speech of 23 March . . . on defensive technologies are not inconsistent with the provisions of the Outer Space Treaty 1967.

(Ibid., vol. 46, col. 362: 20 July 1983.)

Part Eleven: II. A. 1. *Responsibility—responsible entities—States—elements of responsibility*

(See also Part One: II. A., above.)

On 15 July 1982, the United Kingdom ratified the Convention on Long-Range Transboundary Air Pollution, which was signed in November 1979 and which entered into force on 16 March 1983. In the preamble to the Convention, the Parties subscribed to the following recital:

Considering the pertinent provisions of the Declaration of the United Nations Conference on the Human Environment, and in particular principle 21, which expresses the common conviction that States have, in accordance with the Charter of the United Nations and the principles of international law, the sovereign right to exploit their own resources pursuant to their own environmental policies, and the responsibility to ensure that activities within their jurisdiction or control do not cause damage to the environment of other States or of areas beyond the limits of national jurisdiction . . .

(*United Kingdom Treaty Series*, No. 57 (1983) (Cmnd. 9034).)

Speaking on 17 November 1982 in the Sixth Committee of the General Assembly during a debate on the annual report of the International Law Commission, the United Kingdom representative, Mr. F. Berman, stated in the context of the topic of state responsibility that:

As far as the six new draft articles referred to the Drafting Committee were concerned, his delegation had sympathy with the view that the principal focus should be on the position of the State injured by the internationally wrongful act or, in other words, of the State to which the primary obligations in question had been owed. At the same time, it was undoubtedly a fact that certain breaches of international law might in appropriate circumstances be such as to justify a form of collective response not limited to the State whose rights and interests had been most directly affected. However, that was not to say that his delegation necessarily accepted the categorization 'international crime/international delict' which appeared in the Special Rapporteur's third report; it preferred to reserve its judgement for the time being on that question and on the link with the controversial topic of *jus cogens*. He welcomed the fact that the draft articles submitted in the third report avoided the danger implicit in the previous draft of apparently enabling States to choose whether or not to honour their international obligations concerning the treatment to be accorded to aliens.

 . . . He expressed his delegation's appreciation of the imaginativeness and originality which the Special Rapporteur on international liability for injurious consequences arising out of acts not prohibited by international law had brought to the preparation of his 'schematic outline'. It was now abundantly clear that the topic could not be regarded as coming under the heading of 'codification of international law' and that, although it might from a certain point of view fall within the concept of 'progressive development' as defined in the Commission's Statute, there would be obvious difficulties in seeking to apply that concept to what had been referred to as a 'preventive régime'. Whether considered in that light or as a régime of liability, which was potentially a very different concept, the topic clearly raised difficult questions pertaining to the imputability to States of the acts of private individuals and the function of international law in areas frequently covered by domestic law provisions governing liability in actions for damages between private persons and private interests. That was implicit in the Special Rapporteur's references to the concept of foreseeability of damage. In the circumstances, it would be understandable if the Commission were to decide to devote greater attention for the time being to the topic of State responsibility.

(A/C. 6/37/SR. 48, pp. 5–6.)

In reply to a question, the Parliamentary Under-Secretary of State, Department of the Environment, wrote in part:

Acid precipitation is a wider problem for European countries and for that reason the United Kingdom participates fully in joint consideration of it under the UN/ECE convention on long-range transboundary air pollution.

(H.C. Debs., vol. 46, Written Answers, col. *298*: 25 July 1983.)

In the course of a speech to the Security Council on 2 September 1983 on the subject of the destruction by the Soviet Union of a Korean commercial aircraft, the United Kingdom Permanent Representative, Sir John Thomson, stated:

I understand that one United Kingdom national and 13 Hong Kong residents were on the plane when it was shot down. In these circumstances, my Government reserves its right to take any appropriate action in accordance with international law.

(S/PV. 2470, p. 61.)

By a Note dated 12 September 1983, the Secretary of State for Foreign and Commonwealth Affairs wrote to the Soviet Ambassador as follows:

The British Government wishes to state that the actions of the Soviet military authorities in shooting down the unarmed, civilian airliner, Korean Air Lines Flight No 007, with the loss of 269 lives, constituted a grave breach of international law, for which the Soviet Union bears international responsibility.

The British Government accordingly expects the Soviet Government to meet its obligations to provide full compensation for the loss of life and of property occasioned by the wrongful actions of the Soviet military authorities, and in particular requires the Soviet Government to pay such compensation in respect of the pecuniary and other losses suffered by the families of the British citizens and other persons entitled to the protection of the British Government who were killed as a result of the shooting down of the airliner. The British Government will in due course convey to the Soviet Government the details of the amount of compensation due in respect of such losses.

The British Government reserves the right to present further claims to the Soviet Government arising out of this incident, including those arising out of loss of property.

(Text provided by the Foreign and Commonwealth Office.)

In the course of a speech to the Security Council on the same matter, Sir John Thomson stated also on 12 September 1983:

We regard the Soviet action as constituting a grave breach of international law for which the Soviet Union bears international responsibility. I have already reserved my Government's rights before this Council, given that the United Kingdom is one of the States injured by this grave breach of international law. My Government intends to take at the appropriate place and time such action as may be necessary in relation to this breach.

(S/PV. 2476, p. 58.)

In the course of a statement made on 18 October 1983 to the United Nations Special Committee on enhancing the effectiveness of the principle of non-use of force in international relations, the United Kingdom representative, Mr. F. D. Berman, observed:

My delegation has already demonstrated in the Security Council and at the International Civil Aviation Organisation that the Soviet Union's action in shooting down the airliner was grossly disproportionate, that it was not even in accordance with Soviet internal law and that it constituted a grave breach of international law. Yet the Soviet government, instead of responding to this measured argument, have said they would do it again. Once more, what is one to make of this in the present context? Are we really to believe that, in constructing a new world treaty as they have proposed, the Soviet Union would abandon this line and fall in with the overwhelming majority of world opinion about how to treat a foreign airliner which has strayed into one's national airspace? Or is one forced to assume, in the light of statements by Mr Gromyko and others, that the Soviet delegation would be instructed to seek formulae in a new treaty which would indeed allow them to 'do it again'. Here also there are many questions to which the Soviet Union owes us an answer.

(Text provided by the Foreign and Commonwealth Office.)

In the course of a speech to the General Assembly on 19 October 1983, the United Kingdom representative, Mr. Margetson, referred to an observation made by the Foreign Minister of Malta on the problem of the remnants of war in Malta, particularly in Valletta Harbour. Mr. Margetson stated:

While the British Government is under no legal obligation to clear unexploded ordnance or wrecks from Malta's waters much of it the direct result of wartime attacks, it is prepared to examine what assistance it might be possible to offer in the context of specific harbour development plans where it can be shown that wrecks or unexploded ordnance constitute a hindrance to such plans. We have always been and remain willing to discuss any such problems bilaterally. An offer to Malta in this sense is on the table.

(A/38/PV. 33, p. 102; for a previous statement to the same effect, see A/37/PV. 34, pp. 129–30: 15 October 1982.)

Part Eleven: II. A. 2. *Responsibility—responsible entities—States— executive acts*

(See also Part Eleven: II. A. 1., above.)

On 4 March 1983, the Miami, Florida, agency of the Bank of Nova Scotia, a Canadian chartered bank, was served with a grand jury subpoena issued by the United States District Court for the Southern District of Florida upon the application of the United States Government. The subpoena required production of bank records from the Bank's branches in, amongst other places, Georgetown, Cayman Islands, relating to two individuals and three companies in connection with a possible narcotics and tax-evasion prosecution. The laws of the Cayman Islands, a British Crown Colony, make it a criminal offence to disclose such information and the Bank, while expressing its intention to produce the documents in a lawful manner, declined to comply with the subpoena. As a result, the United States Government sought to enforce the subpoena in the above District Court and in October 1983 the Court held the Bank in civil contempt and imposed a daily fine on it until such time as it complied with the subpoena. The Bank appealed to the United States Court of Appeals for the Eleventh Circuit before which the Governments of the Cayman Islands, the United Kingdom and Canada, *inter alios*, each filed an *amicus curiae* Brief.

The United Kingdom Brief, filed in November 1983, contained the following passages:

The United Kingdom's own appearance as amicus curiae, in which it supports the position of the Bank, is in furtherance of critical sovereign interests of the United Kingdom *qua* United Kingdom, as well as in furtherance of the critical sovereign interests of Cayman.

The outcome of this appeal has ramifications far beyond the interests of the Bank and the United States. Many of those ramifications are discussed in the Cayman Brief, the Bank's Brief, Canada's Brief, and the Brief of the Canadian Bankers Association ('CBA') as Amicus Curiae. In addition, the outcome of this appeal will have a substantial impact on the foreign relations between the United States and the United Kingdom. Accordingly, the United Kingdom files this amicus brief so that its interests may be fully expressed to this Court.

. . .

The United Kingdom extended to Cayman the Single Convention [on Narcotic Drugs, 1961], as amended (collectively, the 'Single Convention'). After discussions concerning the mechanics of securing information in certain circumstances, the Governor of Cayman entered into an agreement with the United States government on October 5, 1982, aimed at securing to the United States authorities information in circumstances of strict security (the 'Cayman/U.S. Agreement'). The conduct of the United States in this case has compelled the United Kingdom and the Cayman Islands to disclose the Cayman/U.S. Agreement to this Court, after notice and consultation with, and clearance from, the United States. It is the position of the United Kingdom that in the instant case the

United States (i) failed to use the channels provided by the Single Convention and by the Cayman/U.S. Agreement, and, furthermore, (ii) improperly refused, on the basis of the secrecy of grand jury proceedings, to provide evidence to enable the Cayman authorities to authorize the release of the required information called for by the subpoena directed to the Bank. The United States in this case violated the treaty rights of the United Kingdom and Cayman.

(*Amicus curiae* Brief of the United Kingdom, pp. 4–6 (footnotes deleted): United States Court of Appeals for the Eleventh Circuit: In re *Grand Jury Proceedings the Bank of Nova Scotia*; *United States of America* v. *The Bank of Nova Scotia*.)

Later in its Brief, the United Kingdom Government wrote:

. . . the conduct of the United States in this case, acting through agents of the executive and judicial branches, violated the United Kingdom's rights under the Single Convention and the sovereign rights of the British Crown in the right of Cayman under the Single Convention and the Cayman/U.S. Agreement.

(Ibid., pp. 8–9.)

Part Eleven: II. A. 3. *Responsibility—responsible entities—States—legislative acts*

In the course of his judgment in the Court of Appeal in the case of *British Airways Board* v. *Laker Airways Ltd.*, delivered on 26 July 1983, Sir John Donaldson M.R. stated:

Counsel for the Attorney General has stated that Her Majesty's Government regard the government of the United States as being in breach of its obligations under Bermuda 2 in applying or permitting the application of United States antitrust laws to international commerce and, in particular, to operations carried out under or pursuant to Bermuda 2.

([1983] 3 All E.R. 375, 402.)

Part Eleven: II. A. 4. *Responsibility—responsible entities—States—judicial acts*

(See Part Eleven: II. A. 2., above.)

Part Eleven: II. A. 6. *Responsibility—responsible entities—States—reparation*

(See also Part Three: I. D. 2. (material on Belize), above.)

On 25 February 1982, the Government of the United Kingdom and the Government of the Yemen Arab Republic signed an Agreement for the Promotion and Protection of Investments which came into force on 11 November 1983. Articles 4 and 5 of the Agreement read as follows:

Article 4

Compensation for Losses

(1) Nationals or companies of one Contracting Party whose investments in the territory of the other Contracting Party suffer losses owing to war or other armed conflict, revolution, a state of national emergency, revolt, insurrection or riot in the territory of the latter Contracting Party shall be accorded by the latter Contracting Party treatment, as regards restitution, indemnification, compensation or other settlement, no less favourable than that which the latter Contracting Party accords to its own nationals or companies or to nationals or companies of any third State.

(2) Without prejudice to paragraph (1) of this Article, nationals and companies of one Contracting Party who in any of the situations referred to in that paragraph suffer losses in the territory of the other Contracting Party resulting from:

(a) requisitioning of their property by its forces or authorities, or

(b) destruction of their property by its forces or authorities which was not caused in combat action or was not required by the necessity of the situation,

shall be accorded restitution or adequate compensation. Resulting payments shall be freely transferable.

Article 5

Expropriation

(1) Investments of nationals or companies of either Contracting Party shall not be nationalised, expropriated or subjected to measures having effect equivalent to nationalisation or expropriation (hereinafter referred to as 'expropriation') in the territory of the other Contracting Party except for a public purpose related to the internal needs of that Party and against prompt, adequate and effective compensation. Such compensation shall amount to the market value of the investment expropriated immediately before the expropriation or impending expropriation became public knowledge, shall include interest at a normal commercial rate until the date of payment, shall be made without delay, be effectively realizable and be freely transferable. The national or company affected shall have a right, under the law of the Contracting Party making the expropriation, to prompt review, by a judicial or other independent authority of that Party, of his or its case and of the valuation of his or its investment in accordance with the principles set out in this paragraph.

(2) Where a Contracting Party expropriates the assets of a company which is incorporated or constituted under the law in force in any part of its own territory, and in which nationals or companies of the other Contracting Party own shares, it shall ensure that the provisions of paragraph (1) of this Article are applied to the extent necessary to guarantee prompt, adequate and effective compensation in respect of their investment to such nationals or companies of the other Contracting Party who are owners of those shares.

(*United Kingdom Treaty Series*, No. 79 (1983) (Cmnd. 9096). Similar Agreements with substantially identical Articles to the above were concluded with Saint Lucia on 18 January 1983 and in force on that date (ibid., No. 25 (1983) (Cmnd. 8872)), and signed with Cameroon on 4 June 1982 (Cmnd. 8670) and Costa Rica on 7 September 1982 (Cmnd. 8767).)

In reply to a question, the Minister of State, Foreign and Commonwealth Office, wrote:

On the 28 October 1982, in accordance with the arrangements set out in Cmnd. 8785, which is being published today, we made an ex gratia payment of £4 million to the Government of Mauritius in full and final settlement of all claims made by the Ilois, who formerly lived in the Chagos Archipelago.

(H.C. Debs., vol. 36, Written Answers, col. *382*: 9 February 1983.)

In reply to a question, the Parliamentary Under-Secretary of State, Foreign and Commonwealth Office, wrote:

Some 1,000 United Kingdom citizens submitted personal claims to the Turkish Cypriot Claims Commission, which was established in 1978 to consider claims arising from the Turkish invasion of Cyprus in 1974. It is not possible to give the exact number of claims or the total sum involved as some British nationals have been pursuing their claims directly with the Turkish Cypriot Claims Commission without notifying our high commission in Nicosia. To date, of some 335 ex gratia awards approved, 152 totalling about £472,000 have been paid and a further eight totalling £44,500 will be paid very shortly.

Our high commissioner continues to press the Turkish Cypriot authorities for the remaining claims to be settled as quickly as possible. The latter have recently declared their intention to make regular monthly block payments from now onwards until all approved claims have been cleared.

(Ibid., Written Answers, col. *387*: 9 February 1983; see also H.C. Debs., vol. 46, Written Answers, col. *246*: 22 July 1983 and H.C. Debs., vol. 48, Written Answers, col. *115*: 8 November 1983 (p. 519, below).)

In reply to a question on the subject of compensation by the Ugandan Government to expelled Asians who took refuge in the United Kingdom, the Minister of State, Foreign and Commonwealth Office, wrote:

We have pressed each Ugandan Government since the overthrow of President Amin to pay adequate and effective compensation to those whose assets were expropriated in Uganda. The Ugandan Expropriated Properties Act 1982, which came into force on 21 February 1983, and the accompanying regulations provide that compensation will be paid by the Ugandan Government to those former owners who do not wish to repossess their properties, or whose applications to do so fail to meet the requirements specified in the legislation.

(Ibid., vol. 40, Written Answers, col. *149*: 30 March 1983.)

In reply to a question, the Minister of State, Treasury, wrote:

The Bank of England holds no gold directly on behalf of the Government of Albania, but does hold a certain amount of gold which is the responsibility of the Tripartite Commission for the Restitution of Monetary Gold, on which the Albanian Government have made a claim. The question of the disposal of the gold is discussed by members of the commission from time to time, but, because of several outstanding claims against Albania or on the gold itself, no satisfactory basis has yet been established for making a delivery.

(Ibid., vol. 46, Written Answers, cols. *263–4*: 22 July 1983; see also ibid., vol. 39, Written Answers, col. *346*: 21 March 1983.)

In reply to a question, the Parliamentary Under-Secretary of State, Foreign and Commonwealth Office, wrote:

Of the 1,000 claims registered by private British nationals, there are about 760 who have not received compensation from the Turkish Cypriot authorities. However, 117 of these have accepted ex-gratia awards and are expected to receive payment soon. The remainder covers claims from British nationals with Greek Cypriot origins and connections and claims arising from losses in Varosha—Famagusta—which are not currently being dealt with by the Turkish Cypriot claims commission. It is not possible to give the total sum involved in British claims since some British nationals have been pursuing their claims direct with the Turkish Cypriot claims commission without notifying our high commission in Nicosia. Through the British high commission in Nicosia we are continuing to press the Turkish Cypriot authorities to expedite settlement of all outstanding British claims.

(Ibid., vol. 48, Written Answers, col. *115*: 8 November 1983; see also ibid., vol. 36, Written Answers, col. *387*: 9 February 1983 (p. 518, above).)

Part Eleven: II. A. 7. *Responsibility—responsible entities—States— procedure*

In reply to a question, the Parliamentary Under-Secretary of State, Foreign and Commonwealth Office, wrote:

The Uganda Government have enacted an Expropriated Properties Act which permits persons who were deprived of their property during the military regime in Uganda to apply to repossess their property. Generally speaking, if such application is approved, the applicant will be required to return to Uganda to reside and he will not be able to sell his property for five years without the Minister's permission. The Act also provides for compensation to be paid to persons who do not apply to repossess their properties. The Uganda Government wish to receive written claims for such compensation.

(Ibid., vol. 41, Written Answers, col. *23*: 18 April 1983.)

In reply to a further question, the same Minister wrote:

It is normal British Government policy that a claimant against a foreign State must pay his own, and his agent's and solicitors' costs and expenses incurred on his instructions in preparing or supporting his claim. The British Government could not therefore give either financial or legal assistance to the individual claimants or to the Uganda Evacuees Association.

(Ibid., Written Answers, col. *230*: 25 April 1983.)

Part Eleven. II. A. 7. (a). *Responsibility—responsible entities—States—procedure—diplomatic and consular protection*

(See also Part Eleven: II. A. 1. (material on Korean airliner), above, and Part Thirteen: I. D. (material on Grenada), below.)

The following is the full text of the latest revision of the *Rules regarding the Taking up of International Claims by Her Majesty's Government*, issued by the Foreign and Commonwealth Office in July 1983:

The following are the most important general rules which apply when a United Kingdom national complains of injury suffered at the hands of another State and appeals to HMG to take up his claim under international law. It may sometimes be permissible and appropriate to make informal representations even where the strict application of the following rules would bar the presentation of a formal claim.

RULES REGARDING NATIONALITY

RULE I

HMG will not take up the claim unless the claimant is a United Kingdom national and was so at the date of the injury.

Comment

International law requires that for a claim to be sustainable, the claimant must be a national of the State which is presenting the claim both at the time when the injury occurred and continuously thereafter up to the date of formal presentation of the claim. In practice, however, it has hitherto been sufficient to prove nationality at the date of injury and of presentation of the claim (See 'Nationality of Claims: British Practice' by I M Sinclair: British Year Book of International Law 1950 Vol XXVII pp 125–144).

The term 'United Kingdom national' includes:

(a) individuals who fall into one of the following categories under the British Nationality Act 1981 (or one of the corresponding categories under earlier legislation):

British citizens
British Dependent Territories citizens
British Overseas citizens
British subjects under Part IV of the Act
British Protected Persons

(b) companies incorporated under the law of the United Kingdom or of any territory for which the United Kingdom is internationally responsible.

RULE II

Where the claimant has become or ceases to be a UK national after the date of the injury, HMG may in an appropriate case take up his claim in concert with the government of the country of his former or subsequent nationality.

RULE III

Where the claimant is a dual national, HMG may take up his claim, (although in certain circumstances it may be appropriate for HMG to do so jointly with the other government entitled to do so). HMG will not normally take up his claim as a UK national if the respondent State is the State of his second nationality, but may do so if the respondent State has, in the circumstances which gave rise to the injury, treated the claimant as a UK national.

RULE IV

HMG may take up the claim of a corporation or other juridical person which is created and regulated by the law of the United Kingdom or of any territory for which HMG are internationally responsible.

Comment

This rule rests on the principle that a juridical person (such as a company, corporation or other association having a legal personality distinct from its members) has the nationality of that country whose law has formally created it, which regulates its constitution and under whose law it can be wound up or dissolved. This principle was endorsed by the International Court of Justice in the Barcelona Traction Case (Belgium v. Spain) in 1970. Certain States determine nationality of a corporation by different tests; the place of central administration (siège social) or the place of effective control (to determine which, the residence of the majority of shareholders as well as of the directors may be taken into account). The International Court however said that no one of these tests of 'genuine connexion' has found general international acceptance.

In determining whether to exercise its right of protection, HMG may consider whether the company has in fact a real and substantial connexion with the United Kingdom (This question and other points arising from Rules IV–VI are discussed further in Mervyn Jones's paper 'Claims on behalf of British shareholders in companies having non-British nationality', Library Memo 17793 in AN 4046/91/26/1948[1]).

RULE V

Where a UK national has an interest, as a shareholder or otherwise, in a company incorporated in another State, and that company is injured by the acts of a third State, HMG may normally take up his claim only in concert with the government of the State in which the company is incorporated. Exceptionally, as where the company is defunct, there may be independent intervention.

RULE VI

Where a UK national has an interest, as a shareholder or otherwise, in a company incorporated in another State and of which it is therefore a national, and that State injures the company, HMG may intervene to protect the interests of that UK national.

Comment

In some cases the State of incorporation of a company does not possess the primary national interest in the company. A company may be created for reasons of legal or economic advantage under the law of one State though nearly all the capital is owned by nationals of another. In such circumstances, the State in which the company is incorporated may have little interest in protecting it, while the

---

[1] *Editorial note*: Public Record Office reference F.O. 371/68000A.

State to which the nationals who own the capital belong has considerable interest in so doing. In the Barcelona Traction Case, the International Court of Justice denied the existence under customary international law of an inherent right for the national State of shareholders in a foreign company to exercise diplomatic protection. However, the majority of the Court accepted the existence of a right to protect shareholders in the two cases described in Rules V and VI (when the company is defunct, and where the State in which the company is incorporated, although theoretically the legal protector of the company, itself causes injury to the company).

Where the capital in a foreign company is owned in various proportions by nationals of several States, including the United Kingdom, it is unusual for HMG to make representations unless the States whose nationals hold the bulk of the capital will support them in making representations.

RULE VII

HMG will not normally take up a claim of a UK national against another State until all the legal remedies, if any, available to him in the State concerned have been exhausted.

Comment

Failure to exhaust any local remedies will not constitute a bar to a claim if it is clearly established that in the circumstances of the case an appeal to a higher municipal tribunal would have had no effect. Nor is a claimant against another State required to exhaust justice in that State if there is no justice to exhaust.

RULE VIII

If, in exhausting any municipal remedies, the claimant has met with prejudice or obstruction, which are a denial of justice, HMG may intervene on his behalf to secure redress of injustice.

RULE IX

HMG will not take up a claim if there has been undue delay in its presentation to them unless the delay results from causes outside the control of the claimant, but no time limits are fixed and they are subject to equitable rather than legal definition.

RULE REGARDING REMEDIES UNDER A TREATY

RULE X

Where an express provision in any treaty is inconsistent with one or more of Rules I to IX, the terms of the treaty will, to the extent of the inconsistency, prevail. In case of ambiguity, the terms of any treaty or international agreement will be interpreted according to these rules and other rules of international law.

RULE REGARDING DEVOLUTION OF CLAIMS

RULE XI

Where the claimant has died since the date of the injury to him or his property, his personal representatives may seek to obtain relief or compensation for the injury on behalf of his estate. Such a claim is not to be confused with a claim by a dependent of a deceased person for damages for his death.

Comment

Where the personal representatives are of a different nationality from that of the original claimant, the rules set out above would probably be applied as if it were a single claimant who had changed his national status.

(Text provided by the Foreign and Commonwealth Office.)

In reply to the question whether Her Majesty's Government would establish machinery to expedite claims for repossession of property in Uganda, the Parliamentary Under-Secretary of State, Foreign and Commonwealth Office, wrote:

It will be for the individual claimants to pursue their claims for repossession of property or assets in Uganda through the machinery established by the Ugandan Government. The British high commission in Kampala will be monitoring progress, and if it appears that claimants are encountering particular problems with their claims the high commissioner will be ready to consider making representations to the Ugandan Government on their behalf.

(H.C. Debs., vol. 41, Written Answers, col. *230*: 25 April 1983.)

Part Eleven: II. A. 7. (a). (i). *Responsibility—responsible entities— States—procedure—diplomatic protection—nationality of claims*

On 25 February 1982, the Government of the United Kingdom and the Government of the Yemen Arab Republic signed an Agreement for the Promotion and Protection of Investments, which came into force on 11 November 1983. Article 1 of the Agreement contains the following definitions:

'nationals' means:

    (i) in respect of the United Kingdom: physical persons deriving their status as United Kingdom nationals from the law in force in any part of the United Kingdom or in any territory for the international relations of which the Government of the United Kingdom are responsible;

    (ii) in respect of the Yemen Arab Republic: any natural person possessing the nationality of the Yemen Arab Republic.

'companies' means:

    (i) in respect of the United Kingdom: corporations, firms or associations incorporated or constituted under the law in force in any part of the United Kingdom or in any territory to which this Agreement is extended in accordance with the provisions of Article 10;

    (ii) in respect of the Yemen Arab Republic: corporations, firms, legal entities or associations incorporated or constituted under the law in force in any part of the Yemen Arab Republic.

(*United Kingdom Treaty Series*, No. 79 (1983) (Cmnd. 9096). Similar Agreements with similar Articles were concluded with Saint Lucia on 18 January 1983 and in force on that date (ibid., No. 25 (1983) (Cmnd. 8872)), and signed with Cameroon on 4 June 1982 (Cmnd. 8670) and Costa Rica on 7 September 1982 (Cmnd. 8767).)

In reply to a question on the subject of certain persons arrested in Zimbabwe, the Parliamentary Under-Secretary of State, Foreign and Commonwealth Office, wrote:

> . . . I assume that my hon. Friend is referring to Victor Radmore and Allen Cauvin who were arrested with Frank and Stephen Bertrand. Of these, Stephen Bertrand is the only mono-British citizen. His mother has been repeatedly advised to seek legal advice and assistance with a view to submitting a plea for clemency and deportation. The other three are dual British-Zimbabwean citizens and we cannot intervene officially on their behalf.

(H.C. Debs., vol. 46, Written Answers, col. *194*: 21 July 1983; see also ibid., col. *195*, and ibid., col. *103:* 19 July 1983.)

Part Eleven: II. D. 2. *Responsibility—responsible entities—individuals, including corporations—responsibility of individuals*

(See Part Four: VI. (Written Answer of 9 March 1983), above.)

Part Twelve: II. A. *Pacific settlement of disputes—modes of settlement—negotiation*

In reply to a question on the subject of the Venezuela–Guyana border dispute, the Minister of State, Foreign and Commonwealth Office, wrote:

> We are not a party to the dispute itself but as a party to the Geneva Agreement we have made clear to Venezuela and Guyana the importance we attach to the achievement of a peaceful settlement through the agreement's procedures. We understand that contacts continue to take place directly between Venezuela and Guyana.

(H.L. Debs., vol. 437, col. 1277: 17 January 1983.)

In the course of his argument before the Court of Appeal in the case of *British Airways Board* v. *Laker Airways Ltd.*, Mr. Peter Scott, Q.C., counsel for the Attorney-General, stated on 13 July 1983:

> . . . it is the view of Her Majesty's Government, and no doubt the United States Government, that the contracting parties' obligations to perform treaties in good faith requires them to make a genuine effort to resolve the dispute by negotiation. This Her Majesty's Government is earnestly trying to do, but I must, however, say that Her Majesty's Government has fully reserved their right to take the dispute to arbitration under Bermuda 2, if necessary.

(Text provided by the Foreign and Commonwealth Office.)

In the course of a statement to the General Assembly in a debate on the subject of the Falkland Islands, the United Kingdom Permanent Representative, Sir John Thomson, said on 15 November 1983:

> The word 'negotiations' is an attractive one. We ourselves have frequently urged in one international dispute after another, that the right way to proceed is through negotiations, and we mean it. The word 'negotiation' appears in the

Charter, for example, in Article 33. But what attention did Argentina pay to Article 33 last year when, despite the fact that both Governments were engaged in a process of negotiation, they launched their surprise attack on the Falklands? As I said, our case is based firmly on the Charter and international law, but my delegation cannot accept that the Charter should be interpreted or quoted selectively.

(A/38/PV. 57, p. 46.)

Part Twelve: II. D. *Pacific settlement of disputes—modes of settlement—good offices*

(See Part Three: I. G. 5. (statement of 1 December 1983), above.)

Part Twelve: II. G. 1. *Pacific settlement of disputes—modes of settlement—arbitration—arbitral tribunals and commissions*

(See also Part Twelve: II. A. (item of 13 July 1983), above.)

On 25 February 1982, the Government of the United Kingdom and the Government of the Yemen Arab Republic signed an Agreement for the Promotion and Protection of Investments, which came into force on 11 November 1983. Articles 7 and 8 of the Agreement read:

ARTICLE 7

Reference to International Centre for Settlement of Investment Disputes

Each Contracting Party hereby consents to submit to the International Centre for the Settlement of Investment Disputes (hereinafter referred to as 'the Centre') for settlement by conciliation or arbitration under the Convention on the Settlement of Investment Disputes between States and Nationals of other States opened for signature at Washington on 18 March 1965 any legal dispute arising between that Contracting Party and a national or company of the other Contracting Party concerning an investment of the latter in the territory of the former. A company which is incorporated or constituted under the law in force in the territory of one Contracting Party and in which before such a dispute arises the majority of shares are owned by nationals or companies of the other Contracting Party shall in accordance with Article 25 (2) (b) of the Convention be treated for the purposes of the Convention as a company of the other Contracting Party.

ARTICLE 8

Disputes between the Contracting Parties

(1) Disputes between the Contracting Parties concerning the interpretation or application of this Agreement should, if possible, be settled through diplomatic channels.

(2) If a dispute between the Contracting Parties cannot thus be settled, it shall upon the request of either Contracting Party be submitted to an arbitral tribunal.

(3) Such an arbitral tribunal shall be constituted for each individual case in the following way. Within two months of the receipt of the request for arbitration, each Contracting Party shall appoint one member of the tribunal. Those two

members shall then select a national of a third State who on approval by the two Contracting Parties shall be appointed chairman of the tribunal. The chairman shall be appointed within two months from the date of appointment of the other two members.

(4) If within the periods specified in paragraph (3) of this Article the necessary appointments have not been made, either Contracting Party may, in the absence of any other agreement, invite the President of the International Court of Justice to make any necessary appointments. If the President is a national of either Contracting Party or if he is otherwise prevented from discharging the said function, the Vice-President shall be invited to make the necessary appointments.

If the Vice-President is a national of either Contracting Party or if he too is prevented from discharging the said function, the member of the International Court of Justice next in seniority who is not a national of either Contracting Party shall be invited to make the necessary appointments.

(5) The arbitral tribunal shall reach its decision by a majority of votes. Such decision shall be binding on both Contracting Parties. Each Contracting Party shall bear the cost of its own member of the tribunal and of its representation in the arbitral proceedings; the cost of the Chairman and the remaining costs shall be borne in equal parts by the Contracting Parties. The tribunal may, however, in its decision direct that a higher proportion of costs shall be borne by one of the two Contracting Parties, and this award shall be binding on both Contracting Parties. The tribunal shall determine its own procedure.

(*United Kingdom Treaty Series*, No. 79 (1983) (Cmnd. 9096). See also Agreement with Saint Lucia on 18 January 1983 (ibid., No. 25 (1983) (Cmnd. 8872), and those signed with Cameroon on 4 June 1982 (Cmnd. 8670) and Costa Rica on 7 September 1982 (Cmnd. 8767).)

Part Twelve: II. H. 1. *Pacific settlement of disputes—modes of settlement—judicial settlement—the International Court of Justice*

The Foreign and Commonwealth Office submitted to the Foreign Relations Committee of the House of Commons a memorandum, dated 17 December 1982, on the subject of the Falkland Islands. The memorandum contained the following paragraph on the subject of the British Antarctic Territory:

In December 1947, April 1951 and February 1953 the United Kingdom invited Argentina and Chile to challenge the British title to sovereignty which, *mutatis mutandis*, Argentina and Chile disputed, by invoking the jurisdiction of the International Court of Justice, which the United Kingdom would then accept. Both countries declined the invitation. In December 1954 the United Kingdom invited Argentina and Chile, jointly with the United Kingdom, to refer the dispute to an independent *ad hoc* arbitral tribunal: again, neither government accepted. The United Kingdom then unilaterally made Applications to the International Court of Justice in May 1955 setting out its case relative to the sovereignty over, *inter alia*, what is now the British Antarctic Territory. Again, neither government accepted the jurisdiction of the Court.

(*Parliamentary Papers*, 1982–3, House of Commons, Paper 31-vi, p. 149.)

In reply to the Committee's question why were the Falkland Islands themselves excluded from the reference to the Court, the memorandum stated:

The Dependencies are legally distinct from the Falkland Islands and the proposals we made to refer the issue of the Dependencies as then constituted ... to the International Court of Justice were made in the context of encroachment by Argentina and Chile on some of those territories. The question of the Falkland Islands being excluded from these proposals did not therefore arise.

(Ibid., p. 148.)

In the course of giving evidence to the Committee on 17 January 1983, Sir Ian Sinclair, Legal Adviser, Foreign and Commonwealth Office, stated:

We did make a unilateral application to the International Court of Justice in 1955, bringing proceedings against Argentina and Chile in relation to certain encroachments—what we regarded as encroachments—by Argentina and Chile in territories which are, in fact, now included in the British Antarctic Territory but which were at the time Falkland Islands Dependencies. It was precisely because what we were confronted with was encroachments—actual physical encroachments—that we wished to preserve or strengthen our title to these islands and territories in which encroachments had been made that we made this unilateral application to the Court in relation to the territories concerned. Of course, neither Argentina nor Chile accepted the jurisdiction of the Court, so the proceedings rapidly came to a grinding halt.

(Ibid., p. 168.)

Sir Ian Sinclair then turned to the question why the United Kingdom had not included the Falkland Islands themselves in the reference to the Court. He stated:

There is one additional consideration that we have had to bear in mind: that is that there is this dispute between Argentina and Chile in relation to the Beagle Channel. Now that went to international arbitration, both parties agreed it should go to international arbitration, and an award was handed down which was unfavourable to Argentina and Argentina immediately rejected the award. That frankly does not give us a great deal of confidence as to whether Argentina would comply with any judgment that might be given against it.

(Ibid.)

In reply to the question whether he was confident that the United Kingdom would win before an international court, Sir Ian Sinclair stated:

I am confident we have a very good case to present.

(Ibid.)

Part Twelve: II. I. 1. *Pacific settlement of disputes—modes of settlement— settlement within international organizations—the United Nations*

In the course of a statement made on 29 September 1982 in a general debate before the General Assembly, the Secretary of State for Foreign and Commonwealth Affairs, Mr. Francis Pym, observed:

What are the principles of the Charter whose violation is at the heart of so many of our conflicts? First and foremost is the requirement in Article 2 of the Charter to settle disputes by peaceful means and to refrain from the unlawful use of force. As the drafters of the Manila Declaration—which is to be considered at this session and, we hope, approved—have so aptly put it, neither the existence of a dispute nor the failure of a procedure to settle it peacefully can justify the use of force by any of the parties to it.

(A/37/PV. 9, p. 62.)

Part Thirteen: I. D. *Coercion and use of force short of war—unilateral acts—intervention*

(See also Part Three: I. A. 2. (statement of 18 October 1983), above.)

In reply to a question on the subject of a South African incursion into Lesotho, the Minister of State, Foreign and Commonwealth Office, Lord Belstead, stated:

. . . we supported Security Council Resolution No. 527 which condemned the raid. We also expressed our views directly to the South African Government through their Ambassador in London.

(H.L. Debs., vol. 438, col. 808: 2 February 1983.)

On 23 May 1983, the Secretary of State for Foreign and Commonwealth Affairs, Mr. Francis Pym, issued a statement on the subject of a South African air attack on Maputo, Mozambique. In it, he stated:

. . . I deplore this violation of Mozambique's sovereignty.

(Text provided by the Foreign and Commonwealth Office.)

On 17 October 1983, the Foreign and Commonwealth Office stated in a press release:

We have not yet received full details of this further attack by South African forces on targets in Mozambique. But it is clear that Mozambique's sovereignty has once again been seriously violated. We deplore this.

(Text provided by the Foreign and Commonwealth Office.)

In the course of a debate in the House of Commons on the subject of Grenada, the Secretary of State for Foreign and Commonwealth Affairs, Sir Geoffrey Howe, stated:

. . . we formed the judgment yesterday that circumstances did not justify intervention by the United Kingdom Government to save United Kingdom citizens.

(H.C. Debs., vol. 47, col. 146: 25 October 1983.)

Later in the debate the same Minister remarked:

One of the reasons why a country is entitled to take action in connection with an independent State is the protection of its citizens.

(Ibid., col. 147.)

In the course of a debate on the same subject the next day, the Secretary of State observed:

Those who have spoken from the opposition Benches include the leader of the Liberal party. The right hon. Gentleman showed some understanding of the difficulties of the decision that faced the United States and the Caribbean countries to intervene in Grenada, but he questioned the wisdom of their action and its legal justification. In reply, it must be said that it is primarily for those who have carried out the operation, not Her Majesty's Government, to undertake a detailed justification of their action.

Taking account of all the legal and practical considerations, and of the interests of our citizens and their safety in these circumstances, we came to a different conclusion, as I explained to the House. We would not dispute that a state has the right in international law to take appropriate action to safeguard the lives of its citizens where there has been a breakdown of law and order, nor that there is any provision in the charter of the United [Nations] that makes it unlawful to take such action. Those are the considerations that no doubt the United States and those acting with it must have had in mind. We took a different view of all the circumstances that apply in this case.

(Ibid., cols. 329–30: 26 October 1983.)

In the course of a debate in the House of Lords on the same subject, the Minister of State, Foreign and Commonwealth Office, Baroness Young, stated:

I was also asked about the role of Montserrat. Montserrat a member of the Organisation of Eastern Caribbean States is a dependent territory, and the conduct of its external affairs remains the responsibility of the United Kingdom Government. The Chief Minister reported briefly from Bridgetown to the Governor after the OECS meeting there on 21st October. The Governor told the Chief Minister that he did not have authority to commit Montserrat to any such military venture. On 25th October, after the military intervention, the Montserrat Executive Council requested the United Kingdom Government's approval for participation by volunteer troops from the Montserrat Defence Force. This was sought but was refused. It would have been inconsistent with the United Kingdom Government's policy towards the military intervention to have permitted the dependent territory of Montserrat to have participated.

(H.L. Debs., vol. 444, col. 521: 1 November 1983.)

In a speech to the Security Council on 20 December 1983 on the subject of a complaint by Angola of South African military incursions, the Permanent Representative of the United Kingdom, Sir John Thomson, stated:

The United Kingdom has consistently pressed, both in public and through quiet diplomacy, for the withdrawal of all South African forces from the territory of the Republic of Angola. We believe that the sovereignty and territorial integrity of Angola must be fully respected.

(S/PV. 2508, p. 15.)

Part Thirteen: I. E. *Coercion and use of force short of war—other unilateral acts, including self-defence*

(See also Part Thirteen: II. B., below.)

An Exchange of Notes was concluded between the United Kingdom and Lebanese Governments on 31 January 1983, concerning the deployment of a British contingent for the multinational force in Lebanon. The Lebanese Note stated in part:

In carrying out its duties, the British Force will not engage in hostilities or other operations of a warlike nature. It may, however, exercise the right of self-defence.

(*United Kingdom Treaty Series*, No. 9 (1983) (Cmnd. 8823).)

In the course of a debate on the subject of Lebanon, the Minister of State, Foreign and Commonwealth Office, Mr. Malcolm Rifkind, stated:

. . . the various forces in the multinational force have an inherent right of self-defence, and that right is specifically mentioned in the mandate. When the forces of any member state in the multinational force exercise that right, it is an operational matter. The situation in the Lebanon changes from day to day and from hour to hour. If the American forces are used for proper means of self-defence, that is an operational matter which it is for the American forces and authorities themselves to determine.

(H.C. Debs., vol. 50, col. 25: 5 December 1983.)

In reply to a question, the Prime Minister wrote:

The British contingent of the multinational force in Beirut is entitled to use its ground weapons in self-defence, and can seek air support in self-defence also.

(Ibid., Written Answers, col. *543*: 15 December 1983.)

In reply to a question, the Minister of State, Foreign and Commonwealth Office, pointed out that Panama had for some years maintained a discriminatory levy on the freight revenue of shipping companies from certain non-Panamanian States, including the United Kingdom, when loading and discharging cargoes in Panamanian ports. He went on:

For some time, while diplomatic representations continued, the Panamanian Government kept a moratorium in force, and British shipping companies were not compelled to pay the levy, although their liabilities were accumulating. However, repeated diplomatic representations over a period of years have failed to relieve this discrimination, and it is now apparent that it is causing unacceptable damage to British shipping. Recently, one British shipping line has withdrawn from its Panamanian trade, and another has had to take vessels off the

British register and re-register them under the Panamanian flag in order to avoid the levy.

Naturally Her Majesty's Government cannot instruct British shipping companies as to their payment of financial imposts of foreign jurisdictions under which they trade. But Parliament has provided in section 14 of the Merchant Shipping Act 1974 broad powers against foreign shipping for use when foreign Governments adopt measures damaging the shipping interests of the United Kingdom. I am hopeful, however, that even at this late stage a solution will be found by diplomatic means.

(Ibid., vol. 51, Written Answers, col. *399*: 22 December 1983.)

Part Thirteen: II. A. *Coercion and use of force short of war—collective measures—regime of the United Nations*

In reply to a question, the Parliamentary Under-Secretary of State for Trade wrote:

The United Kingdom complies fully with the mandatory United Nations Security Council's Resolution 418 of 4 November 1977, which prohibits the sale of all arms and related material to South Africa. The necessary legal effect in the United Kingdom is given by The Export of Goods (Control) Order 1981 and The South Africa (United Nations Arms Embargo) (Prohibited Transactions) Order 1978 (as amended).

(Ibid., vol. 39, Written Answers, col. *67*: 14 March 1983.)

In reply to the question whether a consignment of radio equipment to South Africa from Britain would be stopped, the Minister of State, Foreign and Commonwealth Office, Mr. Douglas Hurd, stated:

No Sir. The United Kingdom complies fully with its obligations under Security Council resolution 418. The export of this equipment was approved on the understanding that it is for use in air traffic control in southern Africa and involves no infringement of the United Nations arms embargo. We have no doubt that the system in question has a genuine civil application.

(Ibid., vol. 41, col. *731*: 26 April 1983.)

In reply to a question, the Prime Minister wrote that it remains the policy of Her Majesty's Government to adhere to the United Nations mandatory arms embargo on South Africa.

(Ibid., vol. 45, Written Answers, col. *319*: 12 July 1983; see also ibid., vol. 48, Written Answers, col. *237*: 11 November 1983.)

In reply to a question, the Prime Minister wrote:

There are no mandatory United Nations resolutions on trade with South Africa, other than Security Council resolution 418 imposing an arms embargo. It has been our consistent policy that trade should be determined by commercial considerations. We fully observe the United Nations arms embargo but we are opposed to wider sanctions.

(Ibid., vol. 51, Written Answers, col. *258*: 21 December 1983.)

Part Thirteen: II. B. *Coercion and use of force short of war—collective measures—collective measures outside the United Nations*

(See also Part Thirteen: I. E., above.)

In reply to a question, the Minister of State, Foreign and Commonwealth Office, wrote:

The United Kingdom is a party to the following agreements in the defence field with member countries of the League of Arab States:

Bahrain

Treaty of Friendship, Bahrain, 15 August 1971 (Treaty Series No. 79 (1971); Cmnd. 4828).

Qatar

Treaty of Friendship, Geneva, 3 September 1971 (Treaty Series No. 4 (1972); Cmnd. 4850).

United Arab Emirates

Treaty of Friendship, Dubai, 2 December 1971 (Treaty Series No. 35 (1972); Cmnd. 4937).

Oman

Exchange of Letters concerning Sultan's Armed Forces, Civil Aviation, RAF facilities and Economic Development, London 25 July 1958 (Treaty Series No. 28 (1958); Cmnd. 507).

Lebanon

Exchange of Notes Concerning the Deployment of British Contingent of the Multinational Force in Lebanon (Treaty Series No. 9 (1983); Cmnd. 8823).

Egypt*

Exchange of Notes Concerning the Establishment of a Multinational Force and Observers (MFO) in accordance with the protocol between the Arab Republic of Egypt and the State of Israel Signed at Washington on 3 August 1981 (Treaty Series No. 37 (1982); Cmnd. 8646).

* Egypt is currently suspended from the League of Arab States.

(Ibid., vol. 42, Written Answers, col. *324*: 11 May 1983.)

Lord Skelmersdale, Government Minister in the House of Lords, referred to the British contingent with the multinational force in Lebanon. He said in part:

The multinational force . . . is not a United Nations force. It was set up last year by agreement between the participating countries—the United States, France and Italy—and the Lebanese Government. A British contingent, a later addition to the force, is similarly in Lebanon under the terms of an exchange of letters with the Lebanese Government.

There is no overall commander of the multinational force. Each contingent operates under national command. Political and military control of the British contingent is retained by Her Majesty's Government. Day-to-day tasks of the multinational force are decided by co-ordination between the force commanders, the ambassadors of the countries concerned and the Lebanese authorities.

(H.L. Debs., vol. 442, cols. 550–1: 12 May 1983.)

In reply to the question whether Her Majesty's Government will make representations to the Turkish Government, either directly or through the North Atlantic Treaty Organization, about the reported presence of 15,000 Turkish troops in Iraq as a breach of the North Atlantic Treaty, the Parliamentary Under-Secretary of State, Foreign and Commonwealth Office, wrote:

This is a matter for the Governments of Turkey and Iraq. We do not consider that it is a case where representations should be made under the North Atlantic treaty.

(H.C. Debs., vol. 46, Written Answers, col. 565: 28 July 1983.)

In the course of a debate on the subject of the Falkland Islands in the General Assembly's Special Committee on the Situation with regard to the Implementation of the Declaration on the Granting of Independence to Colonial Countries and Peoples, the United Kingdom Permanent Representative, Sir John Thomson, stated on 1 September 1983:

It is palpably ridiculous to suggest that there is something like a base of the North Atlantic Treaty Organization (NATO) in the South Atlantic. This simply neglects the North Atlantic Treaty, which is a public document that restricts NATO to a specific area in the Northern Hemisphere. There is simply no question of a NATO base anywhere in the Southern Hemisphere, let alone in the Falkland Islands.

(A/AC. 109/PV. 1239, p. 4.)

In a statement made on 12 September 1983, the Secretary of State for Transport, Mr. Tom King, referred to the destruction by the Soviet Union of a Korean airliner. He went on:

I have today suspended for a period of 14 days commencing on 15 September, all operating permits granted to Aeroflot to provide services between the UK and the USSR. I have also suspended the permission for Aeroflot to make flights over UK territory. I have also directed the CAA to withhold permission for flights by British airlines between the UK and the USSR for the same period.

These are the immediate steps which the Government is taking. In addition, since repeated requests for a full explanation of the Soviet action have not resulted in an adequate or credible explanation or assurances that such action will not be repeated, the Government is supporting the important action in the United Nations and in the International Civil Aviation Organisation, aimed at removing such risks to the safety of civil aircraft when flying in the air space of the Soviet Union.

(Text provided by the Department of Transport.)

The following letter, dated 12 September 1983, was sent by the Department of Transport to the General Manager, United Kingdom and Ireland, of the Soviet airline, Aeroflot:

The action of the Government of the USSR in shooting down an unarmed civilian aircraft as a result of which UK nationals were killed was contrary to a fundamental object and purpose of the Chicago Convention on International Civil Aviation which is to ensure the safety of civil aircraft in international flights. This action was a grave breach of international law and calls into question the safety and security of international civil aviation and therefore the basis on which aviation relations between the UK and the USSR are conducted. As a consequence Her Majesty's Government has decided to suspend air services between the USSR and the United Kingdom and the permission granted to Aeroflot to overfly United Kingdom airspace.

Accordingly I am writing on behalf of the Secretary of State to inform you that, in pursuance of the first sentence of Article 59(1) of the Air Navigation Order 1980 the Secretary of State hereby suspends for a period of 14 days commencing on 15 September 1983 all operating permits granted to Aeroflot under Article 80 of the Air Navigation Order 1980.

I have also to inform you that the permission granted to Aeroflot in the letter to Mr Zubkov dated 28 March 1983 to make flights over United Kingdom territory is also suspended for a period of 14 days commencing on 15 September 1983.

If there is any matter you wish to have taken into account by the Secretary of State in his further consideration of the case you should write to me immediately.

(Text provided by the Foreign and Commonwealth Office.)

In reply to the question with which countries has the United Kingdom treaty obligations that might oblige it, in specific circumstances, to provide military assistance, the Minister of State, Foreign and Commonwealth Office, wrote:

We have treaty or similar arrangements with the following countries: Bahrain, Belgium, Belize, Brunei, Canada, Cyprus, Denmark, France, Germany (Federal Republic), Greece, Iceland, Italy, Luxembourg, Malaysia, Netherlands, Norway, Portugal, Qatar, Singapore, Spain, Sri Lanka, Turkey, United Arab Emirates, United States.

The nature of the arrangements varies, from an obligation in some cases to provide military assistance to commitments in other cases to consult on matters of mutual concern in time of need.

(H.C. Debs., vol. 51, Written Answers, cols. *196-7*: 20 December 1983.)

Part Fourteen: I. A. 1. *Armed conflicts—international war—resort to war—definition of war*

In answer to the question whether a state of war still exists between the United Kingdom and North Korea, the Parliamentary Under-Secretary of State, Foreign and Commonwealth Office, wrote:

Although the United Kingdom was among 16 nations which responded to a

Security Council Resolution of 1950 seeking assistance to repel an attack on the Republic of Korea by North Korean forces, a state of war has never existed in connection with hostilities in the Korean peninsula.

(Ibid., vol. 35, Written Answers, col. *202*: 20 January 1983.)

Part Fourteen: I. A. 3. *Armed conflicts—international war—resort to war—limitation and reduction of armaments*

In reply to a question, the Prime Minister wrote:

Among the actions we have taken since May 1979 to encourage arms control and disarmament are the following:

- (i) 1979–80: participation in UK/US/USSR negotiations on a comprehensive test ban treaty;
- (ii) December 1979: participation in NATO's double decision to modernise its theatre nuclear forces and to offer to negotiate reductions with the Soviet Union;
- (iii) December 1979: participation in the formulation of NATO's proposals for associated measures in the mutual and balanced force reduction talks;
- (iv) Since 1980: active encouragement of the renewal of strategic arms control following the non-ratification of SALT II;
- (v) March 1980: participation in biological weapons review conference;
- (vi) June 1980: United Kingdom joined ad hoc committee on the Indian Ocean;
- (vii) August–September 1980: participation in non-proliferation treaty review conference;
- (viii) April 1981: United Kingdom signature of UN weaponry convention;
- (ix) July 1981: United Kingdom co-sponsorship of Western comprehensive programme of disarmament tabled in the committee on disarmament;
- (x) July 1981: participation in the preparation of NATO's proposals in MBFR talks for resolving data discrepancies;
- (xi) November 1981: NATO's agreement to pursue zero option for the intermediate nuclear forces missiles of most concern, prior to the opening of negotiations between the United States and the Soviet Union on intermediate range nuclear forces;
- (xii) February 1982: United Kingdom paper on verification and compliance of a chemical weapons ban tabled in the committee on disarmament;
- (xiii) June–July 1982: participation in second United Nations special session on disarmament, at which I spoke on 16 June;
- (xiv) July 1982: participation in the preparation of NATO's draft MBFR treaty;
- (xv) 1979–82: work of United Kingdom experts in United Nations study groups on Disarmament and Development, United Nations disarmament institutions, and conventional arms.

(Ibid., vol. 32, Written Answers, cols. *101–2*: 16 November 1982.)

In reply to a further question on the same subject, the Parliamentary

Under-Secretary of State, Foreign and Commonwealth Office, referred to the above answer and wrote:

Since then we have taken the following actions to encourage arms control and disarmament.

November 1982: We co-sponsored six resolutions in the First Committee of the United Nations General Assembly. These covered a chemical warfare convention; confidence-building measures; arms control in outer space; the review conference of the Environmental Modification Treaty; Regional Disarmament; and signature of the United Nations Weaponry Convention.

November 1982–April 1983: We continue to seek an effective agreement on the reduction of conventional forces in Europe through the Mutual and Balanced Force Reduction talks.

December 1982–March 1983: Participation in NATO discussion on US–Soviet Strategic Arms Reduction talks in Geneva.

January–March 1983: Extensive consultations with our Allies prior to the offer by the United States to the Soviet Union of an interim agreement on intermediate range nuclear forces.

February 1983: United Kingdom participation in Ad Hoc Committee on the Indian Ocean Peace Zone in New York.

March 1983: United Kingdom paper on verification of non-production of chemical warfare weapons tabled in the Committee on Disarmament in Geneva.

April 1983: United Kingdom paper on definition of radiological weapons and the scope of a radiological weapons treaty tabled in the Committee on Disarmament.

April 1983: United Kingdom participation in Ad Hoc Committee on the Indian Ocean Peace Zone in New York.

November 1982–April 1983: Work of United Kingdom experts in United Nations study groups on conventional arms, research and development and nuclear weapon-free zones.

(Ibid., vol. 41, Written Answers, cols. *175–6*: 21 April 1983.)

Part Fourteen: I. B. 7. *Armed conflicts—international war—the laws of war—humanitarian law*

In reply to a question, the Minister of State, Foreign and Commonwealth Office, wrote:

We have been trying to ensure that Palestinian prisoners held by the Israelis are treated humanely in accordance with the relevant Geneva conventions. To this end the Ten acted in support of the ICRC by making representations to the Israeli Government on 14 June 1982. Bilateral representations to Israeli authorities were also made by Her Majesty's Government four times in June and July 1982. The Government hope that all Palestinian and Syrian prisoners held by Israel, as well as Israeli prisoners held by Syria and the PLO, will be released as soon as possible.

(Ibid., vol. 37, Written Answers, col. *364*: 21 February 1983.)

In the course of answering questions on injuries caused by mines in the

Falkland Islands, the Government spokesman in the House of Lords, Lord Glenarthur, stated:

... some help from volunteers from the Argentine in identifying minefields was forthcoming. But, of course, prisoners were not used in the clearance as this would have been contrary to the Geneva Convention.

(H.L. Debs., vol. 439, col. 753: 23 February 1983.)

In reply to a question on the subject of the deaths of Argentine prisoners on the Falkland Islands, the Secretary of State for Defence referred to the moving of Argentine ammunition by a detail of Argentine prisoners under British supervision at Goose Green. He wrote:

... it has been concluded that the work undertaken by the detail could be classed as dangerous for the purposes of article 52 of the Third Geneva Convention of 1949 but that the prisoners of war undertook the task without coercion.

(H.C. Debs., vol. 40, Written Answers, col. 306: 11 April 1983.)

After considering an injury caused to an Argentine prisoner while marking minefields at Pebbly Pond, Falkland Islands, the Secretary of State continued:

A report, covering both incidents, has been prepared in accordance with article 121 of the Third Geneva Convention on the treatment of prisoners of war. This report has been communicated to Brazil, as the protecting power, and a copy has also been passed to the International Committee of the Red Cross.

(Ibid., col. 307; see also ibid., col. 452: 14 April 1983.)

Draft resolution GC(XXVII)/701 presented to the General Conference of the International Atomic Energy Agency on 13 October 1983 contained a preambular paragraph (e) which recalled 'that Additional Protocol 1 to the Geneva Convention of 1949 prohibits attacks against peaceful nuclear electricity generating stations while other nuclear installations also devoted to peaceful uses are not covered by that prohibition'. Explaining his country's vote against this draft resolution, the United Kingdom representative, Mr. Henderson, stated in part:

... in our view paragraph (e) does not correctly describe the effect of additional protocol 1 to the Geneva Conventions. In any event we consider that this Conference is not the appropriate forum to address this issue.

(Text provided by the Foreign and Commonwealth Office.)

In reply to a question, the Minister of State, Foreign and Commonwealth Office, wrote:

We have tried to ensure that Palestinian prisoners held by the Israelis are treated humanely in accordance with the relevant Geneva conventions. To this end the Ten acted in support of the International Committee of the Red Cross by making representations to the Israeli Government in June 1982 and again in March 1983. We also made bilateral representations to the Israeli authorities.

(H.C. Debs., vol. 49, Written Answers, col. *452*: 29 November 1983.)

The following statement was made in December 1983 to the Third Committee of the General Assembly by the United Kingdom representative in explanation of vote on a resolution on the situation of human rights and fundamental freedoms in Guatemala:

My Delegation has supported the main elements of this Resolution. However, we wish to record our doubts about the reference in operative paragraph 1 to 'non-combatants' and in operative paragraph 5 to 'international humanitarian law'. We remain to be convinced that the situation in Guatemala has reached the point where organised armed groups could be said to exercise control over part of the territory, to carry out sustained and concerted military operations and to be capable of applying international humanitarian law. For these reasons, we must reserve our position over the relevance and applicability of international humanitarian law in the present situation.

(Text provided by the Foreign and Commonwealth Office.)

Part Fourteen: I. B. 8. *Armed conflicts—international war—the laws of war—belligerent occupation*

(See also Part Eight: II. A. (Written Answer of 4 May 1983), above.)

In reply to a question, the Minister of State, Foreign and Commonwealth Office, wrote:

We have often made clear to the Israeli Government our view that Israeli settlements in the occupied territories are both illegal and an obstacle to peace, and have urged them to accept President Reagan's call for a freeze on settlements.

(H.C. Debs., vol. 38, Written Answers, col. *434*: 9 March 1983.)

In reply to a question, the Minister of State, Foreign and Commonwealth Office, wrote:

We regard the establishment of Israeli settlements in the occupied territories as contrary to article 49 of the fourth Geneva convention of 1949 by reason of the consequent transfer of parts of the Israeli civilian population into such occupied territory. The establishment of settlements also runs counter to article 55 of the Hague regulations of 1907, which limits the occupying state's powers over landed property to administration and usufructuary rights.

(Ibid., vol. 42, Written Answers, col. *283*: 10 May 1983.)

In the course of a debate on 2 August 1983 in the Security Council of the United Nations on the subject of the situation in the occupied Arab territories, the United Kingdom delegate, Mr. Margetson, stated:

. . . we consider these settlements to be contrary to international law and to the principle of the inadmissibility of the acquisition of territory by force. This principle is embodied in Security Council resolution 242 (1967).

(S/PV. 2460, p. 36.)

Part Fourteen: I. B. 10. *Armed conflicts—international war—the laws of war—nuclear, bacteriological and chemical weapons*

(See also Part Eight: II. D. (debates on Nuclear Material (Offences) Bill), above.)

In reply to a question, the Government Minister in the House of Lords, Lord Glenarthur, wrote:

The use of nuclear weapons systems operating from United States bases in the United Kingdom is governed by the understanding on joint decision-making between the Governments of the United Kingdom and the United States summarised in the joint communiqué issued in January 1952.

(H.L. Debs., vol. 440, col. 924: 17 March 1983; see also ibid., vol. 441, col. 91: 11 April 1983.)

In reply to a question, the Minister of State, Foreign and Commonwealth Office, Lord Belstead, stated:

. . . the United States custodial force for the Thor missiles which were stationed in this country was provided for the custody of the nuclear warheads which remained in full United States ownership. The cruise missiles force to be based in this country will be owned and operated entirely by the United States. Ownership of the warheads cannot, by international treaty and United States national law, be transferred to the United Kingdom. The question of a United Kingdom custodial force for the warhead does not therefore arise.

(Ibid., col. 1002: 22 March 1983.)

In reply to a question on the subject of the Non-Proliferation Treaty, the Minister of State for the Armed Forces, Mr. Peter Blaker, stated:

The non-proliferation treaty has been an effective check on the further proliferation of nuclear weapons and has contributed to the security of all countries. We welcome the fact that there are now 120 parties to the treaty and we shall continue to encourage more countries to sign.

In reply to further questions, the Minister of State for Defence Procurement, Mr. Geoffrey Pattie, stated:

. . . eight further countries have adhered to the treaty since 1978. The treaty states in article 6 that the parties to it must make their best efforts to secure multilateral nuclear and other disarmament. That is why it is important to support the proposals that President Reagan has made in the INF context and the START negotiations.

. . . Our purchase of Trident is no more a breach of the non-proliferation treaty than the modernisation by other countries, including the Soviet Union, of their existing systems. The treaty does not impose an obligation on existing nuclear states to allow their existing systems to decay.

(H.C. Debs., vol. 40, col. 175: 29 March 1983.)

In reply to a later question on the same subject, the Minister wrote:

My answer of 17th March provided the noble Lord with a full reply to his Question. It explained that any use of nuclear weapons systems operating from United States bases in the United Kingdom would be governed by the understanding summarised in the joint communique issued in January 1952. As the communique makes clear, the understanding provides for a joint decision to be made in an emergency by Her Majesty's Government and the United States Government in the light of the circumstances at the time.

(H.L. Debs., vol. 441, col. 92: 11 April 1983.)

In the course of replying to a question, the Minister of State for the Armed Forces wrote:

It was made clear during the recent South Atlantic campaign that it was inconceivable that we would use or threaten to use nuclear weapons in the dispute with Argentina over the Falkland Islands.

(H.C. Debs., vol. 41, Written Answers, col. *181*: 21 April 1983.)

In replying to the question whether the deployment of cruise missiles would invalidate existing arms control agreements, the Minister of State, Foreign and Commonwealth Office, Lord Belstead, stated in part:

. . . no. The deployment of cruise missiles in Western Europe would invalidate no existing arms control agreement. NATO proposals at the INF talks in Geneva have been for an agreement which would eliminate this class of missile altogether.

(H.L. Debs., vol. 442, col. 273: 6 May 1983.)

On 16 May 1983, Mr. D. Edwards, United Kingdom representative to the Eighth Regular Session of the General Conference of the Agency for the Prohibition of Nuclear Weapons in Latin America, made the following statement:

. . . it is of course for the Member States of the Agency for the Prohibition of Nuclear Weapons in Latin America to settle the Agenda for the Conference in accordance with the Rules of Procedure. My delegation is here representing a non-member State of the Agency, the United Kingdom being a State party to the Additional Protocols. I speak to this matter therefore under Article 20 of the Rules of Procedure of the Conference.

I would wish to make the following points about the item just added to the Agenda of the Conference. This item seems to assume, from its wording, that nuclear weapons have been deployed by my country in the area covered by the Treaty, presumably in contravention of its obligations under Protocols I and II. This is, of course, not correct, as my Government has made clear on a number of occasions. . . . I would draw attention in this connection to Conference document S/INF.261 of 11 May 1983 in which we made it clear that the Government of the

United Kingdom has scrupulously observed its obligations under the Additional Protocols to the Treaty in not deploying nuclear weapons in areas for which the United Kingdom is internationally responsible, which lie within the limits of the geographical zone established in that Treaty and for which the Treaty is in force.

(Text provided by the Foreign and Commonwealth Office.)

The following statement was made on 17 May 1983 by Mr. Edwards at the same Session:

... my Government gives full support to the Treaty of Tlatelolco. The United Kingdom ratified the two Additional Protocols on 6 December, 1969, and was thus the first of the extra-regional states to do so. We would like to see the Treaty in force in the entire region. Like you, Mr. President, we regret that certain states in the region have not yet ratified the Treaty.

We view the Treaty as a valuable piece of international arms control legislation. It has made an important contribution to efforts to curb the spread of nuclear weapons and thereby to reduce the dangers of nuclear war.

(Text provided by the Foreign and Commonwealth Office.)

On 19 May 1983, Mr. Edwards made the following statement at the same Session:

... in the general debate on Tuesday the Argentine delegation made a number of serious allegations against the United Kingdom. Many of these were framed in polemic terms, were based on hypothetical criteria or were largely irrelevant to the real work of this Conference. Most of them have already been made in other fora and my government has repeatedly stated its position on them. As indicated in previous statements, my delegation's intention is to make as constructive a contribution to this Conference as is possible in our capacity as a non-member State of the Agency. I therefore propose to limit this statement in right of reply to those matters raised by the Argentine delegation which may reasonably be considered to be of direct concern to this Agency.

Mr. President, the Argentine delegation has sought to take advantage, in pursuit of its own political ends, of the long standing practice of successive British governments neither to confirm nor to deny the presence or absence of nuclear weapons in a particular place at a particular time. This is a practice which is based on valid reasons of security and weapon safety and is followed also by other nuclear weapon States. However, in recognition of the international legal obligations undertaken under the Additional Protocols to the Treaty of Tlatelolco we have on a number of previous occasions made a clear statement of our position. In Conference Document S/Inf 261 of 11 May 1983 we pointed out that the United Kingdom had scrupulously observed its obligations under the Additional Protocols to the Treaty, firstly, in not deploying nuclear weapons in territories for which the United Kingdom is internationally responsible within the Treaty's zone of application; and secondly, in not deploying such weapons in the territories for which the Treaty is in force.

The delegation of Argentina has accused the United Kingdom of seeking to restrict the scope and applicability of the Zone of the Treaty of Tlatelolco. Mr President, it is not the United Kingdom which has sought to impose any geographical limits to the Zone of application of the Treaty. Rather, it is

Argentina, by her failure to ratify the Treaty, which has placed serious limitations on the Zone of Application.

In addition, the Argentine delegation asserts that the United Kingdom has attempted to restrict and belittle the scope of its obligations in regard to the Latin American nuclear weapons-free zone. Mr President, at least the United Kingdom has obligations. The United Kingdom has accepted formal legal obligations under the Protocols while Argentina has not even ratified the Treaty. The Argentine delegation has said that its country feels committed to the objectives of the Treaty. But this is a very different matter from undertaking specific and clear legally-binding obligations under international law.

The Argentine delegation has said that its nuclear programme is dedicated exclusively to peaceful uses. Why then does she not ratify the Treaty of Tlatelolco or the Non-Proliferation Treaty and conclude a full-scope safeguards agreement with the International Atomic Energy Agency, thus contributing to the international confidence that is necessary in these matters?

. . . the Argentine delegation has referred to the preambular paragraph of the Treaty of Tlatelolco which recalled UN General Assembly Resolution 2028(XX) which established the principle of an acceptable balance of mutual responsibilities and duties for the nuclear and non-nuclear powers. Consistent with the spirit of that resolution, the United Kingdom gave its Negative Security Assurance in 1978 to non-nuclear weapon States parties to the Non-Proliferation Treaty or to other internationally binding commitments not to manufacture or acquire nuclear explosive devices, such as the Treaty of Tlatelolco. Because Argentina has not ratified the Non-Proliferation Treaty or the Treaty of Tlatelolco our Negative Security Assurance does not technically apply to her but we still remained ready to apply our assurance to her in practice. In this connection, the United Kingdom stated categorically at the outset of the Falklands conflict that it was inconceivable that we would use nuclear weapons.

The Argentine delegation have drawn attention to a statement by the British Prime Minister at the Second Special Session on Disarmament. They have of course, taken it out of context. In pointing to the limited value of assurances, Mrs Thatcher was discussing the first use of nuclear weapons between nuclear weapon States. Her remarks were not intended to cast doubt on the assurances we give to non-nuclear weapons States. As Mrs Thatcher pointed out in the same paragraph of her speech, the fundamental risk to peace is not the existence of weapons of particular types. It is the disposition on the part of some States to impose change on others by resorting to force.

In the course of their statement in the general debate, the Argentine delegation made reference to a number of UN General Assembly resolutions. My delegation would wish to recall that Argentine action over the Falkland Islands was a flagrant act of unprovoked aggression and that Argentina refused to act in accordance with a mandatory Security Council resolution to withdraw its forces. British action in self-defence was totally in accord with the United Nations Charter.

The Argentine delegation raised the question of the dangers arising out of the loss of nuclear weapons as a result of an accident or incident. My government has stated categorically, and repeats that statement now, that there has never been any incident anywhere involving a British nuclear weapon leading to its loss or to the dispersal of radioactive contamination.

The Argentine delegation also alleged that the sinking of the *General Belgrano* by a nuclear-powered submarine had constituted the military use of nuclear energy in violation of the Treaty. This allegation had already been made by the Argentine representative at the Plenary meeting of the UN Disarmament Commission on 11 May. In this regard I would point out that vessels propelled by nuclear power are not regulated by the Treaty. The Treaty's full title 'Treaty for the Prohibition of Nuclear Weapons in Latin America' makes it clear what it is intended to cover. In addition, Article 5 of the Treaty excludes means of propulsion and the definition of nuclear weapons in that Article cannot embrace for example nuclear propelled submarines. Mr President, even if the Treaty did apply to nuclear-powered submarines (which, as I have explained, it does not) I would remind the Conference that the United Kingdom's obligations under the Additional Protocols apply, firstly, to the territories for which it is internationally responsible within the Treaty's Zone of Application and, secondly, to the territories for which the Treaty is in force. These obligations did not apply therefore to the site of the sinking of the *General Belgrano*.

The Argentine delegation has pointed out that the United Kingdom's statements concerning the deployment of nuclear weapons cannot be verified by the Parties to the Treaty. I can only say in this connection that the Articles of the Treaty concerned, numbers 6, 15, 16 and 20, do not apply to the United Kingdom as a Party to the Additional Protocols.

Arising out of the statement of the Argentine delegation in the general debate, there was some discussion about the transit of nuclear weapons through the Zone of Application of the Treaty. The United Kingdom considers that such transit of nuclear weapons is consistent with our obligations under the Additional Protocols and that this is clear from the negotiating history of the Treaty. In this respect, therefore, our position is the same as that of the United States and France.

(Text provided by the Foreign and Commonwealth Office.)

In reply to the question whether, in view of the terms of the Treaty of Tlatelolco, Her Majesty's Government would make it their policy not to deploy nuclear submarines in the area covered by the treaty, the Minister of State for the Armed Forces wrote:

The treaty of Tlatelolco does not prohibit nuclear means of propulsion, as its title 'The Treaty for the Prohibition of Nuclear Weapons in Latin America' and article 5 of the treaty make clear.

(H.C. Debs., vol. 45, Written Answers, col. *416*: 14 July 1983.)

In the course of a debate held on 16 November 1983 in the General Assembly on the subject of the Falkland Islands, the United Kingdom Permanent Representative, Sir John Thomson, declared:

In a further flight of fancy the Foreign Minister of Argentina accused the United Kingdom of being in breach of the Treaty of Tlatelolco. I should like to make it clear to this Assembly that the United Kingdom gives full support to this Treaty, which we view as a major and valuable piece of arms control legislation. We have scrupulously observed our obligations under Protocols I and II to the Treaty, first, in not deploying nuclear weapons in territories for which we are internationally responsible within the Treaty's zone of application and, secondly, in not deploying such weapons in the territories in which the Treaty is in force. We would like to see the Treaty of Tlatelolco in force in the entire region. To achieve this, all eligible States in the region must become parties to the Treaty, including Argentina and Cuba.

(A/38/PV. 57, p. 56.)

In the course of a debate in the House of Lords on the subject of the Falkland Islands, the Minister of State, Foreign and Commonwealth Office, Baroness Young, stated:

My noble friend Lady Vickers suggested that a nuclear-free zone should be established in the South Atlantic. She will be aware that the treaty for the prohibition of nuclear weapons in Latin America, the Treaty of Tlatelolco, seeks to establish Latin America, the Caribbean and surrounding waters as a nuclear-free zone.

The intended zone of application includes large areas of international waters and covers the Falkland Islands and the Falkland Island dependencies. Until all eligible states—which include Argentina but not the United Kingdom—have ratified the treaty and its two additional protocols, the treaty is in force only for those states which have ratified and waived the universality provision. Argentina has signed but not ratified the treaty which we should like to see in force in the entire region.

(H.L. Debs., vol. 445, col. 1059: 6 December 1983.)

Part Fourteen: I. B. 12. *Armed conflicts—the laws of war—termination of war, treaties of peace, termination of hostilities*

The following two instruments of surrender by the Argentine forces on South Georgia and Southern Thule respectively are now on display in the Imperial War Museum, together with the instrument of surrender relating to the Falkland Islands themselves the text of which was reproduced in UKMIL 1982, pp. 526-7. The instrument for South Georgia is in typescript form; the instrument for Southern Thule is in illuminated parchment form.

(i)   *Instrument of Surrender*

I [Capitan de Corbeta] LAGOS Commander of the Argentinian Forces in occupation of the islands of SOUTH GEORGIA, hereby unconditionally surrendered those Forces under my command including landed Naval Detachments and the crew of the submarine Santa Fe to the Commander of the British Task Group, HMS ANTRIM.

This Instrument of Surrender is understood to have been proffered by the hoisting of a white flag at KING EDWARD POINT at 1705 [ZULU] 25 April 1982 and to have been effective at 1715 [ZULU] the same day.

I order all Forces under my command to surrender as at 1715 [ZULU] 25 April 1982 and those Forces with whom I am not in direct contact to surrender immediately on notification of this instrument.

I understand that I am obliged to make safe and to notify the Commander

British Task Group any dangerous defence measures for which my Force is responsible or of which they are aware, such as mines, booby traps and similar latent explosives.

It is understood that my Forces will be treated as Prisoners of War and afforded such rights as are applicable under the appropriate Article of the Geneva Convention provided the above conditions are complied with.

Signed . . . Commanding Officer Argentine Submarine Santa Fe
Countersigned . . . Commander Argentine Land Forces
Signed . . . Commander Task Group 317.9 HMS Antrim
Countersigned . . . Second in Command 42 Commando Royal Marines

Dated this 26th day of April 1982

(ii)   *HMS Endurance*

Yo por este medio rindo sin condiciones La Base a Southern Thule South Sandwich Islands y las cercanias en nombre del Gobierno Argentino a los representantes de Her Britannic Majesty's Royal Navy, este 20 dia de junio 1982

[Signed] Teniente de Corbeta Enrique Martinez
        Captain Nicolas Barker
        [Other British officers]

Part Fourteen: III. *Armed conflicts—self-defence*

(See also Part Fourteen: I. B. 10. (statement of 19 May 1983), above.)

In the course of a statement made on 29 September 1982 in a general debate before the General Assembly, the Secretary of State for Foreign and Commonwealth Affairs, Mr. Francis Pym, observed:

Throughout our campaign to repossess the Islands, we took immense care to act strictly within the framework of the Charter, at each point reporting our actions to the Security Council. The force we used in self-defence under Article 51 was the minimum necessary to remove Argentina's occupying forces. We made it clear that in so acting we were showing our absolute determination to implement to the full our obligations towards the populations of our dependent Territories under Article 73. We will not be deflected from that determination and I make that quite clear.

(A/37/PV. 9, p. 66.)

[*Editorial note*: The above item should be read in conjunction with the material under this heading in UKMIL 1982.]

In a memorandum dated 18 January 1983, the Foreign and Commonwealth Office replied to the question posed by the Foreign Affairs Committee of the House of Commons why had it taken six years to remove the Argentine research station established on Southern Thule in 1976:

Following our discovery of the illegal Argentine station on Southern Thule we made repeated protests to the Argentine authorities and left them in no doubt that we consider Southern Thule to be British territory. Our legal position over sovereignty was thus fully protected. However, we took the view that the dispute should if possible be resolved by peaceful means in accordance with the UN Charter. Following the Argentine invasion of the Falkland Islands and South Georgia and our subsequent action to regain the Islands in exercise of our inherent right of self-defence, as recognised by Article 51 of the UN Charter, it was considered anomalous to permit the Argentine station to remain on South Thule. Accordingly, the Argentine personnel were called upon to surrender to British forces which they did on 20 June 1982.

(*Parliamentary Papers*, 1982–3, House of Commons, Paper 31-iv, p. 156.)

In reply to letters from the Permanent Mission of Argentina to the Secretary-General of the United Nations in which Argentina protested against the continuation of the maritime protection zone and against the 'Militarization' of the Falkland Islands, the Chargé d'Affaires at the United Kingdom Permanent Mission to the United Nations in New York, Mr. Hamilton Whyte, addressed a letter dated 28 January 1983 to the Secretary-General in which he wrote:

The critical reference to 'militarization' of the territories in question ignores the unprovoked Argentine invasion of the Islands and our need to defend them from further attacks. The risk of such attacks, despite the assertion in the letter of 24 January from the Argentine Chargé d'Affaires to you, which represents neither a definitive statement of the cessation of hostilities nor a renunciation of the use of force, is underlined by a series of bellicose statements from Argentina in recent weeks.

(A/38/83.)

In the course of a debate on the subject of the Falklands campaign, a question was raised about the sinking of the Argentine cruiser *General Belgrano*. In response, the Parliamentary Under-Secretary of State for the Armed Forces, Mr. Jerry Wiggin, stated:

Our task force was operating with limited air cover thousands of miles from home. Although less powerful than the Royal Navy, the Argentine navy was still a force with which to be reckoned. It had the support of land-based aircraft. It undeniably had the potential to inflict serious losses. On 2 May there were signs that our ships and men were threatened by a pincer attack involving the cruiser General Belgrano and her escorts to the south and other Argentine warships to the north, among them the carrier 25 De Mayo.

. . . on 2 May there were signs that an attack was to be expected. The military appreciation was that the threat was serious. The Belgrano group was operating close to the total exclusion zone around the Falklands. The rules of engagement approved by Ministers prior to 2 May did not permit an attack outside the total exclusion zone. The task force commander, worried that HMS Conqueror might be unable to follow Belgrano over the shallow waters of the Burdwood Bank, sought a change to the rules of engagement to permit an attack outside the zone. In view of the threat to the task force this was agreed.

The Argentine Government had been warned on 23 April that

'any approach on the part of Argentine warships, including submarines, naval auxiliaries or military aircraft which could amount to a threat to interfere with the mission of British forces in the south Atlantic will encounter the appropriate response'.

Establishment of the zone did not give the Argentines licence to operate freely outside it if in so doing they threatened British forces; and they can have been in no doubt of this.

The loss of life resulting from the torpedoing was indeed tragic, as was all loss of life, Argentine as well as British. But the tragedy stemmed directly from Argentina's unprovoked aggression in seizing British territory by force of arms. The opportunity to withdraw under a peaceful settlement before the task force reached the area was not taken. The Argentine Government must bear that heavy responsibility. I assure the House that the military situation thoroughly justified the attack on the cruiser General Belgrano. We have nothing of which to be ashamed.

(H.C. Debs., vol. 39, col. 1116: 24 March 1983.)

In the course of a debate on the subject of the sinking of the Argentine cruiser *General Belgrano*, the Minister of State, Foreign and Commonwealth Office, Mr. Cranley Onslow, stated:

The Government have made it perfectly clear time and again that the General Belgrano was attacked solely for military reasons, because she posed a threat to ships of the task force. The hon. Gentleman [i.e. Mr. Dalyell M.P.] chooses to ignore the warnings that were given not merely about the exclusion zone but in the message on 23 April from our Government, through the Swiss, to the Argentine Government, making it clear that ships of their navy that approached the exclusion zone would be attacked if they threatened to interfere with the mission of the British forces in the South Atlantic. That was a public statement . . .

(Ibid., vol. 42, col. 1006: 12 May 1983; see also H.L. Debs., vol. 442, col. 554: 12 May 1983 and ibid., vol. 443, cols. 882–4: 13 July 1983.)

During a statement made on 19 May 1983 at the Eighth Session of the General Conference of the Agency for the Prohibition of Nuclear Weapons in Latin America, the United Kingdom representative, Mr. D. Edwards, remarked:

In the course of their statement in the general debate, the Argentine delegation made reference to a number of UN General Assembly resolutions. My delegation would wish to recall that Argentine action over the Falkland Islands was a flagrant act of unprovoked aggression and that Argentina refused to act in accordance with a mandatory Security Council resolution to withdraw its forces. British action in self-defence was totally in accord with the United Nations Charter.

(Text provided by the Foreign and Commonwealth Office.)

By a letter dated 10 August 1983 addressed to the President of the Security Council (S/15918), the Permanent Representative of Argentina complained about the United Kingdom's enforcement of its exclusion zone 'in Argentine jurisdictional waters around the Malvinas'. By a letter dated 7 November 1983, the Permanent Representative of the United Kingdom, Sir John Thomson, having dealt with the particular incidents complained of by Argentina, replied:

In its repeated references to 'Argentine jurisdictional waters around the Malvinas', however, the Argentine letter reveals its true purpose. This purpose is not, despite the letter's protestations to the contrary, to reduce tension in the area but, rather, to attempt to bolster Argentine claims to sovereignty over the Falkland Islands and to jurisdiction over their surrounding waters. It is clear that the waters in question are not (not) subject to Argentine jurisdiction but are high seas. Moreover, Argentine pretensions must be seen against the background of the Argentine Government's persistent refusal to declare a definitive end to hostilities more than a year after the repossession by British forces of the Falkland Islands and the surrender of the Argentine forces there. Given this failure to renounce unambiguously the future use of force in pursuit of Argentine claims, the deliberate incursions by Argentine vessels and aircraft, and the attempt in the Argentine letter to turn them into 'incidents provoked in Argentine jurisdictional waters by British military forces', can only be the source of grave concern. As indicated in previous letters, the Government of the United Kingdom will maintain in being the Falkland Islands protection zone, which applies only to Argentine ships, submarines and aircraft, as a necessary and justifiable measure for the defence of the Falkland Islands and the prevention of untoward incidents in present circumstances.

The Argentine letter claims that the real purpose behind the maintenance of the protection zone is to allow the United Kingdom to appropriate to itself unilaterally and exclusively the marine resources of the area. This is manifest nonsense. The purpose of the zone is to defend the Falkland Islands against further attack and to avoid the risk of misunderstandings. The Argentine letter itself acknowledges that vessels of other nationalities were peacefully fishing in the vicinity of the Argentine boats at the time of the latter's interception on 1 August.

(S/16136.)

In a letter dated 25 August 1983 addressed to the Secretary-General of the United Nations, the Permanent Representative of the United Kingdom to the United Nations in New York, Sir John Thomson, referred to two letters sent to the Secretary-General by the Argentine Permanent Representative. He wrote in part:

. . . recent incursions into the Falkland Islands Protection Zone by Argentine military aircraft, as well as by unauthorized civilian vessels, . . . have demonstrated the continuing need for measures to ensure the defences of the Falkland Islands.

It is undeniable that the United Kingdom has the inherent right and indeed the duty to defend the Falkland Islands and its people against further hostile action by Argentina. The United Kingdom remains determined to fulfil that duty. The construction of the new airfield on the Islands is necessary to enable the United Kingdom adequately to do so.

(S/15938.)

In reply to questions, the Minister of State for the Armed Forces wrote:

At the beginning of August three Argentine fishing vessels were challenged in six separate incidents by the Royal Navy within the Falkland Islands protection zone and an Argentine naval air force Electra patrol aircraft was intercepted by two RAF Phantoms. All complied with our instructions to leave the zone and did so without incident.

. . .

There are no foreign vessels currently fishing in the territorial waters of the Falkland Islands and their dependencies. There are, however, about 60 non-Argentine vessels of various nationalities fishing in the Falkland Islands protection zone outside territorial waters. These vessels are not under Royal Navy protection but the zone is kept under continuous surveillance by the Royal Navy and the Royal Air Force to prevent incursions by Argentine vessels.

(H.C. Debs., vol. 48, Written Answers, col. *270*: 11 November 1983.)

In the course of a debate held in the General Assembly on the subject of the Falkland Islands on 15 November 1983, Sir John Thomson stated:

We had to rescue the Falkland Islanders from foreign invaders through our own efforts of self-defence under Article 51 of the Charter.

(A/38/PV. 57, p. 58.)

Part Fifteen: I. A. *Neutrality, non-belligerency—legal nature of neutrality—land warfare*

In reply to a question on the subject of the Iraq-Iran conflict, the Minister of State, Foreign and Commonwealth Office, Mr. Douglas Hurd, observed in part:

We are neutral in this war and we have not supplied lethal equipment to either side.

(H.C. Debs., vol. 36, col. 991: 9 February 1983; see also ibid., vol. 37, Written Answers, col. *277*: 18 February 1983, and ibid., vol. 40, Written Answers, col. *411*: 13 April 1983.)

APPENDICES

I. MULTILATERAL AGREEMENTS SIGNED BY THE UNITED KINGDOM IN 1983[1]

Title	Place and date	U.K. Signature	Text
International Convention on Mutual Administrative Assistance for the Prevention, Investigation and Repression of Customs Offences	Nairobi, 9.6.1977	18.3.1983 (accession to Annex X only)	T.S.[2] No. 10 (1984) (Cmnd. 9153)
Protocol extending the Arrangement regarding International Trade in Textiles (G.A.T.T.)	Geneva, 22.12.1981	21.1.1982 (on behalf of Hong Kong)	Not to be published as a White Paper
Amendment of the Convention relating to International Exhibitions, signed at Paris on 22 November 1928, as modified by the Protocol of 30 November 1972	Paris, 24.6.1982	3.12.1982 (acceptance)	T.S. No. 82 (1983) (Cmnd. 9107)
Convention establishing the European Telecommunications Satellite Organization (EUTELSAT) and Operating Agreement relating thereto	Paris, 15.7.1982	29.9.1982	Misc.[3] No. 25 (1983) (Cmnd. 9069)
International Coffee Agreement 1983	London, 16.9.1982	15.4.1983	Misc. No. 4 (1983) (Cmnd. 8810)
International Agreement on Jute and Jute Products	Geneva, 1.10.1982	6.6.1983	Misc. No. 5 (1983) (Cmnd. 8825)
Convention on the accession of the Hellenic Republic to the Convention on Jurisdiction and Enforcement of Judgments in Civil and Commercial Matters of 27 September 1968 and to the Protocol on its interpretation by the Court of Justice of 3 June 1971	Luxembourg, 25.10.1982	25.10.1982	European Communities No. 46 (1983) (Cmnd. 8973)
Protocol for the amendment of the Agreement on the Joint Financing of certain Air Navigation Services in Greenland and the Faroe Islands done at Geneva on 25 September 1956	Montreal, 3.11.1982	3.11.1982	Misc. No. 8 (1983) (Cmnd. 8844)
Protocol for the amendment of the Agreement on the Joint Financing of certain Air Navigation Services in Iceland done at Geneva on 25 September 1956	Montreal, 3.11.1982	3.11.1982	Misc. No. 9 (1983) (Cmnd. 8845)
International Telecommunication Convention	Nairobi, 6.11.1982	6.11.1982	Not yet published
Optional Additional Protocol to the International Telecommunication Convention 1982 on the Compulsory Settlement of Disputes	Nairobi, 6.11.1982	6.11.1982	Not yet published

[1] Information supplied by the Foreign and Commonwealth Office. The table includes some agreements signed by the United Kingdom before 1983, where information was not previously available. The information is correct as at January 1984, although in some cases information available since that date has been included.

[2] T.S. = United Kingdom Treaty Series.

[3] Misc. = United Kingdom Miscellaneous Series.

Title	Place and date	U.K. Signature	Text
Protocol to amend the Convention on Third Party Liability in the Field of Nuclear Energy of 29 July 1960, as amended by the Additional Protocol of 28 January 1964	Paris, 16.11.1982	16.11.1982	Misc. No. 21 (1983) (Cmnd. 9028)
Protocol to amend the Convention of 31 January 1963 supplementary to the Paris Convention of 29 July 1960 on Third Party Liability in the Field of Nuclear Energy, as amended by the Additional Protocol of 28 January 1964	Paris, 16.11.1982	16.11.1982	Misc. No. 23 (1983) (Cmnd. 9052)
Protocol to amend the Convention on Wetlands of International Importance, especially as Waterfowl Habitat of 2 February 1971	Paris, 3.12.1982	3.12.1982	Misc. No. 1 (1984) (Cmnd. 9113)
Protocol amending the Convention for the Prevention of Marine Pollution by Dumping from Ships and Aircraft signed at Oslo on 15 February 1972	Oslo, 2.3.1983	2.3.1983	Misc. No. 12 (1983) (Cmnd. 8942)
Additional Protocol to the Protocol of 22 January 1965 to the European Agreement on the Protection of Television Broadcasts of 22 June 1960	Strasbourg, 21.3.1983	4.7.1983	Not yet published
Convention on Transfer of Sentenced Persons	Strasbourg, 21.3.1983	25.8.1983	Misc. No. 22 (1983) (Cmnd. 9049)
Convention for the Protection and Development of the Marine Environment of the Wider Caribbean Region, and Protocol concerning Co-operation in Combating Oil Spills in the Wider Caribbean Region	Cartagena De Indias, 24.3.1983	24.3.1983	Not yet published
Agreement terminating the Commonwealth Telecommunications Organization Financial Agreement, 1973	London, 30.3.1983	30.3.1983	Not yet published
Commonwealth Telecommunications Organization Financial Agreement 1983	London, 30.3.1983	30.3.1983	Not yet published
1983 Protocol for the further extension of the Wheat Trade Convention 1971	Washington, 4.4.1983	10.5.1983	Misc. No. 15 (1983) (Cmnd. 8952)
1983 Protocol for the second extension of the Food Aid Convention 1980	Washington, 4.4.1983	10.5.1983	Misc. No. 15 (1983) (Cmnd. 8952)
Exchange of Notes between the Governments of the U.K., France and Switzerland concerning the deposit with the Competent Authority of the Republic and Canton of Geneva of the Archives of the Court of Arbitration on the Delimitation of the Continental Shelf between the U.K. and France	Berne, 17.5.1983	17.5.1983	T.S. No. 49 (1983) (Cmnd. 9020)
Convention for the Establishment of a European Organization for the Exploitation of Meteorological Satellites (EUMETSAT)	Geneva, 24.5.1983	24.5.1983	Misc. No. 9 (1984) (Cmnd. 9202)

Title	Place and date	U.K. Signature	Text
Agreement for Co-operation in Dealing with Pollution of the North Sea by Oil and Other Harmful Substances	Bonn, 13.9.1983	13.9.1983	Misc. No. 26 (1983) (Cmnd. 9104)
Protocol amending the European Agreement on the Restriction of the Use of Certain Detergents in Washing and Cleaning Products of 16 September 1968 (Council of Europe No. 115)	Strasbourg, 25.10.1983	25.10.1983	Not yet published
European Convention on the Compensation of Victims of Violent Crimes (Council of Europe No. 116)	Strasbourg, 24.11.1983	24.11.1983	Misc. No. 5 (1984) (Cmnd. 9167)
Protocol amending the Convention establishing the European Telecommunication Satellite Organization (EUTELSAT) of 15 July 1982	Paris, 15.12.1983	15.12.1983	Misc. No. 4 (1984) (Cmnd. 9154)

II. Bilateral Agreements Signed by the United Kingdom in 1983[1]

Country and Title	Place and date	Text
BARBADOS Agreement concerning Public Officers' Pensions	Bridgetown, 23.3.1983	Not yet published
BELIZE Exchange of Notes extending to Hong Kong, Jersey, Guernsey and the Isle of Man the Agreement for the Promotion and Protection of Investments signed at Belmopan on 30 April 1982	Belmopan, 8/14.3.1983	T.S.[2] No. 43 (1983) (Cmnd. 8993)
BRUNEI Exchange of Notes concerning the Arrangements for a United Kingdom Force in Negara Brunei Darussalam	Brunei, 22.9.1983	T.S. No. 31 (1984) (Cmnd. 9207)
CUBA Agreement on Certain Commercial Debts	Havana, 22.7.1983	T.S. No. 64 (1983) (Cmnd. 9056)
DENMARK Exchange of Notes amending Article 1(c) of the Agreement on the International Carriage of Goods by Road signed in London on 29 June 1972	London, 23.8/5.9.1983	T.S. No. 77 (1983) (Cmnd. 9090)

[1] Information supplied by the Foreign and Commonwealth Office. The table includes some agreements signed by the United Kingdom before 1983, where information was not previously available. The information is correct as at January 1984, although in some cases information available since that date has been included.

[2] T.S. = United Kingdom Treaty Series.

Country and Title	Place and date	Text
EGYPT		
United Kingdom/Egypt Retrospective Terms Agreement 1979	Cairo, 11.4.1979	T.S. No. 17 (1984) (Cmnd. 9200)
Exchange of Notes constituting the United Kingdom/Egypt Loan (No. 1) 1982	Cairo, 16.11.1982	T.S. No. 32 (1984) (Cmnd. 9210)
Exchange of Notes constituting an Agreement amending the United Kingdom/Egypt Loan Agreements 1972 and 1973	Cairo, 24.11.1982/9.2.1983	Not yet published
FINLAND		
Protocol amending the Convention on Social Security of 12 December 1978	London, 24.1.1983	T.S. No. 27 (1984) (Cmnd. 9196)
FRANCE		
Exchange of Notes concerning Exchanges of Information in the event of Emergencies occurring in one of the two States which could have Radiological Consequences for the other State	London, 18.7.1983	T.S. No. 60 (1983) (Cmnd. 9041)
Convention on Maritime Boundaries with detached appendix (map)	Paris, 25.10.1983	France No. 1 (1984) (Cmnd. 9136)
GERMANY, FEDERAL REPUBLIC OF		
Agreement concerning Host Nation Support during Crisis or War	Bonn, 13.12.1983	T.S. No. 30 (1984) (Cmnd. 9202)
ICELAND		
Convention on Social Security	Reykjavik, 25.8.1983	Iceland No. 1 (1983) (Cmnd. 9089)
INDONESIA		
Exchange of Notes amending the Air Services Agreement of 28 June 1973	Jakarta, 10/24.12.1981	T.S. No. 16 (1983) (Cmnd. 8843)
IRAQ		
Agreement on Co-operation in the fields of Education, Science and Culture	London, 26.4.1983	T.S. No. 48 (1983) (Cmnd. 9019)
ISRAEL		
Protocol amending the Convention on Social Security of 25 April 1957	London, 17.6.1983	Not yet published

Country and Title	Place and date	Text
KOREA, REPUBLIC OF		
Exchange of Notes concerning the designation of the British Council as principal agent of H.M.G. for execution of measures falling within the scope of the Cultural Agreement of 21 April 1982	Seoul, 26/31.5.1983	T.S. No. 61 (1983) (Cmnd. 9045)
Exchange of Notes extending the Agreement for the Promotion and Protection of Investments of 4 March 1976 to Jersey, Guernsey and the Isle of Man	Seoul, 23.8/22.9.1983	T.S. No. 14 (1984) (Cmnd. 9159)
KUWAIT		
Exchange of Notes revising the Schedule of the Air Services Agreement of 24 May 1960, as amended	Kuwait, 11.4/2.5.1983	T.S. No. 73 (1983) (Cmnd. 9079)
LEBANON		
Exchange of Notes concerning the Deployment of a British Contingent for the Multi-National Force in Lebanon	Beirut, 31.1.1983	T.S. No. 9 (1983) (Cmnd. 8823)
Exchange of Notes concerning the Extension of the Stay of the British Component of the Multi-National Force in Lebanon	Beirut, 8.5.1983	T.S. No. 40 (1983) (Cmnd. 8982)
Exchange of Notes concerning the further Extension of the Stay of the British Component of the Multi-National Force in Lebanon	Beirut, 7.8.1983	T.S. No. 75 (1983) (Cmnd. 9081)
LESOTHO		
Exchange of Notes extending to Hong Kong, the Bailiwicks of Jersey and Guernsey and the Isle of Man the Agreement for Promotion and Protection of Investments of 18 February 1981	Maseru, 19.1/16.3.1983	T.S. No. 65 (1983) (Cmnd. 9060)
LUXEMBOURG		
Second Protocol amending the Convention for the Avoidance of Double Taxation and the Prevention of Fiscal Evasion with respect to Taxes on Income and Capital signed at London on 24 May 1967, as modified by the Protocol signed at London on 18 July 1978	London, 28.1.1983	Not yet published
MADAGASCAR		
Agreement on Certain Commercial Debts	Antananarivo, 21.5.1983	T.S. No. 50 (1983) (Cmnd. 9021)

Country and Title	Place and date	Text
MALAWI		
Agreement on Certain Commercial Debts	London, 7.7.1983	T.S. No. 54 (1983) (Cmnd. 9036)
MALAYSIA		
Exchange of Notes amending the Route Schedules annexed to the Agreement for Air Services of 24 May 1973, as amended by the Exchange of Notes of 9 October/10 November 1979	Kuala Lumpur, 16.3/11.7.1983	T.S. No. 74 (1983) (Cmnd. 9080)
MAURITIUS		
Exchange of Notes revising the Route Schedules annexed to the Agreement for Air Services of 12 July 1973	Port Louis, 13/17.10.1983	T.S. No. 3 (1984) (Cmnd. 9123)
MISCELLANEOUS ORGANIZATIONS, ETC.		
Headquarters Agreement between the Government of the United Kingdom and the Commonwealth Foundation	London, 14.2.1983	T.S. No. 22 (1983) (Cmnd. 8862)
Headquarters Agreement between the Government of the United Kingdom and the Commonwealth Telecommunication Organization	London, 30.3.1983	T.S. No. 36 (1983) (Cmnd. 8956)
Exchange of Notes regarding Social Security Assessments of Eurocontrol Staff	Brussels, 15.6.1983	Misc. No. 20 (1983) (Cmnd. 9023)
MOZAMBIQUE		
Exchange of Notes constituting the United Kingdom/Mozambique Programme Loan 1977 (Amendment)	Maputo, 29.9/13.12.1983	Not yet published
NETHERLANDS		
Protocol amending the Convention for the Avoidance of Double Taxation and the Prevention of Fiscal Evasion with respect to Taxes on Income and Capital Gains, signed at The Hague on 7 November 1980	London, 12.7.1983	Not yet published
NEW ZEALAND		
Convention for the Avoidance of Double Taxation and the Prevention of Fiscal Evasion with respect to Taxes on Income and Capital Gains	London, 4.8.1983	Not yet published
Convention on Social Security	London, 1.11.1983	T.S. No. 19 (1984) (Cmnd. 9179)

Country and Title	Place and date	Text
NORWAY		
Second Agreement supplementary to the Agreement of 19 October 1979 relating to the Exploitation of the Murchison Field Reservoir and the Offtake of Petroleum therefrom	Oslo, 22.6.1983	T.S. No. 71 (1983) (Cmnd. 9083)
PANAMA		
Agreement for the Promotion and Protection of Investments	Panama City, 7.10.1983	Panama No. 1 (1984) (Cmnd. 9144)
PAPUA NEW GUINEA		
Exchange of Notes extending the Agreement for the Promotion and Protection of Investments of 14 May 1981 to Hong Kong, Jersey, Guernsey and the Isle of Man	Port Moresby, 4.5.1983	T.S. No. 53 (1983) (Cmnd. 9044)
PORTUGAL		
Exchange of Notes amending the Agreement in regard to Tonnage Measurement of Merchant Ships signed at London on 20 May 1926	Lisbon, 26.4/18.5.1983	T.S. No. 9 (1984) (Cmnd. 9146)
ROMANIA		
Agreement on Certain Commercial Debts	London, 8.12.1983	T.S. No. 16 (1984) (Cmnd. 9166)
ST. LUCIA		
Agreement for the Promotion and Protection of Investments	Castries, 18.1.1983	T.S. No. 25 (1983) (Cmnd. 8872)
SRI LANKA		
Exchange of Notes further amending the Air Services Agreement of 5 August 1949	Colombo, 27.10/24.11.1983	T.S. No. 6 (1984) (Cmnd. 9134)
SUDAN		
Agreement on Certain Commercial Debts	Khartoum, 20.8.1983	T.S. No. 70 (1983) (Cmnd. 9082)
SWEDEN		
Convention for the Avoidance of Double Taxation and the Prevention of Fiscal Evasion with respect to Taxes on Income and Capital Gains	Stockholm, 30.8.1983	Not yet published

Country and Title	Place and date	Text
SWITZERLAND		
Exchange of Notes further revising the Route Schedules annexed to the Air Services Agreement signed at London on 5 April 1950	London, 12.1/6.4.1983	T.S. No. 37 (1983) (Cmnd. 8960)
TANZANIA		
Exchange of Notes extending the British Expatriates Supplementation (Tanzania) Agreement 1976	Dar es Salaam, 28.6.1979	T.S. No. 82 (1983) (Cmnd. 9107)
THAILAND		
Exchange of Notes extending to Hong Kong the Agreement for the Promotion and Protection of Investments signed in London on 28 November 1978	Bangkok, 7/28.2.1983	T.S. No. 29 (1983) (Cmnd. 8926)
TRINIDAD AND TOBAGO		
Convention for the Avoidance of Double Taxation and the Prevention of Fiscal Evasion with respect to Taxes on Income	Port of Spain, 31.12.1982	T.S. No. 35 (1984) (Cmnd. 9221)
TURKEY		
Exchange of Notes constituting an Agreement to amend the United Kingdom/Turkey Refinancing Loan (No. 2) 1980	Ankara, 31.3.1983	T.S. No. 38 (1983) (Cmnd. 8970)
Exchange of Letters constituting the United Kingdom/Turkey Project Aid Loan 1983	Ankara, 3.5.1983	T.S. No. 44 (1983) (Cmnd. 8997)
UGANDA		
Agreement concerning Public Officers' Pensions (the Public Officers' Pensions (Uganda) Agreement 1982)	Entebbe, 1.10.1982	Not yet published
Agreement on Certain Commercial Debts	Kampala, 17.6.1983	T.S. No. 63 (1983) (Cmnd. 9051)
Agreement on Certain Commercial Debts	Kampala, 10.11.1983	T.S. No. 8 (1984) (Cmnd. 9141)
U.S.S.R.		
Agreement on Relations in the Scientific, Educational and Cultural Fields for 1983–85	London, 3.3.1983	T.S. No. 39 (1983) (Cmnd. 8981)

Country and Title	Place and date	Text
UNITED NATIONS		
Revised Supplementary Agreement concerning the Provision of Technical Assistance by the International Atomic Energy Agency to the Government of the United Kingdom on behalf of the Government of Hong Kong	Vienna, 4.2.1983	T.S. No. 80 (1983) (Cmnd. 9101)
VENEZUELA		
Basic Convention for Cultural Co-operation	London, 16.12.1983	Venezuela No. 1 (1984) (Cmnd. 9211)
YUGOSLAVIA		
Exchange of Notes constituting the United Kingdom/Yugoslavia Loan Agreement 1983	London, 29.3.1983	T.S. No. 41 (1983) (Cmnd. 8988)
ZAÏRE		
Agreement on Certain Commercial Debts (1979)	Kinshasa, 28.7.1983	T.S. No. 12 (1984) (Cmnd. 9157)
Agreement on Certain Commercial Debts (1981)	Kinshasa, 28.7.1983	T.S. No. 13 (1984) (Cmnd. 9158)
ZAMBIA		
Agreement on Certain Commercial Debts	Lusaka, 30.12.1983	T.S. No. 23 (1984) (Cmnd. 9187)

III. United Kingdom Legislation During 1983 Concerning Matters of International Law[1]

The British Fishing Boats Act (1983 c. 8) provides *inter alia* that the Minister of Agriculture, Fisheries and Food and the Secretaries of State respectively concerned with the sea fishing industry in Scotland, Wales and Northern Ireland may by order prescribe conditions for qualifications for British fishing boats with respect to the nationality of members of the crew. (See Part Nine: IX., above.)

The British Nationality (Falkland Islands) Act (1983 c. 6) provides for the acquisition of British citizenship by certain persons having connections with the Falkland Islands who would otherwise be British Dependent Territories citizens. (See UKMIL 1982, pp. 399-400.)

The Civil Aviation (Eurocontrol) Act (1983 c. 11) makes further provision with respect to the European Organization for the Safety of Air Navigation (Eurocontrol). It amends the Civil Aviation Act 1982 by providing for the enforcement of foreign judgments in respect of route charges and by amending the provisions relating to the immunities and privileges of Eurocontrol. (See Part Ten: II. A. 2., above.)

The International Transport Conventions Act (1983 c. 14) gives effect to the Convention concerning International Carriage by Rail of 9 May 1980 and amends certain Acts giving effect to other international transport conventions so as to take account of revisions of the conventions to which they give effect.

The Nuclear Material (Offences) Act (1983 c. 18) implements the Convention on the Physical Protection of Nuclear Material of 3 March 1980. It provides that if a person, whatever his nationality, does outside the United Kingdom certain acts in relation to or by means of nuclear material which, if done within the United Kingdom, would have made him guilty of any of certain specified offences, he shall be guilty of an offence. It amends, *inter alia*, the Extradition Act 1870, the Fugitive Offenders Act 1967, the Visiting Forces Act 1972, the Internationally Protected Persons Act 1978 and the Suppression of Terrorism Act 1978. (See Parts Four: VI. and Eight: II. D., above.)

---

[1] Compiled by C. A. Hopkins.

TABLE OF CASES[1]

---

[1] The figures in heavier type indicate the pages on which cases are reviewed.

INDEX